INTRODUCTION

TO

SOCIAL

WELFARE

Other Wadsworth Titles of Related Interest in Social Welfare

Marion L. Beaver/Don Miller: *Clinical Social Work*

Ira Colby: *Social Welfare Policy: Perspectives, Patterns, and Insights*

Beulah R. Compton/Burt Galaway: *Social Work Processes*, Fourth Edition

Donald Critchlow/Ellis Hawley: *Poverty and Public Policy in Modern America*

Danya Glaser/Stephen Frosh: *Child Sexual Abuse*

Dean H. Hepworth/Jo Ann Larsen: *Direct Social Work Practice: Theory and Skills*, Second Edition

Bruce S. Jansson: *Social Welfare Policy: From Theory to Practice*

Bruce S. Jansson: *The Reluctant Welfare State*

Albert R. Roberts: *Crisis Intervention Handbook: Assessment, Treatment, and Research*

Albert R. Roberts: *Juvenile Justice: Policies, Programs, and Services*

Allen Rubin/Earl Babbie: *Research Methods for Social Work*

Myron E. Weiner: *Human Services Management*, Second Edition

Charles Zastrow: *The Practice of Social Work*, Third Edition

INTRODUCTION

TO

SOCIAL

WELFARE

SOCIAL PROBLEMS, SERVICES, AND CURRENT ISSUES

Fourth Edition

Charles Zastrow

University of Wisconsin—Whitewater

Wadsworth Publishing Company
Belmont, California
A Division of Wadsworth, Inc.

Social Welfare Editor: Peggy Adams
Production Editor: Deborah Cogan
Designer: MaryEllen Podgorski
Print Buyer: Barbara Britton
Copy Editor: Melissa Andrews
Photo Researcher: Stephen Forsling
Compositor: Thompson Type
Cover Designer: Salinda Tyson
Cover Photographer: H. Mark Weidman

Printed in the United States of America   34

1 2 3 4 5 6 7 8 9 10———94 93 92 91 90

Library of Congress Cataloging-in-Publication Data

Zastrow, Charles.
    Introduction to social welfare: social problems, services, and current issues / Charles Zastrow. — 4th ed.
        p.   cm.
    Rev. ed. of: Introduction to social welfare institutions. 3rd ed. 1986.
    Includes bibliographies and index.
    ISBN 0-534-11544-6
    1. Social service—United States.   2. Social service—Vocational guidance—United States.   3. Public welfare—United States.   4. Social problems.   I. Zastrow, Charles.   Introduction to social welfare institutions.
    II. Title.
HV40.Z27   1990
362—dc20   89-34410
                                                CIP

To Lee

CONTENTS

PART 2   Social Problems and Social Services   75

CHAPTER 3   Poverty and Public Welfare   76

CHAPTER 4   Emotional Problems and Counseling   112

CHAPTER 5   Family Problems and Services to Families   151

PREFACE

This book is designed to stimulate student interest in social welfare and to provide an experiential "flavor" of what the fields of social welfare and social work are really like. Using a social problems approach, the book describes how people are affected by such problems as poverty, child abuse, emotional difficulties, sexism, alcoholism, crime, mental retardation, racism, overpopulation, and sexual dysfunctions. Information on the nature, extent, and causes of such problems is also presented. In teaching introductory courses in social welfare, a number of my colleagues and I have found that students tend to get more interested when they come face-to-face with the tragic social conditions that people experience. This book also includes case examples through which the reader is able to identify with people in need of help.

This information on social problems prepares and motivates the student to read the sections of the text that cover current services, merits and shortcomings of current services, and new programs that are needed to meet service gaps and shortcomings.

In addition, *Introduction to Social Welfare: Social Problems, Services, and Current Issues* is designed to:

- Provoke the reader's thinking about some of the controversial, contemporary issues in social welfare. I believe developing the student's reasoning capacities is much more important than learning unimportant facts to be recited on exams.

- Convey material on counseling techniques and on the analysis of policy issues that the reader can use in working with people and in arriving at policy decisions.

- Provide case examples of the functions, roles, responsibilities, gratifications, and frustrations of social workers that will help the student who is considering a social work major to make an informed career decision.

- Provide a brief historical review of the development of social welfare, social work, and various social services.

- Help the reader "sort out" his or her value structure in relation to welfare recipients, single parents, ex-convicts, the mentally ill, the divorced, abusive parents, minority groups, those who are prejudiced, and so on. The aim is not to sell any particular set of values but to help the reader arrive at a value system that she or he will be comfortable with and find functional in interacting with others.

PLAN OF THE BOOK

Part I introduces the student to the fields of social welfare, social work, and human services. These terms are defined, and their relationships to sociology, psychology, and other disciplines are described. A brief history of social welfare and social work is provided, and the future is examined. A discussion of social work as a career and as a profession is included, and this gives the reader a basis for deciding whether to pursue a career in social work.

Part II focuses on the most common social problems served by the field of social welfare. This part constitutes the main emphasis of the text and describes:

- Contemporary social problems in our society.
- Current social services for meeting these problems.
- Gaps in current services.
- Controversial issues in each service area.
- Proposed new programs to meet current gaps in services.

Numerous case examples are given to provide the reader with a "feeling" awareness of how the problems affect people and to convey what it is really like to be a social worker.

Part II focuses on generalist social work practice and describes three practice areas: casework, group work, and community practice. This part provides considerable usable information on how to counsel individuals, how to work with groups, and how to develop new services and improve existing services in a community.

This fourth edition updates information in all of the chapters, and several chapters have been extensively revised in accordance with the suggestions received from a number of faculty members who have reviewed and commented on the third edition. New topics include the homeless, the farm crisis, eating disorders, blended families, AIDS, generalist practice, and the expanding field of private social work practice.

The book is intended for use in introductory social work and social welfare courses. It serves to introduce prospective social work majors to the field of social welfare, and will help them arrive at career decisions and prepare for future social work courses. For nonmajors, the book provides information about available social services and gives a framework for analyzing policy issues and for making citizenship decisions.

ACKNOWLEDGMENTS

I wish to express my deep appreciation to the various people who made this book possible. Special thanks to the contributing authors, and to the photo researcher, Stephen Forsling. I would like to thank the following colleagues who provided comments on the manuscript for this edition: Lynn Atkinson, Oklahoma State University; Stanley Blostein, Ohio State University; Michael R. Daley, Stephen F. Austin State University; Bettyann Dubansky, University of Missouri, Columbia; Timothy W. Lause, Wichita State University; Keith A. Miller, University of Wyoming; David N. Storm, Central Missouri State University; and Candace Widmer, Elmira College. A sincere thank you to Linda Brown, Kristine Zastrow, Ralph Navarre, Nancy Sienko, and Vicki Vogel, who were "alter egos" for conceptualizing various chapters and helped in a number of ways with the writing of this text.

Charles Zastrow

About the Author

CHARLES ZASTROW, M.S.W. and Ph.D., is Professor in the Social Work Department, University of Wisconsin—Whitewater. He has worked as a practitioner in a variety of public and private social welfare agencies and has chaired several social work accreditation site visit teams for the Council on Social Work Education. He is a member of the National Association of Social Workers and the Council on Social Work Education, and is a member of the Commission on Educational Planning for the Council on Social Work Education. In addition to *Introduction to Social Welfare*, Dr. Zastrow has written four other textbooks: *The Practice of Social Work, Social Work with Groups, Social Problems,* and *Understanding Human Behavior and the Social Environment* (with Dr. Karen Kirst-Ashman).

Contributing Authors

MAUREEN O'GORMAN FOSTER
Executive Director
Rock County Hospice, Inc.
Janesville, Wisconsin

DON NOLAN
Social Worker
Jefferson County Public School System
Wisconsin

LLOYD G. SINCLAIR
Psychotherapist
Midwest Center for Sex Therapy
Madison, Wisconsin

I

INTRODUCTION:

SOCIAL

WELFARE

AND

SOCIAL

WORK

In our industrialized, complex, and rapidly changing society, social welfare activities have become important functions in terms of the money spent, the human misery treated, and the number of people served.[1] This chapter will:

- Define social welfare and describe its goals.
- Describe the relationship between social welfare and the following disciplines: sociology, social work, and human services.
- Provide a history of social welfare.
- Describe how the future of social welfare will be affected by technological advances.
- Indicate that the future of social welfare will also be partially affected by changes in the American family system. A summary of many of the changes that are occurring in the American family is provided.

1

SOCIAL WELFARE: ITS BUSINESS, HISTORY, AND FUTURE

BUSINESS OF SOCIAL WELFARE

The goal of social welfare is to fulfill the social, financial, health, and recreational requirements of all individuals in a society. Social welfare seeks to enhance the social functioning of all age groups, both rich and poor. When other institutions in our society, such as the market economy and the family, fail at times to meet the basic needs of individuals or groups of people, then social services are needed and demanded.

In more primitive societies, people's basic needs were fulfilled in more direct and informal ways. Even in this country, less than 150 years ago, most Americans lived on farms or in small towns with extended families and relatives close by. If financial or other needs arose, relatives, the church, and neighbors were there to "lend a helping hand." Problems were visible and personal; everyone knew everyone else in the community. When a need arose, it was taken for granted that those with resources would do whatever they could to alleviate the difficulty. If, for example, the need was financial, personal acquaintance with the storekeeper or banker usually was sufficient to obtain needed goods

The earthquake that shook Soviet Armenia in 1988 dramatized on a global scale one of the most basic functions of social welfare—to aid those struck by natural disasters. Food, blankets, and medicine poured into Armenia from around the world following the earthquake, which left 25,000 dead and nearly half a million homeless. This sixty-two-year-old woman was rescued by a team of Czech firemen after being trapped under debris for over ten days.

or money. Needless to say, we are now living in a different era. Our technology, economic base, social patterns, and living styles have changed dramatically. Our commercial, industrial, political, educational, and religious institutions are considerably larger and more impersonal. We tend to live in large urban communities, away from families or relatives, frequently without even establishing acquaintances with neighbors. We have become much more mobile, often having few roots and limited knowledge of the community in which we live. Vocationally, we also have specialized and become more interdependent on others, and thereby we have diminishing control over large aspects of our lives. Our rapidly changing society is a breeding ground for exacerbating former social ills and creating new problems, such as the eruption of our inner cities, higher rates of crime, energy crises, and the destruction of the

quality of our environment. Obviously, the old rural-frontier methods of meeting social welfare needs are no longer viable.

It is the business of social welfare:

To find homes for parentless children.

To rehabilitate people who are addicted to alcohol or drugs.

To treat those with emotional difficulties.

To make life more meaningful for the aged.

To provide vocational rehabilitation services to the physically and mentally handicapped.

To meet the financial needs of the poor.

To rehabilitate juveniles and adults who have committed criminal offenses.

To end racial and religious discrimination.

Social welfare institutions attempt to improve the well-being of individuals, groups, and communities. They cover a wide range of services, involving both professionals (family therapy, above) and volunteers (day care and Meals on Wheels home visits, on opposite page and at right).

To provide child-care services for working mothers.

To counteract problems and violence in families, including child abuse and spouse abuse.

To fulfill the health and legal exigencies of those in financial need.

To counsel individuals and groups having a wide variety of personal and social difficulties.

To provide services to persons with AIDS and their families and friends.

To provide recreational and leisure-time services to all age groups.

To educate and provide socialization experiences to children who are mentally retarded or emotionally disturbed.

To serve families struck by such physical disasters as fires and tornadoes.

To provide vocational training services and employment opportunities to the unskilled and unemployed.

To meet the special needs of Native Americans, migrant workers, and other minority groups.

SOCIAL WELFARE AS AN INSTITUTION AND AS A DISCIPLINE

The term *social welfare* has different meanings, as it is both an *institution* and an *academic and professional discipline*. The National Association of Social Workers (the primary professional organization for

BOX 1.1

What It's All About

S hortly after their marriage Frank Lund, age 24, and his wife, Jean, age 22, moved from their rural farm background in northern Wisconsin to a large midwestern city in the fall of 1955. They had bright hopes for their future. Frank obtained a well-paying job on the assembly line of an auto manufacturing company. Jean worked part-time as a file clerk until her first pregnancy in the spring of 1957. In the next four years they had three children and also purchased a three-bedroom home in a suburb. Then in 1962, while on a hunting trip, Frank was accidentally killed. Mrs. Lund was never quite the same. She had periodic moods of depression and had considerable difficulty in finding the energy to care for her three young children.

In 1963 the Lunds' financial resources were depleted. Unable to make the payments on the house, they were forced to move to a rundown two-bedroom apartment closer to the center of the city. In the winter of 1963 Mrs. Lund applied for financial assistance under the Aid to Families with Dependent Children program. The state in which the Lunds lived had negative attitudes toward welfare, and consequently the monthly payments the Lunds received were barely sufficient to meet their basic needs. In addition, the neighbors never attempted to understand the Lunds' plight. They were more concerned about their tax dollars being spent for "such people." Mrs. Lund felt she was a second-class citizen and stigmatized because she was a "charity" case. She also soon became aware that some of her neighbors would not permit their children to play with her children. When the children entered school, they began to feel they were different from other children; they were poorly dressed, the lunch they brought from home usually consisted of cheese sandwiches, and they had no father. A few years later Mrs. Lund dated a salesman for a while; being lonely she permitted him to stay over some evenings at the apartment. The neighbors frowned about this and made moral accusations. Several months later Mrs. Lund ended this relationship when she became aware she would be unable to change the man's drinking problem. (When intoxicated he was sometimes abusive to Mrs. Lund and the children.)

When the oldest child, Tom, was 15 he was arrested for starting three fires in the neighborhood. Perhaps he just wanted attention, or maybe it was his way of demonstrating he needed help. Anyway, he was judged to have emotional difficulties and was sent to a residential treatment center. At the age of 20 he was released. He applied for several semiskilled jobs, but partly because of potential employers' concerns about his past, someone else was always hired. He therefore obtained a series of odd jobs as maintenance man, dishwasher, store clerk, and so forth. Not finding more stimulating work, he began drinking, sometimes to excess. At 25 he married and within the next few years fathered four children. Because of his family responsibilities, low-paying job, and drinking problem, he and his family are now locked into poverty.

The second child, Corine, wanted to escape from her home and from school when she became a teenager. She ran away several times but was always returned by the police. At 16 she became involved with Mike, a high school dropout, and became pregnant. Mike's parents would not give their consent to a marriage. Corine dropped out of school, delivered, and decided to keep the baby. For the next six years she continued to live with her mother, even though there were frequent arguments. At 22 she met and within a year married Bill Loomans, a seasonal construction worker and a widower with three children. Already Bill and Corine were close to being locked into poverty for the rest of their lives. The two additional children they had after marriage did not help.

The youngest child, Dave, was also a problem for Mrs. Lund. In the early years of school he had considerable difficulty learning to read. He soon fell behind the rest of his classmates. By the fourth grade he felt self-conscious about being unable to read. In class he no longer would put forth much effort to do academic work and instead spent most of his time clowning around. Psychological testing indicated Dave had average mental ability and suggested he had developed an "emotional block" to academic work that appeared to be related to his home environment. On entering the fifth grade, he was placed in a special class for the retarded. Dave was very sensitive about this and became involved in several fights when referred to as a "dummy" by his peers. At age 16 he dropped out of school and was fortunate to obtain a job pumping gas. Two years later he was "forced" to marry. Terri and Dave had a stormy marriage, with frequent disputes. Within a year and a half they had two children. Six months later they separated, and Dave was required by the court to pay child support until the children were 18. Two years later, on being named as the father of another child delivered by an unmarried mother, Dave was required by the court to make monthly support payments for this child. He tried to meet these responsibilities, but his income would not stretch, and therefore he wrote some checks that "bounced." Recently he was arrested and placed on probation for two years. He now appears to be solidly locked into poverty for the remainder of his life. His chances of securing a better-paying job are slight because of his past, his lack of training for a skilled job, and his inability to read.

The story of the Lund family raises a number of questions for social welfare. Who is to "blame" for the difficulties of this family—or is no one at fault? Is this cycle of poverty (which has been transmitted from one generation to another, and the social difficulties associated with it) likely to be continued among the grandchildren of Frank and Jean Lund? What should be done, now, to help the members of the Lund family? Who should pay for the help provided? What kind of help (both services and money), if provided to Jean Lund when her husband was accidentally killed, would probably have prevented the social difficulties experienced by her children and likely to be faced by her grandchildren?

social workers) gives the following definition of social welfare as an institution.

Social welfare generally denotes the full range of organized activities of voluntary and governmental agencies that seek to prevent, alleviate, or contribute to the solution of recognized social problems, or to improve the well-being of individuals, groups, or communities. Such activities use a wide variety of professional personnel such as physicians, nurses, lawyers, educators, engineers, ministers, and social workers.[2]

Examples of social welfare programs and services are foster care, adoption, day care, Head Start, probation and parole, public assistance programs such as Aid to Families with Dependent Children, public health nursing, sex therapy, suicide counseling, recreational services such as Boy Scouts and YWCA programs, services to minority groups, services to veterans, school social services, medical and legal services to the poor, family planning services, meals on wheels, nursing home services, shelters for battered spouses, protective services for child abuse and neglect, assertiveness-training programs, encounter groups and sensitivity training, public housing projects, family counseling, Alcoholics Anonymous, runaway services, services to the developmentally disabled, and sheltered workshops.

Social welfare programs and social service organizations are sometimes referred to as "social welfare institutions." The purposes of social welfare institutions are to prevent, alleviate, or contribute to the solution of recognized social problems to directly improve the well-being of individuals, groups, and communities. Social welfare institutions are established by policies and laws, with the programs and services being provided by voluntary (private) and governmental (public) agencies.

The term *social welfare institution* is applied to various levels of complexity and abstraction. It may be applied to a single program or organization: for example, day-care services for the mentally handicapped or Planned Parenthood. Or, the term may be applied to a group of services or programs: For example, child welfare services is a social welfare institution that includes such services as adoption, foster care, juvenile proba-

tion, runaway services, day care, school social services, and residential treatment. The highest aggregate level to which the term *social welfare institution* is applied includes *all* of the social programs and organizations that are designed to prevent, alleviate, or contribute to the solution of recognized social problems.

Another meaning of social welfare derives from its role as an academic and professional discipline. In this context social welfare is "The study of agencies, programs, personnel, and policies which focus on the delivery of social services to individuals, groups, and communities."[3] One of the functions of the social welfare discipline is to educate and train social workers. (Some colleges and universities call their professional preparation programs for social work practice "social work," and others call their programs "social welfare." There are no significant differences between social work and social welfare educational programs that are accredited by the Council on Social Work Education, the national accrediting organization for social work programs in the United States.)

SOCIAL WELFARE'S RELATIONSHIP TO SOCIOLOGY AND TO OTHER ACADEMIC DISCIPLINES

Social welfare has often been confused with "sociology," "social work," and "human services." In addition, many people are confused about how social welfare and social work relate to psychology, psychiatry, and other related disciplines. The next few sections will seek to clarify the relationships between social welfare and these other disciplines.

There are a variety of academic disciplines that seek to obtain knowledge about social problems, their causes, and their alleviation. The most common disciplines are social welfare, sociology, psychology, political science, economics, psychiatry, and cultural anthropology. Figure 1.1 shows the relationship of these disciplines to social welfare.

FIGURE 1.1

Overlap of Knowledge Base of Social Welfare with Other Disciplines

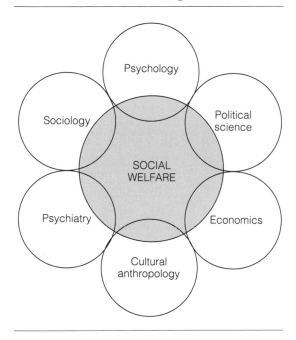

Each of these disciplines has a distinct focus. The following definitions highlight the similarities and differences between these disciplines.

Sociology: The study of human social behavior, especially the study of the origins, organizations, institutions, and development of human society.

Psychology: The study of mental processes and behavior.

Psychiatry: The study of the diagnosis, treatment, and prevention of mental illness.

Political science: The study of the processes, principles, and structure of government and of political institutions.

Economics: The study of the production, distribution, and consumption of commodities.

Cultural anthropology: The study of human culture based on archaeological, ethnographic, linguistic, social, and psychological data and methods of analysis.[4]

Theories and research in these disciplines may or may not, depending on the nature of the content, be considered part of the knowledge base of social welfare. When the theories and research have direct application to the social welfare goal of enhancing the social functioning of people, such knowledge can also be considered to be part of the knowledge base of social welfare. In the past, social welfare has been more of an applied science than a pure science; that is, it has formed its knowledge base primarily from the theories and research of other disciplines and has focused on applying such knowledge through social programs. In recent years the academic discipline of social welfare (called social work at many campuses) has been active in research projects and in theory development. This increased research and theory development activity is an indication that social welfare is a discipline that is maturing, as it is now developing much of its own knowledge base.

A few examples may be useful in illustrating how the knowledge base of other disciplines overlap with social welfare. Sociological research on and conceptualization of the causes of social problems (for example, juvenile delinquency, mental illness, poverty, and racial discrimination) may be considered part of the knowledge base of social welfare. Only through an understanding of such problems can social welfare effectively prevent and control such problems. Sociological studies on the effects of institutions (for example, mental hospitals and prisons) on individuals is currently of considerable interest to and has important application in social welfare. Sociological investigations of other subjects, such as mobility, urbanization, secularization, formation of groups, race relations, prejudice, and the process of assimilation have also become part of social welfare's knowledge base because such investigations are directly applicable to enhancing people's social well-being. However, research in other sociological areas, such as studies of social organizations among primitive tribes, is usually considered outside the knowledge base of social welfare because such research usually does not have direct applications to the goal of social welfare.

Comparable overlap occurs among social welfare and the other previously mentioned disciplines. Using psychology as an example, studies and theory development in such areas as personality growth and therapeutic techniques can be considered part of the knowledge base of social welfare because they have direct social welfare applications. On the other hand, experimental investigations of, for example, the perceptions and thinking processes of animals do not, at least at the present time, have such applications and would not therefore be considered part of the social welfare knowledge base.

SOCIAL WELFARE'S RELATIONSHIP TO SOCIAL WORK

The institutional definition (previously given) of social welfare is applicable when the relationship between social welfare and social work is examined. However, *social welfare* is a more comprehensive term that encompasses social work as well. Social welfare and social work are primarily related at the level of practice. *Social work* has been defined by the National Association of Social Workers as follows:

Social work is the professional activity of helping individuals, groups, or communities to enhance or restore their capacity for social functioning and to create societal conditions favorable to their goals.

Social work practice consists of the professional application of social work values, principles, and techniques to one or more of the following ends: helping people obtain tangible services; providing counseling and psychotherapy for individuals, families, and groups; helping communities or groups provide or improve social and health services; and participating in relevant legislative processes.

The practice of social work requires knowledge of human development and behavior; of social, economic, and cultural institutions; and of the interaction of all these factors.[5]

FIGURE 1.2

Examples of Professional Groups within the Field of Social Welfare

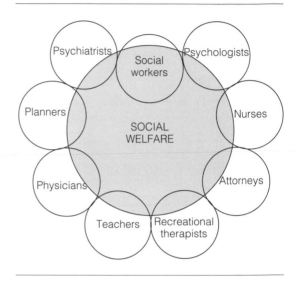

The term *social worker* is generally applied to graduates (either with a bachelor's or master's degree) of schools of social work who are employed in the field of social welfare. A social worker is a "change agent,"— a helper who is specifically employed for the purpose of creating planned change. As a change agent a social worker is expected to be skilled at working with individuals, groups, and families and in bringing about community changes. Almost all social workers are employed in the field of social welfare. There are, however, many other professional and occupational groups that may be employed in the field of social welfare, as illustrated in Figure 1.2. Professional people staffing social welfare services include attorneys providing legal services to the poor; urban planners in social-planning agencies; physicians in public health agencies; teachers in residential treatment facilities for the emotionally disturbed; psychologists, nurses, and recreational therapists in mental hospitals; and psychiatrists in mental health clinics.

SOCIAL WELFARE'S RELATIONSHIP TO OTHER INSTITUTIONS

Social welfare overlaps with such institutions as the family, education, religion, and politics. One of the functions of the family is raising and caring for children. Social welfare assists families by providing such services as counseling, day care, foster care, and adoption. Certain educational courses have both educational and social welfare aspects; for example, social science and physical education courses provide socialization experiences and are important in the social development of youth. Religion has long been interested in people's social well-being and has provided such social welfare services as counseling, financial assistance, day care, and recreation. The overlap between politics and social welfare occurs primarily at the juncture of new social service programs, the point at which our political leaders must decide whether expenditures of tax dollars for these programs are warranted. Some social welfare programs (for example, public assistance) have long been controversial political topics.

SOCIAL WELFARE'S RELATIONSHIP TO HUMAN SERVICES

Human services may be defined as those systems of services and allied occupations and professions that concentrate on improving or maintaining the physical and mental health and general well-being of individuals, groups, or communities in our society. Alfred Kahn has conceptualized human services as being composed of the following four service categories:[6]

1. Personal services (casework, counseling, recreation, rehabilitation, religion, therapy).

2. Protection services (consumer protection, corrections, courts, fire prevention/fire fighting, housing code enforcement, law enforcement, public health services).

3. Information/advising services (consulting, consumer information, education, financial counseling, hot lines, and library services).

4. Maintenance services (child care, unemployment assistance, institutional services, public welfare programs, retirement plans, and social security programs).

Kahn indicates there is a tendency to use the term *human services* for what in the past has been called social welfare.[7] Actually, *human services* is a broader term than *social welfare* because it includes services (such as library services, law enforcement, housing code enforcement, consumer protection, and fire prevention and fire fighting) that are usually not considered social welfare services. The term *social welfare* is thus more limited because it focuses on conceptualizing and resolving social problems. *Human services* is a broader term that encompasses social welfare programs. The two terms relate at a *program* level.

HISTORY OF SOCIAL WELFARE

Two Conflicting Views

The present social welfare scene is being substantially influenced by the past. Currently, there are two conflicting views of the role of social welfare in our society.[8] One of these roles has been termed *residual*—a gap-filling or first-aid role. This view holds that social welfare services should only be provided when an individual's needs are not properly met through other societal institutions, primarily the family and the market economy. With the residual view, it is thought that social services and financial aid should not be provided until all other measures or efforts have failed, including the individual's and his or her family's resources

BOX 1.2

Blaming the Victim

Jerry Jorgenson and Joyce Mantha decided to get married after dating for three years. Both looked forward to a big wedding and a happy future. They had met in college, and now both were working in Mayville, a small town that Jerry had grown up in. Joyce was a kindergarten teacher, and Jerry was manager of an A&P grocery store. Against Jerry's wishes, Joyce drove one weekend to a nearby city to attend a premarriage party with some of her college women friends. The party was still going strong at 2:00 A.M., but Joyce thought it was time to return to her motel in order to return to Mayville early on Sunday. In the parking lot Joyce was sexually assaulted. She tried to fight off the assailant and suffered a number of bruises and abrasions. After the assault, a passerby called the police and an ambulance. Joyce called Jerry the next day. At first he was angry at the rapist. But the more he thought about it, the more he assigned blame to Joyce—she went to the party against his wishes, and he thought that she probably dressed and acted in such a way to interest the rapist, especially since he further assumed she was high on alcohol.

The weeks that followed became increasingly difficult for Jerry and Joyce. Joyce sensed that Jerry was blaming her for being raped. She tried to talk it out with Jerry, but it did not help. Their sexual relationship became practically nil, as Jerry felt his "sexual rights" had been violated, and the few times he made sexual advances he had images of Joyce being attacked by a stranger. They postponed the marriage.

Many townspeople, when they first heard about the rape, also thought that Joyce had "asked for it" while partying in the big city. Postponing the marriage was interpreted by the townspeople as evidence for this belief, and they began shunning Joyce. After several

---

being fully used up. In addition, this view asserts that funds and services should be provided on a short-term basis (primarily during emergencies) and should be withdrawn when the individual or the family again becomes capable of being self-sufficient.

The residual view has been characterized as "charity for unfortunates."[9] Funds and services are not seen as a right (something that one is entitled to) but as a gift, with the receiver having certain obligations; for example, in order to receive financial aid, recipients may be required to perform certain low-grade work assignments. Associated with the residual view is the belief that the causes of social welfare clients' difficulties are rooted in their own malfunctioning—that is, that clients are to blame for their predicaments be-

cause of personal inadequacies or ill-advised activities or sins.

Under the residual view there is usually a stigma attached to receiving services or funds. The prevalence of the residual stigma can be shown by asking, "Have you ever in the past felt a reluctance to seek counseling for a personal or emotional situation that you faced because you were wary of what others might think of you?" For almost everyone the answer is yes, and the reluctance to seek help is due to the residual stigma. The prevalence of this stigma in American society was dramatically shown in 1968 when Senator Thomas Eagleton was dropped as a vice presidential candidate on the Democratic ticket after it became known that he had once received psychiatric counseling.

months of such treatment Joyce began to believe that she was at fault and increasingly blamed herself for her predicament. She became despondent and moved back with her parents for refuge.

This story is only one illustration of the tendency in American culture to blame the victim. Others abound. If an adult is unemployed for a long time, often that person is believed to be "lazy" or "unmotivated." AFDC mothers (mothers receiving Aid to Families of Dependent Children) are erroneously stereotyped as being promiscuous, irresponsible, and desirous of having more children in order to increase their monthly grant. When a marriage breaks up, either the husband or the wife or both are blamed, rather than the relationship viewed as having deteriorated. When unfortunate circumstances occur (for example, lightning striking one's home), some people believe it is a punishment for sinful activity. Slapping one's wife is justified by some segments of the population as being a way to "keep her in line" and to "show her who's boss." People living in poverty are often erroneously viewed as being personally inadequate, incompetent, lazy, or as having a culture that holds them in poverty. The problems of slum housing in inner cities are sometimes traced to the characteristics of "southern rural migrants" not yet "acculturated" to life in the big city. Such blaming of the victim sometimes sadly leads to acceptance by the general public of the victimization, with few efforts then being made to make constructive changes.

But perhaps the saddest feature of victim blaming is that the erroneous explanation often becomes a self-fulfilling prophecy. If a teacher is told that a child is a poor learner, that teacher will interact with the child as if the child were a slow learner. Unfortunately, the child will eventually come to believe the teacher is correct and is likely to learn little. Labeling people as lazy, criminal, immoral, or mentally ill strongly influences the expectations people hold for them and simultaneously influences the victims themselves in their expectations and self-definition.

The opposing point of view, which has been coined the *institutional view*,* holds that social welfare programs are to be "accepted as a proper, legitimate function of modern industrial society in helping individuals achieve self-fulfillment.[10] Under this view there is no stigma attached to receiving funds or services; recipients are viewed as being entitled to such help. Associated with this view is the belief that an individual's difficulties are due to causes largely beyond his or her control (for example, a person may be unemployed because of a lack of employment opportuni-

ties). With this view, when difficulties arise causes are sought in the environment (society), and efforts are focused on improving the social institutions within which the individual functions.

The residual approach characterized social welfare programs from our early history to the depression of the 1930s. Since the Great Depression, both approaches have been applied to social welfare programs, with some programs being largely residual in nature and others being more institutional in design and implementation. Social insurance programs, such as Old-Age, Survivors, and Disability Insurance (described in Chapter 3) are examples of "institutional" programs.

---

*The term *institutional view of social welfare* is distinctly different from, and not to be confused with, the term *social welfare institutions*.

Early European History

One of the problems faced by all societies is to develop ways to meet the needs of those who are unable to be self-sufficient—the orphaned, the blind, the physically disabled, the poor, the mentally handicapped, and the sick. Before the Industrial Revolution, this responsibility was largely met by the family, by the church, and by neighbors. One of the values of the Judeo-Christian religion throughout history having considerable relevance for social welfare is humanitarianism: that is, ascribing a high value to human life and benevolently helping those in need.

With the development of the feudal system in Europe, when a tenant family was unable to meet a relative's basic needs, the feudal lord usually provided whatever was necessary.

The Elizabethan Poor Law

In the Middle Ages, for such reasons as famines, wars, crop failures, recurrences of pestilences, and the breakdown in the feudal system, there were substantial increases in the number of people in need. Former approaches, primarily through the church and the family, were not capable of meeting the needs of many who were unable to be self-sufficient. As a result, many of these people were forced to resort to begging. To attempt to meet this social problem, England passed several Poor Laws between the mid-1300s to the mid-1800s. The most significant of these was the Elizabethan Poor Law of 1601, enacted during the reign of Queen Elizabeth. The fundamental provisions of this Poor Law were incorporated into the laws of the American colonies and have had an important influence on our current approaches to public assistance and other social legislation. (It is interesting to observe that the social problem that these Poor Laws were designed to alleviate was not conceptualized as being poverty, but rather was the ruling class's annoyance with begging.)

The Elizabethan Poor Law established three categories of relief recipients:

1. The able-bodied poor. This group was given low-grade employment, and citizens were prohibited

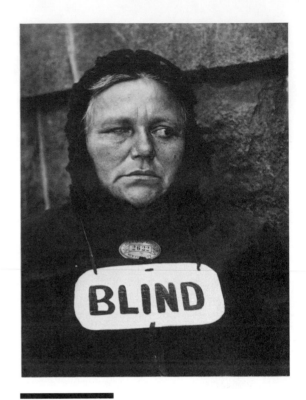

When Paul Strand photographed a blind newspaper dealer in 1916, "charity for unfortunates" was still the widely held view of social welfare. Those who were unable to be self-sufficient were treated—at best—with condescension. As a licensed New York City peddler, this woman's lot may have been only marginally better than other "unfortunates" of her day.

from giving them financial help. Anyone who refused to work was placed in stocks or in jail.

2. The impotent poor. People unable to work composed this group—the elderly, the blind, the deaf, mothers with young children, and the physically and mentally handicapped. They were usually placed together in an almshouse (institution). If the impotent poor had a place to live and if it appeared less expensive to maintain them there, they were permitted to live outside the almshouse, where they were granted "outdoor relief," usually "in kind" (food, clothing, and fuel).

3. Dependent children. Children whose parents or grandparents were unable to support them were apprenticed out to other citizens. Boys were taught the trade of their master and had to serve until their 24th birthday. Girls were brought up as domestic servants and were required to remain until they were 21 or married.

This Poor Law did not permit the registration of a person as being in need of charity if his or her parents, spouse, children, or other relatives were able to provide support. Although the law was passed by the English Parliament, the parish (town or local community) was assigned the responsibility of implementing the provisions of the law, with the program expenses to be met by charitable donations and a tax in the parish on lands, houses, and tithes. The Poor Law also stated that the parish's responsibility only extended to those who had legal residence in the parish, which was variously defined as having been born in the parish to having lived in the parish for three years. (Residency requirements are still part of current public assistance programs.) The Poor Law of 1601 set the pattern of public relief under governmental responsibility in Great Britain and this country for the next 300 years.

Most of the provisions of the Elizabethan Poor Law were incorporated into the social welfare policies of colonial America. Towns were assigned the responsibility of providing for the needy, almshouses were built to house the unemployables, orphaned children were apprenticed out, and a system of legal settlement was established that made it clear that towns were not responsible for meeting the needs of destitute strangers. Conditions in almshouses, it should be noted, were unbelievably deplorable. Into almshouses were packed not only the poor but also the sick, the emotionally disturbed, the blind, the alcoholic, and dependent children. Straw and old cots served for beds, there were no sanitary facilities, and the dilapidated buildings were barely heated in winter.

The Industrial Revolution

In the 17th, 18th, and 19th centuries the Industrial Revolution flourished in Europe and America. A major rea-

son for its development was technological advances, such as the development of the steam engine. But the revolution was also made possible by the *Protestant ethic* and the *laissez-faire economical view*. These two themes also had important effects on social welfare. The Protestant ethic emphasized *individualism*, the view that one is master of one's own fate. Hard work and acting in one's own self-interest were highly valued. An overriding goal for human beings set by the Protestant ethic was to acquire material goods. People were largely judged not so much on the basis of their personalities and other attributes, but on how much wealth they had acquired. To be poor was thought to be one's own moral fault.

The laissez-faire economical theory asserted that the economy and society in general would best prosper if businesses and industries were permitted to do whatever they desired to make a profit. Any regulation by the government of business practices (for example, setting safety standards, minimum wage laws, prohibiting child labor) was discouraged. The Protestant ethic and laissez-faire economical view, together, justified such business practices as cutthroat competition, formation of monopolies, deplorable safety and working conditions, and exploitation of the working class through low pay, long hours, and child labor.

The social welfare implications of the Protestant ethic reached its most inhumane declarations in the theory of *social Darwinism*, which was based on Charles Darwin's theory of evolution. Darwin theorized that higher forms of life evolved from lower forms by the process of survival of the fittest; he had seen in the animal world a fierce struggle for survival that destroyed the weak, rewarded the strong, and produced evolutionary change. Herbert Spencer extended this theory to humanity: struggle, destruction, and survival of the fit were thought to be essential to progress in human society as well. The theory stated in its most inhumane form that the strong (the wealthy) survived because they were superior, whereas the weak (the needy) deserved to perish and that it would be a mistake to help the weak survive. Although leaving the weak to perish was never advocated on a wide scale, the theory did have a substantial influence in curbing the development of innovative and more humane social welfare programs.

Prior to the Industrial Revolution there were few communities in Europe or America with a population larger than a few thousand. One of the consequences of the Industrial Revolution was the development of large urban areas close to where factories were located. Because employment opportunities were limited in rural areas, many workers moved to cities. With such movement, family and kinship ties were broken, and those who were unable to adapt faced a loss of community identity, alienation, and social breakdown. To attempt to meet the needs of people living in urban areas, private social welfare services began to be developed in the 1800s—primarily at the initiation of the clergy and religious groups. (A public social welfare agency receives its funds through tax dollars, whereas a private or voluntary agency generally receives a large part of its funds from charitable contributions.)* Because of the lack of development of public social services, private agencies provided most of the funds and services to the needy until the 1930s. In the 1800s social services and funds were usually provided by upper middle-class volunteers who combined "charity" with religious admonitions.

Turn of the 20th Century

Around 1880 various segments of the population became aware of the evils of unlimited competition and abuses by those with economic power. It became clear that a few captains of industries were becoming very wealthy, whereas the standard of living for the bulk of the population was remaining static and only slightly above the subsistence level. One of the theorists who objected to social Darwinism was Lester Ward, who in *Dynamic Sociology* (1883) drew a sharp distinction between purposeless animal evolution and human evolution.[11] By manipulating the environment, and by

social and economic controls, Ward asserted that everyone could benefit. This new thinking was in direct opposition to the social Darwinism and laissez-faire economical views. It called on the federal government to take on new functions, to establish legislation to regulate business practices, and to provide social welfare programs. As a result, around 1900 there was an awakening to social needs, with the federal government beginning to place some, although limited, funds into such programs as health, housing, and slum clearance.

In the early 1900s, social welfare became more professionalized. Prior to this time such services were generally provided by well-meaning but untrained volunteers (do-gooders) from the middle and upper socioeconomic groups. At this time people with more formalized training were employed in some positions, and there was an increased interest in developing therapeutic skills and methods in counseling clients. In this era some of our present patterns of specialization also developed, such as family services and probation and parole. It was also at this time that the first schools of social work and social welfare were founded in universities.

THE GREAT DEPRESSION AND THE SOCIAL SECURITY ACT

Before 1930 social services were primarily provided by churches and voluntary organizations. Financial assistance for people in need was also largely distributed by churches and voluntary organizations. Some cities and some counties had local relief directors who distributed public tax money financed by local governments. In those days poverty was associated with laziness and immorality. Financial relief was largely designed to keep people from starving. Receiving public relief money was viewed as "pauper aid" and a huge social disgrace.

---

*Some private agencies are now contracting with public agencies to receive public funds to provide services to certain clients. Public agencies are established and administered by governmental units, whereas private agencies are established and administered by nongovernmental groups or private citizens.

Nearly fifteen million people were unemployed at the height of the Great Depression. These San Francisco jobless men, like their counterparts in other cities, lined the streets daily, offering themselves for work.

The roaring 1920s were largely a time of prosperity and festivities. Then, in October 1929 the New York Stock Exchange crashed. Many investors lost their businesses, homes, and life savings. The crash of the stock market was a significant sign that our economy (along with the whole world's economy) was heading for a severe depression.

The number of people who were unemployed rose from 3 million in the spring of 1929 to 15 million in January 1933.[12] More than 20 percent of workers were jobless in 1933.[13] Many banks closed. Many farmers and business owners went bankrupt.

In 1931 some states began providing unemployment relief to prevent starvation among the jobless and their families. Herbert Hoover, who was president at the time, believed that only private charity should meet the needs of the unemployed. He thought public relief (state and federal money) would demoralize people and make them permanently dependent on the state and federal government. His attitude was graphically illustrated in December of 1930 when he approved a $45 million bill to feed starving livestock in Arkansas but opposed a $25 million bill to feed starving farmers and their families in the same state.[14]

Community Chests, Red Crosses, and other voluntary organizations were unable to meet the demand for financial assistance in the early 1930s. Because people were unemployed, private charity also had trouble raising the funds necessary to maintain the jobless.

Local and state funds proved inadequate to protect the growing millions of unemployed against hunger, cold, and despair. Many sick people could not pay for, and therefore did not receive, medical care. Children were passed around among neighbors because their parents had no food or were out looking for jobs. The number of suicides increased. Tuberculosis and malnutrition in children grew dangerously. Many middle-class people became penniless, factories lay idle, and stores had few customers.

In 1933, when President Franklin D. Roosevelt took office, 40 percent of the population in some states was receiving local and state public relief money.[15] Pressure grew for the federal government to bail out the states and counties by helping finance public relief for those living in poverty. Conditions were so desperate that our political leaders became concerned that there might be a socialist or communist revolution in this country.

President Roosevelt immediately proposed, and Congress passed, temporary emergency programs to provide paid work for some unemployed workers. For those unable to obtain a job the federal government provided financial assistance.

The depression of the 1930s brought about profound changes in social welfare. Until that time the belief in individualism was still widely held, that is, the belief that one is master of one's fate. The depression shattered this myth. It became clear that situations and

events beyond individual control can cause deprivation, misery, and poverty. It also became clear that the
federal government must play a role in providing financial assistance and social services.

Categories of Social Welfare Programs

The experience during the Great Depression with
emergency relief and work programs demonstrated
the need for more permanent federal efforts in dealing
with some of the critical problems of unemployment,
aging, disability, illness, and dependent children. As a
result, in 1935 the Social Security Act was passed, which
formed the basis of most of our current social welfare
programs, and federal support for the following three
major categories of programs was enacted.

SOCIAL INSURANCE   This category was set up with an
"institutional" orientation and provided insurance for
unemployment, retirement, or death. It has two main
programs: (*a*) Unemployment Compensation, which
provides weekly benefits for a limited time for workers
who lose their jobs, and (*b*) Old-Age, Survivors, and
Disability Insurance, which provide monthly payments
to individuals and their families when a worker retires,
becomes disabled, or dies. In everyday conversation
this program is generally referred to as *social security*.

PUBLIC ASSISTANCE   This category has many residual
aspects. To receive benefits an individual must undergo a "means test" in which one's assets and expenses are reviewed to determine if there is a financial
need. There were four programs under this category,
with the titles indicating eligible groups: Aid to the
Blind (people of any age whose vision is 20 by 200 or
less with correction); Aid to the Disabled (people between the ages of 18 and 65 who are permanently disabled); Old Age Assistance* (people ages 65 and older);

---

*In January 1974 three programs, Aid to the Blind, Aid to the Disabled,
and Old Age Assistance, were combined into one program entitled
Supplemental Security Income.

and Aid to Families with Dependent Children (AFDC)
(primarily mothers with children under age 18 and no
father in the home). Public assistance programs incorporated several features of the English Poor Laws: for
example, residence requirements, a means test, some
of the aid being "in kind" such as food, and the benefits
being viewed as "charity" rather than aid to which recipients are entitled. Public assistance, particularly the
Aid to Dependent Children program, is frequently criticized and stigmatized by politicians and the general
public. An inaccurate public perception is that "welfare" means public assistance *only*. In actuality, public
assistance is only one of several hundred social welfare
programs. A frequent complaint is that too much
money is being spent on public assistance; yet it is
generally unknown that five to six times more money
is spent annually on social insurance programs than
on public assistance![16]

PUBLIC HEALTH AND WELFARE SERVICES   Whereas the
first two categories provided financial benefits, this category established the role of the federal government
in providing social services (for example, adoption,
foster care, services to disabled children, protective
services, and services to single parents).

Following the enactment of the Social Security Act,
public social welfare services became dominant in
terms of expenditures, people served, and personnel.
The private role shifted from financial aid to certain
specialized service areas. One of the roles of private
agencies has been to test the value of new services and
approaches. If such new services are found to be cost
effective and successful in alleviating human problems,
public funds are sometimes requested to provide them
on a large-scale basis.

The programs established by the Social Security
Act have been controversial. Some authorities credit
the act with bringing economic stability to our country
and helping to bring us out of the worst depression we
have ever seen. Other authorities, including fiscal conservatives, view social security expenditures as perpetuating poverty by making people dependent on
government for their livelihood. It has been claimed
for many years that people would rather live it up on
welfare than work. It is also claimed that the expendi-

The Great Society programs and the Vietnam War protests of the late 1960s helped mobilize public sentiment toward an entire range of social issues, including a new concern for the environment. Ignorance, greed, and self-interest here glower over our planet during rallies commemorating Earth Day, an ecological "teach-in" first held in universities, schools, and communities across the U.S. in 1970.

tures are highly inflationary, as they represent a sizable portion of our federal government's budget.

The basic intent of the Social Security Act was to provide a decent standard of living to every American. President Roosevelt believed that financial security (including public assistance) should not be a matter of charity, but a matter of justice. He asserted that every individual has a right to a minimum standard of living in a civilized society. He believed that liberty and security are synonymous and that without financial security, people will eventually despair and revolt. Therefore, Roosevelt held the conviction that the very existence of a democratic society depended on the health and welfare of its citizens.[17]

From the 1930s to the 1980s the federal government gradually expanded its role in providing financial assistance and social programs to Americans suffering from social problems.

The Great Society and War on Poverty

A major push for expansion of social welfare programs came in the 1960s when President Lyndon Johnson declared War on Poverty and sought to create what he called a "Great Society." In 1964 Johnson noted in his

State of the Union address that one fifth of our population was living in poverty and that nearly half of the nation's blacks were poor. Funding for existing social welfare programs was sharply increased, and many new programs were created (such as Head Start, Medicare, and Medicaid*).

The early 1960s were characterized by optimism; there was a feeling that we were on our way to a golden era in which poverty would gradually disappear, racial integration would occur, and other social problems would be smoothly and painlessly met. The late 1960s were therefore a shock: Martin Luther King, Jr., and Robert Kennedy were assassinated; many of our inner cities were torched and burned to the ground during protests against racial discrimination; there were substantial increases in crime; there were student protests and riots on campuses over the Vietnam War and other issues; racial minorities and poor people organized to demand their piece of the national financial pie; there was a revolution in sexual values and behaviors; and there was a recognition of other social ills such as the drug problem and the need to preserve the environment.

In the social welfare field the late 1960s brought a renewed interest in changing the environment or "the system" to better meet the needs of clients (sociological approach), rather than enabling clients to better adapt and adjust to their life situations (the psychological approach). Social action again became an important part of social work, with some social workers becoming active as advocates of clients, community organizers, and political organizers for social reform.

Recent Years: Conservatism

In the 1970s, after the end of the Vietnam War, the turmoil of the late 1960s was replaced for several years with an atmosphere of relative calm on both the foreign and the domestic level. In contrast to the hope of the 1960s that government programs could cure our social ills, an opposing philosophy emerged that assumed many problems were beyond the capacity of the

government to alleviate. Hence, the liberalism of the 1960s, which resulted in the expansion and development of new social programs, was replaced by a more conservative approach in the 1970s and the 1980s. Practically no new, large-scale social welfare programs were initiated in the 1970s and the 1980s. Unfortunately, other crises (including Vietnam, Watergate, inflation, recession, the Israeli-Arab conflict, energy crises, and political turmoil in Iran, the Iran-Contra affair, and the large federal budget deficit) have received more attention in the last 20 years than our ongoing social problems. Some of these problems are poor living conditions in the inner cities, the emerging problem of AIDS, the homeless, racial discrimination, increasing crime rates, prison conditions, family violence, high divorce rate, overpopulation, the farm financial crisis, and the increasing number of people living in poverty.

During President Jimmy Carter's administration (1976 to 1980) there was increased recognition that the federal government simply did not have the power—no matter how much money it spent—to cure *all* the country's social ills. But instead of a recognition that the government could partially allay *many* of these problems, there appears to have been a 180-degree turn in which many citizens began despairing and demanding that government should sharply reduce the amount of tax money it was spending on social welfare programs.

In 1980 our domestic economy was in a mess. The rates of both unemployment and inflation were high, and the country had been in a recession for several years. Ronald Reagan was elected president that year and proceeded, as he promised during his presidential campaign, to make a number of changes to revitalize the economy and to strengthen the military. The following changes were implemented:

- Taxes were sharply cut for both individuals and corporations. These tax cuts resulted in businesses and consumers having more money to spend, which stimulated the economy and led to a reduction in the unemployment rate.

- Military expenditures were sharply increased, which resulted in a strengthening of our armed forces.

- Expenditures for social programs were sharply cut.

*Medicare and Medicaid are described in Chapter 14.

This massive cutback was the first large-scale federal reduction in social welfare expenditures in our country's history.

Businesses generally prospered during Reagan's presidency. The rich became richer, and the financial gap between the rich and the poor widened.[18] A lot of people, however, were hurt by the federal cutbacks in social welfare expenditures. The ones who were hurt the most, of course, were recipients of federally financed programs. Their financial payments and social services were either sharply reduced or eliminated. The level of health care provided to the indigent was reduced. There were fewer job-training and job-placement programs for the unemployed. Counseling services to the emotionally disturbed, the mentally retarded, the alcoholic, the drug addicted, and the single parent were cut back. Financial payments (food stamps, medicaid, and Aid to Families of Dependent Children) were cut back. Programs to help the elderly remain in their own homes (for example, meals on wheels) were cut back. Family planning services, particularly to the poor, were reduced. Rehabilitative and sheltered workshop programs for the emotionally disturbed, the mentally retarded, and the physically handicapped were cut back. Federal funding for education was reduced. The federal government placed less emphasis on affirmative action programs and on busing programs to achieve school integration.

In 1988 George Bush was elected president of the United States. He campaigned to continue the "peace and prosperity" of the Reagan administration. Bush has pledged to continue the same conservative approach to social welfare programs taken by the Reagan administration. Bush believes, as does Reagan, that the federal government is not a solution to social problems but in fact is part of the problem. By this he means that federally funded social welfare programs tend to make recipients dependent on the government and discourages them from being industrious and productive. With this philosophy it is unlikely that the Bush administration will seek to restore the cuts in social welfare programs that were made by the Reagan administration.

What will the longer-term effects of these cutbacks be? Many of our present social problems are intensifying: The proportion of people who are homeless has increased since Reagan and then Bush became president;[19] more citizens are hungry; in some cities, unemployed people are standing in food lines provided by voluntary organizations; efforts to reduce racial discrimination have slowed; our prisons are overflowing with convicted offenders; many of the chronically mentally ill have been released from mental hospitals and now are living in squalor without receiving supportive services; the plight of the people living in our inner cities is as bleak as when our inner cities erupted in the 1960s; there is a continuing increase in single-parent families; and environmental problems, such as acid rain and chemical waste hazards, are increasing.

Is this what we want? Our federal government has had a history of showing more, and then less, and then more concern for the needy. Presently, we are in a phase where the federal government is spending less for social welfare programs. It is likely that the plight of the needy will again (sometime in the future) become a major national concern. What it will take to reignite this concern is unclear.

There are currently a number of important issues in social welfare, such as: Should some of the cutbacks in federal support for social welfare programs be restored? What services and programs should be developed to combat the AIDS crisis? How can drug abuse (such as alcohol and cocaine abuse) be more effectively controlled? What new programs should be developed for the homeless? What new services should be provided to the chronically mentally ill, especially those who are living on the streets of our cities? How can crime be curbed more effectively and the correctional system be made more rehabilitative? What measures should be taken to eliminate racial discrimination? How can we meet the problems of our inner cities? Should black children-white parents transracial adoptions be encouraged? How should we remedy broken treaties to Native Americans, and what kinds of services need to be developed for Native Americans to alleviate the wide range of social problems they face? Should abortion laws be made more or less restrictive? Should a national health insurance program be established? How can child pornography be prevented? How can we help the physically impaired? How can we prevent the social security system from going bankrupt? How can we curb fraud in medicaid, AFDC, and other social welfare programs? How can child abuse, incest, and spouse abuse be curbed? How can we prevent suicides, especially the increasing number among teenagers? Should prostitution be legalized? What should be done about the teenage runaway problem?

Should busing to achieve racial integration be expanded or cut back? Do some affirmative action programs involve reverse discrimination against white males? What programs are needed to prevent rape? How can retirement living be made more meaningful? Do we really want to provide the funds and services that are necessary to break the cycle of poverty, or do we still believe that many poor people are undeserving in the sense that they would rather be on welfare than working?

The Future

The future direction and nature of social services will largely be determined by technological advances, primarily technological advances in other areas. Changes in our lifestyles are primarily determined by technological advances.[20] In the past 50 years the following advances have resulted in dramatic changes in our lifestyles: auto and air travel, nuclear power, television, birth control devices, automation, new electrical appliances, shopping centers, and the discovery of penicillin and other wonder drugs.

The relationship between technological breakthroughs and changes in social welfare programs generally follows this format: *technological advances largely determine changes in our lifestyles; lifestyle changes largely determine changes in our future social, financial, health, and recreational needs; and the latter changes largely determine what changes will be demanded in social service programs.*

Predicting what technological breakthroughs will occur and how these advances will affect our lifestyles is difficult and undoubtedly filled with error. A number of advances are being predicted: robots that talk and act like humans, space travel, computers capable of thinking, computers that diagnose medical illnesses and recommended treatments, vaccines that will prevent most forms of cancer, artificial hearts and kidneys, shopping from the home with two-way cable television,

weather and climate control, minicomputers in autos that tell the driver how each part of the car is working, lawn mowers and vacuum cleaners with a memory that are programmed to follow a route of mowing or cleaning, and visual telephones. Because there are now more scientists involved in technological research and development than at any other time in the history of civilization, future technological breakthroughs are apt to occur even more rapidly than in the past.[21] In fact, Alvin Toffler in *Future Shock* asserts that adjusting psychologically to rapid lifestyle changes is currently a major problem and will become the most difficult adjustment people will have to make in future years.[22]

In spite of predicted technological advances, it should be noted that environmentalists are predicting our civilization is in serious danger due to overpopulation, depletion of energy resources, likelihood of mass famines and starvation, and dramatic declines in the quality of life.

What the future will hold is difficult to predict accurately. The worst mistake, however, is to take the "ostrich head in the sand" approach in which no effort is made to plan and control the future.

To assist the reader in looking at the future, predicted changes in the American family will be summarized. This area is being selected because it is a key area for social welfare. When there is family breakdown, then social services are generally needed, and as the needs of families change, there is a corresponding demand to change social services.

DRAMATIC CHANGES FORESEEN IN THE AMERICAN FAMILY

In viewing the future of the American family, it is helpful to gain a perspective by taking a quick glance at some of the changes that have occurred in the past. Two hundred years ago marriages were primarily arranged by parents, with economic considerations being the most important determinant of who married whom. Two hundred years ago divorce was practically unheard of; now one out of two marriages ends in divorce or annulment.[23] Two hundred years ago women did not work outside the home, and children were an economic asset; now over 50 percent of married women work outside the home, and children are a financial liability.[24] Since colonial days the family has lost (or there has been a sharp decline in) a number of functions: educational, economic production, religious, protective, recreational, and combative.[25] Today, the two main functions that remain are the affectional or companionship and the childrearing functions.

In our fast-paced society the family is likely to change even more dramatically in the future. As in the past, the family is likely to be affected significantly by technological changes.[26] Labor-saving devices in the home (for example, electrical appliances) have in the past been and currently are an important factor in making it possible for both spouses to work outside the home. Birth control devices have undoubtedly been an important factor in leading to an increase in premarital sexual relationships and in extramarital affairs. Abortions now are important in leading to current reductions in illegitimate and unwanted pregnancies. This reduction has been a factor in sharply reducing the number of children available for adoption. A number of adoption agencies have suspended taking applications from couples desiring healthy white infants. Now, an ethically questionable business has developed where women are paid to deliver and give up their babies for adoption in order to meet the demands of infertile couples who want a child.[27] Women willing to bypass the normal adoption channels may sell an unwanted infant for as much as $20,000.[28]

In the future the American family is likely to be substantially affected by technological breakthroughs in biology and medicine. A few illustrations of scientific developments in these areas will be presented—developments that are as alarming as they are intriguing.

Biomedical Technology

ARTIFICIAL INSEMINATION   There are thousands of babies born annually in the United States through the process of artificial insemination, with the usage expected to continue to increase in the future.[29] Artificial

insemination is used widely in livestock breeding because it eliminates all the problems that can be associated with breeding. A breeder can transport a prized animal's frozen sperm across the world and raise a whole new herd of animals almost effortlessly.

Human sperm can be frozen for long periods of time (the length of time has not been determined; it is generally acknowledged that five years would be safe with close to 100 percent assurance). The sperm can then be thawed and used to impregnate a female. This new technology has led to the development of a unique new institution, the private sperm bank. The sperm bank is usually a private institution that has a couple of functions. It collects and maintains sperm for private citizens for a fee, depending on length of time. Usually, the sperm is withdrawn at some later date to impregnate (with a physician's assistance) a woman.

The sperm used in artificial insemination may be the husband's (called AIH). There may be several reasons for using AIH. It is possible to pool several ejaculations from a man with a low sperm count and to inject them simultaneously into the vaginal canal of his spouse, thus vastly increasing the chance of pregnancy. AIH may also be used for family planning purposes; for example, a man might deposit his sperm in the bank, then receive a vasectomy, and then later withdraw the sperm to have children. High-risk jobs (such as a danger of being exposed to radioactive material) might prompt a man to make a deposit in case of sterility or untimely death.

A second type of artificial insemination is called AID and involves the donor of the sperm being someone other than the husband. AID has been used for several decades to circumvent male infertility. It is also used when it is known that the husband is a carrier of a genetic disease (for example, a condition such as hemophilia). In recent years, an increasing number of single women who want a child but do not (at least for the near future) want a husband are requesting the services of a sperm bank. The usual procedure involves the woman requesting the general genetic characteristics she wants from the father and the bank then trying to match such requests from the information known about donors.

A third type of artificial insemination is of recent origin and has received considerable publicity. Some married couples, in which the wife is infertile, have contracted another woman to be artificially inseminated with the husband's sperm. Under the terms of the contract this "surrogate mother" is paid and is expected to give the infant to the married couple shortly after birth. (Surrogate motherhood is discussed in greater detail in the next section.)

There have been a number of ethical, social, and legal questions raised about artificial insemination. There are the objections from religious leaders that this practice is wrong, that God did not mean for people to reproduce in this way. In the case of AID, there are certain psychological stresses placed on husbands and on marriages, as the procedure emphasizes the husband's infertility and involves having a baby that he has not fathered. On a broader scale, artificial insemination raises such questions as: What are the purposes of marriage and of sex, and what will happen to male/female relationships if we do not even have to see each other to reproduce?

There have also been some unusual court cases that suggest new laws will have to be written to resolve the questions that are arising. For instance, there is the case of Mr. and Mrs. John M. Prutting. Mr. Prutting was medically determined to be sterile as a result of radiation exposure received at work. Without her husband's knowledge, Mrs. Prutting was inseminated. After the birth of the baby, he sued her for divorce on the grounds of adultery.[30]

In another case, a wife was artificially inseminated with the husband's consent by AID. The couple later divorced. When the husband requested child visiting privileges, his wife took him to court on the grounds that he was not the father and thus had no such right. In New York, he won; but she moved to Oklahoma, where the decision was reversed.[31]

And finally, there was a reported case of an engaged couple whose mothers were discovered to have had the same artificial insemination donor and were thus biologically half brother and sister. The marriage would have been incestuous and was therefore canceled.[32]

There are other possible legal implications. What happens if the AIH sperm at a bank is not paid for? Would it become the property of the bank? Could it be auctioned off? If a woman was artificially inseminated

by a donor and the child was later found to have genetic defects, could the parents bring suit against the physician, the donor, or the bank? Does the child have a right to know the identity of the father?

Sperm banks can also be used in genetic engineering movements. In the spring of 1980, it was disclosed that Robert Graham had set up an exclusive sperm bank to produce exceptionally bright children. Graham stated that at least five Nobel Prize winners had donated sperm to inseminate women. Several women have already given birth through the services of this bank.[33] This approach raises questions about whether reproductive technology should be used to produce "superior" children and what characteristics should be defined as superior.

SURROGATE MOTHERHOOD   Thousands of married couples who want children but are unable to reproduce because the wife is infertile have turned to surrogate motherhood. With this type of motherhood, a surrogate gives birth to a baby conceived by artificial insemination, using the husband's sperm. (Often the surrogate mother is paid a fee for her services.) On birth, the surrogate mother terminates her parental rights, and the child is then legally adopted by the sperm donor and his wife.

Couples using the services of a surrogate mother are generally delighted with this medical technique and believe it is a highly desirable solution to their personal difficulty of being unable to bear children. However, there are other groups who assert that surrogate motherhood raises a number of moral, legal, and personal issues.

A number of theologians and religious leaders firmly believe God intended conception to occur only among married couples through sexual intercourse. These religious leaders view surrogate motherhood as ethically wrong because the surrogate mother is not married to the sperm donor and because artificial insemination is viewed as "unnatural." Some religious leaders also assert that it is morally despicable for a surrogate mother to accept a fee (often from $5,000 to $10,000). They maintain that procreation is a blessing from God and should not be commercialized.

Surrogate motherhood also raises complicated legal questions that have considerable social consequences. For example, surrogate mothers usually sign a nonbinding contract stipulating that the mother will give up the child for adoption at birth. What if the surrogate mother changes her mind shortly before birth and decides to keep the baby? Women who have been surrogate mothers usually report that they become emotionally attached to the child during pregnancy.[34]

Most surrogate mothers to date are married and already have children. A number of issues are apt to arise. How does the husband of a surrogate mother feel about his wife being pregnant by another man's sperm? How does such a married couple explain to their children that their half brother or half sister will be given up for adoption to another family? How does such a married couple explain what they are doing to relatives, neighbors, and the surrounding community? If the child is born with severe mental or physical handicaps, who will care for the child and pay for the expenses? Will it be the surrogate mother and her husband, the contracting adoptive couple, or society?

In 1983 a surrogate mother gave birth in Michigan to a baby who was born with microcephaly, a condition in which the head is smaller than normal and mental retardation is likely. At first, neither the surrogate mother nor the contracting adoptive couple wanted to care for the child. The adoptive couple refused to pay the $10,000 fee to the surrogate mother. A legal battle ensued. Blood tests were eventually taken that indicated the probable father was not the contracting adoptive father but rather was the husband of the surrogate mother. Following the blood tests, the surrogate mother and her husband assumed the care of the child.

In 1986 Mary Beth Whitehead was a surrogate mother who gave birth to a child. She refused to give up the baby for adoption by the genetic father and his wife, even though she had signed a $10,000 contract in which she agred to give up the child. The genetic father, William Stern, took the case to court, requesting Whitehead to honor the contract she had signed. Whitehead claimed she was the mother of the child and therefore had maternal rights to the child. The case received national attention. In April 1987 in the nation's first judicial ruling on a disputed surrogate contract, the judge ruled the contract was valid because just as men have a constitutional right to sell their sperm, women

can decide what to do with their wombs.[35] Whitehead appealed this decision to the New Jersey State Supreme Court. In 1988 this court ruled that the contract between Whitehead and the Sterns was invalid because it involved the sale of a mother's right to her child, which violates state laws that prohibit child selling. This decision voided the adoption of the baby by Mrs. Stern; Mr. Stern was given custody, and Whitehead was granted visitation rights. Whether this decision will become the legal guideline for disputed surrogate contracts will be determined by future court decisions about surrogate contracts.

TEST-TUBE BABIES   In England, on July 24, 1978, Mrs. Lesley Brown gave birth to the first "test-tube baby." An egg taken from Mrs. Brown's reproductive system had been externally artificaly impregnated using AIH and then implanted in Mrs. Brown's uterus to complete the normal process of pregnancy. The technique is called embryo transfer and was developed for women whose fallopian tubes are so damaged that the fertilized egg cannot pass through the tubes to the womb as is necessary for it to develop and grow until birth. Following the announcement of this birth, there was a surge of applications from thousands of childless couples to fertility experts asking for similar implants.[36]

Another breakthrough in this area occurred in 1984 when an egg donated by one woman was fertilized and then implanted in another woman. Australian researchers in January 1984 reported the first successful birth resulting from a procedure in which an embryo was externally conceived and then implanted in the uterus of a surrogate.[37] This type of surrogate motherhood is a modern-day twist on the wet nurse of earlier times. An unusual application of this new technology occurred in 1987 in South Africa when a grandmother, Pat Anthony, gave birth to her own grandchildren. The daughter was infertile, so her daughter's eggs (which had been fertilized in the lab) were implanted into Ms. Anthony. Several months later Ms. Anthony gave birth to triplets.[38]

This type of surrogate motherhood differs from the earlier type in which the surrogate mother contributes half of the genetic characteristics through the use of her egg. Here, the surrogate contributes neither her own egg nor any of the genetic characteristics of the child.

BOX 1.3

Embryo Case Gains International Attention

A South American–born couple, Elsa and Mario Rios, amassed a fortune (several million dollars) in real estate in Los Angeles. In 1981 they enrolled in a "test-tube baby" program at Queen Victoria Medical Center in Melbourne, Australia, after their young daughter died. Several eggs were removed from Mrs. Rios and fertilized by her husband's sperm in a laboratory container. One of the fertilized eggs was implanted in Mrs. Rios's womb, but she had a miscarriage ten days later. The two remaining embryos were frozen so that doctors could try later at implantation.

On April 2, 1983, the couple was killed in the crash of a private plane in Chile. Because doctors have successfully thawed and implanted frozen embryos (which have resulted in births) a number of social and legal questions arise. These questions include the following:

Should the embryos be implanted in the womb of a surrogate mother in the hope that they will develop to delivery?

Are the embryos legal heirs to the Rios's multimillion dollar estate?

Does life legally begin at conception? If a surrogate mother carries the embryo to birth is she legally the mother, and is she entitled to some of the inheritance?

Do embryos conceived outside the womb have rights? If so, what rights? Should these rights be the same as those accorded humans? An Australian court ruled in 1987 that the embryo must be thawed and carried to term if a volunteer surrogate can be found; however, the offspring will not be viewed as being legally entitled to inherit their biological parents' estate.

This case highlights how the rapid advance of in vitro fertilization has outstripped attitudes and laws.

Sources: "Embryo Case Opens New Debate," *Wisconsin State Journal*, June 19, 1984, pp. 1–2; Stephen Budiansky, "The New Rules of Reproduction," *U.S. News & World Report*, April 18, 1988, pp. 66–67.

Surrogate pregnancies can, on one hand, be seen as the final step in the biological liberation of women. Like men, women can "sire" children without the responsibility of pregnancy and childbirth.

However, surrogate pregnancies promise to create a legal nightmare. Do the genetic mother and father have any binding legal rights? Can the genetic mother place reasonable restrictions on health, medical care, and diet during the pregnancy? Can the genetic mother require the surrogate mother not to smoke or drink? Could the genetic mother require the surrogate to abort? Could the surrogate abort despite the genetic mother's consent? Whose child is it if both the genetic mother and the surrogate mother want to be recognized as the legal mother after the child is born? Will the lower class and minorities serve as "holding tanks" for upper-class women's children? Legal experts see far-reaching changes in family law, inheritance, and the concept of legitimacy if laboratory fertilization and childrearing by surrogate mothers become accepted practices.

Human embryo transplants, when combined with principles of genetic selection, would allow people who want "superhuman" children to select embryos in which the resultant infant would have a high probability of being free of genetic defects and would also allow parents to choose, with a high probability of success, the genetic characteristics they desired—such as the child's sex, color of eyes and hair, skin color, probable height, probable muscular capabilities, and probable IQ. A superhuman embryo would be formed from combining the sperm and egg of a male and female who are thought to have the desired genetic characteristics. This breakthrough will raise a number of personal and ethical questions. Couples desiring children may be faced with the decision of having a child through natural conception, or of preselecting superhuman genetic characteristics through embryo transplants. Another question that will arise is whether our society will attempt to use this new technology to control human evolutionary development. If the answer is affirmative, decisions will need to be made about which genetic characteristics should be considered "desirable," and questions will arise about who should have the authority to make such decisions. Although our country may not want to control human evolutionary development in this manner, will we not feel it necessary to do so if a rival nation begins a massive evolutionary program? In addition, will parents have the same or somewhat different feelings toward children who result from embryo transplants compared to children who result from natural conception?

GENETIC SCREENING   Practically all states now require mandatory genetic screening programs for various disorders. There are about 2,000 human disorders caused by defective genes, and it is estimated that each of us carries two or three of them.[39] Mass genetic screening could eliminate some of these disorders. One screening approach that is increasingly being used with pregnant women is amniocentesis, a technique used to determine chromosomal abnormality. Amniocentesis is the surgical insertion of a hollow needle through the abdominal wall and uterus of a pregnant female to obtain amniotic fluid for the determination of chromosomal abnormality. More and more pregnant women are being pressured to terminate the pregnancy of a high-risk or proven genetically inferior fetus. Also, some genetic disorders can be corrected if caught in time.

Several years ago *Fortune* magazine carried an article with the heading "How to Save $100 Billion," which urged that genetic screening be used much more extensively to reduce the incidence of persons with genetic diseases. One quote follows: "If we allow our genetic problems to get out of hand by not acting promptly… we can run the risk of overcommitting ourselves to the care of and maintenance of a large population of mentally deficient patients at the expense of other urgent social problems."[40] Genetic screening programs raise serious questions regarding issues such as: Who shall live? Who shall be allowed to have children? Who shall make such decisions? Is this a direction our country ought to take?

The eugenics movement was proposed late in the 19th century and embraced by many scientists and government officials. Similar to today, eugenics was designed to improve humanity or individual races by encouraging procreation by those deemed "most desirable" and discouraging it in those judged "deficient." The movement fell into disfavor for a while when Adolf Hitler used it to justify the Holocaust, which exterminated millions of Jews, Gypsies, mentally retarded people, and others. Are we headed in a similar direction again?

CLONING   This term refers to the process whereby a new organism is reproduced from the nucleus of a single cell. The resultant new organism has the same genetic characteristics of the organism that contributes the nucleus; that is, it probably will be possible to make biological carbon copies of humans from a single cell. Biologically, each cell is a blueprint containing all the genetic code information for the design of the organism. Cloning has already been used to reproduce frogs, mice, cattle, sheep, and other animals.[41]

BOX 1.4

Mr. Mom: Men Can Give Birth

S cientists indicate the technology now exists to enable men to give birth! Male pregnancy
would involve fertilizing a donated egg with sperm outside the body. The embryo
would then be implanted into the bowel area, where it could attach itself to a major organ,
such as a kidney or the wall of the large intestine. In addition, to achieve pregnancy, men
would have to receive hormone treatment to stimulate changes that occur naturally in
women during pregnancy. Because the embryo creates the placenta, the embryo theoretically would receive sufficient nourishment. The baby would be delivered by cesarean
section.

Any attempt at male pregnancy would carry risks (perhaps some as yet unknown risks)
for both the man and the embryo. Will some men try it? If people risk their lives climbing
Mt. Everest, someone is apt to try this.

Source: "Mr. Mom," *Wisconsin State Journal*, May 9, 1986, sec. 1, p. 2.

One type of cloning amounts to a nuclear trans-
plant. The nucleus of an unfertilized egg is destroyed
and removed. The egg is then injected with the nucleus
of a body cell by one means or another. It should then
begin to take orders from the new master, begin to
reproduce cells, and eventually manufacture a baby
with the same genetic features as the donor. The embryo would need a place to develop into a baby—
either an artificial womb or a woman willing to supply
her own. The technology for a complete artificial
womb is not yet in sight. The resultant clone would
start life with a genetic endowment identical to that of
the donor, although learning experiences might alter
the physical development or personality. The possibilities are as fantastic as they are repulsive. Kenneth Denlinger dreams, "Imagine a basketball team of two
Kareem Abdul-Jabbars and three Jerry Wests. Or a football team with three Jim Browns in the backfield and
four Alan Pages on the defensive lines."[42] With a
quarter-inch piece of skin, one could produce 1,000
genetic copies of any noted scientist or of anyone else!

Cloning could, among other things, be used to resolve the ancient controversy of heredity versus environment. On the other hand, there are grave dangers
and undreamed-of complications. What is to prevent
the Adolf Hitlers from making copies of themselves?
Will cloning fuel the population explosion? What legal
rights will clones be accorded (inheritance, for example)? Will religions recognize clones as having a "soul"?
Who will decide who will be able to have clones made
of themselves? Couples may face the choice of having
children naturally or raising children who are copies
of themselves.

BREAKING THE GENETIC CODE   Biochemical genetics is
the discipline that studies the mechanisms whereby
genes control the development and maintenance of the
organism. Current research is focused on understanding more precisely the roles of DNA (deoxyribonucleic
acid) and messenger RNA (ribonucleic acid) in affecting
the growth and maintenance of humans. When genes,
DNA, and RNA are more fully understood, it may be

BOX 1.5

Will Fetal Tissue Be Used for Medical Treatments?

P ioneering surgery has demonstrated that fetal-tissue transplants can be used to replace damaged nerve cells successfully in victims of Parkinson's disease. Parkinson's disease is a neurological disorder that causes severe shaking and eventually death. Transplants of insulin-producing cells from fetuses show promise in treating sugar diabetes as well.

Will some women seek to abort a fetus so that the tissue can be used for such medical purposes? In January 1988 a woman appeared on Ted Koppel's "Nightline" television show and declared that she wanted to get pregnant for the sole purpose of aborting the fetus so that its tissue could be used to treat her father, who has Parkinson's disease. *U.S. News and World Report* (April 18, 1988) notes there is a woman who is seeking to conceive in order to abort the fetus to then use in treating her own diabetes.

Many people would find this use of reproductive technology to be horrifying. Yet, in most states there are no legal means to stop such activities—or to stop the even more outlandish possibility of selling fetal tissue.

Source: Stephen Budiansky, "The New Rules of Reproduction," April 18, 1988, pp. 66–69.

possible sometime in the future to keep people alive, young, and healthy almost indefinitely.[43] It is predicted that aging will be controlled, and any medical condition (for example, an allergy, obesity, cancer, arthritic pain) will be relatively easily treated and eradicated. Such possibilities stagger the imagination. Many legal and ethical issues will arise; perhaps the most crucial issues will be who will live and who will die and who will be permitted to have children. Such a fountain of youth may occur within our lifetime.

New Family Forms

It is hoped that such technological developments provide a perspective for some of the current and future influences on the American family. The current moral and ethical issues resulting from technological advances with birth control and abortion may well look "pale" in comparison to issues that apparently will soon arise.

At present the American family is experimenting with a number of new forms, some of which are apt to be found functional and satisfying and to become widely incorporated gradually. These new forms will briefly be mentioned, with the future determining which ones will endure.

CHILDLESS COUPLES ACCEPTED   In our society there is currently a myth (a belief with no rational basis) that something is wrong with a couple if they decide not have children. Having children is regarded both legally and religiously as one of the central components of a marriage. In some states deceiving one's spouse before marriage about the desire to remain childless is grounds for an annulment. Perhaps in the future this myth will be destroyed by the concern about overpopulation, by the high cost of raising children (the average cost now of raising a child from birth to age 18 is estimated to be over $140,000),[44] and by couples switching their interests from the domestic tasks related to raising children to other types of recreational, cultural, educational, and leisure-time experiences.

POSTPONING RAISING CHILDREN UNTIL MIDDLE AGE OR LATER   Biological innovations, such as growing embryos in laboratory controlled apparatus, will in the future permit couples the freedom to decide at what age they wish to raise children. Young couples today are often torn between a time commitment to their children and to their careers. In our society most couples now have children at the busiest time of their lives. Deferring raising children until later in life provides substantial activity and meaning to old age. A major question, of course, is whether such a family pattern will lead to a large increase in the number of parentless children due to death and perhaps have implications for services involving adoption and foster care. Another important question is whether such a pattern would lead to serious gaps in values between older parents and their young children.

PROFESSIONAL PARENTS   Alvin Toffler predicts that our society will develop a system of professional parents, trained and licensed, to whom a number of natural parents will turn for raising their children.[45] The natural parents would of course be permitted frequent visits, telephone contacts, and time to care for the children when they desired. Toffler states, "Even now millions of parents, given the opportunity, would happily relinquish their parental responsibilities—and not necessarily through irresponsibility or lack of love. Harried, frenzied, up against the wall, they have come to see themselves as inadequate to the tasks."[46] The high rates of child abuse, child neglect, and teenage runaways seem to bear out the assertion that in a large number of families the overall parent-child relationship is more

dissatisfying than satisfying.[47] Many parents are already partially using professional parents to raise their children in day-care centers.

In our society there is currently a myth that bioparents should care for their children, even when they find the responsibility dissatisfying. Only a tiny fraction of bioparents currently terminate their parental rights. Why? Could it be that many parents who have an unsatisfying relationship with their children are reluctant to give up their parenting responsibilities because of the stigma that would be attached? Two hundred years ago divorces were rare, mostly because of a similar stigma. Now, with an increased acceptance of divorce, more than one out of three marriages is being terminated. If a high rate of marital unions eventually becomes unsatisfying, is it not also reasonable to expect that a number of parents who have relatively little choice in the characteristics their children will possess may also find the relationships with their children to be more dissatisfying than satisfying? The point is reinforced when it is remembered that a number of pregnancies are both unplanned and unwanted.

SERIAL AND CONTRACT MARRIAGES   Culturally, religiously, and legally, marriages are still expected to be permanent, for a lifetime. Such a view implies that the two partners made the right decision when they married, that their personalities and abilities supplement and complement each other, and that their personalities and interests will develop in tandem for the rest of their lives. All of these suppositions (along with the permanency concept of marriage) are being called into question, partly by the high divorce rate.

With the high rate of divorce and also of remarriage, a number of sociologists have pointed out that a small proportion of our population is entering (perhaps unintentionally) into marriages that are serial in nature, that is, a pattern of successive, temporary marriages.[48] Serial marriages among movie celebrities have been widely publicized for a number of years. Viewing marriage as temporary in nature may be a factor in reducing some of the embarrassment and pain that is still associated with divorce today and may perhaps result in an increase in the number of unhappily married people who will seek a divorce. Divorce per se is neither good nor bad; if both partners find that their lives are happier and more satisfying following legal termination, the end result may well be viewed as desirable.

The high and increasing divorce rate has resulted in the development of extensive services involving premarital counseling, marriage counseling, divorce counseling, single-parent services and programs, and remarriage counseling for spouses and the children involved. If marriage is increasingly viewed as temporary in nature, divorce may become even more frequent and result in an expansion of related social services.

Several sociologists have proposed that the temporary conception of marriage be legally institutionalized by a contract marriage; for example, a couple would be legally married for a two-year period, and (only in those marriages where there are no children) the marriage would automatically be terminated unless the couple filed legal papers for a continuation.[49]

Another marital arrangement embodying the temporary marriage concept is "trial marriage," which is increasingly being tested out by young people. Living together without a ceremony usually means that a couple lives together on a day-by-day basis and shares expenses. Perhaps more common is the arrangement in which the man and woman maintain separate addresses and domiciles but for several days a month actually live together. (Perhaps this latter form is more accurately described as a "serial honeymoon" rather than a "trial marriage.") Acceptance of trial marriages is currently being advocated by some religious philosophers, and many states no longer define cohabitation as illegal.

There are increasing instances where courts are ruling that cohabiting couples who decide to dissolve their nonmarital living arrangements have certain legal obligations to one another similar to the obligations of a married couple. For example, in a much publicized case in 1979 a California court judge ruled that actor Lee Marvin must pay $104,000 to a woman with whom he cohabited for six years.

OPEN MARRIAGES   George and Nena O'Neill contrast traditional marriages with an emerging new type, "open marriage," which they advocate.[50] A traditional or "closed marriage," the O'Neills assert, embodies such concepts as (*a*) possession or ownership of mate; (*b*) denial or stifling of self; (*c*) playing the couples game by doing everything together during leisure time; (*d*) the man being dominant and out in the world and the woman being domestic, passive, and staying at home with the children; and (*e*) absolute fidelity. An open marriage, in contrast, offers freedom to pursue individual interests, flexible roles in meeting financial responsibilities, shared domestic tasks, and expansion and growth through openness. Such a marriage is based on open communication, trust, and respect. Individual growth and expansion are encouraged, and it is expected that one partner's growth will facilitate the other partner's development.

Marriage counselors are increasingly seeing couples where serious interaction difficulties occur because one spouse has a traditional orientation, whereas the other has an open marriage orientation. The emerging feminist movement and the changing roles of women in our society have brought into public awareness the conflict between open and closed marriages. Marriage counselors are now seeing large numbers of couples where the wife wants a career, her own identity, and a sharing of domestic responsibilities, whereas the husband, having a traditional orientation, wants his wife to stay at home and take care of the domestic tasks.

GROUP MARRIAGES   This form of marriage provides insurance against isolation. In the 1960s and 1970s hundreds of communes composed of young people were in existence. In the later 1970s and 1980s most communes among young people were disbanded. The goals, as well as the structure of these communes, varied widely, involving diverse social, political, religious, or recreational objectives.

Interestingly, geriatric communes (group marriages of elderly people) are now being advocated by a number of sociologists.[51] Such marriages may be a solution to a number of social problems of the aged. They may provide companionship, new meaning and interest to their lives, and an arrangement in which elderly people with reduced functioning capacities can be of mutual assistance to each other. In such a living arrangement the elderly can band together, pool resources, hire nursing or domestic help if needed, and

In the last few years gay parenting has led to an unforeseen kind of baby boom. Although some couples still face legal obstacles as adoptive and foster parents, many others, like this lesbian couple, have chosen to have their own babies, often through artificial insemination procedures.

have the feeling that "life begins at 60." In nursing homes a fair number of the elderly are presently developing relationships that have similarities to a group marriage.

HOMOSEXUAL MARRIAGES AND ADOPTIONS   Gay liberation groups have been formed in this country that seek to inform the public about the "naturalness" of this form of sexual expression and that are attempting to change current legislation.[52] England has already rewritten its statutes; homosexual relations between con-

senting adults in that country are no longer considered a crime. A number of marriages between homosexuals have taken place in churches in this country, in Europe, and in other countries. (It should be noted that no state in this country as yet recognizes homosexual marriages as legal.)

In the future, adoption agencies and the courts may face decisions about whether placing children for adoption with married homosexuals is to be permitted. Such a decision may center around whether homosexual relationships are to be regarded as "natural" or "unnatural," with opponents perhaps being hardpressed to demonstrate that homosexual activities have undesirable consequences. Single people are already being permitted by some agencies and courts to adopt children, so the argument that a child needs both a male and a female figure in the family is diluted.

TRANSRACIAL ADOPTIONS   Oriental and American Indian children have been adopted by white parents for the past four decades.[53] About 25 years ago some white couples began adopting black children. A number of questions have arisen about the desirability of this type of placement, which brings together into a family unit the two polar races in our society. To answer some of these questions, Charles Zastrow compared the satisfactions derived and problems encountered between transracial adoptive parents and inracial adoptive parents.[54] The outcome of transracial adoptions was found to be as satisfying as inracial adoptions. In addition, transracial adoptive children were found to have been accepted by relatives, friends, neighbors, and the general community following placement. The transracial adoptive parents reported that substantially few problems have arisen due to the race of the child than even they anticipated before the adoption. They also indicated they had the parental feeling that the child was really their own following placement, and they reported becoming "color blind" following placement; for example, they came to see the child not as black, but as an individual who is a member of their family.

Unfortunately, none of the children in the study were older than six years. Some observers, a number of whom are black, have raised questions about whether black children reared by white parents will experience serious identity problems as they grow older; for example, will they experience difficulty in deciding which race to identify with, difficulty in learning how to cope with racial discrimination due to being raised in a white home, and difficulty in interacting with both whites and blacks due to a speculated confused sense of who they are. On the other hand, advocates of transracial adoption respond to these questions by asserting that the parent-child relationship is more crucial to identity formation than the racial composition of the members of the family. The question of course is critical, especially because there are a large number of homeless black children and a shortage of black adoptive parents.

Two research studies in the 1980s provide a few answers to some of the many questions that have been raised about the outcome of transracial adoptions. Both studies were conducted on preadolescent and adolescent transracially adopted children. R. J. Simon and H. Altstein conclude:

It is clear that the extraordinary glowing happy portrait that we painted seven years ago now has some blemishes on it. It shows some signs of stress and tension. For every five families in which there are the usual pleasures and joys along with sibling rivalries, school-related problems, and difficulties in communication between parent and child, there is one family whose difficulties are more profound.[55]

One difficulty reported by some parents was that the adopted child had a tendency to steal from other family members. A few parents reported that they experienced guilt either because integrating a child of a different race into the family had absorbed so much of their time that they didn't have enough time for their biological children or because the family had so rearranged its lifestyle that the biological children felt left out. A key finding, however, was that the vast majority of the adoptive families felt their adoptive experiences had brought commitment, happiness, and fulfillment to their lives.

R. G. McRoy and L. A. Zurcher found there were no differences in overall self-esteem between the adolescent transracially adopted children and the adolescent inracially adopted children in their study.[56] However,

Will minority children reared by white parents face identity problems as they grow up? Most adoptive parents will tell you that the parent-child bond is far more important in determining a child's identity than the family's racial composition.

they did find that racial identity seemed to be more of a problem for the black children who were being reared by white parents; such children were more likely to identify themselves as being adopted and to use racial self-referents. In addition, 86 percent of the white parents who adopted racially mixed children in the study stressed that their child was "biracial" and that they were reluctant to accept the notion that the child would be socially and legally defined as belonging to the black race. This finding raises a question whether such parents will be able to fulfill their child's need to feel positive about his or her black identity.

In the 1960s and early 1970s, a number of black children were placed for adoption with white parents. In the 1970s, some of the minority advocacy groups (such as the National Association of Black Social Workers) opposed transracial adoptions, and the number of transracial adoptive placements sharply declined. Now, partly because of the large number of minority children available for adoption and the shortage of black couples applying for black children, there has been a resurgence of interest in transracial adoption. The question of whether transracial adoptions should or should not be encouraged has again become a national issue. Elizabeth Cole notes:

A major research study on transracial adoption, published in 1976, reported that transracial placements had all but ceased to be made in the United States. Since agencies no longer had to grapple with this controversial issue, they turned their attention to other matters. The public's interest in the practice of placing children for adoption across racial lines diminished as well. . . .

The issue of transracial adoption is being debated now. *We hope that it will not cause polarization. What we need is a more balanced view and a search for a clearer perception of the problems and solutions. We must do something to reduce the number of minority youngsters coming into care.*[57]

COMARITAL SEX   The term *comarital sex* refers to mate swapping and other organized extramarital relations in which both spouses agree to participate. Comarital sex is distinctly different from a traditional extramarital affair, which is usually clandestine, as the spouse involved in the affair tries to hide its occurrence from the other spouse.

Although some couples appear to be able to integrate comarital agreements into their lives successfully, others find their marriages breaking up as a consequence.[58] According to marriage counselors a major reason couples drop out of such comarital relationships and sometimes end their marriage is because of

such emotional reactions as jealousy, competition, and possessiveness.[59]

The interest in comarital sex and extramarital sex raises the age-old question of whether any one individual can satisfy all of the intimate sexual and interpersonal needs of another. This question may have become somewhat moot in the new sexual (or nonsexual) climate created by AIDS. That is, an individual may not be having his or her needs met fully in a monogamous relationship, but that individual is now less likely to be inclined to have an affair. (The effect of AIDS on sexuality and relationships is discussed again later in this chapter.)

SINGLE PARENTHOOD   Although marriage and parenthood are in many people's minds viewed as going together, single parenthood is emerging as a prominent form in our society. There are several ways to become a single parent. In many states it is possible for unmarried people to adopt a child. Another way is for an unmarried, pregnant woman to refuse to marry and yet to keep her child after it is born. Some unmarried fathers have been successful in obtaining custody of their child. Today the negative stigma attached to being single and pregnant is not as strong as it once was, but it is still seriously frowned on by some.

A form close to single parenthood is the one-parent family, in which a person divorces or legally separates, assumes custody of one or more children, and chooses not to remarry. Although it has traditionally been the mother who has been awarded custody of the children, today the courts are granting custody to an increasing number of fathers. Another arrangement that is emerging is shared custody, where both the mother and the father have their children part of the time.

Do single parents and one-parent families pose a serious problem for society? Are children adversely affected by being raised in a one-parent family? No definitive answers are yet available. It is clear, however, that one-parent families are increasing.[60]

BLENDED FAMILIES   As reported earlier, one out of two marriages now ends in divorce. A number of divorcees have parented children while married. Most people who obtain a divorce remarry someone else in a few years. Some people are marrying for the first time but have parented a child while single. A variety of blended families are now being formed in our society. In blended families one or both spouses have biologically parented one or more children with someone else prior to the current marriage. In many blended families the newly married couple gives birth to additional children. In some blended families the children are biologically a combination of "his, hers, and theirs."

In blended families a number of adjustments have to be made. The husband or wife (or both) have to adjust to raising children that are biologically parented by someone else. The children in blended families have to form relationships with their biological half brothers and half sisters. The children in such families also often have to adjust to a prior divorce. Many of the children in blended families have to form relationships with a biological parent who is absent from the home and with a new stepparent. An ex-spouse is apt to have visitation rights and thus will have an impact on the family. If ex-spouses are still feuding, they may use the children as "pawns" to create problems, which then generates extensive strife and turmoil in families.

Blended families are increasing in number and proportion in our society, and the family dynamics and relationships are much more complex than in the traditional nuclear family. The stereotypes of stepparents are changing. From Cinderella and other fairy tales we came to view stepparents as being "mean and ugly." Our society is gradually recognizing that stepparents are playing a valuable, positive role in raising the children in our society.

THE SINGLE LIFE   In our society women, and to some extent men, are brought up to believe that one of their most important goals is to marry. Women who remain unmarried are labeled "old maids." Elaborate rituals have been developed to romanticize engagement and marriage. Unfortunately, many couples discover after the honeymoon that marriage is neither romantic nor exciting and that it may even become monotonous, dull, and constricting. A number of people are currently dealing with unfulfilled marriages by a series of divorces and remarriages. In the 1970s and early 1980s an increasing number of adults turned away from the responsibilities and restrictions of marriage by remaining single. Temporary and sometimes long-term deep emotional relationships were entered into without the duties and restrictions imposed by a legal arrangement.

At present there appears to be a shift in sexual values. The sexual revolution that began in the 1960s and that glamorized multiple recreational sexual relationships appears to be on the decline. The current renewed interest in sharply limiting the number of sexual partners is largely due to the fear of acquiring AIDS. People are recognizing that the more sexual partners they have, the greater are their chances of being exposed to the AIDS virus.

It is unclear at this point whether the threat of AIDS will lead to a decline in the number of people who choose to remain single. It should be noted that increases in the number of people who remain single has significant implications for social welfare, as statistics show higher rates of depression, loneliness, alcoholism, suicide, drug abuse, and alienation among those who are single.

To summarize, it appears that the family of tomorrow will face a future shock. Technological developments (particularly in biology and medicine—for example, cloning and human embryo implants) may dramatically affect the family, raising a number of ethical, legal, social, and personal questions. In addition, the family is experimenting with a number of different forms that may dramatically alter the central characteristics of future families. Among the forms are childless couples, postponement of raising children until middle age or later, professional parents, serial and contract marriages, one-parent families, blended families, comarital sex, open marriages, group marriages for all age groups, homosexual marriages and adoptions, transracial adoptions, and remaining single. Other changes being experimented with are interracial marriages and marriages involving partners of unequal ages. Because of technological advances and the experimentation with new family forms, the style of living for all families may be substantially changed. Some will probably find these changes exciting, personally satisfying, and functional; others may be less adaptable and find such changes extremely difficult and perhaps even overwhelming, resulting in personal disintegration. In any case, changes that are made in the American family will have important implications for the field of social welfare.

SUMMARY

The goal of social welfare is to fulfill the social, financial, health, and recreational needs of everyone in a society. The provision of social services has become one of the most important activities in our society in terms of the money spent, the human misery treated, and the number of people served.

Social welfare overlaps with sociology, psychology, and other disciplines on a knowledge base level. When theories and research in other academic disciplines have direct applications to the social welfare goal of enhancing the social functioning of people, then this knowledge is also part of the knowledge base of social welfare.

Social welfare overlaps with social work at a practice (service) level. Almost all social workers are employed in the field of social welfare, but there are also many other professional and occupational groups that are employed within this field. Social welfare is erroneously conceived at times as synonymous with public assistance; yet public assistance is only one of several hundred social welfare programs.

Social welfare institutions are composed of social service programs and social service organizations. The purposes of social welfare institutions are to prevent, alleviate, or contribute to the solution of recognized social problems so as to directly improve the well-being of individuals, groups, and communities.

Currently, there are two conflicting views of the role of social welfare in our society: the residual versus the institutional orientation. The residual approach characterized social welfare programs from early history to the depression of the 1930s, at which time programs with an institutional orientation began to be implemented. Social welfare programs have in the past been influenced, and to some extent still are, by the Protestant ethic, the laissez-faire economical view, social Darwinism, individualism, the Industrial Revolution, and humanitarian ideals.

There are apt to be important changes in the social welfare field in the future, perhaps largely due to anticipated technological advances. In summary form, technological advances largely determine changes in our lifestyles; lifestyle changes largely determine changes in our future social, financial health, and recreational needs; and the latter changes largely determine changes in needed social service programs.

Dramatic changes are anticipated in the American family of the future, due to technological advances in biology and medicine and to the current experimentation with new family forms. Some of these new forms are apt to be found dysfunctional and will be discarded, whereas others will be found satisfying and functional and will probably be incorporated into the "typical" family of the future. The anticipated technological advances and the adoption of new family forms will result in the creation of new social service programs and the expansion of certain existing programs. Unless such changes are carefully examined and planned, our society faces a future shock.

NOTES

1. Ralph Dolgoff and Donald Feldstein, *Undergraduate Social Welfare* (New York: Harper & Row, 1980).
2. National Association of Social Workers, *Encyclopedia of Social Work*, vol 2 (New York: NASW, 1971), p. 1446.
3. *The American Heritage Dictionary*, 2d College Edition (Boston: Houghton Mifflin, 1982).
4. Ibid.
5. National Association of Social Workers, *Standards for Social Service Manpower* (New York: NASW, 1983), pp. 4–5.
6. Alfred Kahn, *Shaping the New Social Work* (New York: Columbia University Press, 1973), pp. 12–34.

7. Ibid., p. 10.

8. Harold Wilensky and Charles Lebeaux, *Industrial Society & Social Welfare* (New York: Free Press, 1965).

9. Ibid., p. 138.

10. Ibid., p. 139.

11. Lester F. Ward, *Dynamic Sociology*, reprint of 1883 ed. (New York: Johnson Reprint, 1968).

12. W. Trattner, *From Poor Law to Welfare State: A History of Social Welfare in America* (New York: Free Press, 1974).

13. Beulah Compton, *Introduction to Social Welfare & Social Work* (Homewood, IL: The Dorsey Press, 1980).

14. Trattner, *From Poor Law to Welfare State*.

15. J. M. Romanyshyn, *Social Welfare: Charity to Justice* (New York: Random House, 1971).

16. U.S. Bureau of the Census, *Statistical Abstract of the United States: 1987* (Washington, D.C.: U.S. Government Printing Office, 1987).

17. Romanyshyn, *Social Welfare: Charity to Justice*.

18. Joseph Julian and Willian Kornblum, *Social Problems*, 5th ed. (Englewood, Cliffs, NJ: Prentice-Hall, 1986), pp. 202–204.

19. Hank Whittemore, "We Can't Pay the Rent," *Parade Magazine*, January 10, 1987, pp. 4–6.

20. W. F. Ogburn and M. F. Nimkoff, *Technology and the Changing Family* (New York: Houghton Mifflin, 1955).

21. Alvin Toffler, *Future Shock* (New York: Bantam Books 1970), p. 27.

22. Ibid.

23. U.S. Bureau of the Census, *Statistical Abstract of the United States, 1987* (Washington, D.C.: U.S. Government Printing Office, 1987), p. 80.

24. Ibid., p. 414.

25. Ogburn and Nimkoff, *Technology and the Changing Family*.

26. Ibid.

27. Ann Rundell, "It's Hard to Find White Babies to Adopt," *Wisconsin State Journal*, February 6, 1972, sec. 7, p. 4.

28. Philip Reilly, *Genetics, Law, and Social Policy* (Cambridge, MA: Harvard University Press, 1977), p. 190.

29. "CBS Reports—The Baby Makers" (television program, October 1979).

30. L. Rifkin, *Who Should Play God?* (New York: Dell Publishing, 1977).

31. Ibid.

32. Ibid.

33. "Exclusive Sperm Bank Rekindles Controversy," *Wisconsin State Journal*, March 1, 1980, sec. 1, p. 7.

34. Ron Seely, "Love for Baby Changed Surrogate's Views," *Wisconsin State Journal*, December 20, 1986, sec. 3, p. 2.

35. "Dad Wins Custody of Baby M," *Wisconsin State Journal*, April 1987, p. 1.

36. "A Rush of Test-Tube Babies," *U.S. News & World Report*, August 7, 1978, p. 22.

37. "Healthy Baby is Born from Donated Embryo," *Wisconsin State Journal*, February 4, 1984, sec. 1, p. 2.

38. Stephen Budiansky, "The New Rules of Reproduction," *U.S. News & World Report*, April 18, 1988, pp. 66–69.

39. Reilly, *Genetics, Law, and Social Policy*.

40. G. Bylinsky, "What Science Can Do about Hereditary Disease," *Fortune*, September 1974, pp. 148–160.

41. William R. Wineke, "Calves Cloned Successfully in UW Experiment," *Wisconsin State Journal*, September 9, 1987, p. 1.

42. Kenneth Denlinger, "Science Could Reproduce a Namath," *Washington Post*, February 8, 1972, p. 7.

43. David M. Rorvik, "Making Men and Women without Men and Women," *Esquire*, April 1969, pp. 110–115.

44. Beth Brophy, "Children under Stress," *U.S. News & World Report*, October 27, 1986, p. 59.

45. Toffler, *Future Shock*.

46. Ibid., pp. 243–244.

47. Alfred Kadushin, *Child Welfare Services*, 3d ed. (New York: Macmillan, 1980).

48. Ethel Alpenfels, "Progressive Monogamy: An Alternate Pattern?" in *The Family in Search of a Future*, ed. Herbert Otto (New York: Appleton-Century-Crofts, 1970), pp. 67–74.

49. Ibid.

50. George O'Neill and Nena O'Neill, *Open Marriage* (New York: M. Evans, 1971).

51. Victor Kassel, "Polygamy after Sixty," *Geriatrics*, vol 21, April 1966.

52. Carl Wittman, "A Gay Manifesto," *Liberation*, February 1970.

53. David Fanshel, *Far from the Reservation* (Metuchen, NJ: Scarecrow Press, 1972).

54. Charles Zastrow, *Outcome of Black Children-White Parents Transracial Adoptions* (San Francisco: R & E Research Associates, 1977).

55. Rita J. Simon and Howard Altstein, *Transracial Adoption: A Follow-Up* (Lexington, MA: D.C. Heath, 1981).

56. Ruth G. McRoy and Louis A. Zurcher, *Transracial and Inracial Adoptees: The Adolescent Years* (Springfield, IL: Charles C. Thomas, 1983).

57. Elizabeth Cole, "Transracial Adoption: A Matter of Balance," *Permanency Report*, Winter, 1987, pp. 1, 4.

58. Brian Gilmartin and D. V. Kusisto, "Some Personal and Social Characteristics of Mate-Sharing Swingers," in *Renovating Marriage*, eds. R. Libby and R. Whitehurst (San Francisco: Concensus Publishers, 1973), pp. 146–166.

59. Duane Denfeld, "Dropouts from Swinging," *The Family Coordinator*, January 1974, pp. 45–49.

60. Julian and Kornblum, *Social Problems*, p. 339.

2

SOCIAL WORK AS A PROFESSION AND A CAREER

S ocial work is one of the primary professions that provides social welfare services. This chapter will:

- Define the profession of social work.

- Provide a brief history of social work.

- Describe the following social work activities: casework, case management, group work, group therapy, family therapy, and community organization.

- Describe the following role models for social work practice: enabler, broker, advocate, and activist.

- Describe the person-in-environment conceptualization for social work practice.

- Summarize societal stereotypes of social workers.

- Summarize the knowledge, skills, and values needed for social work practice.

- Briefly describe educational training for social work practice.

A MULTISKILLED PROFESSION

Social work is the professional activity of helping individuals, groups, or communities to enhance or restore their capacity for social functioning and to create societal conditions favorable to their goals.[1] A social worker is a "change agent" who works with individuals, groups, families, and communities. The term *social worker* is generally applied to graduates (with either a bachelor's degree or a master's degree) of schools of social work who are employed in the field of social welfare.

Social work is distinct from other professions (such as psychology and psychiatry), as it is the profession that has the responsibility and mandate to provide social services.

A social worker needs training and expertise in a wide range of areas to be able to handle effectively the problems faced by individuals, groups, families, and the larger community. Whereas most professions are increasingly becoming more specialized (for example, nearly all medical doctors now specialize in one or two areas), social work continues to emphasize a generic (broad-based) approach. The practice of social work is analogous to the old, now fading practice of general medicine. A general practitioner in medicine had training to handle a wide range of common medical problems faced by people; a social worker has training to handle a wide range of common social and personal problems faced by people. The case example in Box 2.1 highlights some of the skills needed by social workers.

This "success" story (in most cases the outcome is not as fully successful) documents a wide range of abilities displayed by Mr. Tounsend: interviewing skills, knowledge of how to counsel people with sexual problems and feelings of depression effectively, ability to work effectively with other agencies, premarital counseling skills, research and grant-writing skills, program development and fund-raising skills, and knowledge of how to handle ethical/legal issues that arise.

Perhaps the most basic skill that a social worker needs is to be able to counsel clients effectively. If one is not able to do this, one should probably not be in social work, certainly not in direct service. Probably the second most important skill is to be able to interact effectively with other groups and professionals in the area. A social worker, like a general practitioner, should have a wide range of skills and intervention techniques that will enable him or her to intervene effectively with (a) the common personal and emotional problems of clients and (b) the common social problems faced by groups and the larger community. Social workers also need to have an accurate perception of their professional strengths and weaknesses. If a situation arises that a worker knows she or he does not have the training or expertise to handle, then the worker needs to be a "broker" and link those affected with available services.

A BRIEF HISTORY OF SOCIAL WORK

Social work as a profession is of relatively recent origin. To attempt to meet the needs of people living in urban areas, the first social welfare agencies began to be developed in the early 1800s. These agencies, or services, were private agencies that were developed primarily at the initiation of the clergy and religious groups. Up until the early 1900s these services were provided exclusively by members of the clergy and well-to-do "do-gooders" who had no formal training and little understanding of human behavior or how to help people. The focus was on meeting such basic physical needs as food and shelter and attempting to "cure" emotional and personal difficulties with religious admonitions.

An illustration of an early social welfare organization was the Society for the Prevention of Pauperism, founded by John Griscom in 1820.[2] This society aimed to investigate the habits and circumstances of the poor, to suggest plans by which the poor could help themselves, and to encourage the poor to save and economize. Among the remedies used were house-to-house visitation of the poor (a very elementary type of social work).

By the late half of the 1800s there were a fairly large number of private relief agencies that had been established in large cities to help the unemployed, the poor, the ill, the physically and mentally handicapped, and orphans. Programs of these agencies were uncoordinated and sometimes overlapped. Therefore an English invention—the Charity Organization Society (COS)—caught the interest of a number of American cities.[3] Starting in Buffalo, New York, in 1877, COS was rapidly adopted in many cities. In charity organization societies, private agencies joined together to (a) provide direct services to individuals and families—in this respect they were forerunners of social casework and of family counseling approaches—and (b) plan and coordinate the efforts of private agencies to meet the pressing social problems of cities—in this respect they were precursors of community organization and social planning approaches. Charity organizations conducted a detailed investigation of each applicant for services and financial help, maintained a central system of registration of clients to avoid duplication, and used volunteer "friendly visitors" extensively to work with those in difficulty. The friendly visitors were primarily "doers of good works," as they generally gave sympathy rather than money and encouraged the poor to save and to seek employment. Poverty was looked on as the

Early social welfare agencies, developed at the initiation of the clergy, stressed industry and thrift. Dr. Thomas John Barnardo, a British evangelical missionary who opened a house for outcast boys in London in 1871, promoted his programs with "before" and "after" photographs in which little vagrants became little workmen once they received food and shelter. Barnardo's pictures were an important fund-raising tool: some 55,000 images, all taken between 1870 and 1905, helped make the Barnardo Homes one of the largest charity organizations in Victorian England.

result of a personal shortcoming. Most of the friendly visitors were women.

Concurrent with the COS movement was the establishment of settlement houses in the late 1800s. Toynbee Hall was the first settlement house established in 1884 in London; many others were soon formed in larger U.S. cities. Many of the early settlement house workers were daughters of ministers. The workers were from the middle and upper classes who would live in a poor neighborhood so they could experience the harsh realities of poverty. Simultaneously, they sought to develop ways, in cooperation with neighborhood residents, to improve living conditions. In contrast to "friendly visitors" they lived in impoverished

neighborhoods and used the missionary approach of teaching residents how to live moral lives and improve their circumstances. They sought to improve housing, health, and living conditions; find jobs; teach English, hygiene, and occupational skills; and change environmental surroundings through cooperative efforts. Settlement houses used change techniques that are now called social group work, social action, and community organization.

Settlement houses placed their emphasis on "environmental reform," and at the same time "they continued to struggle to teach the poor the prevailing middle-class values of work, thrift, and abstinence as the keys to success."[4] In addition to dealing with local

BOX 2.1

A Case Involving Suicide and Sex Deviancy

D r. John Pritchard referred Dick Cherwenka to the Riverland Counseling Center (a mental health center). Mr. Cherwenka had briefly been hospitalized after slashing his wrists. This case was assigned to Tom Tounsend, MSW (master's degree in social work), who in the recent past had counseled most of the agency's attempted suicide cases. At the first two sessions Mr. Cherwenka presented an unusual account of the events that led to his slashing his wrists.

His main problem centered around his desire to fondle the genitals of young girls (9 to 12 years old) whenever he felt depressed, tense, or at a "low tide." In the past four years he had been arrested on three occasions for this offense. The last time, eleven months ago, he was placed on probation for two years, and the judge warned he would be sentenced to prison for an indeterminate sentence as a "sex deviant" if there were a recurrence of the offense. The afternoon of the evening in which he slashed his wrists, he had felt quite depressed. While driving home from work he stopped at a playground and began talking to a young girl. He offered her a ride home and she accepted. Instead he drove out into the country where he fondled her. The girl was terrified. Mr. Cherwenka then drove her back, dropped her off a few blocks from her home, and informed her that serious harm would come to her if she told anyone. Mr. Cherwenka, after thinking about what he had done, became even more depressed and slashed his wrists a few hours later.

The worker at this point informed Mr. Cherwenka that he (the worker) faced an ethical/ legal question of whether the police should be informed and in the near future would have to discuss his obligations with the director of the agency. Mr. Cherwenka indicated he understood and proceeded to relate the following account of why he believed he developed the desire to fondle young girls.

He had normal childhood experiences until age 8, when his mother died. After his mother's death, his father continued to raise him and his sister, who was 14 months older than he. However, his father changed; he became bitter toward life and began drinking heavily. In the evening he was at times in a drunken stupor. During these times he would be abusive, verbally and physically, to his children. Dick and his sister became very fearful of their father when he was drunk and sought ways to hide from him. Gradually, they learned to hide together under a blanket. While fearful and tense under the blanket, they sought ways to occupy their time and reduce their fear; thereby they began fondling each other. Mr. Cherwenka indicated this activity of hiding and fondling under a blanket when their father was drunk lasted for nearly three years, until an aunt moved into their home and began raising them.

The social worker agreed with Mr. Cherwenka that his present desires to fondle young girls apparently resulted from his past learning experiences of coping with unwanted emotions. The problems that needed to be dealt with now were (*a*) what ethical/legal obligations Mr. Tounsend and the mental health center had in regard to this admitted offense; (*b*) how to prevent Mr. Cherwenka from fondling young girls in the future; (*c*) how to help Mr. Cherwenka handle unwanted emotions; (*d*) how to prevent Mr. Cherwenka from desiring to take his life in the future; and (*e*) because Mr. Cherwenka was engaged and planning to marry in two months, an additional situation that needed to be handled was his future relationship with his fiancée.

After two more meetings, the following treatment plan was developed and then implemented. Mr. Tounsend discussed the ethical/legal obligations of this case with the agency director. It was decided that the probation department needed to be informed. Mr. Tounsend discussed this decision with Mr. Cherwenka. Mr. Tounsend then arranged a meeting with Mr. Cherwenka and his probation officer. Following this meeting it was agreed that the offense would be noted, but proceedings to revoke Mr. Cherwenka's probation would not be initiated as long as Mr. Cherwenka remained in counseling and no other offenses occurred.

The problems of preventing Mr. Cherwenka from fondling young girls and from taking his life in the future were then dealt with. It was agreed that whenever Mr. Cherwenka had strong desires to fondle young girls or to take his life, he should call Mr. Tounsend (day or night), who would then meet with him. (If such immediate counseling could not be arranged, counseling over the telephone would be provided.) If Mr. Cherwenka could not reach Mr. Tounsend, or if after counseling he still had desires to fondle young girls or to take his life, he agreed to admit himself as an inpatient to the mental health center until his desires subsided. (During the next fourteen months, Mr. Cherwenka did voluntarily admit himself on three occasions.)

Gradually, by using rational therapy (described in Chapter 4), Mr. Cherwenka gained better control of his feelings of depression and his other unwanted emotions. Several meetings with Mr. Cherwenka and his fiancée were also held. After the initial shock of learning about Mr. Cherwenka's interest in young girls, the two fully discussed their relationship and agreed to postpone their marriage for a year, while continuing the engagement.

As indicated earlier, this case was only one of several potential suicide cases that Mr. Tounsend was handling. These cases led him to the conclusion that an emergency telephone number was needed that would be widely publicized and would be staffed twenty-four hours a day with professional counselors. He gathered data on the number of suicides in the area in the past year and obtained information from hospitals in the community about the number of attempted suicides. This data supported the need for an emergency counseling service. Mr. Tounsend then wrote a grant proposal, and after ten months of searching for funding, his proposal was funded by a joint grant from the United Way and the Easter Seals Society.

Jane Addams

problems by local action, settlement houses played important roles in drafting legislation, and in organizing to influence social policy and legislation. The most noted leader in the settlement house movement was Jane Addams of Hull House in Chicago (see Box 2.2).

It appears the first paid social workers were executive secretaries of charity organization societies in the late 1800s.[5] In the late 1800s charity organization societies received some contracts from the cities in which they were located to administer relief funds. In administering these programs, COS hired people as executive secretaries to organize and train the friendly visitors and to establish accounting procedures to show accountability for the funds received. To improve the services of friendly visitors, executive secretaries

needed to establish standards and training courses. In 1898 a training course was first offered for charity workers by the New York Charity Organization Society. By 1904 a one-year program was offered by the New York School of Philanthropy. Soon after this time, colleges and universities began offering training programs in social work.

Richard Cabot introduced medical social work into Massachusetts General Hospital in 1905.[6] Gradually social workers were employed in schools, courts, child guidance clinics, and other settings.

Early training programs in social work focused both on environmental reform efforts and on efforts to change individuals to adjust better to society.

In 1917 Mary Richmond published *Social Diagnosis*, a text that presented for the first time a theory and methodology for social work.[7] The book focused on how the worker should intervene with individuals. The process is still used today and involves study (collecting information), diagnosis (stating what is wrong), prognosis, and treatment planning (stating what should be done to help clients improve). This book was important because it formulated a common body of knowledge for casework.

In the 1920s, Sigmund Freud's theories of personality development and therapy became popular. The concepts and explanations of psychiatrists appeared particularly appropriate for social workers, who also worked in one-to-one relationships with clients. The psychiatric approach emphasized intrapsychic processes and focused on enabling clients to adapt and adjust to their social situations. Therefore, social workers switched their emphasis from "reform" to "therapy" for the next three decades. In the 1960s, however, there was a renewed interest in sociological approaches, or reform, by social workers. Several reasons account for this change. Questions arose about the relevance and appropriateness of "talking" approaches with low-income clients, who tend to be nonverbal and who have urgent social and economic pressures. Furthermore, the effectiveness of many psychotherapeutic approaches has been questioned.[8] Other reasons for the renewed interest include the increase in status of sociology and the mood of the 1960s, which raised questions about the relevancy of social institutions in

BOX 2.2

Jane Addams: A Prominent Founder of Social Work

Jane Addams was born in 1860 in Cedarville, Illinois, the daughter of a successful couple who owned a flour mill and a wood mill. Jane graduated from Rockford Seminary (a college in Rockford, Illinois). She briefly attended medical school but was forced to leave because of illness. She then traveled for a few years in Europe, perplexed about what her life work should be. At the age of 25 she joined the Presbyterian Church, which helped her find a focus for her life—religion and humanitarianism and in particular, serving the poor. (Later in her life she joined the Congregational Church, now known as the United Church of Christ.) Addams heard about the establishment of Toynbee Hall in England and returned to Europe to study this approach. Its staff was composed of college students and graduates, mainly from Oxford, who lived in the slums of London to learn conditions first-hand and to contribute to the improvement of life in the slums with their own financial and personal resources.

Addams returned to the United States and rented a two-story house (later called Hull House) in Chicago. Hull House was located in an impoverished neighborhood. With a few friends, Addams initiated a variety of group and individual activities for the community. Group activities included a literature reading group for young women, a kindergarten, and groups with the following foci: social relationships, sports, music, painting, art, and discussion of current affairs. Hull House also provided services to individuals who came asking for immediate help, such as food and shelter and information and referral for other services. A Hull House Social Science Club was formed, which studied social problems in a scientific manner and then became involved in social action efforts to improve living conditions. One of its successful efforts was to work for passage of Illinois legislation to prevent the employment of children in the sweatshops of the area. Addams also became interested in the various nationality groups in the neighborhood around Hull House. She was fairly successful in bringing the various nationalities together at Hull House, where they could interact and interchange cultural values.

The success of Hull House served as a model for the establishment of settlement houses in other areas of Chicago and in many other large cities in the United States. Settlement house leaders believed that by changing neighborhoods, they would improve communities and through altering communities, they would develop a better society. For her extraordinary contributions, Jane Addams received the Nobel Prize for Peace in 1931.

Source: Herbert Stroup, "Jane Addams," in *Social Welfare Pioneers* (Chicago: Nelson-Hall Publishers, 1986), pp. 1–29. Reprinted by permission.

Hull House, the prototype for settlement houses in cities across the United States, is shown in this photograph taken about 1910. The complex is now a part of the campus of the University of Illinois at Chicago.

meeting the needs of the population. Social work at present embraces both the reform approach and the therapy approach.

Not until the end of World War I did social work begin to be recognized as a distinct profession. The depression of the 1930s and the enactment of the Social Security Act in 1935 brought about an extensive expansion of public social services and job opportunities for social workers. Since 1900 there has been a growing awareness by social agency boards and the public that professionally trained social workers are needed to provide social services competently. In 1955 the National Association of Social Workers was formed, which represents the social work profession in this country. The purpose of this association is to improve social conditions in society and promote high quality and effectiveness in social work practice. The association publishes (*a*) several professional journals, with the most noted being *Social Work*; (*b*) *The Encyclopedia*

of Social Work; and (*c*) a monthly newsletter entitled *NASW News*. The newsletter has current social work news information and also a list of position vacancies throughout the country.

Currently, there is considerable interest in developing a system of registration or licensing of social workers. Professionals in medicine, law, teaching, and nursing are required to have an official license or a certificate or to be registered before they can provide a professional service. In Germany, Austria, France, and Sweden social workers need a license to practice. It is being argued that a system of registration or licensing in social work would assure the public that qualified personnel are providing social work services and would also advance the recognition of social work as a profession. Most states have now passed legislation to license or regulate the practice of social work. Although a young profession, social work is growing and gaining increased respect and recognition.

PROFESSIONAL ACTIVITIES

Social work and social welfare activities constitute one of the most important functions in our society in terms of the number of people affected, the human misery treated, and the amount of money spent.[9] There are several types of professional social work activities.

Social casework is aimed at helping individuals, on a one-to-one basis, to meet personal and social problems. Casework may be geared to helping clients adjust to their environment or to changing certain social and economic pressures that are handicapping an individual. A few illustrations of the activities of a caseworker include helping individuals and families with a wide variety of personal difficulties; securing financial aid as well as needed social services; counseling the handicapped, such as the mentally ill, the blind, and the disabled; counseling juveniles and adults in correctional settings; placing children in foster homes or arranging for their adoption; and working in medical and mental hospitals as a member of a rehabilitation team. Casework is practiced in a wide variety of agencies, including hospitals; mental health clinics; courts; family counseling centers; adoption agencies; day-care centers; public welfare departments; child guidance clinics; nursing homes; maternity homes; schools; neighborhood centers; and institutions for the aged, for criminals and delinquents, for the mentally ill and retarded, and for dependent and handicapped children.

Case management, as the term suggests, involves the management of a number of cases by a worker. Case management is increasingly becoming a prominent form of social work practice. In recent years a number of social service agencies have identified their social workers as being *case managers*. The tasks performed by case managers are often similar to those performed by caseworkers. The job descriptions of case managers vary from service area to service area. For example, case managers in a juvenile probation setting are highly involved in supervising their clients, providing counseling, monitoring clients to make certain they are following the rules of probation, linking clients and their families with needed services, preparing court reports, and testifying in court. On the other hand, case managers at a sheltered workshop are apt to be involved in providing job training to clients, counseling clients, arranging transportation, disciplining clients for unacceptable behavior, advocating for clients, and being a liaison with the people who supervise clients during their nonwork hours (which may be at a group home, foster home, residential treatment facility, or with their parents). D. H. Hepworth and J. Larsen describe the role of a case manager as follows:

Case managers link clients to needed resources that exist in complex service delivery networks and orchestrate the delivery of services in a timely fashion. Case managers function as brokers, facilitators, linkers, mediators, and advocates. A case manager must have extensive knowledge of community resources, rights of clients, and policies and procedures of various agencies and must be skillful in mediation and advocacy.[10]

Case management is used in a variety of settings: probation and parole; public welfare; mental health; residential treatment facilities; and sheltered workshops.

Group work is designed to further the intellectual, emotional, and social development of individuals through group activities. In contrast to casework or group therapy, it is not primarily therapeutic, except in a broad sense. Different groups have different objectives: for example, promoting socialization and information exchange, curbing delinquency, facilitating recreation, changing socially unacceptable values, and helping to achieve better relations between cultural and racial groups. For example, a group worker at a neighborhood center may, through group activities, seek to curb delinquency patterns and change socially unacceptable values. Or a worker at an adoption agency may meet with a group of applicants to explain adoption procedures and to help applicants prepare for becoming adoptive parents. Activities and focuses of groups vary: arts and crafts, dancing, games, dramatics, music, photography, sports, nature study, woodwork, first aid, home management, information exchange, and discussion of such topics as politics, sex, marriage, religion, and selection of a career. Group work is used in such settings as Boy Scouts and Girl Scouts, YMCAs and YWCAs, schools, churches, child

Group work is utilized by a wide variety of institutions with equally wide-ranging objectives. This community center offers emergency shelter, counseling, support groups, recreational activities, and educational and career guidance to homeless teenagers in the San Franciso Bay Area.

welfare agencies, Red Cross agencies, community centers, playgrounds, camps, and in most institutions.

Group therapy is aimed at facilitating the social and emotional adjustment of individuals through the group process. Participants in this kind of group usually have personal difficulties. Group therapy has, within the past two decades, been used much more extensively. It has several advantages over one-to-one counseling, such as the operation of the "helper therapy" principle, which maintains it is therapeutic for the helper (who can be any member of a group) to feel she or he has been helpful to others. In contrast to one-to-one counseling, group pressure is often more effective in changing maladaptive behavior of individuals, and group therapy is a time saver because it enables the therapist to treat several people simultaneously. A few examples in which group therapy might be used are situations in which individuals are severely depressed, have an eating disorder, have drinking problems, are victims of a rape, are psychologically addicted to drugs, have a terminally ill relative, are single and pregnant, or are recently divorced. Group therapy is used in such settings as mental hospitals, mental health clinics, family counseling agencies, correctional institutions, maternity homes, hospitals, and residential facilities for youth.

Family therapy can be considered as one type of group therapy and is aimed at helping families with interactional, behavioral, and emotional problems that arise. Examples include parent-child interaction problems, marital conflicts, and conflicts with grandparents. A wide variety of problems are dealt with in family therapy or family counseling, such as disagreements between parents and youth on choice of friends, drinking, pot smoking, domestic tasks at home, curfew hours, communication problems, sexual values and be-havior, study habits and grades received, and choice of dates. Family therapy is used in such settings as family counseling agencies, adoption and foster care agen-cies, mental hospitals, mental health clinics, school social work settings, and residential treatment centers.

Community organization is the process of stimu-lating and assisting the local community to evaluate, plan, and coordinate its efforts to provide for the com-munity's health, welfare, and recreation needs. Perhaps it is not possible to define precisely the activities of a community organizer; but such activities are apt to in-clude encouraging and fostering citizen participation; coordinating efforts between agencies or between groups, public relations, and public education; re-searching; planning; and being a resource person. A community organizer acts as a catalyst in stimulating and encouraging community action. Agency settings where such specialists are apt to be located include community welfare councils, social planning agencies, health planning councils, and community action agen-cies. The term *community organization* is now being replaced in some settings by such terms as *planning, social planning, program development*, and *policy development*.

Administration involves directing the overall pro-gram of a social service agency. Administrative func-tions include setting agency and program objectives, analyzing social conditions in the community and mak-ing decisions about what services will be provided, employing and supervising staff members, setting up an organizational structure, administering financial af-fairs, and securing funds for the agency's operations. In a small-sized agency these functions may be carried out by one person, whereas in a larger agency several people may be involved in administrative affairs.

Other areas of professional activity in social work include research, consulting, planning, supervision, and teaching (primarily at the college level).

There used to be an erroneous conceptualization that a social worker was either a caseworker, a group worker, or a community organizer. Practicing social workers know such a conceptualization is faulty; every social worker is involved as a change agent in working with individuals, groups, families, and community groups. The amount of time spent at these various lev-els varies from worker to worker, but every worker will, at times, be assigned and expected to work at these four levels and therefore needs training at all of them.

ROLE MODELS FOR SOCIAL WORK PRACTICE

In working with individuals, groups, families, and com-munities, a social worker is also expected to be knowl-edgeable and skillful in using a variety of role models. The particular role model that is selected for use (ide-ally) should be determined by what will be most effec-tive given the circumstances.

ENABLER   In this role a worker *helps* individuals or groups to articulate their needs, to clarify and identify their problems, to explore resolution strategies, to se-lect and apply a strategy, and to develop their capacities to deal with their own problems more effectively. This role model is perhaps the most frequently used ap-proach in counseling individuals, groups, and families. The model is also used in community organization primarily when the objective is to "help people orga-nize to help themselves."

BROKER   A broker links individuals and groups who need help (and do not know where help is available) with community services. For example, a wife who is frequently physically abused by her husband may be referred to a shelter care program for battered women. Nowadays, even moderate-sized communities have 200 or 300 social service agencies/organizations pro-viding community services. Even human service pro-fessionals are often only partially aware of the total service network in their community.

ADVOCATE   The role of an advocate has been borrowed from the law profession. It is an active, directive role in which the social worker is an advocate for a client or for a citizen's group. When a client or a citizen's group is in need of help and existing institutions are uninterested (and sometimes openly negative and hostile) in providing services, then the advocate's role may be appropriate. In such a role the advocate provides leadership for collecting information, for arguing the correctness of the client's need and request, and for challenging the institution's decision not to provide services. The object is not to ridicule or censure a particular institution but to modify or change one or more of its service policies. In this role the advocate is a partisan who is exclusively serving the interests of a client or of a citizen's group.

ACTIVIST   An activist seeks basic institutional change; often the objective involves a shift in power and resources to a disadvantaged group. An activist is concerned about social injustice, inequity, and deprivation. Tactics involve conflict, confrontation, and negotiation. Social action is concerned with changing the social environment to meet the recognized needs of individuals. The methods used are assertive and action oriented (e.g., organizing welfare recipients to work toward improvements in services and increases in money payments). Activities of social action include fact finding, analysis of community needs, research, the dissemination and interpretation of information, organization, and other efforts to mobilize public understanding and support in behalf of some existing or proposed social program. Social action activity can be geared at a problem that is local, statewide, or national in scope.

EDUCATOR   In addition to these role models it is important for social workers to be skilled at public speaking and public education. Potential clients and service providers are often unaware of present services or gaps in services. Social workers occasionally talk to a variety of groups (e.g., high school classes, public service organizations such as Kiwanis, police officers, staff at other agencies) to inform them of available services or to advocate the need to develop new services for clients having unmet needs. In recent years new services have been identified as being needed (e.g., runa-

way centers, services for battered women, rape crisis centers, group homes for youth, services to help the elderly remain in their homes rather than go into a nursing home, and services to those who test positive to the AIDS virus and to those who have AIDS). In some settings social workers also have the role of educator/ teacher. For example, social workers who work with functionally or socially impaired individuals at times need to teach clients independent living skills.

GENERALIST PRACTICE

All baccalaureate social work educational programs that are accredited by the Council on Social Work Education (the national accrediting organization for BSW and MSW programs) are required to train their students for *generalist practice*. Generalist practice social workers are trained to assess and treat people (who have a variety of social and personal problems) with a large number of assessment and intervention techniques. D. Brieland, L. B. Costin, and C. R. Atherton define and describe generalist practice as follows:

The generalist social worker, the equivalent of the general practitioner in medicine, is characterized by a wide repertoire of skills to deal with basic conditions, backed up by specialists to whom referrals are made. This role is a fitting one for the entry-level social worker.

The generalist model involves identifying and analyzing the interventive behaviors appropriate to social work. The worker must perform a wide range of tasks related to the provision and management of direct service, the development of social policy, and the facilitation of social change. The generalist should be well grounded in systems theory that emphasizes interaction and independence. The major system that will be used is the local network of services. . . .

The public welfare worker in a small county may be a classic example of the generalist. He or she knows the resources of the county, is acquainted with the key people, and may have considerable influence to accomplish service goals, including obtaining jobs, different housing, or emergency food and clothing. The activities of the urban generalist are more complex, and more effort must be expended to use the array of resources.[11]

Joseph Anderson has identified three assumptions about generalist social work: (*a*) the generalist is often the first professional to see clients as they enter the social welfare system; (*b*) the worker must therefore be competent to assess their needs and to identify their stress points and problems; and (*c*) the worker must draw on a variety of skills and methods in serving clients.[12]

PRIVATE PRACTICE OF SOCIAL WORK

Although the vast majority of social workers are employed by agencies (financed by either public or private funds), a growing number of social workers in the past two decades have provided counseling (also called psychotherapy) and group therapy on a fee basis. This type of practice has been called private practice. The arrangement is similar to the arrangement in which private physicians provide services to patients.

The social worker may conduct a private practice on a part-time basis in addition to working full time for an agency; or, the worker may work full time in private practice. Sometimes social workers form a partnership with psychologists and/or psychiatrists to provide psychotherapy and group therapy through a private, for-profit clinic. In yet another private practice arrangement, social workers may be employed by a private clinic (which may be owned by a psychologist or psychiatrist) to provide therapy to individuals and to groups. Different states have different laws that regulate the structure and operation of private clinics and private practice. Such legislation is intended to protect the public. These laws usually require that the social worker in private practice needs to have a master's

degree from an accredited school of social work, as well as a few years of supervised practice in counseling individuals and groups.

In most cases fees for therapy received are paid by recipients' health insurance policies. If recipients do not have health insurance coverage, they are expected to pay their own fees for the therapy they receive.

A 1988 *Newsweek* article notes there is a renewed interest by undergraduate and graduate students in seeking a degree in social work and makes the following observations:

Today the profession is focusing increasingly on the middle class and its maladies—a shift due in part to the Reagan administration's severe cuts in social-service spending for the poor. The field still appeals to those with a strong social conscience, especially now that problems such as AIDS, homelessness and sexual abuse of children have high visibility. But several new specialties—notably occupational social work and psychotherapy—attract a new breed of professionals who want to help themselves while helping others. Although starting salaries for M.S.W.'s average only about $19,000, a therapist in private practice can make $60,000 or more a year. Says Robert Roberts, dean of the School of Social Work at the University of Southern California: "They have found you can be an altruist and still drive a BMW."[13]

AN ECOLOGICAL MODEL OF HUMAN BEHAVIOR

From the 1920s to the 1960s most social work programs used a medical model approach to assess and change human behavior. The medical model approach was developed by Sigmund Freud.

The medical model approach views clients as being "patients." The task of the provider of services is first to diagnose the causes of a patient's problems and then provide treatment. The patient's problems are viewed as being inside the patient.

In regard to emotional and behavioral problems of people, the medical model conceptualizes such problems as being "mental illnesses." The medical model identifies two major categories of mental illness—psychosis and neurosis—and classifies a number of disorders under each of these. People with emotional or behavioral problems are given medical labels, such as schizophrenic, psychotic, neurotic, or insane. Adherents of the medical approach believe the disturbed person's mind is affected by some generally unknown, internal condition. That unknown, internal condition is thought to be due to a variety of possible causative factors: genetic endowment, metabolic disorders, infectious diseases, internal conflicts, unconscious uses of defense mechanisms, and traumatic early experiences that cause emotional fixations and prevent future psychological growth.

The medical model approach provided a more humane approach to treating people with emotional and behavioral problems. Prior to Freud, the emotionally disturbed were thought to be possessed by demons, viewed as being "mad," blamed for their disturbances, and often treated by being beaten or locked up. The medical model approach emphasized intrapsychic processes and focused on enabling patients to adapt and adjust to their social situations.

In the 1960s social work began questioning the usefulness of the medical model. Environmental factors were shown to be at least as important in causing a client's problems as internal factors. Research also was demonstrating that psychoanalysis was probably ineffective in treating clients' problems.[14]

In the 1960s social work shifted at least some of its emphasis to a reform approach. A reform approach seeks to change systems to benefit clients. The antipoverty programs, such as Headstart and the Job Corps, are examples of efforts to change systems to benefit clients.

In the past several years social work has increasingly focused on using an ecological approach. This ecological approach integrates both treatment and reform by conceptualizing and emphasizing the dysfunctional transactions between people and their physical and social environments. Human beings are viewed as developing and adapting through transactions with all elements of their environments. An ecological model gives attention to both internal and external factors. An ecological model does not view people as being passive reactors to their environments but rather as being involved in dynamic and reciprocal interactions with them.

An ecological model tries to improve the coping patterns of people and their environments so that a better match can be attained between an individual's needs and the characteristics of his or her environment. One emphasis of an ecological model is on the person-in-environment. The person-in-environment conceptualization is depicted in Figure 2.1. People interact with many systems, some of which are shown in the figure. With this conceptualization, social work can focus on three separate areas. First, it can focus on the person and seek to develop his or her problem-solving, coping, and developmental capacities. Second, it can focus on the relationship between a person and the systems he or she interacts with and link the person with needed resources, services, and opportunities. Third, it can focus on the systems and seek to reform them to meet the needs of the individual more effectively.

The ecological model views individuals, families, and small groups as having transitional problems and needs as they move from one life stage to another. Individuals face many transitional changes as they grow older. Examples of some of the transitions are learning to walk, entering first grade, adjusting to puberty, graduating from school, finding a job, getting married, having children, having children leaving home, and retiring.

Families also have a life cycle. The following are only a few of the events that require adjustment: engagement, marriage, birth of children, parenting, children going to school, children leaving home, and loss of a parent (perhaps through death or divorce).

Small groups also have transitional phases of development. Members of small groups spend time getting acquainted, gradually learn to trust each other, begin to self-disclose more, learn to work together on tasks, develop approaches to handle interpersonal conflict, and face adjustments to the group eventually terminating or some members leaving.

FIGURE 2.1

Person-in-Environment Conceptualization

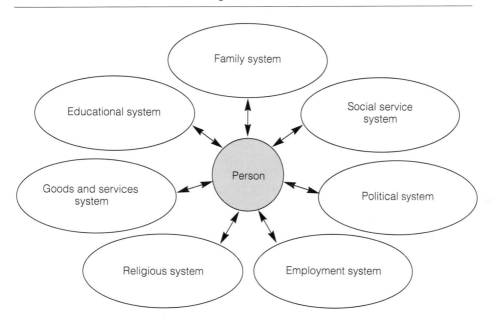

A central concern of an ecological model is to articulate the transitional problems and needs of individuals, families, and small groups. Once these problems and needs are identified, intervention approaches are then selected and applied to help individuals, families, and small groups resolve the transitional problems and meet their needs.

An ecological model can also focus on the maladaptive interpersonal problems and needs in families and groups. It can seek to articulate the maladaptive communication processes and dysfunctional relationship patterns of families and small groups. These difficulties cover an array of areas, including interpersonal conflicts, power struggles, double binds, distortions in communicating, scapegoating, and discrimination. The consequences of such difficulties are usually maladaptive for some members. An ecological model seeks to identify such interpersonal obstacles and then apply appropriate intervention strategies. For example, parents may set the price for honesty too high for their children. In such families children gradually learn to hide certain behaviors and thoughts and even learn to lie. If the parents discover such dishonesty, an uproar usually occurs. An appropriate intervention in such a family is to open up communication patterns and help the parents to understand that if they really want honesty from their children, they need to learn to be more accepting of their children's thoughts and actions.

Two centuries ago people primarily interacted within the family system. Families were nearly self-sufficient. In those days, the "person-in-family" was a way of conceptualizing the main system that individuals interacted with. Our society has become much more complex. Today, a person's life and quality of life are interwoven and interdependent on many systems, as shown in Figure 2.1.

Do-gooders, bleeding hearts, and steely bureaucrats are just a few of the stereotypes many people hold about social workers. Ideally, they are individuals who bring their training, experience, and humanity to bear on the seemingly infinite problems that people face in everyday life.

GOALS OF SOCIAL WORK PRACTICE

Social work practice has been conceptualized as having the following four primary goals.[15]

GOAL 1: *Enhance the Problem-Solving, Coping, and Developmental Capacities of People* Using the person-in-environment concept, the focus of social work practice

at this level is on the person. With this focus a social worker primarily serves as an *enabler.* In the role of an enabler the worker may take on activities of a counselor, teacher, caregiver (that is, providing supportive services to those who cannot fully solve their problems and meet their own needs), and behavior changer (that is, changing specific parts of a client's behavior).

GOAL 2: *Link People with Systems that Provide Them with Resources, Services, and Opportunities* Using the person-in-environment concept, the focus of social work practice at this level is on the relationships between persons and the systems they interact with. With this focus a social worker primarily serves as a *broker.*

GOAL 3: *Promote the Effectiveness and Humane Operation of Systems that Provide People with Resources and Services* Using the person-in-environment concept, the focus of social work practice at this level is on the systems with which people interact. One role a worker may fill at this level is that of advocate. Additional roles at this level are:

Program developer: In this role the worker seeks to promote or design programs or technologies to meet social needs.

Supervisor: The worker seeks in this role to increase the effectiveness and efficiency of the delivery of services through supervising other staff.

Coordinator: The worker seeks in this role to improve a delivery system through increasing communication and coordination between human service resources.

Consultant: The worker seeks in this role to provide guidance to agencies and organizations through suggesting ways to increase the effectiveness and efficiency of services.

GOAL 4: *Develop and Improve Social Policy* Similar to goal 3, the focus of social work practice at this level is on the systems with which people interact. The distinction between goal 3 and goal 4 is that the focus of goal 3 is on the available resources for serving people, whereas the focus of goal 4 is on the statutes and broader social policies that underlie such resources. Major roles of social workers at this level are *planner* and *policy developer*. In these roles workers develop and seek adoption of new statutes or policies and propose elimination of ineffective or inappropriate statutes and policies. In these planning and policy development processes social workers may take on an advocate role and in some instances an activist role.

A PROBLEM-SOLVING APPROACH

In working with individuals, families, groups, and communities, social workers use a problem-solving approach. Steps in the problem-solving process can be stated in a variety of ways. A simple way of describing this process is:

1. Identify as precisely as possible the problem or problems.
2. Generate possible alternative solutions.
3. Evaluate the alternative solutions.
4. Select the solution or solutions to be used, and set goals.
5. Implement the solution(s).
6. Follow up to evaluate how the solution(s) worked.

SOCIAL WORK STEREOTYPES

The image of a social worker has undergone a more rapid change than perhaps any other profession. Fifty years ago there was a stereotype of a social worker as a moralistic upper-middle-class older lady, carrying a basket of food, who had little understanding of the people she tried to help. The image is much more positive today, reflecting the improved professional nature of the training and services provided. The image is also much more varied. Melvin Glasser listed several stereotypes of social workers held by different segments of the population.

- The social worker is a kind, warm, generous, helpful person who makes it possible for people to live richer, more satisfying lives.
- The social worker is a frustrated maiden lady who meddles in other people's business.
- The social worker is a knowledgeable, dedicated crusader for the needs of all people, particularly the underprivileged.
- The social worker is a radical whose real underlying motive is to bring about a change in the social order.
- The social worker is a hardhearted, denying administrator of rules and regulations who checks on people to see that they don't cheat the agency.
- The social worker is a professional whose training and experience enable him or her to help with a wide range of problems people have in everyday living.[16]

Ralph Dolgoff and Donald Feldstein summarize some other social work stereotypes.

Depending upon who is doing the "name calling," social workers are referred to in many ways: do-gooders, bleeding hearts, radicals intent on changing our society, captives of and apologists for "the establishment," organizers of the poor, and servers of the middle class. All these are ways in which people stereotype social workers and the functions they perform in society.[17]

No doubt there are other stereotypes.

KNOWLEDGE, SKILLS, AND VALUES

If a social worker is to provide clients with competent service, the worker must have *knowledge, skills*, and *values* that are consistent with effective practice. (The reader is not expected to have a comprehensive understanding of the material covered in this section. This material is only presented to introduce the reader to the essential knowledge, skills, and values for social work practice.)

Knowledge Base

Knowledge has been defined as the "acquaintance with or theoretical or practical understanding of some branch of science, art, learning, or other area involving study, research, or practice, and the acquisition of skills."[18] To describe the knowledge base a social worker should have, a summary of a conceptual formulation developed by Alfred Kadushin will be presented.[19]

GENERAL SOCIAL WORK KNOWLEDGE   This general knowledge can be categorized into three broad areas:

1. Social welfare policy and services, including content on social problems, social services designed to prevent and treat such problems, service gaps, contemporary social issues; content on how social policy is formulated, forces affecting policies, how to critically analyze and change social policy; and the role of the social worker in formulating policy.

2. Human behavior and the social environment, including content on human growth, personality development (both normal and abnormal); cultural values and norms; community processes; and other aspects influencing the social functioning of individuals and groups.

3. Methods of social work practice, including intervention strategies in casework, group work, and community organization; and content on research and administration.

KNOWLEDGE ABOUT A SPECIFIC PRACTICE FIELD   For example, a worker in the mental health field must have a knowledge of:

- The various theories on why some people develop emotional problems.

- What the contributions of hereditary and social learning factors are.

- How to assess and diagnose emotional disorders.

- The various treatment programs that are available in the community.

- How to assess when a person should be institution-

alized, and the negative effects of labeling and long-term institutionalization on a person.

- How to analyze the merits and shortcomings of various treatment programs critically.

- The effects of psychotropic drugs on people (for example, tranquilizers and antidepressant drugs).

- How to treat clients with contemporary psychotherapy theories, such as psychoanalysis, reality therapy, rational therapy, transactional analysis, and behavior modification.

KNOWLEDGE ABOUT A SPECIFIC AGENCY   A social worker at a mental health center, for example, has to have information about the following:

- What the eligibility requirements are for clients to receive services.

- What the procedures are for admitting a client for inpatient services.

- What the required court procedures are for admitting someone against their consent (involuntary commitment).

- Who is to pay for the services that clients receive.

- What records are to be kept for accountability purposes.

- What the processes are for placing a client in foster care or in a group home.

- What the expected role of a social worker is in working as a team member with psychiatrists, psychologists, nurses, occupational therapists, and other professionals.

- What specific modes of treatment are used by the agency in working directly with individuals, families, and groups.

- What specific treatment programs are provided by the agency and what the expected role of the social worker is in each of these programs.

KNOWLEDGE ABOUT EACH CLIENT   The worker needs to know in detail the following information:

- The specific personal and/or social problems faced by each client.

- Background information on each client, such as age, early childhood development, family relationships, school history, employment history, contact with other social agencies, and general health.

- The contributing factors to the client's problems, such as financial, peer pressure, school or employment relationships, family pressures, racial or ethnic factors, friendship relationships, life goals, interests, and meaningful activities.

- Client's perception and definition of his or her problems.

- Client's set of values and morals that influence these problems.

- Client's strengths, along with shortcomings, in being able to cope with the problems.

- Client's motivation to want to improve his or her circumstances.

- Knowledge about possible treatment strategies for each client's particular problems.

Skill Base

Skill is the *ability* to use knowledge effectively and readily in execution or performance. B. L. Baer and R. Federico have developed an elaborate list of skills needed for beginning-level social work practice, some of which will be listed here.[20]

Observing activities and situations.

Collecting data.

Analyzing data.

Identifying social problems.

Listening.

Communicating effectively.

Interviewing.

Providing information.

Interacting with others.

Clarifying attitudes and feelings.

Clarifying implications of choices.

Supporting and encouraging.

Motivating others.

Teaching others.

Identifying goals.

Selecting appropriate intervention strategies.

Monitoring service delivery.

Contracting.

Mediating.

Advocating.

Referring persons.

Relating to colleagues.

Case recording.

Assessing one's own intervention activities.

Federico has indirectly described social work skills by outlining the following roles and activities:[21]

Outreach worker: Reaching out into the community to identify needs and follow up referrals to service contexts.

Broker: Knowing services available and making sure those in need reach the appropriate services.

Advocate: Helping specific clients obtain services when they might otherwise be rejected, and helping to expand services to cover more needy persons.

Evaluation: Evaluating needs and resources, generating alternatives for meeting needs, and making decisions between alternatives.

Teacher: Teaching facts and skills.

Mobilizer: Helping to develop new services.

Behavior changer: Changing specific parts of a client's behavior.

Consultant: Working with other professionals to help them be more effective in providing services.

Community planner: Helping community groups plan effectively for the community's social welfare needs.

Caregiver: Providing supportive services to those who cannot fully solve their problems and meet their own needs.

Data manager: Collecting and analyzing data for decision-making purposes.

Administrator: Performing the activities necessary to plan and implement a program of services.

The acquisition of social work skills depends partly on innate abilities of people and partly on past learning experiences. In addition, social work educational programs facilitate further learning of such skills by providing theoretical material (for example, material on how to interview), by practicing such skills (for example, videotaping students in simulated counseling situations), and by extensively supervising students in practicum courses.

Unlike many professionals the social worker does not bring many tangible resources to a helping situation. (A physician, for example, has a wide range of equipment to help diagnose problems and a wide range of tangible treatment techniques such as medication.) The social worker, on the other hand, brings a body of knowledge, a repertoire of skills, and a set of values—all of which are fairly abstract. Because there are literally hundreds of intervention strategies that can be used to improve the social functioning of clients, the skill of social work practice requires both the appropriate selection of techniques for a particular situation and the capacity to use the techniques effectively.

Value Base

Should the primary objective of imprisonment be rehabilitation or punishment? Should a father committing incest be prosecuted with the likelihood of such publicity in the community leading to family breakup, or should an effort first be made, through counseling, to stop the incest and keep the family intact? Should a wife who is occasionally abused by her husband be encouraged to remain living with him? Should an abortion be suggested as one alternative for resolving the problems of someone who is single and pregnant? Should youth who are claimed to be uncontrollable by their parents be placed in correctional schools? If a client of a social worker threatened serious harm to some third person, what should the worker do? All of

these questions involve making decisions based not on knowledge but on values. Much of social work practice is dependent on making decisions based on values.

Allen Pincus and Anne Minahan concisely define *values* and describe the differences between values and knowledge:

Values are beliefs, preferences, or assumptions about what is desirable or good for man. An example is the belief that society has an obligation to help each individual realize his fullest potential. They are not assertions about how the world is and what we know about it, but how it should be. As such, value statements cannot be subjected to scientific investigation; they must be accepted on faith. Thus we can speak of a value as being right or wrong only in relation to the particular belief system or ethical code being used as a standard.

What we will refer to as knowledge statements, on the other hand, are observations about the world and man which have been verified or are capable of verification. An example is that black people have a shorter life expectancy than white people in the United States. When we speak of a knowledge statement as being right or wrong, we are referring to the extent to which the assertion has been confirmed through objective empirical investigation.[22]

The National Association of Social Workers (NASW) has formulated a Code of Ethics that summarizes important practice ethics for social workers. A summary of major principles of this code is presented in Box 2.3 with the complete code being presented in the appendix.

Values underlying social work practice will be summarized briefly here.

RESPECT FOR THE DIGNITY AND UNIQUENESS OF THE INDIVIDUAL   This value or principle has also been called *individualization*. Individualization means viewing and treating a person as unique and worthwhile. The social work profession firmly believes each person has inherent dignity, which is to be respected.

Every human being is unique in a variety of ways— value system, personality, goals in life, financial resources, emotional and physical strengths, personal concerns, past experiences, peer pressures, emotional reactions, self-identity, family relationships, and deviant behavioral patterns. In working with a client a social worker needs to perceive and respect the uniqueness of the client's situation.

Individualization is relatively easy for a social worker to achieve when that worker is assisting clients who have values, goals, behavioral patterns, and personal characteristics that are similar to those of the worker. Individualization is harder to achieve when a worker is assigned clients who have values or behavioral patterns that the worker views as disgusting. For example, a worker holding traditional middle-class values may have more difficulty in viewing a client with respect when that client has killed someone, is a homosexual, has raped someone, or is filthy and continually uses vulgar language. A general guideline in such situations is that the worker should seek to accept and respect the client but not accept the deviant behavior that needs to be changed. If a worker is not able to convey that she or he accepts the client (but not the deviant behavior), a helping relationship will not be established. If such a relationship is not established, then the worker will have practically no opportunity to help the client make constructive changes. A second guideline is that if a worker views a client as being disgusting and is unable to establish a working relationship, then that worker should transfer the case to another worker. There should be no disgrace or embarrassment in having to transfer a case for such reasons because it is irrational for a worker to expect to be able to like every client and to expect that every client will like that worker.[23]

Social workers occasionally encounter "raw" situations. For a while I worked in a mental hospital for the "criminally insane" and had a variety of clients who had committed a wide range of asocial and bizarre acts, including incest, rape, murder, sodomy, sexual exhibitionism, and removing corpses from graves. I've worked in a variety of other settings and encountered other raw situations. Achieving an attitude of respect for people who commit bizarre actions is difficult at times, but rehabilitation will not occur unless it is achieved.

Social psychologists have firmly established the theoretical principle that people's image of themselves develops largely out of their interactions and communications with others. A long time ago Charles Cooley called this process the "looking glass self-concept."[24] The "looking glass" says people develop their self-concept in terms of how other people relate to them. For example, if a person receives respect from others and is praised for his or her positive qualities, that person is apt to feel good about himself or herself, gradually will develop a positive sense of worth, will be happier, and will seek responsible and socially acceptable ways to continue to maintain the respect of others.

On the other hand, if a person commits a deviant act and *then* is shunned by others, viewed as different, and treated with disrespect, that person is apt to develop a negative self-concept. It has been found that people with negative self-concepts will withdraw from society, become emotionally disturbed, or express their discontent in delinquent and deviant actions.[25]

The principle of individualization also plays a key role in social work treatment. Various problems, needs, goals, and values of clients involve different patterns of relationships with clients and different methods of helping. For example, a teenage boy who is placed in a group home because his parents have found him to be "uncontrollable" may need an understanding but firm counselor who sets and enforces strict limits. At times the youth may need encouragement and guidance in how to perform better at school. If conflicts develop between the youth and other boys at the group home, the counselor may need to play a mediating role. If the youth is shy, counseling on how to be more assertive may be needed. If his parents are fairly ineffective in their parenting role, the counselor may seek to have the parents enroll in a Parent Effectiveness Training (PET) program.[26] If the youth is being treated unfairly at school or by the juvenile court, the counselor may play an advocate role for the youth and attempt to change the system. If the youth has behavior problems, the reasons need to be explored and an intervention program developed.

CLIENTS' RIGHT TO SELF-DETERMINATION   This principle asserts that clients have the right to hold and express their own opinions and to act on them, as long as in so doing they do not infringe on the rights of others. This principle is in sharp contrast to the layperson's

BOX 2.3

NASW Code of Ethics
(*Summary of Major Principles*)

I. The Social Worker's Conduct and Comportment As a Social Worker
   A. *Propriety.* The social worker should maintain high standards of personal conduct in the capacity or identity as social worker.
   B. *Competence and Professional Development.* The social worker should strive to become and remain proficient in professional practice and the performance of professional functions.
   C. *Service.* The social worker should regard as primary the service obligation of the social work profession.
   D. *Integrity.* The social worker should act in accordance with the highest standards of professional integrity.
   E. *Scholarship and Research.* The social worker engaged in study and research should be guided by the conventions of scholarly inquiry.
II. The Social Worker's Ethical Responsibility to Clients
   F. *Primacy of Clients' Interests.* The social worker's primary responsibility is to clients.
   G. *Rights and Prerogatives of Clients.* The social worker should make every effort to foster maximum self-determination on the part of clients.
   H. *Confidentiality and Privacy.* The social worker should respect the privacy of clients and hold in confidence all information obtained in the course of professional service.

view that a social worker seeks to "remold" clients into a pattern chosen by the worker. Instead, the efforts of social workers are geared to enhancing the capability of clients to help themselves. Client self-determination derives logically from the belief in the inherent dignity of each person. If people have dignity, then it follows that they should be permitted to determine their own lifestyles as far as possible.

Social work believes that making all decisions and doing everything for a client is self-defeating because it leads to increased dependency rather than to greater self-reliance and self-sufficiency. For people to grow, to mature, to become responsible, they need to make their own decisions and to take responsibility for the

consequences. Mistakes and emotional pain will at times occur. But that is part of life. We learn by our mistakes and by trial and error. The respect for the client's ability to make his or her own decisions is associated with the principle that social work is a cooperative endeavor between client and worker (client participation). Social work is done *with* a client, and not *to* a client. Plans imposed on people without their active involvement have a way of not turning out well.

Self-determination implies that clients should be made aware that there are alternatives for resolving the personal or social problems they face. Self-determination involves having clients make decisions, that is, making a choice selected from several courses of ac-

I. *Fees.* When setting fees, the social worker should ensure that they are fair, reasonable, considerate, and commensurate with the service performed and with due regard for the clients' ability to pay.

III. The Social Worker's Ethical Responsibility to Colleagues

J. *Respect, Fairness, and Courtesy.* The social worker should treat colleagues with respect, courtesy, fairness, and good faith.

K. *Dealing with Colleagues' Clients.* The social worker has the responsibility to relate to the clients of colleagues with full professional consideration.

IV. The Social Worker's Ethical Responsibility to Employers and Employing Organizations

L. *Commitments to Employing Organizations.* The social worker should adhere to commitments made to the employing organizations.

V. The Social Worker's Ethical Responsibility to the Social Work Profession

M. *Maintaining the Integrity of the Profession.* The social worker should uphold and advance the values, ethics, knowledge, and mission of the profession.

N. *Community Service.* The social worker should assist the profession in making social services available to the general public.

O. *Development of Knowledge.* The social worker should take responsibility for identifying, developing, and fully utilizing knowledge for professional practice.

VI. The Social Worker's Ethical Responsibility to Society

P. *Promoting the General Welfare.* The social worker should promote the general welfare of society.

---

tion. If there is only one course of action, there is no choice, and therefore clients would not have the right of self-determination. As will be expanded on in later chapters, the role of a social worker in helping clients involves (*a*) building a helping relationship, (*b*) exploring problems in depth with clients, and (*c*) exploring alternative solutions, with clients then choosing a course of action. This third step is the implementation of the principle of self-determination.

Self-determination means that the client, not the worker, is the chief problem solver. Workers need to recognize that it is the client who *owns* the problem and therefore has the chief responsibility to resolve the problem. This is an area where social workers differ markedly from most other professions. Most other professionals, such as physicians and attorneys, advise clients about what they believe clients ought to do. Doctors, lawyers, and dentists are viewed as experts in advising clients. Clients' decision making after receiving the expert's advice in such situations is generally limited to the choice of whether or not to accept the professional's advice.

In sharp contrast, social workers should not seek to establish an expert-inferior relationship but rather a relationship between equals. The expertise of the social worker does *not* lie in knowing or recommending what is best for the client. Rather, the expertise lies in assisting clients to define their problems, to develop and examine the alternatives for resolving the problems, to maximize the client's capacities and opportunities to make decisions for themselves, and to help clients to implement the decisions they make. Many students when they first enter social work, or some other helping profession, mistakenly see their role as being that of "savior" or "rescuer." Mathew Dumont is highly critical of the rescuer role.

The most destructive thing in psychotherapy is a "rescue fantasy" in the therapist—a feeling that the therapist is the divinely sent agent to pull a tormented soul from the pit of suffering and adversity and put him back on the road to happiness and glory. A major reason this fantasy is so destructive is that it carries the conviction that the patient will be saved only through and by the therapist. When such a conviction is communicated to the patient, verbally or otherwise, he has no choice other than to rebel and leave or become more helpless, dependent, and sick.[27]

The principle of self-determination is complex and has some limitations. If a client makes a decision to take a course of action that a social worker believes will adversely affect the client, the social worker has to make a decision whether to intervene. If an elderly female client chooses to live alone in her home when there is a serious concern about her physical capacities to live independently, a social worker has the obligation to point out the dangers and to suggest alternative living arrangements. In this situation the social worker may decide not to take further action to force the woman into a safer living environment. On the other hand, if a client tries to commit suicide, the social worker may seek to do everything possible to prevent this.

Also, if a client decides to take a course of action that will adversely affect another person, a social worker has to make a judgment about whether to intervene to prevent the client from carrying out his or her intended actions. For example, if a client indicates that he intends to shoot someone and then bolts out of the social worker's office, the social worker may choose (and may well have a legal obligation) to inform the police and the intended victim.

CONFIDENTIALITY   Confidentiality is the implicit or explicit agreement between a professional and a client to maintain the private nature of information about the client. An "absolute" implementation of this principle means that disclosures made to the professional will not be shared with anyone else, except when authorized by the client in writing or required by law.

Because of the principle of confidentiality, professionals can be sued if they disclose information that the client is able to document has a damaging effect on him or her.

Confidentiality is important because clients will not be apt to share their "hidden secrets," personal concerns, and asocial thoughts and actions with a professional if they believe that information will be revealed to others. A basic principle of counseling is that clients must feel comfortable in fully revealing themselves to the professional without fear that their secret revelations will be used against them.

Confidentiality is absolute when information revealed to a professional is *never* passed on to anyone or anything in any form. Such information would never be shared with other agency staff, fed into a computer, or written in a case record. A student or beginning practitioner tends to think in absolutes and may even naively promise clients "absolute confidentiality."

Absolute confidentiality is seldom achieved. Social workers today generally function as part of a larger agency. In such an agency much of the communication is written into case records and shared orally with other staff in the system as part of the service-delivery process. Social workers share details with supervisors, and many work in teams where they are expected to share information with other team members. Therefore, instead of absolute confidentiality, it is more precise to indicate that a system of "relative confidentiality" is being used in social work practice.

Confidentiality is a legal matter, and at present there is a fair amount of uncertainty about what is legally a violation and what is not. There have been few test cases in court to determine what is and what is not a violation of confidentiality. Let me provide a brief summary of how agencies are now handling issues related to confidentiality.

At agencies now it is generally permissible to discuss a client's circumstances with other professionals at that agency. At many agencies, such as a mental hospital, the input of many professionals at the agency (psychiatrist, psychologist, social workers, nurses, physical therapist, and so on) is used in assessing a client and developing a treatment plan.

Many agencies feel it is inappropriate to share or discuss a client's case with a secretary. (Yet, the secretary does the typing and usually knows as much about each client as the professional staff.)

Most agencies believe it is inappropriate to discuss a client's case with professionals at another agency, unless the client first signs a release of information form. (Yet, informally professionals employed by different agencies do at times share information about a client without the client's authorization.)

At the present time nearly all agencies share case information with social work interns. (Whether it is legally permissible to share information with student interns has not been determined.)

It is certainly permissible to discuss a case for educational purposes with others if no identifying information about the specific person is given. Yet, this is another "gray" area, as the person talking about the case will not be able to determine precisely when identifying information is being given. Take the following example.

Some years ago I was employed at a maximum security hospital for the criminally insane and had on my caseload a young male who had decapitated his 17-year-old girlfriend. Such a criminal offense is indeed shocking and rare. People in the client's local area will never forget the offense. If I were to discuss this case in a class at a university (which I occasionally do), I would never be fully assured that no one would be able to identify the offender. There is always the chance that one of the students may have lived in the client's home community and recognize the offender.

Another problematic area is the thorny question of when a professional should violate confidence and inform others. Again, there are many "gray" areas surrounding this question.

Most state statutes permit or require the professional to inform the appropriate people when a client admits to a past or intended *serious* criminal act. Yet, the question of how serious a crime must be before there is an obligation to report it has not been resolved.

On the extreme end of the "severity" continuum (for example, when a client threatens to kill someone) it has been established that a professional *must* inform the appropriate people—such as the police and the intended victims.

In regard to the question of how serious a crime must be before it is reported, S. J. Wilson notes:

How serious must a crime be in order for the professional to take protective measures? Obviously, crimes involving someone's life are sufficiently serious. But what about destruction of personal property, theft, and the hundreds of misdemeanors that are so minor that they are rather easily overlooked? Unfortunately, there seems to be no clear-cut definition of what constitutes a serious crime, and it appears that this will have to be determined by the courts in individual case rulings.[28]

Without guidelines a professional has to use his or her own best judgment about when a client's actions or communications warrant protective measures and about what those measures should be. Student interns or beginning practitioners are advised to ask their supervisors when questions in this area arise.

For example, a few years ago I was the faculty supervisor for a student in a field placement at a public assistance agency. The student intern had an unmarried AFDC mother on his caseload. A trusting working relationship between the intern and the mother was developed. The mother then informed the student she was dating a person who was sometimes abusive to her when drunk. The mother further indicated there was a warrant for the boyfriend's arrest in another state for an armed robbery charge. The student intern contacted me, inquiring whether it was his obligation to inform the police, thereby violating confidentiality. My response was to discuss this with his agency supervisor to find out the agency's policy.

Wilson further concludes:

In summary, a professional whose client confesses an intended or past crime can find himself in a very delicate position, both legally and ethically. There are enough conflicting beliefs on how this should be handled, so that clear guidelines are lacking. Social workers who receive a communication about a serious criminal act by a client would be wise to consult an attorney for a detailed research of appropriate state statutes and a review of recent court rulings that might help determine the desired course of action.[29]

There are a number of other areas where a professional is permitted, expected, or required to violate confidentiality.* These areas include:

- When a client formally (usually in writing) authorizes the professional to release information.

- When a professional is called to testify in a criminal case (state statutes vary regarding guidelines on what information may be kept confidential in such criminal proceedings and therefore practitioners must research their own particular state statutes in this area).

- When a client files a lawsuit against a professional (e.g., for malpractice).

- When a client threatens suicide, a professional may be forced to violate confidentiality to save the client's life. Although the treating professional is encouraged to violate confidentiality in such circumstances, there is not necessarily a legal requirement to do so.

- When a client threatens to harm his or her therapist.

- When a professional becomes aware that a minor has committed a crime, when a minor is used by adults as an accessory in a crime, or when a minor is a victim of criminal actions. In such situations most states require that counselors inform the legal authorities. Again, the question arises of how serious the crime must be before it is reported.

- When there is evidence of child abuse or neglect, most states require professionals to report the evidence to the designated child protection agency.

---

*An extended discussion of these areas is contained in Suanna J. Wilson, *Confidentiality in Social Work: Issues and Principles* (New York: Free Press, 1978).

- When a client's emotional or physical condition makes his or her employment a clear danger to himself or herself or others (for example, when a counselor discovers that a client who is an airplane pilot has a serious drinking problem).

In all these areas professional judgment must be used in deciding when the circumstances justify violating confidentiality (for example, making a judgment about when child abuse or neglect may be occurring).

ADVOCACY AND SOCIAL ACTION FOR THE POWERLESS   Social work has recognized an obligation to advocate for those who have little power to ensure their rights and are therefore oppressed or dispossessed. Social work believes that society has a responsibility to all of its members to provide security, acceptance, and satisfaction of basic cultural, social, and biological needs. Only when an individual's basic needs are met is it thought possible for people to develop their maximum potentials. Because social work believes in the value of the individual, it has a special responsibility to protect and secure civil rights for all oppressed individuals and groups. Social workers have a moral responsibility to work toward eradicating discrimination. Civil rights of clients need to be protected in order to preserve human dignity and self-respect.

FOCUS ON FAMILY   Often the focus of social work services is on the family. A family is seen as an interacting interdependent system. The problems faced by any person are usually influenced by the dynamics within a family, as illustrated in the following example.

A school teacher became concerned when one of her pupils was consistently failing and referred the child for psychological testing. Testing revealed a normal IQ, but failure was found to be due to a low self-concept (the girl was reluctant to do her academic work because she saw herself as being incapable of doing it). A school social worker met with the family and observed that the low self-concept was primarily a result of the parents ridiculing and criticizing the child and seldom giving emotional support, encouragement, or compliments.

Because a family is an interacting system, change

in one member affects others. For example, with some abusive families it has been noted that the abused child is at times a scapegoat for the parents to vent their anger and hostility. If the abused child is removed from a home, another child within the family is at times selected to be the scapegoat.[30]

Another reason for the focus on the family rather than on the individual is that the other family members are often needed in the treatment process. For example, other family members can put pressure on an alcoholic to have him or her knowledge that a problem exists. The family members may also need counseling to help them cope with the person when that person is drinking, and these family members may play important roles in providing emotional support for the alcoholic's efforts to stop drinking.

ACCOUNTABILITY   Increasingly federal and state governmental units and private funding sources are requiring that the effectiveness of service programs be measured. Gradually, programs found to be ineffective are being phased out. Although some social workers view accountability with trepidation and claim the paperwork involved interferes with serving clients, social work has an obligation to funding sources to seek to provide the highest quality services. The value of accountability in recent years has been shown by program outcome studies that have demonstrated that orphanages are not the best places to serve homeless children, that long-term hospitalization is not the best way to help those who are emotionally disturbed, that probation generally has higher rehabilitative value than long-term confinement in prison, that the Job Corps program of the 1960s was too expensive for the outcomes achieved, that most mentally retarded children can be better served in their home communities through local programs than by confinement in an institution, and that runaways are better served by placement in runaway centers than in detention or in jail.

Social workers need to become skilled at evaluating the extent to which they are being effective in providing services. At the agency level and program level a wide variety of evaluation techniques are now available to assess effectiveness of current services and to identify unmet needs and service gaps. One of the most useful approaches is management by objectives (MBO). This technique involves identifying at program levels the objectives of each program, specifying in measurable terms how and when these objectives are to be met, and then periodically measuring the extent to which the objectives will be met.

Management by objectives is perhaps also the most useful approach that every social worker can use to assess his or her effectiveness. Many agencies are now requiring each of their workers, *with the involvement of their clients*, to (*a*) identify and specify what the goals will be for each client—generally this is done together with clients during the initial interviews; (*b*) have the client and the worker then write down in detail what each will do to accomplish the goals (deadlines for accomplishing these tasks are also set); and (*c*) assess the extent to which the goals have been achieved when treatment is terminated (and perhaps periodically during the treatment process).

If goals are generally not being achieved the worker needs to examine the underlying reasons. Perhaps unrealistic goals are being set. Perhaps the program or the treatment techniques are ineffective. Perhaps certain components of the treatment program are having an adverse effect. Perhaps other reasons account for the low success rate. Depending on the reason for the goals not being achieved, appropriate changes need to be made.

On the other hand, if the goals are generally being met the worker can use this information to document to funding sources and to supervisors that high-quality services are being provided.

THE INSTITUTIONAL ORIENTATION   There are currently two conflicting views of the role of social welfare in our society: the residual orientation versus the institutional orientation. These two views were described at length in Chapter 1. Social work believes in the institutional approach and seeks to develop and provide programs with this orientation. Social work believes society must provide opportunities for growth and development that will allow each person to realize his or her fullest potential. Social work believes that society has a responsibility to all its members to provide security, acceptance, and satisfaction of basic cultural and biological needs. These beliefs reject the views of rugged individualism and social Darwinism.

SOCIAL WORK EDUCATION

Two-Year Associate Programs

During the past two decades a number of community colleges and technical schools have begun offering two-year associate programs related to social work education. These programs provide training for a wide range of associate degrees with such titles as:

Social Work Aide/Social Service Associate/Social Service Technician.

Probation and Parole Aide.

Mental Health Associate/Mental Health Aide.

Human Services Technician/Human Services Aide.

Child-Care Technician/Residential Child-Care Aide.

Community Service Assistant/Community Services Technician/Community Social Service Worker.

All of these degrees are considered preprofessional degrees and seek to achieve two simultaneous goals—training for employment and provision of some basic courses that *may* transfer to four-year educational programs.

As yet, associate degrees are not accredited by the Council on Social Work Education (CSWE). (This council presently reviews social work baccalaureate and master's programs throughout the United States to determine whether individual programs meet the standards to warrant accreditation.) Standardization of associate programs in social work probably will not be achieved unless CSWE decides to seek to review associate programs for accreditation.

UNDERGRADUATE EDUCATION   Similar to graduate programs, undergraduate programs are accredited by the Council on Social Work Education. This council is a national organization whose purpose is to set standards for social work education and to promote and improve the quality of education in social work programs. Students attending schools with accredited programs have assurance that the quality of education meets national standards and generally have an advantage in securing employment following graduation because social welfare agencies give a hiring preference (ranging from a small to a large amount) to graduates from accredited programs.

Until the early 1970s, undergraduate social work education was generally recognized as an academic or preprofessional degree, with the master's degree being recognized as the professional degree in social work. However, because a majority of people employed in the social welfare field do not have a graduate degree, the need for professional training at the baccalaureate level was recognized. Effective July 1, 1974, accreditation requirements for undergraduate programs were substantially changed to emphasize professional preparation. In fact, the Council on Social Work Education required that an accredited baccalaureate program "shall have as its primary stated educational objective preparation for beginning professional social work practice."[31] Other objectives, secondary in importance, that baccalaureate programs are apt to have include (*a*) preparation of students for graduate professional education in social work, and (*b*) preparation for intelligent, informed citizenship that brings an understanding of a wide range of social problems, intervention techniques on resolving such problems, and an understanding of social welfare concepts.

Along with this change from an academic to a professional preparation focus was an explicit statement of curriculum requirements for undergraduate social work education that:

1. Builds on, and is integrated with, a liberal arts base.

2. Provides content in the areas of
   a. social work practice.
   b. social welfare policy and services.
   c. human behavior and social environment.
   d. social research.

3. Requires educationally directed field experiences.[32]

The curriculum objectives of undergraduate programs are generic (broad based) as they seek to convey and develop a variety of skills, values, and knowledge bases, including:

Ability to counsel individuals effectively on a one-to-one basis and in groups.

Knowledge of the wide range of available social welfare services.

Capacity to analyze social welfare programs, policies, and issues critically.

An understanding of human development and behavior, including biological, psychological, and sociocultural influences.

Capacity to understand and apply social research.

An understanding and appreciation for ethnic, racial, and cultural diversity.

A working knowledge of a variety of intervention techniques that are used in casework, case management, group work, and community organization.

GRADUATE EDUCATION   MSW (Master of Social Work) programs as a rule require two years of academic study. However, a number of graduate programs are granting advanced standing to students holding an undergraduate major in social work. Advanced standing (up to one academic year of credit) is given on the basis of the number of "core" courses taken as an undergraduate. Core courses are those that are required in both undergraduate and graduate programs and include courses in social welfare policy and services, social work practice, human behavior and the social environment, social research, and field placement.*

Because of the professional preparation focus of graduate programs, field work is an important emphasis in all MSW programs, with an average of two to three days per week being spent at an agency while receiving intensive supervision.

Although there is variation in format and structure of master's programs, almost all of the programs have

the following two components: (*a*) Part of the program has a generic social work practice focus. Courses taken to meet this generic practice focus are similar (and at some schools identical) to the core courses of an undergraduate program. Some schools offer this generic focus during the first year, a few offer it during the first semester, and others have course content in this area for both years. (*b*) For the second part of the program the student selects a concentration area from several available options and then takes courses in this study area. There is considerable variation among graduate schools in the concentration options that are offered. The Council on Social Work Education annually publishes *Summary Information on Master of Social Work Programs*, which summarizes the concentration options at each school. Some of the concentration options are policy analysis, planning, research and administration, community organization, direct practice with individuals and small groups, direct practice with large groups, program development, community mental health, family functioning, health care, inner-city neighborhood services, social work in school systems, child welfare, consultation, aging, and crime and delinquency.[33]

Persons with MSW degrees often, within a year or two following graduation, assume supervisory or administrative responsibilities.

At the advanced graduate level two additional programs are offered by some schools: (*a*) a "third-year" program with the aim of strengthening the professional skills of the student and (*b*) a Doctor of Social Work degree (DWS) or a Doctor of Philosophy degree. The doctoral program requires two or more years of postgraduate studies.

Employment Settings and Opportunities in Social Work

There are currently more employment opportunities available in social work than in many other fields. Social services and their delivery are becoming a more integral part of our fast-paced existence, and the de-

---

*Guidelines for granting advanced standing in MSW programs differ between programs; therefore interested students should consult with the graduate schools they desire to attend.

Social work presents professionals and volunteers with numerous opportunities in highly diverse settings. This doctor travels through Newark's poorest neighborhoods in a mobile health van, offering AIDS counseling to drug abusers.

mand for qualified personnel is expected to expand. If you are looking for the challenge of working with people to improve social and personal difficulties, then you should seriously consider a career in social work.

From 1960 to 1987 the number of employed social service workers grew by nearly 400 percent—from 95,000 to 335,000.[34] About two out of five social workers are employed by public social welfare agencies.[35] The Bureau of Labor Statistics projects the following job outlook for social work positions through the mid-1990s.

Employment of social workers is expected to increase faster than the average for all occupations through the mid-1990s, reflecting public and private response to the needs of a growing and aging population.

Demand for social workers is governed by funding; trends in public, private, and third-party spending for social work services are largely responsible for patterns of job growth. . . .

Substantial growth is projected for social work jobs in private agencies that provide services for abused and neglected children, troubled youth, rape and spouse abuse victims, older people and their families, refugees, farm workers, couples with marital difficulties, and so forth.

Opportunities for social workers in private practice will continue to expand, in part because of growing acceptance of private social work practice by the profession and by the public at large, but also because of the anticipated availability of funding from health insurance and from an increasingly affluent population willing to pay for professional help with personal problems. Growing corporate support for employee assistance programs is expected to spur demand for the services of private practitioners, some of whom contract with corporations to run training sessions on group dynamics, or counsel employees on a variety of problems.[36]

There is a wide variation in pay, ranging between approximately $10,000 and $100,000, depending on type of job, geographic location, experience, training, and skills possessed by the employee. Starting salaries for social case workers (positions requiring a BSW) in public agencies averaged about $15,700 in 1984. The average starting salary for positions requiring an MSW in hospitals and medical centers was about $19,300 in 1984. In the federal government, social workers with an MSW and no other experience started at $21,804 in 1985; averge earnings for social workers in the federal service were $30,800 in 1984.[37]

A wide variety of employment settings are available for social workers, including foster care, adoption, probation and parole, public assistance, counseling, services to single parents, day-care services, school social services, services to minority groups and to veterans, recreational services such as Boy Scouts and YWCA programs, social services in a medical or mental hospital, antipoverty programs, social services in a nursing home and other services to the elderly, marital counseling, drug and alcohol counseling, services to the emotionally disturbed or mentally handicapped, abortion counseling, family planning services, services to the blind and disabled, sexual counseling, equal rights services, protective services, services in sheltered workshops, research, social action, and fund-raising. (These settings will be described in detail in the chapters that follow.) In addition to these direct services there are employment opportunities for those with experience and advanced professional training in social planning, community organization, consultation, supervision, teaching, and administration.

At our school we are convinced those who are most likely to secure employment in social work following graduation are those who are outgoing, dynamic, and able to "sell" themselves during an interview as having the competence, confidence, and skills to perform the job they are applying for. Involvement in groups and extracurricular activities while at college facilitates the development of these capacities, as does being a volunteer at one or more social service agencies. A high number of our students secure employment through the relationships they develop with staff during their field placement. If they do well at their field placement and a vacancy occurs, they have an inside track in being hired. Also, through developing acquaintances with staff at an agency, they hear about employment opportunities at other agencies and frequently also receive a positive letter of reference from their field placement.

Students who are considering majoring in social work frequently ask: "Is a graduate degree needed to get a job in social work?" It definitely is not. The vast majority of employed social workers hold only a baccalaureate degree. In addition, there are some agencies who prefer to hire a person with a baccalaureate degree because it is less expensive. However, it should be noted that, as in most fields, a master's degree provides higher status, greater promotion opportunities, and perhaps more gratifying work.

SELF-AWARENESS AND IDENTITY DEVELOPMENT

As said earlier, perhaps the key skill needed to be a competent social worker is the capacity to relate to and counsel individuals.

Increasingly, when training social work students, educators are finding that the students who are best able to counsel others are those who know themselves; that is, they have a high level of self-awareness. A counselor has to be perceptive regarding what clients are thinking and feeling. To be perceptive the counselor has to be able to place himself or herself in the client's situation and determine (with the client's values and pressures), "What is this person really feeling and thinking?" Unless the counselor has a high level of self-awareness, it is very unlikely that she or he will be able to determine what others are thinking and feeling.

There are a variety of approaches that have been developed to increase personal awareness or self-awareness, including biofeedback, transcendental meditation, muscle relaxation, gestalt therapy, identity formation, sensitivity training, and encounter groups.* (Some programs in social work are now offering interpersonal skill courses that are designed to develop self-awareness and interpersonal awareness capacities.)

Identity Formation

One approach to self-awareness—identity formation—will be presented here.† Identity formation is the process of determining who you are and what you want out of life. Arriving at an identity you will be comfortable with is one of the most important tasks you will ever have to face. Whether or not you are interested in a social work career, the following information on identity could have considerable importance for your future. As noted, it is especially significant for those considering a social work career because knowing oneself enhances substantially one's ability to counsel others.

Identity development is a lifelong process, and there are gradual changes in one's identity throughout one's lifetime. During the early years our sense of who we are is largely determined by the reactions of others (the looking-glass self-concept previously mentioned). For example, if neighbors, for whatever reason, perceive a young boy to be a "troublemaker," a "delinquent," they are then likely to accuse the youth of delinquent acts, treat him with suspicion, and label his semidelinquent activities as "delinquent." Although

frequently accused and criticized, the youth, to some extent, soon begins to realize that enacting the delinquent role also brings certain rewards; it brings him a type of status and prestige, at least from other youth. In the absence of objective ways to determine whether he is a "delinquent," he relies on the subjective evaluations of others. Gradually, a vicious cycle develops; the more he is related to as a delinquent, the more he is apt to view himself as a delinquent, and the more apt he is to enact the delinquent role.

Glasser indicates that a useful perspective for viewing identity is in terms of a success versus failure orientation.[38] Those who develop a success identity (view themselves as generally being successful) have two characteristics: (*a*) they feel they are loved by at least one person, and (*b*) they feel they are viewed as being a worthy human being by at least one person. People with failure identities are those who feel they are not loved or who do not have a sense of self-worth. People with failure identities are apt to be depressed, lonely, anxious, reluctant to face everyday challenges, and indecisive. Escape through drugs or alcohol, withdrawal, criminal behavior, or the development of emotional problems are common.

However, because identity is a lifelong process, significant positive changes in one's identity can be achieved even by those with serious failure identities. An important principle is: *Although we cannot change the past, what we want out of the future, along with our motivation to achieve what we want, is more important (than our past experiences) in determining what our future will be.*

Some of the most important questions you will ever have to face are:

1. What kind of person do you want to be?

2. What do you want out of life?

3. Who are you?

Without answers to such questions you will not be prepared to make such major decisions as selecting a career, deciding where to live and what type of lifestyle you want, deciding whether to marry, and deciding whether to have children. Unfortunately, many people muddle through life without ever arriving at answers to these questions. Answers are not easy to arrive at. They require considerable thought and trial and error.

---

*A good review of the specific techniques used in these approaches is contained in Stewart L. Tubbs and John W. Baird, *The Open Person . . . Self-Disclosure and Personal Growth* (Columbus, OH: Charles E. Merrill, 1976).

†This material on identity formation is adapted from an article written by this author entitled "Who Am I: Quest for Identity," in *The Personal Problem Solver*, ed. Charles Zastrow and Dae Chang (Englewood Cliffs, NJ: Prentice-Hall, 1977), pp. 365–370.

During the time you are searching for a sense of who you are, also expect a great deal of anxiety to arise. However, if you are to lead a satisfying, fulfilling life, it is imperative that you seek answers to these questions in order to give direction to your life and to know what will make your life meaningful. To assist you in arriving at a sense of who you are and what you want out of life, a series of more specific questions follows. As you arrive at answers to these specific questions, you will simultaneously be arriving at an increased awareness of who you are.

Questions for Arriving at a Sense of Identity

To determine who you are, you need to work on arriving at answers to the following more specific questions:

1. What do you find satisfying/enjoyable?

2. What are your religious beliefs?

3. What is your moral code? One possible code is to seek to fulfill your needs and to seek to do what you find enjoyable, and to do so in a way that does not deprive others of the ability to fulfill their needs.

4. What are your sexual mores? All of us should develop a consistent code that we are comfortable with, and that helps us meet our needs without exploiting others. There is no one right code— what works for one may not work for another because of differences in lifestyles, life goals, and personal values.

5. What kind of a career do you desire? Ideally, you should seek a career in which you find the work stimulating and satisfying, that you are skilled at, and that earns you enough money to support the lifestyle you desire.

6. What area of the country or world do you desire to live? Variables needing to be considered are climate, geography, type of dwelling, rural or urban setting, closeness to relatives or friends, and characteristics of the neighborhood.

7. Do you desire to marry? If yes, to what type of

person, when, and how consistent are your answers here with your other life goals?

8. Do you desire to have children? If yes, how many, when, and how consistent are your answers here with your other life goals?

9. What kind of image do you want to project to others? Your image will be composed of your dressing style and grooming habits, emotions, personality, degree of assertiveness, capacity to communicate, material possessions, moral code, physical features, and voice patterns. You need to honestly assess your strengths and shortcomings in this area and seek to make improvements in the latter. Seeking counseling in problem areas may be desirable.

10. What do you enjoy doing with your leisure time?

11. Do you desire to improve the quality of your life and that of others? If yes, in what ways, and how do you hope to achieve these goals?

12. What type of people do you enjoy being with and why?

13. What type of relationship do you desire to have with your relatives, friends, neighbors, and people you meet for the first time?

14. What are your thoughts about death and dying?

15. What do you hope to be doing 5 years from now, 10 years, 20 years? What are your plans for achieving these goals in these time periods?

Having answers to most of these questions will provide a reference for developing your views to the remaining unanswered questions. To have a fairly well-developed sense of identity you need to have answers to most, but not all, of these questions. Very few persons are able to arrive at rational, fully consistent answers to all these questions. Be honest about your strengths and shortcomings. For practically any shortcomings there are specific intervention strategies to bring about improvement.

In addition, expect some changes in your life goals as time goes on. As you grow as a person, changes are apt to occur in your beliefs, attitudes and values and in activities that you find enjoyable.

Your life is shaped by different events that are the results of decisions you make and decisions that are made for you. Without a sense of identity, you will not know what decisions are best for you, and your life will be unfulfilled. With a sense of identity, you will be able to direct your life toward goals you select and find personally meaningful.

SUMMARY

A social worker is a multiskilled professional. The social worker needs training and expertise in a wide range of areas to be able to handle problems faced by individuals, groups, and the larger community effectively. Analogous to a general practitioner in medicine, a social worker should have a wide range of skills and intervention techniques.

Ability to counsel clients effectively is perhaps the most basic skill needed by a social worker. Second in importance is probably the ability to interact effectively with other groups and professionals in the community.

Social work as a profession is of relatively recent origin, with formalized training in social work first having been offered at universities in the early 1900s and people first having been hired as social workers around 1900.

A social worker is a "change agent" who works with individuals, groups, families, and communities. There are several types of professional social work activities: casework, case management, group work, group therapy, family therapy, community organization, administration, research, consulting, planning, supervision, and teaching. Role models for social work practice include enabler, broker, advocate, and activist.

Fifty years ago the stereotype of a social worker was that of a moralistic upper-middle-class older lady carrying a basket of food and having little understanding of the people she tried to help. With the rapid development of social work as a profession, there are now many stereotypes (generally more positive) of what a social worker is.

To provide clients with competent service, social workers must have knowledge, skills, and values that are consistent with effective practice. The value base of social work includes respect for the dignity and uniqueness of each individual, clients' right to self-determination, confidentiality, advocacy and social action to ensure the rights of those with limited power, focus on family, accountability, and an institutional orientation.

The primary educational objective for undergraduate social work programs accredited by the Council on Social Work Education is preparation for beginning professional social work practice. A majority of people employed as social workers do not have a graduate degree. As in most fields, however, persons with a master's degree in social work generally have a higher status and greater promotion opportunities.

The chapter concluded with a discussion of the importance for social workers of having a high level of self-awareness and a sense of who they are and what they want out of life.

Arriving at a sense of identity is one of the most important and difficult quests in life—for everyone. With a sense of identity you will be able to direct your life toward goals you select and find personally meaningful.

NOTES

1. National Association of Social Workers, *Standards for Social Welfare Manpower* (New York: National Association of Social Workers, 1973), pp. 4–5.
2. Robert M. Bremner, "The Rediscovery of Pauperism," *Current Issues in Social Work Seen in Historical Perspective* (New York: Council on Social Work Education, 1962), p. 13.
3. Nathan E. Cohen, *Social Work in the American Tradition* (Hinsdale, IL: Dryden Press, 1958), p. 66.
4. Dorothy G. Becker, "Social Welfare Leaders as Spokesmen for the Poor," *Social Casework* 49, no. 2 (February 1968), p. 85.
5. Ralph Dolgoff and Donald Feldstein, *Understanding Social Welfare* (New York: Harper & Row, 1980), pp. 233–234.
6. Ibid., p. 235.
7. Mary E. Richmond, *Social Diagnosis* (New York: Free Press, 1965).

8. H. J. Eysenck, "The Effects of Psychotherapy," in *Handbook of Abnormal Psychology*, ed. H. J. Eysenck (New York: Basic Books, 1961), pp. 697–725.

9. Dolgoff and Feldstein, *Understanding Social Welfare*.

10. Dean H. Hepworth and Jo Ann Larsen, *Direct Social Work Practice: Theory and Skills*, 2d ed. (Chicago: The Dorsey Press, 1986), p. 563.

11. Donald Brieland, Lela B. Costin, and Charles R. Atherton, *Contemporary Social Work: An Introduction to Social Work and Social Welfare*, 3d ed. (New York: McGraw-Hill, 1985), pp. 120–121.

12. Joseph Anderson, *Social Work Methods and Processes* (Belmont, CA: Wadsworth, 1981).

13. Stephen West, "Social Work's New Deal," *Newsweek*, May 1988, p. 38.

14. Richard Stuart, *Trick or Treatment: How and When Psychotherapy Fails* (Champaign, IL: Research Press, 1970).

15. National Association of Social Workers, *Standards for the Classification of Social Work Practice* (Washington, D.C.: National Association of Social Workers, 1982), p. 17.

16. Melvin A. Glasser, "Public Attitudes toward the Profession: What Shall They Be?" *NASW News* 3, no. 4 (August 1958), p. 7.

17. Dolgoff and Feldstein, *Understanding Social Welfare*, p. 223.

18. Alfred J. Kahn, "The Nature of Social Work Knowledge," in *New Directions in Social Work*, ed. Cora Kasius (New York: Harper & Row, 1954), p. 196.

19. Alfred Kadushin, "The Knowledge Base of Social Work," in *Issues in American Social Work*, ed. Alfred J. Kahn (New York: Columbia University Press, 1959), pp. 39–79.

20. Betty L. Baer and Ronald Federico, *Educating the Baccalaureate Social Worker* (Cambridge, MA: Ballinger, 1978), pp. 92–95.

21. Ronald Federico, *The Social Welfare Institution* (Lexington, MA: D. C. Heath, 1973), pp. 146–147.

22. Allen Pincus and Anne Minahan, *Social Work Practice: Model and Method* (Itasca, IL: F. E. Peacock, 1973), p. 38.

23. Albert Ellis and R. Harper, *A New Guide to Rational Living* (North Hollywood, CA: Wilshire Books, 1975).

24. C. H. Cooley, *Human Nature and the Social Order* (New York: Charles Scribner's Sons, 1902).

25. William Glasser, *The Identity Society* (New York: Harper & Row, 1972).

26. Thomas Gordon, *Parent Effectiveness Training* (New York: Wyden, 1973).

27. Mathew Dumont, *The Absurd Healer* (New York: Viking Press, 1968), p. 60.

28. Suanna J. Wilson, *Confidentiality in Social Work: Issues and Principles* (New York: Free Press, 1978), pp. 116–117.

29. Ibid., p. 121.

30. Alfred Kadushin, *Child Welfare Services*, 3d ed. (New York: Macmillan, 1980).

31. "Standards for the Accreditation of Baccalaureate Degree Programs in Social Work" (New York: Council on Social Work Education, 1974), p. 13.

32. Ibid, pp. 13–14.

33. *Summary Information on Master of Social Work Programs: 1983* (New York: Council on Social Work Education, 1983).

34. U.S. Department of Labor, *Occupational Outlook Handbook: 1986–87 Edition* (Washington, D.C.: U.S. Government Printing Office, 1986), p. 113.

35. Ibid., p. 113.

36. Ibid., pp. 114–115.

37. Ibid., pp. 115–116.

38. Glasser, *Identity Society*.

II

SOCIAL

PROBLEMS

AND

SOCIAL

SERVICES

3

POVERTY
AND PUBLIC
WELFARE

P overty has always been one of the most serious social problems in our country. (In most other countries it is even more severe.) In our modern, civilized society one out of seven Americans is poor.[1] This chapter will:

- Describe the extent of poverty and the effects of living in poverty.
- Discuss the income and wealth gaps between the rich and the poor in this country.
- Summarize the causes of poverty, and identify the population groups who have the lowest income levels.
- Outline current programs to combat poverty and discuss their merits and shortcomings.
- Describe and refute some of the myths about public welfare.
- Present strategies to reduce poverty in the future.
- Describe the role of social work in public welfare.

THE PROBLEM

In 1986, over 32 million Americans, 13.6 percent of our population, were living below the poverty line.[2] (The poverty line is the level of income that the federal government considers sufficient to meet basic requirements of food, shelter, and clothing.) A cause for alarm is that the rate of poverty in recent years has been increasing. From 1978 to 1986 the rate went from 11 percent to 13.6 percent. The poverty rate in 1986 was nearly as high as it was in 1966.[3]

Poverty does not simply mean that poor people in the United States are living less well than people of average income. It means that the poor have diets consisting largely of beans, macaroni and cheese, or in severe cases, even dog and cat food. It may mean not having running water, living in substandard housing, and being exposed to rats, cockroaches, and other vermin. It means not having sufficient heat in the winter and being unable to sleep because the walls are too thin to deaden the sounds from the neighbors living next door. It means being embarrassed about the few

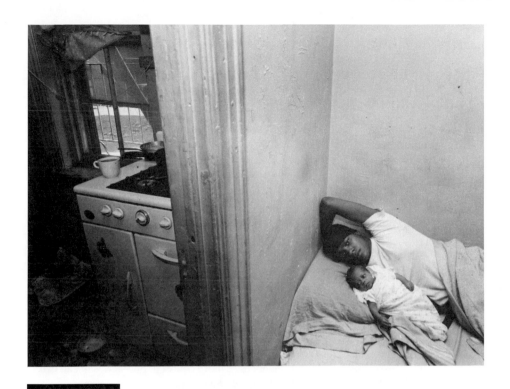

We like to think we live in a land of equal opportunity, and that upward mobility today is open to all those who put forth the effort. But the reality is otherwise: poverty is virtually "escape proof."

ragged clothes that one has to wear. It means great susceptibility to emotional disturbances, alcoholism, and victimization by criminals, as well as having a shorter life expectancy. It means few opportunities to advance oneself socially, economically, or educationally. It often means slum housing, unstable marriages, and little opportunity to enjoy the finer things in life—traveling, dining out, movies, plays, concerts, and sports events.

The infant mortality rate of the poor is almost double that of the affluent.[4] The poor have less access to medical services and receive lower quality care from health care professionals. The poor are exposed to higher levels of air pollution, water pollution, and unsanitary conditions. They have higher rates of malnutrition and disease. Schools in poor areas are of lower quality and have fewer resources. As a result the poor

achieve less academically and are more apt to drop out of school. They are more apt to be arrested, indicted, imprisoned, and given longer sentences for the same offense. They are less likely to receive probation, parole, or suspended sentences.[5]

Poverty also often leads to despair, low self-esteem, and stunting of one's growth—including physical, social, emotional, and intellectual growth. A second level of damage from poverty occurs from the feeling that lack of financial resources is preventing one from having equal opportunities and from the resulting feeling that one is a second-class citizen. Poverty hurts most when it leads to this view of the self as inferior or second class.

We like to think that America is a land of equal opportunity and that there is considerable upward class mobility for those that put forth effort. The reality

BOX 3.1

The Hurt of Being Poor

Homer Burleigh, 33 [and] immobile with resentment, blocked the doorway of his flat. . . . Homer Burleigh finds it hard to stay angry for long and he led the way inside. Four of his five children, ages two, three, five, and seven (a ten-year-old boy was still in school), ran about in bare feet, dressed only in underpants. Mrs. Burleigh, a wan, hard, very pregnant woman, also was barefooted.

He walked into a small kitchen, sat down . . . and sighed. He was in trouble and he knew it. . . . Homer Burleigh was penniless, about to be evicted, maybe even jailed. Much of this was his own fault, the panicked response to crises. . . . Homer Burleigh made mistakes when the margin of safety with which he had to live permitted no mistakes whatever.

The last of the final welfare payment had been spent and in four days he was to be evicted for nonpayment of rent.

"If the arm continues this way, and if they don't give me assistance, I'm going to have to put the kids in a home." His eyes filled.

And so the lines of failure seemed to converge for Homer Burleigh . . . almost no formal education, an impoverished landscape to grow in with no hope for a young man, . . . a drifting of life without heed for the consequences of more children. But he was not an evil man, or a lazy one. His was simply the fragile vessel of endemic poverty, never strong enough to withstand a prolonged storm. And his children seemed doomed to go forth in a similarly brittle craft.

Source: Ben H. Bagdikian, *In the Midst of Plenty: The Poor in America* (Boston: Beacon Press, 1964), pp. 29–40.

is the opposite of the myth. Extensive research has shown that poverty is almost "escape proof." Children raised in poor families are apt themselves to live in poverty in their adult years. Most people have much the same social status as their parents had. Movement to a higher social status is an unusual happening in practically all societies—including the United States.[6]

In testimony before the Senate Select Committee on Nutrition and Human Needs, Robert Coles (a physician) described the plight of those living in poverty.

We had seen . . . not only extreme poverty, but gross, clinical evidence of chronic hunger and malnutrition—evidence that we as doctors found it hard to deal with ourselves, let alone talk about, because we had been unprepared by our own medical training for what we saw. Today's American physicians are simply not prepared by their education to find in this nation severe vitamin deficiency diseases, widespread parasitism, and among infants, a mortality rate that is comparable, say, to the underdeveloped nations of Asia or Africa.

I saw . . . malnourished children, children who are not getting the right amount and kinds of food, who suffer from several diseases and see no physician, who indeed were born in shacks without the help of a

*doctor and under conditions that are primitive, to say
the least. . . . Why . . . must these children go hungry,
still be sick? . . . Why do American children get born
without the help of a doctor, and never, never see a
doctor in their lives? It is awful, it is humiliating for
all of us that these questions still have to be asked in a
nation like this, the strongest and richest nation that
ever was.*

*I do not understand why these things have to
persist and why we have to talk about this again and
again and again, and people like me have to come
and repeat all these findings.*[7]

A BRIEF HISTORY
OF OUR RESPONSE
TO THE POOR

The way a society cares for its needy reflects its values.
In primitive societies the needs of those who were not
self-sufficient were met by family or other tribal members. During the medieval period in Europe, poor relief was a church responsibility.

The famous Elizabethan Poor Law of 1601 in England combined humanitarianism with the Protestant
ethic. This law was enacted because the general public
viewed begging (not poverty) as a social problem. The
law established three separate programs: (*a*) The able-
bodied poor were offered work. If they refused they
were whipped, imprisoned, or sent back to their birthplace. (*b*) The impotent poor (the elderly and disabled) were either given public relief or placed in
almshouses. (*c*) Children whose parents could not provide for them were bound out as apprentices to other
adults. This Poor Law established the principle of categorical relief by distinguishing between the able-bodied (undeserving) poor and the impotent (deserving)
poor. Nearly all the principles contained within this
Poor Law became incorporated into the "relief" programs of colonial America.

In the 19th century a controversy raged in both
England and the United States between advocates of
the workhouse and supporters of "outdoor relief" (as-

sistance to persons in their own homes). Outdoor relief raised concerns about fraud, and citizens feared
cash handouts might destroy moral fiber. On the other
hand, workhouses (also called almshouses) were generally overcrowded and unsanitary, and contrary to
their stated goal they offered no activity for the able-
bodied. Also in the 19th century the first social service
organizations began to develop in urban areas to serve
the needy. These organizations were private and
church sponsored and primarily offered food and shelter. They attempted to meet personal problems with
religious admonitions.

As you will recall from the discussion in Chapters
1 and 2, Americans, until the Great Depression, believed in the myth of individualism, that is, the belief
that each person is master of his or her own fate. Those
in need were viewed as lazy, as unintelligent, or as
being justly punished for their sinful ways.

The Great Depression of the 1930s called into
question the individualism myth. Nearly one third of
the work force was unemployed.[8] With large numbers
of people unemployed, including the middle class, a
new view of relief applicants developed: They were
persons, not essentially different from other people,
who were caught up in circumstances beyond their
own control. Private relief agencies (including private
agencies receiving funding support from local governing entities) were unable to meet the financial needs of
the unemployed. There was a rapid breakdown in traditional local methods of giving aid to the poor.

Harry Hopkins, a social worker from Iowa, was
appointed by President Franklin Roosevelt to oversee
national employment programs and emergency assistance. Hopkins became one of Roosevelt's closest advisers and exerted considerable influence in designing
and enacting the 1935 social security program. As indicated in Chapter 1 this program was of major significance because it initiated the federal government's
role in three areas: (*a*) social insurance programs,
(*b*) public assistance, and (*c*) social services.

After 1935 the economy of our country slowly began to recover, and some of those who were living in
poverty began to enjoy a more affluent lifestyle—even
though many other Americans remained in poverty;
they were left behind and forgotten. Public concern
switched to World War II in the early 1940s and then to

Our response to meeting the needs of the poor is a story of changing values. In the nineteenth century (right) a bowl of soup was likely to have been given with prayers or religious admonitions. During the Great Depression, the public's attitude toward relief shifted; these farmers waiting in line for government checks (below) were beneficiaries of a new belief that financial hardship is a matter often beyond our control. Following a period in the 1950s when the poor were largely ignored, a renewed optimism in the 1960s led to a host of government-sponsored programs designed to eliminate poverty (opposite page). Today the tide seems to have turned back again: virtually no large-scale social welfare programs have been initiated in recent years.

other issues such as halting the spread of communism and the Korean War. From the 1940s through the 1950s, poverty was no longer recognized or addressed as a major problem—although large segments of the population continued to live in abject poverty.

In 1960 John Kennedy saw large numbers of people in many states living in degrading human circumstances due to poverty. He made poverty an issue in his national presidential campaign. Hence, poverty was once again defined as a major social problem.

In 1962 Michael Harrington published *The Other America*, which graphically described the plights of the fifth of our population who were living in poverty.[9] The media publicized the poverty issue, and public concern about poverty increased dramatically.

In 1965 President Lyndon Johnson launched his War on Poverty with the hope of eradicating poverty and creating the "Great Society." Eliminating poverty became one of our nation's highest priorities. A variety of programs were established to try to wipe out poverty: Head Start, VISTA, Job Corps, Title I Educational

Funding, Community Action Program, Youth Corps, and Neighborhood Legal Services.

Although these programs reduced poverty somewhat, the optimistic hope of the early 1960s that poverty could be eradicated was short-lived. The Vietnam War drained resources that would otherwise have been spent on domestic programs. It also turned attention away from poverty, and finally drove Johnson from office. During periods of economic growth it is easier for a society to allocate resources to the poor in an effort to share the national wealth.

In the early 1970s, after the end of the Vietnam War, the turmoil of the late 1960s was replaced for several years with an atmosphere of relative calm on both the foreign level and the domestic level. In contrast to the hope of the 1960s that government programs could cure our social ills, an opposing philosophy emerged that assumed many problems were beyond the capacity of the government to alleviate. Hence, the liberalism of the 1960s, which resulted in the expansion and development of new social programs, was replaced by a more conservative approach in the 1970s and 1980s. Practically no new, large-scale social welfare programs were initiated in the 1970s and 1980s.

It again appears that poverty is taking a backseat to other issues. Government interest in helping the poor has waned considerably. Ronald Reagan was elected in 1980, partly on a program designed to give tax cuts to the rich and to provide decreased funds and services to the poor. Allegations of welfare fraud, high tax rates, and increasing relief roles are replacing poverty as a national concern. Welfare has again become a political "whipping boy." In the 1970s and 1980s there has been a shift away from a liberalized extension of public responsibility to help the poor.

Past history suggests that as government expenditures to help the poor (and the marginally poor) decrease, the proportion of the population living in poverty increases. There is an adage that history tends to repeat itself. In the early 1930s our country became concerned about the large number of people living in poverty, and the social security programs were enacted. Thirty years later, in the early 1960s, our country again became concerned about the large number of people living in poverty, and the War on Poverty programs were initiated. Will this thirty-year cycle be repeated in the early 1990s by a renewed concern about the large number of people living in poverty?

THE RICH AND THE POOR

Poverty and wealth are closely related. Throughout most countries in the world, wealth is concentrated in the hands of a few individuals and families. Abundance for a few is often created by depriving others.

There are two ways of measuring the extent of economic inequality. *Income* refers to the amount of money a person makes in a given year. *Wealth* is a person's total assets—real estate holdings, cash, stocks, bonds, and so forth.

The distribution of wealth and income is highly unequal in our society. Similar to most countries, the United States is characterized by *social stratification*—

that is, it has social classes, with the upper classes having by far the greatest access to the pleasures that money can buy. The income gap between the rich and the poor has widened in the 1980s.

The poorest fifth of American individuals owns only 0.2 percent of the wealth, whereas the richest fifth owns more than three-quarters of the wealth.[10] This means 20 percent of the population has three times as much wealth as all of the rest of the people combined! There are over a million millionaires in this country; there are over 150 families that are worth more than $100 million; and there are about 60 families that are worth more than $500 million.[11] The richest 2 percent of our population owns 62 percent of all privately held corporate stock.[12] It is estimated that approximately one fourth of the wealth in this country is controlled by the richest 1 percent of the population.[13] Almost 20 percent of all American families have a negative net worth, meaning they have more liabilities than assets. Paul Samuelson, an economist, provides a dramatic metaphor of the disparity that exists between the very rich and most people in the United States:

If we made an income pyramid out of a child's blocks, with each layer portraying $1,000 of income, the peak would be far higher than the Eiffel Tower, but almost all of us would be within a yard of the ground.[14]

Given the huge wealth of the richest fifth, it is clear that a simple redistribution of some of the wealth from the top fifth to the lowest fifth could easily wipe out poverty. Of course, that is not politically acceptable to members of the top fifth who have the greatest control of the government. It should also be noted that many of these rich families are able to avoid paying income taxes by taking advantage of tax loopholes and tax shelters.

Similar disparities between the rich and the poor are found when looking at annual income instead of total wealth. The poorest fifth receives only 5 percent of the national income, whereas the richest fifth receives over 40 percent of the national income. This pattern has remained virtually unchanged since World War II.[15]

In our society it is common for heads of major corporations to earn $500,000 or more per year.[16] In 1987, Lee Iacocca, one of the nation's highest-paid ex-

BOX 3.2

The Ideology of Individualism

W ealth is generally inherited in this country. There are few individuals who actually move up the social status ladder. Having wealth opens up many doors (through education and contacts) for children of the wealthy to make large sums of money when they become adults. For children living in poverty there is little chance to escape when they become older. Yet, the individualism myth is held by many. It states that the rich are personally responsible for their success and that the poor are to blame for their failure. The main points of this individualism myth are:

1. Each individual should work hard and strive to succeed in competition with others.

2. Those who work hard should be rewarded with success (such as wealth, property, prestige, and power).

3. Because of widespread and equal opportunity, those who work hard will in fact be rewarded with success.

4. Economic failure is an individual's own fault and reveals lack of effort and other character defects.

   The poor are blamed for their circumstances in our society. Blaming the poor has led to a stigma being attached to poverty, particularly to those who receive public assistance (welfare).

ecutives, earned nearly $18 million in salary, cash and stock bonuses, and exercised stock options—an incredible average of nearly $350,000 per week![17] In addition, these highly paid executives enjoy many other tax-free benefits from their corporations: expense accounts, use of cars and private jets, paid memberships in health clubs, medical care, theater tickets, and vacations.

Millions of Americans regularly do not get enough to eat because they are poor. A 1985 study found that an estimated 20 million Americans are hungry at least some period of time each month.[18] The study concluded that cuts in social programs, particularly in food stamps, have left more people hungry than at any time since the 1930s. The study concluded that "Hunger is a problem of epidemic proportions across the nation." The researchers found that alarmingly some health

clinics in poor areas are seeing cases of kwashiorkor and marasmus, two "Third World diseases of advanced malnutrition," as well as vitamin deficiencies, diabetes, lethargy, "stunting," and other health problems traceable to inadequate food. The brain of an infant grows to 80 percent of its adult size within the first three years of life. If supplies of protein are inadequate during this period, the brain stops growing, the damage is irreversible, and the child will be permanently retarded.[19]

J. W. Coleman and D. R. Cressey describe the effects of having, and not having, wealth:

Differences in income and wealth among the rich, the poor, and the middle class have profound effects on life styles, attitudes toward others, and even attitudes toward oneself. The poor lack the freedom and autonomy so prized in our society. They are trapped

BOX 3.3

Wealth Perpetuates Wealth, and Poverty Perpetuates Poverty

I n this excerpt, C. Wright Mills describes one way in which living in the world of wealth educates wealthy children to be financially successful:

The exclusive schools and clubs and resorts of the upper social classes are not exclusive merely because their members are snobs. Such locales and associations have a real part in building the upper-class character, and more than that, the connections to which they natu-rally lead help to link one higher circle with another. So the distinguished law student, after prep school and Harvard, is "clerk" to a Supreme Court judge, then a corporation lawyer, then in the diplomatic service, then in the law firm again. In each of these spheres, he meets and knows men of his own kind, and, as a kind of continuum, there are the old family friends and the schoolboy chums, the dinners at the club, and each year of his life the summer resorts. In each of these circles in which he moves, he acquires and exercises a confidence in his own ability to judge, to decide, and in this confidence he is supported by his ready access to the experience and sensibility of those who are his social peers and who act with decision in each of the important institutions and areas of public life. One does not turn one's back on a man whose presence is accepted in such circles, even under most trying circumstances. All over the top of the nation, he is "in," his appearance, a certificate of social position; his voice and manner, a badge of proper training; his associates, proof at once of their acceptance and of his stereotyped discernment.

In contrast, Ben Bagdikian describes how living in poverty leads to despair, hopeless-ness, and failure:

It was midafternoon but the tenement was dark. Grey plastic sheeting was tacked to the insides of the living room windows. . . . Plaster was off an expanse of ceiling and walls. . . . In one corner of the kitchen was a small refrigerator, in another a table with three legs and one chair. There was a stained stove bearing a basin full of children's clothes soaked in cold soapy water. . . . Through one kitchen door was a bathroom dominated by a toilet covered by boards; it had frozen and burst during the winter. Through another door was "the kid's room." . . . In this room slept seven children, in two beds. Neither bed had a mattress. The children slept on the springs. . . .

Outside, Sister Mary William . . . said: "You figure out what's going to happen to Harry Martin when he finds out he's never going to be a lawyer. And his brother's never going to be a doctor. And his sister's never going to be a nurse. The worst most of us have to resign ourselves to is that there's no Santa Claus. Wait until this hits those kids."

Sources: C. Wright Mills, *The Power Elite* (New York: Oxford University Press, 1956), pp. 69–70. Ben H. Bagdikian, *In the Midst of Plenty: The Poor in America* (Boston: Beacon Press, 1964), p. 75.

*by their surroundings, living in rundown, crime-
ridden neighborhoods that they cannot afford to
leave. They are constantly confronted with things they
desire but have little chance to own. On the other
hand, wealth provides power, freedom, and the ability
to direct one's own fate. The wealthy live where they
choose and do as they please, with few economic
constraints. Because the poor lack education and
money for travel, their horizons seldom extend
beyond the confines of their neighborhood. In
contrast, the world of the wealthy offers the best
education, together with the opportunity to visit places
that the poor haven't even heard of.*

*The children of the wealthy receive the best that
society has to offer, as well as the assurance that they
are valuable and important individuals. Because the
children of the poor lack so many of the things
everyone is "supposed" to have, it is much harder for
them to develop the cool confidence of the rich. In our
materialistic society people are judged as much by
what they have as by who they are. The poor cannot
help but feel inferior and inadequate in such a
context.*[20]

DEFINING POVERTY IS A POLICY PROBLEM

In spite of all of the time spent on poverty research, we
as yet have not agreed on how to define poverty. A
family of four that earns $9,000 per year on a farm may
not view themselves as being "poverty stricken," especially if they have no rent to pay, are able to grow much
of their own food, and are frugal and creative in securing essential needs. On the other hand, a family of four
that earns $12,000 per year in a city that has a high cost
of living may be deeply in debt, especially if they have
high rent and unexpected medical bills.

The usual definitions of poverty are based on a lack
of money. Income per year is the measure most commonly used. There are two general approaches: the
absolute approach and the relative approach.

The *absolute approach* holds that a certain amount
of goods and services are essential to an individual's or

a family's welfare. Those who do not have this minimum amount are viewed as poor. The fundamental
problem with this approach is that there is no agreement about what constitutes "minimum" needs. Depending on the income level selected, the number and
the percentage of the population who are poor change
substantially, along with the characteristics of those defined as poor.

Another serious problem with the absolute definition of poverty is that it does not take into account the
fact that people are poor not only in terms of their own
needs but also in relation to others who are not poor.
Poverty is relative to time and place. Those Americans
labeled poor today would certainly not be poor by the
standards of 1850, nor would they be viewed as poor
by the standards existing in India or in other underdeveloped countries. In the 1890s people without electricity did not usually view themselves as being poor;
yet today, a family without electricity is usually considered to be poor. Kenneth Boulding adds:

*In the twentieth century, the per capita income of
the richest country is at least forty times that of the
poorest . . . and the gulf widens between them all the
time. It is this gulf which constitutes the main problem
of poverty today. Persons regarded by a rich society as
very poor would be regarded as relatively rich in a
poor society. We see this illustrated in the fact that to
the American, the migrant laborer is the poorest of the
poor and constitutes in his mind a serious problem.
To the Mexican villager, joining the ranks of our
migrant workers is seen as a road to riches and as a
way to lift the grinding burden of the poverty under
which he labors. And yet Mexico is one of the richer of
the poor countries. To hundreds of millions of Asians
and Africans, the standard of life of the Mexican
laborer would seem almost luxurious.*[21]

The *relative approach* in essence states that a person is poor when his or her income is substantially less
than the average income of the population. For example, anyone in the lowest fifth (or tenth, or fourth) of
the population is regarded as poor. By defining poverty
in these terms we avoid having to define absolute
needs, and we also put more emphasis on the inequality of incomes. With a relative approach poverty will
persist as long as income inequality exists. The major

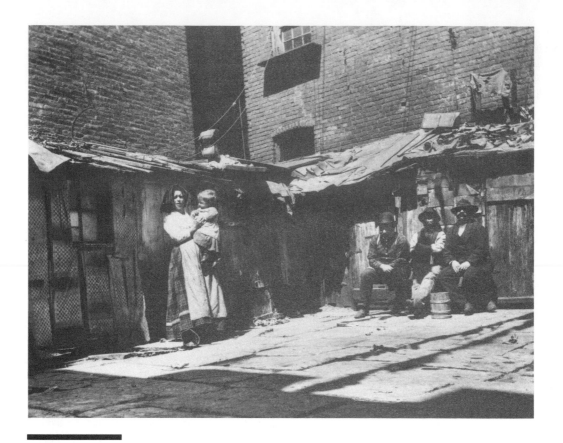

*In the 1880s reporter and social reformer Jacob Riis photographed the slums of the Manhattan's Lower
East Side and shocked complacent New Yorkers with their publication in* How the Other Half Lives.
*"Half" was actually an underestimate: fully three-quarters of all New Yorkers, like these Jersey Street
residents, lived in tenements, and many of these dwelled in abject poverty.*

weakness with a relative approach is that it tells us
nothing about how badly or how well the people at the
bottom of the income distribution actually live. With
poverty measures, ideally, we want to know not only
how many people are poor but also how desperate
living conditions are.

The U.S. government has generally chosen to use
the absolute approach in defining poverty. With the
high inflation rate the poverty line is adjusted upward
each year. In 1987 the government set the poverty line
at $11,203 for a family of four.[22]

WHO ARE THE POOR?

An encouraging trend is that the proportion of people
below the poverty line has gradually been decreasing
in the last 80 years. Prior to the 20th century a majority
of the population lived in poverty. In 1937 President
Franklin D. Roosevelt stated, "I see one third of a nation
ill-housed, ill-clad, ill-nourished."[23] In 1962 the President's Council on Economic Advisors estimated that
one fifth of the population was in poverty.[24] In 1986

13.6 percent of the nation was estimated to be below the poverty line.[25] An alarming concern is that since 1978 there has been an increase in the proportion of the population that is poor.

Michael Harrington points out that the poor are "invisible" in our society; that is, their clothes are not markedly different, our superhighways carry us quickly past their dilapidated homes, and they are such a heterogeneous group that they cannot politically organize to make their needs known.[26]

Population Categories of the Poor

Poverty is concentrated in certain population categories, including one-parent families, children, the elderly, large-sized families, and minorities. Educational level, unemployment, and place of residence are also factors related to poverty.

ONE-PARENT FAMILIES   Most one-parent families are headed by a female. Thirty-four percent of female-headed families are in poverty, compared to 9 percent for two-parent families.[27] Single mothers who are members of a racial minority (for example, blacks, Chicanos, American Indians) are particularly vulnerable to poverty because they are subjected to double discrimination in the labor market because of their race and sex. Women who work full time are paid on the average only about 65 percent of what men who work full time are paid.[28] Many single mothers are unable to work because of lack of transportation and lack or high cost of day-care facilities and because they have received little training for available job openings. Unable to work, they have to rely on public assistance (benefits that are often below the poverty line) in the form of Aid to Families with Dependent Children (AFDC). Of the families living in poverty, *half* are headed by a single mother.[29] About one out of every five children in this country is now living apart from one parent, and because of increasing divorce rates, separations, and births outside of marriage, it is estimated that a majority of the children born today will spend part of their first 18 years in a family headed by a single mother.[30] Single-parent families now compose more than 20 percent of all families in the United States.[31] The increase in one-parent families has led to an increase in the feminization of poverty.

CHILDREN   Approximately 35 percent of the poor are children under the age of 16. More than half of these children live in families where the father is absent.[32] Many of these children rely on AFDC payments for meeting the basic necessities.

THE ELDERLY   About 15 percent of the poor are people aged 65 and older.[33] Many of the elderly depend on social security pensions or public assistance payments (in the form of Supplementary Security Income) to meet basic necessities. Over 43 percent of the elderly have pretransfer incomes below the poverty line.[34]

Since the 1964 War on Poverty programs were enacted, the population group that has benefited most from programs to reduce poverty has been the elderly. Programs such as Medicare, Supplemental Security Income, and increases in monthly payments under the Old Age, Survivors, Disability, and Health Insurance Program have reduced poverty among the elderly from over 25 percent in 1964 to around 12 percent at present.[35]

LARGE-SIZED FAMILIES   Larger-size families are more apt to be poor, partly because more income is needed as family size increases. It now costs an estimated $140,000 to raise a child from birth to age 18.[36]

MINORITIES   Contrary to popular stereotypes, most poor people (over two thirds) are white.[37] But members of most minority groups are disproportionately apt to be poor. Blacks, for example, compose about 12 percent of the total population, yet they constitute over 25 percent of all the poor.[38] One out of every three black persons is poor, compared to one out of ten white persons.[39] Approximately a third of American Indian families live below the poverty line, and about 25 percent of the Mexican Americans (or Chicanos) live in poverty—particularly migrant agricultural workers.[40]

It has become all but impossible to claim that the poor are still "invisible" in our society.

Racial discrimination is a major reason why most racial minorities are disproportionately poor.

Additional Factors Related to Poverty

EDUCATION   Achieving less than a ninth-grade education is a good predictor of poverty. Completing high school, however, is not a guarantee that one will earn wages adequate to avoid poverty because many of the poor have graduated from high school. Obtaining a college degree is an excellent predictor of avoiding poverty because only a small proportion of those with a college degree live in poverty.[41]

EMPLOYMENT   Being unemployed is of course associated with poverty. However, being employed is not a guarantee of avoiding poverty because over a million family heads work full time but earn less than the poverty level.[42]

The general public (and many government officials) wrongly assume that obtaining jobs for unemployed adults is the key to ending poverty. However, jobs alone cannot end poverty.

PLACE OF RESIDENCE   People who live in rural areas have a higher percentage of poverty than people who live in urban areas. In rural areas wages are low, there is high unemployment, and work tends to be seasonal. The Ozarks, Appalachia, and the South have pockets of rural poverty with high rates of unemployment.[43]

People who live in urban slums constitute the largest geographical group in terms of numbers of poor people. The decaying cities of the Northeast and Midwest have particularly large urban slums. Poverty is also extensive on Indian reservations and among seasonal migrant workers.

BOX 3.4

The Farm Crisis

I n the 1980s hundreds of thousands of farmers filed for bankruptcy or quit before creditors closed in. The farm population dropped 11.5 percent between 1980 and 1985. Now, less than 3 percent of working adults are farmers. Less than 3 percent of working adults are now producing all the food to feed the people in this country. Two hundred years ago, most Americans were involved in producing food.

There are a variety of reasons why many farmers are financially in trouble and are living in poverty. Some borrowed money at high interest rates several years ago to buy more equipment, seed, and land; now, with prices for agricultural products being depressed, they have immense difficulty in making mortgage payments. Every summer some areas of the country experience a drought, which sharply reduces crop production. Exportation of agricultural products to other countries is sharply declining, as the "green revolution" (the use of American ideas, personnel and equipment to adopt new grain and livestock varieties with new technology) is blossoming with a vengeance. Countries that once were good customers of U.S. farmers now produce all their own food, and some even sell surpluses in competition with U.S. farmers. India, for example, used to be a good food customer of the United States, but it became self-sufficient in food production in the late 1970s and now is a modest exporter.

Amazingly, the main reason many farmers are in financial trouble is because American farmers are the most efficient in the world. American farming is too successful for its own good. Too many farmers are growing too much food. A growing food surplus at home and abroad is depressing farm income.

Sadly, millions of people are hungry in this country; some are starving. Starvation is a major problem in Ethiopia and many other Third World countries. If surplus food is produced but millions of people are not getting enough to eat, then food distribution systems have not been adequately developed.

What is the answer to the farm crisis? There is a lack of agreement among authorities. The federal government has had a variety of programs over the years. One of the more controversial programs in the past was the Soil Bank Program, which paid farmers to take part of their land out of production for a few years.

What is happening at present is that those farmers who are in greatest financial difficulty are being forced into bankruptcy and thereby compelled to walk away penniless from their land. The hurt of working seven days a week, 52 weeks a year for a number of years and then being forced to leave penniless is one of the severest tragedies in America at the present time.

Source of statistics: Kenneth R. Sheets, "A Bumper Crop in Trouble," *U.S. News & World Report*, August 18, 1986, pp. 14–15.

All these factors indicate that some people are more vulnerable to poverty than others. Michael Harrington, who coined the term "Other America" for the poor in the United States, notes the poor made the simple mistake of:

... being born to the wrong parents, in the wrong section of the country, in the wrong industry, or in the wrong racial or ethical group. Once that mistake has been made, they could have been paragons of will and morality, but most of them would never even have had a chance to get out of the other America.[44]

CAUSES OF POVERTY

There are a number of possible causes of being poor:

- A high unemployment rate
- Poor physical health
- Physical disabilities
- Emotional problems
- Extensive medical bills
- Alcoholism
- Drug addiction
- Large-sized families
- Job displacements due to automation
- Lack of an employable skill
- Low educational level
- Female head of household with young children
- No cost-of-living increases for people on fixed incomes
- Racial discrimination
- Having an "ex-convict" or "crazy" label
- Living in a geographical area where jobs are scarce
- Divorce, desertion, or death of a spouse
- Gambling
- Budgeting problems and mismanagement of resources
- Sex discrimination

- Being a crime victim
- Having an antiwork ethic
- Underemployment
- Low-paying jobs
- Mental retardation
- Being beyond the age of retirement

This list is not exhaustive. However, it serves to show that (*a*) there are a large number of causes of poverty; (*b*) eliminating the causes of poverty would require a wide range of social programs; and (*c*) poverty interacts with almost all other social problems—such as emotional problems, alcoholism, unemployment, racial and sex discrimination, medical problems, crime, gambling, and mental retardation. The interaction between poverty and these other social problems is complicated. As indicated, these other social problems are contributing causes of poverty. Yet, for some social problems, poverty is also a contributing *cause of* those problems (such as emotional problems, alcoholism, and unemployment). Being poor intensifies the effects (the hurt) of all social problems.

THE CULTURE OF POVERTY

To some extent, poverty is passed on from generation to generation in a cycle of poverty (Figure 3.1). Why? Some authorities argue that the explanation is due to a "culture of poverty." Oscar Lewis, an anthropologist, is one of the chief proponents of this cultural explanation.[45]

Lewis examined poor neighborhoods in various parts of the world and concluded the poor are poor because they have a distinct culture, or lifestyle. The culture of poverty arises after extended periods of economic deprivation in highly stratified capitalistic societies. Such economic deprivation is brought about by high rates of unemployment, underemployment for unskilled labor, and low wages for those employed. Such economic deprivation leads to the development of attitudes and values of despair and hopelessness.

FIGURE 3.1

Cycle of Poverty

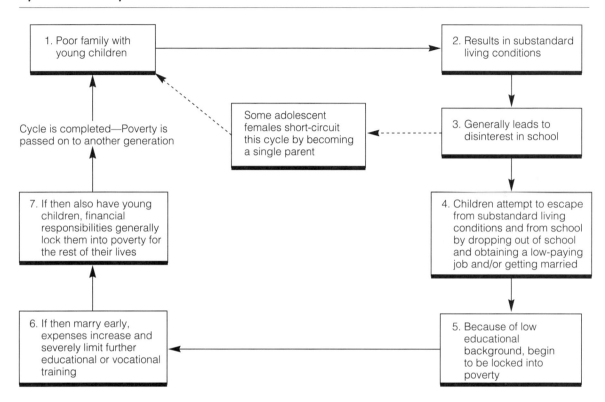

Lewis describes these attitudes and values as follows:

The individual who grows up in this culture has a strong feeling of fatalism, helplessness, dependence, and inferiority, a strong present-time orientation with relatively little disposition to defer gratification and plan for the future, and a high tolerance for psychological pathology of all kinds.[46]

The main reference for poor people living in cultures of poverty is their poor neighbors. A successful person in some neighborhoods is someone who knows where the next meal is coming from, and a "big success" may be someone who gets a job on an assembly line. People with such attitudes become trapped in their own beliefs; they have low-level goals and put

forth little effort to improve their circumstances. Another value they acquire that traps them is instant gratification, in which they are not inclined to defer immediate rewards so that long-range goals, such as a college education, can be reached.

Once developed, this culture continues to exist, even when the economic factors that created it (for example, lack of employment opportunities) no longer exist. The culture's attitudes, norms, and expectations serve to limit opportunities and prevent escape. A major reason the poor remain locked into their culture is that they are socially isolated. They have few contacts with groups outside their own culture and are hostile to the institutions (for example, social services and education) that might be able to help them escape poverty. They reject such institutions because they perceive them as belonging to the dominant class. Furthermore, because they view their financial circumstances as private matters and as hopeless, and because they lack political and organizational skills, they do not take collective action to try to resolve their problems.

The culture of poverty theory has been controversial and widely criticized. Eleanor Leacock argues that the distinctive culture of the poor is not the *cause* but the *result* of their continuing poverty.[47] She agrees that the poor tend to emphasize "instant gratification," which involves spending and enjoying one's money while it lasts. But she argues instant gratification is a result of being poor because it makes no sense to defer gratification when a person is pessimistic about the future. Deferred gratification is only a rational response when one is optimistic that postponing pleasures today by saving the money will reap greater benefits in the future. (Interestingly, studies have found that when ghetto residents are able to obtain a stable, well-paying job, they then display the middle-class value of deferred gratification.[48]) Because of poverty, Leacock argues, the poor are forced to abandon middle-class attitudes and values because such values are irrelevant to their circumstances. If they had stable, well-paying jobs, they would likely take on the values of the middle class.

In an even stronger indictment, William Ryan criticizes the poverty culture theory as simply being a classic example of "blaming the victim."[49] Blaming the poor for their circumstances is a convenient excuse, according to Ryan, for avoiding developing the programs and policies thought necessary to eradicate poverty. The real culprit is the social system that allows poverty to exist. Ryan says bluntly that the poor are not poor because of their culture but because they do not have enough money.

Pro and con arguments for the culture of poverty theory continue to persist. There are many reasons, both external and internal, why a person may be poor. External reasons include high rates of unemployment and underemployment, racial discrimination, automation that causes people to lose their jobs, lack of job-training programs, sex discrimination, a shortage of programs to eradicate poverty, and inflation. Internal reasons include having a physical or mental impairment, being alcoholic, having obsolete job skills, becoming a parent at an early age, dropping out of school, and being uninterested in taking available jobs.

FUNCTIONS OF POVERTY

Obviously, poverty is dysfunctional, mainly to the poor themselves but also to the affluent. However, realizing that poverty also seems to have some functions in society can help us understand why some decision makers are not actively seeking to eradicate poverty. Eleven functions[50] provided by the poor for affluent groups are:

1. They are available to do the unpleasant jobs that no one else wants to do;

2. By their activities, they subsidize the more affluent (an example of such an activity is domestic service for low pay);

3. Jobs are established for those people, such as social workers, who provide services to the poor;

4. They purchase goods, such as those of poor quality, that otherwise could not be sold;

5. They serve as examples of deviance that are frowned on by the majority and that thereby support dominant norms;

6. They provide an opportunity for others to practice their "Christian duty" of helping the less fortunate;

7. They make mobility more likely for others because they are removed from the competition for a good education and good jobs;

8. They contribute to cultural activities by providing, for example, cheap labor for the construction of monuments and works of art;

9. They create cultural forms (for example, jazz and the blues) that are often adopted by the affluent;

10. They serve as symbolic opponents for some political groups and as constituents for others;

Volunteers in Milwaukee prepare fruit salad for a church-sponsored meal program for the needy.

11. They often absorb the costs of change (for example, by being the victims of high levels of unemployment that result from technological advances).

Also, denigrating the poor has the psychological function for some Americans of making them feel better about themselves.

Partly because poverty is functional, our society makes only a halfhearted effort to eradicate or at least reduce it. To eliminate it would mean a redistribution of income from the rich to the poor. Because the rich control the political power, they have generally been opposed to proposals that would eliminate poverty, such as guaranteed annual income programs. Gans emphasizes this point.

Legislation in America tends to favor the interests of the businessman, not the consumers, even though the latter are a vast majority; of landlords, not tenants; of doctors, not patients. Only organized interest groups have the specific concerns and the time, staff, and money to bring their demands before government officials. . . . The poor are powerless because they are a minority of the population, are not organized politically, are often difficult to organize, and are not even a homogeneous group with similar interests that could be organized into a single pressure group. . . . Given the antagonism toward them on the part of many Americans, any programs that would provide them with significant gains are likely to be voted down by a majority. Legislative proposals for a massive anti-poverty effort . . . have always run into concerted and united opposition in Washington.[51]

Our government has the resources to eliminate poverty—but not the will. It has been estimated that it would cost less than one seventh of our annual defense expenditure to raise the income of all Americans above the poverty line.[52]

PROGRAMS TO COMBAT POVERTY

Because poverty interacts with nearly every other social problem, almost every existing social service—to some extent—combats poverty (such as Alcoholics Anonymous, health care programs, vocational rehabilitation, Parents without Partners, foster care, adoption, day care, Head Start, housing programs, urban renewal, and community action programs). Such programs indirectly reduce poverty by alleviating other social problems that happen to interact with poverty. These programs are too numerous to describe fully in this text. This section will instead describe income maintenance programs that are directly designed to alleviate poverty. Income maintenance programs include social insurance programs and public assistance programs.

Social Insurance Programs

OLD AGE, SURVIVORS, DISABILITY, AND HEALTH INSURANCE (OASDHI)   This social insurance program was created by the 1935 Social Security Act. Generally, OASDHI is referred to as "social security" by the public. It is the largest income insurance program and is designed to partially replace income that is lost when a worker retires or becomes disabled. Cash benefits are also paid to survivors of "insured" workers.

Payments to beneficiaries are based on previous earnings. Rich as well as poor are eligible if insured. Benefits are provided to fully insured workers at age 65 or older (age 62 if somewhat smaller benefits are taken). Dependent husbands or wives over age 62 and dependent children under age 18 (no age limit on disabled children who become disabled before 18) are also covered under the retirement benefits.

Participation in this insurance program is compulsory for most employees. The program is financed by a payroll tax assessed equally to employer and employee. The rate has gone up gradually. Eligibility for benefits is based on the number of years in which social security taxes have been paid.

A major concern in recent years has been the financial soundness of OASDHI. Since 1935, the social security (FICA) tax has led to a build-up in the trust fund for OASDHI. But the liberalization of benefits and the increase in recipients in recent years have raised concern about the fact that the system is now paying out more than it is taking in. In times of high unemployment and recession, the number of workers paying into OASDHI is decreased. The decline in the birth rate, with a steadily increasing retired population, is also creating problems for OASDHI because the number of recipients is increasing faster than the number of the younger working population. If OASDHI is not to collapse, benefits may have to be scaled back, taxes increased, or both.

MEDICARE   In 1965 Congress enacted Title XVIII (Medicare) to the Social Security Act. Medicare has two parts: hospital insurance and medical insurance. Hospital insurance helps pay for inpatient hospital care, inpatient care in a skilled nursing facility, home health care, and hospice care. Medical insurance helps pay for medically necessary doctors' services, outpatient hospital services, and a number of other medical services and supplies that are not covered by the hospital insurance part of Medicare. The hospital insurance part is financed by a surcharge on social security taxes that are paid by employers and employees. The medical insurance part is a voluntary insurance plan for which enrollees are charged a monthly premium. (More than two thirds of the costs of the medical insurance premium is paid from general revenues of the federal government.) Medicare, a public health insurance program, is more fully described in Chapter 14.

UNEMPLOYMENT INSURANCE   This program was also created by the 1935 Social Security Act and provides benefits to workers who have been laid off or, in certain cases, fired. Unemployment insurance is financed by a

Despite the existence of unemployment insurance for over fifty years, the suspicion that weekly benefits are a disincentive to seeking work still lingers.

tax on employers. The weekly benefit amount for which the unemployed are eligible, along with the number of weeks, varies from state to state. In many states the unemployed are eligible for benefits for about a year. To be eligible in most states a person must (*a*) have worked a certain number of weeks in covered employment; (*b*) be ready, willing, and able to work; (*c*) file a claim for benefits and be registered in a public employment office; and (*d*) demonstrate that unemployment is due to a lack of work for which she or he is qualified.

Unemployment insurance benefits help individuals and families who become unemployed due to a lack of work. In our society, where employment is valued highly, being without work can be a demeaning experience.

In recent years the unemployment rate has ranged from 5 percent to 11 percent of able-bodied workers. Such a high rate clearly indicates a lack of available jobs.

On the other hand, the unemployment insurance program has received sharp criticism because it has been claimed that some of the unemployed would rather collect insurance benefits (and spend the winter in a warmer climate) than make a concerted effort to obtain employment.[53]

WORKERS' COMPENSATION INSURANCE   This program provides both income and assistance in meeting medical expenses for injuries sustained on a job. The program was enacted after a series of lawsuits by injured employees against employers—the only recourse employees had. The first workers' compensation program was the Federal Employees Compensation Act of 1908. Individual states gradually passed workers' compensation laws modeled after the program for federal employees. By 1920 all but six southern states had such laws, but it was not until 1948 that all states had adequate coverage.[54] Cash benefits are paid for total or temporary disability or death. Medical benefits cover hospital and doctors' fees. Rehabilitation benefits are also available for those needing aftercare and retraining in order to again become employable. Workers' compensation is financed by a tax on employers.

Public Assistance Programs

Public assistance is sometimes viewed as synonymous with "welfare" by the general public; yet there are hundreds of other social welfare programs. Public assistance has primarily residual aspects, and applicants must undergo a "means test" that reviews their assets and liabilities to determine their eligibility for benefits.

Adherents of the residual view of public assistance generally hold the following opinions:

1. Assistance should be made as unpleasant as possible as a deterrent to its use. This is to be accomplished by giving relief in kind rather than money; by threatening prosecution; by continuous reevaluation of need; by making it only temporary; by stopping it if illegitimacy is involved; and by removing children from their own homes when these homes do not come up to standard.

2. Relief should be made unpleasant by requiring recipients to work for it regardless of the nature of the work, or how depressed the wage, or whether the requirement would be used as means for securing cheap labor; notwithstanding, income from this work is still labeled relief.

3. Assistance should be discouraged by making payments too low for anyone to really want it. It is argued by advocates of this approach that assistance in amounts greater than would be received by the lowest paid, most menial worker would encourage individuals to seek assistance in lieu of employment.

4. Outsiders should be prevented from seeking help by extending emergency aid for only short periods of time.

5. People should be forced to remain on their jobs or return to employment; this is accomplished by denying assistance to anyone who is guilty of a "voluntary quit."[55]

In contrast, the institutional view of public assistance (generally held by social workers) assumes or advocates the following:

1. An income floor for all citizens and the elimination of hunger and destitution or their threat should be provided as an instrument of social policy.

2. Relief should be extended to applicants who can qualify under eligibility requirements; that is, subjective, biased, and capricious considerations should be removed. Relief should be based on need as it is determined to exist by objective, rather than subjective, criteria and as a legally determined right.

3. It is assumed that workers generally prefer income from employment rather than from public welfare and that motivations to work are built into the economy in the form of social, cultural, and economic advantages to the employed man or woman.

4. Psychological and social barriers sometimes stand in the way of rehabilitation and employment. Counseling and other services may be needed to restore certain individuals to economic and social self-sufficiency.

5. Preservation of the independence and self-respect of the applicant for assistance is a prime consideration in the administration of programs of relief.

6. A punitive approach defeats the purpose for which assistance is used, namely, the restoration of the individual to normal functioning; it deepens feelings of inadequacy and dependency, causes embarrassment and humiliation, and brings destructive psychological defenses into play.

7. There are many pulls in society that tend to make work more appealing than public welfare—a higher standard of living and the prestige and sense of importance one receives from work, tenure, and emoluments of society.[56]

Public assistance programs have several distinguishing features.

Programs have a means test: Individuals applying for assistance have their income and assets examined in order to determine whether their financial needs meet the eligibility requirements. The means test is designed to ensure that individuals receiving assistance do not already have sufficient resources for a minimum level of subsistence. Resources that are examined include both earned and unearned income. Earned income is money in the form of salary or wages. Unearned income includes benefits from other public and private financial programs, gifts, life insurance annuities, stock dividends, rental income, inheritances, support payments from relatives, and so on.

Case-by-case determination of eligibility and benefit levels: All applicants have their applications for assistance closely reviewed on a case-by-case basis. Although there are federal, state, and local guidelines on eligibility and on how much is allowable as a benefit for eligible persons, the staff who administer public assistance have substantial discretion in deciding whether a client will receive special allowances in addition to basic benefits. Staff also have discretion in deciding which social services and other resources might be mobilized on behalf of the client. Eligibility determination, along with benefit level determination, is a cumbersome, lengthy process involving extensive review of documents.

Benefits are viewed as charity: In contrast to social insurance benefits, which recipients are viewed as legally entitled to, public assistance benefits are viewed as charity. In this country poor persons are not viewed as having a constitutionally established right to a minimum income. (In comparison, some foreign countries, such as Great Britain, recognize the right of those in poverty to be maintained and protected by government.)

Program benefits are paid from general government revenues: Public assistance benefits at the federal, state, and local levels are financed through taxes on personal income and on property.

The main public assistance programs include Supplemental Security Income, General Assistance, Medicaid, food stamps, housing assistance, and Aid to Families with Dependent Children. Each of these programs will be briefly described.

SUPPLEMENTAL SECURITY INCOME (SSI)   Under the SSI program, the federal government pays monthly checks to people in financial need who are 65 years of age and older or who are blind or disabled at any age. To qualify for payments, applicants must have no (or very little) regular cash income, own little property, and have little cash or few assets that could be turned into cash (such as stocks, bonds, jewelry, and other valuables).

The SSI program became effective January 1, 1974 and replaces the following programs that were created by the 1935 Social Security Act: Old-Age Assistance, Aid to the Blind, and Aid to the Permanently and Totally Disabled. SSI is the first federally administered assistance program. All other public assistance programs are administered through state and local governments. The word *supplemental* in the term *supplemental security income* is used because, in most cases, payments *supplement* whatever income may be available to the claimant. Even OASDHI benefits are supplemented by this program.

SSI provides a guaranteed minimum income (an income floor) for the aged, the blind, and the disabled. Aged, blind, and disabled are defined as follows:

Aged: 65 or over.

Blind: Vision no better than 20/200 (even with glasses) or tunnel vision (limited visual field of 20 degrees or less).

Disabled: A physical or mental impairment that prevents a person from doing any substantial, gainful work and is expected to last at least twelve months or result in death.

Administration of SSI has been assigned to the Social Security Administration. Financing of the program is through federal tax dollars, primarily income taxes.

GENERAL ASSISTANCE   The General Assistance (GA) program is supposed to serve those needing temporary, rather than long-term, financial support. It is designed to provide financial help to those in need who are ineligible for any other income-maintenance program. No clearly stated eligibility requirements exist for general assistance. GA is the only public assistance program that receives no federal funds. It is usually funded by property taxes. In large cities, such as New

York and Chicago, the state contributes substantially toward meeting the costs of GA. In most localities, however, the program is financed and administered at the local level, through the county or township or by a village or city. In many local governmental units, a political official has arbitrary jurisdiction over whether an applicant receives help. Most expenditures for GA are for medical care. In-kind payments (food, medical care, clothes, and other items rather than money) are frequent. Whenever feasible, communities usually attempt to move GA recipients into federally funded public aid programs because this reduces local expenses.

Payments for GA tend to be minimal and grudgingly made to discourage people from applying and becoming dependent on welfare. With in-kind and voucher payments, GA conveys to recipients the suspicion that they are incapable of managing their own affairs. Because able-bodied unemployed men and women sometimes find it necessary to seek GA benefits, GA is sometimes viewed as a public assistance program for the "undeserving poor." In some parts of the country, GA has demoralizing effects because many local program directors hold—and convey to recipients—a negative orientation toward providing assistance.

MEDICAID   This program provides hospital and medical care to certain poverty-stricken people. Those eligible are persons who are recipients of Aid to Families with Dependent Children or are SSI recipients. In addition, states have the option to include persons who are able to provide for their own daily living but whose income and resources are not sufficient to meet all their medical costs.

Medicaid is administered by the states, with financial participation by the federal government. Direct payments are made to providers of services. As is required for every public assistance program, Medicaid applicants must undergo a means test.

FOOD STAMPS   Tragically, an estimated 20 million people in the United States (the most powerful and one of the richest countries in the world) do not have enough food to eat.[57] Many of the people with inadequate diets

are poor. Not only does insufficient diet affect the individual, but research suggests also that severe nutritional deficits in expectant mothers may lead to irreversible brain defects in the child.

The food stamp program is designed to combat hunger. Food stamps are available to public assistance recipients and to other low-income families. These stamps are then traded in for groceries. With millions of Americans going hungry, the food stamp program is obviously underfunded.

HOUSING ASSISTANCE   Similar to food stamps and Medicaid, housing assistance is an "in-kind" program, rather than a cash program. Poor families are eligible for housing assistance. Generally, such assistance is provided in the form of public housing, usually large housing projects that are owned and operated by the government. In a public housing project, the tenants enjoy lower, subsidized rents. Because they pay less than the market value of their apartments, they are effectively receiving an income transfer, which, on the average, is approximately $1,000 a year.

In addition to the public housing projects, there are also housing assistance programs for low-income people who are renting and even buying their homes and apartments in the private market. In these programs, the rent or mortgage payment is reduced, with the Department of Housing and Urban Development (HUD) making up the difference.

AID TO FAMILIES WITH DEPENDENT CHILDREN (AFDC)   Originally called Aid to Dependent Children (ADC), AFDC is the most stigmatized public assistance program. The general public's conception of "welfare" is the AFDC program.

Although more money is spent on AFDC than on any other public assistance program, several times as much money is spent on social insurance programs.[58] The stigma attached to AFDC is one reason why the average monthly grant per recipient is lower than for supplemental security income (see Table 3.1).

In 1985 nearly $15 billion was spent on the AFDC program.[59] The reason the AFDC program is so expensive is that a majority of all persons receiving public assistance are on AFDC rolls.[60]

TABLE 3.1

Cash Assistance Programs, 1985

Program	Number of Recipients	Average Benefit per Recipient (per month)	Total Annual Payments (billions)
Supplemental Security Income (SSI)	4,138,000	$226	11
Aid to Families with Dependent Children (AFDC)	10,921,000	$119	15

Source: U.S. Bureau of the Census, *Statistical Abstract of the United States, 1987* (Washington, D.C.: U.S. Government Printing Office, 1987), pp. 362–363.

The precise definition of eligibility for AFDC varies from state to state. Payments are made for both the parent and the children in eligible families. To be eligible, the children must be deprived of parental support or care because of a parent's death, because of a parent's continued absence from the home (desertion, divorce, separation), or because the parent was never married. A change in federal legislation in 1988 now requires that all states must make AFDC payments to two-parent families in which both parents are unemployed. When both parents are unemployed, the breadwinner must agree to seek work actively, to register with the state unemployment service, and to participate in work-training programs. Most AFDC families are headed by a single parent, usually the mother and usually because of the father's absence from the home.[61]

ADC was renamed AFDC in 1962. When first enacted by the 1935 Social Security law, one of ADC's objectives was to enable mothers with young children to remain at home. Since 1935, our values surrounding working mothers have changed. There now is substantial effort, for psychological and financial reasons, to help AFDC mothers obtain gainful employment.

In 1988 the federal government enacted legislation to make significant changes in the AFDC program

that are designed to assist some AFDC recipients to enter the private work force. The major changes are as follows:

1. AFDC parents with children over age 3 have to participate in a new Job Opportunities and Basic Skills (JOBS) program that offers education, training, and work activities ranging from high school to community jobs.

2. States have to concentrate available resources on the toughest cases, which include young parents without a high school education, long-term recipients, and families with older children who are expected to lose eligibility.

3. JOBS participants are eligible to receive transportation and child-care assistance. AFDC recipients working their way off AFDC qualify for a year of transitional child-care and Medicaid benefits. States are permitted to charge for these transitional services on a sliding-scale basis.

4. The federal government now requires all states to make cash payments to two-parent unemployed AFDC families in which the breadwinner or breadwinners are actively seeking work.

5. Starting in 1994, one adult in each two-parent AFDC household will have to participate in a job

BOX 3.5

The Poverty Trap

Elaine Johnson, age 35, has recently become a grandmother. Her oldest daughter, Sylvia, is a 16-year-old unmarried mother. Today, May 13, is a significant day in their lives because Elaine and Sylvia are applying at Chicago's Public Welfare Office to place baby Tony's name on America's welfare rolls. He will represent the third successive generation in the Johnson family to receive AFDC benefits.

Elaine's parents migrated from Mississippi to Chicago in 1952, shortly after Elaine's birth. Her father got a job as a janitor for the school system, and her mother has been a part-time nurse's aide at a hospital. Elaine started high school and received above-average grades. She had hopes of getting a student loan to go to college. She wanted to get out of the ghetto in which she was being raised.

At the age of 17 she became pregnant. Her parents talked her out of an abortion, and she gave birth to Sylvia. Two months after the birth, she signed up for AFDC at the urging of her parents and friends. It would only be temporary, she thought, until she could get a better handle on her life. She found going to school and caring for a baby to be too much work, so she dropped out of high school in her senior year. She no longer had the same interests as her former friends who did not have a baby to care for. At times Elaine found it a joy to care for Sylvia, and at other times she found caring for the baby frustrating. Elaine went out as much as she could, when she had a little extra money and when she could find someone to babysit for her. Over the next fifteen years, Elaine had three other children. Only one of the four different fathers ever married her, and that marriage only lasted two and one-half years. He left home one day, complaining about children and responsibilities. He never returned, and Elaine has never heard from him.

search and, if it fails, spend sixteen hours a week in a state-organized work activity. A young parent can work instead toward a high school diploma.

6. States have to step up child-support collections from noncustodial parents, including automatic wage withholding on the court award of support payments. States will get federal money to set up a computerized tracking and monitoring system for child-support enforcement.

Financing and administering AFDC programs represent a sharing of federal and state control—and in many states, counties participate in the financing and administration. The federal government, through the Department of Health and Human Services, writes regulations to implement the Social Security laws. States, and often counties, then write their own regulations, within federal guidelines, relating to eligibility criteria, benefit standards, and qualifications of public assistance staff. If a state fails to comply with federal guidelines, it may lose federal support.

Decisions about AFDC eligibility are made by the executive, legislative, and judicial branches of government and at federal, state, and local levels. As a result,

Elaine has tried a variety of jobs while on AFDC—nurse's aide, dishwasher, waitress, and service station attendant. She discovered that costs for transportation, clothes, and babysitting left her no better off financially than if she stayed home and received her monthly AFDC checks. Life has been hard for Elaine. Because she is on welfare she feels like a second-class citizen and a "charity" case. She has had to pinch pennies all her life to try to make ends meet. Countless days she has fed her children on beans and rice. She sharply regrets not being able to give her children the material things that many other children have. While some parents are buying computers for their children, she takes her children to Goodwill's clothing store to try to find bargains on second-hand sneakers, shirts, blue jeans, and jackets.

She is living in a ghetto area and is alarmed that her oldest son, Marvin, is experimenting with cocaine and other drugs. The school system is another concern: A high percentage of students drop out, the windows in the buildings are boarded up, vandalism is frequent, physical attacks on teachers sometimes occur, and the educational quality is known to be inferior.

When Elaine discovered Sylvia was sexually active at 15, she pleaded with her not to make the mistake she did. When Sylvia continued to be sexually active, Elaine even took her to Planned Parenthood to receive birth control pills. Elaine's remaining dream is that her children will have a better life than hers. Tears often come to her eyes when she sees her children getting caught in the same poverty trap that she is in. Sylvia took her pills for several months. When the supply ran out, she never got around to going back to Planned Parenthood to get her prescription refilled.

Yes, today is a significant day for Elaine—significant in a sad sense because the third generation in her family is now going on welfare. As Elaine and Sylvia are walking toward the welfare department, Elaine is solemnly pondering why her life has turned out as it has. She also is wondering what it will take to give at least some of her children a chance for a better life.

---

the program is cumbersome, slow to change to meet emerging needs, and heavily involved in paperwork, "red tape," and bureaucratic processes.

The Poverty Cycle Among AFDC Families   A key question is whether our present punitive, residual approach to AFDC is influencing children born in AFDC families to grow up to be recipients themselves. Are we training whole generations for a life of dependency? If we stigmatize and are punitive to a mother who is not gainfully employed, are we not also creating substandard living conditions for her children and thereby increas-

ing the probability of passing dependency on to another generation? Statistics show that many people on public assistance had parents who were also recipients.[62] Also, it has been found that the longer a family receives assistance, the higher the rate of social problems their children manifest in their teenage years—higher rates of births outside of marriage, early marriage, emotional problems, truancy, delinquency, and dropping out of school.[63]

There are some additional serious shortcomings of the AFDC program. Most recipients are kept in poverty by inadequate assistance grants that average well

BOX 3.6

Women Accused of Welfare Fraud

W elfare fraud is rare, but it makes the news, whereas the merits of AFDC do not. Stories like the following help to promote the myth that most welfare recipients are cheaters and frauds.

CHICAGO (AP)—*A woman and her two adult daughters were charged Wednesday with cheating welfare agencies out of $250,000 over the last 11 years, authorities said.*

One of the sisters, ———, 32, used eight names for herself and dozens of names for fictitious children in collecting $150,000 in public aid checks, said James G. Piper, an assistant state's attorney. She was charged with 385 counts of theft.

Her sister ———, 26, was charged with 105 counts of theft and the mother, ———, 51, with 59 counts.

Source: *Wisconsin State Journal*, May 29, 1980, p. 3.

below the poverty level. In addition, the stigma attached to receiving AFDC also keeps many eligible needy people from applying.

Welfare Myths vs. Facts   When welfare programs are criticized, most of the criticism is leveled at the AFDC program. Much of this criticism is unfounded, as it is based on erroneous myths. A number of these myths will be examined:

Myth 1: Most welfare children are illegitimate. *Fact:* A sizable majority of the children receiving AFDC benefits are "legitimate."[64] To help AFDC families avoid unwanted pregnancies, the federal government in recent years has made family planning services available. (The author strongly objects to labeling any child "illegitimate." The marital status of one's parents has nothing to do with one's value as a human being.)

Myth 2: Welfare makes it profitable for women to have illegitimate babies. *Fact:* The size of families on AFDC has actually been declining, particularly since 1967, reflecting a general trend in the birth rate for the population as a whole. Welfare families have an average

of 2.2 children.[65] A majority of AFDC families consist of a mother and one or two children.[66] In the small proportion of AFDC families in which another child is born after the family is receiving benefits, the main reason may well be the lack of availability of appropriate family planning resources. Finally, it is estimated that on the average an AFDC family would experience a boost of $1,400 per year for each additional child.[67] Because it is estimated that it costs an average of over $140,000 to raise a child from birth to age 18, the amount of "profit" a mother might expect to realize from having an additional child is miniscule, even if she minimizes all expenditures for the child.

Myth 3: Give them more money and they'll drink it up. *Fact:* In 1985 the average monthly grant per recipient in the United States was $119.[68] This is hardly enough to meet bare essentials. How would you like to live on $119 per month? Furthermore, most AFDC families report that if they received extra funds, that money would go for essentials.[69]

Myth 4: Most welfare recipients are cheaters and frauds. *Fact:* If fraud is defined as a deliberate and knowing attempt by a client to deceive the agency, then fraud is remarkably low. A national survey found that one out of every twenty AFDC recipients was getting checks for which she or he was ineligible.[70] Less than one half of 1 percent of welfare cases are referred for prosecution for fraud.[71] Because determining eligibility is a cumbersome, complex process, most of these errors were identified as honest mistakes by state and local public assistance agencies or by recipients. The greatest difficulty about money paid out for AFDC is not fraud but error—mistakes unintentionally made either by the agency or by the recipient.[72] There is a substantial need to streamline the management of AFDC and reduce mistakes.

Myth 5: The welfare rolls are soaring out of control. *Fact:* Most of the caseload growth in the AFDC program occurred before 1973, with dramatic increases between 1970 and 1973. Since early in 1976, the number of people on AFDC in the United States has gradually fallen back from a high of 11.4 million to 10.9 million in 1985, a decrease of 4.4 percent.[73] There are many reasons for this recent stabilization, including the declining birthrate and increased use of family-planning resources.

Myth 6: Welfare is just a money handout, a dole. *Fact:* Most families on AFDC receive one or more social services designed to meet personal and social problems and, it is hoped, to make them self-supportive. Social services that are available vary widely from area to area and may include health care, financial counseling, counseling on home management, employment counseling, day care, vocational rehabilitation, homemaker services, consumer education, assistance in childrearing, Head Start, job training, and marriage counseling. The provision of social services to low-income families was one of the three programs enacted by the 1935 Social Security Act.

Myth 7: People on welfare are able-bodied loafers. *Fact:* Contrary to public opinion, there are few able-bodied persons receiving assistance. The vast majority of AFDC recipients are children. Less than 1 percent of welfare recipients are able-bodied, unemployed males.[74] The largest group of able-bodied adults is composed of AFDC mothers, most of whom head families where there is no able-bodied male present. Many of these mothers already work or are actively seeking work, receiving work training, or waiting to be called back after a layoff. Many of the remaining AFDC mothers have serious barriers to obtaining employment: having very young children to rear, needing to obtain a moderate-paying job that would offset the costs of child care, needing job skill training, and needing extensive medical or rehabilitative services before becoming employable. Contrary to the stereotype of the "welfare mother" as shiftless, lazy, and unwilling to take a job, even long-term AFDC mothers continue to have a strong work ethic but lack skills and confidence to obtain a job.[75]

A number of states have AFDC-UP, the program for unemployed or partially unemployed fathers. The number of recipients in this program has always been small. Of the able-bodied males in the program, all are required by law to be actively looking for work, or to be receiving work training to be eligible for benefits.

Myth 8: Most welfare families are black. *Fact:* The number of white families receiving AFDC is approximately the same as the number of black families.[76] Because blacks comprise about 12 percent of the U.S. population and over 40 percent of the AFDC recipients, the stigma attached to AFDC may be partly due to racial prejudice.

Myth 9: Why work when you can live it up on welfare? *Fact:* The average AFDC monthly payment per recipient in 1985 was $119, hardly enough to "live it up."[77] In most states payments to a welfare family of four with no other income are below the established poverty level.

Myth 10: Once on welfare, recipients will spend a lifetime on welfare. *Fact:* Only 10 percent of the households receive AFDC benefits for ten years or longer. Half the families on welfare have been receiving assistance for twenty months or less; two thirds have been receiving it for less than three years.[78]

Myth 11: Welfare is eating up tremendous chunks of our tax money, causing inflation and "bleeding the country dry." *Fact:* At the federal level about 1 percent of the federal budget is allocated to AFDC.[79] The largest single item in the national budget is defense spending.[80]

Myth 12: Welfare is only for the poor. *Fact:* The

United States pays out much more (many times more) to the rich than to the poor. These payments are not called welfare but instead are called research grants, training grants, tax loopholes, compensation, low-interest loans, and parity. Dale Tussing notes that the United States has two welfare systems.

Two welfare systems exist simultaneously in this country. One is well known. It is explicit, poorly funded, stigmatized and stigmatizing, and is directed at the poor. The other, practically unknown, is implicit, literally invisible, is nonstigmatized and nonstigmatizing, and provides vast but unacknowledged benefits for the nonpoor. . . . Our welfare systems do not distribute benefits on the basis of need. Rather, they distribute benefits on the basis of legitimacy. Poor people are viewed as less legitimate than non-poor people. . . . By and large, welfare programs for the poor are obvious, open and clearly labeled, and those for the non-poor are either concealed (as in tax laws, for instance) and ill understood, or are clothed in protective language. . . . Whether or not a person is poor can often be determined by the names of his welfare programs. If his programs are called "relief," "welfare," "assistance," "charity," or the like, he is surely poor; but if they are called "parity," "insurance," "compensation," or "compulsory saving," he is surely a member of the large majority of nonpoor persons who do not even think of themselves as receiving welfare payments.[81]

PROPOSED ALTERNATIVES

In the 1960s and 1970s Presidents Kennedy, Johnson, Nixon, Ford, and Carter advanced a number of proposals to alleviate poverty. Johnson was by far (with his War on Poverty programs) the most successful in getting programs passed and implemented. As noted earlier these programs have had some success in reducing the proportion of people below the poverty line. Yet, over 13 percent of our population (over 32 million

people) still remain in poverty. It appears the efforts of the 1960s and 1970s have dampened (sapped), at least temporarily, America's determination to combat poverty.

Practically everyone agrees that the present welfare system is cumbersome, inefficient, and often unfair. In states not having the AFDC-UP program, unemployed husbands are sometimes forced to desert their families so that the families will become eligible for benefits. (At present only about half of the states have an AFDC-UP program.) The administrative structure of most public assistance programs is very complicated, with decisions being made at federal, state, and local levels and at the three branches of government (executive, legislative, and judicial). It has been estimated that nearly half the money spent on AFDC is spent on administration and eligibility determination.

In recent years there has been a proliferation of new public assistance programs that are available to low-income families. Such programs include Head Start, public housing, Work Incentive (WIN), Medicaid, and Energy Assistance (to pay for heat). The proliferation of these programs has led to some problems in informing eligible recipients and to problems (from a taxpayer's view) that assertive families are receiving more than their "fair share" of assistance. Marilyn Flynn describes this latter problem:

A relatively new problem in benefit standards has arisen . . . as a result of the proliferation of means-tested programs sponsored by the government. A growing number of individuals and families now receive benefits from more than one source. For example, in a large metropolitan environment, an ambitious and assertive poor family might establish eligibility in the following programs: AFDC, food stamps, public housing, Medicaid, free school lunches, Headstart, and community day care. The total value of the benefits to one hypothetical AFDC family in New York City who participated in all these programs would equal the purchasing power of a worker with a gross income of $11,500 per year. On the other hand most American communities do not have all these resources nor are most assistance recipients knowledgeable and confident enough to pursue all the opportunities for public support.[82]

Family Allowances

The United States is the only Western, industrialized country without a family allowance program. Under a family allowance program the government pays each family a set amount based on the number of children. If payments were large enough, such a program would aid in eliminating poverty, particularly in large families.

There are some strong criticisms of a family allowance plan. If payments were made to all children the program would be very expensive, with much of the money going to nonpoor families. This problem could be solved, as Denmark has done, by varying the family allowance payments with income and terminating payments after a certain level of income is reached. (A criticism of such an approach, though, is that it would then involve a means test and continue to stigmatize recipients.) A second criticism of a family allowance program is that it would provide an incentive to increase the birthrate—at a time when overpopulation is a major concern. A final criticism of a family allowance program is that it would not provide payments to single individuals and childless couples who are poor.

Government as Last Resort Employer

The unemployment rate of able-bodied workers in recent years has been between 5 percent and 11 percent. In addition, an estimated million family heads are working full time but earning wages below the poverty line.[83] The government could establish a program in which all able-bodied poor could earn a certain minimum amount above the poverty line.

Yet, there is a question about whether such a program is politically feasible. Public work projects are usually viewed by the general public as being expensive, unproductive, and inefficient. Low-wage employers are also likely to object because such a program is apt to be competitive because workers may earn more by working for the government than by working for them.

Another criticism is that such a program would better serve only a small fraction of AFDC recipients;

as indicated earlier only a small minority of public assistance recipients are presently employable.

Guaranteed Annual Income

A variety of proposals with varying income base levels have been put forth, including proposals by Presidents Nixon and Carter. These proposals guarantee every American a certain annual income. The base level could conceivably be set slightly above the poverty line and be adjusted each year to account for inflation. Such a proposal, if implemented, would eradicate poverty.

Practically all guaranteed income proposals are based on the concept of a "negative income tax." With a negative income tax plan, persons earning above a certain level would pay income tax, whereas persons earning below that level would receive a grant—the negative tax—to bring their income up to the guaranteed level. Most negative income tax plans also contain an incentive to work provision that allows recipients to keep a proportion of their earnings above the guaranteed base level.

Many variations of the negative income tax are possible, and some have been tested by the federal government. The minimum income guarantee for a family of four, for example, could be set at the poverty line, and the incentive to work factor (negative income tax rate) could range widely. But such plans could be very expensive.

Using a hypothetical example, with a guaranteed base level of $4,000 for a family of four and the negative income tax factor at 25 percent—allowing a family to keep $75 out of every $100 earned—the family would receive subsidies until the break-even point of $16,000.

Example: $ 4,000   guaranteed base
          12,000   negative income tax factor at 25 percent—allowing a family to keep 75 percent of, in this case, $16,000 in earnings
    $16,000   break-even point

There are a number of advantages to negative income tax plans. Such plans would shift the focus of income maintenance programs from "charity" to a "right" of entitlement to a guaranteed income. The stigma of being a recipient would be reduced sharply, and the program would be relatively simple to administer, as eligibility would be based on income tax returns. Furthermore, the program would serve everyone who is poor, and if the base level is at the poverty line, poverty would be eradicated. Another advantage would be to reduce equity problems that have occurred under present programs, where nonworking people are eligible for several types of benefits (for example, food stamps and Medicaid) and may be able to achieve a higher standard of living than a low-income employed person who is eligible for few, if any, benefits. A negative income tax plan could also replace practically all other public assistance programs and thereby reduce the expense and complexity of administering a variety of programs.

A number of unanswered questions, however, have been raised by a negative income tax plan: (*a*) Such plans are based on the filing of income tax forms. If a family has little or no income (and no assets) must they wait nearly a year until their tax form is filed before being eligible for benefits? (*b*) Will a guaranteed income destroy the incentive to work? (*c*) The cost of living varies greatly between urban and rural areas and between different parts of the country. Should financial adjustments be made for this? But perhaps the biggest problem with a negative income tax plan is what has been called the "unholy triangle," that is, developing a plan that:

1. Has an adequate guaranteed base level.

2. Allows low-income workers to keep a sufficiently high percentage of their earnings above the guaranteed base level so that the incentive to work is not destroyed.

3. Is not exorbitantly expensive so that our national economy is not severely affected.

The federal government has shown considerable interest in negative income tax programs, as evidenced by the passage in 1973 of the Supplemental Security Income (SSI) program, which has a guaranteed income base. But negative income tax plans proposed by both Nixon and Carter were held up in Congress. Liberals argued that the level of payments was too low, as it would not move families above the poverty line. Conservatives objected that the plans would be too costly, as they would provide financial payments to many more poor families than do current public assistance programs. Conservatives also opposed the plan because they feared it would destroy the incentive to work and would be a handout program that provided "something for nothing."

In 1980 many fiscal conservatives were elected to political leadership positions, including President Ronald Reagan. In the 1980s the federal government focused on cutting back expenditures for public welfare programs rather than giving attention to developing new programs such as a negative income tax program.

Elimination or Reduction of the Causes of Poverty

As noted earlier there are a number of factors that cause and perpetuate poverty. Another way of combating poverty is to develop and expand programs to alleviate its major causes.

Laws to end racial and sex discrimination can be more vigorously enforced. Programs to curb alcohol and drug abuse can be expanded to reach out and serve more of those who are addicted. Higher-quality education programs (and more resources) are needed in pockets of poverty (for example, urban ghettos) to inspire students, to help them stay in school, and to help them achieve higher academic levels. Sex education and family planning services need to be provided to more teenagers and young adults to teach responsible sexuality and prevent unwanted pregnancies, which play a role in locking young people into poverty. Family planning services also need to be expanded to help couples who do not want, and cannot afford, large-sized families. An expanded public housing program is needed to provide adequate living quarters for those in need. A national health insurance program is needed to pay for unusually high medical bills, which at present wipe out the savings of some families and plunge them deep into debt.

Some families need financial counseling to help them more effectively manage and spend within the limits of their financial resources. Many middle-aged adults need educational programs on how to plan for their retirement years—the lifestyle they want, how to remain healthy, and how to prepare financially.

Provision of jobs for able-bodied workers is a key to reducing the number of people in poverty. In recent years unemployment rates have been high, ranging from 5 percent to 11 percent. Such high rates force many of the unemployed and their families into poverty. A variety of suggestions have been advanced to progress toward a full-employment society.

Able-bodied adults who do not have marketable job skills (perhaps because their skills have become obsolete) need to receive training for jobs that are available. (In Germany adults are paid by the government during the weeks or months they are receiving job training and job retraining.) Our government should have a program to financially assist workers and their families to relocate from areas of high unemployment to booming areas where jobs are readily available. Many areas need more quality day-care centers that charge reasonable rates so that single parents (and also two-parent families) can work. For the unemployed able-bodied, the government could be a "last resort" employer. In many other countries the government offers tax incentives to industries to locate in depressed areas. Another suggestion is to encourage industries to hire workers who have been unemployed for a long time by reimbursing employers for a portion of the new workers' salaries.

SOCIAL WORK AND PUBLIC WELFARE

Since the enactment of the 1935 Social Security Act, a wide variety of social services have been provided to public assistance recipients. The particular services provided vary widely from area to area (depending on state and county decisions) but include such services as counseling, day care, protective services, foster home care, services to the physically and mentally handicapped, information and referral, homemaker services, financial counseling, assistance in childrearing, family planning, health services, vocational train-

ing, and employment counseling. A large number of social workers are employed to provide such services.

Until 1972 social services and financial assistance were combined, and social workers were involved in financial eligibility determination. The 1972 Amendments to the Social Security Act separated services and assistance. Now, public assistance recipients are informed of available social services and of their right to request such services. Financial eligibility is now determined by staff who generally are not social workers.

Social work does have its gratifications—as comes from helping someone with a personal or social problem. Yet, social work is at times frustrating. These frustrations occur quite frequently in public welfare and include:

Having extensive paperwork to fill out.

Trying to meet the needs of clients when their needs are not served by existing programs.

Trying to change the huge public welfare bureaucratic structure to meet the needs of clients better. The public welfare system is slow to change to meet emerging needs and is filled with extensive "red tape."

Having a larger caseload than one can optimally and effectively serve.

Trying to keep informed about the numerous changes (program, organizational, and eligibility determination) that occur on an ongoing basis.

Working with discouraged clients who lack the necessary motivation to work toward improving their circumstances. Social work "interns" in field placement and new social workers frequently report this as being their greatest frustration and a severe "reality shock." They anticipated that after carefully working out a "casework plan" with a client to resolve some problem, that the client would follow through. Unfortunately, in many cases this does not happen. Future appointments may be broken by the client, and even if the client responsibly keeps future appointments, she or he is apt to have excuses for not following through on the commitment. These excuses can usually be interpreted to represent a lack of motivation.

Working with Discouraged People

The key variable in determining if clients will make positive changes in their lives is whether they have the motivation to make the efforts necessary to improve their circumstances. Failure in counseling or casework generally occurs when clients do not become motivated.

Many public assistance recipients are discouraged. Continued economic pressures, and generally a long series of past "failure" experiences when they have tried to improve their circumstances, have frequently sapped their motivation. Discouraged people tend to be traveling through life in an unhappy "rut" that is dull, stagnating and generally unfulfilling but that is also seen by them as safe, predictable, and secure. For them to make extensive efforts to improve their circumstances is viewed as risky, frightening, and having unpredictable and uncertain results. Many feel it is safer to remain in their present "rut" than to try something new that might further expose their weaknesses and result in psychological "hurt."

Seeking a job, finding transportation, and making day-care arrangements may be seen as "overwhelmingly" difficult for an unskilled AFDC mother with young children who has never been employed previously. For a wife with five children who periodically is physically beaten by her husband, seeking counseling or making separation arrangements may be seen as highly risky because the future would be uncertain, and she may fear such actions would only make her husband more abusive. For a person with a drinking problem who has recently lost his last two jobs, giving up drinking may be seen as giving up his main support "crutch."

To motivate a discouraged person, the social worker has to be an "encouraging person." According to Lewis Losoncy an encouraging person does the following:[84]

> Has complete acceptance for the discouraged person and conveys "I accept you exactly as you are, with no conditions attached." (She or he should not, however, convey acceptance of the deviant behavior that needs to be changed.)

Has a nonblaming attitude so that the discouraged person no longer feels a need to lie, pretend, or wear a mask.

Conveys empathy that she or he is aware and can to some extent feel what the discouraged person is feeling.

Conveys to the discouraged person that she or he is genuinely interested in the counselee's progress and conveys that the counselee is an important, worthwhile person. In order for discouraged persons to believe in themselves, they generally need an encouraging person who conveys the idea that they are important and worthwhile.

Notices (rewards) every small instance of progress—for example, if the person is wearing something new, the counselor says "That's new, isn't it? It really looks good on you." This is particularly valuable during the beginning of the relationship.

Conveys to the discouraged person that she or he has confidence in that person's capacity to improve.

Conveys sincere enthusiasm about the discouraged person's interests, ideas, and risk-taking actions.

Has the capacity to be a nonjudgmental listener so that the discouraged person's real thoughts and feelings can be expressed freely, without fear of censure.

Has the time to spend listening and understanding the discouraged person as fully as possible. Motivating a discouraged person takes a long, long time. Discouraged people generally have a long history of failures.

Has a sincere belief in the discouraged person's ability to find a purpose in life.

Allows the person to take risks without judging him or her.

Reinforces *efforts* made by the discouraged person. The important thing is that one tries and not necessarily whether one succeeds. By making efforts to improve, there is hope.

Helps the discouraged person to see the falsehood and negative consequences of self-defeating statements, such as "I'm a failure." Every person has skills and deficiencies, and every person should be encouraged to improve both strengths and weaknesses.

Recognizes that all that can be done is to give one's best efforts in trying to motivate a discouraged person. Success in motivating a discouraged person is not guaranteed. To give up hope of motivating a discouraged person means one will no longer be effective in working with that person.

Is skilled at looking for uniquenesses and strengths in an individual. These uniquenesses are communicated to the discouraged person so that the person begins to realize she or he is special and worthwhile. This process leads to a sense of improved self-worth and strengthens the courage to take risks and change.

Helps the discouraged person to develop perceptual alternatives (other ways of looking at life). For example, for a woman who is periodically physically beaten by her husband, it is appropriate to point out that other women in similar situations have separated from their husbands, which has led eventually either to an improved marital relationship or to a happier, independent life.

Is aware of the negative consequences of overdependency in a relationship. When the discouraged person is on the way to taking risks and making constructive changes, one should start to help the discouraged person to develop "self-encouragement," in which the counselee is encouraged to make and trust his or her own decisions and is encouraged to take more risks.

The Future

Programs created by the Social Security Act, along with the War on Poverty programs, have not wiped out poverty as hoped—and such a goal may be unrealistic. But these programs *have* sharply reduced the percentage who are poor and have helped many of those who remain in poverty. These are significant accomplishments and need to be so recognized. If our country continues to retreat by cutting back on social pro-

grams, it is likely that the percentage of the population that is poor will increase.

Poverty is interrelated with most other social problems. Therefore, it may well be that if the poverty problem intensifies, there will be rate increases in crime, emotional disorders, infant mortality, inadequate health care, inner city problems, substandard housing, alcoholism, dropping out of school, malnutrition, child neglect, and suicide. Is this what we want?

SUMMARY

In 1986, over 13 percent of our population was living below the poverty line. Poverty is relative to time and place.

An agreed on definition of poverty does not exist. The usual definitions of poverty are based on a lack of money, with annual income most commonly used to gauge who is poor. Income is defined using either an absolute approach or a relative approach. The pain of poverty involves not only financial hardships but also the psychological meaning that being "poverty stricken" has for a person.

Huge income and wealth gaps exist between the highest fifth and lowest fifth in our society. Social mobility (movement up the social status ladder) occurs rarely in our society. Wealth perpetuates wealth and poverty perpetuates poverty. The ideology of individualism and the Protestant ethic still stigmatize the poor in our society.

Those most likely to be poor include female heads of households, children, nonwhite persons, the elderly, large-sized families, those with limited education, the unemployed, and those living in pockets of poverty and high unemployment.

The causes of poverty are numerous. Poverty is interrelated with all other social problems. Because this is the case, almost every social service, to some extent, combats poverty. Some researchers have noted that the poor have a set of values and attitudes that constitute a culture of poverty. There is now considerable controversy about whether this culture *perpetuates* poverty or is simply an *adaptation* to being poor.

Poverty, to some extent, is functional for society, and because it is functional, some decision makers are not actively seeking to eradicate it.

The major income maintenance programs to combat poverty were created by the 1935 Social Security Act. The federal government's role in providing social insurance programs and public assistance programs was initiated by this act.

Social insurance programs (which are consistent with the institutional view of income transfers) receive less criticism than public assistance programs (which are consistent with the residual view of income transfers). There are many negative myths about public assistance programs, especially the AFDC program. A danger of punitive, stigmatized, public assistance programs is that poverty and dependency may be passed on to another generation.

Our society has the resources to eradicate poverty, but it may not currently have the will. Two alternatives for alleviating poverty are (*a*) enacting a guaranteed annual income plan that would set the base level slightly above the poverty line and (*b*) providing a variety of programs that would eliminate or reduce the causes of poverty.

Although the profession of social work has gratifications, it also has frustrations, including paperwork, red tape, working in a bureaucratic structure that is slow in changing to meet emerging needs, and working with discouraged people who do not follow through on "casework plans" to improve their circumstances.

NOTES

1. Information received from the Institute for Research on Poverty, University of Wisconsin–Madison, May, 1988.
2. Ibid.
3. Ibid.
4. Joseph Julian and William Kornblum, *Social Problems*, 5th ed. (Englewood Cliffs, NJ: Prentice-Hall, 1986), p. 30.
5. Ibid., pp. 158–173.
6. Ibid., pp. 205–207.
7. Robert Coles, Testimony Before the Select Committee on Nutrition and Human Needs of the United States Senate, February, 1969.
8. Marilyn Flynn, "Public Assistance," in *Contemporary Social Work*, ed. Donald Brieland, Lela Costin, and Charles Atherton, 2d ed. (New York: McGraw-Hill, 1980), p. 165.
9. Michael Harrington, *The Other America* (New York: Macmillan, 1962).
10. Ian Robertson, *Social Problems*, 2d ed. (New York: Random House, 1980), p. 177.
11. Ibid., pp. 175–179.
12. Joseph Julian and William Kornblum, *Social Problems*, 4th ed. (Englewood Cliffs, NJ: Prentice-Hall, 1983), p. 238.
13. James W. Coleman and Donald R. Cressey, *Social Problems*, 2d ed. (New York: Harper & Row, 1984), p. 159.
14. Paul Samuelson, quoted in P. Blumberg, *Inequality in an Age of Decline* (New York: Oxford University Press, 1980), p. 34.
15. Coleman and Cressey, *Social Problems*, p. 159.
16. Richard Alm and Robert J. Morse, "Growing Furor Over Pay of Top Executives," *U.S. News & World Report*, May 21, 1984, pp. 79–81.
17. "Iacocca Earns $17.9 Million in '87," *Wisconsin State Journal*, April 20, 1988, p. 6B.
18. "Study Cites Hunger in U.S.," *Wisconsin State Journal*, February 27, 1985, sec. 1, p. 8.
19. Robertson, *Social Problems*, p. 31.
20. James W. Coleman and Donald R. Cressey, *Social Problems* (New York: Harper & Row, 1980), p. 152.
21. Kenneth E. Boulding, "Reflections on Poverty," in *The Social Welfare Forum: 1961* ed. National Conference on Social Welfare (New York: Columbia University Press, 1961), pp. 45–58.
22. David Whitman, "America's Hidden Poor," *U.S. News & World Report*, January 11, 1988, pp. 18–24.
23. Second inaugural address of President Franklin D. Roosevelt (January 20, 1937).
24. President's Council on Economic Advisers, *Economic Report of the President* (Washington, D.C.: U.S. Government Printing Office, 1964), pp. 56–57.
25. Institute for Research on Poverty.
26. Harrington, *The Other America*.
27. "Poverty in the United States: Where Do We Stand Now?" *Focus*, Winter 1984, p. 1.
28. Julian and Kornblum, *Social Problems*, 5th ed., p. 266.
29. Daniel P. Moynihan, "Our Poorest Citizens—Children," *Focus* 11, no. 1 (Spring 1988), pp. 5–6.
30. Ibid.
31. Ibid.

32. Whitman, "America's Hidden Poor," pp. 18–24.
33. U.S. Bureau of the Census, *Statistical Abstract of the United States, 1987* (Washington, D.C.: U.S. Government Printing Office, 1987), p. 446.
34. "Poverty in the United States: Where Do We Stand Now?" *Focus* 7, no. 1 (Winter 1984), p. 6.
35. Moynihan, "Our Poorest Citizens—Children," p. 5.
36. Beth Brophy, "Children Under Stress," *U.S. News & World Report*, October 27, 1986, p. 59.
37. *Statistical Abstract of the United States, 1987*, p. 444.
38. Ibid., p. 444.
39. Ibid., p. 444.
40. "Poverty in the United States," p. 7.
41. *Statistical Abstract of the United States, 1987*, p. 445.
42. Ibid., p. 445.
43. Julian and Kornblum, *Social Problems*, 5th ed., pp. 212–213.
44. Harrington, *The Other America*, p. 21.
45. Oscar Lewis, "The Culture of Poverty," *Scientific American* 215 (October 1966), pp. 19–25.
46. Ibid., p. 23.
47. Eleanor Leacock, ed., *The Culture of Poverty: A Critique* (New York: Simon and Schuster, 1971).
48. Elliott Liebow, *Tally's Corner: A Study of Negro Street-Corner Men* (Boston: Little, Brown, 1967); Ulf Hannertz, *Soulside: An Inquiry into Ghetto Culture and Community* (New York: Columbia University Press, 1969); Leacock, *The Culture of Poverty*.
49. William Ryan, *Blaming the Victim*, rev. ed. (New York: Vintage Books, 1976).
50. Thomas Sullivan et al., *Social Problems* (New York: John Wiley, 1980), p. 390.
51. Herbert J. Gans, *More Equality* (New York: Pantheon, 1968), pp. 133–135.
52. Julian and Kornblum, *Social Problems*, 5th ed., p. 485.
53. Leila Pine, "Good Life on Unemployment," *Wisconsin State Journal*, August 29, 1976, pp. 1, 8.
54. Helen M. Crampton and Kenneth K. Keiser, *Social Welfare: Institution and Process* (New York: Random House, 1970), p. 73.
55. These conservative views are summarized by Samuel Mencher, "Newburgh: The Recurrent Crisis in Public Assistance," *Social Work* 7 (January 1962), pp. 3–4.
56. Rex A. Skidmore and Milton G. Thackeray, *Introduction to Social Work*, 2d ed. (Englewood Cliffs, NJ: Prentice-Hall, 1976), pp. 111–112.
57. "Study Cites Hunger in U.S.," p. 8.
58. *Statistical Abstract of the United States, 1987*, pp. 340–342.
59. Ibid., pp. 362–363.
60. Ibid., pp. 362–363.
61. Moynihan, "Our Poorest Citizens—Children," pp. 5–6.
62. Bradley R. Schiller, *The Economics of Poverty and Discrimination*, 3d ed. (Englewood Cliffs, NJ: Prentice-Hall, 1980).
63. Ibid.
64. Julian and Kornblum, *Social Problems*, 5th ed., p. 214.
65. Ibid., p. 214.
66. *Wisconsin Welfare Facts & Figures, 1984* (Madison, WI: State Dept. of Health & Social Services, 1984), p. 17.
67. *Statistical Abstract of the United States, 1987*, pp. 362–363.
68. Ibid., pp. 362–363.
69. Julian and Kornblum, *Social Problems*, 5th ed., p. 214.
70. Ibid., p. 214.
71. Ibid., p. 214.
72. Ibid., p. 214.
73. *Statistical Abstract of the United States, 1987*, pp. 362–363.
74. Julian and Kornblum, *Social Problems*, 5th ed., p. 214.
75. *Wisconsin Welfare Facts & Figures, 1984*, pp. 18–20.
76. *Statistical Abstract of the United States, 1987*, pp. 362–363.
77. Ibid., pp. 362–363.
78. Julian and Kornblum, *Social Problems*, 5th ed., p. 214.
79. *Statistical Abstract of the United States, 1987*, pp. 293, 362–363.
80. Ibid., p. 293.
81. A. Dale Tussing, "The Dual Welfare System," *Society* 11 (January–February 1974), pp. 50–57.
82. Flynn, "Public Assistance," p. 180.
83. *Statistical Abstract of the United States, 1987*, p. 445.
84. Lewis Losoncy, *Turning People On* (Englewood Cliffs, NJ: Prentice-Hall, 1977).

4

EMOTIONAL
PROBLEMS
AND COUNSELING

Everyone, at times, has emotional and/or behavioral difficulties. This chapter

- Describes the nature and extent of such difficulties.
- Discusses the concept of mental illness.
- Presents a theory about the causes of chronic mental illness.
- Presents information about the homeless.
- Discusses controversial issues in the mental health field.
- Presents research on the relationship between social structure and the rate of mental illness.
- Presents a brief history of our society's treatment of the emotionally disturbed.
- Describes treatment approaches for emotional and behavioral problems.
- Describes the role of social work in the mental health field.

A PERSPECTIVE
ON EMOTIONAL
PROBLEMS

Several years ago this author worked as a counselor at a maximum security hospital for the "criminally insane." A number of the residents at this hospital had committed bizarre crimes due to emotional and behavioral problems. A few of the more bizarre situations will be mentioned to give the reader a "flavor" of situations that arise.

In one case a 22-year-old male decapitated his 17-year-old friend. In another a married male with four children was arrested for the fourth time for exposing himself. In still another a male dug up several graves and used the corpses to "redecorate" his home. Another married man was committed after it was discovered he was involved in incestuous relationships with his 11- and 12-year-old daughters. Another man was committed after several efforts to deliver sermons in local taverns and after he kept maintaining that clouds followed him around in whatever direction he was going. Another brutally killed his father with an ax. Bizarre? Yes, definitely!

Is there a way to explain why these men did what they did? A variety of interpretations have been offered by different authorities—most of whom assert that they acted strangely because they are mentally ill.

Albert Ellis, a prominent psychologist, has advanced a different explanation and one that offers considerable promise in understanding and treating people who commit bizarre offenses. Ellis asserts that through looking at what the offenders were thinking when they committed unusual offenses, we will be able to gain an understanding of (*a*) why the bizarre actions occurred, (*b*) what would have prevented them from happening, and (*c*) what services are now needed to prevent the offenders from again getting into trouble on their release.[1]

At the maximum security hospital Ellis's interpretation was applied to the grave digger's case. Jim Schmidt (the name has been changed) was 46 years old when he began digging up graves and redecorating his home. His mother had died three and a half years earlier. Unfortunately, his mother was the only person who had provided meaning to his life. He was shy and had no other friends, and the two had lived together in a small rural community for the past twenty-two years. After his mother's death he became even more isolated; he lived by himself and had no friends. Being very lonely, he wished his mother were still alive. As happens with many people who lose someone close, he began dreaming his mother was still alive. His dreams appeared so real that on awakening he found it difficult to believe his mother was definitely dead. With such thoughts he began thinking his mother could in fact be brought back to life. He concluded that bringing corpses of females to his home would help bring his mother back. (Now to us, this idea certainly appears irrational, but being isolated he had no way of checking what was real and what was not.) Feeling very deeply the loss of his mother, he decided to give the idea a try. He, of course, needed counseling services (then and now) that would help him adjust to his mother's death, that would help him find new interests in

life, that would help him to become more involved with other people, and that would enable him to exchange thoughts with others to check out what is real and what is not.

EXTENT OF EMOTIONAL AND BEHAVIORAL PROBLEMS

Emotional and behavioral problems are two comprehensive labels covering an array of problems: depression, excessive anxiety, feelings of inferiority or isolation, being alienated, being sadistic or masochistic, marital difficulties, broken romances, parent-child relationship difficulties, being hyperactive, committing unusual or bizarre acts, being overly critical, being overly aggressive, having a phobia, abusing one's child or spouse, being compulsive or having an obsession, feeling guilty, being shy, showing violent displays of temper, being vindictive, having nightmares or insomnia, displaying sexual deviations, and so on.

For each problem there are unique and, in many cases a number of, potential causes. Depression, for example, may be caused by loss of a loved one or loss of someone or something else considered highly valuable, by feelings of guilt or shame, by knowledge of an undesirable impending event (for example, discovery of a terminal illness), by aggression turned inward, by certain physical factors such as menopause, by feelings of inadequacy or inferiority, and by feelings of loneliness or isolation. There have been literally hundreds of thousands of books published on the causes and ways to treat the wide array of emotional and behavioral problems.

Over 18 percent of the U.S. population, or more than 32 million people, are estimated to be suffering from a severe emotional or behavioral disorder.[2] Every year more than 6 million people annually receive mental health care in the United States.[3] In addition, practically all of us experience serious emotional difficulties at some time in our lives: for example, emotional problems surrounding a broken romance or marriage, addiction to alcohol or drugs, being a rape or other crime victim, failing to achieve a goal we've set, and so on.

WHAT IS MENTAL ILLNESS?

Much of the language relating to emotional disturbances has become a familiar part of everyday conversation. We use the following terms to express a judgment (often unfavorable) about the unusual behavior or unusual emotions of another person: *crazy, weird, psychotic, neurotic, having a nervous breakdown, insane, sick, uptight, space cadet,* and *mad.* Whatever the terms we use, we are apt to have only a vague idea as to their meaning. Amazingly, we act as if the label accurately describes the person, and we then relate to that person as if the label was correct and all-encompassing. However, it is impossible to precisely define any of these terms. What, for example, are the specific characteristics that distinguish a "psychotic" or a "space cadet" from other persons? Probably no one can give a precise answer.

There are two general approaches to viewing and diagnosing people who display emotional disturbances and abnormal behaviors—the medical model and the interactional model that asserts mental illness is a myth.

Medical Model

This model views emotional and behavioral problems as a mental illness comparable to a physical illness. The use of mental illness labels involves applying medical labels (for example, schizophrenia, paranoia, psychosis, insanity) to emotional problems. Adherents of the medical approach believe the disturbed person's mind is affected by some generally unknown internal condition. That unknown internal condition, they assert, might be due to genetic endowment, metabolic

disorders, infectious diseases, internal conflicts, unconscious use of defense mechanisms, and traumatic early experiences that cause emotional fixations and prevent future psychological growth.

The medical model has a lengthy classification of mental disorders that are defined by the American Psychiatric Association.

Definitions of some of these disorders follow.[4]

PSYCHOSIS   A major mental disorder of organic or emotional origin in which a person's ability to think, respond emotionally, remember, communicate, interpret reality, and behave appropriately is sufficiently impaired so as to interfere grossly with the capacity to meet the ordinary demands of life.

SCHIZOPHRENIA   A large group of disorders, usually of psychotic proportion, manifested by characteristic disturbances of language and communication, thought, perception, affect, and behavior that last longer than six months.

PARANOIA   A rare condition characterized by the gradual development of an intricate, complex, and elaborate system of thinking based on (and often proceeding logically from) misinterpretation of an actual event. A person with paranoia often considers himself endowed with unique and superior ability, or has systematized delusions of persecution.

HYPOCHONDRIASIS   A chronic maladaptive style of relating to the environment through preoccupation with shifting somatic concerns and symptoms, a fear or conviction that one has a serious physical illness, seeking of medical treatment, inability to accept reassurance, and either hostile or dependent relationships with caregivers and family.

BIPOLAR DISORDER   A major affective disorder in which there are episodes of both mania and depression; formerly called manic-depressive psychosis. Bipolar disorder may be subdivided into manic, depressed, or mixed types on the basis of currently presenting symptoms.

PHOBIA   An obsessive, persistent, unrealistic, intense fear of an object or situation. A few common phobias are:

Acrophobia: Fear of heights.

Algophobia: Fear of pain.

Claustrophobia: Fear of closed spaces.

Erythrophobia: Fear of blushing.

PERSONALITY DISORDERS   Deeply ingrained, inflexible, maladaptive patterns of relating, perceiving, and thinking of sufficient severity to cause either impairment in functioning or distress. Some personality disorders and their characteristics are:

Antisocial: A lack of socialization along with behavior patterns that bring a person repeatedly into conflict with society; incapacity for significant loyalty to others or to social values; callousness; irresponsibility; impulsiveness; and inability to feel guilt or learn from experience or punishment.

Borderline: Instability in a variety of areas, including interpersonal relationships, behavior, mood, and self-image.

Compulsive: Restricted ability to express warm and tender emotions; preoccupation with rules, order, organization, efficiency, and detail; excessive devotion to work and productivity to the exclusion of pleasure; indecisiveness.

Narcissistic: Grandiose sense of self-importance or uniqueness; preoccupation with fantasies of limitless success; need for constant attention and admiration; and disturbances in interpersonal relationships such as lack of empathy, exploitativeness, and relationships that vacillate between the extremes of overidealization and devaluation.

Passive-aggressive: Aggressive behavior manifested in passive ways such as obstructionism, pouting, procrastination, intentional inefficiency, and obstinacy.

Schizoid: Manifested by shyness, oversensitivity, social withdrawal, frequent daydreaming, avoidance of close or competitive relationships, and ec-

centricity. Persons with this disorder often react to disturbing experiences with apparent detachment and are unable to express hostility and ordinary aggressive feelings.

The medical model approach arose in reaction to the historical notion that the emotionally disturbed were possessed by demons, were mad, were to be blamed for having their disturbances, and who were treated by being beaten, locked up, or killed. The medical model led to viewing the disturbed as being in need of help, stimulated research into the nature of emotional problems, and promoted the development of therapeutic approaches.

Interactional Model

Critics of the medical (mental illness) approach assert that medical labels have no diagnostic or treatment value and frequently have an adverse effect.

Thomas Szasz, in the 1950s, was one of the first authorities to assert that mental illness is a myth—that it does not exist.[5] Szasz's theory is an interactional theory; it focuses on the processes of everyday social interaction and the effects of labeling on people. Beginning with the assumption that the term *mental illness* implies a "disease in the mind," Szasz categorizes all of the so-called mental illnesses into three types of emotional disorders and discusses the inappropriateness of calling such human difficulties "mental illnesses":

1. *Personal disabilities*, such as excessive anxiety, depression, fears, and feelings of inadequacy. Szasz says such so-called mental illnesses may appropriately be considered "mental" (in the sense that thinking and feeling are considered "mental" activities), but he asserts they are not diseases.

2. *Antisocial acts*, such as bizarre homicides and other social deviations. Homosexuality used to be in this category but was removed from the American Psychiatric Association's list of mental illnesses in 1974. Szasz says such antisocial acts are only social deviations, and he asserts they are neither "mental" nor "diseases."

BOX 4.1

A Case Example Interpreted in Terms of the Mental Illness Model

D an Vanda was arrested on May 29, 1979, for stabbing to death both his parents. He was 22 years old and had always been described as a "loner" by neighbors. In elementary school, junior high, and high school he was frequently absent, never had any close friends, and received primarily failing grades. School records showed that teachers had informed protective services on three occasions in his younger years that they believed his parents were abusing and neglecting him. Protective service records showed that his parents were uncooperative but that sufficient evidence could never be found to justify placement in a foster home.

At the time of his arrest Mr. Vanda appeared confused. He stated he was in communication with King David (the David in the Bible who slew Goliath), who told him to slay his parents who were out to get him. Mr. Vanda tended to ramble on with incoherent statements from the Bible, and he also stated that cosmic rays were in control of people. At his arrest he appeared to be expecting congratulations for what he had done, rather than incarceration.

The court ordered a 90-day observation period in a maximum security hospital for the mentally ill to determine his sanity.

Neighbors and school officials could add little to explain his actions. He had dropped out of school at age 16. Neighbors felt that he was "weird" and had ordered their children not to associate with him. They reported they sometimes saw him butchering birds, and when they asked him why, he stated he was being advised by Alfred Hitchcock (director of the film *The Birds*) to do this in order to prevent an attack.

Psychiatrists concluded he was insane and labeled him paranoid schizophrenic. It was felt his insanity was such that he would not be able to understand the nature of court proceedings connected with his offense. With this recommendation the court committed him indefinitely to a maximum security psychiatric hospital.

3. *Deterioration of the brain with associated person-ality changes.* This category includes the "mental illnesses" in which personality changes result following brain deterioration from such causes as arteriosclerosis, chronic alcoholism, general paresis, AIDS, or serious brain damage following an accident. Common symptoms are loss of memory, listlessness, apathy, and deterioration of personal grooming habits. Szasz says these disorders can appropriately be considered "diseases" but are diseases of the brain (that is, brain deterioration that specifies the nature of the problem) rather than diseases of the mind.

Szasz asserts that the notion that people with emotional problems are mentally ill is as absurd as the belief that the emotionally disturbed are possessed by demons: "The belief in mental illness as something other than man's trouble in getting along with his fellow man, is the proper heir to the belief in demonology and witchcraft. Mental illness exists or is real in exactly the same sense in which witches existed or were real."[6]

In actuality, there are three steps to becoming labeled mentally ill: (*a*) The person displays unwanted emotions (such as depression) or some strange deviant behaviors; (*b*) the emotions or the behaviors are not tolerated by the family or local community; and (*c*) the professional labeler, usually a psychiatrist, happens to believe in the medical model and assigns a mental illness label. Thomas Scheff and David Mechanic provide evidence that whether the family or community will tolerate the deviant behavior and whether the professional labeler believes in the medical model are more crucial in determining whether someone will be assigned a mentally ill label than the emotions or behaviors exhibited by the person.[7]

The point that Szasz and many other writers are striving to make is that people do have emotional and behavioral problems, but they do not have a mystical mental illness. These writers believe that terms that describe unwanted emotions and dysfunctional behaviors are very useful: for example, *depression, anxiety, an obsession, a compulsion, excessive fear, having hallucinations,* and *feelings of being a failure.* Such terms describe personal problems that people have. But the medical terms, they assert (such as schizophrenia and psychosis), are not useful because there is no distinguishing symptom that would indicate whether a person has, or does not have, the "illness." In addition, Daniel Offer and Melvin Sabshin point out that there is considerable variation between cultures regarding what is defined as a mental illness.[8] The usefulness of the medical model is also questioned because psychiatrists frequently disagree on the medical diagnosis to be assigned to those who are disturbed.[9]

In a dramatic study psychologist David Rosenhan demonstrated that professional staff in mental hospitals could not distinguish "insane" patients from "sane" patients.[10] Rosenhan and seven "normal" associates went to twelve mental hospitals in five different states, claiming they were hearing voices. All eight were admitted to these hospitals. After admission these pseudopatients stated that they stopped hearing voices and acted normally. The hospitals were unable to distinguish their "sane" status from the "insane" status of other patients. The hospitals kept these pseudopatients institutionalized for an average of 19 days, and all were then discharged with a diagnosis of "schizophrenia in remission."

The use of medical labels, it has been asserted, has several adverse effects.[11] The person labeled mentally ill (and frequently the therapist as well) believes that she or he has a disease for which, unfortunately, there is no known "cure." The label gives the labeled person an excuse for not taking responsibility for his or her actions (for example, innocent by reason of insanity). Because there is no known "cure" the disturbed frequently idle away their time waiting for someone to discover a cure rather than assuming responsibility for their behavior, examining the reasons for their problems, and making efforts to improve. Other undesirable consequences of being labeled mentally ill are that people may lose some of their legal rights;[12] may be stigmatized in their social interactions as being dangerous, unpredictable, untrustworthy, or of "weak" character;[13] and may find it more difficult to secure employment or receive a promotion.[14]

The question of whether mental illness exists is indeed important. The assignment of mental illness labels to disturbed people has substantial implications for how the disturbed will be treated, for how others will view them, and for how they will view themselves. Charles Cooley's "looking-glass self-concept" crystallizes what is being said here.[15] The "looking glass" says we develop our self-concept in terms of how other people react to us. People are apt to react to those who are labeled mentally ill as if they were mentally ill. As a result, those who are labeled mentally ill may well define themselves as being different or "crazy," and begin playing that role.

Compared to a physical illness, a diagnosis of a mental illness carries a greater stigma. In 1972 Senator Thomas Eagleton was forced to resign his candidacy for vice president on the Democratic ticket after it was revealed that he had received electroshock treatments for depression. The leaders of the Democratic party feared that the public would conclude that someone who had once received psychiatric help would be too "unstable" and "dangerous" to be president. On the

BOX 4.2

A Case Example Questioning the Usefulness of the Mental Illness Concept

While working at a mental hospital, this author was assigned a case where a 22-year-old male decapitated his 17-year-old girlfriend. Two psychiatrists diagnosed him as schizophrenic, and a court found him "innocent by reason of insanity." He was then committed to a mental hospital.

Why did he do it? Labeling him as insane provides an explanation to the general public that he exhibited this strange behavior because he was then thought to be "crazy." But does such a label explain why he killed this girl rather than someone else, or doing something else that was bizarre? Does the label explain what would have prevented him from committing this act? Does the label suggest the kind of treatment that will cure him? The answer to all these questions is, of course, no.

WHAT IS SCHIZOPHRENIA?

A common definition of schizophrenia is "a psychotic condition usually occurring during or shortly after adolescence and characterized by disorientation, loss of contact with reality, disorganized patterns of thinking and feeling."[a] Let us examine this definition. People who are intoxicated, or stoned on drugs, or who are asleep, or who have not slept for over a day experience a loss of contact with reality, and their feelings and thinking patterns become disorganized. Are they schizophrenic? No. What about the severely and profoundly mentally retarded who have a mental age of less than two? They have the above symptoms but are not considered schizophrenic. What about people who go into a coma following a serious accident? They also fit the definition above but are not considered schizophrenic. The 22-year-old male who committed the bizarre homicide knew the act was wrong, was aware of what he was doing, was in contact with reality, and told me the reasons for doing what he did. Then why was *he* labeled schizophrenic?

Many authorities are now asserting that there is no definition of symptoms that separates people who have this "disease" from those who do not.

This writer generally agrees with Albert Ellis's assertion that the reasons for the occurrence of any deviant act can be determined by examining what the offender was thinking prior to and during the time when the deviant act was being committed.[b]

After this person described what had happened, it was understandable (even though bizarre) why he did what he did, and his account also identified the specific problems he needed help with. He described himself as a very isolated person who, except for his girlfriend, had no close relatives or friends. He came from a broken home and was raised by a series of relatives and in foster homes. Because of frequent moves he attended a number of different schools and made no lasting friends. At age 20 he met the victim and dated her periodically for two years. She provided the only real meaning that he had in life. He held the traditional vision of marrying her and living happily ever after. However, a few months before the fatal day, he became very alarmed that he was going to "lose her." She encouraged him to date others, mentioned that she wanted to date others, and suggested that they no longer see as much of each other.

He thought long and hard about how he could preserve the relationship. He also realized he had rather intense sexual tensions for which he had no outlet. Putting the two together he naively concluded, "If I'm the first person to have sexual relations with her, she will forever feel tied to me." He therefore tried on several occasions to have coitus, but she always managed to dissuade him. Finally, one afternoon during the summer, when he knew they would be alone together, he arrived at the following decision: "I *will* have sex with her this afternoon, even if I have to knock her unconscious." He stated that he knew such action was wrong but said, "It was my last hope of saving our relationship. Without her, life would not be worth living."

He again tried to have sexual relations with her that afternoon, but she continued to dissuade him. Being emotionally excited he then took a soda bottle and knocked her unconscious. He again attempted to have coitus, but was still unsuccessful for reasons related to her physical structure. In an intense state of emotional and sexual excitement, he was unable to rationally consider the consequences of his actions. (All of us, at times, have done things while angry or in a state of intense emotional excitement that we would not have done in a calmer state.) At this point he felt his whole world was caving in. When asked during an interview what he was thinking at this point he stated, "I felt that if I couldn't have her, no one else would either." He sought and found a knife, became further carried away with emotions, and ended up slaying her. He knew it was wrong, and he was aware of what he was doing.

From talking with this person (and identifying his thinking before and during this bizarre murder) certain factors are pinpointed that help explain why this murder took place, including this man's loneliness and isolation, his feeling that continuing a romantic relationship with this girl was the only source of meaning in his life, his naive thinking that a forced sexual relationship would make the girl feel tied and attracted to him, his having no outlet for his sexual drives, and his jealous and possessive desires to go to extreme lengths to prevent this girl from developing a romantic relationship with another male. Such reasons help to explain why the bizarre behavior took place, while the label *schizophrenia* does not.

If the above problems had been known prior to the murder the slaying might have been prevented. What he needed was to find other sources of interest and other meaningful relationships in his life. Joining organizations in the community and developing hobbies may well have helped. An appropriate sexual outlet probably would have also been helpful. Better control of his passions and other sources of finding meaning might have prevented him from losing control of his emotions that afternoon. Reducing the intensity of his jealous and possessive feelings, along with developing more mature attitudes toward romance and sexuality, might also have been preventive. These specific problems are also the areas in which he needs help while in a mental hospital, rather than finding a cure for schizophrenia. In no way does the author feel that this person should be excused for his actions, as implied

Continued

BOX 4.2 *Continued*

by the term "innocent by reason of insanity." But he does need help for the specific problems identified. (In 10 or 15 years he will probably be released and return to society.)

If the reader wonders how someone could arrive at a point where he does something as bizarre as taking the life of someone he loves, remember it is necessary to attempt to view the situation from the deviant person's perspective. In order to understand such a perspective, it is essential to try to consider all the circumstances, pressures, values, and belief systems of the deviant person.

Another example may help the reader to become aware that practically anyone will do something bizarre when circumstances become desperate. Several years ago a passenger plane crashed in the Andes Mountains in the wintertime. A number of people were killed, but there were nearly 30 survivors. Rescue efforts initially failed to locate the survivors, who took shelter from the cold in the wreckage of the plane. The survivors were without food for over 40 days until they were finally rescued. During this time they were faced with the choice of dying of starvation, or cannibalizing those who had died. It was a desperate, difficult decision. (Psychologically, many people who commit a bizarre act feel they face a comparably desperate decision.) In this situation all but one of the initial plane crash survivors chose cannibalism. The one who refused died of starvation.

---

[a]Louis P. Thorpe and Barney Katz, *The Psychology of Abnormal Behavior* (New York: Ronald Press, 1948), p. 849.
[b]Albert Ellis, *Reason and Emotion in Psychotherapy* (New York: Lyle Stuart, 1962).
Source: Adapted from an article written by Charles Zastrow, "When Labeled Mentally Ill," in *The Personal Problem Solver*, eds. Charles Zastrow and Dae H. Chang. © 1977 by Prentice-Hall, Inc. Published by Prentice-Hall, Inc., Englewood Cliffs, NJ 07632.

---

other hand, Franklin Roosevelt was partly disabled from polio but was elected president for four terms.

Szasz also argues that the mental illness approach is used (perhaps unintentionally) as a means of exerting social control over people who do not conform to social expectations.[16] The Soviet Union has a long history of labeling dissenters (including poets, writers, and intellectuals who would be respected in this country) as mentally ill and then sending them to concentration camps or insane asylums. Psychiatrists in Russia find it relatively easy to conclude that people who do not accept the Marxist-Leninist philosophy must be psychologically impaired. Are some psychiatrists using mental illness labels to control the behavior of noncon-

formists in our country? Szasz asserts they are. As an example he cites that homosexuality was listed (until 1974) as a mental disorder by the American Psychiatric Association. As another example Szasz cites a quote from Dana L. Farnsworth, a Harvard psychiatrist and an authority on college psychiatric services:

Library vandalism, cheating and plagiarism, stealing in the college or community stores or in the dormitories, unacceptable or anti-social sexual practices (overt homosexuality, exhibitionism, promiscuity), and the unwise and unregulated use of harmful drugs, are examples of behavior that suggest the presence of emotionally unstable persons.[17]

Mental illness labels do have a "boundary" effect, since they determine what behaviors a society defines as "sick," with pressures then being put on citizens to avoid such behaviors. Szasz's point is that a number of nonconformists are adversely affected by the use of the medical model to control their behavior.

LABELING AS THE CAUSE OF CHRONIC "MENTAL ILLNESS"

A question that is frequently raised about Szasz's assertion that mental illness is a myth is, "If you assert that mental illness doesn't exist, why do some people go through life as if they are mentally ill?" Thomas Scheff has developed a sociological theory that provides an answer.[18] Scheff's main hypothesis is that labeling is the most important determinant of people displaying a chronic (long-term) mental illness.

Scheff begins by defining how he will determine, for his research purposes, who is mentally ill. Before giving his definition, he notes:

One source of immediate embarrassment to any social theory of "mental illness" is that the terms used in referring to these phenomena in our society prejudge the issue. The medical metaphor "mental illness" suggests a determinate process which occurs within the individual: the unfolding and development of disease. In order to avoid this assumption, we will utilize sociological, rather than medical concepts to formulate the problem.[19]

He goes on to state that the symptoms of mental illness can be viewed as violations of social norms and that for his research purposes the term *mental illness* will be used to refer to those assigned such a label by professionals (usually psychiatrists).

Scheff indicates that literally thousands of studies have been conducted in recent years that seek to identify the origins of long-term mental disorders. Practi-cally all of these studies have sought to identify the causes as existing somewhere inside a person (for example, metabolic disorders, unconscious conflicts, heredity factors). These research efforts have been based on medical and psychological models of human behavior. Yet, amazingly, in spite of this extensive research, the determinants of chronic mental disorders (for example, schizophrenia) are largely unknown.

Scheff suggests that researchers may well be looking in the wrong direction for determinants. Instead of seeking causes inside a person, he suggests the major determinants are in social processes—that is, in interactions with others.

Scheff's theory will briefly be summarized. He suggests that everyone, at times, violates social norms and commits acts that could be labeled as symptoms of mental illness. For example, a person may occasionally angrily get in fights with others, experience intense depression or grief, be highly anxious, use drugs or alcohol to excess, have a fetish, be an exhibitionist, or commit a highly unusual and bizarre act.

Usually, the person who has unwanted emotions or who commits deviant acts is not identified (labeled) as mentally ill. Such emotions and deviant actions are typically not classified as symptoms of a mental illness but instead are ignored, unrecognized, or rationalized in some other manner.

Occasionally, however, such norm violations are perceived by others as "abnormal." The offenders are then labeled mentally ill and consequently related to as if they were mentally ill. At the time when people are publicly labeled they are highly suggestible to cues from others. They realize they have done something unusual and turn to others for an assessment of why they have unwanted emotions or are engaging in deviant actions. In the absence of objective measures of their sanity they rely on others for this assessment. If others relate to them as if they are mentally ill they begin to define and perceive themselves as such.

Traditional stereotypes of mental illness define the mentally ill role, both for those who are labeled mentally ill and for the people they interact with. Those labeled mentally ill are often rewarded for enacting that social role. They are given such rewards as sympathy and attention and are excused from being expected to hold a job, from fulfilling other role requirements, and from being held responsible for their wrongdoings.

In addition, those labeled mentally ill are punished for attempting to return to conventional roles. They are viewed with suspicion and implicitly considered to be still insane. They also have considerable difficulty in obtaining employment or in receiving a job promotion.

Such pressures and interactions with others gradually lead to changes in their self-concept; they begin to view themselves as different, as being insane. Often a vicious circle is created. The more they enact the mentally ill role, the more they are defined and treated as mentally ill; the more explicitly they are defined as mentally ill, the more they are related to as if they are mentally ill; and so on. Unless this vicious circle is interrupted, Scheff suggests, it will lead to a career of long-term mental illness. Scheff's conclusion is that with this process, labeling is the single most important determinant of chronic mental illness.

If labeling is an important determinant of chronic functional mental illness, significant changes are suggested in diagnostic and treatment practices. Mental health personnel are frequently faced with uncertainty in deciding whether a person has a mental disorder. An informal norm has been developed to handle this uncertainty; when in doubt it is better to judge a well person ill than to judge an ill person well. This norm is based on two assumptions taken from treating physical illnesses: (*a*) A diagnosis of illness results in only minimal damage to the status and reputation of a person, and (*b*) unless the illness is treated it will become progressively worse. However, both these assumptions are questionable. Unlike medical treatment psychiatric treatment can drastically change a person's status in the community; for example, it can remove rights that are difficult to regain. Furthermore, if Scheff is right about the adverse effects of mental illness labeling, then the exact opposite norm should be established to handle uncertainty; namely, when in doubt do not label a person mentally ill. This would be in accord with the legal approach that follows the norm, "When in doubt, acquit," or "A person is innocent until proved guilty."

If labeling is indeed a major determinant of mental illness, then certain changes are suggested in treating

violators of social norms. One is to attempt to maintain and treat people with problems in their local community without labeling them mentally ill or sending them to a mental hospital where their playing the role of the mentally ill is apt to be reinforced. The field of mental hygiene has, in the past several years, been moving in this direction. Another outgrowth of Scheff's theory would be increasing public education efforts to inform the general population of the nature of emotional problems and the adverse effects that result from inappropriate labeling.

OTHER ISSUES

There are other issues at stake in the field of mental health. These include care for the homeless, civil rights of those labeled mentally ill, the improper use of the insanity plea to excuse criminals from their actions, and the use (or misuse) of drugs in "treating" supposedly mentally ill persons.

The Homeless

One of the population groups that has received considerable media attention in recent years is the homeless. Having hundreds of thousands of people homeless in the richest nation in the world is a national disgrace. The number of homeless Americans is large and growing larger. The exact number is unknown, but the Department of Housing and Urban Development (HUD) estimates the number is over half a million.[20] Many of the homeless are living on the street, in parks, in subways, or in abandoned buildings. Food is often sought from garbage.

An estimated 25 to 50 percent of the homeless are thought to suffer from serious and chronic forms of mental illness.[21] Discharged from institutions without the support they need, tens of thousands of former patients live on the street in abominable conditions. Instead of providing support services for discharged patients, many states have a deinstitutionalization program of simply drugging people and dumping them into the street. Such an approach is a far cry from what was envisioned twenty years ago when federal authorities embarked on an ambitious program to phase out large state hospitals and move the disturbed to more humane and convenient treatment in communities. This commendable goal has not been fulfilled. Federal, state, and local governments have failed to provide enough housing, transitional care, and job training to integrate patients into society. In many areas of the country, a revolving-door policy prevails. Patients are discharged from state hospitals, only to return again because of a lack of community support. It is true that institutional care is not only highly expensive, about $50,000 per year,[22] but frequently also stifles the intellectual, social, and physical growth of patients. But, tragically, the necessary supportive services have not been developed in most communities to serve discharged patients.

In past decades the homeless tended to be white, alcoholic, middle-aged, single males. Such a stereotype is not an accurate description of homeless people today. Today, the homeless tend to have the following characteristics:

- Most are single, but 20 to 30 percent are in family groups, including children.

- Most are male, but 15 to 25 percent are women, and this percentage appears to be increasing.

- The average age of most is the mid-thirties, which is considerably younger than in the past.

- Half to two thirds have completed high school, and 25 to 30 percent have attended college, indicating that lack of education is not as prevalent as might be expected.

- A majority tend to live in the same area rather than constantly drifting from area to area and from town to town.[23]

There are a variety of reasons for the large increase in the number of homeless. Deinstitutionalization of state mental hospitals is one reason. Cutbacks in social services by the federal government is another. Urban renewal projects have demolished low-cost housing in many areas. The shift from blue-collar jobs to service and high-tech jobs in our society has reduced sharply the demand for unskilled labor. Another factor has been a recent trend in our society to ignore members of society who are unable to fend for themselves. Most of the homeless are homeless because they cannot afford the housing that is available; our country does not have a commitment to a social policy of providing affordable housing to the poor.

The answers to the dismal conditions in which the homeless are living include low-cost housing, job-training and placement programs, and community services for those with emotional problems. Is our society willing to provide the necessary resources to meet the needs of the homeless? Deplorably, the answer is "No, not at present."

Civil Rights

State laws permit the involuntary hospitalization of people in mental health hospitals, which can be seen as an infringement of their civil right to liberty. Although state laws differ, in many jurisdictions people can be hospitalized without their consent and without due process.[24] In some jurisdictions a person may be sent to a mental hospital without his or her consent, based on the statement of a physician.[25]

When this author worked at a hospital for the "criminally insane" there was a patient who was originally arrested on a disorderly conduct charge for urinating on a fire hydrant. Some neighbors thought he might be mentally ill, so the judge ordered that he be sent to a mental hospital for a sixty-day observation period to determine his sanity. The hospital judged him "insane" and "incompetent to stand trial" on the charge. He was not considered a threat to himself or to others. But, with the hospital's finding, the judge confined him to a maximum security hospital for the criminally insane, and when I worked there he had already been hospitalized for nine years—for committing an offense for which, if found guilty, he probably would only have been required to pay a small fine. Involuntary confinement has been a controversial practice for years.

Another problem in some mental hospitals is that patients do not receive adequate treatment even after several years of confinement. Inadequate treatment is a civil rights violation because in 1964 Congress

Although the exact number of homeless people in America is unknown, recent government estimates indicate that over half a million people are sleeping in streets, subways, parks, and abandoned buildings and cars in cities and towns across the United States. Many suffer from alcoholism and serious mental illness and desperately need medical attention or psychiatric care; others, until recently the "working poor," have fallen victim to federal cutbacks in housing and social service programs. As we move into a new century, the plight of the homeless—already a problem of epidemic proportions—may be the biggest challenge our nation will face.

The holiday shopping season that many of us take for granted can ignore the hard realities that others of us experience.

Soup kitchens serve meals to thousands of the hungry every day. These people enjoy a free Thanksgiving dinner in Washington, D.C.

Up to a third of homeless people live in family groups. Until recently residents of a derelict schoolbus outside Fort Worth, Texas, this family now has their own home.

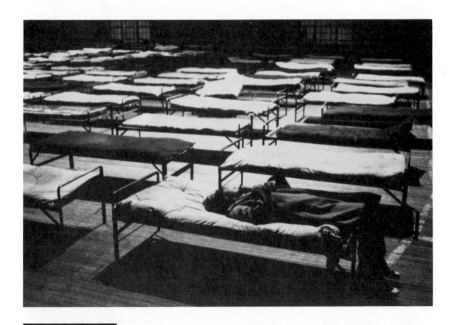

Many shelters in large cities offer bleak, barracks-style conditions to those seeking temporary refuge. Because some shelters are crowded, violent, unsanitary, and prone to violent incidents, many homeless people prefer to live in the streets.

established a statutory right to treatment in the Hospitalization of the Mentally Ill Act.[26]

Decisions about providing treatments such as electroconvulsive therapy (which has questionable value and may cause brain damage) also raise civil rights questions. The severely disturbed are often unable to make rational choices about their own welfare. Permission of relatives is sometimes obtained, but this still denies patients their fundamental rights.

The above problems caused the President's Commission on Mental Health in 1978 to recommend that due process be followed in arriving at decisions involving enforced hospitalization and treatment.[27] Federal court decisions have also reflected these concerns; they have held that mental illness is not a sufficient basis for denying liberty and that hospitalized mental patients have a right either to adequate treatment or to release.[28]

Plea of Innocent by Reason of Insanity

In 1979 a jury found Dan White innocent by reason of insanity on charges of the premeditated murder of city mayor George Moscone and city supervisor Harvey Milk. This verdict was rendered even though testimony presented clearly showed that these murders had been carefully planned and carried out by White.[29] The general public was as shocked by the jury's decision as it was by the crime. With this jury's decision White was confined in a mental hospital for a few years and then released in 1984.

In 1982 John Hinckley, Jr. was found innocent by reason of insanity for the attempted assassination of President Reagan a year earlier. Three other people were also injured by Mr. Hinckley in the assassination attempt. Mr. Hinckley is currently receiving treatment in a mental hospital.

In another recent case Kenneth Bianchi (called the Hollywood "Hillside Strangler"), was accused of murdering thirteen women in the Los Angeles area and two more in Washington state. Six different psychiatrists examining Bianchi came to three different conclusions

about his mental state: Two judged him sane, two judged him insane, and two were undecided.[30]

Cases such as those of White, Hinckley, and Bianchi have forced the courts and psychiatrists to begin to examine more carefully the plea of innocent by reason of insanity. As indicated earlier the terms *mental illness* and *mental health* are poorly defined. Mental illness (insanity) may not even exist. In a number of trials involving the insanity plea, it has become routine for the prosecuting attorney to use as witnesses those psychiatrists who are apt to judge the defendant "sane," whereas the defendant's attorney uses as witnesses those psychiatrists who are apt to arrive at an "insane" recommendation. An authority notes:

Among psychiatrists, there is nothing remotely approaching a consensus on what constitutes insanity. Moreover, psychiatrists themselves concede that they lack reliable means for determining whether a person was insane in any sense at the time of a crime. All too often, they must rely heavily on the accused's behavior and on what he tells them—two types of data that a shrewd defendant can carefully orchestrate.[31]

Defendants are increasingly becoming aware that they can probably get a psychiatrist to label them insane by "acting crazy," such as by openly performing indecent acts or by claiming to hear voices.

The argument for eliminating the insanity plea is that people are literally using it to get away with murder and other serious felonies. Instead of forcing people to take responsibility for their felonies, the insanity plea excuses people for their crimes. The plea enables a clever defendant or his or her attorney to seek refuge from criminal punishment.

When a person is acquitted by reason of insanity, she or he is generally sent to a mental institution. Under the law a person is kept there until doctors determine the person is no longer dangerous and the judge concurs. Sadly, the measures for determining "no longer dangerous" are as untrustworthy as those used to assign a mental illness label.

For example, E. E. Kemper III spent five years in a hospital for the criminally insane after murdering his grandparents. Mr. Kemper convinced psychiatrists and the judge that he was cured by giving rational answers to a battery of psychological tests. (He memorized the answers prior to the tests.) Three years after his release he was again arrested for brutally killing eight women during this time—including his mother.[32]

Psychiatrist Lee Coleman urges that the insanity defense be eliminated altogether in courts in order to resolve this dilemma. Eliminating the insanity defense would allow courts to deal with the guilt or innocence of an individual without interference from psychiatrists. Coleman states, "Victims are no less injured by one who is mentally sound and violent."[33] Coleman further urges that if the individual convicted later wishes help for emotional or behavioral problems, he or she can then request it.

Because of the controversy over the insanity plea a number of states are revising their laws surrounding this plea. One approach adopted by several states is to have a two-step process in which the jury first determines whether the defendant is innocent or guilty. If they find the defendant guilty the jury then decides if that person is sane or insane. (If found insane the defendant is usually sent to a maximum security mental hospital.)

Use of Psychotropic Drugs

Psychotropic drugs include tranquilizers, antipsychotic drugs (such as thorazine), and antidepressant drugs. The use of psychotropic drugs, since their discovery in 1954, has been given substantial credit for the marked decrease in the number of patients in state and county hospitals, from 550,000 in 1955 to 146,000 in 1985.[34] Psychotropic drugs do not "cure" emotional problems but are useful in reducing high levels of anxiety, depression, and tension.

Americans make extensive use of psychotropic drugs, particularly tranquilizers. Valium, Librium, Miltown, and other mild tranquilizers are widely used. Most general practitioners prescribe tranquilizers for the large number of patients who complain of tension and of being emotionally upset. Librium has been found to be fairly effective in reducing depression in a

number of clients and is now being widely prescribed by physicians. "Popping pills" (both legal and illegal) has become fashionable. The dangers of excessive drug use include physical and psychological dependence and unwanted side effects. There is also the danger that because drugs provide temporary symptom relief, users may focus their attention on taking pills rather than on making the necessary changes in their lives to resolve the problems causing the anxiety, depression, or tension. Physicians face a dilemma in balancing the benefits of psychotropic drugs against the dangers of abuse, particularly when such drugs are sought by patients for extended periods of time. Because psychotropic drugs only provide temporary relief for the *symptoms* (such as anxiety and depression) that patients have, many authorities urge that patients also receive counseling or psychotherapy to help resolve their emotional difficulties.

SOCIAL STRUCTURE AND MENTAL ILLNESS

Sociologists have conducted a number of studies examining the relationships between social factors and the rate of mental illness. Questions investigated include, Is social class status related to the rate of mental illness? Does illness occur more in urban areas, in suburbs, or in rural areas? Which age groups are more prone to be affected? Are men or women more apt to be affected? (As indicated earlier there is a question as to whether mental illness exists. Instead of continually repeating this question, the term *mental illness* will be used in this section to refer to those who are labeled mentally ill.)

SOCIAL CLASS   A classic study was conducted by A. B. Hollingshead and F. C. Redlich in New Haven, Connecticut.[35] The study examined the social class status of patients who were treated for a mental illness in hospitals and in private and public agencies. The researchers used a socioeconomic scale ranging from class I (highest) to class V (lowest). The results showed that

BOX 4.3

Eating Disorders: An Emerging Problem

I n the early 1980s Karen Carpenter died from complications resulting from anorexia nervosa. In 1984 Jane Fonda acknowledged she was bulimic for a number of years. Eating disorders have recently become recognized as being very serious. Estimates are that as high as 20 percent of college females have an eating disorder. Most of the people who have an eating disorder are female.

The two primary eating disorders are anorexia nervosa and bulimia. Both anorexics and bulimics have a fear of fatness, but their techniques for staying thin vary greatly.

An anorexic eats very little food. She is near starvation much of the time. Bulimics, on the other hand, binge and purge themselves. The average American's food intake is around 3,500 calories a day. Bulimics eat substantially more. They may devour as much as 40,000 to 60,000 calories a day. They typically binge on high-calorie junk foods—such as sweets and fried foods. Bulimics also want to stay thin. So they purge themselves through a variety of ways. The most common method of purging is vomiting. Vomiting may initially be induced by putting the fingers down the throat. Some bulimics rely on Q-tips or on drinking copious amounts of fluids. Many bulimics, with practice, gain control of their esophageal muscles and are able to induce vomiting at will.

Although vomiting is the most common method used by bulimics for purging, there are other methods. These methods include laxatives, fasting, enemas, chewing food and then spitting it out, and compulsive exercise—such as swimming many laps, running many miles, and working out with barbells and weights.

The widespread incidence of bulimia has gone unrecognized until recently. Bulimia is much more common than anorexia. Bulimia has gone unrecognized for so long because binging and purging is almost always done in secret. Bulimics dread the possibility that their habit will be revealed. Very few will tell the whole story to their doctors, therapists, or family.

Anorexics and bulimics have some similarities. Both are likely to have been brought up in middle-class, upwardly mobile families, where their mothers are overinvolved in their lives and their fathers are preoccupied with work outside the home. For the most part, bulimics and anorexics were good children, eager to comply and eager to achieve in order to obtain the love and approval of others. Both tend to lack self-esteem, feel ineffective and have a distorted body image in which they view themselves as being fatter than others view them as being. Both have an obsessive concern with food.

Anorexics and bulimics are different. Anorexics are generally younger, far less socially competent, and much more isolated from and dependent on the family. The anorexic stays away from food. In contrast, bulimics, during times of stress, turn toward food. They binge and then purge. Bulimics, for the most part, are able to function in social and work contexts. Their health may be gravely affected by binging and purging, but their lives are not necessarily in imminent danger, as is often the case with anorexics. Anorexics are also *very* thin, whereas bulimics are not as underweight and may even be overweight.

One societal reason for the increased incidence of anorexia and bulimia may be the increasing value that our society places on being slim and trim.

Bulimics tend to have few friends. Much of their time is spent on binging and purging and keeping others from knowing about it. Bulimics are often overachievers and in college tend to attain high academic averages.

Purging for bulimics often becomes a purification rite, as it is frequently viewed as a way to overcome self-loathing. They tend to believe they are unlovable and inadequate. Through purging, they feel completely fresh and clean again. These feelings of self-worth are only temporary. They are extremely sensitive to minor insults and frustrations, which are often used as excuses to initiate another food binge.

Why are bulimics and anorexics primarily women? One important reason is that in our society there are many more pressures on women to be slender and trim than on men.

Both anorexia and bulimia lead to serious health problems. Stating the obvious, nutritious meals are needed for good health and survival. Anorexics risk starvation, and both bulimics and anorexics risk serious health problems. Fat synthesis and accumulation are necessary for survival. Fatty acids are a major source of energy. When fat levels are depleted, the body must draw on carbohydrates (sugar). When sugar supplies dwindle, body metabolism decreases, which often leads to drowsiness, inactivity, pessimism, depression, dizziness, and fatigue.

Bulimics and anorexics are taking a number of dangerous health risks. Psychotropic drugs (such as tranquilizers and antidepressant drugs) may affect the body differently due to changes in body metabolism. Abnormalities in the electroencephalograms of people with eating disorders have been found. Chronic vomiting may lead to gum disease and innumerable cavities, due to the hydrochloric acid content of vomit. Vomiting can also lead to severe tearing and bleeding in the esophagus. Chronic vomiting may result in a potassium deficiency, which then may lead to muscle fatigue, weakness, numbness, erratic heartbeat, kidney damage, and in severe instances, paralysis. Additional medical problems associated with eating disorders are described in Marlene Boskind-White and William C. White, *Bulimarexia*.

A variety of treatment programs are available for anorexics and bulimics. Individual and group therapy programs have been developed to change the psychological thinking patterns that initiated and are sustaining the undesirable eating patterns. For those for whom severe health problems have already developed, medical care is essential. Therapy for eating disorders includes instruction in establishing and maintaining a nutritious diet. Some elementary, secondary, and higher education school systems are now developing preventive programs that seek to inform students about the risks of eating disorders and that seek to identify and provide services for students who are beginning to develop an eating disorder.

Source: Marlene Boskind-White and William C. White, *Bulimarexia* (New York: W. W. Norton, 1983).

the rate of mental illness was significantly higher in the lower classes than in the upper classes. Class V, by far, had the highest rate, with schizophrenia being eleven times more prevalent for class V than for class I if measured in terms of hospitalization rates. The study also found that the types of treatment and opportunities for rehabilitation for the lower classes were of a lower quality and less satisfactory than for the upper classes.

A second research project by William Rushing studied 4,560 males admitted for the first time to mental hospitals in Washington, D.C.[36] Similar to the Hollingshead and Redlich study, hospitalization rates were found to vary inversely with class. Hospitalization rates were particularly high for the lowest class.

A third study was conducted in midtown Manhattan in the 1950s by Leo Srole and his associates.[37] The study involved conducting extensive interviews with 1,660 randomly selected people to find out if they had ever had a nervous breakdown, sought psychotherapy, or shown neurotic symptoms. They then gave the information to a team of psychiatrists who rated each case on the degree of psychiatric impairment. The study found almost 23 percent of the sample was considered "significantly" impaired in mental functioning, including many persons not under treatment. In addition, psychological impairment was found to correlate closely with social class. Nearly one person in every two in the lowest class was considered psychologically impaired, whereas the rate fell to one in eight for the highest class.

These studies clearly suggest that the poor are more apt to be labeled mentally ill. There are a variety of explanations, however, that shed light on these results. Perhaps the poor are less likely to seek treatment when emotional problems first begin to develop and they therefore become mentally ill before receiving help. Perhaps they are under greater psychological stress, which leads to a higher rate. Perhaps their attitudes, values, kind and amount of education, and living conditions make them more susceptible to becoming mentally ill. Perhaps mental illness leads to a lower status. And finally, there may be no actual difference in severity and rate of emotional problems between social classes. It is possible that psychiatrists are less likely to assign a mental illness label to a person of a higher status because of the stigma associated with the label.

In addition, psychiatrists may have less understanding of the value systems of the poor and therefore be more apt to label lower-class behavior as deviant or mentally ill.

A number of studies have also found social class differences in quality of treatment for those labeled mentally ill.[38] Lower-class patients are likely to receive lower quality care (often just custodial care when hospitalized) and to have lower rates of release when hospitalized in a mental institution.

URBANIZATION   There is some evidence that cities, particularly the inner city areas, have a higher rate of mental illness than rural areas.[39] One explanation is that in cities (particularly inner city areas) the higher incidence is due to overcrowding and to the deteriorated quality of life—dirt, noise, crime, transportation problems, inadequate housing, unemployment, drugs—which creates a higher level of emotional problems. Another explanation is that the higher rate in cities is due to mental health facilities being located in and around urban areas, which increases the probability that urban dwellers with emotional problems will be identified and treated.

AGE   The elderly are more likely to have emotional problems, particularly depression (which is partially due to the low status that the elderly have in our society, since it leads to a crushing sense of uselessness and isolation). An additional category of mental disorder that the elderly are apt to have is disturbances associated with degeneration of brain cells from such causes as arteriosclerosis and chronic alcoholism.[40]

MARITAL STATUS   People who are single, divorced, or widowed have higher rates of mental disorder than married people. Unmarried men have somewhat higher rates than unmarried women.[41]

SEX   Men and women are equally likely to be treated, but the nature of the diagnosis varies. Women are more likely to be labeled neurotic, more likely to be hospitalized in a mental institution, and more likely to have higher rates of depression. Men are more likely to be diagnosed as psychotic.[42] (Why more men are labeled psychotic but less often hospitalized compared to women is unclear.)

The vast majority of psychiatrists are men, and there is evidence that psychiatrists are more apt to consider sexual promiscuity or aggressive behavior in women a mental disorder but to overlook such behavior in men.[43]

RACE   Blacks are more likely to be diagnosed mentally ill compared to whites, and their rate of hospitalization is about 33 percent higher than the rate for whites.[44] There are several sociological explanations for these trends. Blacks may be under greater psychological pressure due to discrimination. Or, the higher rates may be due to their lower social status, as a greater proportion of people in the lower social classes is diagnosed mentally ill. Or, because most psychiatrists are white, they may have less awareness of the lifestyles of blacks. This lack of awareness may lead psychiatrists to more readily assign mentally ill labels to blacks, who generally differ in class, status, cultural values, and cultural background from whites.

TREATMENT

Brief History

Although the history of treatment for the emotionally disturbed is fascinating, it is also filled with injustices and tragedies. George Rosen documents that most societies have developed unique ways of viewing mental illness and treating those so labeled.[45] In some societies deviants have been valued highly, even treated as prophets having supernatural powers. In others the emotionally disturbed have been viewed as being evil and have even been feared as people possessed with demonological powers. For instance, during a brief period in our colonial history, certain of the disturbed were viewed as "witches" and were burned at the stake. Prior to the 19th century the severely disturbed were confined in "almshouses"; received only harsh, custodial care; and were often chained to the walls.[46]

In the 19th century a few mental institutions in France, England, and the United States began to take a more humanitarian approach to treating the disturbed. Although the severely disturbed were still confined in institutions, they began to be viewed either as having an illness or as having an emotional problem. The physical surroundings were improved, and there were efforts to replace the harsh, custodial treatment with a caring approach that recognized each resident as a person deserving of respect and dignity. Unfortunately, these humanitarian efforts were not widely accepted, in part because they were considered too expensive. Most of the severely disturbed continued to be confined in overcrowded, unsanitary dwellings, with inadequate care and diet.

In 1908 Clifford Beers's book, *A Mind that Found Itself*, was published.[47] Beers had been confined as a patient, and the book recounted the atrocities occurring in this "madhouse." The book reached a wide audience and sensitized the public to the emotional trauma being experienced by those confined. Under Beers's leadership mental health associations were formed that advocated the need for improved inpatient care and initiated the concept of outpatient treatment.

Between 1900 and 1920, Sigmund Freud developed his psychoanalytic theories about the causes of and ways to treat emotional problems. According to Freud, emotional problems were mental illnesses that resulted from early traumatic experiences, internal psychological conflicts, fixations at various stages of development, and unconscious psychological processes. Most segments of the counseling professions (psychiatry, clinical psychology, social work) accepted, from the 1920s to the 1950s, Freud's and other psychoanalytic theorists' views in regard to diagnosing and treating the disturbed. Due to Freud's influence the public accepted a more humanitarian approach to treating the disturbed.

However, in the 1950s questions began to arise about the effectiveness of the psychoanalytic method. It was expensive, an analysis took four or five years, and research studies appeared that showed that the rate of improvement for those undergoing analysis was no higher than for those receiving no treatment![48] Since the 1950s a variety of counseling approaches have been developed that reject most or all of the

BOX 4.4

Asylums and Total Institutions

In 1961 Erving Goffman wrote *Asylums*, which described life inside state mental hospitals. Goffman indicates that such mental hospitals are "total institutions." (Other total institutions are prisons, boot camps, monasteries, and convents.) In a total institution a resident is cut off from society for appreciable periods of time and required to lead a regimented life. Inside an asylum residents are stripped of their clothing and cut off from contact with the outside world. Total institutions seek to control residents fully and to resocialize and remake their lives. In such institutions the fear of expulsion is a major control mechanism. Long-term confinement in asylums tends to result in people losing their capacities to respond in an independent, rational fashion. Confinement gradually undermines their capacities to cope with the outside world.

Total institutions teach residents to accept the staff's view of right and wrong and erode residents' capacities to think independently. Goffman points out that in mental hospitals an act of assertiveness or rebellion by residents is not taken as a sign of mental stability but as a symptom of sickness. The "good" patient, from the staff's point of view, is one who is undemanding, docile, and obedient. In general, mental hospitals downgrade patients' feelings of self-esteem and emphasize their failures and inadequacies. Uniform furniture and clothing, a regimented routine, and a custodial atmosphere encourage patients to be docile and unassertive. The use of the medical model approach to emotional problems encourages patients to view themselves as sick and in need of help. Such "resocialization" actually hinders residents from being able to make a successful return to society. There is a high probability that long-term hospitalization will do more harm than good. The film *One Flew over the Cuckoo's Nest* vividly illustrates the resocialization process described by Goffman.

Source: Erving Goffman, *Asylums: Essays on the Social Situation of Mental Patients and Other Inmates* (New York: Doubleday, 1961).

concepts underlying psychoanalysis; these newer approaches include behavior modification, rational therapy, reality therapy, transactional analysis, radical therapy, gestalt therapy, and client-centered therapy.[49]

It should be mentioned that certain segments of the medical profession have continued to maintain, since the 19th century, that mental illness is akin to other physical illnesses. They assert that infectious diseases, genetic endowment, and metabolic disorders are the causes of mental disorders.[50] However, only a few specific organic causes have been identified. General paresis, for instance, which is a progressive emotional disorder, has been linked to syphilis; and pellagra, another disorder, has been found to result from dietary deficiency. The notion that mental disorders are physiological led to certain medical treatments that now appear to be tragedies. In the 18th century bloodletting was widely used. In the early 20th century prefrontal lobotomies (surgical slashing of the frontal section of the brain) were performed to "remove" the mental illness. Lobotomies have little therapeutic value, cause lasting brain damage, and result in patients becoming docile and retarded.

Current Trends

In the past thirty years there have been two major developments in the treatment of the severely disturbed. The first development has been the discovery and use of psychoactive drugs, both tranquilizers and stimulants. The initial hope was that such drugs would cure severe disturbances, but it was soon realized that they provide primarily symptom relief and thereby enable the disturbed person to be more accessible to other therapy programs and approaches.[51] The second development has been deinstitutionalization. Mental health practitioners realized that mental hospitals, instead of "curing" the disturbed, were frequently perpetuating disturbed behavior via long-term hospitalization. The disturbed were labeled mentally ill and through long-term hospitalization would define themselves as "different" and enact the insane role.[52] Also, they became adapted to the relaxed, safe life of a hospital, and the longer they stayed the more they perceived the outside world as threatening.

Mental health professionals now only use hospitalization for those whose emotional problems pose a serious threat to their own well-being or to that of others. Psychotherapy is the main treatment approach used in mental hospitals. In most cases now, hospitalization for an emotional problem is brief. The concept of deinstitutionalization has brought about a significant expansion of services designed to meet the needs of the disturbed in their home community, including community-based mental health centers, halfway houses, rehabilitation workshops, social therapeutic clubs, and foster-care services for the disturbed.

A criticism of the deinstitutionalization approach has been that some communities have returned long-term hospitalized patients to society *without* developing adequate community-based support services. The result is that many of the patients who have been discharged are living with families, friends, or on the street and are receiving little or no counseling and/or medical services.

Recent investigations reveal incidents of discharged mental patients living in squalor in unlicensed group homes and low-quality hotels.[53] Many are victims of crime, fire, and medical neglect. Some are fed rancid food and exposed to rats and cockroaches. Sometimes such former patients set fires, abuse others, and a few commit homicide or suicide.

TREATMENT FACILITIES: COMMUNITY MENTAL HEALTH CENTERS

Treatment services for emotional problems are provided by nearly every direct-service social welfare agency, including public welfare agencies, probation and parole agencies, penal institutions, school social services, family service agencies, adoption agencies, sheltered workshops, social service units in hospitals, and nursing homes. However, in many communities mental health centers are a primary resource for serving those with emotional problems.

Community mental health centers were given their impetus with the passage by the federal government of the Community Mental Health Centers Act of 1963. This act provided for transferring the care and treatment of the majority of "mentally ill" persons from state hospitals to their home communities. The emphasis is on local care, with provision of comprehensive services (particularly to underprivileged areas and people).

Other emphases are (*a*) early diagnosis, treatment, and early return to community; (*b*) the centers being located "near and accessible to" the populations they serve; (*c*) the establishment of centers on the basis of "catchment areas" containing between 75,000 and 200,000 people; and (*d*) the provision of comprehen-

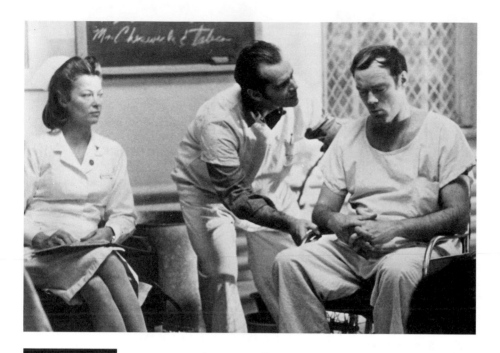

The film One Flew Over the Cuckoo's Nest *vividly portrayed life inside a state mental hospital. Like the residents of other "total institutions," the patients are controlled by an authoritarian staff whose sole objective is to keep them as docile and obedient as possible. While the accuracy of the story is open to debate, there is no question that both the book and the movie exploited the view that psychiatric institutions are little more than jails—a belief probably held by most Americans today.*

sive care having five basic components: inpatient care, outpatient care, partial hospitalization (that is, day, night, and weekend care), emergency care, and consultation/education. Services provided are expected to relate to a wide range of problem areas and population groups, such as the disturbed, the aged, minorities, and those with alcohol and other drug-related problems.[54]

Professionals in a community mental health center represent all the helping professions, including psychiatrists, social workers, psychologists, psychiatric nurses, specialized consultants, occupational and recreational therapists, paraprofessionals, and volunteers. Typical services include outpatient care, inpatient care, alcohol and chemical abuse treatment, work evaluation, occupational therapy, family and group therapy,

transportation services, counseling of children and adults, crisis intervention (including twenty-four-hour emergency care), community education, and field training of students in the helping professions.

Community mental health services have in recent years received increasing criticism. Studies have found that some community mental health services are ineffective and inadequate.[55] Patients still have high readmission rates and inadequate levels of adjustment to the community.[56] Many centers have been ineffective in dealing with the personal and societal problems of large numbers of poor people, with many of these so-called comprehensive centers providing little more than traditional inpatient and outpatient care for middle-class patients.[57]

Many social agencies offer counseling and therapy to people with emotional problems. Art therapy is one activity these professionals use in working with children at a private medical center.

On the other hand, proponents of community mental health centers argue that the results of such centers have been impressive. They point out that their programs have reduced the number of people in state and county mental hospitals from 550,000 in 1955 to 146,000 in 1985.[58]

SOCIAL WORK AND MENTAL HEALTH

Social workers were first employed in the mental health field in 1906 to take social histories of newly admitted patients to Manhattan State Hospital in New York.[59] Since then they have been involved in providing a variety of preventive, diagnostic, and treatment services.

Over the years the treatment emphasis has moved from treating the individual to treating the family. Social workers, psychologists, and psychiatrists now function interchangeably as individual, family, and group therapists. All three professional groups are also involved in designing and administering mental health programs. Other professionals involved in working as a team in mental health facilities include psychiatric nurses, occupational therapists, and recreational therapists.

It has been estimated that half the professionals who provide mental health services in the United States today are social workers.[60] Many social agencies, in addition to community mental health centers, provide counseling and psychotherapy to people having emotional problems. Such agencies include schools, family counseling agencies, public welfare departments, hospitals, adoption agencies, and probation and parole departments. An increasing number of clinical social workers are opening private practices to furnish individual, family, and group therapy for a variety of emotional problems. Increasingly, payments from public and private insurance programs reimburse social workers for providing therapy on a private basis.

The National Association of Social Workers (NASW) has been promoting state licensing (or registration) requirements to ensure the public that social work practitioners meet high standards of competence. With the expansion of private practices by clinical social workers, the need for licensing is increasing.

NASW has also established a national Registry of Clinical Social Workers. Requirements for membership are:

A master's or doctoral degree in social work from a graduate school of social work accredited or recognized by the Council on Social Work Education; two years or 3,000 hours of post-master's clinical social work practice under the supervision of a master's degree level social worker, or, if social work supervision could be shown to have been unavailable, supervision by another mental health professional with the added condition of giving evidence of continued participation and identification with the social work profession; at least two years or 3,000 hours of direct clinical practice within the last ten years; be a member of the Academy of Certified Social Workers (ACSW) or be licensed in a State at a level at least equivalent to ACSW standards. The clinical social worker has specialized knowledge of human growth and behavior and of internal, interpersonal, and environmental stress on social functioning. This knowledge must be combined with practice skills in treatment modalities which alleviate such problems.[61]

Until several years ago social work in the mental health field was generally practiced in a subordinate role to psychiatry. But with a growing recognition that emotional problems are primarily problems in living rather than organic in nature, social workers are increasingly being employed in agencies to provide counseling and psychotherapy, without being supervised by a psychiatrist.

The primary therapy approach used to treat people with emotional or behavioral problems is psychotherapy or counseling (the author will use these two terms interchangeably, as there do not appear to be clear-cut distinctions between the two). Counseling is a broad term covering individual, family, and group therapy. A skilled counselor has knowledge of (*a*) interviewing principles and (*b*) comprehensive and specific treatment approaches. Material in these two areas will briefly be presented. This material is designed to give the reader a "flavor" of what counseling is composed of. Additional theoretical material covering these two areas is presented in social work methods and field placement courses. Through role playing of contrived counseling situations and, later, through working with clients, social work students gain skill and confidence in putting this material into practice. Sharpening and further developing one's counseling skills do not end with acquiring a degree in a counseling field; it is an ongoing, lifelong process.

COUNSELING

Counseling services are provided by practically every direct service social welfare agency. Some agencies, such as welfare departments and mental health centers, provide counseling services covering almost all emotional or interpersonal problems. Other more specialized agencies provide counseling designed for specific problems that require considerable background knowledge and training in using highly developed treatment techniques. (Such areas include drug abuse counseling, abortion counseling, sexual counseling, genetic counseling, and parent effectiveness training.)

Capacity to counsel effectively is one of the key skills needed in social workers; in fact, it may be *the* most important skill. Acquiring in-depth skill at counseling in one area (for example, marriage or adoption counseling) prepares that person for counseling in other areas. The key learning variable is acquiring skill at in-depth counseling, as this skill is transferable. Because in-depth counseling is transferable to other areas, undergraduate and graduate social work programs are able to take a generic (broad-based) approach to social work training. The emphasis is placed on in-depth training in counseling rather than on training students for specialized counseling areas.

How to Counsel*

Counseling someone with personal problems is neither magical nor mystical. Although training and experience in counseling is beneficial, everyone has the potential of helping another by listening and talking through difficulties. Counseling with a successful outcome can be done by a friend, neighbor, relative, yourself, the local barber, hairdresser, banker, and bartender, as well as by social workers, psychiatrists, psychologists, guidance counselors, and the clergy. This is not to say that everyone will be successful at counseling. Professional people, because of their training and experience, have a higher probability of being successful. But competence and concern, rather than degrees or certificates, are the keys to desirable outcomes.

There are three phases to counseling: (*a*) building a relationship, (*b*) exploring problems in depth, and (*c*) exploring alternative solutions. Successful counseling gradually proceeds from one phase to the next, with some overlapping of these stages. For example, in many cases, while exploring problems, the relationship between the counselor and the counselee continues to develop; and while exploring alternative solutions, the problems are generally being examined in greater depth.

BUILDING A RELATIONSHIP   The following suggestions are guidelines for building a relationship with a client:

1. The counselor should seek to establish a nonthreatening atmosphere where the counselee feels safe to communicate fully his or her troubles while feeling accepted as a person.

2. In initial contacts with the counselee, the counselor needs to "sell" himself or herself, not arrogantly, but as a knowledgeable, understanding person who may be able to help and who wants to try.

3. Be calm; do not express shock or laughter when the counselee begins to open up about his or her problems. Emotional outbursts, even if subtle, will lead the counselee to believe that you are not going to understand his or her difficulties, and she or he will usually stop discussing them.

4. Generally be nonjudgmental, nonmoralistic. Show respect for the counselee's values, and do not try to sell your values. The values that work for you may not be best for someone else in a different situation. For example, if the counselee is premaritally pregnant, do not attempt to force your values toward adoption or abortion, but let the counselee decide on the course of action after a full examination of the problem and an exploration of the possible solutions.

5. View the counselee as an equal. "Rookie" counselors sometimes make the mistake of thinking that because someone is sharing his or her intimate secrets, the counselor must be very important, and they end up arranging a superior-inferior relationship. If counselees feel that they are being treated as inferior, they will be less motivated to reveal and discuss personal difficulties.

6. Use "shared vocabulary." This does not mean that the counselor should use the same slang words and the same accent as the counselee. If the counselee sees the counselor as artificial in use of slang or accent, it may seriously offend him or her. The counselor should use words that the counselee understands and that are not offensive.

7. The tone of the counselor's voice should convey the message that the counselor empathetically understands and cares about the counselee's feelings.

8. Keep confidential what the counselee has said. People unfortunately have nearly irresistible urges to share "juicy secrets" with someone else. If the counselee discovers that confidentiality has been violated, a working relationship may be quickly destroyed.

9. If you are counseling a relative or a friend, there is a danger that, because you are emotionally involved, you may get upset or into an argument with the other person. If that happens it is almost always best to drop the subject immediately, as tactfully as possible. Perhaps after tempers cool the subject can be brought up again, or perhaps it may be best to refer the counselee to someone else. When counseling a friend or relative, you should be aware that when you find yourself becoming upset, further discussion will not be

---

*This section on "How to Counsel" is reprinted from an article written by this author with the same title in *The Personal Problem Solver*, ed. Charles Zastrow and Dae Chang (Englewood Cliffs, NJ: Spectrum Books, 1977). Reprinted by permission of Prentice-Hall, Englewood Cliffs, New Jersey.

productive. Many professional counselors refuse to counsel friends or relatives because they are aware that they are emotionally involved. Emotional involvement interferes with the calm, detached perspective that is needed to help clients explore problems and alternative solutions.

EXPLORING PROBLEMS IN DEPTH   Following are suggestions to guide counselors in helping a client explore his or her problems in depth:

1. Many "rookie" counselors make the mistake of suggesting solutions as soon as a problem is identified, without exploring the problem area in depth. For example, an advocate of abortions may advise this solution as soon as a single female reveals that she is pregnant, without taking the time to discover whether this person is strongly opposed to abortions, really wants a baby, or intends to marry soon.

2. In exploring problems in depth the counselor and counselee need to examine such areas as the extent of the problem, how long the problem has existed, what the causes are, how the counselee feels about the problem, and what physical and mental capacities and strengths the counselee has to cope with the problem, before exploring alternative solutions. To illustrate, if a single female is pregnant, the counselor and counselee need to explore the following questions: How does the person feel about being pregnant? Has she seen a doctor? About how long has she been pregnant? Do her parents know? What are their feelings and concerns if they know? Has the girl informed the father? What are his feelings and concerns if he knows? What does she feel is the most urgent situation to deal with first? Answers to such questions will determine the future direction of counseling. The most pressing, immediate problem might be to inform her parents, who may react critically, or it might be to secure medical services.

3. When a problem area is identified there are usually a number of smaller problems that may occur. Explore all these. For example, planning how to tell the father, obtaining medical care, obtaining funds for medical expenses, deciding where to live, deciding whether to leave school or work during the pregnancy, deciding whether to keep the child, and making plans for what to do after the child is delivered or the pregnancy terminated.

4. In a multiproblem situation, the best way to decide which problem to handle first is to ask the counselee which problem she or he perceives as most pressing. If the problem can be solved, start with exploring that subproblem in depth and developing together a strategy for the solution. Success in solving a subproblem will increase the counselee's confidence in the counselor and thereby will further solidify the relationship.

5. Convey empathy, not sympathy. Empathy is the capacity to show that you are aware of and can to some extent feel what the counselee is saying. Sympathy is also a sharing of feelings, but it has the connotation of offering pity. The difference is subtle, but empathy is oriented toward problem solving, whereas sympathy usually prolongs problems. Giving sympathy usually causes the counselee to dwell on his or her emotions without taking action to improve the situation. For example, if one gives sympathy to a depressed person, that person wil keep telling you his or her sad story over and over, each time having an emotional outpouring supported by your sympathy, without taking any action to improve the situation. Telling the story over and over only reopens old wounds and prolongs the depression.

6. "Trust your guts." The most important tool that a counselor has is himself or herself (his or her feelings and perceptions). A counselor should continually strive to place himself or herself in the client's situation (with the client's values and pressures). To use the earlier example, if the client is 17 years old, single, pregnant, and has parents who are very critical of the situation and who want her to have an abortion, a competent counselor would continually strive to feel what she is feeling and to perceive the world from her perspective, with her goals, difficulties, pressures, and values. It probably never happens that a counselor is 100 percent accurate in placing himself or herself in the counselee's situation, but 70 percent to 80 percent is usually sufficient to gain an awareness of the counselee's pressures, problems, and perspectives. This information is very useful in assisting the counselor in determining what additional areas need to be explored, in deciding what

she or he should say, and in figuring out possible solutions. Stated in a somewhat different way, a counselor should ask himself or herself, "What is this person trying to tell me and how can I make it clear that I understand not only intellectually but empathetically?"

7. When you believe that the client has touched on an important area of concern, further communication can be encouraged by

a. Nonverbally showing interest.

b. Pauses: "Rookie" counselors usually become anxious when there is a pause, and they hasten to say something, anything, to have conversation continue. This is usually a mistake, especially when it leads to a change in the topic. A pause will also make the counselee anxious, give him or her time to think about the important area of concern, and then usually motivate him or her to continue conversation in that area.

c. Neutral probes: for example, "Could you tell me more about it?" "Why do you feel that way?" "I'm not sure I understand what you have in mind."

d. Summarizing what the client is saying: for example, "During this past hour you made a number of critical comments about your spouse; it sounds like some things about your marriage are making you unhappy."

e. Reflecting feelings: for example, "You seem angry" or "You appear to be depressed about that."

8. Approach socially unacceptable issues tactfully. Tact is an essential quality of a competent counselor. Try not to ask a question in such a way that the answer will put the respondent in an embarrassing position. Suppose, for instance, that you are counseling a male with poor personal hygiene who has been discharged from a variety of jobs and does not know why. The man explains that employers initially compliment him on his work productivity and then tend a few weeks later to discharge him without informing him why. After exploring several possible reasons for the dismissals for which the client is able to present refuting evidence, you as the counselor may tactfully say, "I'm wondering if your personal appearance and hygiene may be a reason for the dismissals. I notice you haven't

shaved for a few days, and I sense you may not have bathed for a few days either. Do you think your hygienic habits may be an explanation?" It is very important to confront clients with those ineffective actions that are having substantial negative effects on their lives.

9. When pointing out a limitation that a counselee has, mention and compliment him or her on any assets. When a limitation is being mentioned, the counselee will literally feel that something is being laid bare or taken away. Therefore, compliment him or her in another area to give something back.

10. Watch for nonverbal cues. A competent counselor will generally use such cues to identify when a sensitive subject is being touched on, as the client will generally become anxious and show anxiety by changing tone of voice, fidgeting, yawning, stiff posture, and a flushed face.

11. Be honest. A untruth always runs the risk of being discovered. If that happens, the counselee's confidence in the counselor will be seriously damaged and perhaps the relationship seriously jeopardized. But being honest goes beyond not telling lies. The counselor should always point out those shortcomings that are in the counselee's best interest to give attention to. For example, if someone is being fired from jobs because of poor grooming habits, this needs to be brought to that person's attention. Or if a trainee's relationship skills and personality are not suited for the helping profession, that trainee needs to be "counseled out" in the interest of clients and in the trainee's own best interests.

12. Listen attentively to what the counselee is saying. Try to view his or her words, not from your perspective but from the counselee's. Unfortunately, many people are caught up in their own interests and concerns, and they do not "tune out" those thoughts while the counselee is speaking. This guideline seems very simple, but it is indeed difficult for many to follow.

EXPLORING ALTERNATIVE SOLUTIONS The following suggestions provide guidelines for counselors in exploring alternative solutions with a client:

1. After (or sometimes when) a subproblem is explored in depth, the next step is for the counselor and

the counselee to consider alternative solutions. The counselor's role is generally to indicate the possible alternatives and then to explore with the counselee their merits, shortcomings, and consequences. For example, with the case of the premaritally pregnant girl, if she decides to continue the pregnancy to full term, possible alternatives for the subproblem of making plans for living arrangements include keeping the child, getting married, seeking public assistance, finding foster care after delivery, filing a paternity suit, placing the child for adoption, and obtaining the assistance of a close relative to help care for the child.

2. The counselee usually has the right to self-determination, that is, to choose the course of action among possible alternatives. The counselor's role is to help the counselee clarify and understand the likely consequences of each available alternative but generally not to give advice or choose the alternative for the counselee. If the counselor were to select the alternative, there are two possible outcomes: (*a*) The alternative may prove to be undesirable for the counselee, in which case the counselee will probably blame the counselor for the advice, and the future relationship will be seriously hampered. (*b*) The alternative may prove to be desirable for the counselee. This immediate outcome is advantageous, but the danger is that the counselee will then become overly dependent on the counselor, seeking the counselor's advice for nearly every decision in the future, and generally being reluctant to make decisions on his or her own. In actual practice, most courses of action have desirable and undesirable consequences. For example, if the unmarried mother is advised to keep her child, she may receive considerable gratification from being with and raising the child, but at the same time she may blame the counselor for such possible negative consequences as long-term financial hardships and an isolated social life.

3. Counseling is done *with* the counselee, not *to* or *for* the counselee. The counselee should have the responsibility of doing many of the tasks necessary to improve the situation. A good rule to follow is that the counselee should take responsibility for those tasks that she or he has the capacity to carry out, and the counselor should only attempt to do those that are beyond the capacities of the counselee. Doing things

for counselees, similar to giving advice, runs the risk of creating a dependency relationship. Furthermore, successful accomplishment of tasks by counselees leads to personal growth and better prepares them for taking on future responsibilities.

4. The counselee's right to self-determination should be taken away only if the selected course of action has a high probability of seriously hurting others or the counselee. For example, if it is highly probable that a parent will continue to abuse a child, or if the counselee attempts to take his or her own life, intervention by the counselor is suggested. For most situations, however, the counselee should have the right to select his or her alternative, even when the counselor believes that another alternative is a better course of action. Frequently, the counselee is in a better position to know what is best for him or her, and if the alternative is not the best, the counselee will probably learn from the mistake.

5. The counselor should attempt to form explicit, realistic "contracts" with counselees. When the counselee does select an alternative, the counselee should clearly understand what the goals will be, what tasks need to be carried out, how to do the tasks, and who will carry out each of them. Frequently, it is desirable to write the "contract" for future reference, with a time limit set for the accomplishment of each task. For example, if the unmarried mother decides to keep her child and now needs to make long-range financial plans, this goal should be understood and specific courses of action decided on—seeking public assistance, seeking support from the alleged father, securing an apartment within her budget, and so on. Furthermore, who will do what task within a set time limit should be specified.

6. If the counselee fails to meet the terms of the "contract," do not punish, but do not accept excuses. Excuses let people off the hook; they provide temporary relief, but they eventually lead to more failure and to a failure identity. Simply ask, "Do you still wish to try to fulfill your commitment?" If the counselee answers affirmatively, another time deadline acceptable to the counselee should be set.

7. Perhaps the biggest single factor in determining whether the counselee's situation will improve is the counselee's motivation to carry out essential tasks. A

counselor should seek to motivate apathetic counselees. One of the biggest reality shocks of new trainees entering into the helping professions is that many clients, even after making commitments to improve their situation, do not have the motivation to carry out the steps outlined.

8. One way to increase motivation is to clarify what will be gained by meeting the commitment. When counselees meet commitments, reward them verbally or in other ways. Seldom punish if commitments are not met. Punishment usually increases hostility, without positive lasting changes. Also, punishment only serves as a temporary means of obtaining different behavior; when a person no longer believes that she or he is under surveillance, she or he will usually return to the "deviant" behavior.

9. For a number of tasks in which the counselee lacks confidence or experience in carrying them out, it is helpful to "role-play" the tasks. For example, if a pregnant single girl wants help in deciding how to tell her boyfriend about the pregnancy, role-playing the situation will assist the girl in selecting words and developing a strategy for informing him. The counselor can first play the girl's role and model an approach, with the girl playing the boy's role. Then the roles should be reversed so that the girl practices telling her boyfriend.

Other helpful hints to counseling could be given here, but the basic format is to develop a relationship, explore problems in depth, and then to explore alternative solutions. These guidelines are not to be followed dogmatically; they will probably work 70 to 80 percent of the time. The most important tool that a counselor has is himself or herself (feelings, perceptions, relationship capacities, and interviewing skills).

One final important guideline is that the counselor should refer the counselee to someone else, or at least seek a professional counselor to discuss the case with, for any of the following situations: if the counselor feels that she or he is unable to empathize with the counselee; if the counselor feels that the counselee is choosing unethical alternatives (such as seeking an abortion) that conflict with the counselor's basic value system; if the counselor feels that the problem is of such a nature that she or he will not be able to help; and if a working relationship is not established. A competent counselor

knows that she or he can work with and help some people but not all and that it is in the counselee's and the counselor's best interests to refer the person to someone else who can.

Comprehensive and Specialized Counseling Approaches

In addition to having a working knowledge of interviewing principles, an effective counselor needs to have a knowledge of comprehensive counseling theories and of specialized treatment techniques to be able to diagnose precisely what problems exist and how to intervene effectively. There are a number of contemporary comprehensive counseling approaches: psychoanalysis, Adlerian psychotherapy, client-centered therapy, rational therapy, behavior modification, gestalt therapy, reality therapy, transactional analysis, neurolinguistic programming, and encounter approaches.* These therapy approaches generally present theoretical material on (*a*) personality theory, or how normal psychosocial development occurs; (*b*) behavior pathology, or how emotional problems arise; and (*c*) therapy, or how to change disturbed behavior.

An effective counselor generally has a knowledge of several treatment approaches and, depending on the unique set of problems being presented by the client, is able to pick and choose from his or her "bag of tricks" which intervention strategy is apt to have the highest probability of success. In addition to comprehensive counseling approaches, there are a number of specialized treatment techniques for specific problems: for example, assertiveness training for people who are shy or overly aggressive, relaxation techniques for people experiencing high levels of stress, specific sexual counseling techniques for such difficulties as premature ejaculation or orgasmic dysfunction, and

---

*A good summary of contemporary global counseling approaches is provided in *Current Psychotherapies*, ed. Raymond Corsini (Itasca, IL: F. E. Peacock, 1984); *Social Work Treatment*, ed. Francis J. Turner (New York: Free Press, 1979); and Charles Zastrow, *The Practice of Social Work* (Chicago, IL: Dorsey Press, 1989).

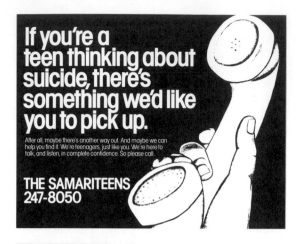

Anyone can be of potential help to others by listening and talking through difficulties. The Samariteens are teenaged volunteers from the Boston area who befriend their lonely, depressed, and suicidal peers.

parent effectiveness training for parent-child relationship difficulties.* An effective counselor strives to gain a working knowledge of a wide variety of treatment techniques in order to increase the likelihood of being able to help clients.

For illustrative purposes, one comprehensive therapy approach, rational therapy, will be summarized.

RATIONAL THERAPY   The two main developers of this approach are Albert Ellis and Maxie Maultsby.[62] The approach has the potential to enable those who become skillful in rationally analyzing their self-talk to control or get rid of any undesirable emotion they encounter.

It is erroneously believed by most people that our emotions and our actions are primarily determined by our experiences (that is, by events that happen to us). On the contrary, rational therapy has demonstrated that the primary cause of all our emotions and actions is what we tell ourselves about events that happen to us.

---

*A summary of a number of specialized treatment techniques is contained in Charles Zastrow, *The Practice of Social Work* (Chicago, IL: Dorsey Press, 1989).

All feelings and actions occur according to the following format:

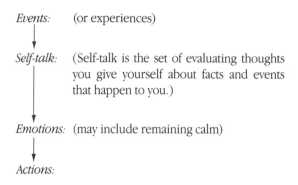

Events:	(or experiences)
↓	
Self-talk:	(Self-talk is the set of evaluating thoughts you give yourself about facts and events that happen to you.)
↓	
Emotions:	(may include remaining calm)
↓	
Actions:	

An example will illustrate the above process.

Event:	Cheryl, the 5-year-old daughter of Mr. and Mrs. Shaw, is playing with her brother and knocks over and breaks a lamp.
↓	
Mr. Shaw's self-talk:	"That lamp was our favorite; we bought it on our honeymoon—it's irreplaceable. This is awful."
	"Spare the rod and spoil the child—some stiff discipline will make her shape up."
	"As head of this household it's my duty to make her shape up. I'll teach her a lesson she'll never forget by giving her the spanking of her life."
	"She's always breaking things. I think this might have been intentional! I'll teach her to have respect for me and for our valuable items."
↓	
Emotions:	Anger, disappointment, frustration.
↓	
Actions:	Spanking and yelling at Cheryl, with the severity of the spanking bordering on abuse.

If, on the other hand, Mr. Shaw gives himself a

different set of self-talk, his emotions and actions will be quite different:

Event: Cheryl, the 5-year-old daughter of Mr. and Mrs. Shaw is playing with her brother and knocks over and breaks a lamp.

Mr. Shaw's   "This was a lamp we cherished, but I know
self-talk: she didn't break it intentionally. It was an accident. My getting angry at this point won't help."

               "I might have prevented this accident by informing Cheryl and our son that they can only horse around in this house in the rec room and in their bedrooms."

               "With young children some accidents are bound to happen."

               "The most constructive thing I can do at this point is to say that I understand that it was an accident, that all of us are disappointed that the lamp broke, and tell them in the future their horsing around should be limited to the rec room and the bedrooms."

Emotions: Some disappointment but generally remaining calm.

Actions: In an understanding fashion talking to the children and expressing his thoughts in line with his self-talk.

The most important point about the above processes is that our self-talk determines how we feel and act; by changing our self-talk we can change how we feel and act. Generally we cannot control events that happen to us, but we have the power to think rationally and thereby change *all* of our unwanted emotions and ineffective actions.*[63]

The rehabilitative aspect of this conceptualization of self-talk is that any unwanted emotion and any ineffective behavior can be changed by identifying and then changing the underlying self-talk.

The self-talk we give ourselves about specific events that happen to us is often based on a variety of factors, including our beliefs, attitudes, values, wants, motives, goals, and desires.[64] For example, the self-talk a married woman might give herself on being informed by her husband that he wants a divorce would be influenced by her desires (or lack of desires) to remain married, by her values and beliefs about being a divorcée, by her attitudes toward her husband, by how she believes getting a divorce would be consistent or inconsistent with her present goals, and by her beliefs about the reasons why her husband says he wants a divorce.

Another important point about self-talk is that with repeated occurrences of an event, a person's emotional reaction becomes nearly automatic because the person rapidly gives himself or herself a large set of self-talk gradually acquired through past experiences. For example, a few years ago I counseled a woman who became intensely upset and depressed every time her husband came home intoxicated. In examining her emotional reactions it became clear that because of the repeated occurrences she would rapidly tell herself the following on seeing him inebriated:

"He's making a fool of himself and of me."

"He's foolishly spending money we desperately need."

"For the next few hours I'm going to have to put up with his drunken talk and behavior—this is awful."

"He loves drinking more than he loves me because he knows I do not want him to get drunk."

"Woe is me."

The use of rational therapy is demonstrated in Box 4.5.

---

*According to Maultsby rational thinking and rational behavior (*a*) is consistent with the facts, (*b*) helps you protect your life, (*c*) helps you achieve your short- and long-term goals more quickly, (*d*) helps you get out and stay out of significant trouble with other people, and (*e*) helps you prevent significant unwanted emotions.

BOX 4.5

A Case Example Using Rational Therapy: Coping with a Sexual Affair

A 21-year-old coed, Cindy, sought counseling after she was informed by the person she was dating, Jim, that a few months earlier he had become sexually involved with another woman, Linda. Jim and Cindy had dated fairly steadily for the past two years. Both were attending the same college. Prior to their summer break they were having frequent arguments and decided not to see each other during the summer. When they returned to college in the fall they again felt strongly about each other and resumed their relationship. A few weeks later Jim (after Cindy questioned him) informed her that he, on one evening, did become sexually involved with Linda.

Cindy told the counselor that she wanted to handle the emotions she was having about this affair better. After discussing her feelings in some depth, the counselor informed her that she could counter her undesirable emotions by doing a rational self-analysis (based on rational therapy). Doing a rational self-analysis involves writing down:

A. The facts and events that occurred.

B. The self-talk a person gives himself or herself.

C. The emotions that are experienced.

D. The self-talk statements found in the A section—which should be in the B section (these self-talk statements are identified after looking at the A section to judge whether the statements are factual or whether some are self-talk statements).

E. Positive and rational self-talk challenges to the negative and irrational self-talk in the B section (this segment is the main therapeutic part of the process).

F. The emotional and behavioral goals that a person has.

The format is presented below. For this process to be therapeutic, the person must practice replacing the irrational self-talk with rational self-talk.

COMBATING ANGER AND HURT FEELINGS

A	D
Facts and Events	*Camera Check of A*
My boyfriend Jim informed me that he had sexual relations with a girl, Linda, after a party at which they had both been drink- ·ing.	D. This is all factual. I know this be- cause Jim told me himself. Jim and I are very close, and I know he would not lie to me.

B	E
My Self-Talk	*My Rational Debates of B*

B–1.   It's not fair! How could Jim do such a thing to me? (bad)

E–1.   Jim had sex with Linda. I'll just have to accept that. Because people are human and fallible, it is a mistake to expect that I will always be treated with fairness by others. Besides, Jim and I had broken up, so I'm sure they didn't have me in mind when they did it. At the time they were sexually involved, neither Jim nor I had any commitment to each other. In truth I also considered getting sexually involved this summer and perhaps would have if I had met the right guy.

B–2.   That creep just had sex with Linda because he wanted a piece of _____. (bad)

E–2.   Jim probably had sex with Linda for other reasons. I know he's not the type that "uses" a girl merely for relief of his sexual tensions. It is also a mistake to label him a creep. No one is a creep. People are humans. If I mislabel him a creep, it may lead me to view him in terms of an inaccurate label.

B–3.   Jim and Linda had no good reasons for doing what they did. They only did it because they were both drunk. What a couple of jerks! (bad)

E–3.   I do believe that the alcohol had a little to do with the fact that Jim and Linda had sex. I know for a fact that Jim becomes much less inhibited when he has had a few drinks. I don't know about Linda, though. The drinking can't be the only reason they had sex. Maybe they felt attracted to each other and wanted to have sex. I've got to remember that this summer Jim and I had no commitments to each other, and therefore I do not have the right to expect that he would be celibate to please me. Also it is a mistake for me to refer to Jim or Linda as being a "jerk." People are people.

Continued

BOX 4.5 *Continued*

B–4.   Linda must be some kind of cheap girl. Only a loose girl would have sex with a guy she didn't love. (bad)

E–4.   I don't even know Linda so I shouldn't judge her like this. Furthermore, I have no way of knowing how Linda felt about Jim. Maybe she felt she loved him at the time. A girl isn't necessarily loose if she has sex with a guy.

B–5.   Jim must think he's some kind of stud now. (bad)

E–5.   Jim has told me that he has had sex with only two girls. My idea of a "stud" is a guy who thinks he can have sex with any girl who comes along. I know Jim better than that. He doesn't think he could, nor would he try to, conquer just any girl.

B–6.   Jim and I will never again be able to have a good sexual relationship of our own now that he has someone else to compare me to. I just know that he'll be thinking of Linda from now on. (bad)

E–6.   Jim and I love each other. Jim told me that he does not love Linda. Just because Jim had sex with Linda does not mean our relationship will always be adversely affected. We can communicate easily during sex, and it has always been satisfying so far. It would be silly for Jim to compare our entire relationship to the one night he spent with Linda.

B–7.   This is the worst thing that Jim could have done. (bad)

E–7.   This is not the worst thing that Jim could have done. What he did was not a crime, like murder or rape, which would have been worse. The situation would be worse if Jim had slept with Linda while he was still seeing me. I'm glad to know that he would never do that.

B–8.   Now that I know Jim had sex with Linda, our whole relationship will be ruined. (bad)

E–8.   The fact that Jim had sex with Linda does not have to ruin our relationship. The event occurred in the past.

It's over. Past sexual experiences have no bearing on the future of our relationship. I want the relationship to continue, and I don't want to see it ruined.

B–9. I should never have broken up with Jim. Then he would never have slept with Linda. It's all my fault. (bad)

E–9. It's not my fault at all. I broke up with Jim because I felt it was the best thing to do at the time. I know Jim would not have been unfaithful to me had we still been dating, but we weren't dating at the time this happened. I had no way of knowing he would some day go to bed with Linda, and knowing would not have changed my decision to break up with him. It's not my fault because I wasn't even involved.

B–10. From now on, whenever I hear Linda's name mentioned I'm going to have a fit! I won't be able to handle it! (bad)

E–10. When I hear Linda's name mentioned, I don't have to respond by having a fit. I can handle my feelings by being calm and not letting the mention of her name bother me.

C
My Emotions

I feel guilty, hurt, angry, upset, and jealous. (very bad)

F
My Emotional and Behavioral Goals

I want to get over my unwanted emotions that I have had about this affair. I want to put this affair in our past. At the time it happened Jim and I had no commitments to each other. What is important to Jim and me is our present and future relationship and not what happened one evening when Jim and I had broken up.

SUMMARY

Emotional and behavioral problems are two comprehensive labels covering an array of problems. All of us, at times, experience emotional and behavioral problems. Serious or severe emotional problems are sometimes labeled "mental illnesses."

The history of treatment for the emotionally disturbed is fascinating but is also filled with injustices and tragedies. In the past the disturbed have been viewed in a variety of ways, ranging from prophets to evil people possessed by demonological powers. Recent major treatment developments are the discovery and use of psychoactive drugs and the trend toward deinstitutionalization.

A major controversy is whether mental illness exists. Adherents of the medical approach believe the disturbed person's mind is affected by some generally unknown, internal condition. Critics of the medical model assert that disturbed people display a social deviation or have an emotional problem but do not have a disease of the mind. Further, they assert that mental illness labels have no diagnostic or treatment value and frequently have an adverse effect.

The large number of homeless people in our nation is a national disgrace. Many of the homeless are thought to suffer from serious and chronic forms of mental illness. Discharged from mental institutions without the support they need, tens of thousands of former mental patients live on the street in abominable conditions.

Another major issue in the mental health field is civil rights concerns over involuntary confinement, inadequate treatment, and enforced use of treatment approaches that have adverse side effects. Other issues include the usefulness of the innocent-by-reason-of-insanity plea, the extent to which psychotropic drugs should be used, and whether local communities are providing adequate services for the emotionally disturbed who are no longer (because of deinstitutionalization) being sent to state mental hospitals.

Sociologists have found a number of associations between social factors and mental illness. Higher rates of diagnosed mental illness have been found in the lower socioeconomic classes, in inner cities as compared to rural areas, among the elderly, among unmarried people, and among blacks as compared to whites. Men and women are about equally likely to be diagnosed mentally ill, with women more apt to be labeled neurotic and men more apt to be labeled psychotic. Lower-class patients are likely to receive lower quality care.

The main therapy approach used to treat people with emotional and behavioral problems is psychotherapy or counseling. Counseling services are provided by practically every direct service social welfare agency. Capacity to counsel others effectively is perhaps the most important skill needed by social workers. To be a competent counselor it is essential to have a working knowledge of interviewing principles and of a wide range of treatment approaches. There are three distinct phases to counseling: building a relationship, exploring problems in depth, and exploring alternative solutions.

NOTES

1. Albert Ellis, *Reason and Emotion in Psychotherapy* (New York: Lyle Stuart, 1962).
2. Joseph Julian and William Kornblum, *Social Problems*, 5th ed. (Englewood Cliffs, NJ: Prentice-Hall, 1986), p. 53.
3. Ibid., p. 53.
4. American Psychiatric Association, *DSM-III (Diagnostic and Statistical Manual of Mental Disorders*, 3rd ed.) (Washington, D.C.: APA, 1980).
5. Thomas S. Szasz, *The Myth of Mental Illness* (New York: Hoeber-Harper, 1961).
6. Thomas S. Szasz, "The Myth of Mental Illness," in *Clinical Psychology in Transition*, comp. John R. Braun (Cleveland: Howard Allen, 1961).
7. Thomas Scheff, *Being Mentally Ill* (Chicago: Aldine Publishing, 1966); and David Mechanic, "Some Factors in Identifying and Defining Mental Illness," *Mental Hygiene* 46, pp. 66–74.
8. Daniel Offer and Melvin Sabshin, *Normality: Theoretical and Clinical Concepts in Mental Health* (New York: Basic Books, 1966), p. 253.
9. Lawrence C. Koll, Viola Bernard, and Bruce P. Dohrenwend, "The Problem of Validity in Field Studies of Psychological Disorder," in *Urban Challenges to Psychiatry*, eds.

Bruce P. Dohrenwend and Barbara Snell Dohrenwend (New York: John Wiley, 1969), pp. 429–460.

10. David L. Rosenhan, "On Being Sane in Insane Places," *Science* 179 (January 1973), pp. 250–257.

11. Scheff, *Being Mentally Ill.*

12. Thomas S. Szasz, *Law, Liberty, and Psychiatry* (New York: Macmillan, 1963).

13. Derek L. Phillips, "Rejection: A Possible Consequence of Seeking Help for Mental Disorder," *American Sociological Review* 28 (1963), pp. 963–973.

14. Edwin M. Lemert, *Social Pathology* (New York: McGraw-Hill, 1951).

15. Charles H. Cooley, *Human Nature and the Social Order* (New York: Scribner, 1902).

16. Thomas S. Szasz, "The Psychiatrist as Double Agent," *Trans-action* 4 (October 1967), p. 16.

17. Scheff, *Being Mentally Ill.*

18. Scheff, *Being Mentally Ill*, p. 17.

19. Ibid., p. 31.

20. Cited in "Homeless: A Problem for Many Mentally Ill," in *The Human Touch*, December, 1985, p. 2.

21. Ibid., p. 2.

22. Lawrence D. Maloney, "Take Mental Patients Off Streets, Back to Hospitals?" *U.S. News & World Report*, July 1, 1985, p. 56.

23. "Homeless: A Problem for Many Mentally Ill," pp. 2–3.

24. Anthony J. Vattano, "Mental Health," in *Contemporary Social Work*, eds. Donald Brieland, Lela B. Costin, and Charles R. Atherton, 2d ed. (New York: McGraw-Hill, 1980), p. 292.

25. Ibid., p. 292.

26. The President's Commission on Mental Health, *Report to the President from The President's Commission on Mental Health*, vol. 1 (Washington, D.C.: U.S. Government Printing Office, 1978).

27. Ibid., pp. 69–72.

28. Franklin D. Chu and Sharland Trotter, *The Madness Establishment* (New York: Grossman, 1974), p. 40.

29. "Psychiatric Testimony Clouds Justice in the Courtroom," *Freedom*, February 1980, p. 1.

30. Ibid., p. 4.

31. "Behind Growing Outrage over Insanity Pleas," *U.S. News & World Report*, May 1979, p. 41.

32. Ibid., p. 42.

33. "Psychiatric Testimony Clouds Justice in the Courtroom," *Freedom*, p. 4.

34. U.S. Bureau of the Census, *Statistical Abstract of the United States, 1987* (Washington, D.C.: U.S. Government Printing Office, 1987), p. 93.

35. August B. Hollingshead and Frederick C. Redlich, *Social Class and Mental Illness: A Community Study* (New York: John Wiley, 1958).

36. William Rushing, "Two Patterns in the Relationship between Social Class and Mental Hospitalization," *American Sociological Review* 34 (August 1969), pp. 533–541.

37. Leo Srole et al., *Mental Health in the Metropolis: The Midtown Manhattan Study*, rev. ed. (New York: Harper & Row, 1975).

38. For example, see Jerome K. Meyers, Lee L. Bean, and Max P. Pepper, "Social Class and Psychiatric Disorders: A Ten-Year Follow-Up," *Journal of Health and Social Behavior* (Summer 1965), pp. 74–79.

39. Jonathan Freeman, "The Effects of Crowding on Human Performance and Social Behavior," in *Contemporary Studies in Psychology*, eds. F. J. Mogulgan and Paul J. Woods (Englewood Cliffs, NJ: Prentice-Hall, 1972), pp. 195–219.

40. Robert C. Atchley, *The Social Forces in Later Life: An Introduction to Social Gerontology*, 2d ed. (Belmont, CA: Wadsworth, 1977).

41. National Institute of Mental Health, *Statistical Note* 104, 1974.

42. Phyllis Chesler, *Women and Madness* (New York: Avon, 1972).

43. Ibid.

44. George J. Warheit, Charles E. Holzer, and Sandra A. Arey, "Race and Mental Illness: An Epidemiological Update," *Journal of Health and Social Behavior* 16 (September 1975), pp. 243–356.

45. George Rosen, *Madness in Society, Chapters in the Historical Sociology of Mental Illness* (New York: Harper & Row, 1969).

46. Ibid., pp. 172–195.

47. Clifford W. Beers, *A Mind that Found Itself* (New York: Longmans, Green, 1908).

48. H. J. Eysenck, "The Effects of Psychotherapy: An Evaluation," *Journal of Consulting Psychology* 11, 1955, pp. 319–324.

49. A good summary of these therapies is provided in *Current Psychotherapies*, ed. Raymond Corsini (Itasca, IL: F. E. Peacock, 1984); and James O. Prochaska, *Systems of Psychotherapy* (Homewood, IL: Dorsey Press, 1979).

50. Miriam Siegler and Mumphrey Osmond, *Models of Madness, Models of Medicine* (New York: Harper & Row, 1974).

51. Joseph Mehr, *Human Services* (Boston, MA: Allyn & Bacon, 1980), p. 88.

52. Erving Goffman, *Asylums: Essays on the Social Situation of Mental Patients and Other Inmates* (New York: Doubleday, 1961).

53. "Mental Patients: A 'Forgotten Minority' in U.S.," *U.S. News & World Report*, May 1979, p. 41.

54. William Glasser, *Reality Therapy* (New York: Harper & Row, 1965).

55. Vattano, "Mental Health," p. 283.

56. "Special Report: Schizophrenia, 1976," *Schizophrenia Bulletin* 2, no. 4 (1976), pp. 44–45.

57. Chu and Trotter, *The Madness Establishment*.

58. U.S. Bureau of the Census, *Statistical Abstract of the United States, 1987*, p. 93.

59. Vattano, "Mental Health," p. 293.

60. Ibid., p. 294.

61. *NASW Register of Clinical Social Workers, Supplement to the First Edition* (Washington, D.C.: National Association of Social Workers, 1977), p. x.

62. Ellis, *Reason and Emotion*; and Maxie Maultsby, *Help Yourself to Happiness* (Boston: Marborough/Herman, 1975).

63. Maultsby, *Help Yourself to Happiness*.

64. From the book *Talk to Yourself* by Charles Zastrow © 1979 by Prentice-Hall, Inc. Published by Prentice-Hall, Inc., Englewood Cliffs, NJ 07632.

5

FAMILY PROBLEMS AND SERVICES TO FAMILIES

The family is a social institution that is found in every culture. A family is a group of people who live together and who are related by marriage, ancestry, or adoption. This chapter will:

- Present a brief history of changes in the American family since colonial days.

- Describe current problem areas in the American family, including divorce, empty shell marriages, family violence, and births outside of marriage.

- Describe current social services for family problems.

- Describe current issues involving family problems.

First, a brief look will be taken at the wide diversity of family patterns that exist in the world.

DIVERSE FAMILY FORMS

Families in different cultures take a variety of forms. In some societies husband and wife live in separate buildings. In others they are expected to live apart for several years after the birth of a child. In many societies husbands are permitted to have more than one wife. In a few countries wives are allowed to have more than one husband. Some cultures permit (and a few encourage) premarital and extramarital intercourse.

Some societies have large communes where adults and children live together. There are also communes in which the children are raised separately from adults. In some cultures without communes surrogate parents rather than the genetic parents raise the children. Some societies encourage certain types of homosexual relationships, and a few recognize homosexual as well as heterosexual marriages.

In many cultures marriages are still arranged by the parents. Some societies do not recognize the existence of romantic love. Some cultures expect older men to marry young girls. Others expect older women to marry young boys. Some expect a man to marry his

Extended families, like this one in Bangladesh, are still the predominant pattern in many developing countries.

father's brother's daughter; others insist that he marry his mother's sister's daughter. Most societies prohibit the marriage of close relatives, yet a few subcultures encourage marriage between brothers and sisters or between first cousins. In a few societies infants are married before they are born (if the baby is of the wrong sex, the marriage is dissolved). In some societies a man, on marrying, makes a substantial gift to the bride's father; in others the bride's father gives a substantial gift to the new husband.

There are indeed substantial variations in family patterns. People in each of these societies generally feel strongly that their particular pattern is normal and proper; many feel the pattern is divinely ordained. Suggested changes in their particular form are usually viewed with suspicion and defensiveness and are often sharply criticized as being unnatural, immoral, and a threat to the survival of the family.

In spite of these variations, practically all family systems can be classified into two basic forms: the extended family and the nuclear family.

An *extended family* consists of a number of relatives living together, such as parents, children, grandparents, great-grandparents, aunts, uncles, in-laws, and cousins. The extended family is the predominant pattern in preindustrial societies. The members divide various agricultural, domestic, and other duties among themselves.

A *nuclear family* consists of a married couple and their children living together. The nuclear family emerged from the extended family. Extended families are particularly functional in agricultural societies where many "hands" are needed. The nuclear family is more suited to the demands of complex, industrialized societies because its smaller size and potential geographic mobility enable it to adapt more easily to changing conditions—such as the need to relocate to obtain a better job.

THE AMERICAN FAMILY: PAST AND PRESENT

The Family in Preindustrial Society

We often view the family as being a stable institution in which few changes have occurred. Surprisingly, a number of changes have taken place since colonial and frontier days.

Prior to the 1800s, the economy in our country was predominantly agricultural. The majority of people lived on small farms in rural areas. In preindustrial society transportation was arduous and travel was constricted. The family was nearly self-sufficient; most of what it consumed was produced on the farm. The house and the farm were the center of production. The most common family type was the extended family. Each family member had specific roles and responsibilities. Because there were many tasks to be performed on small farms, the extended family was functional, as it contained a number of family members to carry out those tasks.

Economic considerations influenced a variety of family patterns. Marriage was highly valued, as was having a number of children. A large-sized family was needed to do the wide variety of tasks involved in planting and harvesting crops and in raising cattle and other animals. With more children a married couple could cultivate more acreage and thereby become more profitable. Children were therefore important economic assets. Parents wanted their sons to marry robust, industrious women who could substantially contribute to the work that needed to be done.[1]

John F. Cuber et al. have noted that preindustrial American society developed a *monolithic code* of cultural beliefs that were accepted by most people during this era.[2] A monolithic code permits only one accepta-

ble pattern of behavior. Components of this code were:

1. Adults were expected to be married. Women were expected to marry in their teens or early 20s. Those who delayed marriage or did not marry were referred to as "old maids" and "spinsters."

2. Marriage was considered permanent—for life. Divorce was rare and highly disapproved.

3. An individual was expected to place the welfare of the family unit ahead of his or her individual preferences. For example, an individual's preferences about who she or he wanted to marry was considered less important than the parents' notions about what was best for the family as a unit.

4. Sexual relations were to be restricted to marriage. There was a double standard: Women who had premarital or extramarital affairs were more harshly criticized and stigmatized than men.

5. Married couples were expected to have children. Children were not only considered an economic asset but were also viewed as a religious obligation, based on the biblical ethic, "Be fruitful and multiply."

6. Parents were expected to take care of their children, whatever the cost. Children were expected to be obedient to their parents and to honor them. When parents became partially disabled (for example, grew old), children were expected to care for them.

7. The father was the head of the family and made the important decisions. Women and children were expected to be subordinate to him. There were numerous advantages to being male. Women left their family on marriage and moved into their husband's home. (Male children were more highly valued than female children, partly because male children would remain home after marrying.) The woman's place was in the home, and she was expected to do the cooking, washing, cleaning, and a variety of other domestic tasks. Thus, American preindustrial society was clearly patriarchal.

These beliefs were so strongly held by most people that they were considered the morally decent way to live. To violate them was viewed as going against nature and against God's will. (As we shall see, remnants of this code still remain in American society.)

The Family in Industrial Society

The Industrial Revolution, which began roughly 200 years ago, has greatly changed family life. Factories and large-scale business organizations have replaced the small family farm as centers of economic production. Most people now live in urban and semiurban areas. Urbanization has accompanied industrialization. Products produced on small family farms or in small family shops are no longer competitive with products that are mass produced on assembly lines or produced using complex equipment and technology.

With the advent of the Industrial Revolution the family gradually began losing its economic-productive function, and with the loss of this function, the family began making other changes. Fewer people were needed in families to fill essential economic roles. There was a sharp decline in the economic need for extended families. In fact, smaller-sized families became more functional for industrialized societies because small families could more readily relocate to fill the employment openings that arose.

Gradually, there was a shift toward individualism. A key component of individualism is the belief that the desires of the individual should take precedence over those of the family. As part of individualism and the loss of the economic-productive function, it became increasingly recognized that the choice of a mate should be based more on personal preference.

Also, with the loss of the economic-productive function, it became recognized that children had become economic liabilities; that is, they did nothing to increase family income but still had to be clothed, fed, and sheltered. As a response, parents began having a smaller number of children.

There have been numerous other changes. No longer is the wisdom of the elderly as highly valued, as children are now trained and educated in educational settings. In a rapidly changing industrial society the job skills of older workers often become obsolete. As a result, the elderly are no longer held in the esteem they once were.

Gradually, women won the right to vote, and in the past three decades the feminist movement has been calling into question the "double standards" of sexual morality. Women are also seeking equalitarian relationships with men. An increasing number of women are entering the labor force and seeking employment in settings (such as police departments) that were once considered only appropriate for men. Sexuality is more openly discussed today, and there has been an increase in the rate of sexual relations outside of marriage.[3] However, recent concern about acquiring AIDS has led many adults to reduce the number of sexual partners they have. (The chances of acquiring AIDS increase with the number of sexual partners that one has.)

Still, remnants of the monolithic code remain. Some people think something is "mentally wrong" if a married couple decides not to have children. Those who obtain a divorce are still stigmatized by some. Those who decide never to marry are looked on as "strange" by some. Becoming pregnant while single is still stigmatized.

In 1934 sociologist William Ogburn noted that the American family has undergone a number of changes in family functions as a result of industrialization and technological advances.[4]

1. The economic-productive function has been lost. In most families the financial resources are now acquired outside of the home.

2. The protective function has been lost. The protective function is now being met by such agencies as police departments, hospitals, insurance companies, and nursing homes.

3. The educational function has been sharply reduced. Schools, day-care centers, and Head Start programs have taken on much of this function.

4. The family is less likely to be the center for religious activity.

5. The recreational function has largely been reduced. Each family member is now more apt to join recreational groups outside of the home, which has reduced family-centered recreation.

Over the last century many of the functions of the American family have been sharply reduced. Today's family, however, still plays a key role both in socializing new members and in providing the affection, recognition, and emotional support we all need.

6. The status recognition function has been sharply reduced. Individuals now receive recognition through their own achievements in organizations outside of the family, such as at school, at place of employment, and in social and religious groups.

7. The family has retained its affectional function. Family members receive social and emotional gratification from the family and also have many of their companionship needs met by the family.

Most authorities agree with Ogburn's assessment that many of the functions of the American family have been lost or sharply reduced. It has been noted, however, that the modern family retains certain functions that Ogburn overlooked. Families in modern industrial societies perform the following five essential functions that help maintain the continuity and stability of society.[5]

1. REPLACEMENT OF THE POPULATION   Every society has to have some system for replacing its members. Practically all societies consider the family as the unit in which children are to be produced. Societies have defined the rights and responsibilities of the reproduc-tive partners within the family unit. These rights and responsibilities help maintain the stability of society, although they are defined differently from one society to another.

2. CARE OF THE YOUNG   Children require care and protection until at least the age of puberty. The family is a primary institution for the rearing of children. Modern societies have generally developed supportive institutions to help in caring for the young—for example, medical services, day-care centers, parent training programs, and residential treatment centers.

3. SOCIALIZATION OF NEW MEMBERS   To become productive members of society, children have to be socialized into the culture. Children are expected to acquire a language, to learn social values and mores, and to dress and behave within the norms of society. The family plays a major role in this socialization process. In modern societies there are a number of other groups and resources that are involved in this process. Schools, the mass media, peer groups, the police, movies, books, and other written material are important

influences in the socialization process. (Sometimes these different influences clash by advocating opposing values and attitudes.)

4. REGULATION OF SEXUAL BEHAVIOR Failure to regulate sexual behavior would result in clashes between individuals due to jealousy and exploitation. Unregulated sexual behavior would probably result in large numbers of births outside of marriage—children for whom no fathers could be held responsible. Every society has rules that regulate sexual behavior within family units. Most societies, for example, have incest taboos, and most disapprove of extramarital sex.

5. SOURCE OF AFFECTION Spitz has demonstrated that humans need affection, emotional support, and positive recognition from others (including approval, smiles, encouragement, and reinforcement for accomplishments).[6] Without such affection and recognition, a person's emotional, intellectual, physical, and social growth would be stunted. The family is an important source for obtaining affection and recognition, as family members generally regard each other as among the most important people in their lives and gain emotional and social satisfaction from their relationships with one another. (As noted above, Ogburn identified this function as the primary one remaining in modern families.)

This brief sketch of American family history shows that a number of changes have occurred. Yet, the family retains several important functions. We will now turn to examining problem areas for today's American family: divorce, empty shell marriages, family violence, and births outside of marriage.

PROBLEMS IN THE FAMILY

Divorce

Our society places a higher value on romantic love than most other societies. In societies where marriages are arranged by parents, being in love generally has no role in mate selection. In our society, however, romantic love is a key factor in forming a marriage.

American children are socialized from an early age to believe in the glories of romantic love. "Love conquers all," it is asserted. Magazines, films, TV programs, and books continually portray "happy ending" romantic adventures. All of these breathtaking romantic stories suggest that every normal person falls in love with that one special person, gets married, and lives happily ever after. This "happily ever after" ideal rarely happens.

Now, nearly one out of two marriages ends in divorce.[7] This high rate has gradually been increasing. Before World War I divorce seldom occurred.

Divorce usually leads to a number of difficulties for those involved. First, those who are divorcing face a number of emotional concerns, such as a feeling that they have failed, concern over whether they are able to give and receive love, a sense of loneliness, concern over the stigma attached to getting a divorce, concern about the reactions of friends and relatives, concern over whether they are doing the right thing by parting, and concern over whether they will be able to make it on their own. Many people who part or are considering parting feel trapped because they believe they can neither live with their spouse nor live apart from their spouse. Dividing up the personal property is another area that frequently leads to bitter differences of opinions. If there are children, there are concerns about how the divorce will affect them.

There are also other issues that need to be decided. Who will get custody of the children? (Joint custody is now an alternative—with joint custody, each parent has the children for part of the time.) If one parent is awarded custody, controversies are apt to arise over visiting rights and over how much (if any) child support should be paid. Each spouse often faces the difficulties of finding a new place to live, making new friends, doing things alone in our couple-oriented society, trying to make it on one's own financially, and thinking about the hassles connected with dating.

Studies show that going through a divorce is very difficult. People are less likely to perform their jobs well and are more likely to be fired during this time period.[8] Divorced people have a shorter life expectancy.[9] Suicide rates are higher for divorced men.[10]

Divorce per se is no longer automatically assumed to be a social problem, although some of its consequences still are. On the other hand, there is increasing recognition that in some marriages where there is considerable tension, bitterness, and dissatisfaction, divorce is sometimes a solution; it may be a concrete step that some people take to end the unhappiness and to begin leading more productive and gratifying lives. It is also increasingly being recognized that a divorce may be better for the children because they may no longer be subjected to the tension and unhappiness of a marriage that has gone sour.

Mary Jo Bane has noted that the rising divorce rate may not be as serious a threat to the institutions of marriage and family as some people believe.

It is distressing in and of itself . . . only if staying together at all costs is considered an indicator of healthy marriages or healthy societies . . . Some things are fairly clear. The majority of marriages do not end in divorce. The vast majority of divorced people remarry. Only a tiny proportion of people marry more than twice. We are thus a long way from a society in which marriage is rejected or replaced by a series of short-term liaisons. . . . Society may be changing its attitudes toward the permanence of marriage and its notions of the roles of husbands and wives. It may simply be recognizing that there is no particular benefit to requiring permanence in unhappy marriages.[11]

The rising divorce rate does not necessarily mean that more marriages are failing. It may simply mean that in an unhappy marriage more people are dissolving the marriage than continuing to live in it.

REASONS FOR MARITAL UNHAPPINESS   There are many sources of marital breakdown. Some of the major reasons will briefly be mentioned: alcoholism, economic strife caused by unemployment or other financial problems, incompatibility of interests, infidelity, jealousy, verbal or physical abuse of spouse, and interference in the marriage by relatives and friends.

As noted earlier many people marry because they believe they are romantically in love. If this romantic love does not grow into rational love, the marriage is apt to fail. Unfortunately, young people are socialized in our society to believe that marriage will bring them continual romance; resolve all their problems; be sexually exciting, thrilling, full of adventure and excitement; and always be as wonderful as the good moments of the courtship. (Most young people only need to look at their parents' marriage to realize such romantic ideals are seldom attained.) Unfortunately, living with someone in a marriage involves carrying out the garbage, washing dishes and clothes, being weary from work, putting up with one's partner's distasteful habits (for example, poor hygiene or belching), changing diapers, and dealing with conflicts over such things as how to spend a vacation and differences in sexual interests. *To make a marriage work requires that each spouse puts considerable effort into that marriage.*

Another factor that is contributing to an increasing divorce rate is the unwillingness of some men to accept the changing status of women. Many men still prefer a traditional marriage in which the husband is dominant and the wife plays a supportive (subordinate role) as childrearer, housekeeper, and the husband's and family's emotional support. Many women are no longer accepting such a status and are demanding equalitarian marriages in which making major decisions, doing the domestic tasks, raising the children, and bringing home paychecks are shared responsibilities.

Over half of today's adult women are now in the labor force.[12] This increase in the percentage of women in the labor force means women are no longer as heavily reliant financially on their husbands. Women who are able to support themselves financially are more likely to seek a divorce if their marriages go sour.

Another factor contributing to the increasing divorce rate is the growth of individualism. Individualism involves the belief that people should seek to actualize themselves, to be happy, to develop their interests and capacities to the fullest, and to seek to fulfill their own needs and desires. With individualism the interests of the individual take precedence over the interests of the family. People in our society have increasingly come to accept individualism as a way to go through life. In contrast, people in more traditional societies and in extended families are socialized to put the interests of the group first, with their own individual interests being viewed as less important. In extended families

BOX 5.1

Romantic Love versus Rational Love

A chieving a gratifying, long-lasting love relationship is one of our paramount goals. The experience of feeling "in love" is exciting, adds meaning to living, and psychologically gives us a good feeling about ourselves. Unfortunately, few people are able to maintain a long-term love relationship. Instead, many people encounter problems with love relationships, including falling in love with someone who does not love them, falling out of love with someone after an initial stage of infatuation, being highly possessive of someone they love, and having substantial conflicts with the loved one because of differing sets of expectations about the relationship. Failures in love relationships are more often the rule than the exception.

The emotion of love, in particular, is often viewed (erroneously) as being a feeling over which we have no control. A number of common expressions (erroneously) connote or imply that love is a feeling beyond our control, such as, "I *fell* in love," "It was love at first sight," "I just couldn't help it," and "He swept me off my feet." It is more useful to think of the emotion of love as being primarily based on our self-talk (that is, what we tell ourselves) about a person we meet. Romantic love can be diagramed as follows.

Event

Meeting or becoming acquainted with a person who has
some of the overt characteristics you adore in a lover.

Self-talk

"This person is attractive, personable;
has *all* of the qualities I admire in a lover/mate."

Emotion

Intense infatuation, being romantically in love;
a feeling of being in ecstasy.

Romantic love is often based on self-talk that stems from intense, unsatisfied desires and frustrations rather than on reason or rational thinking. Unsatisfied desires and frustrations include extreme sexual frustration, intense loneliness, parental and personal problems, and extensive desires for security and protection.

A primary characteristic of romantic love is to idealize the person with whom we are infatuated as being a "perfect lover"; that is, we notice this person has some overt characteristics we desire in a lover and then conclude that this person has *all* the desired characteristics.

A second characteristic is that romantic love thrives on a certain amount of distance. The more forbidden the love, the stronger it becomes. The more social mores are threatened, the stronger the feeling. (For example, couples who live together and then later marry often report that living together was more exciting and romantic.) The more the effort necessary to be with each other (for example, traveling large distances), the more intense the romance. The greater the frustration (for example, loneliness or sexual needs), the more intense the romance.

The irony of romantic love is that if an ongoing relationship is achieved, the romance usually withers. Through sustained contact, the person in love gradually comes to realize what the idealized loved one is really like—simply another human being with certain strengths and limitations. When this occurs, the romantic love relationship either turns into a rational love relationship or is found to have significant conflicts and dissatisfactions and then is terminated. For people with intense unmet needs, the latter occurs more frequently.

Romantic love thus tends to be of temporary duration and based on make-believe. A person experiencing romantic love never loves the real person—only an idealized imaginary person.

Rational love, in contrast, can be diagramed in the following way.

Event

While being aware of and comfortable with your own needs, goals,
identity, and desires, you become well acquainted with someone who fulfills,
to a fair extent, the characteristics you desire in a lover or spouse.

↓

Self-talk

"This person has many of the qualities and attributes
I seek in a lover or spouse. I admire this person's strengths,
and I am aware and accepting of his or her shortcomings."

↓

Emotion

Rational love.

The following are ingredients of a rational love relationship: (*a*) You are clear and comfortable about your desires, identity, and goals in life; (*b*) you know the other person well; (*c*) you have accurately and objectively assessed the loved one's strengths and shortcomings and are generally accepting of the shortcomings; (*d*) your self-talk about this person is consistent with your short- and long-term goals; (*e*) your self-talk is realistic and rational so that your feelings are not based on fantasy, excessive need, or pity; (*f*) you and this person are able to communicate openly and honestly so that problems can be dealt with when they arise and so that the relationship can continue to grow and develop; (*g*) rational love also involves giving and receiving; it involves being kind, showing affection, knowing and doing what pleases the other person, communicating openly and warmly, and so on.

Continued

BOX 5.1 *Continued*

Because love is based on self-talk that causes feelings, it is we who create love. *Theoretically*, it is possible to love anyone by making changes in our self-talk. On the other hand, if we are in love with someone, we can gauge the quality of the relationship by analyzing our self-talk to determine the nature of our attraction and to determine the extent to which our self-talk is rational and in our best interests.

Source: Adapted from the book *Talk to Yourself* by Charles Zastrow. © 1979 by Prentice-Hall, Inc. Published by Prentice-Hall, Inc., Englewood Cliffs, NJ 07632, pp. 44–51.

people view themselves as members of a group first and as individuals second. With America's growing belief in individualism, people who conclude they are unhappily married are much more apt to dissolve the marriage and seek a new life.

Another reason for the rise in the divorce rate is the growing acceptance of divorce in our society. With less of a stigma attached to divorce, more people who are unhappily married are now ending their marriages.

An additional factor in the increasing divorce rate is that modern families no longer have as many functions as did traditional families. Education, food, production, entertainment, and other functions once centered in the family are now largely provided by outside agencies. Kenneth Keniston notes:

In earlier times, the collapse of a marriage was far more likely to deprive both spouses of a great deal more than the pleasure of each other's company. Since family members performed so many functions for one another, divorce in the past meant a farmer without a wife to churn the cream into butter or care for him when he was sick, and a mother without a husband to plow the fields and bring her the food to feed their children. Today, when emotional satisfaction is the bond that holds marriages together, the waning of love or the emergence of real incompatibilities and conflicts between husband and wife leave fewer reasons for a marriage to continue. Schools and doctors and counselors and social workers provide their supports whether the family is intact or not. One loses less by divorce today than in earlier times, because marriage provides fewer kinds of sustenance and satisfaction.[13]

Box 5.2 presents facts about divorce today. These facts identify variables that predict whether a marriage will or will not last.

DIVORCE LAWS   In the past, society attempted to make the breakup of marriages almost impossible. One way it did this was by having laws that made a divorce difficult to obtain. Once one of the spouses petitioned the court for a divorce, there were long waiting periods before that divorce could be obtained. Divorce courts also followed the "adversary" judicial procedures in which the spouse seeking the divorce had to document that the other spouse was guilty of some offense, such as adultery, desertion, or cruel and inhuman treatment. In many cases the actual reasons for the divorce (such as no longer finding the relationship satisfying) bore little relationship to the grounds on which the court allowed that divorce. Often the marital partners contrived a story that fit the legal reasons for granting the divorce.

In most divorces, both partners contribute to the marital breakdown. Yet traditional divorce laws erroneously assume that one partner is the guilty party and the other the innocent party. Traditional divorce laws often intensify the trauma that both partners are

BOX 5.2

Facts about Divorce

Age of spouses: Divorce is most likely to occur when the partners are in their 20s.

Length of engagement: Divorce rates are higher for those having a brief engagement.

Age at marriage: People who marry at a very young age (particularly teenagers) are more apt to divorce.

Length of marriage: Most divorces occur within two years after marriage. There is also an increase in divorce shortly after the children are grown. This may be partly because some couples wait until the children are ready to leave the nest before dissolving an unhappy marriage.

Social class: Divorce occurs more frequently at the lower socioeconomic levels.

Education: Divorce rates are higher for those with fewer years of schooling. Interestingly, divorce occurs more frequently when the wife's educational level is higher than the husband's.

Residence: Divorce rates are higher in urban areas as compared to rural areas.

Second marriages: The more often individuals marry, the more likely they are to get divorced again.

Religion: The more religious individuals are, the less apt they are to become divorced. Divorce rates are higher for Protestants than for Catholics or Jews. Divorce rates are also higher for interfaith marriages than for intrafaith marriages.

Sources: William J. Goode, "Family Disorganization," in *Contemporary Social Problems*, eds. Robert K. Merton and Robert Nisbet 4th ed. (New York: Harcourt Brace Jovanovich, 1976) pp. 511–556; Goode, *After Divorce* (New York: Free Press, 1956); Paul C. Glick, *American Families* (New York: John Wiley & Sons, 1957); J. Richard Udrey, *The Social Context of Marriage*, 2d ed. (Philadelphia: J. B. Lippincott, 1971); Joseph Julian and William Kornblum, *Social Problems*, 5th ed. (Englewood Cliffs, NJ: Prentice-Hall, 1986), pp. 338–341.

undergoing. The traditional divorce process pits both partners against each other—and the process is highly expensive.

Because of these difficulties, most states have now passed "no fault" divorce laws, which allow the couple to obtain a divorce fairly rapidly by stating to the court that they both agree their marriage has irreparably broken down. (The adversary process is still available for any spouse who chooses to use it.)

Issues that are still often contested between the two partners in divorce proceedings involve the division of property, alimony (a financial allowance paid to one spouse by the other for support after the divorce), child-support payments, and custody of the children. In the past the court invariably awarded to the woman the custody of the children, child-support payments, and alimony (particularly if she was not employed). A large percentage of the men failed to make some, or all, of their child-support and alimony payments, which left their former wives in dire financial straits.

Changes in sex roles and the increasing employment of women are leading to changes in divorce settlements. Most states have enacted legislation that allows courts to require that the woman make alimony payments to her former husband, although few courts have as yet issued such orders. Custody of the children is still generally given to the mother. Yet, this assignment is no longer automatic. An increasing number of fathers are requesting custody of their children and are making it known that they resent the sexist bias of many courts, which assumes that a mother is automatically better qualified to raise children.

A critical point about divorce is that when it occurs, many of the costs of a divorced family's shattered lives are paid by society. In families of average income or less, the burden of divorce-related poverty falls on society as a whole. Thirty-four percent of all previously married female heads of household are on welfare, whereas less than 2 percent of married women from similar backgrounds are on welfare.[14] Additional expenses for society that often occur when lower-income people divorce include subsidized housing, public sector make-work jobs, and payments to lawyers who are involved in collecting support for women and children.

The recent willingness of courts to consider giving custody to the father is having a hidden cost to society. Fathers can and do threaten a protracted custody battle. As a result, mothers who wish to get custody of their children without a fight are routinely forced to "barter" custody in exchange for reduced child-support payments. Because such payments are so low, these women and their children then qualify for being welfare recipients. Richard Neely, a state Supreme Court justice notes:

Most of us begin with a political conviction that women ought *to be equal to men economically, and then leap to a conclusion that they* are. *It then logically follows that women can support children as well as men and that whoever wants the children can pay for them.*

The fact is that women are much poorer than men, and this pattern appears highly resistant to change. The mean wage for women who work full

time is 59 percent of the mean wage for men. Once a man and a woman are married, if both are working full time, the woman's wage on average amounts to 34.7 percent of the family's earnings.[15]

Custody battles between fathers and mothers are currently becoming more common in divorce cases. Typical custody battles may take as long as two years. It is common for parents in such custody battles to spend thousands of dollars on attorneys, expert witnesses, and court costs. During this process the parents are apt to use the children as "pawns" against each other. They bribe the children with large allowances, relax discipline, and indulge outrageous whims of their children. At the same time they are apt to seek to turn their children against the other parent by "bad mouthing" him or her. Custody battles are not only costly but also are emotionally damaging to all family members.

In many states, now, children over age 14 are allowed to select the parent with whom they wish to live if that parent is "fit." To avoid custody battles and the process in which women barter reduced child-support payments for custody, Ralph Neely recommends that for children under age 14, custody be awarded to the primary caretaker parent, who is defined as:

. . . the parent who: (1) prepares the food; (2) changes the diapers, dresses and bathes the child; (3) takes the child to school, church, and other activities; (4) makes appointments with a doctor and generally watches over the child's health; and (5) interacts with the child's friends, the school authorities, and other adults engaged in activities that involve the child. It is not surprising that the "primary caretaker" is usually the mother, but that need not be the case.[16]

In 90 percent of divorce cases, the mothers are awarded custody of the children.[17] On divorce, the mother's standard of living sharply declines, whereas the father's standard of living generally increases because he has fewer financial responsibilities.[18] Women are awarded alimony in only 15 percent of divorce cases.[19] When there are children, the fathers are usually required to pay child support. But the amounts awarded are generally insufficient to meet the financial needs of the children. In addition, 50 percent of divorced fathers fail to pay the full amount of child-support payments, and 24 percent do not make any court-ordered child-support payments.[20] As a result, the income for the divorced mother and her children often plunges below the poverty level. In many cases taxpayers wind up supporting the mother and her children through the welfare system.[21]

Empty Shell Marriages

In empty shell marriages the spouses feel no strong attachments to each other. Outside pressures keep the marriage together, rather than feelings of warmth and attraction between the members. Such outside pressures include business reasons (for example, an elected official wanting to convey a stable family image); investment reasons (for example, husband and wife may have a luxurious home and other property that they do not want to lose by parting); and outward appearances (for example, a couple living in a small community may remain together to avoid the reactions of relatives and friends to a divorce). In addition, a couple may believe that ending the marriage would harm the children or that getting a divorce would be morally wrong.

John F. Cuber and Peggy B. Harroff have identified three types of empty shell marriages.[22] In a *devitalized relationship* husband and wife lack excitement or any real interest in each other or their marriage. Boredom and apathy characterize this marriage. Serious arguments are rare.

In a *conflict habituated relationship* husband and wife frequently quarrel in private. They may also quarrel in public or put up a facade of being compatible. The relationship is characterized by considerable conflict, tension, and bitterness.

In a *passive-congenial relationship* both partners are not happy but are content with their lives and generally feel adequate. The partners may have some interests in common, but these interests are generally insignificant. The spouses contribute little to each other's real satisfactions. This type of relationship generally has little overt conflict.

The number of empty shell marriages is unknown: It may be as high (or even higher) than the number of happy marriages. The atmosphere in empty shell marriages is without much fun or laughter. Members do not share and discuss their problems or experiences with each other. Communication is kept to a minimum. There is seldom any spontaneous expression of affection or sharing of a personal experience. Children in such families are usually starved for love and reluctant to have friends over because they are embarrassed about having their friends see their parents interacting.

The couples in these marriages engage in few activities together and display no pleasure in being in one another's company. Sexual relations between the partners, as might be expected, are rare and generally unsatisfying. Visitors will note that the partners (and often the children) appear insensitive, cold, and callous to each other. Yet closer observation will reveal that the members are highly aware of each other's weaknesses and sensitive areas, as they manage to mention these areas frequently in order to hurt one another.

William J. Goode compares empty shell marriages to marriages that end in divorce.

Most families that divorce pass through a state— sometimes after the divorce—in which husband and wife no longer feel bound to each other, cease to cooperate or share with each other, and look on one another as almost a stranger. The "empty shell" family is in such a state. Its members no longer feel any strong commitment to many of the mutual role obligations, but for various reasons the husband and wife do not separate or divorce.[23]

The number of empty shell marriages ending in divorce is unknown. It is likely that a fair number eventually do. Both spouses have to put considerable effort into making a marriage work in order to prevent an empty shell marriage from gradually developing.

MARRIAGE COUNSELING   The primary social service for people who are considering a divorce or who have an empty shell marriage is marriage counseling. (Those who do obtain a divorce may also need counseling to work out adjustment problems—such as adjusting to single life. Generally such counseling is one-on-one but at times may include the ex-spouse and the children, depending on the nature of the problem.)

Marriage counseling is provided by a variety of professionals including social workers, psychologists, guidance counselors, psychiatrists, and members of the clergy. Marriage counseling is provided (to a greater or lesser extent) by most direct social service agencies.

Marriage counselors generally use a problem-solving approach in which (*a*) problems are first identified, (*b*) alternative solutions are generated, (*c*) the merits and shortcomings of the alternatives are examined, (*d*) the clients select one or more alternatives to implement, and (*e*) the extent to which the problems are being resolved by the alternatives is later assessed. Because the spouses "own" their problems they are the primary problem solvers.

A wide range of problems may be encountered by married couples. A partial list of such problems includes sexual problems, financial problems, communication problems, problems with relatives, interest conflicts, infidelity, conflicts on how to discipline and raise children, and drug abuse problems. Marriage counselors seek to have spouses precisely identify their problems and then use the problem-solving format to seek to resolve the issues. In some cases couples may rationally decide that a divorce is in their best interest.

In marriage counseling there is considerable effort by the counselor to see both spouses together during sessions. Practically all marital conflicts involve both partners and therefore are best resolved when both partners work together on resolving the conflicts. (If the spouses are seen separately, each spouse is apt to become suspicious of what the other is telling the counselor.) By seeing both together the counselor can facilitate communication between the partners and have the partners work together on resolving their concerns. (When spouses are seen individually, they are also more apt to compose exaggerated stories of the extent to which their mate is contributing to the disharmony.) Seeing both partners together allows each partner the opportunity to refute what the other is saying. Only in rare cases is it desirable to hold an individual session with a spouse. For example, if one of the partners wants to work on unwanted emotions concerning a past incestuous relationship, it may be desirable to meet individually with that spouse. (When an individual session is held, the other spouse should

be informed of why the session is being held and of what will be discussed.)

If some of the areas of conflict involve other family members (such as the children), it may be desirable to include these other family members in some of the sessions. For example, if a father is irritated that his 14-year-old daughter is often disrespectful to him, the daughter may be invited to the next session to work on this subproblem.

Although marriage and divorce counseling are the primary social services that are available for resolving marital conflicts, there are a variety of other related services. A few of these will be noted.

Premarital counseling services are designed for those considering getting married. Such services help such clients assess whether marriage is in their best interest, and also help them to prepare for the realities of marriage. Conflicts that people are having while dating are also worked on, and other topics, such as birth control, are explored.

The self-help organization *Parents without Partners (PWP)* serves divorced people, unwed mothers or fathers, and stepparents. It is partially a social organization, but it is also an organization to help members with the adjustment problems of raising a family alone.

A recent development in social services is *divorce mediation*, which helps spouses who have decided to obtain a divorce to resolve (as amicably as possible) such issues as dividing the personal property, resolving custody and child-support issues, and working out possible alimony arrangements.

Some agencies are now offering *relationship workshops* and *encounter couple groups*, which are designed to help those who are dating or who are married to improve their relationships through sharing concerns and improving communication patterns.

Violence in Families

We tend to view the family as a social institution in which love and gentleness abound. Sadly, the opposite is often true, with violence being pervasive in American families.

 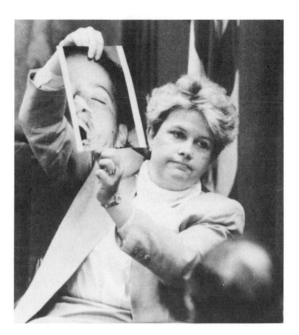

A recent case of child abuse that received national attention involved the beating death of young Lisa Steinberg, whose adoptive parents, Joel Steinberg and Hedda Nussbaum (left), were charged with her murder. Steinberg was convicted of first-degree manslaughter in January 1989. Nussbaum, Steinberg's lover, was originally also implicated in Lisa's death. Charges against Nussbaum were dropped, however, on the grounds that Steinberg had so severely beaten her that she was physically unable to either harm—or save—their daughter (whose battered face is shown in a hospital photo, right). Steinberg, a disbarred lawyer, has since been sentenced to a jail term of from 8⅓ to 25 years. This disturbing case has served to create greater public consciousness of the potential for family violence at all levels of American society.

Child abuse, spouse abuse, and other physical violence occur in more than half of all U.S. households.[24] An estimated 50 million people fall victim annually to physical harm at the hands of another family member.[25] Studies show that in 20 percent of child abuse cases, a spouse is also abused.[26]

Violence in families is not limited to child abuse and spouse abuse. Statistics from a study funded by the National Institute of Mental Health found that the number of children who assault their parents is greater than the number of children who are abused by their parents.[27] Violence between children is also common: A 1979 study found that 138,000 children ages 3 to 17

used a weapon on a brother or sister during a one-year period.[28]

Parent abuse is a new term that is increasingly receiving attention. This term primarily refers to elderly parents who are abused by their children with whom they live with or on whom depend. The public is virtually unaware of the battered aged, but it is estimated that there may be a million or more who are abused by their adult children.[29] Lewis and Joanne Koch provide one case example.

In Chicago, a 19-year-old woman confessed to torturing her 81-year-old father and chaining him to a toilet for seven days. She also hit him with a hammer when he was asleep: "I worked him over real good with it. Then after I made him weak enough, I chained his legs together. After that I left him and rested. I watched TV for a while."[30]

A Cleveland study found the following four types of abuse to be the most prevalent:

- *Physical abuse, which included direct beating and the withholding of personal care, food, medicine, and necessary supervision.*

- *Psychological abuse—verbal assaults and threats provoking fear.*

- *Material abuse or theft of money or personal property.*

- *Violation of rights—forcing a parent out of his or her own dwelling usually into a nursing home.*

    Three fourths of the cases in the Cleveland study involved physical abuse; almost half included psychological abuse; and in almost every case, there was a violation of rights.[31]

The victims of family violence—battered children, battered parents, and battered wives—have common disadvantages. They are generally smaller in size, have less physical strength, and usually feel helpless in relation to the aggressors. Often they feel helpless because they depend on their aggressors for physical, financial, and emotional support.

Before the 1960s little attention was given to violence in families, partly because the family was viewed as a sacred institution and a private domain: What goes on within families was viewed as a personal concern and the responsibility of family members alone—not outsiders. Over the past three decades there has been an increasing awareness that violence in families is a major social problem.

Family fights constitute the largest single category of police calls, and more police fatalities result from trying to handle these situations than from any other.[32] Suzanne Steinmetz and Murray Straus have noted: "It would be hard to find a group or an institution in American society in which violence is more of an everyday occurrence than it is within the family."[33] Vio-

lence not only causes physical harm in families; each incident also weakens the loyalty, attraction, and trust between members that are basic to positive family functioning.

One explanation of why family violence occurs is based on the theory that frustration often provokes an aggressive response. A husband or wife who is frustrated at work may come home and take out that frustration on the spouse or the children. A young child frustrated by the action of his or her sibling may take a poke at the sibling. Steinmetz and Straus observe: "In a society such as ours, in which aggression is defined as a normal response to frustration, we can expect that the more frustrating the familial and occupational roles, the greater the amount of violence."[34]

In another explanation John O'Brien has noted that family members often use physical force to gain an advantage.[35] A parent spanks a child for disciplinary reasons. A sister may shove her brother out of the way to attempt to obtain something they both are seeking. O'Brien suggests that family members are apt to resort to physical force when other resources are nonexistent, diminished, or exhausted. Thus, an alcoholic husband who feels he has lost the respect of his family may resort to physical abuse as a last-ditch effort to assert his authority.

SPOUSE ABUSE   Spouse abuse, particularly wife beating, has become an issue of national concern only relatively recently. Before this recognition, spouse abuse was, unfortunately, tolerated.

It is not just wives who are abused. Husbands are slapped or shoved with about the same frequency as are wives.[36] The greatest physical damage, however, is usually sustained by women. Studies show that men cause more serious injuries, largely because they are physically stronger.[37] Nearly 11 percent of all murder victims are killed by their spouses.[38] It should be noted that women also tend to endure cruelty and abuse much longer than men, at times because they feel trapped due to unemployment and financial insecurity. Spouse abuse is sometimes precipitated by the victim; that is, the recipient of the abuse may be the first to use verbal or physical violence in the incident.[39] However, the dominant theme in American spouse abuse is the systematic use of violence and the threat of violence by some men to "keep their wives in line." That is to say, there is a traditional belief held by some segments of our society that husbands have a right to control what their wives do and to force them to be submissive.

Incidents of physical abuse between spouses are not widely isolated but tend to reoccur frequently in the marriage. Moreover, Murray Straus et al. have noted spouse abuse occurs as often among the well educated as among those less educated.[40]

In 1979 Straus and his associates conducted a survey for the National Commission on the Causes and Prevention of Violence. Interviews were held with over 2,000 couples who represented a cross section of American families.[41] The study concluded that each year 7.5 million couples in this country have a violent episode in which one spouse seeks to hurt the other physically. Wives use knives and other weapons more often than husbands and are as likely to murder their spouses as husbands are. Disturbingly, the study found that one man in four, and one woman in six, approved of a husband slapping his wife under certain conditions. Most wives who are severely beaten by their husbands do not seek to end the marriage. Wives are more likely to remain in the home if (*a*) the violence is infrequent, (*b*) they were abused by their parents when they were children, or (*c*) they believe they are financially dependent on their husbands.

Many authorities believe spouse abuse is related to a norm of tolerating violence in American families. Straus notes:

There seems to be an implicit, taken-for-granted cultural norm which makes it legitimate for family members to hit each other. In respect to husbands and wives, in effect, this means that the marriage license is also a hitting license.[42]

A number of studies have found that a sizable number of both men and women believe it is appropriate for a husband to hit his wife physically "every now and then."[43]

A surprising number of battered women do not permanently leave their husbands. There appear to be a variety of reasons for this. Many are socialized to play a subordinate role to their husbands. And their hus-

bands use violence and psychological abuse to make them feel too inadequate to live on their own. Some women believe it is their moral duty to stick it out to the end—that marriage is forever, for better or for worse. Many hope (in spite of the continuing violence) that their husbands will change. A fair number do not view leaving as a viable alternative because they feel financially dependent on their husbands. Many have young children and do not believe they have the resources to raise children on their own. Some believe the occasional beatings are better than the loneliness and insecurity connected with leaving. Some dread the stigma associated with separation or divorce. These women are captives in their own homes.

Fortunately, new services in recent years have been developed for battered women. Shelter homes for battered women have been established in many communities. These shelters give abused women an opportunity to flee from the abusive situation, with shelter being provided for the women and their children. Such women also generally receive counseling, assistance in finding a job, and legal help. In some areas programs are also being established for the husbands. These programs include group therapy for batterers, marriage counseling for both spouses, and twenty-four-hour "hot lines" that encourage potential spouse abusers to call when they are angry. (Unfortunately, many batterers refuse to participate in such programs.) Many communities also have public information programs (for example, short television announcements) to inform battered women that they have a legal right not to be abused and that there are resources (for example, shelter homes and counseling services) to stop the abuse. As services for battered wives become more widely available, we may expect an increasing number of these women to flee from their homes and to refuse to return until they have some guarantee of their safety.

CHILD ABUSE AND NEGLECT   Although definitions of child abuse and neglect vary somewhat from state to state, Alfred Kadushin and Judith Martin summarize the kinds of situations as including:

Physical abuse.

Malnourishment; poor clothing; lack of proper

shelter, sleeping arrangements, attendance, or supervision. (Includes "failure to thrive" syndrome, which describes infants who fail to grow and develop at a normal rate.)

Denial of essential medical care.

Failure to attend school regularly.

Exploitation, overwork.

Exposure to unwholesome or demoralizing circumstances.

Sexual abuse.

Somewhat less frequently, the definitions include emotional abuse and neglect involving denial of the normal experiences that permit a child to feel loved, wanted, secure, and worthy.[44]

Physical Abuse   In the past thirty years, there has been considerable national concern about the "battered-child syndrome." The Children's Division of the American Humane Society conducted a nationwide survey of newspaper reports on child abuse and concluded:

The forms or types of abuse inflicted on these children is a negative testimony to the ingenuity and inventiveness of man. By far the greater number of injuries resulted from beatings with various kinds of implements and instruments. The hairbrush was a common implement used to beat children. However, the same purpose was accomplished with deadlier impact by the use of bare fists, straps, electric cords, TV aerials, ropes, rubber hose, fan belts, sticks, wooden shoes, pool cues, bottles, broom handles, baseball bats, chair legs, and, in one case, a sculling oar. Less imaginative, but equally effective, was plain kicking with street shoes or with heavy work shoes.

Children had their extremities—hands, arms, and feet—burned in open flames as from gas burners or cigarette lighters. Others bore burn wounds inflicted on their bodies with lighted cigarettes, electric irons, or hot pokers. Still others are scalded by hot liquids thrown over them or from being dipped into containers of hot liquids.

Some children were strangled or suffocated by pillows held over their mouths or plastic bags thrown

over their heads. A number were drowned in bathtubs, and one child was buried alive.

To complete the list—children were stabbed, bitten, shot, subjected to electric shock, were thrown violently to the floor or against a wall, were stamped on, and one child had pepper forced down his throat.[45]

This survey went on to report that these abused children incurred various kinds of injuries:

The majority had various shapes, sizes, and forms of bruises and contusions. There was a collection of welts, swollen limbs, split lips, black eyes, and lost teeth. One child lost an eye.

Broken bones were common. Some were simple fractures; others compound. There were many broken arms, broken legs, and fractured ribs. Many children had more than one fracture. One five-month-old child was found to have 30 broken bones in his little body.

The grimmest recital of all is the listing of internal injuries and of head injuries. The head injuries particularly were a sizable group. Both the internal injuries and the head injuries were responsible for a great many of the fatalities. In this group, we find damage to internal organs such as ruptured livers, ruptured spleens, and ruptured lungs. Injuries to the head were concussions or skull fractures, with brain hemorrhage and brain damage a frequent diagnosis.

This is indeed a grim, sad, sordid, and horror-filled recital of what happens to children in communities in almost every state of the Union.[46]

Physical abuse involves beating a child to the point where some physical damage is done. The line between physical abuse and harsh parental discipline is difficult to define. Silver et al. note:

If a parent punishes a child with a belt, is it after the fourth slash with the belt that parental rights end and child abuse begins; is it after the belt raises a welt over two millimeters that it becomes abuse versus parental rights?[47]

Definitions of abuse vary. Definitions that are narrow in scope restrict abuse to actual serious injury sus-

BOX 5.3

A Case of Physical Abuse and Murder

Chicago—Jody Marie Olcott lived only 102 days. She died on November 16, 1988. The coroner's report showed she had suffered more injuries than most people who live into later adulthood. Charged with second-degree murder in her death is her father, Malcom Olcott, age 34.

Jody Marie was born on August 5, 1988. Her unmarried parents lived together. Her mother, Judy Forbes, worked as a waitress. Her father was unemployed and felt considerable "pressure" over being unemployed and now having parental responsibilities.

Jody's first two months were quite normal. Her pediatrician saw her early in October and reported she had gained nearly 2 pounds and appeared in good health. Shortly after that, Jody's nightmare began. The pathologist who examined Jody after her death noted that she suffered from at least five broken ribs, caused about a month ago by kicking or by punching from a fist.

The pathologist noted that about ten days before her death she had received bruises to her head, chest, and left elbow. Also, at about the same time she had received burn marks on her buttocks and her head. The district attorney acknowledged that Mr. Olcott had admitted (at the time of his arrest) to setting Jody on top of a space heater.

The pathologist's report also noted one of Jody's knees was broken, and the other was badly sprained, "possibly resulting from the child being picked up by her legs and then her legs were snapped." At the time of her death Jody's weight had dropped to 6 pounds— 1 pound less than when she was born.

The blow that caused Jody's death occurred during the night of November 15. Ms. Forbes was at her waitressing job at a fast-food restaurant. The district attorney stated that Mr. Olcott was feeling on edge with his financial and family responsibilities. He began drinking. Jody was crying, as she had done for the past several days (probably from the pain from all of her injuries). Mr. Olcott stated he just couldn't take the incessant crying. He grabbed Jody and tossed her about 10 feet—hoping she'd land on the sofa. Jody missed the sofa and landed on her head on a hardwood floor. Mr. Olcott told the police that during the next few hours Jody stopped crying but appeared to have trouble breathing and sometimes vomited. When Ms. Forbes came home that evening, she found that Jody did not appear to be breathing. She called for a ambulance. Jody was pronounced dead on arrival, with the cause of death being a blood clot caused by a skull fracture. Ms. Forbes was asked by the police why she did not report the violence occurring to Jody over the past several weeks. Ms. Forbes stated, "Malcom told me if I went to the police, he would leave me and have nothing more to do with me."

tained by the child; broader definitions include intent to harm the child and verbal abuse.

In the late 1960s, in response to a growing national concern about child abuse, all states adopted child abuse and neglect reporting laws. Such laws are essentially a case-finding device. The laws require that professionals (such as physicians, social workers, hospital administrators, school administrators, nurses, and dentists) must report suspected cases of child abuse to certain specified agencies, such as the local police department and the county welfare department.

The true national incidence of child abuse is unknown. Accurate data are difficult to get for two reasons: the failure of citizens and professionals to report suspected cases and the reluctance of abused children to talk. Many battered children, believing their punishment is deserved, keep mute when interviewed by those who might help, and they develop negative self-images.

Estimates of the number of abused children each year range widely from 60,000 to 6.5 million children in America.[48] Jerome E. Leavitt notes: "More children under five years of age die from mistreatment by parents than from tuberculosis, whooping cough, polio, measles, diabetes, rheumatic fever, and appendicitis combined."[49]

Another danger of child abuse is that violence breeds violence. George C. Curtis reports there is evidence that abused children may "become tomorrow's murderers and perpetrators of other crimes of violence."[50] When they become parents, there is also a higher probability they will become abusive parents.[51] Theoretically, abuse generates an unusually high degree of hostility, which, in future years, may well be channeled into violence. A disproportionate number of rapists, murderers, robbers, and spouse abusers were child abuse victims when they were younger. Abused children are high risks to become runaways, which exposes them to other kinds of victimization and sometimes results in their being involved in criminal activity, such as shoplifting, theft, or prostitution.

Although in rare cases abuse is nonrecurrent, generally it is repeated. Nonrecurrent abuse is usually difficult to document, as the abuser can contrive a plausible explanation for the one-time injuries received by the child.

Statistics on abused children compiled from state reports by the National Center on Child Abuse and Neglect found the following:[52]

Over two thirds of the abused children required no medical treatment, with the most frequent injury being welts and bruises.

The fatality rate is 0.5 percent.

Six percent of the children required hospitalization.

Sixty-five percent were 6 years of age or older. Boys were more frequently abused than girls, particularly for children under age 10. (Teenage girls, however, were more frequently abused than teenage boys—a finding that was attributed to the inclusion of sexual abuse in the statistic and to sexual abuse being much more frequently reported among teenage girls.)

The National Center on Child Abuse and Neglect also compiled data on the parents involved in the abuse[53] and found the following:

Abuse was more apt to occur among parents with limited education and employment skills, among nonwhite families, and among mother-headed, single-parent families.

Fathers were somewhat more often the abusers than were the mothers (55 percent to 45 percent respectively), despite the fact that they commonly spend much less time with their children.

There was evidence of "family discord" and stress due to limited financial resources in many of the families. (It is possible that the higher incidence of abuse in lower classes may partly result from the fact that middle- and upper-class parents are in a better position to conceal the abuse.[54]) Most abused children (over two thirds) are permitted to remain in their homes by protective service even after abuse is determined.[55] (Protective service is described later in this section.)

Physical Neglect   In contrast to child abuse, child neglect is more apt to be a problem of omission than of commission. Specific types of physical neglect include (*a*) child abandonment; (*b*) letting a child live in filth, without proper clothing, unattended, unsupervised, and without proper nourishment; (*c*) educational neglect, in which a child is allowed to be excessively absent from school; and (*d*) medical neglect, in which no effort is made to secure needed medical care for the child.

Although child neglect has received less national attention than child abuse, it is the most common situation in which protective service agencies must intervene. The National Clearinghouse on Child Abuse and Neglect has found child neglect to occur in twice as many families as child abuse.[56]

In rare cases, such as child abandonment, the parent rejects the parental role. In most child neglect cases, however, the parent inadequately performs the role. Alfred Kadushin defines a typical neglectful mother as being physically exhausted, mentally impoverished, emotionally deprived, and socially isolated.[57] Parental neglect is more likely to be found among those who are poverty stricken or live on marginal incomes.

Vincent De Francis provides the following description of what a social worker encountered in investigating a neglect complaint:

What I saw as I entered the room was utter, stark disorganization. The room was a combined kitchen-dining room. At the other end of the room, two scrawny, owl-eyed, frightened children—a girl of about four and a boy of three—stared silently at me. Except for thin cotton undershirts, they were stark naked. They had sore crusts on their legs and arms. They were indescribably dirty, hair matted, body and hands stained and covered with spilled food particles. Sitting on a urine-soaked and soiled mattress in a baby carriage behind them was a younger child—a boy about two.

The floor was ankle-deep in torn newspapers. There were feces in about a half-dozen spots on the floor, and the air was fetid and saturated with urine odor.

There were flies everywhere. What seemed like giant roaches were crawling over the paper-strewn floor. The kitchen sink and gas stove were piled high with greasy and unwashed dishes, pots, and pans.[58]

Emotional Neglect   Meeting a child's affectional needs is as important to normal growth and development as meeting a child's physical needs. Yet, emotional neglect is difficult to define and document in the precise terms required by law.

The National Clearinghouse on Child Neglect and Abuse defines emotional neglect as:

. . . failure to provide the child the emotional nurturing or emotional support necessary for the development of a sound personality, as for example, subjecting the child to rejection or to a home climate charged with tension, hostility, and anxiety-producing occurrences which result in perceivable problems in children.[59]

Interpreted broadly, the problem with this definition of emotional neglect is that practically every parent at times is guilty of such neglect. Other definitions of emotional neglect encounter the same problem.

Although there is general agreement that writing an acceptable definition of emotional neglect is difficult, there is also solid agreement that some children do suffer from emotional neglect—even when they are adequately cared for physically.

Emotional neglect is very difficult to document in court. When emotional neglect is accompanied by physical neglect, protective service agencies make a case based on physical neglect.

Sexual Abuse   Sexual abuse within families has in recent years become an issue of national concern. It is discussed at length in Chapter 6.

Unwholesome or Demoralizing Conditions   Children who are exposed to the following situations are also considered in need of protective services: parents who are involved in continued prostitution, criminal activity, drug addiction, and severe alcoholism. Such exposure is considered injurious to the moral development of children.

Exploitation   This category involves forcing a child to work for unreasonably long hours and encouraging a child to beg, steal, or engage in prostitution.

BOX 5.4

Is This Emotional Neglect?

T he following case example raises a number of yet unanswered questions surrounding emotional neglect.

Gary, age 9, was the only child of Mr. and Mrs. Jim N. The N. family lived in a suburb of a metropolitan area, and Gary's physical needs were adequately met. Yet Gary was not doing well in school. He repeated the first grade and now is repeating the third grade.

Gary was referred for psychological testing and was found to have a very low self-concept. His self-concept was so negative that he refused to study math for fear of failing and would not participate in any competitive games with peers. He instead preferred to play by himself, with toys appropriate to children of an age level of five.

A home study found that Mr. N. was a stoic, unaffectional person who was seldom at home, as he spent long hours in operating a service station he owned. Mrs. N. had such a distasteful personality and disposition that she was unable to hold a job and had no close friends. Below average in intellectual functioning, she only completed the ninth grade. In her interactions with Gary she was observed to have a short tolerance level, would frequently berate and criticize him, and call him "stupid" and "an idiot." Gary appeared somewhat fearful of her and tried to avoid interacting with her. Both parents refused to take parent effectiveness training or to receive counseling.

Are Gary's personal problems (negative self-image) a result of interactions with his parents or due to some other factors (for example, school environment, a past traumatic experience, or an inherited disposition)?

Even if it is assumed his problems are due to his parental interactions, how can this be proved in court?

Would his personal problems be reduced or intensified if he were to be removed from home and placed in a foster home?

Abusive and Neglectful Parents   Why do some parents abuse or neglect their children? Abuse and neglect cover a wide variety of behaviors that have diverse effects on children. No single cause can fully explain why parents abuse or neglect their children. Available research indicates abusive and neglectful parents may have little in common. The following factors[60] have been found to be associated with parents who abuse their children:

Some abusive parents were themselves abused as children. If not abused, they generally had a lack of stable love relationships in their childhood and an inadequate gratification of early emotional needs.

Although abuse, like neglect, is more heavily concentrated among lower classes, it is more randomly distributed than neglect throughout the population.

Frequently, one child is singled out to be the target of the abuse. A variety of reasons appear to account for this. The child may be viewed as mentally slow or a potential delinquent. Where there is marital conflict, one child may be chosen as the victim because of a resemblance to the disliked spouse. One child may cry more, be more hyperactive, or be more demanding of parental care. The child may be punished because he or she was conceived prior to marriage, is illegitimate, or is the result of an unwanted pregnancy.

In some cases, the abused child contributes to the selection process by making greater than normal burdens on parental patience: by having severe temper tantrums; by having feeding, speech, or toilet-training problems; and/or by being restless, negative, unresponsive, listless, whiny, or fussy.

The child who is the victim may, in disturbed families, be essential for the psychic stability of the family. It appears some disturbed families need a "whipping boy" or "scapegoat" to maintain an equilibrium within the family. Sometimes when an abused child is removed, another is selected to be the victim and thereby fulfill this "stability" role.

Abusive parents often show an absence of guilt, have a tendency toward social isolation, have a high level of overall aggressiveness, are prone to impulsivity, tend to have emotional problems, have feelings of inadequacy, and have a low tolerance of criticism.

Environmental stress factors (for example, marital problems), economic pressures, and social isolation sometimes help trigger abuse.

Abusive parents tend to believe in strict discipline and tend to view misbehavior by their children as willful, deliberate disobedience. Also, they are characterized by a high demand for the child to perform to gratify the parent.

Alcohol/drug abuse plays an important contributing role in some cases.

The following factors[61] have been identified as being associated with child neglect:

The preponderance of families come from the lower socioeconomic classes. Financial deprivation is a major contributing factor. Many also have inadequate housing.

A high percentage (60 percent in some studies) are one-parent families, generally headed by a female.

Neglectful parents have also been found frequently to have an atypically large number of children.

A fair number of neglectful mothers are below normal in intellectual capacity.

Neglectful parents (particularly the mothers who have most contact with children) are physically and emotionally exhausted, have health problems, are socially withdrawn or isolated, are frustrated, are apathetic, and lack hope. Such factors lead them to be "indifferent" toward their children.

Neglectful parents tend to have had emotionally deprived early childhood experiences. Similar to abusive parents, they failed to have stable affectional relationships when they were young. Such early childhood experiences appear to lead to current "emotional inadequacies" and then, when combined with severe financial and environmental stress, result in physical and emotional exhaustion.

Neglectful families are not without intrapsychic distress but are generally less emotionally disturbed than abusive parents. Similar to abusive parents, they tend to be socially isolated.

PROTECTIVE SERVICES

Brief History   Under the concept of *parens patriae*, the state is ultimately a parent to all children. When the natural parents neglect, abuse, or exploit a child, the state has the legal right and responsibility to intervene. Protective services has been defined as "a specialized casework service to neglected, abused, exploited, or rejected children. The focus of the service is preventive and nonpunitive and is geared toward rehabilitation through identification and treatment of the motivating factors which underlie" the problem.[62]

In colonial days a child was regarded as chattel (an item of personal property). In its fullest expression, this gave parents the right to sell the child, exploit his or her labor, offer the child as a sacrifice, and even to kill the child at birth. Although most communities regulated and restricted such rights, it was not until the era of industrialization that children were considered to have certain rights. These rights have gradually been expanded. Until the early 20th century, when child labor laws were finally enacted, parents were allowed to exploit the labor of their children.

Agencies providing protective services in America trace their origin to the case of Mary Ellen in 1875. Mary Ellen was severely beaten and neglected by a couple who had raised her since infancy. Concerned community citizens were unaware of any legal approach to protect her. In desperation, they appealed to the Society of the Prevention of Cruelty to Animals. (It's interesting to note that organizations existed to protect animals at this time, but not children.) Mary Ellen was brought to the court's attention by this society. The court accepted the complaint, partly because laws existed that protected animals from abuse. Protection was given to Mary Ellen, and the abusive couple was sentenced to prison. Following this dramatic case, a Society for the Prevention of Cruelty to Children was formed in New York. Gradually, other similar societies throughout the United States were formed, laws protecting children from abuse and neglect were enacted, and agencies providing protective services were established.

Almost from the start, two focuses for protective services were initiated: a law enforcement approach and a rehabilitative approach. The law enforcement focus emphasized punishment for the abusive or neglecting parents, whereas the rehabilitative approach emphasized the importance of helping the parents and keeping the family together rather than disrupting it. Since the early 1900s, protective services have generally taken the rehabilitative approach.

Since the late 1960s there has been a dramatic growth of interest in services to prevent and treat child abuse. With this interest came passage of Title XX to the Social Security Act in 1975, making protective services mandatory for each state and providing federal reimbursement for most costs. A federal Child Abuse Prevention and Treatment Act was passed in January 1974, which provides direct assistance to states to help them develop child abuse and neglect programs.

Processes in Protective Services   Extensive efforts have been made to encourage parents who have maltreated their children (or feel they may maltreat them) to request agency services voluntarily. Radio and TV announcements, along with posters, announce the availability of parental stress hot-line services that parents may call in many communities.

Parents who maltreat their children, however, do not generally apply for help. Currently, initiation of services frequently results from the legal requirement of mandatory reporting by professionals of suspected abuse, physical neglect, sexual abuse, and emotional injury. The list of professionals required to report includes, among others, social workers, school personnel, doctors, day-care center personnel, legal personnel, nurses, and dentists. The agencies to which reports are to be made are generally the local police department, the county welfare department, or the county sheriff. These laws grant civil and criminal immunity to the professionals required to make such reports and also specify penalties for failure to report.

Each state has the legal right and responsibility to intervene when a child is being abused, neglected, or exploited. This right and responsibility are delegated to protective services (in many states protective services are located within public welfare departments).

Case finding is almost always through a complaint referral. Complaints generally are filed by neighbors, relatives, public health nurses, physicians, school authorities, police, or another social agency. A complaint is a report of a possible neglect or abuse situation that needs exploration. The complainant may remain anonymous (not provide his or her own name). Occasionally, unfounded complaints are made to "harass" a parent.

Some complainants feel guilty about having made a report, and they are given reassurance that they are performing a very useful function that is necessary to protect and safeguard children. They are also informed that their identity (name) will not be revealed to the family against which the report has been made.

All complaints are then investigated by the protective service agency. Some agencies make the initial contact by letter. This letter identifies the agency, gives a general explanation of the service, and indicates that a concern has been expressed that needs to be looked into. Such a letter gives parents a chance to react privately and prepare for a meeting with a social worker.

BOX 5.5

Letter to Parents in Which a Complaint of Child Abuse or Neglect Has Been Filed

July 26, 1977

Mr. and Mrs. _____
Racine, WI

Dear Mr. and Mrs. _____:

Information which raises question about the care your child is receiving has come to our attention. When such reports reach our agency, it is our legal responsibility to explore them. We realize there are always two sides to any such report, and therefore, we would like to talk with you in person about this information. If there is any need for help, this contact with you should assist us in determining in what way we could be most helpful to you.

I have been assigned as your social worker in this matter. I would appreciate it if you would contact me within forty-eight (48) hours after you receive this letter about an appointment to discuss this situation. My office hours are from 7:30 A.M. to 4:00 P.M. Monday through Friday, and my telephone number is 636-3348. If I am not in when you call, please leave your name and number, and I will return your call.

Thank you for your anticipated cooperation.

Sincerely,

Protective Service Intake Worker
Racine County Department of Social Services

Source: Reprinted with permission of Racine County Department of Social Services (Wisconsin).

Some agencies make arrangements for the initial visit by telephone, which usually reduces the length of time that elapses before the initial visit is held.

Other agencies prefer an unannounced visit. This approach has the advantage of allowing the social worker to view the home environment in its day-to-day appearance. Whether or not a letter is used, the initial approach is direct and frank. The social worker conveys that a situation of potential danger to a child has been expressed and needs to be explored; if a potential danger does exist, the worker's responsibility and interest are to be helpful to both the parents and their children.

The social worker attempts to obtain an objective and accurate description of the situation. Specific information relevant to the complaint is sought. For example, if the complaint is that a child appears malnourished and is frequently absent from school, specific questions are asked about the daily diet of the child, what illnesses he or she has had and when, and the specific dates and reasons why the child has been absent from school. Such details are necessary to determine if the child is in fact in danger and what help (if any) is needed. Such detailed information is also essential as evidence if a petition is made to the court for removal of the child from the home. Obtaining this information has to be done tactfully because it is also important that the social worker seeks to develop a working relationship with the parents.

During this evaluation process the social worker almost always seeks to see the child who has been alleged to be in an endangered situation. If abuse or neglect exists, the objective is to convey to the parents that the focus of protective services is to prevent further neglect or abuse and to alleviate the factors that are now a danger to the child. Because many families charged with abuse or neglect have multiproblems, services may be far ranging (for example, health, educational, financial, housing, counseling, employment, parent effectiveness training, homemakers, day care, and so on).

If there is no evidence of neglect or abuse, the case may be closed after the initial interview. For families with serious problems, continued services may be provided for years.

If the child is clearly in danger (for example, repeated severe abuse) or if the parents are unable or unwilling to make changes essential for the long-term well-being of the child, the child may have to be removed from the home. Protective service agencies view court action as "a means of protecting the child rather than prosecuting the parents."[63]

If the social worker decides it is necessary to remove the child from the home, the parents' voluntary consent is first sought. If this is not received, a petition is made to the court that the child needs protection (court action is atypical in protective services; studies suggest roughly 80 percent of cases are closed without it).[64]

After a petition is filed a preliminary hearing is held within a few weeks. Parents are permitted to be represented by an attorney, and the normal adversary court procedures are followed. The social worker has to support the petition with documented facts. The judge has the responsibility of protecting the rights not only of the child but also of the parents. At the preliminary hearing the parents are asked if they will consent to or contest the petition. If they decide to contest and if evidence of abuse and neglect is substantiated, a trial is held.

In making a disposition a number of avenues are open to the judge. She or he may decide there is not sufficient evidence of neglect or abuse to warrant any action. Or, the judge can place the child under supervision of the court, while permitting the child to remain at home. Such supervision puts pressure on the family to make needed changes, with the threat of the child being removed if the changes are not made. The judge also has the option of placing the child under protective legal custody. Under this arrangement, legal custody of the child is assigned to a social agency who then has the authority to remove the child if essential changes are not made. The judge can also terminate the parents' legal rights and place the child under guardianship of the agency. Under this disposition, the child is automatically removed from the home.

For children who are in imminent danger, many jurisdictions have provisions that allow either the protective service agency or the family court to remove the child immediately. Such children are then usually placed in a foster home for a temporary period of time. When a child is removed for emergency reasons, a court hearing must be held within twenty-hour hours to determine the appropriateness of the action. Unless the court is satisfied that protection of the child requires his or her removal from the home, the child must be returned to his or her parents.

Involuntary Services   Protective services cannot withdraw from the situation if it finds that the parents are uncooperative or resistant. For most social services, clients are voluntary recipients; generally they are interested in receiving services. Protective services is one of the few services where participation is involuntary (probation and parole is another).

Because protective services are involuntary and because provision of services is based on an "outside" complaint, the recipients are apt to view the services as an invasion of privacy. The initial contact by the social worker is therefore likely to arouse hostility, be viewed as a threat to their family autonomy, and perhaps raise some guilt about incidents where they have mistreated their children in the past. Having one's functioning as a parent questioned and explored arouses substantial emotional feelings. Although the focus of protective services is rehabilitative and nonpunitive, Edith Varon found in a study that former protective service clients generally viewed the service as punitive and investigatory.[65]

Some recipients of protective services remain hostile and resistant throughout the time period in which services are provided. Others, in time, form a productive, working relationship with the agency, with positive changes being much more apt to occur. A few are cooperative from the beginning, perhaps because they recognize their family needs help.

In working with parents who neglect or abuse their children, the social worker has to show respect for the parents as people, while in no way conveying acceptance of their mistreatment. The worker needs to convey empathy with their situation, be warm, and yet be firm about the need for positive changes. This approach is illustrated in the following interview:

The C. family was referred to the child welfare agency by a hospital which treated the 6-year-old boy, Wade,

for a broken arm suffered in a beating by his mother.

Both parents said they whipped the children because they believed in firm discipline, and they challenged the worker's right to question this. Mr. C. again attempted to avoid the subject of Wade's beating by describing at length how strict his parents had been with him.

Again the worker brought the conversation back to the C.'s own disciplinary practices by saying that children had to be dealt with firmly, but the injury of a child was a serious matter. He added, "I can understand that one may be so upset he has trouble controlling himself." Mrs. C. hesitatingly said, "I was so upset and too angry," and broke into tears. The worker replied that, if together they could try to understand why Mrs. C gets so upset, perhaps the behavior would not continue. Mr. C., who had been silent for a while, said he realized it was serious and that he did not approve of Mrs. C. beating the children but did not know what to do. He had told her that this was bad for the youngsters, but she continued. Mrs. C. remarked that looking back on Wade's beating was a terrible experience. She did not realize she had injured him until his arm became swollen. She supposed it was her anger and her temper that did it. She would like to talk to someone and she does need help.[66]

In working with families who maltreat their children the protective service worker has to be ready to perform a variety of roles: teacher, enabler, adviser, coordinator of treatment, intervener, supporter, confidante, and expediter. The focus has to be on constantly identifying concrete needs, selecting intervention approaches, and providing concrete services. Workers must also be ready to work with other professional groups: the doctors treating the child, schoolteachers, lawyers, and judges.

A wide variety of treatment resources have been used in attempting to make the needed changes. Crisis nurseries, extended day-care centers, and emergency foster homes provide short-term shelter to relieve a potentially damaging crisis situation. Parent effectiveness training programs, group therapy, and family life education programs sometimes are useful in curbing the abuse or neglect. Homemakers relieve the frustrated, overburdened mother of some of the daily load of child care. Emergency relief funds are sometimes provided to meet immediate rent, heat, food, and electricity needs. Behavior modification programs, such as modeling and role playing, have been used to change the behaviors of parents toward their children. "Emergency parents" have been used in some communities to go into a home and stay with a child who has been left unsupervised and unprotected. Psychotherapy and counseling have also been provided by protective service workers and other professionals. A self-help group, Parents Anonymous, is described in Box 5.6. (It should be noted that very few communities have the resources to provide all of the above listed services. In many communities the primary intervention resource available to protective service workers is their own counseling capacities.)

Kadushin has reviewed studies on the effectiveness of protective services and concludes:

In summary, the evaluation studies suggest that the agencies have achieved some modest measure of success. The amount of change one might reasonably expect the agencies to effect must be assessed against the great social and personal deprivation characteristic of the client families. Even the modest success achieved may have been more than could have been expected initially.

The resources available to treat these families are limited. The technology available to the worker in trying to effect change in such families is blunt and imprecise.

Scarce resources backed by a weak technology applied to a group of involuntary, disturbed clients resistive to change and living in seriously deprived circumstances would seem to guarantee the likelihood of limited success.[67]

Social workers have found protective services to be demanding. "Burnout" occurs at a higher rate among protective service workers than in many other social welfare areas.

Rights of Children versus Rights of Parents   The rights of parents have had a long history. Earlier in American history the law guarded the rights of parents but gave little attention to the rights of children. In recent years, defining and protecting the rights of children has received national attention, as indicated by a variety of child advocacy efforts and the specification of various "bill of rights for children" proclamations. Protective services, particularly in contested court cases, encounters the problem of defining the respective rights of parents and children. Henry Maas and Richard Engler found the balance of rights between parents and children varies from community to community.[68]

Some of the situations where this balance becomes an issue are the following. If parents, for religious reasons, are opposed to their child receiving medication for a serious health problem, should the state intervene? Should the state intervene where an unmarried parent is sexually promiscuous yet is meeting his or her children's basic physical and emotional needs? Should the state intervene where a child is being raised in a homosexual environment or in a commune where lifestyles and mores are substantially different? Should the state intervene in families in which a child has serious emotional problems and the parents refuse to seek professional help? Should the state intervene in certain ethnic or minority settings where educational needs are not being met? Should intervention occur when a father uses harsh discipline by whipping a child two or three times a week? Should the state intervene in families where there is long-term alcoholism and serious marital discord? Should the state intervene where a child is living in filth, has ragged clothing, and seldom bathes, but where the child's emotional and social needs are being met?

Different workers, different judges, and different communities would probably disagree on what should be done. The reluctance to intervene may have tragic consequences, as indicated in the following case:

In 1953, a boy of 13 was referred to a children's court because of chronic truancy. A psychiatric examination established the fact that the boy was "drawn to violence" and represented "a serious danger to himself and to others." Psychiatric treatment was recommended by the psychiatrist and social workers concerned with the boy's situation. The mother refused to accept the recommendation and refused to bring the boy back for treatment. Should

BOX 5.6

Parents Anonymous (PA)

P arents Anonymous is a national self-help organization for parents who have abused or neglected their children. Because self-help organizations (such as Parents Anonymous, Alcoholics Anonymous, Parents of Gays and Lesbians, Overeaters Anonymous, and Weight Watchers) have had considerable rehabilitative success, PA will be described in this section. It is one of several approaches that can be used in helping parents who abuse their children.

PA was originally established in 1970 in California by Jolly K., who was desperate to find help to meet her needs. For four years prior to this time, she struggled with an uncontrollable urge to punish her daughter severely. One afternoon, she attempted to strangle her daughter. Desperate, she sought help from the local child-guidance clinic. She was placed in therapy. When asked by her therapist what she could do about this situation, she developed an idea as she explained, "If alcoholics could stop drinking by getting together, and gamblers could stop gambling, maybe the same principle would work for abusers, too."[a] With her therapist's encouragement, she therefore formed Mothers Anonymous in 1970 and started a few local chapters in California. The organization has grown to over 1,000 chapters in the United States and Canada, and the name has been changed to Parents Anonymous, since fathers who abuse their children are also eligible to join.

PA uses some of the basic therapeutic concepts of Alcoholics Anonymous. PA is a crisis intervention program that offers two main forms of help:

1. A weekly group meeting in which members share experiences and feelings and learn to control their emotions better.

2. Personal and telephone contact among members during periods of crisis, particularly when a member feels a nearly uncontrollable desire to take his or her anger or frustration out on a child.

Parents may be referred to PA by a social agency (including protective services) or may be self-referrals as parents who are aware they need help.

Cassie Starkweather and S. Michael Turner describe why some parents who abuse their children would rather participate in a self-help group than receive professional counseling:

It has been our experience that most (abusive) parents judge themselves more harshly than other more objective people tend to judge them. The fear of losing their children frequently diminishes with reassurance from other members that they are not the monsters they think they are.

Generally speaking, PA members are so afraid they are going to be judged by others as harshly as they judge themselves that they are afraid to go out [to] seek help. Frequently, our members express fears of dealing with a professional person, seeing differences in education, sex, or social status as basic differences that would prevent easy communication or mutual understanding.

Continued

BOX 5.6 *Continued*

Members express feelings of gratification at finding that other parents are "in the same boat." They contrast this with their feelings about professionals who, they often assume, have not taken out the time from their training and current job responsibilities to raise families of their own.[b]

PA emphasizes honesty and directness. In the outside world, parents who are prone to abuse their children learn to hide this problem, as society finds it difficult to stomach. In contrast, the goal in PA is to help parents admit and accept the fact that they are abusive. The term *abuse* is used liberally at meetings. PA has found that this insistence on frankness has a healthy effect. Parents are relieved because finally they have found a group of people who are able to accept abusive parents for what they really are. Furthermore, once they are able to admit they are abusive, only then can they begin to find ways to cope with this problem.

During PA meetings, parents are expected to say why they believe they are beating their child, and the members challenge each other to find ways to curb the abuse. Members also share constructive approaches that each has found useful, and efforts are made to help each other develop specific plans for dealing with situations that have resulted in abusive episodes in the past. Members learn to recognize danger signs and then to take the necessary action to curb the potential abuse.

PA stresses protecting members' anonymity and confidentiality. This protection permits group members to discuss their experiences and asocial thoughts without risk of public disclosure. The fact that they are sharing their experiences with other parents who have abused children assures their being able to "confess" without danger of humiliation, recrimination, or rejection.

Group members develop a sense of "oneness," and often the group becomes a "surrogate family." Each group member is given the phone numbers of all others in the group and is urged to reach for the phone instead of the child when feeling distressed. Members are gradually transformed into "lay professionals" who are able to help other abusers and who perceive themselves skillful at this because they have, at one time, been child abusers.

The group leader or chapter chairperson is always a parent who at one time abused a child. Members can identify more readily with such a person than they can with a professional therapist. Among the reasons PA is successful is that it diminishes the social isolation of abusive parents and provides them with social supports.

[a]Phyllis Zauner, "Mothers Anonymous: The Last Resort," in Jerome E. Leavitt, *The Battered Child* (Morristown, NJ: General Learning Press, 1974), p. 247.

[b]Cassie L. Starkweather and S. Michael Turner, "Parents Anonymous: Reflections on the Development of a Self-Help Group," in *Child Abuse: Intervention and Treatment*, eds. Nancy C. Ebeling and Deborah A. Hill (Acton, MA: Publishing Sciences Group, 1975), p. 151.

the mother have been forced to accept treatment for the boy? This is the question of limits of protection intervention. Nothing was done. Ten years later the boy, Lee Harvey Oswald, assassinated President Kennedy.[69]

Birth Outside of Marriage

Women between the ages of 15 and 24 compose about 40 percent of the total population of women of childbearing age, yet they account for roughly 80 percent of births outside of marriage.[70] More than a million teenage women become pregnant each year. Most of these pregnancies are unplanned, are generally unwanted, and often result from misinformation or lack of access to birth control. Roughly 60 percent of these teenagers have babies, with the remainder ending the pregnancy through abortion or miscarriage.[71] Over half of the teenagers who carry the pregnancy to full term are still unmarried at the time of birth. Four out of five teenage marriages end in divorce; many of these marriages were preceded by a pregnancy.[72] For those who are unmarried when the child is born, over 90 percent decide to keep the child rather than to give it up for adoption.[73] The United States' yearly pregnancy rate—one teenage girl in every ten—is the highest of any developed country.[74] By age 20, nearly 40 percent of white girls and 63 percent of black girls become pregnant.[75]

In the late 1950s only about 5 percent of all births were to unmarried mothers; by 1984 21 percent were.[76] Although teenage women compose roughly 25 percent of the population of childbearing age, they account for 35 percent of all births outside of marriage.[77] These statistics emphasize that birth outside of marriage is a problem that is disproportionately faced by teenagers. Teenagers who marry when pregnant are nearly as likely to be single parents sometime in the future (due to divorce) as are those who are unmarried at the time of birth.

Many teenagers are not adequately informed about the reproductive process and tend not to use contraceptives. Some teenage women think that if you take a pill once a week, you're protected; some believe it's safe to have sex standing up; some are afraid birth control will harm them or their future babies.[78]

Many unmarried mothers are simply not prepared, by education, work experience, or maturity, to undertake the dual responsibility of parenthood and economic support. As a result, society inevitably has to contribute to the support of these children through public assistance payments and social welfare services.

The number of births outside of marriage is disproportionately higher for nonwhites.[79] This higher rate does not necessarily mean that unmarried nonwhites are more likely to be promiscuous. It may simply mean nonwhites have less access to contraceptives, or they may be less likely to seek an abortion, or they may be less apt to marry the father before the birth of the child. The reason the rate of births outside of marriage is higher among nonwhites is unclear.

Fifty years ago both premarital intercourse and births outside of marriage were stigmatized in our society. (In fact, children born outside of marriage were labeled "illegitimate" and were usually stigmatized as much as the mother. The terms *illegitimate* and *illegitimacy* last today, even though they stigmatize innocent persons.) In the 1940s, Alfred Kinsey found, however, that high percentages of the population had experienced premarital intercourse.[80] Since the Kinsey studies, attitudes toward premarital intercourse have become more tolerant. Now, few people are virgins when they marry.

Attitudes toward birth outside of marriage have also become somewhat more tolerant. Few parents now send their pregnant daughter off to a maternity home to avoid "disgracing" the family. Today, we have the unusual situation in which many parents tolerate premarital intercourse, yet if their daughter happens to become pregnant, there is considerable turmoil.

Why are births outside of marriage seen as a social problem by most Americans? There are many answers to this question. Some parents still feel "disgraced" if their daughter becomes pregnant. Some single pregnant women (and their parents) view it as a problem because difficult decisions have to be made about whether to end the pregnancy. If it is decided not to have an abortion, decisions have to be made about adoption, whether to stay in school or continue employment, a possible marriage, living arrangements, and possibly going on welfare. The father of the child has to make decisions about his role and the extent to which he will seek to provide emotional and financial support.

Some people see birth outside of marriage as a social problem because they assert that it is a sign of a breakdown in the traditional family and a symptom of moral decay. Others assert that birth outside of marriage is a problem because the great majority of these children are born to women who are simply not yet prepared—by experience, education, or maturity—to be a parent or to provide for a family financially. Authorities who view birth outside of marriage as a problem for this reason are concerned about the effects on the child of being raised by a mother who is in many ways merely an older child herself. They are also concerned about the effects on the mother of seeking to maintain a one-parent family with limited financial and personal resources. Finally, some authorities view birth outside of marriage as a problem because of the high cost to society of having to make welfare payments to large numbers of single-parent families (generally through the Aid to Families of Dependent Children program, which is described in Chapter 3).

Is the social stigma attached to birth outside of marriage functional? Certainly it is not to either the child or the mother. On the other hand, some authorities have argued that the stigma is functional to society, since it discourages out-of-wedlock pregnancies and thereby helps perpetuate the nuclear family, which provides a structure for the financial support and socialization of children. In response to this view, it can be argued that the punitive, stigmatization approach may not be the optimal way to reduce the incidence of births outside of marriage. Ursula Myers asserts that a more effective approach would be quality educational programs about responsible sexuality. Components of sex education programs for teenagers would include:

1. Basic biological information about reproduction, pregnancy, birth control, venereal disease, childbirth, abortion, and the medical risks of premature pregnancy and parenthood.

2. An examination of some of the consequences of single parenthood, such as economic dependency,

A nurse explains to a teenager how birth control pills are used. Educational programs about responsible sexuality are the most effective means of reducing the number of births outside marriage.

turmoil with parents, interruption and/or dropping out of educational programs, inadequate housing, and difficulties in meeting the role requirements of being both a mother and a teenager.

3. Information on alternatives to sexual intercourse— for example, petting.

4. Parenting skills training—that is, training on how to raise a child.

5. Family living training, role expectations of children and of husband and wife, conflict resolution, decision making, financial counseling, and dating and marriage responsibilities.[81]

Even with over one million teenagers becoming pregnant each year, the question of whether to provide sex education is still a controversial issue in many school systems. Apparently, many people believe sex education will lead to promiscuity and to teenage pregnancies. Advocates of sex education argue that such programs reduce the number of teenage pregnancies.

Authorities who track what is happening to young people across the United States are noticing an encouraging trend. The pregnancy rate among teenagers, which rose sharply in the 1970s, has leveled off, and teen birth rates and the number of abortions have dropped somewhat.[82] The major reason for these declines appears to be the increased use of contraceptives. Health clinics located in or near high schools appear to be particularly effective. Such clinics provide birth control information and also prescribe contraceptives for sexually active persons. In Baltimore, pregnancy rates dropped 30 percent in three years at two schools served by health clinics, whereas pregnancy rates in similar schools in Baltimore not served by health clinics shot up 58 percent.[83]

SINGLE-PARENT SERVICES   Services to single women who become pregnant have become known as single-parent services. A high proportion of pregnant single women decide to carry the baby to full term and to then keep their child. The scope of single-parent services includes not only services prior to the delivery but also services after the delivery. Single-parent services are provided by certain public agencies (generally the public welfare department) and by private agencies (such as Catholic Social Services and Lutheran Social Services).

Typical services provided by single-parent units include the following:

Alternatives counseling: The pregnant single woman is helped to make decisions about carrying the baby to full term, having an abortion, keeping the child, terminating parental rights, deciding on foster placement, and undergoing adoption counseling. (Single-parent workers generally refrain from revealing their values about abortion and the other alternatives to the clients because clients have the right to make their own decisions in these areas.)

Physical and mental preparation of client for giving birth to a child: Clients are informed about the effects of drug and alcohol abuse on the embryo, prepared for childbirth, given pre- and postnatal counseling, and provided with information on the effects of venereal diseases. Clients also receive mental and physical health counseling.

Counseling on legal issues: Areas covered include paternity action, procedures for termination of parental rights, legitimation and/or adoption procedures, rights to attend school, and procedures involved in receiving public assistance.

Counseling on interpersonal relationships: Such counseling focuses on the client's relationships with the alleged father, parents and other relatives, and significant others.

Alternative living arrangements: Alternatives include a maternity home, living with parents or other relatives, and foster home care.

Alleged-father counseling: This involves informing him about his rights and responsibilities, counseling on his concerns, birth control counseling, and perhaps premarital counseling.

Family planning counseling: Birth control information is provided for both sexes, and perhaps referral to a family planning clinic is made.

Educational and employment counseling: Here, information is provided about remaining in educational programs (including home study programs) or about employment opportunities and work-training programs.

Self-development counseling: This may include a variety of areas: identity formation, assertiveness training, sexual counseling, rape counseling, and so on.

Financial and money management counseling: This includes eligibility for AFDC, food stamps, and medicare.

Child development counseling: Areas covered are counseling on caring for young children and meeting their physical, social, and emotional needs.

In providing social services to single parents, social workers seek first to establish a helping relationship (see Chapter 4). If the client is single and pregnant, the worker seeks to convey that the client (not her parents) has the right and responsibility to decide among the alternatives of carrying the child to delivery, having an abortion, keeping the baby after delivery, placing the baby in foster care, and putting the baby up for adoption. In helping a client to make such decisions a problem-solving approach is used in which the worker helps the client:

1. Define her problems.

2. Identify the alternatives.

3. Make a pro-con list for each alternative.

4. Evaluate the alternatives.

5. Select one or more alternatives.

6. Implement, and later evaluate, the alternatives that are chosen.

Most single parents decide to keep their baby. The proportion who are making this decision has been increasing. Abortions have become more acceptable and available; therefore some single women who are pregnant and know they do not as yet want the responsibilities of motherhood are terminating the pregnancy. The social stigma of single parenthood has also lessened. In addition, unmarried single parents are not as visible as they have been in the past because we now have single foster parents, single adoptive parents, and a large number of one-parent families following a divorce. Support systems have also become more available to help unmarried mothers who keep their babies. Such services include financial aid through public assistance, programs in schools that help school-age parents complete their education and also provide training in being a parent, homebound education to help high school-age parents complete their education, child-care monies that are available to single parents who are in school or in training programs,

programs to help young parents learn parenting skills, and counseling services.*

Ursula Myers (a supervisor of a single-parent unit at a social services agency) describes the small minority of single parents who decide to terminate parental rights.

In our experience, the woman who terminates her parental rights is generally long-range goal, reality oriented. The stigma of single parenthood is for her perceptually more marked. She sees the coming child as an encumbrance or as totally out of place in her present and future world, her immediate culture, and her internal mental health system. She is usually aware that her pregnancy is untimely and that she cannot cope with the vital needs of an infant at this point in her life. The separation process can result in a broad spectrum of responses, all perfectly normal and human. Both or either parent may feel a sense of loss, grief, emptiness, and unreality. There may be a sense of relief and even pleasure at terminating for some, while others may become depressed and withdrawn. Some work through the grief process to a point of rational and emotional acceptance, while others may completely sever themselves from the pregnancy by "cutting out" that part of their lives and/or totally denying its reality.[84]

Foster Care and Adoption   If a single parent relinquishes her parental rights, the child is usually placed temporarily in foster care. Some single parents who are unsure about whether to give up parental rights

---

*The author wishes to note that he does not want to take a position on whether, in general, unmarried mothers should keep their babies. Being a parent at a young age has some rewards. But it is certainly an immense responsibility. An unmarried mother often has little time to enjoy young adulthood. Dating, pursuing a career, and having the necessary funds to meet wants and desires are more or less restricted. Most single-parent workers feel it is usually in the long-range best interest of the child and the mother to consider placing the child for adoption. In working with unmarried mothers, however, single-parent workers seek to refrain from expressing their views on termination. They instead seek to have the single mother carefully analyze the pros and cons of the available alternatives. Deciding whether to keep the baby is a very difficult, emotionally taxing task.

may also place their child in foster care until they make a decision. (Foster care, as was discussed earlier, is also used for children who are removed from their parents for neglect or abuse.)

The goals of foster care are to protect the children, to rehabilitate the parents, and generally to return the children to their genetic parents as soon as it is feasible to do so. Foster care is the temporary provision of substitute care for children whose parents are unable or unwilling to meet the child's needs in their own home. Except for emergency placement, legal custody of the child is usually transferred, by court action, from the child's parents to the agency responsible for foster placement. (Removal of a child from the parents' legal custody is carefully weighed by the court in an effort to protect the parents' rights while at the same time seeking to provide protection to the child.)

Foster parents face the difficult task of being expected to provide love and affection to foster children, without becoming too emotionally attached. The placement is temporary in nature, and separating is easier when strong emotional bonds have not been established between foster parents and foster children. One of the tragic aspects of some foster placements is that the genetic parents do not, over a period of years, attain the capacity to care for their children. If they do not relinquish parental rights, the children may end up being raised in a series of foster homes. When this happens a serious question arises about whether a child's right to be raised in a stable, healthy environment is being met. Children who are raised in a series of foster homes are apt to experience considerable emotional trauma over relating to and later separating from a variety of parental figures.

Foster placement agencies seek to attain quality care in foster placements by studying and selecting applicants for foster parenthood, licensing foster parents, and monitoring foster placements after a child is placed. While the children are in foster care the genetic parents have visitation rights. In neglect and abuse cases the hours of visitation are usually arranged through the court and supervised by the foster placement agency. Single parents who decide to relinquish their parental rights often choose not to visit the foster home, as they are in the process of separating emotionally from their child.

If the genetic mother relinquishes her rights, the alleged father does not automatically receive custody of the child. He must first be adjudged the father of the child by a court of law. Then, to obtain custody of the child he must also convince the court of his fitness and ability to care for the child. (If the mother decides to keep her child, she does not have to demonstrate her fitness and ability to care for the child to a court.) For a child to be eligible for adoptive placement, both the genetic mother and the alleged father must relinquish their parental rights. In recent years many more people have applied for adoptive parenthood than there are children available for adoption. In particular, there are many more applicants for white, healthy infants than there are available babies.

Adoptive placement agencies carefully study, select, and prepare for parenthood applicants who want a child. After a child is placed, the agency monitors the placement until it is finalized by court action. Courts generally wait several months after a child is placed before finalizing a placement. Only in very rare circumstances is a child removed from an adoptive placement. The purpose of this waiting period is to ascertain, as thoroughly as possible, that the placement is working out well.

As fully as possible, the medical histories of both biological parents are compiled to provide physical health and genetic information to the adoptive parents. Efforts are also made by placement agencies to meet the wishes of the biological parents concerning the physical characteristics, religious affiliation, racial characteristics, and geographical location of the adoptive parents.

A recent trend in adoptions is "open adoptions," whereby some genetic and adoptive parents are officially known to each other. (In the past, adoptive placement agencies usually did not tell the adoptive parents who the genetic parents were, nor did they tell the genetic parents who the adoptive parents were.) At present a few adoptive and genetic parents are even maintaining contact with each other. Another trend is for some adoptive children (when they become young adults) to seek to find and make contact with their genetic parents.

It should be noted that not all adoptions are arranged by state-licensed adoption agencies. Although professionally frowned on, some attorneys (for a substantial fee) arrange adoptions for couples seeking a child. These attorneys sometimes pay a fee (which they charge to the adoptive couple) to the single, pregnant woman for agreeing to carry the pregnancy to delivery and then relinquishing parental rights.

SUMMARY

The family is a social institution that is found in every culture. Yet there are substantial variations in family patterns and forms. Most families throughout the world can be classified as either an extended or a nuclear family. Our culture has moved from an extended family system (before the Industrial Revolution) to a nuclear family system.

No society has ever existed without the institution of the family. Five essential functions performed by the modern family are replacement of the population, care of the young, socialization of new members, regulation of sexual behavior, and an important source of affection.

Four problems in the American family were examined: divorce, empty shell marriages, family violence, and birth outside of marriage.

Now, one out of two marriages end in divorce. Divorce per se is not a social problem, but the consequences sometimes are. Reasons for the high divorce rate in our society include the extensive emphasis on romantic love, the changing status of women (who are now increasingly more financially independent), the growth of individualism, the growing acceptance of divorce, and the loss of certain functions in the modern family.

In empty shell marriages the spouses feel no strong attachments to each other. Three types were described: devitalized relationships, conflict habituated relationships, and passive-congenial relationships. Some empty shell marriages eventually end in divorce. Marriage counseling is the primary service available to spouses contemplating a divorce, and to spouses with an empty shell marriage.

Spouse abuse, child abuse, and parent abuse occur in more than half of all U.S. households. In the past twenty years family violence has become recognized as one of our major social problems.

With spouse abuse, the greatest physical damage is usually sustained by women. Although husbands are slapped or shoved with about the same frequency as wives, husbands are not controlled through violence to the extent that battered wives are. Spouse abuse appears to be related to a norm of tolerating violence in American families. A sizable number of men and women believe it is acceptable for a husband to occasionally hit his wife. Services (for example, shelter homes) are increasingly being developed in many communities for battered wives.

Large numbers of children are victims of child abuse or neglect. Physical abuse is dramatic and has received considerable national attention. Child neglect has received less national attention, even though it occurs more frequently than physical abuse. *Physical abuse, physical neglect,* and particularly *emotional neglect* are terms that are somewhat ambiguous and difficult to define precisely. The primary service designed to curb child abuse and neglect is protective services.

Premarital intercourse is fairly common, and is now often tolerated in our society. If a single woman becomes pregnant, however, there is often considerable turmoil within families. Birth outside of marriage has become somewhat more accepted in our society, yet it is still viewed as a social problem. There is considerable variation in the reasons why it is viewed as a problem—ranging from the assertion that it is a sign of the moral decay and collapse of the family, to concern about the difficulties that the single parent and her child will encounter. A disproportionately high number of births outside of marriage occur among teenagers, suggesting a need for quality educational programs about responsible sexuality. Single-parent services is the primary social service for women who are single and pregnant and for unmarried mothers and fathers.

NOTES

1. Philippe Aries, "From the Medieval to the Modern Family," in *Family in Transition*, ed. Arlene S. Skolnick and Jerome H. Skolnick (Boston: Little, Brown, 1971), pp. 90–104.

2. John F. Cuber, Martha Tyler John, and Kenrick S. Thompson, "Should Traditional Sex Modes and Values Be Changed?" in *Controversial Issues in the Social Studies: A Contemporary Perspective*, ed. Raymond H. Muessig (Washington, D.C.: National Council for the Social Studies, 1975), pp. 87–121.

3. Morton Hunt, *Sexual Behavior in the 1970s* (Chicago: Playboy Press, 1974).

4. See William F. Ogburn, "The Changing Family," *The Family* 19 (July 1938), pp. 139–143.

5. George P. Murdock, *Social Structure* (New York: Free Press, 1949); William F. Ogburn, "The Changing Family," *The Family* 19 (July 1938), pp. 139–43; William J. Goode, "The Sociology of the Family," in *Sociology Today*, eds. Robert K. Merton, Leonard Broom, and Leonard J. Cottrell (New York: Basic Books, 1959); and Talcott Parsons and Robert F. Bales, *Family, Socialization and Interaction Process* (Glencoe, IL: Free Press, 1955).

6. Rene Spitz, "Hospitalism: Genesis of Psychiatric Conditions in Early Childhood," *Psychoanalytic Study of the Child*, 1945, pp. 53–74.

7. U.S. Bureau of the Census, *Statistical Abstract of the United States, 1987* (Washington, D.C.: U.S. Government Printing Office, 1987), p. 80.

8. William J. Goode, *After Divorce* (New York: Free Press, 1956).

9. Alexander A. Plateris, *Increases in Divorces: United States—1967* (Washington, D.C.: U.S. Government Printing Office), p. 14.

10. Ibid.

11. Mary Jo Bane, *Here to Stay: American Families in the Twentieth Century* (New York: Basic Books, 1976), pp. 31–33.

12. *Statistical Abstract of the United States, 1987*, p. 382.

13. Kenneth Keniston, *All Our Children: The American Family under Pressure* (New York: Harcourt Brace Jovanovich, 1977), p. 21.

14. Richard Neely, "Barter in the Court," *The New Republic*, February 10, 1986, p. 13.

15. Ibid., p. 14.

16. Ibid., p. 16.

17. "NBC News White Paper: Divorce is Changing America," June 3, 1986.

18. Ibid.

19. Ibid.

20. Ibid.

21. Ibid.

22. John F. Cuber and Peggy B. Harroff, "Five Types of Marriage," in *Family in Transition*, eds. Arlene S. Skolnick and Jerome H. Skolnick (Boston: Little, Brown, 1971), pp. 287–299.

23. William J. Goode, "Family Disorganization," in *Contemporary Social Problems*, eds. Robert K. Merton and Robert Nisbet, 4th ed. (New York: Harcourt Brace Jovanovich, 1976), p. 543.

24. "Battered Families: A Growing Nightmare," *U.S. News & World Report*, January 15, 1979, p. 60.

25. Ibid., p. 60.

26. Ibid., p. 62.

27. Ibid., p. 60.

28. Ibid., p. 62.

29. Lewis Koch and Joanne Koch, "Parent Abuse—A New Plague," *Parade*, January 27, 1980, p. 14.

30. Ibid., p. 14.

31. Ibid., p. 14.

32. Federal Bureau of Investigation, *Uniform Crime Reports for the United States, 1986* (Washington, D.C.: U.S. Government Printing Office, 1987).

33. Suzanne K. Steinmetz and Murray A. Straus, *Violence in the Family* (New York: Dodd, Mead, 1974), p. 3.

34. Ibid., p. 9.

35. John O'Brien, "Violence in Divorce Prone Families," *Journal of Marriage and the Family* 33 (November 1971), pp. 692–698.

36. "Battered Families: A Growing Nightmare," p. 62.

37. Ibid., p. 62.

38. Ibid., p. 62.

39. Richard J. Gelles, *The Violent Home: The Study of Physical Aggression between Husbands and Wives* (Beverly Hills, CA: Sage, 1974).

40. Murray A. Straus, Richard Gelles, and Suzanne Steinmetz, *Behind Closed Doors: A Survey of Family Violence in America* (Garden City, NY: Doubleday, 1979).

41. Ibid.

42. Murray A. Straus, "Wife Beating: How Common and Why?" *Victimology* 2, no. 3–4 (Fall–Winter 1977), pp. 443–458.

43. Gelles, *The Violent Home*; Murray A. Straus, "Leveling, Civility, and Violence in the Family," *Journal of Marriage and Family* 36 (February 1974), pp. 13–30.

44. Alfred Kadushin and Judith A. Martin, *Child Welfare Services*, 4th ed. (New York: Macmillan, 1988), pp. 218–327.

45. Vincent De Francis, *Child Abuse—Preview of a Nationwide Survey* (Denver: American Humane Association, Children's Division, 1963), pp. 5–6.

46. Ibid., p. 6.

47. Larry Silver et al., "Does Violence Breed Violence? Contribution from a Study of the Child-Abuse Syndrome," *American Journal of Psychiatry*, September 1969, pp. 404–407.

48. Kadushin and Martin, *Child Welfare Services*, pp. 243–247; and "Battered Families: A Growing Nightmare," p. 60.

49. Jerome E. Leavitt, *The Battered Child* (Morristown, NJ: General Learning Press, 1974), p. 3.

50. George C. Curtis, "Violence Breeds Violence—Perhaps?" in Leavitt, *The Battered Child*, p. 74.

51. Leavitt, *The Battered Child*, p. 183.

52. Alfred Kadushin, *Child Welfare Services*, 3d ed. (New York: Macmillan, 1980), p. 160.

53. Ibid., p. 161.

54. LeRoy Pelton, "Child Abuse and Neglect—The Myth of Classlessness," *American Journal of Orthopsychiatry* 48, no. 4 (October 1978), pp. 608–616.

55. Kadushin and Martin, *Child Welfare Services*, pp. 277–282.

56. American Humane Society, *National Analysis of Official Child Neglect and Abuse Reporting* (Denver: American Humane Society, 1978).

57. Kadushin, *Child Welfare Services*.

58. Vincent De Francis, *Special Skills in Child Protective Services* (Denver: American Humane Association, 1958), p. 11.

59. American Humane Society, *National Analysis of Official Child Neglect and Abuse Reporting*.

60. C. Henry Kempe and Ray E. Helfer, *Helping the Battered Child and His Family* (Philadelphia: J. B. Lippincott, 1972); Kadushin, *Child Welfare Services*; Kadushin and Martin, *Child Welfare Services*; and Leavitt, *The Battered Child*.

61. Ibid.

62. Vincent De Francis, *The Fundamentals of Child Protection* (Denver: American Humane Association, 1955), p. 2.

63. Ellen Thomson, *Child Abuse—A Community Challenge* (Buffalo, NY: Henry Stewart, 1971), p. 44.

64. Kadushin and Martin, *Child Welfare Services*, p. 278.

65. Edith Varon, "Communication: Client, Community, and Agency," *Social Work*, April 1964.

66. Anna Mae Sandusky, "Services to Neglected Children," *Children*, January–February 1960, p. 24.

67. Kadushin, *Child Welfare Services*, p. 212.

68. Henry Maas and Richard Engler, *Children in Need of Parents* (New York: Columbia University Press, 1959).

69. Kadushin, *Child Welfare Services*, p. 274.

70. *Statistical Abstract of the United States, 1987*, p. 61.

71. "Fact Sheet on Adolescent Pregnancy" (Milwaukee: Planned Parenthood of Wisconsin, 1986).

72. Lacey Fosburgh, "The Make-Believe World of Teenage Maternity," *New York Times Magazine*, August 7, 1977, p. 7.

73. Ibid., p. 7.

74. Art Levine, "Taking on Teen Pregnancy," *U.S. News & World Report*, March 23, 1987, p. 67.

75. Ibid., p. 67.

76. *Statistical Abstract of the United States, 1987*, p. 61.

77. Ibid., p. 61.

78. C. P. Green and K. Poteteiger, "Major Problems for Minors," *Society*, 1978, pp. 10–13.

79. *Statistical Abstract of the United States, 1987*, p. 61.

80. Alfred C. Kinsey et al., *Sexual Behavior in the Human Male* (Philadelphia: W. B. Saunders, 1948); and *Sexual Behavior in the Human Female* (Philadelphia: W. B. Saunders, 1953).

81. Ursula S. Myers, "Illegitimacy and Services to Single Parents," in *Introduction to Social Welfare Institutions*, ed. Charles Zastrow, 2d ed. (The Dorsey Press: Homewood, IL: 1982), p. 189.

82. Levine, "Taking on Teen Pregnancy," p. 67.

83. Ibid., p. 67.

84. Myers, "Illegitimacy and Services to Single Parents," p. 176.

I regard sex as the central problem of life. . . . Sex lies at the root of life, and we can never learn to reverence life until we know how to understand sex.

HAVELOCK ELLIS[1]

6

HUMAN SEXUALITY VARIATIONS, SEX COUNSELING, AND SEX THERAPY

Amazingly, we were able to put a person in space before we understood the physiology of sexual orgasms.[2] This chapter:

- Presents a brief look at sexual expression in history and in other cultures.

- Presents a historical review of scientific studies of sexuality.

- Describes three types of sexual variances:
  Tolerated sex variances—sexual actions such as premarital intercourse and masturbation that are generally tolerated in our society.
  Asocial sex variances—sexual actions such as incest and rape that are highly disapproved of in our society.
  Structural sex variances—sexual actions such as homosexuality that are also disapproved of in our society yet have supportive social structures.

- Discusses personal sexual concerns—sexual difficulties or concerns such as premature ejaculation among males and painful intercourse among females.

- Describes sex counseling and sex therapy.

SEX IN HISTORY AND IN OTHER CULTURES

Practically every conceivable sexual activity and conjugal arrangement, to some degree, has been socially acceptable to at least some people. Sex only to

This chapter was coauthored by Lloyd G. Sinclair, MSSW, ACSW. Mr. Sinclair is a psychotherapist at Midwest Center for Sex Therapy (Madison, Wisconsin) and is certified as a sex educator and a sex therapist by the American Association of Sex Educators, Counselors, and Therapists (AASECT).

procreate, oral-genital relations, premarital sex, adultery, anal intercourse, monogamy, polyandry (more than one husband), polygyny (more than one wife), homosexuality, lifelong celibacy—each has been a method of responding to sexual desire that has been socially approved by some human community. Not even incest, which is among the most widely prohibited of sexual relationships, has been universally tabooed.[3] Some ancient cultures encouraged incest among royal families as a way to maintain the wealth and power among a small number of people, and as a way to ensure the purity of the royal line.

Male and female homosexuality in ancient Greece was not only acceptable but was encouraged. Today, homosexual practices are acceptable in some subcultures of the United States and Europe.

In northern Sumatra, all youths are taught homosexual techniques from older adolescents of the same sex. Interestingly, most of these young people easily make the transition to heterosexual relationships as they become older and marry.[4]

Only a small minority (the United States is one) of the 190 contemporary societies studied by Clellan Ford and Frank Beach discourage or prohibit sexual expression by children.[5] Inhabitants of the Trobriand Islands encourage premarital sex because it is thought to be an important preparation for marriage. Some societies permit young boys and girls to play husband and wife even before puberty. In Asia the Lepcha society believes that girls need sexual intercourse in order to mature.[6] In contrast, in many Moslem and South American cultures, premarital chastity for women is highly revered: A woman who has premarital sex is apt to be shamed and ostracized. However, in some other developing countries it has even been the practice of some low-income parents to sell their adolescent daughters as prostitutes, particularly to tourists.

There are some cultures in which rape is practically nonexistent, as among the Arapesh of New Guinea. In that society males are socialized to be peaceful and nonaggressive. In contrast, in the Gussi tribe in Kenya the rate of rape is at least five times higher than in the United States. In this tribe both men and women are socialized to be aggressive and competitive—and women often resist sexual relations, even with their husbands.[7]

It has been fairly common throughout history for soldiers to rape the women of the societies they conquered. In the past some Eskimo husbands offered male guests the privilege of spending the night with their wives, and it was considered a serious insult for guests to refuse. White slave owners in our past history often prohibited their slaves from marrying, and some attempted to improve the characteristics of black children by mating female slaves with a black male who was considered to have desirable characteristics. Some of the mentally retarded in various societies have been sterilized in an effort to prevent them from having children. Hitler, in Nazi Germany in the 1930s and 1940s, mated women with certain soldiers in an effort to "breed" offspring with the characteristics he considered desirable.

Some parents in Europe suggest fathers should have intercourse with their daughters to teach them about sex, although this is most often viewed as an excuse for incest or sexual abuse. Although there is a myth in our society that the elderly do not and should not get involved in sexual activity, many elderly persons are sexually active and may have more than one sexual partner. In many cultures males greet one another with a kiss and a hug.

Sex-change operations have been occurring since the early 1930s. They became publicized in 1952 when Christine Jorgensen announced to the world that she had undergone transsexual surgery to change her from being biologically male to biologically female. As is often the case with sexual matters that are little understood by the larger society, Jorgensen's surgery met with widespread disapproval. Nonetheless, several thousand people have since undergone such operations.[8]

Clearly, what is defined as acceptable and unacceptable sexual behavior varies from culture to culture and from one time period to another. Let us look briefly at the history of our changing sexual attitudes and mores. Perhaps the major influence on the current beliefs of Western culture related to sex has been the Judeo-Christian tradition. The Old Testament approved of sexual intercourse only within marriage. The purpose of intercourse, it was asserted, should only be to conceive children. The Jewish religion was somewhat more liberal, as it stated that heterosexual intercourse

BOX 6.1

Sexuality in Mangaia

M angaia is an island in the South Pacific. The Mangaians have elaborate rituals that use sex for pleasure and for procreation.

Mangaian boys are instructed on how to masturbate at around the ages of 7 and 8. At around age 13 they have a superincision ritual (in which a slit is made on the full length of the skin on the top part of the penis). This ritual initiates them into manhood. During this ritual they are also given instruction in how to kiss and suck breasts, on how to bring a female partner to orgasm several times before they have an orgasm themselves, and on how to perform cunnilingus. Approximately two weeks later each boy is introduced to sexual intercourse with an experienced woman. She shows him intercourse in various positions and further instructs him on how to delay ejaculation in order to have simultaneous orgasms with his partner.

Mangaian girls also receive sexual instruction from adult women. Following such instruction, Mangaian boys and girls actively seek each other out, and many have coitus nearly every night. Teenage girls are raised to believe virility in a male is proof of his desire for her. In particular, a male is valued who is able to vigorously continue in-and-out action of intercourse for fifteen to thirty minutes or longer while the female moves her hips back and forth in a rhythmic motion. A male who is unable to perform this act is looked down on.

By age 20 the average male is likely to have had ten or more girlfriends, and the average "nice" girl will have had three or four successive boyfriends. Mangaian parents encourage such sexual experiences because they want their daughters and sons to find a marriage partner with whom they are sexually compatible. At around age 18 Mangaians typically have sex every night. Men are brought up to believe that bringing their partner to orgasm is one of the chief sources of sexual pleasures for males.

Source: John C. Messinger, "The Luck of the Irish," and Donald S. Marshall, "Too Much in Mangaia," both in *Human Sexual Behavior*, eds. D. S. Marshall and R. C. Suggs (New York: Basic Books, 1971).

for pleasure within a marriage was not sinful. Masturbation, homosexuality, and all other sexual expressions outside of marriage were viewed as sinful.

Early Christianity took a more conservative position. It regarded sex as evil and degrading and asserted that it should only be indulged in by married couples for the purpose of procreation. This remains the official position of the Roman Catholic Church.

The Protestant Reformation, which began in the 16th century, advocated a strict and repressive sexual code. The Protestant ethic, which was prominent at this time, emphasized the importance of hard work and asserted that it was morally wrong to engage in pleasurable activities of any kind. Denying sexual interests and refraining from sexual activities except to procreate were seen as virtues. A major immigrant group that began colonizing America in the 17th century were the Puritans, who rigidly adhered to this ascetic (self-denial of pleasurable activities) life.

The views promulgated by the Protestant ethic be-

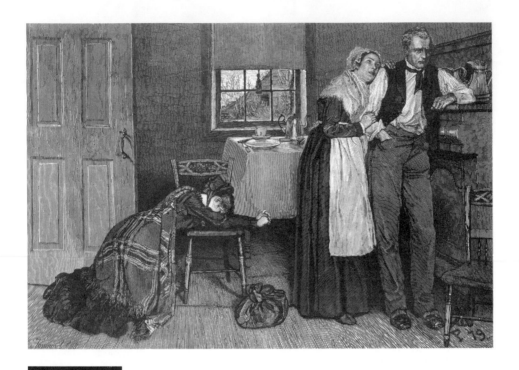

"Fallen women" are the stuff of melodrama today, but less than a century ago, middle-class morality absolutely forbade sex for women before marriage. This late Victorian print, entitled The Outcast's Return, *makes us wonder how any young woman would consider even a moment's indiscretion when faced with parental reactions like these.*

came incorporated into what has become known as "Victorian morality." The name is derived from the reign of Queen Victoria of England. Victorian morality was prominent in the 19th and early 20th centuries. John Gagnon and Bruce Henderson note: "The Puritan-dominated sex ethic became that of penny-pinching Adam Smith.... The moral values of the new middle classes, with their belief in hard work, delayed gratification, and avoidance of pleasure, including the sexual, were to triumph during the Victorian age, not only in England but in most of Western Europe."[9]

Victorian morality all but banished sexuality from discussions in respectable relationships. Modesty was stressed to the point of extreme prudishness. In polite conversations simple anatomical terms such as *leg* or *breast* were taboo, and instead were referred to as limbs and bosoms. The limbs (legs) of tables were

often covered by long tablecloths so that sexual feelings would not be aroused. Women did not "get pregnant"; they were "in a family way" and were expected to remain at home during their "condition." In Philadelphia men and women were not allowed to visit art galleries together for fear their modesty might be offended by the classical statues—and plastic fig leaves were added to the genital areas of the statues to minimize their offensiveness.[10]

Middle- and upper-class women, before marriage, were expected to be virgins. There were considered to be two types of women. The good women were virgins—undamaged property—who were fit to marry. The bad were "fallen women" who were premaritally sexually active. They were pitied, but not consoled, since their "fall" was attributed to their own weakness. They were no longer considered fit to marry but were

Sexual attitudes have been profoundly affected by the onset of AIDS. Many sexually active adults now limit the number of their sexual partners. This pamphlet, published by the San Francisco AIDS Foundation, promotes condom use and open communication between partners as additional means of reducing the risk of contracting AIDS.

nevertheless considered available for nonmarital relations with men. A popular myth throughout this period held that men were inherently more sexual than women. This led to the development—still very prevalent today—of two standards of acceptable behavior, the so-called double standard. Although it was hoped that men would remain chaste, it was thought that men had "animal natures." Men were seldom criticized for having premarital and extramarital relations. They were thought to have much stronger sexual drives than women, and it was thought that prostitutes and lower-class women were proper outlets for those excessive sexual urges, too beastly to impose on their wives.

Palen notes:

From this division of women—good and bad, mothers and whores—came the double standard that implicitly allowed men to be sexually active but that forbade "nice girls" even to think about such things. Overt sexuality was condemned, while covert premarital or extramarital sex among men was tolerated as a necessary evil, given the male's more pressing sexual urges.[11]

Researchers have since found that the female sex drive is as strong as that of the male. Interestingly, even during the repressive years of the Puritan and Victorian eras there were always certain segments advocating more liberal expressions of sexuality. For example, in the Victorian era there was a profitable trade in erotic drawings and novels.

Since the turn of the last century there have been dramatic changes in sexual attitudes and behaviors. For example, in 1974 Morton Hunt found that most men and women have premarital sex, and most young women (ages 18 to 24) are not virgins at marriage.[12] Hunt also found the percentage of those having oral sexual experiences is increasing. The decade of the 1970s in the United States was viewed as a time of sexual permissiveness and experimentation, in which many people engaged in sexual behaviors that were previously uncommon. The 1980s has ushered in some reversal of this permissive trend, with a general movement toward fewer partners, more emphasis on long-term relationships, and a slower development of the sexual aspects of a relationship. This trend has been a response to a general dissatisfaction with sexual behavior divorced from intimacy, as well as to the very real threat of increased susceptibility to disease (such as AIDS) for the person who has sexual contact with multiple partners.

At present there is ambiguity and confusion about what ought to be the sexual code and behavior of Americans. On the conservative end of the spectrum are certain groups, such as the Catholic Church and some fundamentalist religious organizations, that advocate that sex should only be for procreation and should be restricted to heterosexual, married people. The so-called missionary position (man on top) is considered the only acceptable position for intercourse. Such groups express considerable alarm that increased sexual permissiveness will destroy the moral fiber of the family and will ultimately result in the destruction of our society.

At the liberal end of the spectrum are groups and organizations that advocate that sex can legitimately be enjoyed for recreation as well as for procreation; how sex is expressed should be of no concern except to those consenting adults who participate.

Over the past several decades in Western culture more permissive attitutdes toward sex have emerged.

Sexual topics are presented more frankly and openly by the mass media, including by television, magazines, and newspapers. Nudity is displayed more—in movies, in magazines, and on television. No longer are women who have premarital sex considered unfit for marriage. One factor that appears to have led to increases in premarital and extramarital relations is the increased availability of birth control devices, particularly the pill.[13]

On the other hand, since the 1970s our country has become more conservative, and the sexual revolution appears to have slowed. There is less interest in recreational sex and more emphasis on a code that asserts that sexual relations should first have a base of love and commitment between the partners. Fear of acquiring such sexually transmitted diseases as genital herpes and AIDS has also led some segments of our population to turn to more conservative views of sexual behavior.

At present each individual goes through considerable personal turmoil in arriving at a sexual code of behavior that he or she is comfortable with and will seek to live by—particularly because there is a wide range of conflicting codes that peers, parents, and other pressure groups advocate be followed.

FORMAL STUDY OF SEX

Prior to the 20th century there were practically no scientific studies of sexuality. Since the turn of the century there have been a considerable number of studies, with three having profound effects: the studies by Sigmund Freud, Alfred Kinsey, and the team of William Masters and Virginia Johnson.

Sigmund Freud

Sigmund Freud was a psychoanalyst who theorized in his writings (from 1895 to 1925) that the sex drive was

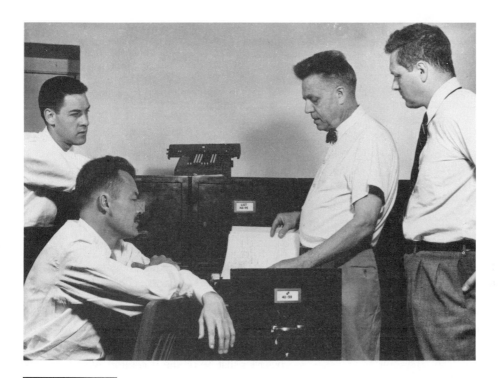

Pioneer Sexologist Alfred Kinsey (second from right) and his associates review case histories for Sexual Behavior in the Human Female *(1953). Kinsey's studies revealed the discrepancy between Americans' sexual mores and their sexual practices.*

a fundamental part of human life. Freud realized that many people had sexual conflicts. He made sexuality a central focus of his theories and defined most emotions and behaviors as being primarily sexual in nature. He thought sexuality included physical love, affectionate impulses, self-love, love for parents and children, and friendship associations. He advanced a number of controversial theories. He asserted that everyone, from birth on, has sexual interests. He stated that boys at an early age (around age 3) fall sexually in love with their mother and fear their father will discover this interest and then castrate them. Thus, he believed boys suffer from castration anxiety at this age. Girls, on the other hand, at about the same age (age 3) fall sexually in love

with their father. Freud asserted that girls discover they do not have a penis, and their desire to have one leads to penis envy. Girls conclude they lost their penis at an earlier age when their mother discovered their sexual interest in their father developing. Young girls believe their mother castrated them because of their love for their father. Girls, Freud believed, also suffer from castration anxiety, but the source and nature of the anxiety is different from boys. Girls have castration anxiety because they believe having been castrated makes them inferior to males.

Freud's notion that sexuality was a critical part of human development initially provoked shock and outrage. Before his time it was thought that sexual interests played only a minor role in human development. Gradually, his theories had a liberating effect, as sexuality slowly became recognized as playing a key role in personality development. Freud's theories also led to increased communication about sexuality and stimulated scientific investigations of this topic. Perhaps Freud's greatest contribution was this liberating effect on sexuality. Unfortunately, Freud developed a number of hypotheses and advanced them as "truths," without scientifically testing their validity. Consequently, some of Freud's specific hypotheses about sexuality have been hotly disputed and widely challenged—for example, his hypotheses involving castration anxiety in boys and his hypotheses about castration anxiety and penis envy in girls.

Alfred Kinsey

In 1948 Alfred C. Kinsey, an American zoologist, published *Sexual Behavior in the Human Male*, which was based on interviews with 5,300 white American men. This study investigated sexual practices and found that the sexual behavior of males differed substantially from the stated moral values of the time. One third of the respondents had had at least one homosexual experience since puberty; 83 percent had had premarital relations; half of those who were married had had extramarital affairs; and 92 percent had masturbated to orgasm.[14]

Five years later, in 1953, Kinsey published *Sexual Behavior in the Human Female*, which was based on interviews with 5,940 white American women.[15] This study showed, to some extent, that the double standard was still operating. But it also found that women were not as asexual as was commonly thought. More than half of these respondents had had premarital relations, and one fourth of those who were married had had extramarital relations.

Kinsey's findings were widely publicized by the mass media and directly confronted many people for the first time with the wide gaps that existed between sexual mores and sexual practices. Kinsey's studies may have led people to become freer in their sexual behav-

ior, or at least to feel less guilt about sexual behavior that was inconsistent with traditional sexual mores. The studies certainly challenged the belief that women were basically uninterested in sex.

William Masters and Virginia Johnson

In 1957 William Masters and Virginia Johnson began their study of the physiology of human sexual response, which culminated in the publication of their classic text, *Human Sexual Response*.[16] Their contribution to the scientific understanding of human sexual response has been enormous. Their findings have generally stood the test of others' replications. Masters and Johnson were the first to provide accurate information about the physiology of human sexual response based on laboratory observation of people's responses rather than their personal reports. Their findings destroyed a number of myths. Freud, for example, had asserted that vaginal orgasm in women was superior to clitoral orgasm. Masters and Johnson found that the clitoris was the area having the most nerve endings (and therefore the area of greatest pleasure) in a female's genitals. The clitoris was essentially the main area being stimulated in both clitoral orgasm and vaginal orgasm, and therefore there were no physiological differences between these orgasms. This finding enhanced the sex lives of many women who were fruitlessly searching for the vaginal orgasm—many of whom felt inadequate or that they were missing out on something. Other important findings were that men and women are able to enjoy sexual activity into advanced age and that some women have numerous orgasms in succession.

On completion of this research Masters and Johnson began to treat persons with sexual dysfunctions, such as premature ejaculation in males and failure to achieve orgasm in females. They departed radically from the prevailing thinking of the day, which viewed sexual dysfunction as a by-product of other individual or relationship problems. Instead, Masters and Johnson primarily dealt with the sexual problem and treated persons in short-term (two weeks) therapy. Extremely successful results were achieved, and their methods and outcomes were subsequently published in *Human Sexual Inadequacy*.[17] Most contemporary forms of sex therapy are based on Masters and Johnson's original work.

VARIANCES RATHER THAN SEXUAL PROBLEMS

Human beings are capable of expressing their sexuality in an amazing variety of ways due to both biological determinants and learning. Everyone has some form of a sex drive, but how it is expressed will be shaped by biological predispositions, the attitudes of others, rituals, schools, parents, acceptable role models, trial and error as to what is pleasurable and what is not, peers, and so on. Gagnon and Henderson note that the learning of ways to express our sexuality is closely related to the process of forming our gender identity (our self-concept of maleness or femaleness):

We assemble our sexuality beginning with gender identity, and we build upon that the activities we come to think of as fitting to ourselves. Our belief in what is correct and proper results more from our social class, religion, style of family life, and concepts of masculinity and femininity than from the specifically sexual things that we learn.[18]

If we were to use a social problem approach to studying the wide variety of sexual behaviors, some difficulties would arise. A social problems approach would seek to classify as social problems all sexual behaviors that differ from a norm to such an extent that a significant number of people (or a number of significant people) feel that something should be done about it. Using this approach requires delineating the code or norm that specifies which sexual acts are acceptable and which are unacceptable. The difficulty with this

approach is that there is no general consensus about which are acceptable sexual expressions and which are not. In addition, as the Kinsey study showed, there is a vast difference between the purported sexual norms of society and people's actual sexual behavior.

Another shortcoming in using the social problems approach is that those acts that would be identified as social problems would then be stigmatized as "sick," "degenerate," or "perverted." During the Victorian era, our society suffered too much from the efforts of some to make value judgments about what is inappropriate sexual behavior. This text will not attempt to force a specific sexual code onto readers—too many other groups are still trying to do this. Instead of the term *social problems*, the term *sex variances* will be used to refer to sexual expressions that are of concern to certain segments of our society.

Definitions of acceptable and nonacceptable sexual behavior tend to change over time. Certain sexual behaviors, which were once widely condemned, are now generally accepted. Masturbation, for example, used to be viewed as sinful, immoral, and unhealthy, but is now widely practiced and is recommended by sex therapists as a way to learn about one's sexuality. Not long ago oral sex was considered immoral or wrong, but now a large majority of young people have engaged in oral sex.[19]

It may be argued that laws in a society can be used to determine acceptable and nonacceptable sexual expressions. Sexual acts that are prohibited, it might be argued, identify nonacceptable sexual behaviors.

However, present laws relating to sexual behaviors were primarily enacted during the Victorian era. As such, existing laws relating to sex remain highly conservative. There is a considerable time lag between laws relating to sexuality and existing attitudes and norms about sexuality. Herant Katchadourian and Donald T. Lunde note: "Almost all sexual activity that may occur between husband and wife, with the exception of kissing, caressing, and vaginal intercourse, is defined as criminal in every state of the union."[20]

Some acts that are currently fairly widely practiced, but are still illegal, include premarital sex, oral sex, masturbation, extramarital sex, cohabitation, and (in some states) sex in any position other than the missionary position. Historically, many laws imposed severe penalties for those found guilty. For example, the 17th century Puritans made extramarital sex a crime punishable by death.

Laws, to some extent, are an indicator of how societies feel about certain sexual behaviors. For example, the stiff penalties assigned to rape and child molestation suggest strong disapproval. Yet, for the reasons cited above, laws cannot be used as the only measure of prevailing views about acceptable sexual behavior in a society.

TYPES OF SEXUAL VARIANCES

A useful classification of sexual variances is provided by Joseph Julian and William Kornblum, who identify three categories: tolerated sex variance, asocial sex variance, and structural sex variance.[21] Tolerated sex variances are sexual behaviors, such as masturbation, that are generally tolerated in our society. Asocial sex variances are behaviors that our society strongly disapproves of and that do not have supportive social structures. Behaviors in this category include incest and rape. Structural sex variances are also generally disapproved of in our society but differ from the previous category by having supportive social structures. Behaviors in this category include homosexuality, prostitution, and pornography.

Tolerated Sex Variance

Included in this category are masturbation, premarital intercourse, sex between consenting adults in a variety of positions, and heterosexual oral-genital contact. There are a few groups (such as certain fundamentalist religious groups) who assert such acts are immoral and ought to be prohibited. Laws in some states prohibit such sexual behavior but are seldom enforced. Most segments in our society, however, tolerate these acts.

John Gagnon and William Simon note these acts "are generally disapproved, but . . . either serve a socially useful purpose and/or occur so often among a population with such low social visibility that only a small number are ever actually sanctioned for engaging in."[22] Because these sexual behaviors tend to be tolerated in our society, we will move on to examine sexual variances that are disapproved.

Asocial Sex Variance

This category of sex variance includes those acts that elicit widespread, strong disapproval and at the same time do not have a social structure that supports such acts. Acts in this category include child molestation, incest, rape, voyeurism, and exhibitionism. People who engage in these behaviors usually act alone; that is, they do not have a social group that encourages and rewards such acts. All of these sex variances are prohibited by laws.

CHILD MOLESTATION   Child molestation involves an adult sexually abusing a child. Sexual abuse not only includes sexual intercourse (genital or anal) but also oral-genital contact, fondling, and exposing oneself to a child. An unambiguous definition of abuse is not available. Sexual intercourse is definitely abuse, but some forms of contact are harder to judge as being abuse. At some point, hugging, kissing, and fondling become inappropriate.

Child molestation is generally regarded as one of the most despicable sexual offenses in our society. The public fears this type of sexual abuse will destroy the "innocence" of the child and may lead to severe psychological trauma for the child.

How extensive is child molestation? McCaghy cites a survey of 1,800 university students that reported 35 percent of the women and 30 percent of the men had had childhood experiences of being sexually molested.[23] Julian and Kornblum report that an estimated 20 to 25 percent of girls and 10 to 12 percent of boys are sexually molested before the age of 13, usually by family members or adults who are trusted by the family.[24]

BOX 6.2

Learning Sexual Behavior via Scripts

Sociologists have made a major contribution to an understanding of human sexuality by asserting that sexual behavior (as well as most other human behavior) is developed through learning "scripts." *Scripts* (as in a play in a theater) are plans that we learn and then carry around in our heads. These scripts enable us to conceptualize where we are in our activities and provide us with direction for completing our activities and accomplishing our goals. Scripts are also devices for helping us to remember what we have done in the past.

Sexual scripts result from elaborate prior learning in which we acquire an etiquette of sexual behavior. According to this script approach, little in sexual behavior activity is spontaneous. Scripts tell us who appropriate sexual partners are, what sexual activity is expected, where and when the sexual activity should occur, and what the sequence of the different sexual behaviors should be.

Scripts vary greatly from one culture to another. Hortense Powdermaker provides the following description of a script about female masturbation that is generally held by the Lesu of the South Pacific:

A woman will masturbate if she is sexually excited and there is no man to satisfy her. A couple may be having intercourse in the same house, or near enough for her to see them, and she may thus become aroused. She then sits down and bends her right leg so that her heel presses against her genitalia. Even young girls of about six years may do this quite casually as they sit on the ground. The women and men talk about it freely, and there is no shame attached to it. It is a customary position for women to take, and they learn it in childhood. They never use their hands for manipulation.[a]

---

[a]Quoted from Hortense Powdermaker, *Life in Lesu* (New York: W. W. Norton, 1933), pp. 276–277.

In the past few decades there have been several well-publicized cases of child molestation. In the 1960s, a Houston man was arrested for killing nearly 30 runaway male adolescents after having homosexual experiences with them. In 1979 John Gacy was arrested in Chicago for enticing 33 male adolescents into his home, sexually assaulting them, and then killing and burying them under his home. On March 11, 1977, Roman Polanski (a noted film director) was arrested in Los Angeles and charged with unlawful sexual inter-course, child molestation, supplying a minor with the drug Quaalude, oral copulation, sodomy, and rape via the use of drugs. A teenage girl was the alleged victim of these charges. He confessed to and was found guilty of only the first charge through plea bargaining. While awaiting sentencing, he fled the United States. In 1984 several members of the staff of a Los Angeles day-care center, most of whom are women, were charged with dozens of sexual assaults on the children entrusted in their care.

Who are child molesters? The stereotype is that a molester is a stranger who lurks in the dark, waiting to pounce on a child who is walking or playing alone. The fact is that in most cases the offender is an acquaintance, friend, or relative.[25] (If the offender is a relative, the abuse is called incest.) Force is rarely used, and violence probably occurs in no more than 3 percent of all cases.[26] The abuser generally gains sexual access to the child by manipulation and enticement rather than by use of a threat of force or harm. Actual intercourse is also rare, with the abuse usually being limited to genital fondling.[27] In a small proportion of cases the child may even initiate the contact—although such initiation does not justify the adult becoming an active participant.

A. Nicholas Groth has identified two categories of child molesters: fixated and regressed.[28] A *fixated* child molester's primary sexual object choice is children and, as such, he would always prefer a child as a sexual partner over an adult. A *regressed* child molester is a person whose usual sexual interest is in another adult, but when faced with massive stress (marital difficulty, loss of job, death in family, and so on), he "regresses" emotionally (becomes a psychologically younger person) and acts out sexually toward children to meet his needs. Regressed child molesters generally seek female children as partners; fixated molesters are generally interested in male children. Most incest perpetrators are of the regressed type; they generally function well in society, are in a stable heterosexual relationship, but manage stress inappropriately by acting out sexually toward children.

There is a tendency for child molesters who are arrested to be members of the lower class. This tendency may be due to class differences in the willingness to report molestation to the police, or it may represent a "true class difference." The average age is between 30 and 40, which contradicts the stereotype that molesters are "dirty old men." Only about 20 percent of child molesters target young males as victims.[29]

How traumatic is the molesting for the child? Some authorities believe a brief, nonviolent experience with a molester is often only mildly upsetting to the child.[30] The factors that determine how traumatic the molestation will be for the child include (*a*) the relationship between the child and the adult (it is more damaging to the further development of trust to be abused by someone you are close to than by a stranger); (*b*) the frequency and duration of the abuse; (*c*) the actual sexual behaviors engaged in; (*d*) the reactions of persons if the abuse becomes revealed; (*e*) the child's general mental and emotional health and coping strategies; and (*f*) the availability and use of professional intervention by the abuser, the victim, and others (such as the parents).

INCEST   Incest is defined as sexual relations between blood relatives. Typically, the definition is extended to include sex between certain nonblood relatives, such as between a stepparent and a child. In the past, families generally attempted to "hide" this type of abuse, and it usually was not reported. Now, with an increasing openness about human sexuality, there is a rising willingness for family members to seek professional help.

In the largest proportion of incest cases reported to the police, the sexual abuse is between father or stepfather and daughter.[31] However, most incest cases are never reported to the police. Brother-sister incest is actually the most common form of incest.[32] This may or may not be sexual abuse. If the children are approximately the same age and the sexual activity is mutual and not coerced, this type of incest may be considered normal sexual experimentation. However, if the children are more than a few years apart in age, the potential exists for the younger child to be coerced into activity she or he is not comfortable with. At that point consent no longer exists, and nonconsenting sex is sexual abuse.

It is extremely difficult to determine the true incidence of child sexual abuse. The incest taboo has been extremely effective in preventing its widespread reporting but much less effective in preventing its occurrence.

Most often incest occurs in the child's home. The child is usually enticed or pressured, rather than physically forced, to participate. The age range of the abused child is from several months to adulthood, although most reports involve teenagers.[33] Children are unlikely to report sexual abuse because they often have loyalties toward the abuser and realistically fear the consequences for themselves, for the abuser, and for the family.

Causes of Incest   Why does incest occur? Students of sexology have long known that people frequently use sexual behavior to achieve nonsexual rewards. For example, a teenage boy might wish to have intercourse with his girlfriend (sexual behavior) not primarily because he loves her or for the sexual gratification, but rather to enhance his status with his friends, and therefore his ego (nonsexual reward).

Adults who are threatened by and fearful of the rejection of other adults often turn to children, who are nonthreatening and generally unconditionally loving, for reassurance. This need for acceptance can develop into the adult initiating sexual behavior (especially if the adult was sexually abused as a child, as is often the case), since many people view sexual behavior as the ultimate acceptance and ego validation. Most child molesters intend no harm to their victims; they are psychologically needy people who use children in their own battle for emotional survival.

Effects of Incest   Blair and Rita Justice have studied the consequences of incest at three different points in time: while the incest is going on, when the incest is discovered, and the long-term effects in future years.[34] It is important to bear in mind that incest is a symptom of a disturbed family system.

First, we will look at the effects while the incest is occurring. A daughter who has sex with her father often gains special power over him; she controls the power of a very important secret. The daughter can receive special privileges from the father, which makes the other siblings (and even the mother) jealous. Role confusion often occurs. The daughter is still a child, but at times she is a lover and an equal to her father. The daughter often does not know if her father is going to act as a parent or as a lover, so she is confused about when or whether she should respond to her father as a child or as an equal. The mother may become both a parent and a rival to her daughter. Siblings may also become confused about who is in charge and how to relate to their sister who is receiving special privileges.

Fathers in an incestuous family may become jealous and overpossessive of their daughters.

As the daughter grows older she wants to be more independent and to spend more time with other teenagers. Often, she grows more resentful of her father's possessiveness. To make a break from the father she may run away or tell someone about the incest. Or, she may passively resist the father's rules by, for example, staying out later at night than the time he sets. In a small number of cases incest is discovered when the daughter becomes pregnant. At times incest is discovered by the mother who then may seek to stop the incest by reporting it to the police. (Sometimes the mother discovers the incest, but remains quiet.)

If the incest is reported to the police and criminal charges are filed against the father, the entire family is usually caught up in a traumatic, time-consuming, confusing, and costly legal process. When there is legal involvement, questions that the daughter is asked often result in embarrassment and humiliation. The daughter feels, at times, that her account of the incest is not believed. Or, she may feel blame is being placed on her rather than on her father. Once she is recognized as a victim of incest, she may, at times, be approached sexually by other men who now view her as "fair game."[35] Often she is removed from the home to prevent further abuse. In addition, the mother and father suffer considerable embarrassment and humiliation. Their marriage may become so conflictful that it ends in divorce.

The long-term effects of incest vary from child to child. Younger children usually do not as fully realize the significance of the sexual behavior and tend to suffer less guilt than adolescent victims. However, with young children there is always the danger that as they grow older and recognize that society condemns incest, they may start blaming themselves for having participated. Possible long-term effects on the daughter include low self-esteem, guilt, and depression.

The daughter may also become angry at times with both parents for not protecting her and angry at the father for exploiting her. Moreover, she may believe she is somehow to blame for what happened; she may feel tainted by the experience and see herself as worthless, or as "damaged goods." Because of her guilt and

*Many communities now have rape crisis centers that offer counseling and medical and legal services
to rape victims.*

anger, she may in future years develop sexual difficulties and experience difficulty in relating to men. She may also have difficulty in trusting men, since she was betrayed and severely hurt by her father whom she deeply trusted. Some victims seek to blot out their pain and loneliness through self-destructive behavior such as prostitution, drug abuse, or suicide.

Some victims during their childhood years seek to deny or suppress the traumas associated with incest. When such victims become adults they are apt to experience difficulties in sexual performance and in other areas of their lives. Many of these adult victims finally acknowledge the traumas they experienced as children. Therapy is highly recommended for these adult victims to help them come to terms with these traumas and the fact that they were violated by someone they trusted.

Treatment of Incest   Because incest is but one symptom of a disturbed family, treating these families is difficult and complex. In the past when incest was reported, the victim (usually a teenage girl) was generally placed in a foster home, thus further victimizing her. Such action was likely to expose the sexual abuse to the local community. Often, neighbors, relatives, and friends expressed shock and began shunning all members of the family. The disruption usually intensified the marital conflict between husband and wife and generally led to permanent dissolution of the family. In some communities the husband was also prosecuted, which even further intensified the family conflicts.

In recent years a number of social service agencies have been seeking to keep the family intact, particularly when all three of the members involved (husband, wife, and victim) express a desire to maintain the family. A typical intervention requires the father's removal from the home for a period of six months to a year, during which time all family members are involved in individual and group treatment. During this time the incest perpetrator must acknowledge to his wife and daughter that he was entirely responsible for the sexual abuse, that he is sorry it happened, and that he will make the necessary lifestyle and value changes to ensure that the abuse will not recur. The nonabusing parent (typically the mother) is taught assertiveness. Intervention with the mother and daughter is also geared to improving their relationship, which is usually very damaged. The victim (typically the daughter) is helped in processing her anger, guilt, and confusion. Eventually all family members are seen in therapy together to help them build, perhaps for the first time, a healthy, functional family system.

FORCIBLE RAPE   Forced intercourse is a commonly committed violent crime in the United States.[36] More than 70,000 cases are reported annually, and many more cases go unreported. Victims of rape are hesitant to report cases for a variety of reasons. They feel that reporting the case will do them no good because they already have been victimized. They fear they may be humiliated by the questions the officer will ask. They are reluctant to press charges because they fear the reactions of the general public and of people close to them, including their boyfriends or husbands. Many fear that if they report the offense, the attacker will be more likely to attack them again. Some try to forget about it by not thinking or doing anything about it. Others fail to report it because they do not want to testify in court.

(In many states rape is defined as a crime that only males can commit. Several years ago there was a former beauty pageant winner who kidnapped a Mormon minister with whom she was infatuated. She tied him up, held him for a few days, and forced him to have sexual relations.[37] More cases where the woman is the attacker are now being reported.)

There is no profile that fits all rapists. Rapists vary considerably in terms of motivations for committing the rape, prior criminal record, education, occupation, marital status, and so on. In a majority of cases the rapist and his (or her) victim know each other on a first-name basis. A significant proportion of rapes are date rapes.

Rape is first an aggressive and second, a sexual act. Rape is a sexual expression of aggression, not an aggressive expression of sexuality. Many people wrongly believe rape occurs because the rapist manages his sexual arousal poorly or because he is "oversexed." Rape is, instead, the mismanagement of aggression where the rapist's gratification (if any) comes not from

the sexual act but rather from the expression of anger or control through the extreme violation of another's body. Most rapes occur between persons who know each other, contrary to the myth of the rapist who is a stranger.

There are a number of typologies for classifying rapists, depending on numerous variables. Perhaps the most useful was developed by A. Nicholas Groth,[38] who describes rapists as falling into one of three categories: the anger rapist, the power rapist, and the sadistic rapist.

The *anger rapist* performs his act to discharge feelings of pent-up anger and rage. He is brutal in the commission of his assault, using far more force than is necessary to gain sexual access to his victim. His aim is to hurt and debase his victim; forced sex is his ultimate weapon in degrading his victim.

The *power rapist* is interested in possessing his victim sexually, not harming her. He acts out of underlying feelings of inadequacy and is interested in controlling his victim. He uses only the amount of force necessary to gain her compliance. Often he will kidnap his victim and hold her under his control for a long period of time, perhaps engaging in sexual intercourse with her numerous times.

The *sadistic rapist* eroticizes aggression; that is, aggressive force creates sexual arousal in him. He is enormously gratified by his victim's torment, pain, and suffering. His offenses often are ritualistic and involve bondage and torture, particularly to the sexual organs.

We live in a society that promotes aggression and represses sexuality. In the United States males are socialized to be aggressive, including in seeking sexual gratification. Men, for example, are often expected to play the "aggressive" role in sex. In our culture sex and aggression are frequently confused and combined. In Swedish culture, where sexual information is readily available in the media but depictions of aggression are not, the rate of rape offenses is low. According to Janet Hyde, the confusion of sex and aggression in socialization practices may lead males to commit rape.

It may be, then, that rape is a means of proving masculinity for the male who is insecure in his role. For this reason, the statistics on the youthfulness of rapists make sense; youthful rapists may simply be young men who are trying to adopt the adult male role, who feel insecure about doing this, and who commit a rape as proof of their manhood. Further, heterosexuality is an important part of manliness. Raping a woman is a flagrant way to prove that one is a heterosexual. Interestingly, some rapists have a history of passivity, heterosexual inadequacy, and being called "queers" or "pansies" by their peers in adolescence. Rape for them may establish their heterosexual manliness.[39]

Effects on Victims   Ann Burgess and Lynda Holmstrom have found that rape is generally a severe crisis for the victims and that adjustment effects often persist for six months or longer.[40] They analyzed the reactions of 92 victims of forcible rape and found that victims undergo a series of emotional changes that they labeled the "rape trauma syndrome."[41]

This syndrome occurs in two phases: an acute phase and a long-term reorganization phase. The *acute phase* begins immediately after the rape (or attempted rape) and may last for several weeks. Victims have an expressive reaction in which they are apt to cry and have feelings of anger, fear, humiliation, tension, anxiety, and a desire for revenge. During this phase victims also usually have periods of controlled reaction in which they mask or deny their feelings and appear calm, composed, or subdued. Victims also experience many physical reactions during this phase, such as stomach pains, nausea, headaches, insomnia, and jumpiness. In addition, some women who were forced to have oral sex reported irritation or damage to the throat. Some who were forced to have anal intercourse report rectal pain and bleeding. Two feelings were especially common: fear and self-blame. Many women feared future physical violence or continued to suffer from the fear of being murdered during the attack. The self-blame is related to the tendency on the part of the victim and others to "blame the victim." Victims often spent hours agonizing over what they thought they had done to bring on the attack or over what they could have done to fight off the attacker. Common self-criticisms are, "If only I hadn't walked alone," "If only I had bolt-locked the door," "If only I hadn't worn that tight sweater," "If only I hadn't been dumb enough to trust that guy."

The *long-term reorganization phase* follows the acute phase. During this phase victims may experience a variety of major disruptions. These disruptions vary among victims. Some women who have been raped outdoors may develop fears about going outdoors; others who have been raped indoors may develop fears about being indoors. Some are unable to return to work, particularly if the rape occurred at work. Some quit their job and remain unemployed for a long time. Many fear the rapist will find them and assault them again. To attempt to avoid an assault by the same rapist, some move (sometimes several times), change their telephone number, or get an unlisted number. Some develop sexual phobias and have severe difficulties in returning to their regular sexual lifestyle. In some cases it takes several years before the victim returns to her previous lifestyle.

In addition, if the victim reports the rape, the police investigation and the trial (if it occurs) are further crises that are experienced. Police and the courts have a history of abusive and callous treatment of rape victims. The police have, at times, conveyed the idea that the victim may be fabricating the assault or suggested that she willingly agreed to have sex but then changed her mind. The police often ask embarrassing questions about the details of the assault, without showing much understanding and sympathy. In court it is common for the defense attorney to imply that the victim seduced the defendant, who then decided to call it rape. Victims are sometimes made to feel as if they are the ones who are on trial. Recently, fortunately, many police departments have developed sensitive crime units with specially trained officers to intervene in cases of rape and child sexual assault. With such units, victims are less likely to be further victimized by authorities. Also, a number of states have enacted "shield" evidence laws, which prohibit defense attorneys from asking questions about the victim's previous sexual experiences (except with the alleged rapist) during a rape trial. (In the past, defense attorneys at times sought to imply that the victim was promiscuous and therefore probably seduced the defendant.)

Because rape and its aftereffects are likely to be extremely traumatic, Burgess and Holmstrom urge counseling be made available to victims in order (*a*) to provide support and allow the victims to ventilate their

BOX 6.3

How to Attempt to Prevent Rape

There have been a number of suggestions to help women prevent rape and fight off an attacker. These suggestions include having and using secure locks on doors, not walking alone at night, and learning self-defense measures such as judo, aikido, tae kwon do (Korean karate), or jujitsu. Presenting oneself in an assertive fashion may be another way to stop a potential rape from occurring; being assertive is particularly useful in preventing acquaintance rape. Exercising regularly and keeping in shape are also recommended to give the potential victim the strength to fight back and the speed to run fast. Some experts recommend poking an attacker in the eyes or snapping a knee into his groin. Other experts recommend that every woman have a psychological strategy to use if attacked, such as telling the rapist that she has cancer of the cervix or a contagious venereal disease or that she is a carrier of the AIDS virus. If other preventive measures fail, some experts urge dissuading the attacker by regurgitating on him, which can be accomplished by sticking one's finger in one's throat. Another last-ditch strategy is to urinate on him. *It is important that each woman have a strategy, or set of defensive measures, she would seek to use if an attack occurred.* No one set of advice can apply to all situations because the rapist may respond quite differently to the victim fighting back, depending on whether he is primarily a power, anger, or sadistic rapist.

On a broader, sociological level, feminists urge certain sex role socialization practices be changed so that attacks would seldom, if ever, occur. Margaret Mead has noted rape does not occur in certain societies where males are socialized to be nurturant rather than aggressive. To reduce rape sharply, Janet S. Hyde recommends the following changes in socialization practices:

If little boys were not so pressed to be aggressive and tough, perhaps rapists would never develop. If adolescent boys did not have to demonstrate that they are hypersexual, perhaps there would be no rapists. . . .

Changes would also need to be made in the way females are socialized, particularly if women are to become good at self-defense. Weakness is not considered a desirable human characteristic, and so it should not be considered a desirable feminine characteristic, especially because it makes women vulnerable to rape. . . . While some people think that it is silly for the federal government to rule that girls must have athletic teams equal to boys' teams, it seems quite possible that the absence of athletic training for girls has contributed to making them rape victims. . . .

Finally, for both males and females, we need a radical restructuring of ideas about sexuality. As long as females are expected to pretend to be uninterested in sex and as long as males and females play games on dates, rape will persist.[b]

[a]Margaret Mead, *Sex and Temperament in Three Primitive Societies* (New York: Morrow, 1935).

[b]Janet S. Hyde, *Understanding Human Sexuality* (New York: McGraw-Hill, 1979), pp. 389–390.

feelings, (*b*) to lend support and guidance during the medical tests and while the police are questioning them, (*c*) to be similarly supportive during the trial, (*d*) and to provide follow-up counseling for emotional reactions to the rape.

Burgess and Holmstrom also note that because a majority of rapes are not reported, many of the nonreporters have a *silent rape reaction*. These nonreporters not only fail to report the rape to the police, but many tell no one about it. Nonreporters are apt to experience the same adjustment problems as victims who report the rape experience. However, the trauma for nonreporters is often intensified because they have no way of expressing or venting their feelings. Some nonreporters eventually seek professional counseling for other problems such as depression, anxiety, or inability to have orgasms. Often, such problems are then found to stem from the rape. Women who have had secret rape experiences should be helped to talk about the rape experience so they can gradually learn to deal with it. A number of communities now have rape crisis centers that provide counseling, medical services, and legal services to victims.

EXHIBITIONISM AND VOYEURISM   Exhibitionists and voyeurs are frequently referred to as "flashers" and "Peeping Toms." They are often considered nuisances rather than serious threats to society or to individuals. There is, of course, more alarm and disdain when exhibitionists disrobe in front of children. Having someone peek into our homes is also alarming. Of greater concern is the recent scientific revelation that exhibitionists and voyeurs are also apt to engage in more assaultive sex offenses, such as sexual abuse of children and even rape.[42] This finding contradicts the traditional view that exhibitionists and voyeurs are unlikely to commit harmful sexual acts.

To some extent all of us have probably become involved in displaying our bodies to others. Nude swimming (skinny-dipping) has been popular for a long time. Some people go to beaches to display their physiques. A number of years ago streaking (running nude on college campuses and other places) was popular. "Mooning" (displaying one's buttocks in public) has been a common fad among high school and college students.

Voyeurism is defined as watching persons undress, viewing them in the nude, and observing them performing sexual acts without their knowledge or consent. To some extent most of us have found enjoyment in at least one of the following: looking at magazines containing pictorials of people who are nude or seminude, going to night clubs featuring nude dancers, going to X-rated movies, watching our sex partner undress, and observing the attractive physiques of others out in public. Again, it should be noted that invasion-of-privacy voyeurism is demeaning and threatening to an unwilling victim.

Exhibitionism and voyeurism involve behaviors that differ only in degree from the kinds of showing and looking that are considered "normal" in our society.

Structural Sex Variance

Behaviors in this category include prostitution, pornography, and homosexuality. Similar to the previous category (asocial sex variance), sexual behaviors in this category run counter to prevailing norms and legal statutes. The differences are that the behaviors in this category have supportive social structures and are participated in by substantial numbers of persons. In this section we will focus on homosexuality, since this area has in recent years had the greatest interest among social workers.

HOMOSEXUALITY   A homosexual is a person who has and prefers sexual contact with members of the same gender. This is a pervasive pattern that occurs over a long period of time rather than occasional sexual experimentation with someone of the same gender. Teenagers, in experimenting with sexuality, may, for example, have some homosexual experiences. People isolated from the other gender (in prisons, segregated schools, sailors, juveniles in correctional schools) often have sexual experiences with members of their own sex when members of the other gender are not available.

On the other hand, it is possible to be a homosexual without adopting the homosexual lifestyle—by ignoring one's homosexuality, denying it, or simply pretending to be heterosexual.

It is important to note that most Americans disapprove of homosexuality. Surveys have found that a majority of Americans regard homosexuality as "very obscene and vulgar" and as being a "curable disease."[43] Homosexuals are also often viewed as being harmful to American life. The negative view of homosexuality in this country is indicated by the array of derogatory slang terms for homosexuals. (It should be noted that similar attitudes and different derogatory terms have been applied in the past to various ethnic minorities including the Irish, Italians, blacks, and Hispanic Americans.) Many heterosexuals are *homophobic*: They have feelings of personal anxiety and disgust of homosexuals and seek to avoid contact with homosexuals.

Such negative attitudes can have considerable psychological impact on a homosexual. It is distressing for a homosexual to realize that a majority of Americans consider him or her vulgar and obscene. Some homosexuals therefore seek to hide their sexual orientation, and they live in constant fear of being "discovered." Some believe (often correctly) that discovery will result in being fired from their job or being ostracized by friends and relatives.

There are several erroneous myths about homosexuality:

Myth 1: People are either homosexual or heterosexual. *Fact:* Alfred Kinsey found that homosexuality and heterosexuality are not mutually exclusive categories. Most people have had sexual thoughts, feelings, and fantasies about members of the same sex as well as about members of the opposite sex. Kinsey proposed a seven-point rating scale to categorize sexuality, with exclusive heterosexuality at one end and exclusive homosexuality at the other (Table 6.1). Kinsey noted:

The world is not divided into sheep and goats. . . .
Only the human mind invents categories and tries to
force facts into pigeonholes. The living world is a
continuum in each and every one of its aspects. The
sooner we learn this concerning human sexual
behavior, the sooner we will reach a sound
understanding of the realities of sex.[44]

Myth 2: Homosexuality is universally disapproved in all cultures. *Fact:* Some cultures accept, and others

encourage, homosexuality. A young boy in ancient Greece was sometimes given a boy slave who served as a sexual partner until the boy was old enough to marry a woman. Once married, it was common for older married men to form a homosexual relationship with a young boy. Today, all males among the Siwans of North Africa are expected to engage in homosexual relationships throughout their lives. Among the Aranda of Central Australia, there are relationships between young boys and unmarried men, with these liaisons generally ending at marriage.[45]

Myth 3: Male homosexuals are generally "effeminate," and female homosexuals are generally "masculine." The erroneous stereotype is that male homosexuals are supposed to be limp-wristed, talk with a lisp, and have a "swishy" walk; lesbians are erroneously believed to have short hair and wear clothes that are normally worn by males. *Fact:* Most homosexuals are indistinguishable in appearance and mannerisms from heterosexuals.[46] This myth probably comes from confusing homosexuality with transvestism—wearing the clothing of the opposite sex for sexual arousal. Transvestism and homosexuality are in fact quite different: It appears that transvestite behavior is not any more common among homosexuals than among heterosexuals.[47] Interestingly, whereas our culture erroneously associates male homosexuality with effeminacy, the ancient Greeks and Romans associated homosexuality with aggressive masculinity (as among the Spartan warriors).

Brian Garner and Richard Smith found further evidence contradicting the stereotype that male homosexuals are generally effeminate. In a study of male university athletes, they found that 40 percent had engaged in homosexual behavior to orgasm in the previous two years.[48]

Myth 4: Homosexuals are "sick" and different in personality characteristics from heterosexuals. *Fact:* Evelyn Hooker gave a battery of personality and psychological adjustment tests to a homosexual group and to a matched group of heterosexuals. The study found no differences between the two groups in personality traits or in general adjustment. The only difference was their sexual orientation.[49]

Myth 5: One partner in a homosexual liaison generally plays the "active" or masculine role in sexual

TABLE 6.1

Kinsey's Conceptualization of Homosexuality and Heterosexuality as Being Variations on a Continuum

0	1	2	3	4	5	6
Exclusive heterosexual	Heterosexual with incidental homosexual experience	Heterosexual with substantial homosexual experience	Equal heterosexual and homosexual experience	Homosexual with substantial heterosexual experience	Homosexual with incidental heterosexual experience	Exclusive homosexual

Source: Adapted from Alfred C. Kinsey et al., *Sexual Behavior in the Human Male* (Philadelphia: W. B. Saunders, 1948), p. 638.

activity, and the other plays the "passive" or feminine role. *Fact:* Most homosexuals play both roles and (similar to heterosexuals) experiment with a variety of sexual arousal roles and techniques. (The question is sometimes asked: "What do homosexuals do in bed?" Most of their activities are similar to those in which heterosexuals engage. Preliminary activities generally include kissing, hugging, and petting. Male homosexuals may engage in mutual masturbation, oral-genital sex, interfemoral intercourse (in which one man's penis moves between the thighs of the other), and anal intercourse. Lesbians may engage in mutual masturbation, oral-genital sex, and more rarely tribadism (one partner lying on top of the other and making thrusting movements so that both receive genital stimulation); a rarer practice among lesbians is the use of a dildo by one person to stimulate the other.

Myth 6: Male homosexuals primarily seek out young boys. *Fact:* Homosexuals are no more attracted to children than are heterosexuals, and homosexual child molesting is less common than its heterosexual counterpart.[50] Charles McCaghy found that 80 percent of all reported child molesting is done by heterosexual men to young girls.[51] (And there is reason to believe that same-sex child molesting is often not homosexual but is committed frequently by otherwise heterosexual men.) Strangely, people who worry that homosexual male teachers will try to seduce young boys in a

school do not seem to worry that heterosexual male teachers will try to seduce young girls—and it is the latter that occurs much more frequently.

Myth 7: AIDS is a punishment from God for the homosexual activity of gays and lesbians, and homosexuals are to blame for AIDS. *Fact:* Although gay males are a high-risk group for the AIDS virus in our society, very few cases have been reported among lesbians.[52] (Gay men are at high risk for acquiring AIDS because of the transfer of body fluids that occurs during anal intercourse.) AIDS is not only a life-threatening disease for gay men; it is now a disease whose incidence is increasing rapidly among heterosexuals.[53] In many African countries the majority of people afflicted with AIDS are heterosexuals.

Homosexuals are not the cause of AIDS. Blaming a deadly disease on the group who, in the United States, has suffered and died disproportionately from AIDS is a classic and regrettable case of blaming the victims. Although it is true that the largest single "risk group" of persons with AIDS is male homosexuals, it is ludicrous to assume this group caused this health crisis. AIDS is caused by a virus. It is further ludicrous to assert that male homosexuals would want to deliver the disease on the world after first delivering it on themselves. Quite to the contrary, the gay male community in the United States has been in the forefront of educating people about behavior that minimizes the transmission of the disease. Gay men have radically altered their sexual behavior patterns, as evidenced by a substantial drop in the rate of transmission of this disease among this group in the past few years. No group in the United States would benefit more from a cure or treatment for AIDS than would male homosexuals.

Incidence of Homosexuality   Determining the extent of homosexuality is difficult. First, there are definitional problems because most people are not exclusively heterosexual or homosexual. Second, because of the stigma attached to homosexuality, some people are reluctant to acknowledge homosexual thoughts, feelings, or acts.

Kinsey found that 4 percent of white males and 2 percent of white females were exclusively homosexual—that is, never had sex with someone of the opposite sex. He further estimated that 37 percent of American males have had one or more homosexual experiences to orgasm and that 10 percent of American males have long periods of more or less exclusive homosexuality.[54] Other studies have resulted in similar estimates.[55] After reviewing several studies, Janet Hyde concludes:

How many people are homosexual?—is complex. Probably about 75 percent of men and 85 percent of women are exclusively heterosexual. About 2 percent of men and slightly less than 1 percent of women are exclusively homosexual. And the remaining 25 percent of men and 15 percent of women have had varying amounts of both heterosexual and homosexual experience.[56]

Causes   People are often curious about the causes of homosexuality—that is, why some persons are erotically attracted to members of the same gender, and others are attracted to members of the other gender. Social, behavioral, and biological scientists have examined and argued this question for decades. Let us see what they have learned.

First, you cannot study the question of why one becomes homosexual without studying the larger question; that is, what determines sexual object choice for anyone, heterosexual or homosexual? Why do we

get aroused by a woman, or a woman with particular attributes, or a man of a certain body type? Is this something we've learned? Are we born with a "script" that determines our sexual object choice?

Many researchers and theoreticians have advanced hypotheses in an effort to explain this complex and important question. Some believe that the biology of an individual determines heterosexuality or homosexuality. Some studies have shown chemical differences between these two groups, but it is impossible to determine causation from the results of these studies. In other words, are the chemical differences between people responsible for this behavior, or does their behavior somehow alter their body chemistry?

Other theorists posit that childhood experiences determine heterosexuality or homosexuality. Here we have the causation question again. If we determined that a certain child had more sex play with a child of the same gender and grew to be a homosexual in adult life, can we say that this sex play led to homosexuality? Perhaps the increased sex play grew out of an inborn desire and erotic potential toward gratification from such play; that is, the behavior grew out of a predisposition toward homosexuality; the predisposition did not grow out of the behavior.

The most comprehensive study of this question to date was undertaken by researchers at the Alfred C. Kinsey Institute for Sex Research.[57] The researchers, Alan P. Bell, Martin S. Weinberg, and Sue Kiefer Hammersmith studied 979 homosexual and 477 heterosexual men and women, gathering a large amount of information about their lives in an effort to determine critical and statistically significant differences between these two groups. They analyzed their data using a method called "path analysis," which enabled them to examine a large number of independent variables (such as parental traits, parent and sibling relationships, and gender conformity) to determine *causation* of sexual orientation, and not merely association between variables. Their significant findings were: (*a*) by the time boys and girls reach adolescence, their sexual orientation is likely to be already determined, even though they may not yet have become sexually very active; (*b*) the homosexual men and women in the study were not particularly lacking in heterosexual experiences during their childhood and adolescent years. They were distinguished from their heterosexual counterparts, however, in finding such experiences ungratifying; (*c*) among both the men and the women in the study, there was a powerful link between gender nonconformity and the development of homosexuality. (Gender nonconformity refers to children who prefer engaging in activities generally associated in this culture with the other gender, that is, boys playing with dolls.) This factor of gender nonconformity was more significant for males than for females, with variables related to family relationships more important for females.

What do these findings suggest? First, they show that sexual orientation is established early in life, perhaps long before adolescence. Although every person has the potential to behave sexually in the manner he or she chooses one's true sexual orientation may be set before birth or at a very early age, and then no longer be influenced by the environment. Many homosexually oriented persons behave as if they are heterosexual in this society because there are so many sanctions against homosexuality. However, their true sexual orientation and preferred sexual partner, in the absence of these negative sanctions, would be someone of the same gender. Human beings certainly have the ability to respond sexually to persons who are not their most preferred sexual partner, but to do so requires going against the current of their innermost inclinations. We can freely choose various behaviors; we cannot freely choose who or what "turns us on." The question of what causes a person's sexual orientation to be set (either as homosexual or heterosexual) before birth or at a very early age has not as yet been answered. (Some people are naturally left-handed, and others are naturally right-handed; it appears that some people are naturally heterosexual in orientation and others are naturally homosexual.)

Life as a Homosexual   Homosexual behavior between males is illegal in most states. Lesbianism (female homosexuality) is prohibited in fewer states than is male homosexuality. There appear to be several reasons for this. Fewer females are homosexual than males. Lesbians keep their sexual behavior more hidden and are not as likely to form obvious homosexual

communities as are males. In addition, most legislators have been males and perhaps see male homosexuality as more of a threat to them than female homosexuality.

The Gay Liberation Movement has been seeking to change negative attitudes and end discriminatory acts toward homosexuals. Yet, many people still view homosexuals as being psychologically "sick"—having a form of mental illness. (Until 1974 the American Psychiatric Association defined homosexuality as a mental illness.)

The Gay Liberation Movement is a coalition of such groups as the Gay Liberation Front, the National Gay Task Force, and the International Union of Gay Athletes. The movement contends (along with many social scientists) that homosexuality is not a perversion or sickness but is simply a different lifestyle. Their arguments have met with mixed reactions. Some states have repealed antihomosexual legislation, and several cities have passed homosexual civil rights ordinances that prevent discrimination against police officers, teachers, and other city employees.

Other cities and states have rejected bills that sought to ban discrimination against homosexuals. The armed services (officially, at least) still discharge anyone found to be homosexual. In 1977, the Washington State Supreme Court ruled it was constitutional to fire a teacher with a homosexual orientation, as it was concluded a homosexual teacher may (allegedly) adversely affect the education of children.

Because of negative attitudes and discriminatory acts, some homosexuals go to extensive lengths to hide their sexual behavior. They fear discrimination and even being discharged from their place of employment. They also fear the stigma and embarrassment that they and their families would receive if they "came out" (publicly acknowledged their sexual orientation). Some homosexuals marry someone of the opposite sex and may even hide their homosexual encounters from their spouses. Leading a double life, with fear of criminal penalties if one's sexual orientation is discovered, is stress producing.

Many larger cities now have homosexual communities that provide an escape from the pressures of leading such a double life. Community activities are usually recreational and leisure-time in nature.

Despite the negative and even hostile view many Americans still have of homosexuality, more gay men and women now openly acknowledge their sexual preference.

Homosexual communities also serve to socialize new entrants into the homosexual subculture. These communities are often located in a certain geographical area of a city and generally have shops, restaurants, and hotels that are owned and patronized primarily by homosexual customers. The "gay bars" are perhaps the most visible establishments in such communities. Evelyn Hooker describes the social and socialization functions served by gay bars.

The young man who may have had a few isolated homosexual experiences in adolescence, or indeed

none at all . . . may find the excitement and opportunities for sexual gratification appealing and thus begin active participation in the community life. Very often, the debut, referred to by homosexuals as "coming out," of a person who believes himself to be homosexual but who has struggled against it, will occur in a bar when he, for the first time, identifies himself publicly as a homosexual in the presence of other homosexuals. . . . He may be agreeably astonished to discover a large number of men who are physically attractive, personable, and "masculine"-appearing, so that his hesitancy in identifying himself as a homosexual is greatly reduced. . . . He becomes convinced that far from being a small minority, the "gay" population is very extensive indeed. Once he has "come out," that is, identified himself as a homosexual to himself and to some others . . . they assist him in providing justifications for the homosexual way of life as legitimate.[58]

Increasingly, homosexuals are "coming out" and acknowledging their sexual orientation. A respondent interviewed by Barry Dank described the functions served by gay bars in this process.

I knew that there were homosexuals, queers, and whatnot: I had read some books, and I was resigned to the fact that I was a foul, dirty person, but I wasn't actually calling myself a homosexual yet. . . . The time I really caught myself coming out is the time I walked into this bar and saw a whole crowd of groovy, groovy guys. And I said to myself, there was the realization, that not all gay men are dirty old men or idiots, silly queens, but there are some just normal-looking and acting people, as far as I could see. I saw gay society and I said, "Wow, I'm home."[59]

It should be noted that there is a wide variation in homosexual lifestyles, as is true for heterosexuals. Also, lesbians and male homosexuals differ somewhat in their sexual attitudes and practices. Lesbians are more likely to equate sex with love. They tend to engage in sex with fewer partners than do male homosexuals. Their homosexual relationships tend to last longer and to be based more on love and affection. Female homosexuals may be less likely to acknowledge their sexual orientation publicly, and to participate in a homosexual community.

Lesbians are better able to conceal their sexual orientation because the public is less suspicious of two women living together or otherwise being close to each other. Most female homosexuals have had sexual relationships with men. Jack H. Hedblom notes, "The female homosexual does not prefer sex with a woman because she has had no experience with a man."[60]

The specter of AIDS has had a tremendous impact on homosexual communities, particularly on gay men. Homosexual communities have been active in encour-

aging federal and state governments to (*a*) recognize the dangers of AIDS, (*b*) provide research funds to learn more about the disorder and to seek to develop treatments for those who are infected with the AIDS virus, and (*c*) provide research funds to develop approaches to prevent the spread of AIDS.[61] Homosexual communities have also been advocates of safer sex practices, and many gay men have made responsible and dramatic changes in their sexual practices. Homosexual communities have also developed support systems for people who have AIDS. (Unfortunately, the larger society has been slow in developing services and programs for people who have AIDS. Persons with AIDS are often shunned and victimized by discrimination in our society.[62])

Current Issues   As mentioned earlier, a major issue is whether civil rights laws should be enacted to protect homosexuals from discrimination in housing, employment, and other areas. Homosexuals argue that they are refused jobs in teaching, in the military service, and in many private corporations. They also note they are commonly the targets of blackmailers who know of the sexual orientation they are seeking to hide. They assert that legal protection for gay rights will not turn heterosexuals (for example, school children) into homosexuals. They maintain they have been the victims of abuse and exploitation and now want the same protection that other minorities receive. Two prominent social work organizations, the National Association of Social Workers and the Council on Social Work Education, have taken strong positions to help protect the rights of homosexuals and are actively working to end discriminatory practices against homosexuals.

Those who oppose civil rights laws for homosexuals assert that homosexuals are not like other minority groups who are discriminated against based on physical characteristics (blacks, women, the handicapped). It is argued that homosexuals, by contrast, choose their sexual behavior, which can be changed if they so desire. A number of other objections are also given by opponents. Legislation to protect gay rights would indicate approval of homosexual behavior, when in fact opponents assert that such behavior is unnatural. Permitting homosexuals to teach in school, it is asserted, would unwisely expose children to homosexual attitudes and activities and would probably lead to increased homosexual experimentation. Because most members of society are heterosexual, and many are confused or threatened by their lack of information and understanding of homosexuality, homosexuality is viewed by many heterosexuals as being morally wrong and socially damaging. The belief is that if sanctions against homosexuality were relaxed, homosexuality would flourish, the stability of the family would be threatened, birthrates would fall drastically, and society would be severely damaged. This is, of course, highly unlikely because with or without social sanctions, homosexuals compose only a small minority of any society. And social support is unlikely to increase significantly behavior so constitutional to one's being as his or her sexual orientation.

As can be seen, arguments on both sides of this issue are intense—and there are other issues as well.

Some churches are now marrying homosexual couples who request this ceremony. These marriages are recognized by certain religious groups but not by state laws, which still prohibit homosexuals from marrying one another. Proponents of such marriages assert that homosexuals ought to be permitted to receive the same personal gratifications and financial advantages through marriage that are available to heterosexuals. Opponents assert that such marriages are sacrilegious, are a violation of the purpose of marriage, and are a threat to the stability of the traditional family.

Related issues involve whether married homosexuals ought to be allowed to adopt children and whether homosexual fathers or mothers ought to be allowed to retain custody of their children after divorce. In some court cases lesbian mothers have won custody of their children after divorce. In other cases courts have decreed that lesbian behavior is sufficient evidence that a person is unfit to be a parent. At issue in homosexual adoptions and custody battles is whether homosexuals would pass on their sexual orientation to the child. Initial findings from studies suggest that this is unlikely to occur.[63] We as a society continue to be confused about how sexual orientation might influence, if at all, other important aspects of life, such as childrearing or work performance.

In the past, psychotherapists who counseled homosexuals generally had the goal of switching the sexual orientation to heterosexuality. This goal was seldom achieved. Homosexuals often became more anxious and uncomfortable about their sexual orientation but continued to maintain homosexual behavior. In counseling the emphasis has shifted in recent years. Most therapists now seek to have homosexuals examine their concerns and arrive at a sexual identity they can be comfortable with. Most choose to continue their homosexual behavior, and counseling is then geared to helping them deal with discrimination they may face, and helping them with concerns they have (such as whether to inform their relatives or employer and whether to "come out" in other ways).

A number of issues involving homosexuality have been debated for decades and undoubtedly will continue to be national issues. Over time, our society has become more tolerant of homosexuality. Thirty-five years ago, efforts to suppress homosexuality were so strong that no newspaper even dared to print the word *homosexual*.

PERSONAL SEXUAL CONCERNS

All of us at one time or another have had sexual concerns. The kinds of sexual concerns are probably infinite. A few will be listed. A 17-year-old male may wonder if he should seek to become sexually involved with someone he is dating. A male who has had relations with a prostitute may be concerned he has acquired AIDS. Adolescents may feel guilty about masturbating. A wife may feel guilty about having had an extramarital affair. Men may worry about premature ejaculation, failure to have an erection, or failure to become sexually aroused. Some women are concerned because they seldom achieve orgasm. Some people who are married or dating over an extended period of time may become alarmed because their sex life appears to be becoming boring and routine. Some people may be unhappy with various sexual techniques and approaches used by their partners. Some people have been the victims of rape or incest and still have uncomfortable emotions associated with those traumatic experiences. Some people may strongly admire someone of their own sex and wonder if this attraction means they are a homosexual. Middle-aged people may fear losing their sexual capacities in the future. Some may find intercourse painful, and be concerned. Some know their current sexual partner has had previous sexual experiences with others and may feel angry, hurt, or threatened. Sex counseling and sex therapy are directly designed to resolve personal sexual problems.

Sex counseling is short-term, often crisis-oriented counseling directed toward the alleviation of some immediate sexual concern. Sex therapy, on the other hand, tends to be somewhat more comprehensive and longer in duration and focuses on resolving specific sexual dysfunctions (such as premature ejaculation and erectile difficulties in men and failure to achieve orgasm and painful intercourse in women). Sex therapy involves several stages: problem identification, history gathering, physical examination, information giving, assignment of sexual experiences designed to resolve the dysfunction, and ongoing evaluation.[64] In actual counseling, the distinctions between sex counseling and sex therapy are not clear-cut. Sex counseling and sex therapy treatment programs are now developing in many communities. Counselors and psychotherapists at most social service agencies occasionally counsel clients with sexual concerns. Private sex therapy centers, often based on the treatment programs pioneered by Masters and Johnson, are now providing services in many larger communities.

SEX COUNSELING*

Social workers have long been recognized as resources for persons suffering from problems related to sex. Alfred Kinsey observed that social workers were

*The remainder of this chapter was written by Lloyd G. Sinclair.

sought out by persons with sexual concerns more than any other professional group.[65] Further, most sex counseling done by social workers is performed by persons whose primary professional role is not that of sex counselor. Probation and parole officers; group home supervisors; and school, medical, and psychiatric social workers are frequently confronted by persons with problems related to sex, requesting their skills as sex counselors.

Prerequisites to Effective Counseling

In addition to the requirements of the specific professional position, there are two basic prerequisites to becoming an effective sex counselor: comfort and knowledge.

To be effective as a social worker, one must be professionally comfortable with the subject matter. This is absolutely essential in the area of sex, where most people tend to be anxious and embarrassed. This certainly doesn't mean the counselor would feel comfortable *experiencing* all the various sexual behaviors her or his clients might report. Rather, it means the counselor should be comfortable enough with her or his own sexuality that the behaviors reported by clients, however aberrant, don't threaten the worker's personal sexuality or identity. Further, as in all helping relationships, when the counselor is confronted with a situation that demands additional expertise or comfort, ethics dictate that the worker identify the situation honestly and make an appropriate referral. Social workers can be effective as role models to their clients, demonstrating that sex can be addressed directly, clearly, and without embarrassment.

Because social workers aren't inherently more comfortable in the area of sex than anybody else, comfort needs to be developed. Although there are many ways to do this, some of the most effective include examining one's own sexual history and values, talking frankly with others about sex, exposing oneself to sexually explicit material, and gaining as much knowledge—the second prerequisite—as possible.

It is generally assumed that knowledge and training about a subject are a requirement if one is to be helpful to others in that area. Surprisingly, many people seem not to apply this premise to sex. They consider themselves to be self-taught *"sexperts,"* believing that their own personal experience provides them with as much knowledge as they need. This assumption is not only incorrect but is downright dangerous and unethical. Particularly in the past two decades, we have learned a great deal about sex: The responsible, competent sex counselor will take it on herself or himself to gain as much of this knowledge as possible.

Box 6.4 presents four specific examples of professional sex counseling. As you read them, think about the comfort and knowledge that would be required to most effectively resolve the problems presented.

Words

When talking with clients about sex, careful consideration should be given to the use of words. Sex words can be categorized roughly into three groups: slang, colloquial, and scientific. Slang words and expressions, such as *tits* and *getting laid*, are used to describe things vigorously and often demeaningly. Colloquial language, such as *making love* or *coming*, define things clearly, relatively uneuphemistically, and usually with a pleasant tone. Scientific language, like *coitus* and *testicles*, connotes precision and a certain value-free detachment.

It is important to realize that most people use slang terms when talking about sex. Warren R. Johnson captured this when he wrote, "Fuck, screw, jack-off, cock, pussy, wet dream, and the like are, perhaps, regrettably vulgar, but they are the dominant linguistic sex vehicles of American English."[66]

This is not to suggest that helping professionals should necessarily use slang terms when talking with clients. Sex counselors must, however, *understand* the meaning of slang terms and be *comfortable* when hearing them. This is particularly critical when working with certain groups of people, such as mentally retarded persons, where the language barrier may be severe. The vocabulary that is most comfortable to the counselor may be completely misunderstood by the client. In these cases, the use of slang terms may be essential to communicate effectively.

Most counselors develop a vocabulary that is comfortable for them, somewhere between slang and scientific. When the words used are overly technical, they tend to be misunderstood, or the language may be a mask for the counselor's discomfort. The major problem with slang words is that they may be interpreted as vulgar by many clients.

Emma Lee Doyle, a sex therapist from Dallas, Texas, illustrates the problem of sex words in a colorful case example. When interviewing a woman client, Doyle asked her what her husband did sexually that she really disliked. The woman replied, "He insists on referring to my genital area as my 'pussy.' I hate the word 'pussy,' it's so demeaning and vulgar." When Doyle asked what words she preferred for him to use, she said, "I wish he'd call it my 'cunt'; it's so much more refined." The sensitive therapist is cautious in her or his use of words, taking care to listen to clients for the connotations they place on the words they use.

Levels of Therapeutic Intervention

Jack S. Annon, a psychologist and sex therapist from Honolulu, Hawaii, has developed an extremely useful conceptual scheme for the treatment of sexual problems.[67] He rejects the notion that the alleviation of sexual dysfunction demands, in every case, intensive therapy. Rather, he suggests a model providing four levels of intervention. This model is called the PLISSIT model. The acronym stands for the following:

P   Permission

LI   Limited information

SS   Specific suggestions

IT   Intensive therapy

Annon suggests the largest number of sexual problems can be treated effectively by the counselor simply giving the client well-placed, accurate *permission*.

BOX 6.4

Four Case Examples of Sex Counseling

BEN, A NURSING HOME RESIDENT

Fran was a social worker in a nursing home. A nurse who worked nights had become very upset the previous evening because she had walked into the room of an elderly resident, Ben, and found him masturbating. She had scolded him for his behavior and had made the incident known to several other people.

Fran decided that this was something that shouldn't be ignored. She spoke first to the nurse to learn more about the incident. The nurse thought the behavior was abhorrent, using words like "perverted," "juvenile," and "animalistic" in her description. Fran then spoke to Ben. He expressed regret and embarrassment about the incident, felt his privacy had been severely violated, but concluded that "he really should act his age."

Fran knew that masturbation was a healthy, normal sexual outlet for all people, regardless of age. Indeed, for this man, masturbation was perhaps the only reasonable means presently available to express his sexuality; his wife of 45 years had died a few years before. Fran was also aware that many people, including older persons themselves, believe that sex is for the young and that the only legitimate sexual expression is that which is shared by a heterosexual couple.

Fran offered Ben information about the normalcy of self-stimulation and reassurance that it was not his behavior, but the nurse's, that was the problem. They discussed ways that he could enjoy more privacy, in order to honor his right to personal, solitary space. Ben appeared grateful for the recognition of his personhood. Fran spoke again to the nurse. She obviously had strong ideas about masturbation, and Fran knew she wasn't going to change them. She knew that people who have fixed, powerful emotions in response to behavior that is enjoyable *to others*, and doesn't affect them, are often responding to something in themselves that is threatening.

Fran's goal, instead, was to encourage the nurse to recognize the resident's need for privacy to maintain self-esteem. The nurse agreed that living in a nursing home stripped residents of most of what they had enjoyed throughout their adult lives—self-determination, property, privacy. Because the nursing home was, in part, a medical care facility, there were good reasons why many of the residents' personal needs had to be compromised— but there were also simple ways to respect their rights. Fran and the nurse agreed that residents should not lock themselves into their rooms, but a closed door could be respected by a knock and an invitation to enter, rather than the staff's current habit of merely barging in. They took this idea to the nursing home director who agreed to have the staff implement the policy for a trial period.[a]

---

[a]Two books that address the sexual concerns and habits of older persons are Edward M. Brecher, *Love, Sex and Aging* (Boston: Little, Brown, 1984) and Bernard D. Starr and Marcella Bakur Weiner, *The Starr-Weiner Report on Sex and Sexuality in the Mature Years* (New York: McGraw-Hill, 1981). A film that portrays many issues related to intimacy, sexuality, and loneliness in institutions among older persons is *Rose By Any Other Name*, available from Adelphi University Center on Aging, Garden City, NY.

TINA, AN ADOLESCENT GROUP HOME RESIDENT

Pat, a social worker in a group home for adolescent women, became concerned about Tina, a 16-year-old resident. Tina had confided to some of the other women in the house that she and her friend, Dennis, were having intercourse regularly. Pat was faced with several dilemmas: (*a*) in wanting to respect their privacy, was it appropriate to confront her on the subject? (*b*) if she did confront her, should Pat try to change her behavior by attempting to stop Tina from having intercourse? or (*c*) should she respect Tina's right to make her own decisions and suggest that they use a contraceptive to reduce the chance of Tina becoming pregnant or contracting a sexually transmitted disease?

Pat decided that although ignoring the entire issue would certainly be easiest for *her*, it probably would not be in Tina's best interests. Pat was most concerned that Tina might become pregnant or contract a disease, causing negative consequences for herself, Dennis, the potential child, and others.

Pat examined her values and her knowledge about teenage sexuality. She was aware that Tina might be, among her immediate peer group, in the majority in that she was having intercourse. In one recent study, 45 percent of teenage girls had had intercourse, and the average age of first intercourse for the girls in this study was 16.2 years.[b] Although a 16-year-old might be viewed by Pat as inappropriately young to be sexually active, she realized that Tina's values were different from hers and that, practically speaking, there was little that Pat could do to force Tina to stop, even if she wanted to.

But birth control and disease prevention seemed like another matter. Pat believed that the aspects of Tina's behavior that affected her alone were largely her business. But the prospect of a child being born to a 16-year-old was another concern. Pat knew that 1 million teenagers in the United States became pregnant each year and that 13 percent of all births in this country are to teenage women.[c] She didn't want Tina to be among these statistics. And although it was admittedly unlikely, the possibility of Tina becoming infected with the AIDS virus and passing it on to her child was too horrible to imagine. She decided it was appropriate to encourage Tina to protect herself from an unwanted pregnancy and disease.

Pat approached Tina to discuss the issue. Although Tina was initially reluctant to talk about it, Pat was able to draw her out with some perseverence. Tina confided that she was, indeed, engaging in regular sexual activity with Dennis, that they were not using a contraceptive, and that she certainly did not want to get pregnant. She felt they were very much in love with each other and considered their sexual activity to be a testimony of their love. In regard to the possibility of contracting a disease, she thought only gay people got AIDS.

Tina's statements seemed reasonable to Pat—most people believe that sex *is* a statement

Continued

---

[b]Centers for Disease Control, "Morbidity and Mortality Weekly Report," January 29, 1988, vol. 37, S2.

[c]Cheryl D. Hayes, ed., *Risking the Future: Adolescent Sexuality, Pregnancy and Child Bearing* (Washington, D.C.: National Academy Press, 1987).

BOX 6.4   *Continued*

of love. But Tina was only 16. Could her love be as real as someone's who was older? Pat reflected on her own history, remembering when she was 16, feeling very much in love. She had waited to have intercourse until later—she hadn't even considered it at age 16—but Tina was living in a different environment.

Pat encouraged Tina to talk more about love and sex. Was the sexual aspect of their relationship enhancing other aspects? Did she feel it was good for each of them as individuals?

After considerable discussion, Tina observed that sex really wasn't that important to her and that although it was somewhat pleasurable from an emotional standpoint, it wasn't as physically exciting as it had been early in the relationship. Lately she had felt trapped by the expectation of intercourse whenever she and Dennis were alone together. Sex had, in her mind, taken on entirely too much importance. She feared that their sexual life was the major reason for Dennis's interest in her.

The more she talked, the clearer it became that Tina wanted permission *not* to have intercourse. Both she and Dennis had been under tremendous peer pressure to "grow up," and she thought they had become involved in intercourse because it was expected behavior. She wondered if Dennis was really that interested in sex, or if perhaps he just had to act out a role. This uncertainty had allowed her to put off decision making about birth control—she might stop having intercourse, so she wouldn't need it—and confronting Dennis directly—if sex *was* that important to him, maybe he would break up with her if he knew her true feelings.

Pat suggested that Tina discuss her feelings with Dennis and to stop assuming sex was something too volatile to talk about. She encouraged Tina to be assertive about what was good for her, and pointed out that no one should engage in sexual activity primarily for *someone else*. Pat further encouraged Tina to think about possible alternatives to intercourse—sexual and nonsexual—that Tina might feel more comfortable with and Dennis would enjoy. She agreed to bring it up with Dennis the next weekend, and she and Pat would talk further after that. In the meantime, Tina agreed that if intercourse occurred, she would insist they use a condom.

Counselors should be aware that often a sexual problem is really another kind of problem. This is particularly common with children, adolescents, or persons who live in institutions who may be deprived of adequate attention.

Children learn quite early in life that perhaps the most effective way to generate attention is to do something that is sexual and inappropriate. Because many adults are anxious about sexual matters, the tendency is to overreact when forced to confront them. When one adds the fact that most persons, particularly the young, have very limited access to good information about appropriate sexual behavior, the result is often sexual experimentation, which is seen by society as inappropriate.[d]

---

[d]For an excellent discussion of adolescent sexuality see Lorna J. Sarrel and Philip M. Sarrel, *Sexual Unfolding* (Boston: Little, Brown, 1979). A book that is helpful to parents in talking with their adolescent children is Carol Cassell, *Straight From the Heart: How to Talk to Your Teenagers Above Love and Sex* (New York: Simon and Schuster, 1987).

JIM, A FOSTER HOME RESIDENT

Jim was a 14-year-old boy who lived in a foster home. His history included many short-term living situations with relatives and foster and group homes. Jim's foster parents became aware, through the parents of 10-year-old Steve, that Jim had repeatedly pressured Steve into exploring and touching each other's genital areas, and Jim had suggested that they experiment with oral sex. Steve was frightened but couldn't seem to say "no" to Jim.

Jim's social worker intervened in this situation by talking first with Steve's parents to determine what their reaction had been when Steve first reported the incidents to them. They had not, fortunately, overreacted with alarm (a not uncommon reaction that can be more damaging to the child than the behavior itself). They commended Steve for telling them about it, assured him that he was not at fault, answered his questions, and told him that while it wasn't that serious, he shouldn't do anything that was being forced on him or otherwise did not seem right. The social worker chose not to meet directly with Steve and encouraged his parents to continue to be *askable* with Steve. They could, further, suggest ways for Steve to avoid a compromising situation with Jim, should the incident recur.

The social worker then met with Jim's foster parents. When informed of Jim's behavior, they had reacted with alarm, reprimanded him, and confined him to the house afternoons and evenings for several days. The parents remained confused, upset, and angry about Jim's behavior. The social worker acknowledged that forced sexual behavior is clearly inappropriate but encouraged the parents to view same-sex behavior as relatively normal for an inquisitive, maturing adolescent. In fact, in boys under the age of 15, homosexual contact is more common than heterosexual contact.[e] They seemed relieved when the social worker offered to meet with Jim.

When talking to Jim, the social worker informed him of his awareness of the situation and asked him about it. Jim told the worker that he had explored genitals with Steve but initially denied having been the aggressor. When Jim realized that he would not be punished by the social worker for being honest, he conceded that the behavior had been at his initiation.

The social worker pondered the most appropriate method of approaching the problem. What was Jim's behavior indicating? Was he merely curious? Was he a homosexual? Was he exercising power and dominance over his young friend? Did he not know the behavior was inappropriate? Is this behavior that could be an early indication that Jim might grow into a child molester or even a rapist?

The social worker knew that persons who are child molesters as adults often begin their sexually abusive behaviors as adolescents,[f] and boys who are sexually assaulted sometimes

Continued

---

[e]Ira L. Reiss, *Journey Into Sexuality* (Englewood Cliffs, NJ: Prentice-Hall, 1986).

[f]David Finkelhor, *A Sourcebook on Child Sexual Abuse* (Beverly Hills, CA: Sage, 1986).

BOX 6.4   *Continued*

become child molesters as adults.[g] So although it was important not to overreact to this incident, it should not just be ignored as "boys will be boys." If Jim was particularly focused on sex with younger persons, professional intervention would be appropriate.

After a lengthy, frank discussion, the social worker concluded that Jim did, indeed, know that forcing sexual behavior on someone else was wrong. The social worker stressed the importance of consent in sexuality. There did seem to be elements of curiosity operating, but they didn't seem to account entirely for the behavior.

Jim stated that he was as interested sexually in girls as he was in boys, and his preference would be to have a consenting sexual relationship with a teenage girl. The choice of Steve seemed to be more due to accessibility than anything. The social worker was aware that a majority of adolescents engage in sex play with members of their own gender and that the label *homosexual* can safely be applied only to adults who have and prefer sexual relationships with members of their own sex.[b]

Jim seemed to have chosen Steve partly because, being older, he had more likelihood of pressuring him to get what he (Jim) wanted. But the most important element seemed to be the attention he was likely to generate in adults—foster parents, social workers, and others—when the behavior was reported.

Had the social worker seen these incidents solely as a sexual problem, or indeed primarily as a sexual problem, he would likely have experienced little success in dealing with Jim. (If attention is the reward, Jim is likely to act out more and more to continue the shower of concern and attention from significant adults. The more therapy the social worker does the more Jim is likely to continue, even if punishment was involved.)

The social worker was aware that human beings' need for attention and recognition is one of the strongest emotional needs. When people are feeling unnoticed, rejected, or discounted, they have been known to experience huge amounts of pain, to the point of threatening their lives to gain attention.[i] This is a process the person is usually not consciously aware of. Punishment is not necessarily a negative consequence: At least when one is being punished, she or he is being recognized by the punisher.

The treatment plan developed by the social worker was designed to encourage Jim's foster parents to give him attention for appropriate, positive behavior. If inappropriate sexual incidents were to occur, the parents agreed to reprimand Jim briefly and drop further discussion or punishment. The social worker further encouraged the foster parents to talk with Jim about sex, independent of the incidents, to give him information and help him make healthy decisions.[j]

---

[g]Ann Wolbert Burgess and Christine A. Grant, *Children Traumatized in Sex Rings* (Washington, D.C.: National Center for Missing and Exploited Children, 1988).

[b]Sol Gordon, "Ten Heavy Facts about Sex" (Syracuse, NY: Ed-U Press, 1975). This is an exceptionally creative pamphlet designed for adolescents, which answers frequently asked questions about sex.

[i]A. J. Bachrach, W. J. Erwin, and J. P. Mohr, "The Control of Eating Behavior in an Anorexic by Operant Conditioning Techniques," in *Case Studies in Behavior Modification*, eds. L. P. Ullman and L. Krasner (New York: Holt, Rinehart & Winston, 1965), pp. 153–163.

[j]An excellent book to suggest to young people to learn more about sex is Eleanor S. Morrison, Kay Starks, Cynda Hyndman, and Nina Ronzio, *Growing Up Sexual* (New York: D. Van Nostrand, 1980).

The social worker informed the parents of the possibility of increased attention-getting sexual acts, particularly once the activity following the most recent one died down. A well-known pattern for behavior that gains a reward (in this case, attention) is to undergo a radical increase once the reward is removed.[k] Sometimes persons, desperate for attention, escalate their behavior in a vain attempt to force the response they are seeking when they are deprived of it. Usually the behavior will disappear quickly once the previously expected reward is consistently withheld.

In fact, this escalation did not occur. The social worker continued to be in contact with Jim and his foster family, and no further inappropriate sexual acts were reported.

CARRI, SINGLE AND PREGNANT

Carri came to an abortion clinic requesting to speak to someone regarding her pregnancy. She had missed her period and received a positive pregnancy test.

Carri told the counselor she had been in a relationship with Bruce for two years, and lately they had been distant and argumentative. She was feeling little support from him in general and had, for that reason, not revealed to him that she was pregnant. It was clear to her that she hadn't wanted to conceive, but they had been irregular users of birth control, assuming a pregnancy wouldn't happen to them.

The counselor asked her to discuss her thoughts about her alternatives. Carri was 19, a sophomore in college, and was interested in continuing her studies through a graduate degree in journalism. One of her major concerns was that her pregnancy, if continued, would interrupt her career goals.

She was worried about her relationship with Bruce. They had discussed ending it, but neither seemed to have the courage to do so. Carri felt that if the relationship had continued like it started—warm, loving, supportive—she would consider getting married to Bruce. But not now. Besides, she felt that a pregnancy was a poor reason to get married.

Carri talked about putting the child up for adoption. Although this would allow her to resume her studies relatively quickly without feeling pressure to get married, she was terrified of her parents' reactions. She felt they might reject her, or influence her to get married, or, at the very least, be extremely disappointed. Carri feared those reactions greatly.

The circumstances seemed to point to abortion as the best alternative. But was abortion murder? She had always abhorred the idea of abortion and never thought she would consider it for herself. Abortion was certainly not an alternative she would feel good about.

The counselor spent a great deal of time simply listening. Carri needed to talk with someone and had not yet trusted her dilemma with a friend. It was also clear that she had spent a large amount of time probing her predicament. The counselor helped Carri sort her alternatives—*Would* her parents reject her? *Would* suspending her studies for a semester or

Continued

_____

[k]James Deese and Steward H. Hulse, *The Psychology of Learning* (New York: McGraw-Hill, 1967).

BOX 6.4   *Continued*

two be that serious of a problem? What about the option of keeping the child and returning to school once the child could be taken care of by a babysitter?

Carri worried about whether getting an abortion was selfish, or if it meant she disliked children. They talked about the quality of life as being important, and if Carri were to raise the child herself, she might not be as able to give time, love, and energy as fully as if she had planned the pregnancy. Another stark reality was economic; Carri was aware that her lack of financial resources would pose an ongoing problem should she decide to keep the child. They agreed it wasn't exactly an act of selflessness to give birth to someone she didn't have time for, couldn't feed or read to, someone who might grow to feel lonely and resented. The counselor encouraged Carri to recognize her own needs as important and the validity of wanting what seemed best for herself.

The counselor raised the question of whether to share the dilemma with Bruce. Although Carri feared rejection from him, they both agreed he had some right to know about the pregnancy. Because Carri was the one who was ultimately likely to be most affected by the pregnancy, the primary decision should rest with her. But a part of her decision might be determined by his response. Further, Carri felt she needed someone close to talk with about her feelings and share her burden. With some encouragement from the counselor, Carri decided to discuss it with Bruce. The counselor suggested, further, that it might be helpful to talk with another close friend.

After an intense, 90-minute discussion, the counselor suggested that Carri go home, talk with Bruce, think about it more, and come back in a couple of days for further discussion. She was early enough in her pregnancy that time was not critical. Although Carri was eager to make her decision, additional time would probably help her find the best one.

As the counselor left the session, she was aware of being emotionally drained. Although she had talked with many women in a similar predicament before, she was struck by the pain in each individual. These are almost never simple decisions, and she realized how important it was to present options fairly and accurately, guiding the client but not deciding for her.

Occasionally the decision seemed pretty obvious—the 16-year-old rape victim, the 13-year-old incest case, the woman who had been exposed to German measles. But these cases were rare. Most of the persons the counselor saw who were coping with an unintended pregnancy would be able to have the child and would probably be at least adequate parents. But should they be forced into parenthood because they had accidentally become pregnant? The court has said they shouldn't, but each individual needs to decide for herself.

Carri returned one week later, had talked several times with Bruce, and decided to have an abortion. He accompanied her on the day of her appointment. They decided to postpone any decisions about the future of their relationship until this crisis had passed. The counselor explained the medical procedure to them and discussed birth control. Carri had decided to start on oral contraceptives following the abortion.

Although the question of whether abortion should be available to persons remains a hotly contested issue because of people's deep moral and religious feelings, abortion remains available to those who are able to pay for the procedure.

Most abortion counseling is done immediately prior to the medical procedure. Counseling should involve the discussion of at least three areas: the decision to terminate the pregnancy, the medical procedure, and birth control. Because abortions were, until recently, often performed by unqualified persons in unsafe surroundings, many people have fears and misinformation about the safety of the medical procedure. The abortion counselor can point out that abortion, when performed early in pregnancy by a physician, is considerably safer than carrying the pregnancy to term.[1] She or he should answer whatever questions the patient has about the medical procedure—how she is likely to feel, for what amount of time, what her recovery will involve, aftercare, and so forth.

The decision to terminate a pregnancy is a difficult one for most persons, although not for everyone. A sensitive counselor will probe the patient's feelings and thoughts regarding her options. Particularly for the woman who is undecided, it is critical to provide a calm and supportive atmosphere to facilitate her making the best decision.

---

[1]U.S. Department of Health and Human Services, Center for Disease Control, "Abortion Surveillance Report: 1981," 1985, and National Center for Disease Statistics, "Health, United States: 1987," 1988.

Permission, as it is used in this model, implies a kind of professional reassurance, letting clients know they are normal, OK—not perverted or deviant. Many people are not bothered by the specific behavior they are engaging in but are concerned that it is seen by most other people as wrong or aberrant. These concerns frequently involve masturbation ("it's only for kids"), fantasies and dreams ("to think about it is equal to doing it"), or behaviors expected by society but not desired by the individual ("anal intercourse is the latest thing"). The case example of Tina, discussed above (Box 6.4), is an illustration of a client seeking permission *not* to engage in a certain sexual activity.

A smaller group of persons suffering from sexual problems can be treated by the helping professional disseminating *limited information*. Limited information, usually expanding on permission, provides the client with "specific factual information directly relevant to the particular sexual concern."[68] An example of this was presented by a 68-year-old client who had believed, for as long as he could remember, that human beings were capable of a certain number of orgasms in life, and no more. So he had *rationed* them,

always confining orgasms to a single intercourse experience each weekend. The therapist informed him that what he had believed was incorrect. In fact, he could enhance his ability to respond sexually by maintaining a frequency and regularity of response. Since this client received this information, he has been making up for a great deal of lost time. His need in this area was for a specific piece of accurate information. Because so many people suffer from misinformation about sex, examples of persons needing this level of intervention abound. Often they involve myths about averages (sizes, frequencies), masturbation, menstruation, and aging.

A still smaller number of clients need intervention at Annon's next level, *specific suggestions*. The therapist offers the suggestions only after she or he has taken a *sexual problem history*. The sexual problem history includes (*a*) description of the current problem, (*b*) onset and course of the problem, (*c*) client's concept of the cause and maintenance of the problem, (*d*) past treatment and outcome, and (*e*) current expectancies and goals of treatment.[69]

This history, short of a complete sexual history but

providing more background than is generally needed for permission or limited information, is important to maximize the likelihood that the specific suggestions will be effective in the alleviation of the sexual distress. Specific suggestions are often given to relieve performance problems. For example, the woman who finds intercourse painful due to lack of lubrication might benefit from suggestions encouraging the couple to slow down, allowing her adequate time for arousal, and identifying verbally to her partner behaviors that are pleasurable to her.

The final level, *intensive therapy*, is required by a very small number of persons with sexual complaints. Their dysfunctions are sufficiently involved and complicated that intervention using permission, limited information, and specific suggestions is not sufficient to alleviate the dysfunction.

SEX THERAPY

Until the late 1960s, most helping professionals assumed that sexual functioning was an entirely natural activity and any dysfunction was merely a by-product of other individual or relationship problems. Therefore, the resolution of sexual problems would be a natural outcome of the resolution of other problems. Indeed, if one set out to resolve *only* the sexual problem, and was successful, some other problem would surface, since the sexual problem was seen as a symptom of a larger pathology.

Depending on the therapist's theoretical framework and philosophical beliefs, these psychological problems might be the result of unresolved conflicts, incomplete growth in a particular stage, communication problems, or perhaps faulty learning. When a client sought therapeutic help with a sexual problem, the therapist set out to improve functioning in her or his life in general, assuming sexual functioning would follow suit. Often it did.

But alarmingly, often it did not. Persons would undergo psychoanalysis or another form of psychotherapy, would gain insight into themselves and their problems, but would continue to suffer from premature ejaculation, inability to experience orgasm, or some other sexual problem.

Masters and Johnson

In 1957, William Masters and Virginia Johnson began their classic study of the physiology of human sexual response. Their research in this area was the finest performed ever before or since.

On completion of their research on human sexual response, Masters and Johnson began, in 1959, to treat persons with sexual dysfunctions. They departed radically from the prevailing thinking of the day, discussed above, which suggested that sexual problems were merely manifestations of other problems. They identified the relationship of the two partners as the client, rather than one person or the other, and indeed *required* both partners to participate in the process of therapy. They did what many others had thought untenable—they isolated the sexual problem, dealt with it directly in short-term therapy, and generated extremely successful results.

Masters and Johnson's methods are reported in *Human Sexual Inadequacy*[70] (a condensation for the lay person is *Understanding Human Sexual Inadequacy*[71]). Virtually all forms of sex therapy developed after Masters and Johnson published their approach have been variations on their original approach. Further, there is no evidence that relief of a sexual problem leads to ~~the formation of a~~ replacement problem.

Anxiety as a Cause of Sexual Dysfunction

It is generally agreed that all sexual dysfunctions (except the minority caused by physical problems such as diabetes or spinal cord injury) are the result of a single, pervasive cause: anxiety. This anxiety can be as straightforward as a fear of a specific sexual failure, such as an inability to reach orgasm. It may be much more complex, such as a fear of becoming close to another person, which relates back to negative experiences in early childhood. Or, perhaps most commonly, it may be a combination of a variety of anxiety-producing factors, which may be exacerbated by physical problems. In any case, anxiety is the common element that, for almost everyone, interrupts the ability to fully function sexually.

Every person defends against anxiety-producing situations differently. Some people are quick to respond; others are slow. Some have many physical reactions such as palm sweating or mouth dryness; others want to talk or be quiet. These differences account for why anxiety can result in a problem of erectile difficulty for one person, inability to have orgasm for another, and a lack of sexual interest for a third. We all choose to avoid unsafe situations, so as we approach danger, we avoid. If you have learned that being sexual with a particular partner is "dangerous," you are likely to feel little desire to be with that person. If you have found that being sexual with all partners is dangerous, you might develop an inhibition of sexual desire for partner sex and instead express your sexuality, anger, and low self-esteem by looking in windows, exposing your genitals to strangers, becoming sexually aroused by certain objects, or a multitude of other variations.

Helen Singer Kaplan, a noted psychiatrist and sex therapist, has identified three phases of sexual response: desire, excitement, and orgasm.[72] Anxiety can produce dysfunctions in each phase. The principal desire phase disorder is hypoactive desire—lack of sexual interest. Excitement phase disorders include erectile difficulty in men and lack of arousal in women, which results in little vaginal lubrication or other normal physical responses to sexual stimulation. (These are discussed later in this chapter). Orgasm phase dysfunctions include premature ejaculation or retarded ejaculation in men and orgasmic dysfunction in women. Two dysfunctions that are not associated with a particular phase of sexual response are (*a*) vaginismus in women—a painful, spastic contraction of the pelvic muscles that prohibits vaginal penetration and (*b*) the male counterpart to vaginismus, ejaculatory pain due to muscle spasms.

Because some situations may be perceived as safe and others dangerous, all these dysfunctions can be present in some situations or with some partners and absent at other times or with other partners. And because sexual problems are almost always relationship problems, the dynamics of the relationship have a profound effect on the success or failure of treatment. This is why treating some sexual problems is straightforward and simple and treating others is extremely complex.

Principles of Sex Therapy

The basic tenets of most common forms of sex therapy are outlined below:

1. Sexual behavior, although a natural physiological process, is largely governed by learned behavior. Many persons who suffer from sexual dysfunction have experienced inadequate or inaccurate learning. Further, the more information one has (about sex or anything else), the more likely is that individual to make healthy decisions and function in the most satisfying way.

2. The vast majority of sexual problems are psychological in origin, not organic. Although most have physical manifestations (spastic contractions of the pelvic musculature, erectile difficulty), they originate from mental preoccupations that interrupt sexual response: performance anxiety, fear of failure, unreasonable expectations, focusing on a goal, and so on. Some sexual problems are caused by a combination of psychological and physical deficits; for example, a man may have difficulty achieving erection *partly* because of performance anxiety and *partly* because of poor blood flow to his genitals.

3. Persons benefit from verbal communication with their partners regarding their sexual behavior preferences.

4. The most effective way to learn about one's own sexual response is through masturbation, an activity that provides immediate, accurate feedback.

Only when one is familiar with her or his own response can one accurately communicate it to a partner.

5. In a sexual relationship, both persons contribute positively and negatively to the interaction. There is no such thing as an uninvolved partner.[73]

6. Virtually all sexual dysfunctions are either correctable or adaptable; the symptoms can be reversed, or behaviors can be adapted to accommodate performance problems, thereby enabling the persons to obtain sexual gratification.

The Sex Therapy Clinic

The following section describes the experience a couple might have during the course of sex therapy.*

Bill, age 36, and Mary, age 33, had been married for ten years when they first telephoned the sex therapy clinic. Bill is an attorney; Mary is, at present, primarily responsible for the care of their children, ages 6 and 3, and is active in civic organizations.

Bill and Mary were each aware of sexual problems in their marriage from almost the beginning, but for years they were never discussed, except in an argument. Mary was quite sure she had never experienced orgasm, and Bill had, early in their sexual relationship, been unable to control his ejaculation. His response resulted in his reaching orgasm almost immediately at the commencement of intercourse. More recently, Mary had become almost completely turned off to sex, and Bill found he was experiencing increasing difficulty maintaining his erection so that intercourse could occur at all. Both seemed aware, although it had not been stated outright, that the tensions in the sexual area were carrying over into other areas of their rela-

---

*This case history illustrates the method used by the author when seeing couples in intensive sex therapy. As stated above, virtually all forms of sex therapy currently in practice are based on psychotherapeutic techniques pioneered by William Masters and Virginia Johnson and described in *Human Sexual Inadequacy*. These techniques have been expanded on by many sex therapists, the most notable of whom is Helen Singer Kaplan. Her ideas are described in *The New Sex Therapy* and *Disorders of Sexual Desire and Other New Concepts and Techniques in Sex Therapy*. I wish to credit them.

tionship. Further, if the sexual problems did not get resolved, the relationship would probably continue to deteriorate and eventually end in separation and divorce.

Acknowledging these rather grim realities, Mary finally gathered enough courage to ask her gynecologist for help. He examined her, found no physical problems, reassured her that help was available, and suggested that she call a sex therapy clinic where he had referred patients before.

Mary and Bill discussed the doctor's advice and agreed that something needed to be done. Because Mary felt the problem was largely *hers*, she made the telephone call.

Mary's inquiry was referred to a woman therapist. The therapist, realizing the anxiety that almost always accompanies the initial contact, projected a reassuring tone as she briefly explored the problems with Mary. She explained that both of them would be seen by a male-female cotherapy team should they decide to participate in sex therapy. After answering all of Mary's questions, the therapist suggested that she discuss it with Bill and, if they desired, set up an evaluation meeting.

THE EVALUATION SESSION   Bill and Mary made a preliminary decision to proceed, so the evaluation session was scheduled. The purposes of this initial meeting were (*a*) to provide an opportunity for the clients to meet the cotherapists who would be seeing them should they enter therapy; (*b*) to provide for the therapists, through discussion with each client, the background and current assessment of the problems to determine if therapy would likely be helpful, what level might be most appropriate, or if referral to another agency might be more fruitful; (*c*) to describe the treatment plan that might be used; and (*d*) to answer all questions before a further decision to proceed was made. The male therapist suggested a physician for Bill to see to rule out any organic or physiological reason for his erectile difficulty. Although he suspected strongly that the erectile problems were anxiety related and not caused by physical problems, he wanted to be sure he wasn't attempting to treat a biological problem with counseling. Bill agreed to see this physician. Bill and Mary left the sex therapy office feeling greatly relieved; they had begun to deal with the situation after ten years of avoidance, and the therapists had reassured them that their problems were neither unique nor hopeless.

THE SEXUAL HISTORY   In the next therapy meeting, the sexual history was gathered. The couple was separated, each meeting with the therapist of their own gender. Each therapist explored the client's childhood and adolescent experiences, goals of therapy, patterns in their family of origin, sexual value systems, the history of the sexual problems, strengths and weaknesses of the marriage, and much more.[74] The purposes of the history-taking session are twofold: (*a*) for the therapist to understand, as accurately and completely as possible, the client she or he will be principally representing in treatment (the client of the same gender) and (*b*) for the client to establish "comfort" with that therapist, which will facilitate the entire treatment process.

During the history-taking session, the therapists were particularly careful to ask specific questions and press for specific, detailed answers. A very important rule for sex counselors and therapists to observe is to avoid *assuming* anything. Because specific, personal sexual experiences are not something people tend to talk about, particularly if there is a sexual problem involved, persons often assume their behaviors are similar to everybody else's. The thorough, careful therapist will avoid serious pitfalls that will sabotage the success of therapy if they are not noticed. Two examples, drawn from my clinical experience, illustrate this point.

One couple reported that when the woman had an orgasm, she "really came." The therapists pressed for more information: The man said she "ejaculated so much it made a puddle on the bed." If the therapists had assumed he was talking about copious lubrication, they might have been pleased to know her body was responding so well. She was, to the couple's shock, suffering from urinary incontinence; her pelvic musculature was so poor that when she experienced orgasm she was voiding her bladder. Although, with the correct diagnosis, this turned out to be a relatively simple problem to treat, the couple would not have known what to do without the therapists' guidance, which begins with specific, accurate information.[75]

Another client who had recently been divorced, in part because of the couple's inability to have children, reported that he could have orgasms through masturbation and intercourse. When the therapist asked for more specific information, he learned that what the man was defining as orgasm and ejaculation was, in fact, the secretion of Cowper's gland fluid, a clear substance that drops out of the end of the penis during arousal but *prior to* ejaculation and orgasm. He had developed a lifelong pattern of stimulation to arousal but always stopped prior to orgasm; he didn't realize there was more he could experience. Previous psychotherapists had taken his report of orgasm at face value. The sex therapist suggested that he continue the stimulation, and he reported a very pleasant surprise with his next sexual experience.

It may be tempting to assume that people who suffer from such gross misinformation would be people who might be misinformed in a lot of other areas. Beware—general intelligence is not a measure of sex intelligence. The couple in the incontinence example were college graduates; the man who was misinformed about his orgasm was a prominent and highly respected professional person.

THE ROUNDTABLE   Bill and Mary met with the therapists for the next meeting, the roundtable. The purposes of the roundtable meeting are (*a*) to review each client's history as it relates to the sexual problem, (*b*) to trace and account for the development of the problem, (*c*) to outline the treatment plan, (*d*) to dispel myths and correct misinformation that were uncovered in previous meetings, and (*e*) to assign the initial home experiences and communication exercise.

The male therapist, in reviewing Bill's history, discussed how Bill had *learned* a pattern of quick ejaculation from his sexual experiences as a teenager. Because he was fearful at that time that he might be caught, it was functional for him to come to orgasm quickly. This was long before he learned that prolonging his arousal would be more pleasurable for both his partner and himself. When he entered marriage, he expected his response to slow down as he became more familiar with Mary. But Bill seemed to have learned the pattern of speedy response so thoroughly that he was utterly unable to respond any other way.

The more he worried about the problem, the more anxiety he experienced, causing him to have even less control. Eventually, he started experiencing difficulty with erection. He had become so preoccupied with his performance that he was blocking all erotic stimulation—a necessary condition for erection to occur in a sexual encounter.

Mary, on the other hand, had learned as a teenager to be *sexy*, but not *sexual*. That is, she was expected to attract men but not to "go too far." She became adept at kissing, hugging, and petting—becoming very aroused—but then stopping the sexual encounter. This pattern, arousal followed by turnoff, later victimized her in marriage, long after she had to worry about getting pregnant, venereal disease, or ruining her reputation. Not surprisingly, she described her teenage petting experiences as the best sexual encounters of her life.

For the first several years of marriage, Mary remembered experiencing high arousal, but coming short of orgasm, and then "going numb, feeling nothing." In the more recent past, her body felt less and less aroused, as if to say, "I'm not going to reach orgasm anyway, so why bother?"

The therapists pointed out these patterns, emphasizing that the sexual problems were neither person's fault. New, more functional patterns could be learned to replace the old, dysfunctional ones.

The woman therapist gave Mary a beginning self-pleasuring assignment. This was to help her learn her own sexual response, so that later she could share it with and teach it to Bill. Both agreed there was no way Bill could automatically *know* what was pleasurable to Mary, particularly if she didn't know herself. Mary had never masturbated, and with encouragement and specific, graduated instructions, she agreed to try.[76]

The male therapist instructed Bill to continue masturbating, something he had been doing since childhood. He suggested that Bill slow down, however, to learn as much about his various levels of arousal as possible.

TOUCHING   The couple was instructed to abstain from intercourse, in order to eliminate the anxiety that had invariably surrounded that activity. In place of intercourse, they were given the following instructions:

To many persons, the idea of touching any part of the body is thought of only as a preliminary to orgasm. Thinking of touching in this way often causes the touching to become less valued in and of itself. Although the entire body may be pleasant to touch and to have touched, emphasis is usually placed on the breasts, vaginal area, penis, and testicles. Touching need not be explicitly genital or goal oriented to be pleasurable. Touching, by yourself or with a partner, can be a joyful expression of discovery and exploration, of giving and getting.

Plan ahead and prepare, together, a quiet, private, warm, and comfortable place. Create an atmosphere that is pleasant for you. It may include soft-colored lights, or candles and music, or other things that help you relax. Get really comfortable by removing your clothing and assuming positions that will permit relaxation during long periods of touching. Give yourselves a lot of time. Slowly become very familiar with your partner's entire body. Remember, this experience is not one of trying to arouse one's partner sexually; but it is an experience that is designed to give you time and space to explore your own feelings about touching and being touched. Touch, stroke, squeeze, and caress your partner for your own pleasure. The feeling you receive need not be an arousing one. You will feel something; get in touch with whatever that feeling is.

You may wish to shower together, using pleasant soaps on one another's body, or try a shower in the dark (you must then really rely on touch). When you do come together for a touching experience it is suggested you use a pleasant-tasting, nonalcohol-based lotion or oil, or a baby powder, which is particularly nice in warm weather. These facilitate the movement of skin on skin and reduce friction. Oils or lotions should first be poured in your hands to be warmed, or warmed on a stove or candle stand.

Use your fingers, your fingertips, your palms, and your full hand to touch and caress in different ways. This is not a message. Massage is designed primarily to give pleasure to the other person. Remember, the major purpose of this touching experience is to discover feelings for yourself through touching your partner. It may be pleasant to close your eyes while touching so you can "get into" your own feelings without observing your partner's response. Try a joyful fantasy, if you like; or pretend you've lost the use of your sight for awhile and must rely on touch alone. The person being touched has only to lie there and concentrate on his or her own feelings of being touched. Sometimes, too, you may want to explore your partner's body visually while you are touching and would feel more comfortable if your partner were to close his or her eyes. If so, ask your partner to do so. If it would be pleasant to comb your partner's hair, do so. Because you are touching your partner for yourself, you need not concern yourself with your partner's reaction, unless it is one of discomfort or pain (if so, your partner must tell you). After each touching experience discuss your feelings with one another; not in a directive or accusatory fashion but with an effort toward understanding each other's feelings about touching and being touched. Do not make assumptions about your partner's feelings. It is important to remember to communicate with one another and not to move faster than your comfort levels.

The first week we ask you to have "touching experiences" a minimum of three times during the week to reinforce comfortable feelings. We will discuss with you which partner should initiate the first touching experience. After the "initiator" has fully explored his or her partner's body for his or her own pleasure, she or he will change off and the person who was touching for his or her own pleasure will then become the one who is touched. During this first week we do not want the man to touch his partner's breasts, nipples, or vaginal area, not do we want the woman to touch her partner's nipples, penis, or testicles. Touching should be done only with the hands during this week.

VERBAL COMMUNICATIONS   Bill and Mary were also given the following instructions to enhance their verbal communications.[77]

Most sexually intimate couples think they know considerably more about each other's feelings, attitudes, and behaviors than they, in fact, really do know. They take pride in outguessing and in predicting their partner's responses without adequately communicating with each other. They believe "If he or she loved me, he or she would know how I feel."

Responsibility for Self

We are each responsible for our own sexuality. We should not wait for someone else to discover it for us. We need to explore, discover, and understand our own sexual responses. We are then free to share or not to share our sexuality with another person. If we decide to share our sexuality, we need to be willing to communicate with our partner what we have learned about ourselves, to be open and vulnerable, to risk. We also need to be willing to learn about our partner's sexuality from our partner. We cannot make assumptions about his or her needs, feelings, or thoughts, without asking. Too often we are wrong. In order to share a sexual experience on an equal basis, we must both have and express knowledge, comfort, and responsibility for our own sexuality. This responsibility is necessary to take ownership for our own feelings, attitudes, and ideas, as well as our behavior.

Representation of Self

Once we are responsible for our own sexuality and have made a decision to share our sexuality with another person, we need to learn functional ways to represent ourselves clearly to our partner. Perhaps the simplest and most effective verbal communication method is "I language."

I Language

a. "You make me so angry when you don't pick up your clothes."
    (an accusatory statement, which is most likely to place your partner on the defensive)

b. "I'm angry because in addition to picking up
    my own clothes I feel I have to pick your clothes
    up too."
    (permits further communication and represents
    your feelings)

a. "Let's go out to dinner."
    (a confused message that takes over your partner's
    response)

b. "I'd like to go out to dinner and wonder if you
    would like to also."
    (much clearer)

a. "You're so clumsy when you touch my breasts."
    (another accusatory message likely to shut down
    communication—not open it up)

b. "I get turned off when you touch my breasts that
    way because it hurts; I'd like to show you what
    kind of touch feels good."

a. "Do you want to go to the movies tonight?"
    (answer: "I don't know, do you?"—next response:
    "I don't know, I asked you first."—result:
    confusion)

b. "I would like to see _____ tonight, and
    wonder if you would also like to see that film?"
    (extremely clear)

*The purpose of "I language" is not to promote
agreement but rather to promote accurate
communication and understanding. Only with
accurate understanding can you ever know if you
agree or disagree. When you use "I language" you
must first be aware of your own feeling, attitude, idea,
or thought, before you can clearly state it to your
partner. Thus, the use of "I language" helps you to get
in touch with your own feeling first. All feelings are
real for you—they exist—they may not always be
rational—but you have them; it is your responsibility
to represent your feeling. Do not expect your partner
to know your feelings clearly unless you represent
them. Through the use of "I language" you minimize
putting your partner in a defensive position. You also
optimize opening further communication. You speak
for you, not for someone else. It is hoped you know
yourself better than anyone else because you have
given yourself permission to know and to represent
yourself. By honestly expressing your feelings you
encourage your partner to do the same. Honesty*

*often seems risky when used with someone you care
about; but the alternative may be confusion.*

THE PHYSIOLOGY SESSION   The next therapy meeting
followed the roundtable by one week. The purposes
of this meeting were (*a*) to review and evaluate the
couple's experiences in touching and communication,
(*b*) to make new assignments, and (*c*) to discuss the
physiology of human sexual response.

The therapists asked Bill and Mary about their first
week's assignments, focusing on relaxation, learning,
and comfort as the goals—not sexual arousal. Both
reported feeling awkward during the first touching experiences, but the awkwardness soon passed and both
enjoyed the experience of performance-free touching.

Because Bill and Mary seemed comfortable, they
were given the next touching assignment. They were
instructed to do exactly as they had done the previous
week, except now they could include breasts, nipples,
and genitals in the touching. These areas were not to
become the focus of the sessions, nor was there an
expectation of arousal. In fact, if arousal did occur, they
were instructed to move the touching to another area.
And, of course, they were not to have intercourse.

The therapists asked about "I language." Mary had
found it particularly useful in communicating anger to
Bill; he had largely forgotten to use it. The therapists
reemphasized its importance, particularly following a
touching experience.

Bill reported that he was able to slow his arousal
in masturbation as much as he wanted. This didn't
seem significant to him—his lack of control was associated with intercourse—but he was becoming more
aware of his levels of arousal. He was learning to recognize the point of ejaculatory inevitability—the few
seconds immediately preceding orgasm. The therapist
informed him that his efforts at slowing his response
need to be focused prior to ejaculatory inevitability;
once he is in that stage, orgasm is, as it states, inevitable.

Mary had spent some private time each day exploring her body. She had many questions for the
woman therapist and seemed eager to continue her
exploration.

The therapists gave Bill and Mary two additional
assignments. They taught the couple the use of the
squeeze technique for controlling premature ejacula-

tion,[78] and Mary was given exercises designed to strengthen her vaginal muscles, thereby increasing vaginal sensations.[79] They were also asked to read *For Each Other*, by Lonnie Barbach, to learn more about sharing sexual intimacy.[80]

The therapists then presented, using slides, factual information on human sexual response. (This educational experience is used to promote knowledge and understanding of physical changes that occur in the body as a result of sexual arousal. Much of this data was gathered by Masters and Johnson in their studies of the physiology of human sexual response.)

In their discussion of sexual response, the male therapist assumed primary responsibility for presenting male response, the female therapist for presenting female response. They paid particular attention to the physiological components of Bill and Mary's sexual dysfunctions—nonorgasmic response, premature ejaculation, and erectile dysfunction.

Masters and Johnson identified four stages of sexual response in females and males: excitement, plateau, orgasm, and resolution. There are many similarities in the physical responses of men and women. These include the two major body changes that result from sexual stimulation—myotonia, or muscle tension, and vasocongestion, or blood engorgement.

The male therapist explained the genital response in the male, using slides and models to illustrate the physical changes. In *excitement*, blood flows into the erectile tissue of the penis (vasocongestion), resulting in erection. The scrotum (the sac surrounding the testicles) becomes thicker, more wrinkled, and the testicles move up closer to the body.

Plateau response is characterized by the continuation of erection, although it often waxes and wanes during sex play with a partner. The testicles become fully elevated, rotate toward the front, and become blood engorged causing expansion in their size. The Cowper's gland secretes a small amount of clear fluid that comes out the tip of the penis. The purpose of this fluid is generally thought to be to cleanse the urethra of urine, thereby neutralizing the chemical environment for the passage of sperm.

The *orgasm* stage in men consists of two phases. The first is ejaculatory inevitability, a short period dur-

ing which stimulation sufficient to trigger orgasm has occurred and the resulting ejaculation becomes inevitable. The second phase, ejaculation, results from rhythmic contractions (myotonia) forcing sperm and semen through the urethra. Simultaneous with this is the very pleasant physical sensation of orgasm.

The final stage, *resolution*, represents a return to the unstimulated state. In resolution, the penis loses its erection, and the testicles lose their engorgement and elevation.

In women, the *excitement* stage of sexual response ushers in many changes. The process of vaginal lubrication begins. This response is analogous to the male erection; it is caused by sexual stimulation and is, physiologically, a blood engorgement response. The uterus and cervix begin to move up and away from the vagina. The clitoris and labia minora (inner lips) enlarge and the labia majora (outer lips) spread. Breast size increases slightly and the nipples become erect.

In *plateau*, the uterus continues in its movement up and back, the vagina lengthens and balloons at the rear, and the outer third of the vagina contracts, causing a gripping effect. The clitoris retracts under its hood, making it seem to disappear.

At *orgasm*, the uterus and vagina become involved in wavelike muscular contractions. This response, as well as the subjective pleasure of orgasm, are very similar to the experience of the male.

In *resolution*, the cervix and uterus drop to their normal positions and the outer third of the vagina returns to normal, followed by the inner two thirds. The clitoris and the breasts also return to normal.

The therapists also discussed the many involuntary *extragenital* physical responses in men and women. These include muscle tension responses such as facial grimace, spastic contractions of the hands and feet, and pelvic thrusting. Extragenital blood engorgement responses include sex flush, blood pressure and heart-rate increases, and perspiration on soles of feet and palms of hands.

Finally, the therapists discussed how aging affects sexual response. They emphasized that persons are capable of experiencing pleasurable sexual response throughout life; although their bodies may slow down, they do not need to stop. The effects of aging on sexual response are summarized in Figures 6.1 and 6.2.

FIGURE 6.1

Aging Aspects of Sexual Responses in Men

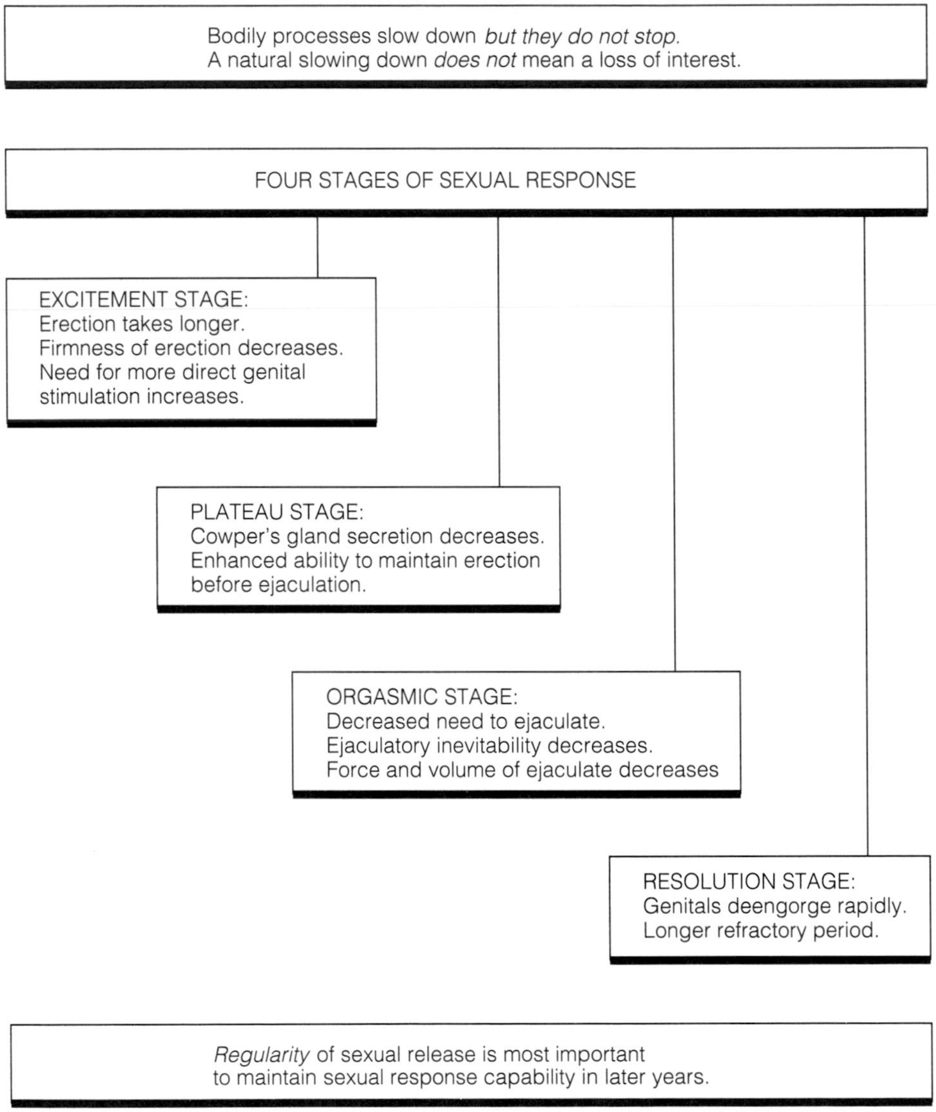

Bodily processes slow down *but they do not stop.*
A natural slowing down *does not* mean a loss of interest.

FOUR STAGES OF SEXUAL RESPONSE

EXCITEMENT STAGE:
Erection takes longer.
Firmness of erection decreases.
Need for more direct genital
stimulation increases.

PLATEAU STAGE:
Cowper's gland secretion decreases.
Enhanced ability to maintain erection
before ejaculation.

ORGASMIC STAGE:
Decreased need to ejaculate.
Ejaculatory inevitability decreases.
Force and volume of ejaculate decreases

RESOLUTION STAGE:
Genitals deengorge rapidly.
Longer refractory period.

Regularity of sexual release is most important
to maintain sexual response capability in later years.

FIGURE 6.2

Aging Aspects of Sexual Response in Women

Bodily processes slow down *but they do not stop.*
A natural slowing down *does not* mean a loss of interest.

FOUR STAGES OF SEXUAL RESPONSE

EXCITEMENT STAGE:
Lubrication occurs more slowly.
Amount of lubrication decreases.
Clitoris may become smaller.

PLATEAU STAGE:
Vagina increases less in size.

ORGASMIC STAGE:
Usually a shorter orgasmic phase.
Occasionally a painful spastic contraction
of uterus at orgasm (indicates sex
hormone levels are below normal).

RESOLUTION STAGE:
Genital area deengorges rapidly.

Regularity of sexual release is most important
to maintain sexual response capability in later years.

Sex therapy for Bill and Mary continued for eight additional weekly meetings. Mary progressed dramatically in the fourth week; she experienced her first orgasm in self-stimulation, and she continued in her ability to stimulate herself to orgasm.

During one of the couple-touching experiences, Mary stimulated herself to orgasm. Sporadically at first, and then consistently by week six, each was able to bring the other to orgasm through hand stimulation. Touching experiences in the later weeks of therapy emphasized whole-body touching, genital touching, female-active intercourse with simultaneous clitoral stimulation, and lots of verbal feedback.

Bill practiced the penile squeeze (the technique to delay ejaculation) in self-stimulation, and Mary applied it during their couple experiences. They found he could experience increased stimulation with less need for the squeeze. In the seventh week, Bill was able to control his orgasm, assuming there had not been a period of abstinence from orgasm, as he desired.

Not surprisingly, once Bill understood the mechanisms that had previously precluded his having an erection, and once he and Mary were comfortable in their sexual interactions, erectile difficulty was seldom a problem. When a problem did occur, Bill was able to identify the cause, take it in stride, and have a better experience the next time.

At the termination of therapy, Mary and Bill reported that they were both enjoying their sexual experiences and that improvement in their sexual intimacy had relieved many other tensions in the relationship. Their communication had also improved greatly. They were interested in Mary achieving orgasm in intercourse through penile thrusting alone, but this certainly wasn't an all-important goal. Further, they knew what they could do to work toward that and looked forward to the process.

A major thesis of this chapter is that almost all social workers, regardless of their specific professional responsibilities, are sometimes called on to be sex counselors. Further, the levels of treatment of sexual problems require varying degrees of knowledge, comfort, and experience. Because most social workers are not sex therapists, the need for responsible referral arises. To assist persons in locating competent, experienced sex therapists, the American Association of Sex, Educators, Counselors, and Therapists (AASECT) certifies qualified sex therapists. The association will, by writing their office at Eleven Dupont Circle, N.W., Suite 220, Washington, D.C. 20036, provide the names of knowledgeable, ethical, and experienced sex therapists.

SUMMARY

Practically every conceivable sexual activity is socially acceptable to some groups of people. What is defined as acceptable and unacceptable sexual behavior varies from culture to culture and from one time period to another. Judeo-Christian values, the Puritan influence, and Victorian morality have sought in our history to repress sexual expression. At present there is ambiguity and confusion about what ought to be the sexual code and behavior of Americans. For the past several decades our society has been undergoing a revolution in sexual values and mores. Three formal studies have made immense contributions to improving our understanding of sexuality—those of Freud, Kinsey, and the team of Masters and Johnson.

This text uses a social variance approach to examining sexual concerns rather than a social problems approach, since there is, as yet, no general consensus about which sexual acts are acceptable and which are not. Three categories of sexual variances were discussed: tolerated sex variance, asocial sex variance, and structural sex variance. Tolerated sex variance includes masturbation, premarital intercourse, and heterosexual oral-genital contact between consenting adults.

Asocial sex variance includes those acts that elicit strong disapproval and at the same time do not have a social structure that supports them. Acts in this category include incest, child molestation, rape, voyeurism, and exhibitionism.

Structural sex variance refers to those acts that run counter to prevailing norms and legal statutes while at the same time having supportive social structures. Homosexuality is in this category and was discussed at some length.

Personal sexual concerns (for example, men worrying about premature ejaculation and women experiencing painful intercourse) were also described.

The chapter ended with an examination of the role of the social worker as a helping agent to persons suffering from sexual problems. The social worker is frequently called on to step out of her or his primary professional role to become a sex counselor. In this role the worker performs short-term, often crisis-oriented counseling directed toward the alleviation of some immediate difficulty related to sex. Issues specific to effective sex counseling, such as the counselor's vocabulary, were highlighted in this section.

Sex therapy focuses on the alleviation of sexual dysfunction, implying a planned change sequence involving several contacts between the client(s) and the therapist(s). The stages of intensive sex therapy are problem definition, history gathering, physical examination, information dissemination, prescribed sexual and communication experiences, and ongoing evaluation. The historical and theoretical underpinnings of current sex therapy were discussed. Critical issues in sex therapy, such as the therapist's need to avoid making assumptions, were examined. An example of intensive sex therapy was given that paid particular attention to prescribed sexual and communication experiences.

NOTES

1. Havelock Ellis, *Sex and Marriage: Eros in Contemporary Life* (Westport, CT: Greenwood Press, 1977).
2. David A. Schulz, *Human Sexuality* (Englewood Cliffs, NJ: Prentice-Hall, 1979), p. 4.
3. *New York Times*, March 7, 1976.
4. John Gagnon and Bruce Henderson, *Human Sexuality: The Age of Ambiguity* (Boston: Little, Brown, 1975), p. 10.
5. Clellan S. Ford and Frank A. Beach, *Patterns of Sexual Behavior* (New York: Harper & Row, 1951).
6. Gagnon and Henderson, *Human Sexuality: The Age of Ambiguity*, p. 14.
7. Duncan Chappell et al., "Forcible Rape: A Comparative Study of Offenses Known to the Police in Boston and Los Angeles," in *Studies in the Sociology of Sex*, ed. James H. Henslin (Englewood Cliffs, NJ: Prentice-Hall, 1971), pp. 174–175.
8. Richard A. Maier, *Human Sexuality in Perspective* (Chicago: Nelson-Hall, 1984), pp. 391–393.
9. Gagnon and Henderson, *Human Sexuality: The Age of Ambiguity*, p. 16.
10. J. John Palen, *Social Problems* (New York: McGraw-Hill, 1979), p. 544.
11. Ibid.
12. Morton Hunt, *Sexual Behavior in the 1970s* (Chicago: Playboy Press, 1974).
13. W. G. Steglich and Margaret K. Snooks, *American Social Problems: An Institutional View* (Santa Monica, CA: Goodyear Publishing Co., 1980).
14. Alfred C. Kinsey et al., *Sexual Behavior in the Human Male* (Philadelphia: W. B. Saunders, 1948).
15. Alfred C. Kinsey et al., *Sexual Behavior in the Human Female* (Philadelphia: W. B. Saunders, 1953).
16. William H. Masters and Virginia E. Johnson, *Human Sexual Response* (Boston: Little, Brown, 1966). For a layperson, an excellent summary is Ruth Brecher and Edward Brecher, *An Analysis of Human Sexual Response* (New York: Signet Books, 1966).
17. William H. Masters and Virginia E. Johnson, *Human Sexual Inadequacy* (Boston: Little, Brown, 1970). For a layperson, an excellent summary is Fred Belliveau and Lin Richter, *Understanding Human Sexual Inadequacy* (New York: Bantam Books, 1970).
18. Gagnon and Henderson, *Human Sexuality: The Age of Ambiguity*, p. 14.
19. Maier, *Human Sexuality in Perspective*, pp. 145–147.
20. Herant Katchadourian and Donald T. Lunde, *Fundamentals of Human Sexuality*, 2d ed. (New York: Holt, Rinehart & Winston, 1975).
21. Joseph Julian and William Kornblum, *Social Problems*, 5th ed. (Englewood Cliffs, NJ: Prentice-Hall, 1986), pp. 81–83.
22. John H. Gagnon and William Simon, "Introduction: Deviant Behavior and Sexual Deviance," in *Sexual Deviance*, eds. John H. Gagnon and William Simon (New York: Harper & Row, 1967), p. 8.

23. Charles H. McCaghy, "Child Molesting," *Sexual Behavior* 1, 1971, pp. 16–24.

24. Julian and Kornblum, *Social Problems*, p. 79.

25. McCaghy, "Child Molesting," pp. 16–24.

26. Ibid.

27. Paul H. Gebhard, J. H. Gagnon, W. B. Pomeroy, and Cornelia Christenson, *Sex Offenders: An Analysis of Types* (New York: Harper & Row, 1965).

28. A. Nicholas Groth, "The Incest Offender," in *Intervention in Child Sexual Abuse*, ed. Suzanne M. Sgroi (Lexington, MA: Lexington Books, 1982), pp. 215–239.

29. McCaghy, "Child Molesting," pp. 16–24.

30. John C. Gagnon, "Female Child Victims of Sex Offenses," *Social Problems* 13, 1965, pp. 176–192.

31. Edward Sarafino, "An Estimate of Nationwide Incidence of Sexual Offenses Against Children," *Child Welfare* 58, no. 2 (February 1979), pp. 127–133.

32. Hunt, *Sexual Behavior in the 1970s*.

33. Sarafino, "An Estimate of Nationwide Incidence of Sexual Offenses against Children," pp. 127–133.

34. Blair Justice and Rita Justice, *The Broken Taboo: Sex in the Family* (New York: Human Sciences Press, 1979).

35. Ibid., p. 177.

36. Federal Bureau of Investigation, *Crime in the United States: Uniform Crime Report, 1987* (Washington, D.C.: U.S. Government Printing Office, 1988).

37. Wisconsin State Journal, November 6, 1982, sec. 1, p. 2.

38. A. Nicholas Groth, *Men Who Rape* (New York: Plenum Press, 1979).

39. Janet S. Hyde, *Understanding Human Sexuality* (New York: McGraw-Hill, 1979), p. 387.

40. Ann W. Burgess and Lynda Holmstrom, *Rape: Victims of Crisis* (Bowie, MD: Robert J. Brady, 1974).

41. Ann W. Burgess and Lynda Holmstrom, "Rape Trauma Syndrome," *American Journal of Psychiatry* 131, 1974, pp. 981–986.

42. Gene G. Abel et al., "Self-Reported Sex Crimes of Nonincarcerated Paraphiliacs," *Journal of Interpersonal Violence* 2, no. 1, March 1987, pp. 3–25.

43. Hyde, *Understanding Human Sexuality*, p. 317.

44. Kinsey et al., *Sexual Behavior in the Human Male*, p. 639.

45. Thomas Sullivan et al., *Social Problems* (New York: John Wiley, 1980), p. 537.

46. C. A. Tripp, *The Homosexual Matrix* (New York: McGraw-Hill, 1975), p. 99.

47. H. T. Buckner, "The Transvestic Career Path," *Psychiatry* 33, 1970, pp. 381–389.

48. Brian Garner and Richard W. Smith, "Are There Really Any Gay Male Athletes? An Empirical Survey," *Journal of Sex Research* 13, 1977, pp. 22–34.

49. Evelyn Hooker, "The Adjustment of the Male Overt Homosexual," *Journal of Projective Techniques* 21, 1957, pp. 18–31.

50. Ian Robertson, *Social Problems*, 2d ed. (New York: Random House, 1980), p. 414.

51. McCaghy, "Child Molesting," pp. 16–24.

52. "10 Million May Have AIDS Virus," *Wisconsin State Journal*, June 3, 1987, p. 2.

53. Ibid.

54. Kinsey et al., *Sexual Behavior in the Human Male*; and Kinsey et al., *Sexual Behavior in the Human Female*.

55. Hyde, *Understanding Human Sexuality*, pp. 332–334.

56. Ibid., p. 334.

57. Alan P. Bell, Martin S. Weinberg, and Sue Kiefer Hammersmith, *Sexual Preference* (Bloomington, IN: Indiana University Press, 1981).

58. Evelyn Hooker, "The Homosexual Community," in *Proceedings of the XIV International Congress of Applied Psychology*, vol. 2, *Personality Research* (Copenhagen: Munksgaard, 1962), pp. 52–53.

59. Barry M. Dank, "Coming Out in the Gay World," *Psychiatry* 34 (May 1971), p. 186.

60. Jack H. Hedblom, "The Female Homosexual: Social and Attitudinal Dimensions," in *Deviance: Studies in Definition, Management, and Treatment*, eds. Simon Dinitz, Russell R. Dynes, and Alfred C. Clarke, 2d ed. (New York: Oxford University Press, 1975), p. 246.

61. C. Patton, *Sex and Germs: The Politics of AIDS* (Boston: South End Press, 1985).

62. Kathleen A. Rounds, "AIDS in Rural Areas: Challenges to Providing Care," *Social Work* 33, no. 3 (May–June 1988), pp. 257–261.

63. Jane E. Brody, "Sex Research Has Earned Respectability," *New York Times*, January 8, 1978, sec. 4, p. 20.

64. Belliveau and Richter, *Understanding Human Sexual Inadequacy*.

65. Kinsey et al., *Sexual Behavior in the Human Male*; and Kinsey et al., *Sexual Behavior in the Human Female*.

66. Warren R. Johnson, "Sex Education of the Mentally Retarded," in *Human Sexuality and the Mentally Retarded*, eds. Felix de la Cruz and Gerald D. LaVeck (New York: Brunner-Mazel, 1973), p. 64.

67. Jack S. Annon, *Behavioral Treatment of Sexual Problems* (Hagerstown, MD: Harper & Row, 1976).

68. Ibid., p. 65.

69. Ibid., p. 77.

70. Masters and Johnson, *Human Sexual Inadequacy.*

71. Belliveau and Richter, *Understanding Human Sexual Inadequacy.*

72. Helen Singer Kaplan, *The New Sex Therapy* (New York: Brunner-Mazel, 1974), p. 290; and Helen Singer Kaplan, *Disorders of Sexual Desire and Other New Concepts and Techniques in Sex Therapy* (New York: Simon & Schuster, 1979).

73. Masters and Johnson, *Human Sexual Inadequacy*, pp. 2–3.

74. An excellent outline for a sexual history can be found in Masters and Johnson, *Human Sexual Inadequacy*, pp. 34–51.

75. Raymond Rosen and J. Gayle Beck, *Patterns of Sexual Arousal* (New York: Guilford, 1987).

76. Lonnie Garfield Barbach, *For Yourself* (Garden City, NY: Doubleday, 1975).

77. "I language" is a communication technique suggested by many helping professionals. For a more thorough treatment, see Thomas Gordon, *Parent Effectiveness Training (The Tested New Way to Raise Responsible Children)* (New York: Wyden, 1970).

78. Masters and Johnson, *Human Sexual Inadequacy*, pp. 101–115.

79. Sandra R. Lieblum and Lawrence A. Pervin, eds., *Principles and Practice of Sex Therapy* (New York: Guilford, 1980).

80. Lonnie Barbach, *For Each Other* (Garden City, NY: Anchor Press/Doubleday, 1982).

7

DRUG ABUSE
AND DRUG
TREATMENT
PROGRAMS

P ractically everyone has taken one or more drugs. Most people have, on a few occasions, used a drug to excess. A large proportion of our population, as we will see, is currently abusing one or more drugs. This chapter will:

- Define drugs and drug abuse.
- Provide a brief history of our drug-taking society.
- Present sociological theories of drug abuse.
- Describe drug subcultures.
- Summarize facts about and effects of commonly used drugs.
- Describe rehabilitation programs for drug abuse.
- Present suggestions for curbing drug abuse in the future.

DRUGS AND
DRUG ABUSE

Pharmacologically, a drug is any substance that chemically alters the function or structure of a living organism.[1] Such a definition includes food, insecticides, air pollutants, water pollutants, acids, vitamins, toxic chemicals, soaps, and soft drinks. Obviously this definition is too broad to be useful. For our purposes a definition based on context is more useful. In medicine, for example, a drug is any substance that is manufactured specifically to relieve pain or to treat and prevent diseases and other medical conditions.

In a social problem approach, a *drug* is any habit-forming substance that directly affects the brain and nervous system. It is a chemical substance that affects moods, perceptions, body functions, or consciousness, and that has the potential for misuse as it may be harmful to the user.

Drug abuse is the regular or excessive use of a drug when, as defined by a group, the consequences endanger relationships with other people, are detrimental to a person's health, or jeopardize society itself. This definition identifies two key factors that determine what is considered drug abuse in a society: The first is the actual drug effects, and the second is a group's perception of the effects.

Society's perceptions of the ill effects of a drug are often inconsistent with the actual effects. In our society moderate use of alcohol and tobacco is generally accepted. Yet moderate use of both can cause serious health problems. Excessive drinking of coffee (containing caffeine) is accepted in our society but can also lead to health problems. In the 1930s, our society was convinced that marijuana was a dangerous drug; it was said to cause insanity, crime, and a host of other ills. Now, available evidence suggests that it may be less dangerous than alcohol.[2] The occasional use of heroin has been thought for years to be highly dangerous, even though available evidence indicates that occasional users suffer few health consequences and can lead productive lives.[3]

The dominant social reaction to a drug is influenced not only by the actual dangers of the drug but also by the social characteristics and motives of the groups that use it. Heroin is considered to be dangerous because its use has been popularly associated with inner-city residents and high crime rates. Society is more accepting of the use of pills for middle-aged people to reduce stress and anxiety but less accepting of college students using the same pills "to feel good" and "to get high." Surprisingly, legal drugs are more often abused and cause more harm in our society than illegal drugs.

One of the most widely used drugs in our society is aspirin. Millions of Americans use aspirin to relieve pain and other discomforts. Taken in excessive amounts, however, it can be harmful because it can cause gastrointestinal bleeding, ulcers, and other ailments.

Other over-the-counter drugs (available without a physician's prescription) can and are being abused. Laxatives, for example, taken for constipation, can damage the digestive system. Large doses of vitamins A and D are toxic.

Prescription drugs are also frequently abused. Among the most abused prescription drugs are tranquilizers, pain killers, sedatives, and stimulants. Amer-

icans are obsessed with taking pills. More than 1.5 billion drug prescriptions at a cost of over $25 billion are filled each year.[4] Many of these prescribed drugs have the potential to be psychologically and physiologically addicting. Drug companies spend millions in advertisements in an effort to convince consumers that there is something wrong with them—that they are too tense, that they are taking too long to fall asleep, that they should lose weight, that they are not "regular" enough—and then the companies suggest their medications will solve these problems. Unfortunately, many Americans accept this easy symptom relief approach and end up depending on pills rather than making the necessary changes in their lives to be healthy. Such changes include learning stress reduction techniques, changing their diets, and deciding to exercise regularly.

Because a drug is legal and readily available does not mean it is harmless. Alcohol and tobacco are legal, but both may be more harmful than marijuana. The rationale determining the acceptability of a drug is often illogical. Drugs favored by the dominant culture (such as alcohol in our society) are generally acceptable, whereas those favored by a small subculture are usually outlawed. It is interesting to note that in many parts of North Africa and the Middle East marijuana is a legal drug, and alcohol is outlawed. Many Americans believe heroin is the most harmful drug in our society; yet most authorities now believe that the use of barbiturates and amphetamines is more widespread and harmful than the occasional use of heroin.[5] Our country imposes severe penalties on the use of cocaine, but in certain areas of the Andes Mountains it is legal and widely used.[6]

A characteristic of habit-forming drugs is that they lead to a *dependence* as the user develops a recurring craving for them. This dependence may be physical, psychological, or both. When physical dependence occurs the user will generally experience bodily withdrawal symptoms, which may take many forms and range in severity from slight tremblings to fatal convulsions. When psychological dependence occurs the user feels psychological discomfort if use is terminated. Users also generally develop a *tolerance* for the drug, in which case they have to take increasing amounts over time to achieve a given effect. Tolerance partly depends on the type of drug, since some drugs (such as aspirin) do not create tolerance.

Why are Americans so involved in using and abusing drugs? There are numerous reasons: to feel good, to get high, to escape from reality, to obtain relief from pain or anxiety, and to relax or sleep. Drugs definitely meet a functional need for a person (such as providing temporary relief from unwanted emotions) but can have serious side effects. On a broader level it should be noted that many segments of our society encourage and romanticize the use of drugs. Senator Frank Moss, for example, comments on the role played by advertisements and commercials.

It is advertising which mounts the message that pills turn rain to sunshine, gloom to joy, depression to euphoria, solve problems, and dispel doubt. Not just pills: cigarette and cigar ads; soft drinks, coffee, tea, and beer ads—all portray the key to happiness as things to swallow, inhale, chew, drink, and eat.[7]

A BRIEF HISTORY OF OUR DRUG-TAKING SOCIETY

When the Pilgrims set sail for America they loaded on their ships 14 tons of water—plus 10,000 gallons of wine and 42 tons of beer.[8] Ever since, Americans have been widely using and abusing drugs.

During and after the Civil War thousands of injured soldiers were treated with narcotics to relieve their pain; many became addicted. Narcotics addiction was a serious problem from the 1860s to the first decade of the 20th century. At the turn of the century about 1 percent of the population was addicted to a narcotic drug—the highest rate in our history.[9] At that time opiates (including heroin and morphine) were fairly available for a variety of purposes. They were used to treat such minor ailments as stomach pains and to

ease the discomfort of infants during teething. Pharmacies, grocery stores, and mail-order houses did a prosperous business in selling opiates. Such sales were legally stopped in 1914 by the Harrison Narcotics Act, which required that narcotic drugs be dispensed only through prescriptions by licensed physicians.

Tobacco was widely chewed in colonial times. After 1870 it was also frequently smoked. Since that time it has been commonly used—and often abused. For a brief time shortly after the turn of the century its sale was prohibited in fourteen states because it was thought to be a "stepping stone" to alcohol use and was also believed to lead to sexual deviance, insanity, and impotence. The laws proved ineffective in banning the sale and were repealed after World War I. Today, we are increasingly becoming aware of the health hazards of smoking.

Marijuana has been used throughout our history. In the mid-19th century it was often smoked by writers and artists in the larger cities. Shortly after the beginning of the 20th century, blacks and Mexican-Americans began smoking it. The drug was then thought to lead to "unruly" behavior, and the first laws prohibiting its use and distribution were rapidly passed in southern states. The rest of the states soon enacted similar legislation. In 1937 the director of the Federal Bureau of Narcotics claimed marijuana was the "assassin of youth." The mass media jumped on this campaign and began publishing stories stereotyping marijuana users as "crazed drug fiends." Later, to continue receiving funds for his narcotics bureau, the director asserted that marijuana was dangerous as it was a "stepping stone" to using narcotic drugs.[10] Marijuana, in the 1960s and 1970s, became increasingly used by youths, college students, drug subcultures, and the general population. Its use and effects remain a controversial issue.

The use of alcohol has continued unabated ever since the Pilgrims landed. The first governor of Massachusetts began complaining of excessive drunkenness in his colony, and since that time there have always been some segments of American society that have viewed its use as a social problem. The American Temperance Union was formed in the early 1800s. It was

*Since colonial times some segments of American society have viewed the consumption of alcohol as a
social ill. By the early 1900s members of organizations such as the Women's Christian Temperance
Union (above) were a political force to be reckoned with: several states had passed laws prohibiting
the manufacture and sale of alcoholic beverages. The temperance movement culminated in 1920
with the ratification of the eighteenth amendment to the Constitution prohibiting the sale of liquor
and ushering in an era of speakeasies, bootleg liquor, and "bathtub gin."*

later joined by the Women's Christian Temperance
Union, the Anti-Saloon League, and several other temperance organizations. Alcohol was viewed as responsible for many social ills: crime, the collapse of the
family, and unemployment. Immigrants, the poor, and
certain minority groups were the major consumers of
alcohol at this time. Under such pressure several states
passed legislation prohibiting the sale and distribution
of alcoholic beverages in the later half of the 19th century. By the start of World War I, nearly half the population resided in "dry" areas.

The 18th Amendment to the Constitution, which
prohibited the sale of alcohol, was ratified in 1920.
Prohibition began. But people continued to drink, and
the law was nearly unenforceable. It gave organized
crime its impetus to develop. Moonshine and speakeasies (places where illegal alcoholic beverages were
sold) flourished. Prohibition became a political embarrassment and a laughing stock around the world. In
1933 the 18th Amendment was repealed. Following
Prohibition the use of alcohol became more widespread.[11] Middle- and upper-middle classes also began

drinking it on a rather large scale. No longer was it viewed as the scourge of society.

It is interesting to note that whereas narcotics made a transition from respectability to disrepute in the past 100 years, alcohol made exactly the opposite transition.

SOCIOLOGICAL THEORIES OF DRUG ABUSE

Three theories are summarized in this section: anomie theory, labeling theory, and differential association.

Anomie Theory

This theory was developed by such theorists as Emile Durkheim[12] and Robert Merton.[13] Merton used anomie to explain deviant behavior. Merton viewed deviance as occurring when there is a discrepancy between socially approved goals (such as making considerable money) and the availability of socially approved means (such as high-paying jobs) of achieving them. Applied to drug abuse this theory asserts that if people are prevented from achieving their goals, they may be "driven to drink" or to use other drugs. According to this theory drugs may be used as an escape to avoid the suffering caused by failing to achieve goals, or they may be used as a substitute for the "highs" and "feeling good" that users had originally hoped to experience from successfully accomplishing their goals.

Merton asserts that drug abuse can be reduced by having society set realistic goals that people can attain and by society then establishing legitimate means, which are available to everyone, for attaining these goals. It should be noted that anomie theory fails to explain drug abuse by people who appear to be achieving their goals.

Labeling Theory

This theory was developed by a number of researchers.[14] Labeling theorists view drug abuse as largely due to the process in which occasional users are labeled "abusers." Initially, occasional users indulge in drug use that is disapproved of by others—such as getting drunk or smoking marijuana. These users do not at this point view themselves as abusers. However, if their use is discovered and made an issue by significant other people (such as parents, police, or high school teachers), and if they are then publicly labeled as a "drunkard," "pot head," or "dope user," they are more closely watched. Under closer surveillance, if they continue to occasionally be found using drugs, the label is gradually confirmed. If these significant others begin relating to them in terms of the label, the occasional users may come to view themselves as people who "are" whatever label is applied. When this happens the occasional user is apt to embark on a "career" as a habitual drug abuser.

Labeling theory asserts that drug abuse can be reduced by avoiding labeling: that is, by refusing to treat occasional drug users as if they were "abusers." It should be noted that labeling theory fails to explain drug abuse among "secret alcoholics" and others who are already abusing drugs before being labeled as such.

Differential Association

Their theory was developed by Edwin Sutherland.[15] It asserts that behavior is primarily determined by learning the values and actions that are considered important by the small, intimate groups that one interacts with. Applied to drug abuse, differential association theory asserts that people are apt to learn and take on the drug use norms of the small, intimate groups they associate with. These groups include family, neighborhood peer groups, and religious and social groups. Differential association has been used to explain differences in alcoholism rates among ethnic and religious groups.

There are, for example, marked differences between the alcohol use norms of the Irish as compared to the Italians and Jews in the United States. The Italian subculture (both in Italy and in this country) widely accepts the moderate use of alcohol, particularly at mealtimes. Serving wine at mealtimes is part of the dietary customs, which even the young participate in. Excessive drinking, however, is frowned on. As a result, although alcohol is widely used in the Italian community, drunkenness and alcoholism are relatively rare.[16]

Similarly, the Jewish community uses alcohol widely, including as a component in religious rituals. As with Italian families, the use of alcohol in controlled social settings minimizes its potential negative effects. But because there are strong norms against drunkenness and abuse, alcoholism among American Jews is also rare.[17]

In contrast, the Irish subculture tolerates periodic episodes of excessive drinking, particularly by single males. Such drinking is seen as a way to relieve tension and frustration. With such norms there is a relatively high rate of alcoholism among Irish-American males.[18]

It is, of course, possible for people to be resocialized into the drug use norms of another subculture. For example, a teenager raised in a family opposed to marijuana use may become attracted to a high school group having somewhat different values toward marijuana. This teenager may then, through the principles of differential association, become resocialized into using marijuana by this new group.

No single theory of drug abuse is sufficient for identifying all the causes, and each theory may or may not apply in any given case.

DRUG SUBCULTURES

A person's decision about whether to use a drug depends not only on his or her personality characteristics and family background but also on the views of peers. These views play an important role in which drugs are used, how often they are used, the amount used at any one time, and the other activities that will be engaged in when drugs are used.

A group of peers who advocate the use of one or more drugs can be called a *drug subculture*. Most drug taking occurs in a social group that approves the use of the drug. In a classic study, "Becoming a Marijuana User," Howard Becker found that the peer group plays crucial roles in learning to smoke marijuana.[19] The group introduces the novice to smoking and teaches the new smoker to recognize the pleasant experiences associated with a "high." Membership in this group (drug subculture) also encourages further drug use and instructs the newcomer to reject established norms against using marijuana and instead to accept the norms of the drug subculture.

Drug subcultures appear to play similar roles in learning to use other drugs. Drug subcultures are more apt to develop around the use of illegal rather than legal drugs. Alcohol use among teenagers, marijuana use, heroin use, LSD use, and PCP use generally occur in drug subcultures.

Although drug subcultures are often dysfunctional for society, they do serve important functions for the user. They provide instructions on how to use the drug and guidelines on the safety limits of dosages. They help handle adverse effects, assist in obtaining the drug, and provide protection from arrest when the drug is being used. They also provide a party-type atmosphere to help a person enjoy the effects of the drug.

FACTS ABOUT AND EFFECTS OF COMMONLY USED DRUGS

Depressants

In this section we will examine the following drugs, which are classified as depressants: alcohol, barbiturates, tranquilizers, Quaalude, and PCP.

BOX 7.1

Jokes about Drunks

J okes about drunks are common. They suggest that our society does not take alcohol abuse seriously. Here are two examples.

A man walked into a pub with a duck under his arm, and a drunk remarked, "What are you doing with that pig in here?" The man said, "That isn't a pig, it's a duck." The drunk said, "I was talking to the duck."

A drunk staggered out of a bar and started to get into her car. An officer stopped her and stated, "You really don't intend to drive that car home do you?" The drunk replied, "Of course officer, I'm in no condition to walk."

ALCOHOL Alcohol is the most abused drug in American society. Yet the use of alcohol is so accepted that few Americans view it as a serious social problem. Social drinking is highly integrated into the customs of our society. In many areas of the country the local pub is the center (particularly for men) of meeting and socializing with friends and neighbors. Going out and getting "high" or even "smashed" is a favorite pastime of college students. In many communities, taverns and nightclubs are the centers for meeting and entertaining dates. Businesses frequently use cocktail lounges to wine and dine customers. In some communities it is the custom to have "a second church service" at a local watering hole after the weekly church service is over. (Because alcohol is the most abused drug, considerable attention will be given in this chapter to its use, abuse, and treatment.)

Alcohol is a colorless liquid that is in beer, wine, brandy, whiskey, vodka, rum, and other intoxicating beverages. The average American over the age of 14 consumes the equivalent of 591 cans of beer or 115 bottles of wine or 35 fifths of whiskey, gin, or vodka each year.[20] The vast majority of teenagers and adults in our society drink.

Drinking has become so entrenched into our customs that, unfortunately, those who do not drink are sometimes viewed as "weird," "stuck up," or "killjoys" and are often assumed "to have something wrong with them." The serving of alcoholic beverages is expected at many rituals and ceremonies for adults: weddings, birthday parties, Christmas parties, graduations, and the like. Some formal religious rites also include alcohol (for example, wine as the blood of Christ). Many popular songs (such as "Scotch and Soda," "Tiny Bubbles," and "Kisses Sweeter than Wine") highlight drinking. It is, however, not the use of alcohol at rituals and ceremonies that causes most alcohol problems. Most American alcohol use is informal and relatively uncontrolled and therefore can easily become excessive without the safeguards that are built into the drinking patterns of many ethnic groups.

The type of alcohol found in beverages is ethyl alcohol. (It is also called grain alcohol, as most of it is made from fermenting grain.) Many drinkers believe alcohol is a stimulant, since it relaxes tensions, lessens sexual and aggressive inhibitions, and seems to facilitate interpersonal relationships. It is, however, very definitely a depressant to the central nervous system. Its chemical composition and effects are very similar to ether (an anesthetic used in medicine to induce unconsciousness).

Alcohol slows mental activity, reasoning ability,

speech ability, and muscle reactions. It distorts perceptions, slurs speech, lessens coordination, and slows memory functioning and respiration. In increasing quantities it leads to stupor, sleep, coma, and finally death. A hangover (or aftereffects of too much alcohol) includes having a headache, thirst, muscle aches, stomach discomfort, and nausea.

The effects of alcohol vary with the percentage of alcohol in the bloodstream as it passes through the brain. Generally, the effects are observable when the concentration of alcohol in the blood reaches $\frac{1}{10}$ of 1 percent. Five drinks (with each drink being 1 ounce of 86-proof alcohol, 12 ounces of beer, or 3 ounces of wine) in two hours for a 120-pound person will result in a blood alcohol concentration of $\frac{1}{10}$ of 1 percent. (The heavier a person, the more drinks it takes to increase the level of alcohol in the blood.) Table 7.1 shows the effects of increasing percentages of alcohol in the blood.

Who Drinks   Several factors are related to whether an individual will drink and how much a drinker will use. These factors include socioeconomic factors, gender, age, religion, urban-rural residence, and geographical region.[21]

Socioeconomic factors: College-educated persons are more apt to drink than those with only high school educations. Young men at the highest socioeconomic level are more apt to drink than young men at lower socioeconomic levels. However, drinkers at the lower socioeconomic levels are more apt to drink more than those at higher socioeconomic levels.

Gender: Men are more apt to use and abuse alcohol than are women. Yet recent decades have seen a dramatic increase in alcoholism among adult women. Why? One explanation is that cultural taboos against heavy drinking among women have weakened. Another explanation is that increased drinking is related to the changing roles of women in our society.

Age: Older people are less likely to drink than younger people, even if they were drinkers in their

TABLE 7.1

Percent of Alcohol in the Blood and Its Effects

Alcohol	Effects
.05%	Lowered alertness and a "high" feeling
.10	Decreased reactions, reduced coordination (legally drunk in most states)
.20	Massive interference with senses and motor skills
.30	Perceptions are nearly gone, understanding is nearly gone
.40	Unconsciousness occurs
.50	Death may occur

Sources: Adapted from Oakley S. Ray, *Drugs, Society, and Human Behavior* (St. Louis: C. V. Mosby, 1972), p. 86; and Erich Goode, *Drugs in American Society* (New York: Alfred A. Knopf, 1972), pp. 142–143.

youth. Heavy drinking is most common at ages 21 to 30 for men and ages 31 to 50 for women.

Religion: Nonchurchgoers drink more than regular churchgoers. Heavy drinking is more common among Episcopalians and Catholics, whereas conservative and fundamentalist Protestants are more apt to be nondrinkers or light drinkers.

Urban/rural residence: Urban residents are more apt to drink than rural residents.

Geographical region: People who live in the Northeast and along the West Coast are more apt to drink than people who live in the South and Midwest.

Recently there has been a marked decline in drinking, especially of hard liquor, in many segments of the American public.[22] For example, some business executives have switched from martini luncheons to jogging and working out. In recent years the federal government has put considerable financial pressure on states to raise the drinking age to 21; if a state does not raise the age to 21, federal highway funds are withheld. Practically all states have now raised the drinking age to 21. Many secondary schools, colleges and universities have initiated alcohol awareness programs. Many businesses and employers have developed Employee Assistance programs, which are designed to provide treatment services to alcoholics and problem drinkers. Many states have passed stricter drunk driving laws, and police departments and the courts are more vigorously enforcing such laws. Organizations, such as Mothers Against Drunk Driving and Students Against Drunk Driving, have been fairly successful in creating greater public awareness of the hazards of drinking and driving. A cultural norm is emerging in many segments that it is stylish not to have too much to drink. Despite these promising trends, rates of alcohol use and abuse in the United States remain extremely high.

Reasons for Drinking   As discussed earlier, a major reason for alcohol use is that our social patterns influence people to drink socially in a wide variety of situations. Happy hours, a cocktail or beer before and after dinner, and parties where alcoholic beverages are served are common.

There are also individual reasons for drinking. Some people drink because alcohol acts as a "social lubricant" in that it relaxes them so that they feel more at ease interacting with others. Some drink simply to relax. Others use alcohol as a kind of anesthetic to dull the pain of living and to take their minds off their problems. Some excessive drinkers seek a continual "buzz" to avoid facing life. Others occasionally drink to be "high." Some insomniacs drink so that they will sleep (often they pass out). Drinking before flying is common for those who have fears about flying, since alcohol has a tranquilizing effect.

People often drink to temporarily get rid of unwanted emotions such as loneliness, anxiety, depression, feelings of inadequacy, insecurity, guilt, and resentment.

Alcoholism is a rather imprecise term, as there is no clear-cut distinction between a problem drinker and an alcoholic. An imprecise but useful definition of alcoholism is *the repeated and excessive use of alcohol*

to the extent that it is harmful to interpersonal relations, to job performance, or to the drinker's health.

Whether a person will be labeled an alcoholic depends to a large extent on the reactions of one's employers, family, friends, associates, and community. For example, the "drier" the community in which one lives, the less alcohol and the fewer the problem incidents involving alcohol it takes for someone to be defined as an alcoholic.

People's reactions to drinking vary considerably. Some people can drink large amounts quite regularly while appearing sober—although their driving is affected, and they may have a high likelihood of becoming alcoholic in the future. Some can drink large amounts and not experience hangovers—although hangovers are functional because they let people know when they have ingested too much alcohol and discourage further binges. Generally, the greater the weight of the drinker, the more she or he can consume before becoming intoxicated. Many alcoholics who stop drinking have to refrain *totally*: If they start again they will have a compulsive, uncontrollable urge to go on a series of binges. Because of this Alcoholics Anonymous assumes, "Once an alcoholic, always an alcoholic." There is some evidence (highly controversial) that some alcoholics can, after treatment, return to social drinking.[23] This finding has been highly criticized by a number of treatment organizations because it has led some alcoholics who quit drinking to try to drink lightly, with the result that they immediately returned to excessive drinking.

There are over 10 million alcoholics in America, and each one affects at least four other people close to him or her—including spouse, family, or employer. Approximately two out of three alcoholics are male, but the proportion of female alcoholics has risen sharply in the past twenty years.[24] Contrary to popular stereotypes, only an estimated 5 percent are "skid-row bums."[25] Most are ordinary people. One out of ten social drinkers becomes an alcoholic.[26]

Some people become alcoholic quite soon after they start drinking. Others may drink for ten, twenty, or thirty years before becoming addicted. An alcoholic may be only psychologically dependent on alcohol, but a sizable number are also physically dependent.

BOX 7.2

Polydrug Abuse Is Becoming a Serious Problem

I n recent years such well-known people as Elvis Presley, John Belushi, and former First Lady Betty Ford have been dependent on two or more drugs. Drug abuse contributed to the early deaths of Presley and Belushi. Betty Ford publicly acknowledged that she was dependent on Valium, alcohol, and the medication she was taking for arthritis. She received treatment at the Naval Hospital in Long Beach, California.

Health Problems Caused by Alcohol   The life expectancy of alcoholics is ten to twelve years lower than that of nonalcoholics.[27] There are several reasons why the life span is shorter. Alcohol, over an extended period of time, gradually destroys liver cells, leaving scar tissue in their place. When the scar tissue is extensive, a medical condition called cirrhosis of the liver occurs. This condition is the eighth most frequent cause of death in America (about 27,000 per year).[28]

Alcohol has no healthy food value, although it contains a high number of calories. Heavy drinkers, as a result, have a reduced appetite for nutritious food, frequently suffer from vitamin deficiencies, and are more susceptible to infectious diseases.

Heavy drinking also causes kidney problems, contributes to a variety of heart ailments, is a factor that leads to sugar diabetes, and also appears to contribute to cancer. Heavy drinking is also a contributing cause of ulcers and impotency in males. In addition, heavy drinking is associated with over 10,000 suicides annually.[29] Death may result from drinking an excessive amount of alcohol—for example, from depression of the respiratory system or from the drinker choking on vomit while unconscious.

Interestingly, for some as yet unknown reason, the life expectancy age for light to moderate drinkers exceeds that for nondrinkers.[30] Perhaps an occasional drink helps people to relax and thereby reduces the likelihood of life-threatening psychosomatic illnesses developing.

Combining alcohol with other drugs can have disastrous and sometimes fatal effects. Sometimes, two drugs taken together have a *synergistic* interaction in that they create an effect much greater than either would produce alone. For example, sedatives like barbiturates (often found in sleeping pills) or Quaaludes, when taken with alcohol, can so depress the central nervous system that a coma or even death can result.

Other drugs tend to have an *antagonistic* response to alcohol, in that one drug negates the effects of the other. Many doctors now caution patients not to drink while taking certain prescribed drugs, as the alcohol will reduce, and even totally negate, the beneficial effects of these drugs.

Whether drugs will interact synergistically or antagonistically depends on a wide range of factors: the properties of the drugs, the amounts taken, the amount of sleep of the user, the kind and amount of food that has been eaten, and the user's overall health and tolerance. The interactive effects may be minimal one day and extensive the next.

Withdrawal from alcohol, once the body is physically addicted, may lead to delirium tremens (DTs) and other unpleasant reactions. The DTs include rapid heartbeat, uncontrollable trembling, severe nausea, and profuse sweating.

BOX 7.3

Fetal Alcohol Syndrome

P rior to the 1940s it was thought that the uterus was a glass bubble that totally separated the fetus from the outside world and fully protected the fetus from whatever drugs the mother happened to be using. Since the 1940s medical science has learned that chemical substances are readily transferred from the mother's uterine arteries, across the placental membrane, into the baby's umbilical vein, and then to the baby's entire body.

When a pregnant woman drinks any alcoholic beverage (including beer and wine), the alcohol easily crosses the placenta, and the fetus attains blood alcohol levels that are similar to those in the mother. Heavy alcohol consumption by pregnant mothers can cause a variety of malformations in the new baby that have been labeled the fetal alcohol syndrome. These malformations include mental retardation and developmental delays; overall growth retardation before and after birth; and various congenital malformations of the face, head, skeleton, and heart. Such babies also are more apt to be born prematurely, to have a low birth weight, to be hyperirritable, and to have neurological defects and poor muscle tone. Such babies have a higher infant mortality rate. The chances of microcephaly (a condition in which the baby has a small brain and skull and is mentally retarded) occurring is also much higher.

The more alcohol a pregnant woman ingests, the higher the chances that her baby will have fetal alcohol syndrome. Studies suggest that if a pregnant woman has five or more drinks at any one time, her baby has a 10 percent chance of having fetal alcohol syndrome. Also, if she drinks lightly over a prolonged period, the syndrome may also occur. An average of one ounce per day results in a 10 percent risk; an average of two ounces per day results in a 20 percent risk.

The U.S. Public Health Service recommends that pregnant women should not drink alcohol. Just as a mother would not give a glass of wine to her newborn, she should not give it to her unborn baby. It is not just alcohol but also the use of other drugs (such as tobacco, marijuana, cocaine, and heroin) during pregnancy that endanger the unborn child.

Source: Mike Samuels and Mary Samuels, "Pregnancy: How Smoking and Drugs Endanger Baby," *Wisconsin State Journal*, July 2, 1986, sec. 2, p. 1.

Drinking and Driving Alcohol is a significant contributing factor in at least half of all fatal automobile accidents and in many serious automobile accident injuries. Each year over a million people in the United States are arrested for driving under the influence of alcohol.[31] More people are killed by intoxicated drivers than are killed through violent crimes! Drunk drivers kill an average of twenty-seven people every ten hours in the United States.[32] Mothers against Drunk Drivers (MADD) is an organization that was formed several

BOX 7.4

Courts Are Getting Tougher on Drunk Drivers

L arry Mahoney was a 34-year-old father who was described by a friend as "somebody who wouldn't hurt anybody for the world." On Sunday evening, May 14, 1988, while drunk, Larry climbed into his pickup truck and drove the wrong way down a Kentucky interstate. He had 0.24 percent alcohol in his blood, more than twice Kentucky's statutory level. He slammed head-on into an old school bus carrying sixty-seven passengers, mainly teenagers, on a church outing from Radcliff, Kentucky. Twenty-four teenagers and three adults were killed in this crash. Larry Mahoney was charged with "capital murder," which carries the death penalty. The charge is one more indication that the court system is taking a tougher stand on drunk driving. (Lawyers anticipate the charge may be reduced to manslaughter, as premeditation to kill would have to be proved.) Many states have enacted legislation to suspend drivers' licenses for offenders immediately and have mandated jail terms for repeat offenders. Many states now also mandate instant suspension of the driver's license for those failing, or refusing to take, a breath test.

Source: "Kentucky's Textbook Case in Drunk Driving," *U.S. News & World Report*, May 30, 1988, pp. 7–8.

years ago and is having considerable success in getting states to enact and enforce stricter drunk-driving laws. In an attempt to prevent some of the fatalities associated with drunken driving, a number of states have raised the minimum drinking age from 18 to 21.

Alcohol and Crime   About a third of the arrests for minor crimes are alcohol related: public drunkenness, violations of liquor laws, disorderly conduct, and vagrancy.[33]

Alcohol is a contributing factor in many major crimes. In a majority of homicides, aggravated assaults, sexual crimes against children, and sexually aggressive acts against women, the offender had been drinking.[34] This is not to say that alcohol is the main cause of these crimes. The use of alcohol appears to be a contributing factor that increases the likelihood of such crimes occurring.

Effects of Alcohol Abuse on the Family   In the past if there was a problem drinker in the family, it was almost always the husband. Now, it is still apt to be the husband, but it may also be the wife or one or more of the teenagers.

Heavy drinking is a contributing factor to many problems in a family: child abuse, child neglect, spouse abuse, parent abuse, financial problems, unemployment of wage earners, violent arguments, and unhappy marriages. Marriage to an alcoholic often ends in divorce, separation, or desertion. Children of an alcoholic parent have higher rates of severe emotional and physical illnesses.[35]

Alcohol and Industry   It is estimated that alcoholism costs businesses and industry over $6.5 billion annually.[36] This figure reflects losses in terms of sick leave, absenteeism, missed or late work assignments,

Heavy drinking contributes to many other family problems. Studies show that children of alcoholic parents have higher rates of emotional and physical illnesses.

and on-the-job accidents. It is further estimated that 6 to 10 percent of the work force experiences drinking problems to such a degree that their job performance is affected.[37]

Seeking Treatment for Alcoholism   Many alcoholics (perhaps the majority) do not seek help because they *deny* they have a drinking problem. They seek to prove they can drink like any other person, and wind up sneaking drinks, excusing their drinking behavior, or blaming others ("if you had a job like mine, you'd drink too!"). There are many reasons alcoholics deny they have a drinking problem. Alcoholism is highly stigmatized, so alcoholics do not like to admit they have a drinking weakness and are different from others. Alcoholism is viewed as a disease, and they do not want to acknowl-

edge that they have this illness. Drinking often becomes the central interest of their life. They socialize through drinking and are also able to relax, fall asleep, or escape from their problems. For them to acknowledge that they have a drinking problem means they would have to stop drinking. Because they believe drinking is essential to their lives, they often choose to keep drinking even though they are aware it is ruining their health, destroying their reputation in the community, getting them fired at a variety of jobs, and breaking up their family. Many alcoholics believe that the freedom to continue to drink is the most important need in their lives, and they will sacrifice their marriage, their children, their career, and their health to alcohol.

If an alcoholic is to be helped, this denial of a

problem must be confronted. (We will discuss denial further in the section on rehabilitation programs.)

BARBITURATES   Barbiturates are derived from barbituric acid and depress the central nervous system. Barbiturates were first synthesized in the early 1900s, and there are now over 2,500 different barbiturates. They are commonly used to relieve insomnia and anxiety. Some are prescribed as sleeping pills, and others are used during the daytime by tense and anxious persons. They are also used to treat epilepsy and high blood pressure and to relax patients before or after surgery. Barbiturates are illegal, unless obtained by a physician's prescription.

Taken in sufficient doses, barbiturates have effects similar to strong alcohol. Users experience relief from inhibitions, have a feeling of euphoria, feel "high" or in good humor, and are passively content. However, these moods can change rapidly to gloom, agitation, and aggressiveness. Physiological effects include slurred speech, disorientation, staggering, appearance of being confused, drowsiness, and reduced coordination.

Prolonged high use of barbiturates can cause physical dependence, with withdrawal symptoms similar to those of heroin addiction. Withdrawal is accompanied by body tremors, cramps, anxiety, fever, nausea, profuse sweating, and hallucinations. Many authorities believe barbiturate addiction is more dangerous than heroin addiction, and it is considered more resistant to treatment than heroin addiction. Abrupt withdrawal can cause fatal convulsions. One forensic pathologist noted: "Show me someone who goes cold turkey (the sudden and complete halting of drug use) on a bad barbiturate habit, and I'll show you a corpse."[38]

Barbiturate overdose can cause convulsions, coma, poisoning, and sometimes death. Barbiturates are particularly dangerous when taken with alcohol because alcohol acts synergistically to magnify the potency of the barbiturates. Accidental deaths due to excessive doses are frequent. One reason for this is that the user becomes groggy, forgets how much has been taken, and continues to take more until an overdose level has been reached. Barbiturates are also the number one

suicide drug. A number of famous people, such as Marilyn Monroe, have fatally overdosed on barbiturates.

Barbiturates are generally taken orally, although some users also inject them intravenously. Use of barbiturates, like alcohol, may lead to traffic fatalities.

TRANQUILIZERS   Yet another depressant is the group of drugs classified as tranquilizers. Common brand names are Librium, Miltown, Serax, Tranxene, and Valium. They reduce anxiety, relax muscles, and are sedatives. Users have moderate potential of becoming physically and psychologically dependent. They are usually taken orally, and the effects last four to eight hours. Side effects include slurred speech, disorientation, and behavior resembling intoxication. Overdoses are possible, with the effects including cold and clammy skin, shallow respiration, dilated pupils, weak and rapid pulse, coma, and possibly death. Withdrawal symptoms are similar to those from alcohol and barbiturates: anxiety, tremors, convulsions, delirium, and possible death. The extent of tranquilizer use is indicated by the nearly 100 million prescriptions written each year.[39]

QUAALUDE AND PCP   Both Quaalude and PCP are depressants. (PCP also produces effects similar to those of hallucinogens.)

Methaqualone (better known by its patent name Quaalude) has effects similar to barbiturates and alcohol, although it is chemically different. It has the reputation of being a "love drug," since users believe it makes them more eager for sex and enhances sexual pleasure. These effects are probably due to the fact that it lessens inhibitions (similar to alcohol and barbiturates). Quaaludes also reduced anxiety and give a feeling of euphoria. Users can become both physically and psychologically dependent. Overdose can result in convulsions, coma, delirium, and even death. Most deaths occur when the drug is taken together with alcohol, which vastly magnifies the drug's effects. Withdrawal symptoms are severe and unpleasant. Abuse of the drug may also cause hangovers, fatigue, liver damage, and temporary paralysis of the limbs.

The technical name for PCP is phencyclidine, and its street name is "angel dust." PCP was developed in the 1950s as an anesthetic. This medical use was soon terminated as patients displayed symptoms of severe emotional disturbance after receiving the drug. PCP is used legally today to tranquilize elephants and monkeys, since they apparently do not have the adverse side effects.

PCP is primarily used by young people who are unaware of its hazards. It is usually smoked, often after being sprinkled on a marijuana "joint." It may also be sniffed, swallowed, or injected. PCP is a very dangerous drug. It distorts senses, disrupts the sense of balance, and leads to an inability to think clearly. Larger amounts of PCP can cause a person to become paranoid, can lead to aggressive behavior (in some cases it has led to committing violent murder), and can cause the user to display symptoms of a severe emotional disturbance temporarily. Continued use can lead to the development of a prolonged emotional disturbance. Overdose can result in coma or even death. Research has not as yet concluded whether it induces physical or psychological dependence. The drug has a potential to be used (and abused) extensively because it is relatively easy to prepare in a home laboratory and because the ingredients and recipes are widely available. An additional danger of PCP is that even one-time users sometimes have flashbacks in which the hallucinations are reexperienced, even long after use has ceased. It may be that the cause of many accidents and unexplained disasters may be due to the unknown use by a person of PCP or some other undetectable hallucinogenic substance.

Stimulants

In this section we will examine the following drugs, which are classified as stimulants: caffeine, amphetamines, cocaine, crack, amyl nitrate, and butyl nitrate.

CAFFEINE   Caffeine is a stimulant to the central nervous system. It is present in coffee, tea, cocoa, Coca-Cola, and many other soft drinks. It is also available in tablet form (for example, No-Doz). Caffeine is widely used—practically all Americans use it on a daily basis. It reduces hunger, fatigue, and boredom and improves alertness and motor activity. The drug appears addictive, since many users develop a tolerance for it. A further sign that it is addictive is that heavy users (for example, habitual coffee drinkers) will experience withdrawal symptoms of mild irritability and depression.

Excessive amounts of caffeine cause insomnia, restlessness, and gastrointestinal irritation. Excessive doses can even, surprisingly, cause death.

Because caffeine has the status of a "nondrug" in our society, users are not labeled criminals, there is no black market for it, and no subculture is formed to give support in obtaining and using the drug. Because caffeine is legal, its price is low compared to other drugs. Users are not tempted to resort to crime to support their habit. Some authorities assert that our approach to caffeine should serve as a model for the way we react to other illegal drugs (such as marijuana) that they feel are no more harmful than caffeine.[40]

AMPHETAMINES   Amphetamines are called "uppers" because of their stimulating effect. When prescribed by a physician they are legal. Some truck drivers have obtained prescriptions in order to stay awake and more alert while making a long haul, with a few becoming addicted. Dieters have received prescriptions to help them lose weight and have also found that the pills tend to give them more self-confidence and buoyance. College students have used them to stay awake and more alert while studying. Others who have used amphetamines to increase alertness and performance for relatively short periods of time include athletes, astronauts, and executives. Additional nicknames for this drug are *speed, ups, pep pills, black beauties,* and *bennies.*

Amphetamines are synthetic drugs. They are similar to adrenalin, a hormone from the adrenal gland that stimulates the central nervous system. The better known amphetamines include Dexedrine, Benzedrine, and Methedrine. Physical reactions to amphetamines are extensive: Consumption of fat stored in body tissues is accelerated, heartbeat is increased, respiratory processes are stimulated, appetite is reduced, and in-

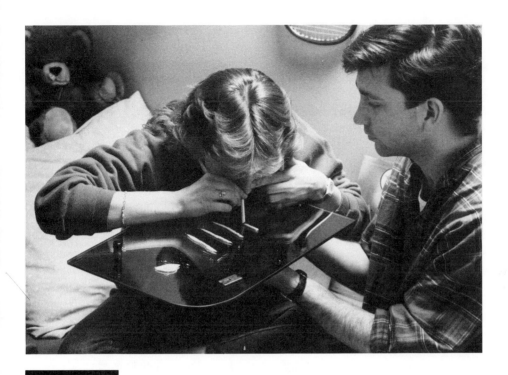

In recent years cocaine has obtained a chic status in this country, particularly among the young, affluent, and well educated.

somnia is common. Users feel euphoric, stronger, and have an increased capacity to concentrate and to express themselves verbally. Prolonged use can lead to irritability, deep anxiety feelings, and an irrational persecution complex that can lead to sudden acts of violence.

Amphetamines are usually taken orally in tablet, powder, or capsule form. They can also be sniffed or injected. "Speeding" (injecting the drug into a vein) produces the most powerful effects and can also cause the greatest harm. An overdose can cause a coma, with possible brain damage, and in rare cases death may occur. There are other dangers, as speeders may develop hepatitis, abscesses, convulsions, hallucinations, delusions, and severe emotional disturbances. Another danger is that when sold on the street, the substance may contain impurities that are health hazards.

An amphetamine high is often followed by mental depression and fatigue. Continued amphetamine use leads to psychological dependence. It is unclear whether amphetamines are physically addicting, since the withdrawal symptoms are uncharacteristic of withdrawal from other drugs. Amphetamine withdrawal symptoms include sleep disturbances, apathy, decreased activity, disorientation, irritability, exhaustion, and depression. Some authorities believe such withdrawal symptoms indicate that amphetamines may be physically addicting.[41]

One of the legal uses of certain amphetamines is in the treatment of hyperactivity in children. Hyperactivity (also called hyperkinesis) is characterized by a short attention span, extensive motor activity, restlessness, and shifts in moods. Little is known about the causes of this condition. When children become older, the symptoms tend to disappear, even without treatment. Interestingly, some amphetamines (Ritalin is a popular one) have a calming and soothing effect on children: the exact opposite effect occurs when Ritalin is taken by adults. It should be noted that treating "uncontrollable" children with amphetamines in the past has frequently been abused. Joel Fort and Christopher Cory note:

Many of the children for whom Ritalin is prescribed are not really hyperactive to begin with. They are normal children who simply refuse to submit to what their teachers and parents consider orderly school and family routines. Categorizing children who are different as hyperactive often is a seductively convenient way to blame the victims of teachers' and parents' own shortcomings. Drugging these children, however, brands them as troublemakers and helps to further institutionalize drug use.[42]

COCAINE AND CRACK   Cocaine is obtained from the leaves of the South American coca plant. It has a chic status in this country and is rapidly replacing other illegal drugs in popularity. Although legally classified as a narcotic, it is in fact not related to the opiates from which narcotic drugs are derived. It is a powerful stimulant and antifatigue agent.

In America, cocaine is generally taken by sniffing and is then absorbed through the nasal membranes. The most common method is sniffing through a straw or a rolled-up bank note; this is known as "snorting." It may also be injected intravenously, and in South America the natives chew the coca leaf. It may be added in small quantities to a cigarette and smoked. Cocaine has been used medically in the past as a local anesthetic, but other drugs have now largely replaced it for this purpose.

Cocaine constricts the blood vessels and tissues and thereby leads to increased strength and endurance. It also is thought by users to increase creative and intellectual powers. Other effects include a feeling of euphoria, excitement, restlessness, and a lessened sense of fatigue. It is claimed by some that use of cocaine heightens or restores their virility and enables them to extend the sex act for long periods.[43]

Larger doses, or extended use, may result in hallucinations and delusions. A peculiar effect of cocaine abuse is *formication*—the illusion that ants, snakes, or bugs are crawling on or into the skin. Some abusers have such intense illusions that they literally scratch, slap, and wound themselves trying to kill these imaginary creatures.

Physical effects of cocaine include increased blood pressure and pulse rate, insomnia, and loss of appetite. Heavy users may experience weight loss or malnutrition due to appetite suppression. Physical dependence on cocaine is considered to be a low to medium risk. However, the drug appears to be psychologically habituating; terminating use usually results in intense depression and despair, which drives the person back to taking the drug.[44] Additional effects of withdrawal include apathy, long periods of sleep, extreme fatigue, irritability, and disorientation. Serious tissue damage to the nose can occur when large quantities of cocaine are "sniffed" over a prolonged time period. Regular use may result in habitual sniffing and sometimes leads to an anorexic condition. High doses can lead to agitation, increased body temperature, and convulsions. A few people who overdose may die if their breathing and heart functions become too depressed.

Crack (also called rock) is obtained from cocaine by separation of the adulterants from the cocaine by mixing it with water and ammonium hydroxide. The water is then removed from the cocaine base by means of a fast-drying solvent, with ether being the most commonly used solvent. The resultant mixture resembles large sugar crystals, similar to rock sugar. Crack is highly addictive. Some authorities claim that one use is enough to lead to addiction. Users generally claim that after they have finished one dose, they crave another.

Crack is usually smoked, either in a specially made glass pipe or mixed with tobacco or marijuana in a cigarette. The effects are similar to cocaine, but the "rush" is more immediate, and the drug gives an intensified high and has an even greater orgasmic effect.

An overdose is more common when crack is injected than when it is smoked. Withdrawal effects include an irresistible compulsion to have it, as well as apathy, long periods of sleep, irritability, extreme fatigue, depression, and disorientation.

BOX 7.5

Tragic Cocaine Overdoses

On June 17, 1986 Len Bias was the first pick by the Boston Celtics in the college draft of the National Basketball Association. He was the second player chosen in the draft. The Celtics were his favorite team, and he looked forward to signing a contract for around one million dollars per year. Len Bias was an All-American forward at the University of Maryland. Two days later he was partying and died of heart failure induced by cocaine intoxication.

Eight days after the death of Len Bias, Don Rogers was having a bachelor's party on June 27, 1986. He was to be married the next day. Don Rogers was a pro football player for the Cleveland Browns. He had played at UCLA and was the number one selection by the Browns in the 1984 college draft. He was selected that year as the Defensive Rookie of the Year in the American Football Conference. He died at his bachelor's party of heart failure induced by cocaine intoxication.

Communal use of needles spreads AIDS. Cocaine and crack can have serious effects on the heart, straining it with high blood pressure, with interrupted heart rhythm, and with raised pulse rates. Cocaine and crack may also damage the liver. Severe convulsions can cause brain damage, emotional problems, and sometimes death. Smoking crack may also damage the lungs.

AMYL NITRATE AND BUTYL NITRATE   Amyl nitrate ("poppers") is prescribed for patients who risk certain forms of heart failure. It is a volatile liquid that is sold in small bottles. When the container is opened, the chemical begins to evaporate (similar to gasoline). If the vapor is sniffed, the user's blood vessels are immediately dilated, and there is an increase in heart rate. These physical changes create feelings of mental excitation ("head rush") and physical excitation ("body rush"). The drug is supposedly sold only by prescription, but (as with many other drugs) the illicit drug market has obtained access to distributing it.

Butyl nitrate is legally available in some states without a prescription and has an effect similar to amyl nitrate. Trade names under which it is sold are Rush and Locker Room. Similar to amyl nitrate, the vapor is sniffed. It is available at some sexual aid and novelty stores.

Both these drugs have been used as aphrodisiacs and as stimulants while dancing. The drugs have some short-term, unpleasant side effects that may include fainting, headaches, and dizziness. A few deaths have been reported due to overdoses. Both these drugs are classified as stimulants.

Narcotics

The most commonly used narcotic drugs in the United States are the opiates (such as opium, heroin, and morphine). The term *narcotic* means sleep inducing. In actuality, drugs classified as narcotics are more accurately called analgesics, or painkillers. The principal effect produced by narcotic drugs is a feeling of euphoria.

The opiates are all derived from the opium poppy. The opium poppy grows in many countries; Turkey,

Stories of drug seizures regularly dominate newspaper headlines. These U.S. Customs agents guard some 700 pounds of cocaine found on a pleasure boat near Miami.

Southeast Asia, and Colombia have in our recent past been major sources of the opiates. The drug opium is the dried form of a milky substance that oozes from the seed pods after the petals fall from the purple or white flower. It has been used for centuries.

Morphine is the main active ingredient of opium. It was first identified early in the 1800s and has been used extensively as a painkiller. Heroin was first synthesized from morphine in 1874. It was once thought to be a cure for morphine addiction but later was also found to be addicting. Heroin is a more potent drug than morphine.

Opium is usually smoked, although it can be taken orally. Morphine and heroin are either sniffed (snorted) or injected into a muscle or into a vein (called "mainlining"), which maximizes the drugs' effects.

Opiates affect the central nervous system and produce feelings of tranquility, drowsiness, or euphoria. It produces a sense of well-being, which makes pain, anxiety, or depression seem unimportant. Tony Blaze-Gosden notes:

It has been described as giving an orgasmlike rush or flash that lasts briefly but memorably. At the peak of

the euphoria, the user has a feeling of exaggerated physical and mental comfort and wellbeing; a heightened feeling of buoyancy and bodily health, and a heightened feeling of being competent, in control, capable of any achievement, and being able to cope.[45]

Overdoses can cause convulsions and coma and, in rare cases, death by respiratory failure. All opiates are now recognized as being highly addicting.

Heroin is the most widely abused opiate. In addition to the above-mentioned effects, heroin slows the functioning parts of the brain. The user's appetite and sex drive tend to be dulled. After an initial feeling of euphoria, the user generally becomes lethargic and stuporous. Contrary to popular belief, most heroin users take the drug infrequently and do not as a rule become addicted,[46] although frequent use is highly addicting.

Opiate addiction occurs when the user takes the drug regularly for a period of time. Whether addiction will occur depends on the opiate drug taken, the strength of the dosages, the regularity of use, the characteristics of the user, and the length of time taken— sometimes as short as a few weeks. Users rapidly develop a tolerance and may eventually need a dose that is up to 100 times stronger than a dose that would have been fatal during the initiation to the drug.[47]

The withdrawal process is very unpleasant. Symptoms include chills, cramps, sweating, nervousness, anxiety, running eyes and nose, dilated pupils, muscle aches, increased blood pressure, severe cramps, sometimes extreme nausea, and a fever. Most addicts are obsessed with securing a fix to avoid these severe withdrawal symptoms.

Addiction to opiates is extremely difficult to break, partly because intense craving for the drug may recur periodically for several months afterward. Edward Brecher et al. note that the opiate drug

. . . is one that most users continue to take even though they want to stop, decide to stop, try to stop, and actually succeed in stopping for days, weeks, months, or even years. It is a drug for which men and women will prostitute themselves. It is a drug to which most users return after treatment. . . . It is a drug

which most users continue to use despite the threat of long-term imprisonment for its use—and to which they promptly return after experiencing long-term imprisonment.[48]

Most opiate addicts are under age 30, are of low socioeconomic status, and are poorly educated. A disproportionate number are black. Distribution and addiction to narcotic drugs primarily occur in large urban centers.

When heroin was first discovered in the late 1800s, it was initially used as a pain killer, as a substitute for people addicted to morphine, and as a drug taken by many to experience euphoria. A fair number of people became addicted, and in the early 1900s laws were passed to prohibit its sale, possession, and distribution.

Heroin abuse continues to be regarded by many Americans as our most serious drug problem. This stereotype does not appear warranted, since only a tiny fraction of the U.S. population has ever tried heroin, and the number of people addicted to heroin is miniscule compared to the number addicted to alcohol or tobacco. In addition, such drugs as alcohol and barbiturates contribute to many more deaths.

One reason heroin has the reputation it does is because users are thought to be "dope fiends" who commit many violent crimes and who reject the values of contemporary society. Addicts, however, are unlikely to commit such violent crimes as rape or aggravated assault. They are more apt to commit crimes against property (shoplifting, burglary, pickpocketing, larceny, and robbery) in order to support their habit.[49] Prostitution for female addicts is also common. Because the severe withdrawal symptoms begin about eighteen hours after the last fix, addicts who have experienced these symptoms will do almost anything to avoid them.

Contrary to popular belief, heroin addiction in itself has few adverse effects on the user.[50] A person who uses heroin daily (while avoiding excess doses) may continue using the drug for decades without detectable physical side effects. Alcohol and tobacco unquestionably damage the human body much more than heroin. (It should be noted that unsanitary injections of heroin may cause hepatitis and other infections. Communal use of needles can spread AIDS. Also, the high cost of maintaining a heroin habit—often over $100 daily—may create huge financial problems for the user.)

Then why is heroin so feared? The Consumers Union concluded that practically all the undesirable effects of the opiates are not due to the drugs themselves but to narcotic laws, which label and treat users as "dope fiends."

By far the most deleterious effects of being a narcotics addict in the United States today are the risks of arrest and imprisonment, infectious disease, and impoverishment—all traceable to the narcotics laws, to vigorous enforcement of those laws, and to the resulting excessive black-market prices for narcotics.[51]

Because the price of illicit narcotic drugs is so high, organized crime has made huge profits in the smuggling and distribution of these drugs. Often such drugs are diluted with dangerous impurities, which pose serious health hazards for the users. And, unfortunately, addicts are often forced, for economic reasons, into illegal activities to maintain their daily supply in order to avoid the withdrawal symptoms.

Hallucinogens

Hallucinogens were popular as psychedelic drugs in the late 1960s. These drugs distort the user's perceptions, creating hallucinations consisting of sensory impressions of "sights and sounds" that do not exist. The four hallucinogens most commonly used in this country are Mescaline (peyote), psilocybin, psilocin, and LSD. All are taken orally—for example, in capsule form, on a sugar cube, or licked from the back of a stamp.

Peyote is derived from a cactus plant. Mescaline is the synthetic form of peyote. Psilocybin and psilocin are found in approximately ninety different species of mushrooms. They have been called "magic mushrooms." Both peyote and psilocybin have had a long history of use by certain American Indian tribes. Members of the Native American Church, a religious organization, have won the legal right to use peyote on ceremonial occasions.[52]

By far the most popular hallucinogen is LSD (lysergic acid diethylamide). LSD is a synthetic material derived from a fungus (ergot) that grows on rye and other plants. It is one of the most potent drugs known; a single ounce will make up to 300,000 doses.

The effects of LSD vary a great deal depending on the expectations and psychological state of the user and the context in which it is taken. A given person may experience differing reactions on different occasions. The effects that can be experienced include the apparent "seeing" of sounds, "hearing" of colors, colors seeming unusually bright and shifting kaleidoscopically, exaggerations of color and sound, and objects appearing to expand and contract. Users become highly suggestible and easily manipulated; seduction of males and females alike becomes easier.

Bizarre hallucinations are also common. The experience may be peaceful or may result in panic. Some users have developed severe emotional disturbances that resulted in long-term hospitalization.[53] Usually a "trip" will last eight to sixteen hours. Physical reactions include increased heartbeat, goose bumps, dilated pupils, hyperactivity, tremors, and increased sweating. Aftereffects include acute anxiety or depression. Flashbacks sometimes occur after the actual drug experience. Flashbacks may happen at any time and place, with no advance warning. If the user is driving a car when a flashback occurs, a life-threatening condition is present for the user and for others in the vicinity.

There is no evidence of physical or psychological dependence on LSD by users. Users do develop tolerance to the drug very rapidly; effects can only be achieved in the future by larger doses. Cessation of use, even for a few days, will restore sensitivity to the drug, enabling the user to take smaller quantities to experience the effects.

The effects and dangers of mescaline, psilocybin, and psilocin are similar to LSD. LSD is, however, the most potent of these hallucinogens.

Tobacco

The use of tobacco has now become recognized as one of the most damaging drug habits in America. Smoking can cause emphysema, cancer of the mouth, ulcers, and lung cancer and reduces life expectancy. It significantly increases the risk of strokes and heart disease,

particularly in women who use birth control pills.[54] Smoking by a pregnant woman sometimes leads to miscarriages, premature births, and the child being born underweight. Yet, in spite of these widely publicized hazards, over one third of the adult population continues to smoke.[55]

In 1988 the Surgeon General of the United States, C. Everett Koop, declared that tobacco is as addictive as heroin or cocaine.[56] More people die from the health hazards of using tobacco than from all other illegal drugs combined. Koop noted that people addicted to tobacco are drug addicts.

Tobacco is highly habit-forming. Nicotine is the primary drug in tobacco. Nicotine has remarkable capacities, as it can act as a depressant, a stimulant, or a tranquilizer. Smokers quickly develop a tolerance for nicotine and often gradually tend to increase consumption to one or two packs or more a day.

There are special clinics and a variety of other educational and therapeutic programs to help people quit smoking. Studies show that less than 20 percent of smokers who make determined efforts to quit actually succeed.[57] Tobacco is indeed a very habit-forming drug. Withdrawal from use leads users to become restless, irritable, and depressed and to have an intense craving to smoke.

At the same time the Health Department is widely publicizing the hazards of drugs, the Department of Agriculture is subsidizing tobacco farmers. Educational programs urge people not to smoke, while tobacco companies are permitted to advertise that cigarette smoking is "cool" and "sexy," connoting rugged manliness in men and social sophistication in women.

Marijuana

Marijuana, "grass," or "pot" comes from the hemp plant, *cannabis sativa*. This hemp plant grows throughout the world, and its fibers are legally used to produce rope, twine, paper, and clothing.

The main use of the plant now, however, centers on its dried leaves—marijuana—and on its dried resin—hashish. Both may be taken orally but are usually smoked. Hashish is several times more potent than marijuana.

The effects of marijuana (and hashish) vary, as with any other drug, according to the mood and personality of the user, according to circumstances, and according to the quality of the drug. The effects are rather complicated and may induce a variety of emotions. Many of the effects are produced because marijuana has sedative properties and creates in the user a sense of relaxed well-being and freedom from inhibition. There may also be mild hallucinations that create a dreamy state in which the user may experience fantasies. Smokers become highly suggestible and may engage in actions (such as sexual activities) in which they may not otherwise be involved. The drug may induce feelings of joyousness, hilarity, and sociability. It may lead to talkativeness, disconnected ideas, a feeling of floating, and laughter. It may also intensify sensory stimulation, create feelings of enhanced awareness and creativity, and increase self-confidence. A person may gradually experience some of these emotions, followed by others.

The threat of physical dependence is rated low; the threat of psychological dependence is rated as moderate. Withdrawal, however, may be very unpleasant, with the user suffering from insomnia, hyperactivity, and loss of appetite.

The short-term physical effects of marijuana are minor: a reddening of the eyes, dryness of the throat and the mouth, and a slight rise in heart rate. There is some evidence that continued use by young teenagers will result in these users becoming apathetic, noncompetitive, and uninterested in school and other activities. For years, heated debates have raged about the hazards of long-term marijuana use. Some studies claim it may cause brain damage, chromosome damage, irritation of the bronchial tract and lungs, and a reduction in male hormone levels. These findings have not been confirmed by other studies, and the controversy rages on.[58]

Frequent users may have impairments of short-term memory and concentration and of judgment and coordination. They may find it difficult to read, to understand what they read, or to follow moving objects with their eyes. Users may feel quite confident that their coordination, reactions, and perceptions are quite normal while they are still experiencing the effects of the drug; under such conditions such activities as driving a vehicle may have tragic consequences to them

and to others. Marijuana use by pregnant women may also be a contributing factor to malformations in fetuses, much like the effects of alcohol use.

An overdose of the active ingredients of cannabis can lead to panic, fear, confusion, suspiciousness, fatigue, and sometimes aggressive acts. One of the most voiced concerns about marijuana is that it will be a "stepping stone" to using other drugs. This fear appears to be groundless.[59] Other factors, such as peer pressure, are more crucial determinants of what mind-altering drugs people will use. The overwhelming majority of marijuana users do not progress to using other mind-altering drugs.[60]

The attempt to restrict the use of marijuana through legislation has been described as a "second prohibition,"[61] which has had similar results as the first; a large number of people are using the drug in disregard of the law. The unfortunate effect of laws that attempt to regulate acts (crimes as defined by law) without victims is that they criminalize the private acts of many people who are otherwise law abiding. Such laws also foster the development of organized crime and the illicit drug market.

After reviewing studies conducted on its use, the National Commission on Marijuana and Drug Use in 1972 recommended that possession of marijuana for personal use no longer be a criminal offense.[62] Commissions in Britain, Canada, and Scandinavia have also made similar recommendations. Since 1972 several states decriminalized the possession of small amounts of marijuana. When marijuana was used by a small subculture of youths and young adults, it was easy for the dominant culture to impose harsh penalties. However, when marijuana became more widely used by the middle and upper classes, it was inevitable that federal and state governments deemphasized their efforts to control marijuana use.

In 1982 the National Academy of Science completed a fifteen-month, extensive study on marijuana. The study found that 25 percent of our population has tried marijuana at least once and that 7 percent of high school seniors are daily users. The study found no evidence that marijuana causes permanent changes in the nervous system and concluded that the drug probably does not break down human chromosomes. It also found that marijuana may be useful in treating glaucoma, asthma, certain seizure disorders and spastic conditions and in controlling severe nausea caused by cancer chemotherapy. The study warned, however, that the drug presents a variety of short-term health risks and justifies "serious national concern." One of the reversible, short-term health effects is impairment of motor coordination, which adversely affects driving or machine-operating skills. The drug also impairs short-term memory, slows learning abilities, and may cause periods of confusion and anxiety. The study also found evidence that smoking marijuana may affect the lungs and respiratory system in much the same way that to-bacco smoke does and may be a factor in causing bron-chitis and precancerous changes. Thus, the study found some evidence that marijuana may lead to certain ad-verse, long-term health problems. The major recom-mendation was that "there be a greatly intensified and more comprehensive program of research into the effects of marijuana on the health of the Ameri-can people."[63]

REHABILITATION PROGRAMS

Rehabilitation programs for alcohol abuse are very similar to rehabilitation programs for most other drugs. We will begin by looking closely at the treatment of alcoholism.

Alcohol Treatment Programs

We mentioned earlier that before an alcoholic may be helped, the alcoholic's denial of the problem must be confronted. If the alcoholic cannot or does not con-front the situation, the confrontation can be done by family members, friends, employers, alcoholic coun-selors—or all of these together. Tim Bliss briefly de-scribes guidelines for this confrontation.

In confronting the alcoholic, documentation of incidents that occurred while drinking becomes

extremely important. This is particularly important because the alcoholic may have blackouts. These are periods of amnesia as opposed to passing out or unconsciousness. Both are due to excessive drinking. Many times during confrontation it is important that the entire family be present to reinforce the incident. In documenting the incident, one should be instructed to write down the date and time, and to be as specific as possible in describing the situation. The counselor can be present during this confrontation to act as a facilitator; however, the primary responsibility in breaking through denial is with the spouse, family, or employer.

Many times the practicing alcoholic has been threatened with divorce, job discipline, and so on. It is important not to continue these threats; action must occur if the alcoholic continues to drink after confrontation.[64]

If the alcoholic continues to deny that a problem exists, there are some guidelines for what family mem-bers should and should not do. "Nagging" the alco-holic will only increase family arguments and may provoke the alcoholic into verbally or physically abus-ing someone, particularly when he or she is inebriated. Family members often make the mistake of assuming they are responsible for getting the alcoholic to stop drinking and feel guilty or frustrated if the person con-tinues to drink. They, however, do not *own* the drink-ing problem—the alcoholic is the one responsible for his or her drinking and is the one that determines whether he or she will stop drinking. When a person is drunk, yelling and screaming at him or her will ac-complish nothing; it usually results in the other family members becoming more upset. More productive for the other family members is to isolate themselves from the alcoholic when she or he is drunk—perhaps by going shopping, taking a walk, or, if need be, locking themselves in a room.

There are two self-help groups that family mem-bers can attend. Al-Anon is for spouses and other family members of alcoholics. The program reaches out to people affected by another person's drinking regard-less of whether the alcoholic recognizes his or her problem. It helps members learn the facts about alco-holism and how to cope with an alcoholic. Alateen is for teenage children of alcoholics and helps teenagers to understand alcoholism and to learn effective ways to cope with problems.

If the alcoholic does acknowledge a drinking problem, there are many treatment programs available. The best-known and most successful program is Alcoholics Anonymous, which is further described in Box 7.6.

There appear to be several reasons why such self-help groups are successful. The members have an internal understanding of the problem that helps them to help others. Having experienced the misery and consequences of the problem, they are highly motivated and dedicated to find ways to help themselves and others who are fellow sufferers. The participants also benefit from the "helper therapy principle"; that is, the helper gains psychological rewards by helping others.[65] Helping others makes a person feel "good" and worthwhile and also enables the helper to put his or her own problems into perspective as he or she sees that others have problems that may be as serious, or even more serious. From the viewpoint of the new member who is still drinking, having people around who have successfully stopped drinking provides role models of abstinence behavior and gives them reason to think they too can break the grip of alcohol abuse.

At one time intoxicated people were just thrown in jail to sober up. Today, practically all community mental health centers offer both inpatient and outpatient treatment programs for alcoholics. Outpatient treatment usually serves clients who can work and live at home without any significant problems. If the client is unable to live at home, or is still drinking excessively, usually inpatient treatment will be recommended. Those going through an inpatient program are followed up on an outpatient basis. Inpatient treatment can last anywhere from two weeks to three months depending on the patient's problems and the treatment program at the mental health center. Inpatient treatment is usually intense, including one-on-one therapy, group therapy, an orientation to Alcoholics Anonymous, and occupational and recreational therapy. Outpatient treatment is not as intense, usually lasts from three to six months, and offers the same forms of treatment.

Outpatient and inpatient services are also provided in some medical hospitals. Many larger cities now have specialized rehabilitation centers and clinics to serve the chemically dependent. Many communities have halfway houses that serve the alcoholic who is unable to live with family members and who is not yet ready to live alone.

Most larger companies are now sponsoring alcohol treatment programs for their employees (often called Employee Assistance programs). These programs seek to identify problem drinkers in their early stages and then to intervene before severe problems arise. Such programs refer problem drinkers to appropriate community resources. If the employee uses such help, there are no adverse work consequences. There is considerable pressure on the employee to participate in receiving help, since there is the threat of eventual discharge if she or he refuses help and continues to display lowered work productivity due to drinking.

In treating alcoholics, most therapists now believe that drinking meets some of a person's needs—a way to socialize, to relax, to escape from unwanted emotions, and so on. If treatment is to be successful it must find alternatives to meeting these needs—by helping the alcoholic to find a new circle of friends, to learn other ways to relax, to learn to handle life's problems better—whatever the unique need of the drinker. This is known as the theory of functional need equivalents and has been applied to other addictions as well as to alcohol abuse.

Other Drug Treatment Programs

Rehabilitation programs for abuse of most drugs parallel those programs that have already been described for alcohol abuse.

There is a stereotype, "Once an addict, always an addict." This attitude has hampered efforts to rehabilitate those who are dependent. Statistical evidence in the past tended to confirm this myth. More recent evidence, however, suggests that those dependent on drugs can successfully kick the habit. Martin Kasindorf found, for example, that American soldiers addicted to heroin in Vietnam could successfully terminate use on returning home.[66]

BOX 7.6

Alcoholics Anonymous

I n 1929 Bill Wilson was a stock analyst. When the stock market crashed that year he lost most of his money and took to the bottle. A few years later his doctor warned him that his continued drinking was jeopardizing his health and his life. Bill W. underwent what he perceived as a spiritual experience, and he made a commitment to stop drinking. He also discovered that through discussing his drinking problem with other alcoholics, he was helped to remain sober. One of the people he discussed his problem with was Robert Smith, an Ohio doctor, and also an alcoholic. Together they formed Alcoholics Anonymous (AA), a self-help group composed of recovering alcoholics.

AA stresses: (*a*) a confession to the group that the member has a drinking problem, (*b*) a testimony to the group recounting past experiences with the drinking problem and his or her plans for handling the problem in the future, and (*c*) a phone call to another member of the group when a member feels an intense urge to drink. The person called will do whatever can be done to keep the caller "dry," including coming over to stay with the caller until the urge subsides.

Today AA has chapters in about 100 countries. In the United States AA has a membership of over 600,000 recovering alcoholics.[a] (The term *recovering* is used, as AA believes there is no such thing as a permanently recovered alcoholic.) The local chapters (around twenty-five persons per chapter) meet once or twice a week for discussions. These groups resemble traditional group therapy meetings without the presence of a trained professional leader.

Bill W. and Dr. Bob, as they were known within AA, remained anonymous until their deaths. Local chapters still follow treatment procedures similar to the ones originally initiated—the sharing of similar experiences in order to abstain from the first drink (which is one too many) and from the thousand drinks, which are not enough.

AA is still widely recognized as the treatment approach that has the best chance of helping an alcoholic. Testimony to its value is that hundreds of other self-help groups, having treatment principles based on the AA model, have now been formed to deal with other personal problems—for example, Weight Watchers, Prison Families Anonymous, Parents without Partners, Debtors Anonymous, Gamblers Anonymous, Emotions Anonymous, Emphysema Anonymous, and many more.

---

[a]Alan Gartner and Frank Riessman, *Help: A Working Guide to Self-Help Groups* (New York: New Viewpoints, 1980), p. 8.

BOX 7.7

Antabuse Treatment

Antabuse is a drug that is useful in helping an alcoholic stay sober. When taken it makes a patient's system react adversely to even small quantities of alcohol. Shortly after a person drinks an alcoholic beverage, antabuse causes the person to become intensely flushed, the pulse to quicken, and the person to feel intensely nauseated, often to the point of regurgitation.

Antabuse was developed in Copenhagen in 1947. Before beginning to administer Antabuse treatment, the patient is detoxified. Treatment then begins by giving the drug to the patient for several consecutive days, along with small doses of alcohol. The small amounts of alcohol are used to help the patient recognize the strong and uncomfortable effects that will occur while drinking.

Antabuse is not a cure-all for drinking because the reasons for drinking still remain. An alcoholic, if she or he chooses, can simply stop taking Antabuse and resume drinking. Antabuse, however, is useful as part of a comprehensive treatment program involving counseling, vocational and social rehabilitation, and AA. By taking Antabuse a person is forced to remain sober and is thereby more apt to respond to other therapies.

Source: Stanford L. Billet, "Antabuse Therapy," in *Alcoholism: The Total Treatment Approach*, ed. Ronald J. Cantanzaro (Springfield, IL: Charles C. Thomas, 1974), pp. 167–174.

The physical dependence on practically any drug can be ended with detoxification programs. Generally, the user will undergo some intense and highly painful withdrawal symptoms for the first few days, or even for a few weeks. The psychological dependence is often more difficult to end. Users of drugs receive certain psychic rewards (feelings of relaxation, euphoria, more alertness, less pain, escape from reality and their problems). The psychological needs met by taking a drug are often unique to each user. Because drugs meet psychological needs, they are functional. To end psychological dependence it is necessary for drug treatment programs to discover what psychological needs are being met for each user and then to teach the user new ways (drug-free ways) to meet such needs.

INPATIENT PROGRAMS   Community mental health centers, specialized chemical abuse rehabilitation centers, and some medical hospitals provide inpatient treatment programs. Detoxification lasts from twenty-four hours to three weeks depending on the severity of withdrawal. Additional inpatient care lasts two to three more weeks in a chemically free environment. Inpatient care is designed for those chemically dependent individuals who are unable to end the dependence while remaining in the community. Inpatient treatment is highly expensive; it may cost $10,000 or more for a thirty-day stay.

OUTPATIENT PROGRAMS   Outpatient care is usually not as intense as inpatient care and generally lasts three to

Many therapeutic communities see unrelenting confrontation in encounter groups as an integral part of the drug rehabilitation process.

six months. Outpatient care serves people who no longer need inpatient care, as well as people who have a fair chance of terminating their habit without having to be hospitalized as an inpatient. Outpatient care consists of counseling, medical services, and vocational services. Outpatient services are provided by community mental health centers, specialized rehabilitation centers for treating chemical abuse, medical hospitals, and outpatient clinics for chemical abuse.

SELF-HELP PROGRAMS   Modeled after Alcoholics Anonymous, there are many self-help programs for abusers. Such programs include Narcotics Anonymous, Synanon, Potsmokers Anonymous, Pills Anonymous, Delancey Street Foundation, and Renaissance Project.[67]

THERAPEUTIC COMMUNITIES   These are long-term residential treatment programs, with patients usually staying from 12 to 18 months. Therapeutic communities

focus on making lifestyle changes so that the person will learn to find rewards for staying drug free and will also learn to function more appropriately in society. Tim Bliss further describes the focus.

The environment is one of constant confrontation that aims at breaking down walls that cover up the real person. An individual might, for example, come on as a "tough guy" as a result of leading the street life. Actually, this image needs to be broken down. Feelings that are painful (for example, loneliness, fear, depression) are allowed to be expressed, eventually allowing the individual to be honest with himself or herself, and thus not needing to wear a mask. Many graduates of therapeutic communities remain in close contact for support purposes. It is difficult to measure the success of these programs because there is a high rate of dropouts. However, for those that graduate there is evidence they are successful in obtaining employment and remaining chemically free.[68]

Programs that realistically stress the dangers of drugs are more effective than scare tactics with elementary and high school students.

HALFWAY HOUSES   Halfway houses assist those who have been hospitalized (and detoxified) to reenter the community at their own pace. Halfway houses also serve those who are psychologically dependent and want to kick a habit but do not need to be hospitalized. Halfway houses provide counseling services (both one-to-one and group) to help residents remain drug free and to work on resolving other personal problems they face. Residents also receive vocational training, assistance in finding a job, and room and board. Many halfway houses employ staff who were former addicts. Recovered drug abusers are often more effective than professional staff in relating to the residents and in breaking down the barriers of denial, anger, isolation, and hostility that addicts feel. Former addicts also pro-

vide a model, since they are evidence that addiction is a curable disease. Halfway houses emphasize the importance of residents assuming responsibility for their actions and behaviors.

TREATMENT USING DRUGS   Analogous to the use of Antabuse with alcoholics, there are some chemicals that are used in therapeutic programs to treat certain drug addictions.

Methadone has received by far the most publicity and is sometimes used to treat heroin addiction. Methadone is a synthetic narcotic and is sufficiently similar to heroin to satisfy the addict's physical craving. It prevents the anguish of heroin withdrawal symptoms but does not induce a high. Methadone thus allows a

BOX 7.8

Therapy with a Heroin Addict

Tim Bliss, a drug counselor, describes the efforts made to treat an addict.

Many times the drug counselor feels he or she isn't making any progress in the recovery process of the heroin addict. Counseling the heroin addict takes a special type of counselor—one who can walk the walk and talk the talk so to speak. To counsel, first off, it takes an extreme amount of dedication, concentration, and effort.

The client I worked with was a 30-year-old black, married male with three children. The history was as follows. The client will be referred to as Bob. Bob was raised in an urban area; he was the middle child and seemingly led a normal childhood. As he reached his early teens he got more and more involved with drinking and drugs. He graduated from high school and went into the army soon after graduation. This is where many problems arose. Bob had several bouts with the army ranging from insubordination to disorderly conduct. He started chipping heroin and became quite involved in the drug culture overseas in Germany. He then married a white German girl and brought her back to the United States where they have lived for the past 10 years. Bob then became involved in an armed robbery and claimed he was innocent; yet he spent three years in prison. After his prison time ended, Bob secured a job at a local factory; this lasted approximately one and one-half years at which time he was fired for excessive absenteeism. The excessive absenteeism was a result of episodic drinking and drug abuse.

Prior to Bob's going to prison he was involved in the Black Panthers. What was interesting was that he was married to a white, which had to be a conflict with Bob.

In general Bob seemingly had quite a conflict being black. He wanted at times to be white, and yet at other times wanted to be married to a black instead of a white.

Bob became increasingly involved with drugs, and in time developed a habit with heroin. This led to his involvement in both the criminal justice system and treatment.

Fortunately, there was a federal grant at this time that could divert criminal justice clients to alcohol or drug treatment centers. Bob became involved in a local alcohol treatment center while on probation. However, due to the fact he was a heroin addict, treatment was ineffective. Within a very short period of time after discharge, Bob was back to "junk." He was then involved in another armed robbery and this time was facing 7 to 10 years for several counts of armed robbery and burglary. At this point I became involved with the client. Bob was out on bond and was awaiting his court date. Throughout this time period Bob was seen on an outpatient treatment basis. Urine drug screens were taken and all turned up negative for opiates for about four weeks. Then Bob started chipping (using heroin on occasion). A therapeutic community which treated heroin addicts had been contacted to arrange an intake interview with Bob. The therapeutic community was a six- to nine-month intensive inpatient treatment program. Their philosophy was that the drug of choice was only a symptom and what needed to be changed was the lifestyle.

The court date was finally reached and it was time for Bob to "face the music." The therapeutic community had interviewed Bob and he was accepted into their program. I had arranged for a psychologist to run a series of tests on Bob to determine statistically his chances for succeeding in treatment. The results of this testing were that Bob would have one third of a chance of succeeding in treatment, one third not succeeding, and one third of no change at all. Obviously statistics were against Bob, but in outpatient treatment he had demonstrated that he was sincere and did want to change. So with that, this counselor and Bob's probation officer felt treatment was the best alternative rather than incarceration. The presiding judge was approached with this alternative and he accepted it. However, Bob was found guilty so the judge imposed a stayed sentence of seven years to be served if Bob did not successfully complete treatment.

The following week Bob was transferred to the therapeutic community. He stayed there approximately six months at which time the community voted that he be terminated, unsuccessfully completing treatment. Bob was voted out for a number of reasons: (a) he wasn't following instructions when reprimanded by staff, (b) overall he was an extremely bad influence on the rest of the community as he was always gaming people, not being able to be honest with himself or others, (c) he was breaking cardinal rules which meant that when he would get angry other members of the community were actually afraid to be around him as they were afraid he might get physically violent. The incident that resulted in Bob's termination was that he was reprimanded for an incident that involved a female client. Supposedly Bob had intercourse with the female and the female admitted this to staff in one of the community's "cop to" groups. (A "cop to" simply means people in the community that have done something wrong, or are feeling guilty, talk about it in one of these groups.)

The staff told Bob he was on a communication ban (no talking) the following day; they also requested he wear a five-foot sign with some writing on it. This kind of reprimand might seem ineffective or silly to some of us; however, it is quite effective in an atmosphere like a therapeutic community, especially on a long-term basis. Bob didn't follow through the next day and a vote was taken and he was transferred to the county jail where he would await a decision by the probation officer, the judge, and the original referring agent.

We had decided Bob was still amenable to treatment. However, this would entail a more highly structured treatment environment, a facility that dealt more with the hard-core heroin addict.

Meanwhile Bob was becoming increasingly bitter sitting in jail thinking about what had occurred, and also becoming anxious due to the fact he was facing seven years in prison.

The probation officer and original treatment staff involved with Bob found a treatment facility that would be most favorable to any kind of successful treatment for Bob. The judge also went along with this.

Bob, after about two weeks of sitting in jail was transferred on a Friday afternoon to this treatment facility. Friday evening he called his wife and absconded from treatment. He has not been heard of since, and consequently his probation has been revoked and when caught, he will be sent to prison.

I have heard unofficial reports he is still around, back to heroin in his old way of life.

This is not a success story, obviously, but all too often that's all we ever hear. The field is

Continued

BOX 7.8 *Continued*

challenging; however, this case history is also a real part of treatment that oftentimes a therapist has to realize his or her own limitations and accept reality as it is. Not everyone is a success and no matter what you do, you can't change that. All we can do is seek as much knowledge about the field as possible and utilize every tool available to motivate clients in changing their behavior. Only after this can we say, "I gave it my best shot, and that's all there is."

Source: Tim Bliss, "Drugs—Use, Abuse, and Treatment," in *Introduction to Social Welfare Institutions* (Homewood, IL: Dorsey Press, 1978), pp. 315–316. Used with permission.

heroin addict to function fairly normally in a community. (It is usually not effective for heroin users who seek to become "high.")

Methadone itself is addictive. It also does not cure a heroin addict of his or her addiction to heroin. It simply *maintains* heroin addicts in their communities without their having to use heroin. Methadone is controversial, as some authorities object to treating heroin addicts by having them become dependent on another drug.

Methadone is only available (legally) through approved programs. In the first few weeks of treatment addicts are usually required to report daily to the treatment center to receive the drug. As with any other drug that is in demand, an illicit market has also developed in methadone. Some heroin addicts use it to tide them over when they cannot obtain heroin, and other heroin addicts sometimes seek to treat themselves by taking methadone instead of heroin. As with heroin, an overdose of methadone can result in death.

Scientists have also developed narcotic antagonists that prevent opiate users from experiencing euphoria. Some opiate (morphine and heroin) addicts have a psychological craving to become euphoric. Two of the best known opiate antagonists are Naloxone and Cyclazocine. These drugs prevent opiate addicts from experiencing pleasurable sensations when taking opiates and thereby help motivated addicts to kick the habit.

SUGGESTIONS FOR CURBING DRUG ABUSE IN THE FUTURE

Although it is important to treat current drug abusers, perhaps even more important is a prevention approach that is designed to keep nonabusers from becoming abusers. We will consider five approaches: educational programs, prevention of illegal drug trafficking across borders, employee drug-testing programs, revision of drug laws, and the British system.

Educational Programs

Gradually, more programs are appearing that give students in schools and the general public a realistic understanding of drug use and abuse. Quality programs inform people of (*a*) the nature and effects of commonly used drugs, (*b*) how to recognize signs of abuse, (*c*) how to responsibly decide when and when not to use drugs, (*d*) how to help someone who overdoses, (*e*) how to seek to help friends and relatives who are abusing drugs, (*f*) what treatment resources and programs are available in the community, (*g*) what to do if you think you may have a drug problem, (*h*) what to do if a relative or friend refuses to acknowledge the existence of a drug problem, and (*i*) how to help abusers learn drug-free ways of meeting their psychological needs.

Educational programs in the past tried to use scare tactics—showing pictures of fatal automobile crashes after drug use, suggesting that drug users would end up on "skid row," and indicating that experimenting in small quantities with drugs would drive them crazy and forever ruin their lives. Such scare tactics are now viewed as ineffective. The young see their parents, other adults, and peers using drugs (particularly alcohol) with generally no tragedies occurring. Such alarmist approaches wound up destroying the credibility of the educators.

Fortunately, books, curriculum guides for teachers, and audiovisual materials now available give a more realistic approach to drug use and abuse. It is hoped the ineffective scare approach is on its way out.

The United States will never become drug free. Drugs do have considerable valid use for medical purposes. They also meet certain psychological needs. But the abuse of drugs can certainly be curbed. Quality education about how to use drugs responsibly and about the realistic dangers of drugs appears to be a key to curbing abuse.

Prevention of Illegal Drug Trafficking across Borders

John S. Lang summarizes the extent of the illegal drug business in the United States:

Americans now consume 60 percent of the world's production of illegal drugs. An estimated 20 million are regular users of marijuana, 4 million to 8 million more are cocaine abusers and 500,000 are heroin addicts.

Drugs are flooding the nation. This year, more than 12 tons of heroin, 65 tons of marijuana and 150 tons of cocaine will spread across the land— from big cities to rustic hamlets. Sales of illegal narcotics total $100 billion annually, more than the total net sales of General Motors, more than American farmers take in from all crops.[69]

Small drug dealers are rich, middlemen are millionaires, and the top drug barons are billionaires. Illegal drug trade across borders of countries is a big, highly profitable business. One way of combating the illegal drug trade business is to take the kind of action that will put drug barons out of business.

The United States and other countries have spent millions of dollars on trying to prevent illegal drugs from being smuggled across borders. A few drug shipments are confiscated, and a few transporters of drugs are arrested. But drug barons are generally successful in finding creative ways to smuggle drugs across borders. It appears that drug barons, if allowed to do business in drug-producing countries, will continue to find ways to smuggle drugs across borders. If drug trafficking across borders is to be stopped, other actions need to be taken.

One way to combat drug trafficking across borders would be for countries of the world to agree amongst themselves to treat drug trafficking across borders as being an international crime. International law could make it an indictable offense to be involved in drug trafficking across borders.

An international court to administer this law could be established as a division of the United Nations. This court could have an investigative force that would have the authority to enter drug-producing countries to gather evidence about the drug barons who are masterminding the production, manufacture, and distribution of illegal drugs across borders. Countries would be expected to arrest and extradite for trial to this international court those who are indicted as masterminding drug trafficking across borders. Those found guilty could be penalized with a life sentence, with no chance of parole. The United Nations could be empowered to impose trade sanctions against any country who refused to arrest and extradite indicted drug barons. (No country can survive nowadays without international trade and finance.) Gradually stiffer trade sanctions could be levied against countries who make little or no effort to arrest and extradite indicted drug barons. In addition, armed forces of the United Nations could be made available to those governments who are too weak to combat the private armies employed by some of the notorious drug barons.

Employee Drug-Testing Programs

In 1986 the President's Commission on Organized Crime recommended that both government and private industry should launch drug-testing programs for employees. The Commission asserted that such examinations would help curb a drug abuse epidemic that drains billions of dollars annually from American society and erodes the nation's quality of life.[70]

Dozens of major U.S. companies already require applicants or employees to provide urine for an analysis that can detect the use of such drugs as cocaine, marijuana, heroin, and morphine. The tests are also given in the military, in a few sensitive federal agencies, and in many drug treatment facilities.[71]

The commissioner of baseball, Peter Ueberroth, and team owners are seeking to require major league baseball players to submit to drug testing.[72] Professional basketball and football leagues are also seeking to expand their drug-testing programs for professional athletes. In 1986, the commissioner of the National Football League, Peter Rozelle, announced that all players in the league will be required to take a mandatory urine test prior to the start of the regular season and two unscheduled tests during the regular season. If a player tests positive, he will first be required to receive treatment. If a player relapses twice (as identified by three positive tests over a period of time), he will be permanently banned from the league. A few players have already been banned from the NBA.

Drug-testing programs are being recommended in the interest of safety, in the interest of health, and in the interest of increased productivity. These programs are a clear signal that companies are serious about addressing the hazards caused by drugs. Employees who test positive are generally given an opportunity to enter treatment programs. If further drug tests show that an employee is continuing to use illegal drugs, the employee is generally discharged.

Opponents of drug-testing programs assert that

The AIDS crisis has prompted a new look at our drug laws, and in particular the current philosophy that emphasizes punishment over treatment of drug addicts. In an effort to curb the spread of AIDS, New York City launched the first government-sponsored program to give free sterile needles to intravenous drug addicts in 1988. Some critics have argued that needle-exchange programs condone and even encourage further drug abuse.

such programs raise serious civil-liberty concerns, including the Constitution's ban on unreasonable searches.[73]

Revision of Drug Laws

During the last century a number of laws were enacted prohibiting the use of a variety of drugs. Penalties also became harsher. Yet the proportion of the population using drugs has steadily increased. In every jail and prison there are a number of people who have been arrested for drug-law violations. Helen Nowlis notes: "Drug legislation makes possession of a 'potentially dangerous' substance a crime with penalties in some cases equivalent to or in excess of those for such criminal acts as grand larceny and second-degree murder."[74] Some states in the past have sentenced people for up to twenty-five years, or even life, for selling or giving small quantities of marijuana to another person. Such harshness discredits the criminal justice system and is a factor leading to disrespect for the law.

Until recently drug legislation in this country has been designed to punish users rather than to treat drug abuse or to prevent the use of drugs. Does it really do any good to arrest and jail (sometimes weekly) habitual drunks? The public's general lack of accurate information about drugs has led to irrational fears about drug use and abuse. For example, there is the fear that the use of marijuana will always be a stepping stone to using narcotic drugs, and there are unwarranted fears about the negative effects of such drugs as heroin and opium. These irrational fears have led citizens to demand that stiff legislation be passed to attempt to curb the use of drugs.

However, it is increasingly being recognized that punitive legislation is not working. Prohibition demonstrated that outlawing alcohol would not end its use. Analogous to laws prohibiting the use of alcohol, laws prohibiting the use of other drugs have been largely responsible for the enormous growth of organized crime and the illicit drug trade.

A number of authorities are now urging that drug laws be revised to emphasize treatment rather than punishment of addicts and to make the penalties for the possession of drugs more consistent with the actual dangers. It seems irrational to send to prison (at a huge expense to taxpayers) a person who possesses one joint of marijuana (a drug that may be less dangerous than alcohol).

Recent changes in certain drug laws are beginning to emphasize rehabilitation and to reduce harsh penalties for the sale and possession of certain drugs. Many of these revisions have centered on marijuana.

In 1972 the National Commission on Marijuana and Drug Abuse recommended changes in state and federal laws regarding marijuana. It was urged that the private possession of marijuana for personal use and the distribution of small amounts without profit to the distributor no longer be considered offenses. Public use would still be a criminal offense, but the maximum penalty would be reduced to a fine of $100.[75] Since this 1972 report a number of states have passed laws decriminalizing the use of marijuana.

Laws have also been passed mandating that those arrested for public drunkenness receive treatment rather than simply being thrown into jail. In some areas of the country people who acknowledge they are addicted to a hard drug (such as heroin) are now given treatment without risking arrest or incarceration. Such programs are experimental and are often controversial.

Although the treatment approach is still controversial here, the British have been successfully using such an approach for several decades.

The British Approach

The United States in the last century has primarily used a punitive approach to anyone found guilty of possessing or using prohibited drugs.

In contrast, the British for many years have avoided labeling drug users as criminals and have viewed drug use as a disease that should be treated. Because of this rehabilitative emphasis, the British have formulated a very different set of laws and government policies to curb drug abuse. The British regard narcotic addicts as "sick" instead of "criminal." Rather than sending narcotic addicts to prison, they allow them to buy drugs at a low cost. If the addict cannot afford it, she or he is given the drug free of charge. The system does not allow an addict to have an unlimited supply of narcotics. Extensive precautions are taken to regulate the distribution of narcotic drugs carefully.

The British program applies to heroin, morphine, and cocaine. (The program does not involve marijuana, barbiturates, amphetamines, or hallucinogens.) To qualify, the narcotics user must demonstrate to a physician certified by the government that she or he is an addict. The person is then officially registered as an addict and receives a steady supply of the drug. The supply is not enough to get "high," but is sufficient to prevent withdrawal symptoms. There is a central registry, so it is difficult for addicts to register with more than one clinic to obtain duplicate supplies. If a registered addict is discovered to be receiving a narcotic drug from more than one source, she or he is prosecuted. Also, anyone found possessing a narcotic who is not a registered addict is also prosecuted. Efforts are made to rehabilitate the addicts. For example, with heroin addicts attempts are made to decrease gradually the amount of heroin that is given or to switch the addicts to methadone.

The British approach appears to be working well for them. The rate of addiction is far lower than in the United States, and the illicit market is far smaller and less profitable. British addicts have less need to obtain large amounts of money to support their habits, and as a result they commit fewer property crimes. Organized crime has few profit incentives to smuggle narcotics into the country, and as a result there are few narcotics available for nonaddicts to experiment with. Because the prescription drug is of uniform strength and is distributed in small dosages, there are few overdoses. Because the prescription drug does not contain impurities, drug fatalities and other health hazards are lessened. In addition, a higher percentage of British addicts (compared to American addicts) are able to keep their jobs and be productive.[76]

Whether the British system would work in this country is questionable. The idea of giving heroin and other drugs to addicts runs counter to American values that people should not be drug dependent, that users should be punished to deter others, and that the government should not be involved in distributing potentially harmful drugs. With organized crime's strong position in this country there is also the danger that it will find a way to gain access to the government's supply of drugs and then sell them to nonaddicts at inflated prices. However, because the British system is rather successful, it warrants careful consideration for adaptation here.

SUMMARY

A drug is any habit-forming substance that directly affects the central nervous system; it affects moods, perceptions, bodily functions, or consciousness. Drug abuse is the regular or excessive use of a drug when, as defined by a group, the consequences endanger relationships with others, are detrimental to a person's health, or jeopardize society itself. The dominant social reaction to a drug is influenced not only by the actual dangers of the drug but also by the social characteristics and motives of the groups that use it. Legal drugs are more often abused and cause more harm in our society than illegal drugs. Many drugs produce psychological or physical dependence (addiction) or both. Often, users develop a tolerance for a drug, which is the need for steadily increasing dosages.

Social costs of drugs include property crime (generally committed to support a habit), automobile accidents, economic losses, health problems, disrespect for the law, family disruption, spouse and child abuse, financial crises for users, and adverse psychological effects on individuals.

Our society romanticizes and encourages the use of several drugs through commercials, films, books, and TV programs. Widely advertised drugs include alcohol, tobacco, caffeine, and over-the-counter drugs.

Facts about and effects of many drugs are described in this chapter, including depressants (alcohol, barbiturates, tranquilizers, Quaalude, PCP); stimulants (caffeine, amphetamines, cocaine, crack, amyl nitrate, butyl nitrate); narcotics (opium, heroin, morphine); hallucinogens (peyote, psilocybin, psilocin, LSD); tobacco; and marijuana. Alcohol is by far the most widely abused drug in our society.

Treatment programs for drug abuse include inpatient and outpatient services provided by community mental health centers, some medical hospitals, and specialized chemical abuse rehabilitation centers. Additional programs include self-help groups, halfway houses, and therapeutic communities.

Drug abuse will probably never cease in this country, but the extent of the abuse can certainly be reduced. Punitive laws, as Prohibition demonstrated, do not deter drug use for many people and often encourage the development of organized crime and an illicit drug market. Suggestions for curbing abuse include expanding quality educational programs that give accurate information about drugs, indicting drug barons who mastermind the production and distribution of illegal drugs, using employee drug-testing programs, and revising drug abuse laws to use a treatment approach rather than a punitive approach.

NOTES

1. *Webster's New Collegiate Dictionary* (Springfield, MA: G. & C. Merriam, 1981).

2. Bertram S. Brown, "The Decriminalization of Marijuana," *Hearings of the House Select Committee on Narcotic Abuse* (March 14, 1977), First Session, 95th Congress.

3. Herbert C. Modlin and Alberto Montes, "Narcotics Addiction in Physicians," *The American Journal of Psychiatry* 121 (October 1964), pp. 358–365.

4. U.S. Bureau of the Census, *Statistical Abstract of the United States, 1987* (Washington, D.C.: U.S. Government Printing Office, 1987), pp. 88, 105.

5. Erich Goode, *Drugs in American Society* (New York: Alfred A. Knopf, 1972).

6. Richard Ashley, *Cocaine: Its History, Uses, and Effects* (New York: St. Martin's Press, 1975).

7. Quoted in Earle F. Barcus and Susan M. Jankowski, "Drugs and the Mass Media," *The Annals of the American Academy of Political and Social Science* 417, 1975, p. 89.

8. Ian Robertson, *Social Problems*, 2d ed. (New York: Random House, 1980), p. 438.

9. Leon G. Hunt and Carl D. Chambers, *The Heroin Epidemics* (New York: Spectrum Books, 1976).

10. Alfred R. Lindesmith, *The Addict and the Law* (Bloomington: Indiana University Press, 1965), p. 228.

11. Joseph Gusfield, *Symbolic Crusade: Status Politics and the American Temperance Movement* (Urbana, IL: University of Illinois Press, 1963).

12. Emile Durkheim, *Suicide: A Study in Sociology*, trans. John Spaulding and George Simpson (New York: Free Press, 1951).

13. Robert Merton, *Social Theory and Social Structure*, 2d ed. (New York: Free Press, 1968).

14. See Charles H. Cooley, *Human Nature and the Social Order* (New York: Charles Scribner's Sons, 1902); and Howard S. Becker, *Outsiders: Studies in the Sociology of Deviance* (New York: Free Press, 1963).

15. Edwin H. Sutherland and Donald R. Cressey, *Principles of Criminology*, 7th ed. (Philadelphia: J. B. Lippincott, 1966).

16. U.S. Department of Health, Education, and Welfare, *Alcohol and Health* (Rockville, MD: Public Health Service, 1975), pp. 15–16.

17. Joseph Julian and William Kornblum, *Social Problems*, 5th ed. (Englewood Cliffs, NJ: 1986), p. 122.

18. Richard Stivers, *A Hair of the Dog: Irish Drinking and the American Stereotype* (University Park, PA: Pennsylvania University Press, 1976).

19. Howard S. Becker, "Becoming a Marijuana User," *American Journal of Sociology* 59 (November 1953), pp. 235–242.

20. Julian and Kornblum, *Social Problems*, p. 120.

21. The material in this section is summarized from studies that were reviewed in Julian and Kornblum, *Social Problems*, pp. 119–124.

22. Ibid., p. 123.

23. See David J. Armor, J. Michael Polich, and Harriet G. Stambul, *Alcoholism and Treatment* (New York: Wiley Interscience, 1978).

24. Julian and Kornblum, *Social Problems*, p. 121.

25. Ibid., pp. 119–124.

26. Ibid., pp. 120–121.

27. Ibid., p. 125.

28. U.S. Bureau of the Census, *Statistical Abstract of the United States, 1987*, p. 75.

29. Ernest P. Noble, ed., *Alcohol and Health: Third Special Report to the United States Congress* (Rockville, MD: U.S. Public Health Service, June 1978), pp. 10–12.

30. Ibid., pp. 10–12.

31. Ibid., p. 13.

32. Federal Bureau of Investigation, *Crime in the United States, 1986: Uniform Crime Report* (Washington, D.C.: U.S. Government Printing Office, 1987).

33. Ibid.

34. Robertson, *Social Problems*.

35. Julian and Kornblum, *Social Problems*, p. 127.

36. Lewis J. Lord, "Coming to Grips with Alcoholism," *U.S. News & World Report*, November 30, 1987, p. 56.

37. Julian and Kornblum, *Social Problems*, p. 127.

38. Wayne W. Dunning and Dae H. Chang, "Drug Facts and Effects," in *The Personal Problem Solver*, eds. Charles Zastrow and Dae H. Chang (Englewood Cliffs, NJ: Spectrum Books, 1977), p. 177.

39. National Institute on Drug Abuse, *Sedative-Hypnotic Drugs: Risks and Benefits* (Washington, D.C.: U.S. Government Printing Office, 1977), p. 63.

40. John Timson, "Is Coffee Safe to Drink?" *Human Nature* (December 1978), pp. 57–59.

41. National Clearinghouse for Drug Abuse Information, *Amphetamine* (Rockville, MD: Alcohol, Drug Abuse, and

Mental Health Administration, Report Series 28, no. 1, February 1974), pp. 9–10.

42. Joel Fort and Christopher T. Cory, *American Drug Store* (Boston: Little, Brown, 1975), p. 41.

43. Tony Blaze-Gosden, *Drug Abuse* (Birmingham, Great Britain: David & Charles Publishers, 1987), p. 99.

44. George Andrews and David Solomon, eds., *The Coca Leaf and Cocaine Papers* (New York: Harcourt Brace Jovanovich, 1975).

45. Blaze-Gosden, *Drug Abuse*, p. 95.

46. Leon G. Hunt and Norman E. Zinberg, *Heroin Use: A New Look* (Washington, D.C.: Drug Abuse Council, 1976).

47. Ibid.

48. Edward M. Brecher et al., *Licit and Illicit Drugs: The Consumers Union Report on Narcotics, Stimulants, Depressants, Inhalants, Hallucinogens, and Marijuana—Including Coffee, Nicotine, and Alcohol* (Boston: Little, Brown, 1972), p. 84.

49. S. Mushkin, "Politics and Economics of Government Response to Drug Abuse," *Annals of the American Academy of Political and Social Science* 417 (January 1975), p. 30.

50. Brecher et al., *Licit and Illicit Drugs*, pp. 71–79.

51. Ibid., p. 22.

52. Robertson, *Social Problems*, p. 450.

53. "Hallucinogens and Narcotics Alarm Public," *Chemistry and Engineering News* 48, no. 47 (1976), pp. 44–45.

54. U.S. Department of Health, Education, and Welfare, *Surgeon-General's Report on Smoking and Health* (Washington, D.C.: U.S. Government Printing Office, 1979).

55. Ibid.

56. Lynn Rosellini, "Rebel with a Cause: Koop," *U.S. News & World Report*, May 30, 1988, pp. 55–63.

57. William A. Hunt and Joseph D. Matarazzo, "Habit Mechanisms in Smoking," in *Learning Mechanisms of Smoking*, ed. William A. Hunt (Chicago: Aldine Publishing, 1970), p. 76.

58. Edward M. Brecher, "Marijuana: The Health Questions," *Consumer Reports*, March 1975, pp. 143–149.

59. *Marihuana: A Signal of Misunderstanding, First Report of the Commission on Marihuana and Drug Abuse* (Washington, D.C.: U.S. Government Printing Office, 1972), p. 109.

60. Ibid.

61. John Kaplan, *Marijuana: A New Prohibition* (New York: World, 1970).

62. National Commission on Marihuana and Drug Abuse, *Drug Use in America: Problem in Perspective*, Second Report (Washington, D.C.: U.S. Government Printing Office, March 1973).

63. National Academy of Sciences, *Marijuana and Health* (Washington, D.C.: U.S. Government Printing Office, 1982).

64. Tim Bliss, "Drugs—Use, Abuse, and Treatment," in *Introduction to Social Welfare Institutions* (Homewood, IL: Dorsey Press, 1978), p. 301.

65. Frank Riessman, "The 'Helper Therapy' Principle," *Journal of Social Work*, April 1965, pp. 27–34.

66. Martin Kasindorf, "By the Time it Gets to Phoenix," *New York Times Magazine*, October 26, 1975, p. 30.

67. For descriptions of these self-help groups see Gartner and Riessman, *Help: A Working Guide to Self-Help Groups* (New York: New Viewpoints, 1980).

68. Bliss, "Drugs—Use, Abuse, and Treatment," p. 314.

69. John S. Lang, "America on Drugs," *U.S. News & World Report*, July 28, 1986, p. 48.

70. "A Test-Tube War on Drugs?" *U.S. News & World Report*, March 17, 1986, p. 8.

71. Ibid.

72. Alvin P. Sanoff, "Baseball's Drug Menace," *U.S. News & World Report*, March 17, 1986, p. 57.

73. Ibid.

74. Helen H. Nowlis, *Drugs on the College Campus* (New York: Doubleday, 1969), p. 51.

75. *Drug Use in America: Problem in Perspective*.

76. *The Prevention and Treatment of Drug Dependence in Britain* (New York: British Information Services, 1973), pp. 4–6.

8

CRIME, JUVENILE DELINQUENCY, AND CORRECTIONAL SERVICES

On August 9, 1969, actress Sharon Tate was slain in her home, along with four other people. The next night Leno LaBianca (a wealthy president of a grocery chain company) and his wife were brutally stabbed to death. In the weeks that followed, Charles Manson and several of his followers were arrested and later convicted for these murders. Charles Manson was head of a commune, "The Family," that lived in Death Valley, California. Why did Manson and his followers commit these bizarre murders? What can be done to prevent these, and other offenses, from being committed?

These questions highlight the focus of this chapter. The main topics to be covered are:

- Nature and extent of crime.
- Crime causation theories.
- Types of crime.
- The criminal justice system (the police, the courts, and the correctional system).
- How to reduce crime and delinquency.
- The role of social work in providing correctional services.

NATURE AND EXTENT OF CRIME

What Is Crime?

A *crime* is simply an act committed or omitted in violation of a law. A *law* is a formal social rule that is enforced by a political authority. Usually the state (or the power elite that controls the state) specifies as crimes those acts that violate certain strongly held values and norms. Not all behaviors that violate such norms are prohibited by law; in some cases informal processes such as social disapproval regulate norm violations. A swimmer's failure, for example, to aid a drowning person is not a criminal act, although it is usually considered morally wrong.

Norms and values change over time, and therefore so do laws. When norms change, there is often a time

In the early hours of September 22, 1988, a five-alarm blaze destroyed the construction site of a drugstore and seriously damaged nine other buildings in San Francisco's Haight-Ashbury district. Although at this writing no one has been charged with a crime, investigators immediately suspected that the fire was the act of an arsonist. The chain drugstore had been actively opposed by many local residents, who feared it would permanently alter the character of the neighborhood famous as the birthplace of the 1960s hippie movement. Arson is one of eight crimes reported annually in the FBI's Serious Crime Index; the Haight Street fire was one of over 13 million serious crimes reported to law enforcement agencies in 1988.

lag before laws based on the outdated norms are changed: For example, there are obsolete laws remaining in some areas that still prohibit card playing on Sundays and prohibit sexual intercourse (even among married couples) in any position other than the missionary position. Certain norms and values differ between cultures and societies, therefore, so do laws. In South Africa it is a serious crime, punishable by whipping and incarceration, for persons of different races to have, or to attempt to have, sexual intercourse with one another.[1] In many Arab countries the use of alcohol is illegal, but the use of marijuana is acceptable; in the United States the reverse is generally the law.

Everyone, at one time or another, has violated some laws. A survey in the New York area found that in response to a list of forty-nine criminal offenses, over 90 percent of the anonymous respondents acknowledged

that they had committed one or more offenses for which they could have received a jail or prison sentence.[2] Whether a law violator becomes a convicted offender depends on a number of factors, including whether she or he is arrested, how forcefully the prosecuting attorney wants to present the case, the legal skills of the defense attorney, whether there are witnesses, and how the offender presents himself or herself in court.

With thousands of laws on the books, police, prosecuting attorneys, and judges have considerable discretion over which laws to ignore, which to enforce, and how strongly to enforce. This discretionary power offers many opportunities for criminal justice officials to choose which laws to enforce, who to arrest, and who to release. The act of applying the law often involves issues of political power and more favorable treatment being given to certain groups and classes. Because criminal justice power usually resides with the white middle and upper classes, the poor and minority groups are often (intentionally or unintentionally) treated more harshly. For example, authorities are substantially less vigorous in enforcing white-collar crime than they are in enforcing vagrancy laws in middle-class neighborhoods. (The middle-class power structure generally seeks to enforce vagrancy laws in order "to keep bums and other undesirables off the streets, or at least out of respectable neighborhoods."[3])

What Is the Extent of Crime?

Crime is one of the most serious problems facing our nation. Former President Nixon remarked on several occasions that crime is our "number one enemy" and that "we must declare war against it." (Ironically, President Nixon and many of his top administrative officials later faced criminal charges—with some being imprisoned—in connection with the Watergate affair.*)

The most comprehensive statistical summary of crime in America is the annual publication of the Uniform Crime Reports (UCR) by the FBI. This report lists the crimes and arrests in this country, as reported by law enforcement agencies. One part of this report is the Serious Crime Index, which is constructed to show the amount of, and trends in, serious crimes. The Serious Crime Index is composed of four types of property crimes (burglary, larceny over $50, motor vehicle theft, and arson) and four types of crimes against persons (willful homicide, forcible rape, aggravated assault, and robbery.)

There are over 13 million Serious Crime Index offenses reported annually to law enforcement agencies in the United States.[4] Serious Crime Index offenses are listed in Table 8.1.

---

*The Watergate affair involved a break-in in the early 1970s into the Democratic Presidential Campaign headquarters (housed in the Watergate building in Washington, D.C.) by people who were clandestinely employed to help reelect President Richard Nixon. Nixon and some of his top aides then committed a variety of offenses in an effort to cover up this break-in. President Nixon was eventually forced to resign from the presidency after the coverup was revealed.

TABLE 8.1

Number of Reported Serious Crimes— 1986

Crime	Number
Arson	(Statistics unavailable)
Murder	20,610
Forcible rape	90,430
Robbery	542,780
Aggravated assault	834,320
Burglary	3,241,400
Larceny theft	7,257,200
Motor vehicle theft	1,224,100
Total	13,210,800

Source: *Crime in the United States, 1986, FBI Uniform Crime Reports* (Washington, D.C.: U.S. Government Printing Office, 1987), p. 41.

It is generally agreed that serious, violent crime has reached alarming proportions in the United States. A survey by the Law Enforcement Assistance Administration (LEAA) found that 61 percent of all women feel unsafe in their own neighborhood at night; that 45 percent of the population is afraid to walk alone at night near their own homes; and that 47 percent own their own guns, largely for self-protection.[5] Table 8.2 demonstrates graphically why people are so fearful today.

Who Is Arrested?

Those arrested for crimes are disproportionately likely to be male, young, a member of a racial minority, and a city resident.

Males are arrested about five times as often as females.[6] Only in juvenile runaway and prostitution cases are females arrested more often than males. There are two major reasons why males are more often arrested.

TABLE 8.2

Crime Clock (Occurrence of Reported Crimes according to Time in the United States)

1. Murder—one every 25 minutes

2. Forcible rape—one every 6 minutes

3. Robbery—one every 58 seconds

4. Aggravated assault—one every 38 seconds

5. Motor vehicle theft—one every 26 seconds

6. Violent crime—one every 21 seconds

7. Burglary—one every 10 seconds

8. Larceny-theft—one every 4 seconds

9. Property crime—one every 3 seconds

Source: *Crime in the United States, 1986, FBI Uniform Crime Reports* (Washington, D.C.: U.S. Government Printing Office, 1987), p. 6.

One is the sex role stereotyping, which encourages males to be more aggressive and daring, whereas females are encouraged to be more passive and conforming to rules and norms. The second reason is the tendency of police officers and the courts to deal more leniently with female offenders.[7] However, it should be noted that in the past two decades crime among females has been increasing at a faster rate than among males,[8] which may be a negative side effect of women challenging the traditional sex roles of passivity and conformity.

Young people appear to commit far more than their share of crime, including the crimes that are classified by the FBI as most serious—rape, murder, robbery, arson, burglary, aggravated assault, auto theft, and larceny. In 1986, 31 percent of all arrests were under age 21, and 45 percent of all arrests were under age 25.[9] A partial explanation of the high arrest rate among juveniles and young adults is that they may be less

skillful than older adults in avoiding arrest. Another reason is that they tend to commit crimes, such as auto theft, that are highly visible to the police. Even when all these factors are taken into account it is still the case that the young commit more crimes than the old.

Members of racial minority groups have a disproportionately higher rate of arrests. For example, a black person is three times more likely to be arrested than a white person.[10] One reason for this higher rate is that a higher proportion of the black population is poor or unemployed; and there are high correlations between poverty (and unemployment) and the types of crime classified by the FBI as most serious. An additional reason for the higher arrest rates among minority groups may be racial prejudice. A number of studies have shown that the probability of arrest, prosecution, conviction, and incarceration for an offense that is committed decreases as the social status of the offender increases. In one study, thirty-six judges were given fact sheets on a hypothetical case and asked to recommend an appropriate sentence. The fact sheets contained the following information:

"Joe Cut," 27, pleaded guilty to battery. He slashed his common-law wife on the arms with a switchblade. His record showed convictions for disturbing the peace, drunkenness, and hit-run driving. He told a probation officer that he acted in self-defense after his wife attacked him with a broom handle. The prosecutor recommended not more than five days in jail or a $100 fine.[11]

Half the fact sheets identified "Joe Cut" as white, and the other half identified him as black. The judges who thought he was white recommended a sentence of three to ten days, whereas those who thought he was black recommended a sentence of from five to thirty days.

A majority of reported crimes and reported arrests are in large cities, as compared to suburbs and rural areas.[12] Within large cities crime tends to occur in those sections that are changing rapidly and those having a high concentration of low-income and transient inhabitants. Arrest rates are substantially lower in more stable, higher-income, residential areas.

TABLE 8.3

Most Crimes Remain Unsolved

For every 100 reported crimes:

20 persons are arrested
14 persons are charged
 7 persons are referred to juvenile court
 2 persons are acquitted
 1 person is fined
 1 person is found guilty of a lesser offense
 3 persons are placed on probation
 3 persons are imprisoned

Source: Joseph Julian and William Kornblum, *Social Problems*,
4th ed. (Englewood Cliffs, NJ: Prentice-Hall, 1983), p. 159.

How Accurate Are Official Crime Statistics?

As described earlier the Federal Bureau of Investigation annually compiles the Uniform Crime Reports (UCR), receiving reports from law enforcement agencies throughout the country of crimes committed and arrests made. The Serious Crime Index is a part of UCR.

There are a number of problems connected with this Index. The precise rates of serious crimes are unknown. The actual crime rates are substantially higher than the official rates. A survey of five large American cities found that the actual rates for violent personal and property crime were several times higher than the number reported; many victims do not report crimes to the police because (among other reasons) they feel that nothing can be done.[13] As indicated in Table 8.3, most crimes remain unsolved.

The Serious Crime Index of UCR focuses on crimes that are more apt to be committed by persons of lower social and economic status. It does not contain the types of crimes typically committed by higher-income groups: fraud, false advertising, corporate price fixing, bribery, embezzlement, industrial pollution, tax eva-

sion, and so on. If white-collar crimes were included in the Crime Index, and if law enforcement authorities would be more vigorous in enforcing such laws, the profile of a typical criminal would very likely be older, wealthier, whiter, and more suburban than suggested by the Crime Index.

Self-report studies in which respondents are asked anonymously the details of any crimes they may have committed reveal that "close to 100 percent of all persons have committed some kind of offense, although few have been arrested."[14] In what way then, do those who are arrested differ from those who are not? One explanation is that those who are not caught only rarely commit a crime, whereas those who are arrested are breaking the law more frequently. Perhaps a better explanation, however, is in the types of crimes committed. Those arrested may be committing the types of crimes that are more strictly enforced by law enforcement agencies. The poor, for example, may be more apt to commit the high-risk, low-yield crimes such as larceny, burglary, or robbery. In contrast, the wealthier are more apt to commit crimes that are less strictly enforced and have a higher yield, such as income tax evasion and false advertising.

In the past twenty years there have been dramatic increases in the rate of reported Serious Crime Index offenses. Yet it is uncertain whether this rate increase actually represents an increase in the rate of serious crime offenses. Perhaps crime victims are reporting more offenses. Or perhaps the increase is due to improvements in police-reporting practices. In the past two decades police departments have given extensive attention to training police in more accurate crime-reporting practices and are increasingly using computers, clerical personnel, and statisticians to improve the accuracy of police reports.

Strictly speaking, the Crime Index is not fully comparable between jurisdictions and, at times, is even inconsistent from one year to the next within the same reporting unit. A major reason for this difficulty is that each of the fifty states has its own unique criminal code. For example, an offense that is classified as burglary in one state may be classified as larceny or robbery in another. What is classified as sexual assault in one state may be considered a less serious offense in another. Because states occasionally make changes in their criminal codes, inconsistencies may arise from one year to the next within the same reporting unit because of changes in definitions of offenses. Furthermore, individual officers interpret the law differently as they carry out their duties.

Finally, it should be noted that crime statistics are at times manipulated by the police and public officials. Sometimes the data are manipulated to show higher rates of crime, perhaps to help document the need for a federal or state grant or to politic for a budget increase in personnel or facilities. More often than not, however, police and public officials are under considerable pressure to keep the crime rate low. One way to manipulate statistics is to reclassify certain serious crimes into different, less serious categories.

In summary, the Serious Crime Index of the FBI provides an indication of the rates and trends of certain crimes in the United States. Yet these statistics overlook white-collar crime, are affected by police-reporting practices, and have to be viewed against the fact that many crimes are unreported. It further appears that the poor, the undereducated, and minorities have been the victims not only of selective law enforcement but also of misleading statistics on crime. Some sociologists have contended that because higher-income classes are far more involved in white-collar crime (which is often ignored by law enforcement agencies), the higher classes may actually have a higher rate of crime than the lower classes.[15]

CRIME CAUSATION THEORIES

A variety of theories about the causes of crime have been advanced by several disciplines. Space limitations permit only a summary of the more prominent theories. Table 8.4 identifies the names of these prominent theories and gives the approximate date of origin. As you read each of these theories, ask yourself the following questions: "Is this theory helpful in understanding why a person committed a rape (or a burglary, a mur-

der, a drug-traffic offense, engaged in prostitution, an aggravated assault, kidnapping, or embezzled funds), and is the theory useful in suggesting a correctional plan to prevent a recurrence of the offense?"

Early Theories

Three of the earliest theories on the cause of crime were *demonology*, the *classical/neoclassical theory*, and the *Marxist-Leninist theory.*

DEMONOLOGY   For centuries, many primitive societies conceived of crime as being caused by evil spirits. This is commonly referred to as *demonology.* It was thought that those who engaged in deviant behavior were possessed by the devil. The only way to cure the criminal act, it was believed, was to remove the evil spirit through prayer, through a ritual, or by torture. Sometimes the entire body would be destroyed to remove the evil. This theory is no longer prominent, partly because scientific study has found no evidence that law breakers are possessed by evil spirits. Remnants of this theory, however, remain. There are satanic cults, some rock groups produce records with satanic themes, and some moves (such as "Friday the 13th" and "The Exorcist") have had themes of people being possessed by demons.

CLASSICAL AND NEOCLASSICAL THEORY   The *classical* and *neoclassical* schools were based on hedonistic psychology. Classical theory asserted that a person makes a decision regarding whether to engage in criminal activity based on the anticipated balance of pleasure minus pain. Each person was assumed to have a free will and to act solely on the basis of the anticipated hedonistic calculations. Advocates of this school assumed this explanation was a full and exhaustive explanation of causality. Applied to corrections, this approach urged that definite amounts of punishments be assigned to each offense so the prospective offender could calculate anticipated pleasures and pains. The penalties assigned were to be slightly more severe than anticipated pleasures in order to discourage criminal activity. The neoclassical school accepted the basic no-

TABLE 8.4

Prominent Theories of Crime

School	Approximate Date of Origin
Early theories	
Demonology	Primitive societies
Classical–Neoclassical	1775
Marxist–Leninist	1850
Physical and mental trait theories	
Phrenology	1825
Lombrosian	1900
Mental deficiency	1900
Morphological	1920
Psychological theories	
Psychoanalytic	1900
Psychodynamic problem solving	1920
Frustration-aggression	1950
Self-talk	1975
Sociological theories	
Labeling	1900
Differential association	1939
Control	1950
Deviant subcultures	1955
Anomie	1957

tion of hedonistic calculations but urged that children and "lunatics" be exempt from punishment because of their inability to calculate pleasures and pain responsibly. Judicial discretion was also urged for certain mitigating circumstances (for example, an offense now referred to as involuntary manslaughter).

Although correctional systems in the 19th century were primarily based on the neoclassical approach, the classical/neoclassical approach has waned in popularity. Remnants, however, are still to be found in our legal/judicial system—particularly the emphasis on using punishment to deter crime. The theory has been severely criticized because it does not allow for other causes of crime and because the punitive approach it advocates has not been very successful in curbing further criminal activity. In addition, hedonistic psychology ignores the fact that much of human behavior is determined by values and morals rather than by the pleasure-over-pain calculation.

MARXIST-LENINIST THEORY   Marxist-Leninist theory assumes that all crime results from the exploitation of workers and from severe competition among people. Crime disappears, according to neoMarxists, when society achieves a "classless" status. The basic tenet of communism is, "from each according to his ability, to each according to his need." Socialist countries (such as Russia and Cuba) have moved in the direction advocated by Marx. Class differentials are much less prominent in socialist countries as compared to capitalistic nations. Although Marx asserted that crime would be sharply reduced in socialist countries because there would be less class conflict, substantial criminal activity is occurring in these countries. The extensiveness of criminal activity is difficult to determine, since these countries publish almost no crime-rate reports. The continued existence of crime in these countries is not taken by socialists as evidence that socialist theory is defective but is explained as being the result of old capitalistic traditions and ideologies and from the imperfect application of Marxist theory.

Physical and Mental Trait Theories

You may have noticed in Table 8.4, "Prominent Theories of Crime," that the first mentioned "physical and mental trait theory," *phrenology*, actually originated before the Marxist theory mentioned previously. Although it falls into the date category of "early theories," it is more closely related to "trait theories" and will be discussed in this section along with three other trait theories, the *Lombrosian*, the *mental deficiency*, and the *morphological* theories.

PHRENOLOGY   Phrenology was popular until the turn of this century. Phrenologists maintained that crime was related to the size and shape of the human skull. The grooves, ridges, and number of bumps of a skull were closely scrutinized. The shape of the brain, which was influenced by the exterior of the skull, was thought to be sufficient to predict criminal behavior. Although there were isolated incidents in which offenders whose skulls fit the guidelines of being "criminal prone" were more harshly treated, this approach was not widely incorporated into correctional systems. Scientific studies have found no evidence of correlations between criminal behavior and the shape of the skull.

LOMBROSIAN THEORY   Around the beginning of the 20th century, biological/constitutional theories were popular. The prototype of such theories was Cesare Lombroso's theory of the "born criminal." This school maintained that a criminal inherits certain physical abnormalities or stigmata, such as a scanty beard, low sensitivity to pain, a distorted nose, large lips, or long arms. The more such stigmata a person had, the more he or she was thought to be predisposed to a criminal career. Persons with several stigmata were thought to be unable to refrain from criminal activity unless their social environment was unusually favorable. The theory that criminals have distinct physical characteristics was refuted by Charles Goring, who found no significant physical differences in a study comparing several thousand criminals to several thousand noncriminals.[16]

MENTAL DEFICIENCY THEORY   The mental deficiency theory replaced the Lombrosian school when the latter fell into disrepute. The mental deficiency theory, which was popular until the 1930s, asserted that criminal behavior resulted from "feeblemindedness," which was alleged to impair the capacity to acquire morality and self-control or to appreciate the meaning of laws. As mental tests became standardized and widely used, it was discovered that many criminals achieved average or above average intelligence scores, and the theory

waned in popularity. Neither the Lombrosian nor the mental deficiency approach had a lasting, significant effect on corrections.

MORPHOLOGICAL THEORY   Closely related to the mental deficiency and Lombrosian theories is morphological theory, which asserted there is a fundamental relationship between the psychological makeup and the physical structure. The most popular variant of this theory has been William Sheldon's categories, which were developed in the 1940s. Sheldon set up three body categories: endomorph (obese), mesomorph (muscular), and ectomorph (lean). To the mesomorph, he ascribed an unusual propensity to criminal activity. He did not assert that mesomorphs were inherently criminally prone. Rather, he asserted that this physique was associated with a distinctive type of temperament that is characterized by such traits as love of physical adventure, abounding and restless energy, and enjoyment of exercise. Mesomorphy, it was asserted, produced energetic, aggressive, and daring types of people, persons such as generals, athletes, and politicians, as well as criminals. Morphological approaches (such as Sheldon's theory) are still popular in southern European and South American countries. Scientific studies, however, have found little evidence that muscular people are more apt to commit crimes than people who are lean or overweight.

Psychological Theories

Psychological theories about crime try to explain the cause or causes of crime as having to do with the criminal's thought processes, relatively unrelated to overall societal conditions. These theories include *psychoanalytic, psychodynamic problem-solving, frustration-aggression,* and *self-talk* approaches to understanding criminal behavior.

PSYCHOANALYTIC THEORY   Psychoanalytic theory is not a single coherent theory but a variety of hypotheses developed by psychoanalysts since the turn of the century from the pioneering work of Sigmund Freud. Generally, these theories postulated that delinquent behavior results when the restraining forces in the superego (one's conscience and self-ideal) and the ego (mediator between the superego, the id, and reality) are too weak to curb the instinctual, antisocial pressures from the id (source of psychic energy). Psychoanalytic theory asserted that human nature was largely determined by id instincts, which were basically antisocial and immoral in character. This theory postulated that current behavior was largely controlled by early learning experiences. Deviant behavior was viewed as stemming from unconscious conflicts, fixations, and repressed traumatic experiences.

The psychiatric school, of which psychoanalysis is a large component, has had a significant influence on corrections, since it asserts that some offenders commit illegal acts because they are insane. Criminal justice systems frequently request psychiatrists to determine the "sanity" of accused offenders. If an offender is judged by the court to be "innocent by reason of insanity," the offender is sent to a mental hospital, instead of to a jail, to recuperate.

Psychiatry has also classified individuals into numerous categories in terms of their "mental" functioning. One category, *sociopath*, has had considerable relevance for corrections. A sociopath is thought to be a person who has no moral constraints against engaging in criminal activity and will do so whenever it is personally advantageous, even though others may be hurt.

Since 1950, Thomas Szasz and others have seriously questioned the medical model approach to emotional problems and have asserted that mental illness is a myth.[17] Szasz asserts that people have emotional problems, but not a "disease of the mind," as implied by the medical model (see Chapter 4). Courts, however, continue to use the mental illness model.

Psychoanalytic theory is increasingly falling into disfavor. One reason is that people with emotional problems who undergo psychoanalysis are no more likely to improve than a comparable group who receive no therapy.[18]

PSYCHODYNAMIC PROBLEM-SOLVING THEORY Psychodynamic problem-solving theory views deviant behavior as being contrived by the personality as a way of dealing with some adjustment problem. The problem is generally viewed as a conflict among various ingredients of the personality: wishes, drives, fears, strivings, loyalties, codes of ethics, and so on. Situational factors are generally deemphasized, since the problem is commonly thought of as a conflict within the personality. For example, the following internal desires have all been advanced for committing rape: unfilled sexual desires, a desire for violence, and feelings of inferiority, which are temporarily alleviated during rape as the offender feels a sense of power and superiority.

A serious shortcoming of the theory is that it is often extremely difficult (if not impossible) to determine precisely which wishes, drives, fears, or ethics motivated someone to commit a crime. Frequently, while using this theory, only speculations can be made about why a crime occurred, with there being few "tools" to check out the accuracy of the speculations.

FRUSTRATION-AGGRESSION THEORY Frustration-aggression theory is at times used to explain violence. The theory asserts that frustration often provokes an aggressive response; that is, violence is seen as a way to release tension produced by a frustrating situation. An unemployed husband unable to pay his bills or obtain a job, for example, may explode by beating his wife. Some authorities saw the burning and rioting in our inner cities in the 1960s as being a reaction by blacks to the frustration of living in a society that promises equality but does not provide it. Frustration-aggression theory only provides an explanation for violent crimes. It does not attempt to explain the occurrence of other crimes, such as prostitution, fraud, and forgery.

SELF-TALK THEORY Self-talk theory presents a psychological approach for identifying the underlying motives for committing a crime.[19] This theory asserts that the reasons for any criminal act can be determined by examining what the offender was thinking prior to and during the time the crime was being committed. A shortcoming of this theory is that when offenders discuss what they were thinking when they committed a crime, they often seek to slant what they reveal in a socially acceptable way.

BOX 8.1

Self-Talk Theory Explanation of the Manson Murders

W hy (in August of 1969) did Charles Manson and several members of his commune murder Sharon Tate and six other prominent persons? Vincent Bugliosi, prosecuting attorney for the state of California, was able to document that the following thinking processes led Manson to order these killings.

Manson hoped that brutal murders of the prominent and wealthy would create fear and panic among whites. Manson thought whites, unable to determine who actually killed these people, would conclude these murders were committed by blacks. Manson theorized that whites, out of fear, would go into the ghettos and start killing black people, thus causing a race war. Such a war, he thought, would also lead to a split between white liberals and conservatives, who would then begin killing each other. During this time, Manson thought the "true black race" (at various times identified by Manson as the "Black Panthers" or the "Black Muslims") would go into hiding and would be unaffected. After almost all whites had perished, the "true black race" would come out and kill the remaining whites, except for Manson and his followers, who would be in hiding in Death Valley. Manson further thought the remaining blacks would not have the capacities to govern the nation and that, after failing to govern, would then turn to him to be the leader of the nation. (Manson was found to be "sane" and was convicted of first-degree murder.)

Thus, it appears that this strange, somewhat unrealistic belief system led Manson and his followers to kill seven people. Having an unrealistic belief system does not in any way make a person "crazy." All of the defendants in this case were considered to be "sane." While living together in isolation in a commune, the members apparently gave mutual support to each other for the correctness of Manson's beliefs, probably partly because objective evidence was not available to refute Manson's interpretations.

Source: Vincent Bugliosi and C. Genty, *Helter Skelter* (New York: Norton, 1974).

Sociological Theories

Sociological theories focus on societal processes that influence people to commit crimes. For ease in understanding these theories, we will examine them out of chronological order (see Table 8.4) as follows: *differ-*

ential association theory, anomie theory, deviant subcultures theory, control theory, and *labeling theory*.

DIFFERENTIAL ASSOCIATION THEORY   Edwin Sutherland is perhaps the best known criminologist in contemporary sociology. In 1939, he advanced his famous theory of differential association. The theory asserts that criminal behavior is the result of a learning process that primarily stems from small, intimate groups—family, neighborhood peer groups, friends, and so on. In essence, the theory states, "A person becomes delinquent because of the excess of definitions favorable to violation of law over definitions unfavorable to violation of law."[20] Whether a person decides to commit a crime is based on the nature of present and past associations with significant others. People internalize the values of the surrounding culture. When the environment includes frequent contact with criminal elements and infrequent contact with noncriminal elements, a person is apt to engage in delinquent or criminal activity. Past and present learning experiences in intimate personal groups thus define whether a person should violate laws, and, for those deciding to commit crimes, the learning experiences also include which crimes to commit, the techniques of committing these crimes, and the attitudes and rationalizations for committing these crimes. Thus, a youth whose most admired person is a member of a gang involved in committing burglaries or in drug trafficking will seek to emulate this model, will receive instruction in committing these crimes from the gang members, and will also receive approval from the gang for successfully committing these crimes. The theory has difficulty in explaining such crimes as arson and embezzlement, where the offender often has little or no exposure to others who have committed such crimes.

ANOMIE THEORY   Robert Merton applied anomie theory to crime.[21] This approach views criminal behavior as resulting when an individual is prevented from achieving the high status goals in a society. Merton begins by noting that every society has both approved goals (for example, wealth and material possessions) and approved means for attaining these goals. When certain members of society want these goals but have insufficient access to the approved means for attaining them, a state of anomie results. (Anomie is a condition in which the acceptance of the approved standards of conduct is weakened). Unable to achieve the goals through society's legitimately defined channels, indi-

vidual's respect for these channels is weakened, and they then seek to achieve the desired goals through illegal means. Merton asserts that higher crime rates are apt to occur among those groups discriminated against (that is, those groups facing additional barriers to achieving the high status goals). These groups include the poor and racial minorities. Societies with high crime rates (such as America) differ from those with low crime rates because, according to Merton, they tell all their citizens they can achieve, but in fact they block achievement for some people. Anomie theory has difficulty explaining why white-collar crime (which is primarily committed by individuals who are seldom discriminated against) is perhaps the most common type of crime committed in this country.[22]

DEVIANT SUBCULTURES THEORY   Deviant subcultures theory is another explanation for crime. This theory asserts that some groups have developed their own attitudes, values, and perspectives that support criminal activity. Walter Miller, for example, argues that American lower-class culture is more conducive to crime than middle-class culture.[23] He asserts that lower-class culture is organized around six values—trouble, toughness, excitement, fate, smartness (ability to con others), and autonomy—and he states that allegiance to these values produces delinquency. Miller concludes the entire lower-class subculture to be deviant in the sense that any male growing up in it will accept these values and almost certainly violate the law.

Albert Cohen advanced another subculture theory.[24] He contended that gangs develop a delinquent subculture that represents solutions to the problems of young male gang members. A gang gives them a chance to belong, to amount to something, to develop their masculinity, to fight middle-class society. In particular, the delinquent subculture, according to Cohen, can effectively solve the status problems of working-class boys, especially those who are rejected by middle-class society. Cohen contends that the main problems of working-class boys revolve around status.

The above deviant subculture theories are unable to explain white-collar crime and other crimes committed by the middle and upper classes.

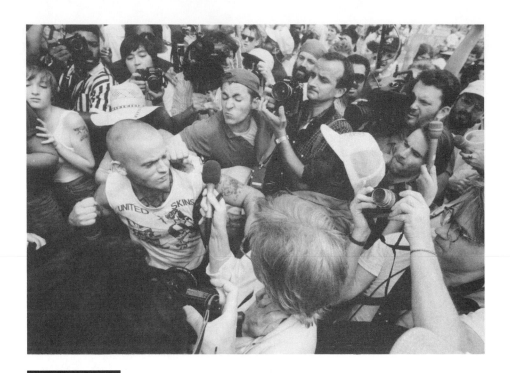

According to one theory, gangs develop delinquent subcultures that solve the status problems of working-class adolescents, especially those rejected by middle-class society. Thirty years ago, motorcycle gangs were a typical deviant subculture; today's counterpart to the Hell's Angels of the 1950s are the far more menacing Skinheads and other white supremacist youth gangs. At left, a Skinhead throws a punch in a confrontation on the eve of the 1988 Democratic National Convention in Atlanta.

SOCIETAL CONTROL THEORY   Control theories ask the question, "Why do people *not* commit crimes?" Theories in this category assume that all people would "naturally" commit crimes and therefore must be constrained and controlled by society from breaking the law. Control theorists have identified three factors for preventing crime. One is the internal controls through the socialization process that society builds up in an individual; it is believed that developing a strong conscience and a sense of personal morality will prevent most people from breaking the law. A second factor is thought to be a strong attachment to small social groups (for example, the family), which is thought to prevent individuals from breaking the law because they fear rejection and disapproval from the people who are

important to them. A third factor (taken from the classical school) is that people do not break the law because they fear arrest and incarceration.

Control theories assume the basic nature of humans is asocial or evil. Such an assumption has never been proved. Theories that assume humans have an evil nature are unable to explain altruistic and other "good" deeds performed by people.

LABELING THEORY   Labeling theorists, similar to differential association theorists, assert that criminals *learn* to break the law. Labeling theory focuses on the processes of branding people as criminals and on the effects of such labeling. Contrary to control theory, this theory asserts labeling a person a delinquent or a

BOX 8.2

The Saints and the Roughnecks:
A Study Showing the Effects
of Labeling and the Effects
# of Expectations of Significant Others

William Chambliss, in a dramatic study, examined factors affecting delinquency among two groups of adolescents at the same high school: one group was composed of middle- and upper-class boys (the Saints), and the other was composed of lower-class boys (the Roughnecks). The Saints were often truant from school, harassed citizens and the police, openly cheated on exams, vandalized homes, drank excessively, and drove recklessly. Teachers, school officials, and the police largely ignored their acts, since they were viewed as being basically "good boys." They were almost never arrested by the police, and hardly anything negative appeared in their school records. These youth were regarded as harmless pranksters, were allowed to "sow their wild oats," and were expected to succeed in life. Interestingly, the success expectations appeared to be a major factor in determining their futures, as practically all of the Saints went on to college and white-collar careers.

On the other hand, the Roughnecks, who committed fewer, although similar, offenses were labeled "deviants." Because they didn't have cars as the Saints did, the Roughnecks were confined to an area where they were more easily recognized and substantially more often arrested. The police and school officials expected they would fail—and they did. They were labeled "delinquents," did poorly in school, and went on to low-status jobs or criminal careers. The study of the Saints and Roughnecks demonstrates that the expectations of significant others and "labeling" can have a substantial effect.

One additional factor that led to fewer arrests for the Saints was their apologetic nature whenever they were stopped by a police officer. They were polite, penitent, and pled for mercy when stopped. In contrast, there was a high level of dislike and distrust between the police and the Roughnecks. When stopped by police they came across as "tough" kids who displayed disdain and hostility—and as a consequence were more frequently arrested.

Source: William Chambliss, "The Saints and the Roughnecks," *Society* 2, no. 11 (November–December 1973), pp. 24–31.

criminal encourages rather than discourages criminal behavior.

Charles Cooley developed a labeling theory with his "looking-glass self" approach.[25] This theory argues that people develop their self-concept (sense of who and what they are) in terms of how others relate to them. For example, if a neighborhood identifies a young boy as being a "troublemaker," a "delinquent," neighbors are apt to relate to the youth as if he were not to be trusted. They may accuse him of delinquent acts, and they will label his semidelinquent and aggressive behavior as being "delinquent." This labeling process, the youth begins to realize, also results in a type of prestige and status, at least from his peers. In the absence of objective ways to gauge whether he is, in fact, a "delinquent," the youth will rely on the subjective evaluations of others. Thus, gradually, as the youth is related to as being a "delinquent," he is apt to begin to perceive himself in that way and will begin to enact the delinquent role.

Labeling theory is unable to explain why some offenders stop committing crimes after being arrested and convicted. The theory is also unable to explain why offenders initially begin breaking the law.

Usefulness of Theories

There are many other sociological as well as psychological theories. The above discussion is, of course, not exhaustive. These theories identify some of the reasons why crime occurs, especially why crime rates are higher among some groups than others.

One of the most important questions in criminology is, Do these theories identify the reasons why an offender committed a specific crime (for example, an aggravated rape)? The answer, unfortunately, is that most of the above theories are not very useful in identifying the causes for specific crimes. Also, the theories reviewed are generally not very useful in describing why one individual may commit forgery, whereas another may commit rape, and another may burglarize someone. Without knowing why a crime occurs, it is extremely difficult to develop an effective rehabilitation approach to curb the offender from committing a similar crime in the future.

Theories that attempt to explain all types of crime have a built-in limitation. Crime is a comprehensive label covering a wide range of offenses, including such different offenses as purse snatching, auto theft, rape, check forgery, prostitution, drunkenness, possession of narcotics, and sexual exhibition. Obviously, since the natures of these crimes vary widely, the motives or causes underlying each must vary widely. Therefore, it is unlikely that any theory can adequately explain the causes of all crimes. In developing theories about the causes of crime in the future, it may be more productive to focus on developing more limited theories that

attempt to identify the causes of specific offenses (for example, drunkenness, incest, auto theft, rape, or fraud) rather than to develop additional comprehensive theories.

To better understand crime, the specific types of criminal offenses will now be described.

TYPES OF CRIMES

We tend to think that crime is a well-defined phenomenon, and we tend to have stereotyped views about who criminals are. Actually, criminal offenses and the characteristics of lawbreakers are almost as varied as noncriminal offenses and law-abiders. Many diverse forms of behaviors are classified as crimes, with the only major common thread being a violation of a criminal statute. Although it is impossible to look at all crimes, we will examine the more important ones. (It will be noted that the following categories are not mutually exclusive. There is overlap between the categories.)

Organized Crime

Organized crime is a large-scale operation in which illegal activities are carried out as part of a well-designed plan developed by a large organization that is seeking to maximize its overall profit. Illegal activities that lend themselves to organized crime include illegal gambling, drug dealing, fencing (receiving and selling stolen goods), prostitution, bootlegging, and extortion (in the form of selling protection). Large-scale operations are more cost efficient than small-scale operations in certain illegal activities. For example, in drug trafficking, drugs must be smuggled into a country and distributed on a large scale, with corrupt officials being paid off to reduce the risks of arrest and prosecution.

It appears that most organized crime efforts start on a small scale, generally by developing a small organization to carry on a particular crime, such as extortion or gambling. The group then expands to control this activity within a given neighborhood or city, by absorbing or destroying the competition. Eventually, the organization expands its activities into other crimes and becomes large scale when it operates in a region or even nationwide.

A major characteristic of organized crime is that many of its activities are not predatory (such as robbery, which takes from its victims). Instead, organized crime generally seeks to provide to the public desired goods and services that cannot be legally obtained. Such goods and services include drugs, gambling, prostitution, and loan money. For its success, organized crime relies on public demand for illegal services.

Organized crime also involves syndicates, which are large-scale, coordinated, illegal operations involving several criminal groups. The exact extent of organized crime is unknown, but authorities agree that organized crime has a large impact on the public in terms of the volume of crimes committed and in terms of the cost to taxpayers. The major organized crime efforts are gambling, drug trafficking, loan sharking, infiltrating legitimate businesses, labor racketeering, and prostitution.

GAMBLING   The extent of and profits from illegal gambling are enormous. Illegal operations include lotteries, off-track betting, illegal casinos, "numbers," and dice games. Such operations can be located practically anywhere—in a restaurant, garage, or tavern; in an apartment complex; on business premises.

DRUG TRAFFICKING   It has been estimated that a $20 purchase of a kilo (2.2 pounds) of opium in Turkey, Mexico, or Southeast Asia can be sold for $500,000 in the United States.[26] With such profits, it is little wonder that organized crime is involved in the importation and distribution of such drugs as cocaine, heroin, marijuana, amphetamines, and hallucinogens.

LOAN SHARKING   This crime involves lending money at interest rates above the legal limit. Interest rates have been reported to go as high as 150 percent a week.[27] Syndicated crime can ensure repayment by the threat of violence. Major borrowers from loan sharks include gamblers who need to cover losses, drug users, and small business owners who are unable to obtain credit from legitimate sources.

INFILTRATING LEGITIMATE BUSINESSES   The huge profits from illegal activities provide organized crime with the capital to enter into legitimate operations, including the entertainment industry, banking, insurance, restaurants, advertising firms, bars, the automotive industry, and real estate agencies—to name but a few.

Marshall Clinard and Richard Quinney describe the legal and illegal ways in which organized crime infiltrates legitimate businesses:

The control of (legitimate) business concerns is secured through (1) investing concealed profits acquired from gambling and other illegal activities, (2) accepting business interests in payment of the owner's gambling debts, (3) foreclosing on usurious loans, and (4) using various forms of extortions. A favorite operation is to place a concern (that organized crime has acquired) into fraudulent bankruptcy after milking its assets.[28]

Infiltrating legitimate businesses provides organized crime with tax covers for its members, gives them a certain respectable status in the community, and offers additional profit-making opportunities. With its cash reserves, a syndicate can temporarily lower prices in order to bankrupt competitors. It can also use strong-arm tactics to force customers to buy its goods and services.

LABOR RACKETEERING   This activity involves the systematic extortion of money from labor unions and businesses. Racketeers can extort money from union members by forcing them to pay high union dues and fees in order to obtain and secure employment. Racketeers can short-change employees by paying less than union wages and by misusing the union's pension and welfare funds. Finally, racketeers can extort money from employers by forcing them to make payoffs for union cooperation (for example, to avoid a strike).

PROSTITUTION   Because prostitutes offer a service for which some people are willing to pay high prices, prostitution offers an opportunity for profit making; and organized crime has taken advantage of it. Organized crime draws its profits from being a broker for prostitutes and customers and from providing arrest and prosecution protection for prostitutes by bribing law enforcement officials. Organized crime has also gotten involved in other sex-related forms of crime, such as the illegal distribution of pornographic films and magazines.

Because of the obvious emphasis on secrecy in organized crime, relatively little is known about the extent of offenses, the leaders and members of organized crime, or the nature of the internal organization. In this regard, Thomas Sullivan et al. note:

There is a great deal of myth about the Mafia or Cosa Nostra. Evidence available to social scientists suggests that they are not *international syndicates operated by groups outside the United States, nor is there a single syndicate controlling all (or even most) organized crime in this country. American syndicates are very much American in their goals and organization. . . . In addition, just as there is competition between the giants in most legitimate business sectors, there is competition in drug dealing, illegal gambling, racketeering, and the other financial ventures involving organized crime.*[29]

Organized crime is thought to be primarily organized around the Mafia (also called the Cosa Nostra). The leadership of the Mafia is Italian American, with the lower ranks drawn from a variety of other ethnic groups. The Mafia largely developed during the 1920s and 1930s, when criminal groups organized to supply illegal alcohol during Prohibition. The Mafia has grown into a loose network of American regional syndicates or groups. These syndicates coordinate their efforts through a "commission," composed of the heads of the most powerful "families." There are thought to be twenty-four Mafia families that employ over 50,000 people in illegal activities that gross more than $150 billion each year.[30] At the head of each family is a "don," who has absolute authority over the family unless overruled by the commission. Each don is assisted by an underboss and a counselor. Next in the hierarchy are "lieutenants," each of whom supervises a group of "soldiers" who are involved in illegal enterprises. Contrary to public opinion, the Mafia is not an international syndicate of Sicilian law breakers but rather is a network of syndicates that were developed and organized in this country. The *Godfather* books and films portray a fairly realistic picture of the structure and operations of organized crime.

The costs to society and to our economy from organized crime are enormous. Through gambling and drug traffic, the lives of many individuals and their families are traumatized. Labor racketeering and infiltration of legitimate businesses lead to higher prices for goods, lower-quality products, the forced closing of some businesses, the establishment of monopolies, the unemployment of workers, misuse of pension and welfare benefits, and higher taxes. Through corruption of public officials (a necessary component of many illegal ventures), organized crime leads to public cynicism about the honesty of public officials and the democratic process. It also leads to higher taxes and mismanagement of public funds.

In recent years the FBI has made immense progress in its battle against organized crime. The heads of sixteen of the nation's twenty-four Mafia families were indicted from 1983 to 1986.[31] In 1985 the federal government obtained more than 4,190 organized crime indictments.[32] Experts credit this breakthrough to a number of factors. The FBI now devotes about one-quarter of its work force to combating organized crime[33] and has been making increased use of electronic eavesdropping. The FBI is working more closely with state law-enforcement authorities and with Italy to curb organized crime. Law enforcement agencies have recently been successful in getting large numbers of gang members to violate the traditional code of *omertà*—conspiracy of silence. Fearing lengthy stays in prison, where they could be vulnerable to mob-ordered murders, many underworld figures are joining a witness-protection effort that provides informants with new identities, houses, and fake biographies.

Despite these efforts, no one sees an end to the mob's influence anytime soon. Many of the old leaders are being replaced by a "new breed" of leadership, who have a greater familiarity with the world of high finance and legitimate business. Organized crime is developing new marketplace scams, including counterfeiting of consumer credit cards, counterfeiting airline tickets, producing and distributing record albums, bootlegging gasoline and thereby avoiding to pay federal and state gasoline taxes, and selling fraudulent tax shelters.[34]

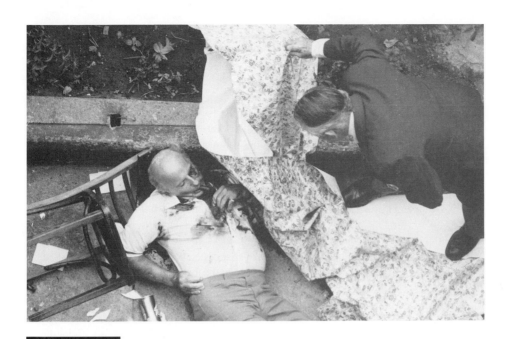

Just as there is competition among the giants of legitimate business, so are there power struggles in the world of organized crime. Carmine Galante, one of the most powerful underworld figures in recent years, smoked his last cigar in the garden of this Brooklyn restaurant in 1979. According to law enforcement officials, Galante had been marked for gangland slaying for over a year because of his ambitions to succeed the late Carlo Gambino, once called the "boss of all bosses."

White-Collar Crime

John Johnson and Jack Douglas have noted that the most costly crimes, and perhaps the most frequent crimes, are committed by "respectable" middle-class and upper-class citizens.[35] White-collar crimes are offenses committed by persons of respectability and high status in the course of their occupations.[36] A number of common white-collar offenses are discussed in the following paragraphs.

Offenses against customers include false advertising, stock manipulation, violations of food and drug laws, release of industrial waste products into public waterways, illegal emissions from industrial smokestacks, and price-fixing agreements. In 1977, for example, General Motors committed consumer fraud by placing Chevrolet engines in certain Oldsmobile auto-mobiles without informing the public. Their advertisements implicitly indicated the Oldsmobiles really had the larger, more expensive, and powerful Oldsmobile engines.

Embezzlement is the offense where an employee fraudulently converts some of the employer's funds for personal use through altering the employer's records. Embezzlers who take large sums of money are usually thought to be respectable citizens and trusted employees. A motivating force in the lives of embezzlers is encountering financial problems that their regular income is insufficient to handle—such as gambling debts, financial demands of a lover or spouse, and extensive medical bills for a relative.[37] Sullivan et al. note:

Embezzlers rationalize their theft by convincing themselves that they are merely "borrowing" the

BOX 8.3

Kepone—A Case Example of Industrial Pollution

In the late 1970s, Life Science Products Company and Allied Chemical Corporation were found guilty of safety violations in producing Kepone and of contaminating the James River in Virginia with Kepone through dumping. Kepone is a chemical pesticide and a hydrocarbon similar to DDT (DDT has been banned from use because of the adverse side effects it produces in humans.)

Life Science Products Company was producing Kepone in Hopewell, Virginia, in the mid-1970s, under contract for Allied Chemical Corporation. Hopewell is a small town located on the James River. On July 23, 1975, a Virginia health official, Dr. Robert Jackson, inspected the facilities of Life Science Products Company. Dr. Jackson was appalled at what he found. The "plant" consisted of a metal building and an abandoned service station. Safety precautions were atrocious. Kepone dust was everywhere in the town—in the air and on the soil. Traffic on streets was slowed by Kepone dust when the wind blew.

Examinations of employees revealed a number of medical problems, with the danger that other disorders such as cancer might develop in the future from exposure to the chemical. The most common symptom was called "Kepone shakes," in which the entire body shook. Other symptoms included difficulty in breathing, tension, skin rash, and psychological disorientation. The plant was immediately closed. Yet further examination revealed additional alarming disclosures. Kepone was found to cause cancer in rodents, to cause reproduction problems and infertility in birds, and to have the potential to kill both rodents and birds—and perhaps also humans. It was also found that 100,000 pounds of waste products containing Kepone had been dumped into the James River. The James River empties into Chesapeake Bay, which has since been found to be contaminated with Kepone.

The Governor of Virginia closed the lower James River to fishing in 1975 after the Kepone contamination was discovered. Unfortunately, Kepone accumulates in fish, and if the fish are eaten by humans, Kepone can cause cancer, liver problems, and reproductive problems. The Virginia fishing industry lost at least $10 million in 1976 alone. Many businesses associated with the fishing industry have since been forced to close.

A particular difficulty with Kepone is that it is bioaccumulative, which means the body retains all that it consumes rather than passing it off in wastes. Therefore, the greater the exposure, the greater the accumulation in the body, and the greater the probability of future disorders, such as cancer. The long-term effects of Kepone contamination are as yet unknown.

A number of criminal and civil suits were filed against Life Science, the City of Hopewell, and Allied. The City of Hopewell was fined $10,000, and Life Science was fined $3.8 billion and went bankrupt. Allied Chemicals was fined $13.4 million (Allied's fine was reduced to $5 million, with Allied pledging another $8 million for cleanup efforts.) As is often the case with white-collar crime, no one served a prison sentence.

money, that their employers are really crooks who deserve to lose the money, or that the employers will not miss the funds.[38]

Embezzlement occurs at all levels of business, from a clerk stealing from petty cash to the president of a company stealing large investment sums. Many cases go undetected. Even when detected, few are prosecuted. An informal arrangement is often worked out in which the embezzler agrees to pay back the amount and seek employment elsewhere—a solution that is often more effective than prosecution for recovering the stolen funds. Because a scandal involving employee dishonesty threatens the employer's public image and hurts future business, employers often seek to handle the offense informally and privately.

Other examples of white-collar crime include income tax evasion, expense-account fraud, misuse of government funds by business organizations, and corporate bribes.

American society, unfortunately, is generally tolerant of white-collar crime. A pickpocket who repeatedly steals small sums of money may well go to prison, whereas someone who repeatedly fails to report large earnings for income tax purposes is unlikely to face prosecution. This tolerance for white-collar crime appears largely due to the feeling that the victim is a large, impersonal organization (for example, the government) that will be unaffected. For example, most people would never think of taking an item from a private home, yet many of these same people steal "souvenirs" (towels, sheets, ashtrays) from hotels.

White-collar crime raises serious questions about our conceptions of crime and criminals. It suggests crime is not necessarily concentrated among the young, the poor, and racial minorities and in our inner cities. In our society, burglars and pickpockets are severely punished and stigmatized, whereas white-collar criminals committing offenses that are far more costly are seldom prosecuted or viewed as criminals. Why? Could it be due to the power structure of our society in which the middle and upper classes define their own offenses as being "excusable," whereas those offenses committed by powerless groups are viewed as being "intolerable"?

Victimless Crimes

With most crimes, there is an identifiable victim, as with embezzlement or robbery. However, there are several crimes in which no one suffers, except perhaps the person who willfully decides to engage in the illegal activity. Victimless crimes include prostitution, vagrancy, pornography, gambling, drunkenness, curfew violations, loitering, drug abuse, fornication, and homosexuality between consenting adults. (Some of these are illegal in certain jurisdictions and legal in others.) Laws that make such behaviors criminal are designed to regulate people's private lives rather than to protect some citizens from others. These laws exist because powerful groups within society regard these acts as "undesirable."

The United States invests enormous resources in controlling victimless crime, as evidenced by arrest statistics that show that nearly one fourth of all arrests annually involve victimless crimes.[39] Organized crime makes much of its money from victimless crimes by providing illegal goods and services for which certain customers willingly pay. Prohibition is the classic example, as organized crime supplied illegal alcoholic beverages at inflated prices.

Because victimless crimes are considered less serious (by at least some segments of the population) and because these crimes consume excessive money and time that police and courts could devote to reducing more serious crime, there is an effort to decriminalize or repeal some of these laws. Alexander Smith and Harriet Pollack state:

For every murderer arrested and prosecuted, literally dozens of gamblers, prostitutes, dope pushers, and derelicts crowd our courts' dockets. If we took the numbers runners, the kids smoking pot, and winos out of the criminal justice system, we would substantially reduce the burden on the courts and the police. . . . Moral laws that do not reflect contemporary mores or that cannot be enforced should be removed from the penal code through legislative action because, at best, they undermine respect for the law.[40]

Criminal penalties for such crimes may also do more harm than good. For example, treating someone arrested for homosexual activity as a hardened criminal may well damage the person's self-concept and status in the community. Criminal penalties may also force the offenders to form a subculture in order to continue their illegal activity with greater safety. Such subcultures, for example with homosexuals and drug users, serve to separate them even further from the rest of society.

Sex Offenses

There are a number of sex offenses, with forcible rape, prostitution, soliciting, statutory rape, fornication, sodomy, homosexuality, adultery, and incest being among the most common.

In most states, only males are legally liable for rape by force. Forcible rape is a highly underreported crime, with less than one quarter of the victims reporting the rape to the police.[41] Why? It is estimated that in about half of the cases the attacker is a friend or acquaintance of the victim, and therefore some victims think police action will only create more interpersonal problems. Many victims are also reluctant to report the offense because they believe (perhaps realistically) they have nothing to gain and more to lose by making a report, including social humiliation, interrogation by sometimes unsympathetic law enforcement officials, and humiliating public testimony in court about the offense. A danger to society of underreporting of rape is that the rapist is more apt to seek out other victims, since he is less likely to fear apprehension.

Statutory rape involves sexual contact between a male who is of a legally responsible age (usually 18 years) and a female who is a willing participant but is below the legal age of consent (16 years in some states and 18 years in others). In most states, females are not defined as being liable for committing statutory rape. In some states, a charge of statutory rape can be made on the basis of sexual contact other than sexual intercourse, such as oral-genital contact.

There is considerable variation in homosexuality laws among states. Most states define male homosexual acts between consenting adults as being illegal, although some states have now legalized such relations. Some states that prohibit male homosexuality between consenting adults do not prohibit such acts between adult females. (Homosexuality is further discussed in Chapter 6.)

Increased attention is now being given to sexual abuse of children. Such abuse includes sexual intercourse (genital or anal), masturbation, oral-genital contact, fondling, and exposure. An unambiguous definition of sexual abuse is not available. Sexual intercourse with children is definitely abuse, but other forms of contact are harder to judge as being abusive. At some point, hugging, kissing, and fondling become inappropriate. The abusers may include parents, older siblings, extended relatives, friends, acquaintances, or strangers. (Sexual abuse is discussed in greater length in Chapter 6.)

Certain sex offenses (such as incest, rape, and homosexual contact with a minor) incite considerable repugnance among the general public, which results in harsh punishments being assigned to the offender. Unfortunately, less attention is given to help the victims cope with their exploitation or to rehabilitate the offenders.

Homicide and Assault

Criminal homicide involves the unlawful killing of one person by another. Criminal assault is the unlawful application of physical force on another person. Most homicides are unintended outcomes of physical assaults. People get into physical fights because one (or both) is incensed about the other's actions and so retaliates. Initial actions may include ridicule, flirting with the other's spouse or lover, and anger over failure to pay a debt. Getting into a fight is often an attempt by one or both to save face when challenged or degraded. Homicides are often "crimes of passion," occurring during a violent argument or other highly charged emotional situation.

Although most homicides are unintended, there are some that are carefully planned and premeditated, including most gangland killings, killings to obtain an inheritance, and mercy killings. Some homicides are also associated with robberies, in which the robbery victim, the robber, or a law enforcement official is shot.

Contrary to public stereotypes, the vast majority of murders occur between relatives, friends, and acquaintances. People statistically have more to fear in terms of assaults and homicides from people they know than from strangers. For example, one study of homicides found that the murderer was a spouse in 27 percent of the cases, a relative other than a spouse in 10 percent of the cases, and an acquaintance in 40 percent of the cases.[42]

Because of the overt physical damage from assault and homicide, these crimes are among the most feared. The police have a higher success rate (around 70 percent) in making arrests in homicide cases than with any other crime—partly because they devote extensive attention to murders and partly because the questioning of the friends, neighbors, and relatives usually identifies the killer.[43]

Theft

This category of crimes involves the illegal taking of another's property without the person's consent. Offenses under this category range from pickpocketing and burglary to sophisticated forms involving multi-million-dollar swindles. Types of thieves range from grocery store clerks who take small amounts of food to people who concoct highly professional confidence schemes to swindle someone out of thousands of dollars.

The most successful thieves have been labeled professional thieves by the noted criminologist Edwin Sutherland.[44] Professional thieves become involved in confidence games, forgery, expert safe cracking, counterfeiting, extortion (for example, blackmailing others who are engaging in illegal acts), and organized shoplifting. Most such crimes require that professional thieves appear personable and trustworthy and that they be good actors to convince others they are somebody who they are not. Professional thieves use sophisticated, nonviolent techniques. Their crimes are carefully planned, and they tend to steal as a regular business. They define themselves as thieves, have a value system supportive of their career, and tend to be respected by their colleagues and by law-enforcement officials. Because of their cunning and skill, they seldom are arrested. They often justify their activities by claiming that they are simply capitalizing on the fact that all people are dishonest and would probably also be full-time thieves if they had sufficient skills.

Semiprofessional thieves become involved in armed robberies, burglaries, holdups, and larcenies that do not involve much detailed planning. Some semiprofessional thieves work alone, holding up service stations, convenience stores, liquor stores, and the like. Semiprofessional thieves often wind up spending substantial portions of their lives in prison, since they commit the types of crimes that are harshly punished by courts. They also tend to be repeat offenders for similar crimes. They often define themselves as products and victims of a corrupt and unjust system, with many starting their careers in low-income and ghetto neighborhoods. They adjust fairly well in prison, as other inmates often have similar backgrounds, lifestyles, and views on life. As a group they are poor parole risks.[45]

Amateur thieves are individuals who steal infrequently. In contrast to professional and semiprofessional thieves, these individuals generally define themselves as respectable, law-abiding citizens. Their criminal acts tend to be crude and unsophisticated, with some offenders being juveniles. Examples of offenses by this group include stealing from employers, shoplifting, stealing an unguarded bicycle, taking an auto for a joy ride, taking soda from a truck, and breaking into a home to take records or beer. Violations of property laws by this group often are opportunistic, unplanned, and amateurish. Although amateurish, businesses and industries suffer substantial losses from amateur thieves who are either employees or customers.

Juvenile Delinquency

According to official crime statistics, 17 percent of all persons arrested are under age 18.[46] A fair number of

BOX 8.4

A Prison Inmate Describes the Crimes
for Which He Was Arrested

Here a man describes how he was arrested for assault and other crimes. This vignette illustrates the ease with which some Americans turn to violence, and the horrors experienced by innocent victims who are assaulted.

I was arrested in Chicago for "Aggravated Kidnapping, Rape, Aggravated Battery, etc." I was at this time 17 years old. I will not claim my innocence or guilt in this paper, since I am telling only one side of the story (my own), but I will relate the facts of my arrest.

I left work at the warehouse at approximately 5 P.M. on the evening of my arrest and returned home. At home I changed clothes, picked up a friend a couple of blocks from my home, and together we went to a tavern on 31st Street. We arrived at the tavern shortly after six o'clock, and began drinking. We drank, and played the juke box, until midnight. Both of us were very drunk by this time, but I felt well enough to drive. My new car was parked outside the tavern. It was raining quite hard, and had been for several hours.

We jumped into my car, with the intention of going somewhere to eat. My friend was only 18 years old, and looked it, so I ran into another tavern and bought more beer, then we drove to a popular drive-in restaurant. At the restaurant we ordered hamburgers, and ate them in the car with our beer. It was 1:15 when we left the restaurant, I remember the time because I was listening to the car radio as we pulled out of the parking lot. Only one block from the restaurant my friend asked me to pull into an alley so he could urinate. I pulled into an A&P parking lot, and left the car parked under a floodlight so no one would accidentally run into it. From the parking lot I ran down an alley to an overhanging garage roof, to get out of the rain while I urinated, and I didn't see which way my friend Bob ran.

As I stood under the garage overhang I heard two screams, and pulling my pistol I ran back toward the car. When I arrived at the car, Bob and a girl were in the back seat, so I

---

these arrests are for crimes that have already been discussed—thefts, robberies, assaults, and rapes. Yet it should be noted that one reason juveniles have such a high arrest rate is because a majority of the arrests are for status offenses—that is, acts that are defined as illegal if committed by juveniles, but not for adults. Status offenses include being truant, having sexual relations, running away from home, being ungovernable, violating curfew, and being beyond the control of parents.

Police arrests of lower-class juveniles are far higher than for middle- and upper-class juveniles.[47] But the arrest rate does not necessarily mean that members of the lower class commit more crimes; it may only mean they are arrested more often. One nationwide self-report study of youths found little association between social class and delinquency, except that higher-status boys reported that they committed slightly more offenses (including more assaults and thefts) than lower-status boys.[48]

jumped into the car. I recognized the girl immediately, she was the girlfriend of the leader of a rival gang. She didn't know Bob but she knew me, so she ceased her struggling with Bob. Bob shouted for me to start the car and "Let's go!" Knowing the screams, at that time of the morning, would bring people, I started the car and drove away. I was also shocked at the way the girl was dressed. All she had on was a pair of "baby-doll pajamas" and I figured Bob had taken her out of her home. Bob was telling her to take off her clothes, which she did, but she was asking me to make Bob let her alone. I pulled into another alley, about six blocks from where we had picked her up, and stopped to talk to her and Bob. Bob in the time I was driving had attempted to rape her, but hadn't succeeded. I told him to cool it while I talked to her. She wasn't frightened while I talked, but Bob was getting mad. She told me that her boyfriend and her Grandmother would "pay lots of money" if we didn't kill her. Bob really hated her boyfriend, and that remark set him off. He punched the girl in the face.

At that moment a police car entered the alley, and swept my car with a spotlight. I immediately fired a shot thru the windshield of the police car, and pushed the gas pedal to the floor. The police car gave chase. The alley was a long one, and I was traveling at approximately 60 miles per hour before leaving it. Near the mouth of the alley Bob cut the girl's throat and threw her out of the car in front of the police car. Naturally the police stopped. But other police cars were already attempting to block the area. Bob left the car about 15 minutes later, jumping out to run on foot, but I remained with the car until I wrecked it against a telephone post. Then I ran for approximately a mile, before becoming exhausted and taking shelter in the passageway between two homes. This is where the police arrested me. Needless to say, my treatment by the police was somewhat rough (an understatement).

The girl, who had somehow survived serious injury, was treated at the hospital and released.

Source: This vignette first appeared in *The Prison: Voices from the Inside*, eds. Dae Chang and Warren Armstrong (Cambridge, MA: Schenkman Publishing Co., 1972), pp. 40–42. Permission to reprint has gratefully been received from the copyright owners.

THE CRIMINAL JUSTICE SYSTEM

The criminal justice system is composed of the police, the courts, and the correctional system. This system is perceived by many Americans as being cumbersome, ineffective, irrational, and unjust because it appears "crime does pay." A 1978 Gallup Poll found that only 47 percent of the population had favorable attitudes toward police officers, only 19 percent had positive attitudes toward the court system, and only 14 percent had favorable attitudes toward the prison system.[49]

Some segments of the population are suspicious of the police and fear the police may abuse their powers. Other segments, particularly among the middle and upper classes, believe the police are unduly hampered in their work by cumbersome arrest and interrogation procedures that are designed to protect the civil rights of suspected offenders.

Courts are sharply criticized for their long delays in bringing cases to a conclusion and for their sentencing procedures. Opinion polls show that over 80 percent of the population believes that courts are not harsh enough on offenders. Courts are also criticized (*a*) for varying widely in the harshness of sentences assigned for apparently similar offenses and (*b*) for giving harsher sentences to "ordinary offenders," but giving light fines to white-collar offenders.

Prisons, too, have been sharply criticized; they are viewed as failing to prevent those who are incarcerated from committing additional crimes after their release. The rate of recidivism (that is, a convicted person's return to crime) is alarmingly high. Nearly two thirds of those arrested have been convicted of a crime in the previous five years.[50] Far from rehabilitating offenders, prisons are accused of being breeders or schools for crime.

In all societies criminal justice systems face a conflict between two goals: crime control versus due process. The crime control goal involves the need to curb crime and protect society from lawbreakers. It includes an emphasis on speedy arrest and punishment for those who commit crimes. The due process goal involves the need to protect and preserve the rights and liberties of individuals. Some societies are police states that use strong-arm tactics to control their citizens and display little concern for individual rights. At the other extreme are societies in which individuals run wild in breaking the law, with the government having neither the power nor the respect of its citizens in upholding the law. American society seeks to strike a balance between the conflicting goals of crime control and due process. There is a constant struggle between these goals. At times the same individual may seek to have one goal emphasized in one situation but the opposite goal emphasized in a different setting. For example, a home owner may want speedy justice when his or her home is burglarized (or when a daughter is raped) but may seek to use all the due process protections when accused of income tax evasion.

We will now take a closer look at each of these three components of the criminal justice system.

The Police

Police officers are the gatekeepers for the criminal justice system. Who they arrest determines who the courts and corrections will have to deal with. As we have seen, nearly everyone commits an occasional crime. Police cannot arrest everyone, as the jails, courts, and prisons would be overloaded, and our society would probably collapse. Therefore, police have considerable discretion in which laws they will vigorously seek to enforce and which types of offenders they will seek to arrest: For example, police are more apt to arrest lower-income as compared to middle-income youths.

It should be noted that only a small part of a police department's effort is directly focused on arresting offenders. Police officers classify as "criminal" only about 10 to 20 percent of the calls and incidents they handle on a given day.[51]

David Peterson has noted that the role of a police officer is usually best conceptualized as that of a "peace officer" or even "social worker" rather than a "law enforcement officer."

A prominent theme in the literature dealing with the work behavior of the police stresses that the role of the uniformed patrol officer is not a strict legalistic one. The patrol officer is routinely involved in tasks that have little relation to police work in terms of controlling crime. His activities on the beat are often centered as much on assisting citizens as upon offenses; he is frequently called upon to perform a "supportive" function as well as an enforcement function. Existing research on the uniformed police officer in field situations indicates that more than half his time is spent as an amateur social worker assisting people in various ways. Moreover, several officers have suggested that the role of the uniformed patrol officer is not sharply defined and that the mixture of enforcement and service functions creates conflict and uncertainties for individual officers.[52]

Police have such service functions as giving first aid to injured persons, rescuing trapped animals, and directing traffic. When police do perform law enforcement functions, they squarely face trying to achieve the proper balance between the crime control model and the due process model. There is considerable pressure to swiftly apprehend certain lawbreakers—murderers, rapists, and arsonists. Yet they are expected to perform according to the due process model so that the legal rights of those arrested are not violated. James Coleman and Donald Cressey note: "Police officers operate more like diplomats than like soldiers engaged in a war on crime."[53]

In many areas of the nation police do not have sufficient resources to do their job effectively. There is also considerable hostility toward police officers. Part of this hostility may result from the fact that everyone commits an occasional crime, and perhaps most are suspicious of police officers because they fear possible apprehension. In addition, in the past some people (particularly the poor and minority group members) have been harassed by being picked up for crimes they clearly did not commit and by being subjected to long "third-degree" interrogations. There is also hostility toward the police because there have been well-publicized incidents of police corruption (for example, taking bribes), particularly in larger cities.

The Courts

Criminal justice in the United States is an adversary system. A person is presumed innocent until proved guilty. It is an adversary system in the sense that the prosecuting attorney first presents the state's evidence against a defendant, and that defendant then has an opportunity to refute the charges with the assistance of a defense attorney. There are four key positions in a court: the prosecuting attorney, the defense attorney, the judge, and the jury.

It should be noted, contrary to public opinion, that over 90 percent of the convictions for offenses in the United States are not obtained in court but through plea bargaining between the prosecuting attorney and the defendant, who is often represented by a defense attorney in the plea-bargaining process.[54] For a plea of guilty, suspects may receive more lenient sentences, have certain charges dropped, or have the charge reduced to a lesser offense. Plea bargaining is not legally

binding in court, but the judge usually goes along with the arrangement. Plea bargaining is highly controversial. It does save taxpayers considerable expense, as court trials are costly. But, it may in some cases circumvent due process protections because an innocent person charged with some serious offenses may be pressured into pleading guilty to reduced charges.

Prosecuting attorneys have considerable discretionary authority in choosing whether to seek a conviction for those arrested by the police and considerable discretion in choosing how vigorously they will seek to prosecute a defendant. Prosecuting attorneys are either elected or appointed to office and are therefore political figures, since they must periodically seek reelection or reappointment. As such, they seek to prosecute vigorously those cases they perceive the community is most concerned about. Prosecuting attorneys usually set a focus for police departments about which law violations to enforce, as they decide which arrested persons and which law violations will be further processed by the criminal justice system.

Defense attorneys are supposed to represent their clients' interests before the criminal justice system. Impoverished people are provided, at the state's expense, a court-appointed attorney. The skills and competence of the defense attorney are major factors in determining whether a defendant will be found innocent or guilty if there is a trial. The wealthy are able to retain higher skilled attorneys and can afford the resources (such as a private investigator) to prepare a better defense.

The poor have at times been shortchanged by court-appointed defense attorneys, as such attorneys tend to be young, inexperienced practitioners or less competent older persons who resort to this type of practice in order to survive professionally. Because these defense attorneys depend on the good opinion of their legal colleagues (including judges and prosecuting attorneys) to stay in practice, the client's best interest sometimes receives secondary priority to an emphasis on retaining respect from colleagues.[55]

If a prosecuting attorney decides to prosecute a person charged with a minor offense, the case is generally presented before a lower-court judge, without a jury. For a serious offense the defendant first receives a preliminary hearing. This hearing is solely for the benefit of the suspect. At the hearing the prosecuting attorney presents evidence against the suspect, and the judge decides whether the evidence is sufficient to warrant further legal proceedings. If the evidence is insufficient the suspect is discharged. If the evidence is judged sufficient the accused is held over to await a court trial in the future. (Often the held-over cases are then decided prior to the court trial by plea bargaining.)

Under the bail system, accused persons are allowed to deposit money or credit with the court to obtain a release from jail while awaiting the court trial. The amount of bail is set by the court and gives assurance that the suspect will appear for trial. The amount of bail varies according to the offense and partially on the judge's attitudes toward the suspect. The bail system severely discriminates against the poor. Poor people, unable to raise enough money, stay in jail while awaiting trial—which may take several months. Those unable to post bail have less opportunity to prepare a good defense because they are locked up. Also, their case is further prejudiced when they do appear in court because they are brought into the courtroom in handcuffs and have less opportunity to be properly groomed for their court appearance. Being locked up before the court trial is a form of punishment that runs counter to the notion that the suspect is innocent (and should be treated as such) until proved guilty. In some cases a suspect spends more time in jail awaiting trial than she or he spends in jail if found guilty.

After defendants have been found guilty, or have pleaded guilty, they return to the courtroom for sentencing. Judges usually have fairly wide discretion in assigning sentences; for example, they can place one murderer on probation, commit another to prison, and in those states having capital punishment they can order the execution of a third. Judges base their sentences on such factors as the seriousness of the crime, the motives for the crime, the background of the offender, and their attitudes toward the offender.

Judges vary greatly in the extent to which they send convicted offenders to prison, use probation, or assign fines. Concern about disparities in sentences has grown in recent years. Coleman and Cressey note:

Judges and other sentencing authorities are on the spot. They are supposed to give equal punishments, no matter what the social status of the defendants involved. Yet they are supposed to give individual punishments because the circumstances of each crime and the motivations of each criminal are always different and a just punishment for one burglar or car thief may be completely inappropriate for another. . . . As judges try to satisfy these conflicting demands, they are bound to be denounced as unfair. The judge's task, like the police officer's task, is to walk a thin line between the crime control model and the due process model, balancing demands for repressing crime against demands for human rights and freedom.[56]

JUVENILE COURTS   The first juvenile court was established in Cook County, Illinois, in 1899. The philosophy of the juvenile court is that it should act in the best interests of the child, as parents should act. In essence, juvenile courts have a treatment orientation. In adult criminal proceedings the focus is on charging the defendant with a specific crime, on holding a public trial to determine if the defendant is guilty as charged, and on sentencing the defendant if he or she is found to be guilty. In contrast, the focus in juvenile courts is on the current psychological, physical, emotional, and educational needs of children, as opposed to punishment for their past misdeeds. Reform or treatment of the child is the goal, even though the child or his or her family may not necessarily agree that the court's decision is in the child's best interests. Figure 8.1 presents a model of the operations of a typical juvenile justice system.

Of course, not all juvenile court judges live up to these principles. In practice some juvenile judges focus more on punishing than on treating juvenile offenders. There is also a danger that court appearances by children can have adverse labeling effects. A Supreme Court decision in the famous Gault case of May 15, 1967 restored to juveniles procedural safeguards that had been ignored—including notification of charges, protection against self-incrimination, confrontation, and cross-examination.[57] Because of the adverse labeling effects of court appearances, especially with the increased formality of court procedures, there is currently considerable effort to have juvenile probation officers provide informal supervision for youth who commit "minor" violations. With informal supervision, youthful offenders receive counseling and guidance and do not appear in court.

Correctional Systems

Current correctional systems in America and throughout the world contain conflicting objectives. Some components are punishment oriented, whereas others are treatment oriented. A manifestation of this confusion is the existence, side by side, of correctional programs intended primarily for deterrence and retribution and other programs designed to reform offenders. Only rarely do punitive and treatment components complement each other. Generally, the two components, when combined, result in a system that is ineffective and inefficient in curbing criminal activity. In the past several years correctional systems have moved toward using a more punitive approach.

THE PUNITIVE APPROACH   Throughout history various approaches have been used to punish offenders. These methods can be summarized as physical torture, social humiliation, financial loss, exile, the death penalty, and imprisonment.

Physical Torture   Most societies have at one time or another used this method. Specific examples of corporal (bodily) punishment have included stocks, whipping, flogging, branding, hard labor, confinement in irons and cages, arm twisting, and mutilation of body parts. Corporal punishment was particularly popular during the medieval periods. Practically all types of corporal punishment are no longer assigned by European or United States' courts.

Social Humiliation   Actions to reduce the social status of an offender is another method of punishment. This approach flourished in the 16th and 17th centuries, and remnants exist today. Specific techniques included some that also had corporal punishment facets: the stocks, the pillory, the ducking stool, branding, and the

brank. The brank was a small cage that was placed over the offender's head. The brank had a bar that was inserted into the mouth of the offender to prevent him or her from talking; occasionally this bar had spikes in it. Some of these methods were temporary—for example, the stocks—whereas others had a permanent effect on the offender—for example, branding. Although one of the objectives of the permanent methods was to curb future crime, they frequently had the opposite effect, as they overtly labeled the offender, thereby making it difficult for him or her to secure employment and earn a living in a law-abiding manner.

Deprivation of civil rights is another approach that has been used for centuries to humiliate the convicted offender socially. The principal rights that are taken away from convicted felons by most states in this country are (*a*) the right to vote while in prison or while on probation or parole; (*b*) the right to hold public office; (*c*) the right to practice certain professions, for example, the right to practice law; and (*d*) the right to own or possess any firearms.[58]

Financial Penalties   The use of fines in criminal law became widespread in this country about a century ago and is now by far the most frequent court approach to reacting to offenders. Sutherland and Cressey estimate that more than 75 percent of all penalties imposed at present are fines.[59] The advantages of a fine are: (*a*) it provides revenue to the state; (*b*) it costs the state almost nothing to administer, especially in comparison to the cost of imprisonment; (*c*) the amount of the fine can easily be adjusted to the enormity of the offense, to the reaction of the public, and to the wealth and character of the offender; (*d*) it inflicts a material type of suffering; and (*e*) it can easily be paid back if the alleged offender is later found innocent. A serious disadvantage is that it is highly discriminatory toward the poor, since they have less ability to pay. Sweden has found a way to curb this discrimination by the creation of day fines in which the offender pays the equivalent of the amount earned in a specified number of days of work rather than a flat amount as a fine.

Courts are also increasingly requiring, in their sentencing decisions, that the offender make restitution payments to the victim that are in line with the

FIGURE 8.1

Operations of the Juvenile Justice System

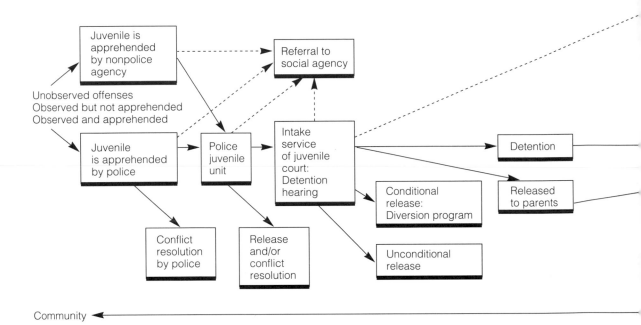

Source: Galan M. Janeksela, "Youth, Delinquency, and the Juvenile Justice System," *Fundamentals of Criminal Justice*, ed. Dae H. Chang, 2d ed. (Geneva, IL: Paladin House, 1977), pp. 269–295. Permission to reprint has gratefully been received from Dae Chang and Galan Janeksela.

amount of injury. This kind of reaction to crime is more treatment oriented, as it attempts to give the offender an opportunity to "make good." Restitution is, of course, also advantageous to the victim. Restitution and reparation are used more frequently for minor offenses. Generally, the offender is placed on probation, with restitution being a condition of probation. Much of the work of probation departments is now centered around being a collection agency to obtain restitution payments from probationers.

Exile   Almost all societies have exiled some offenders, but deportation on a large scale has only been used

since about the 16th century. Most societies have at times exiled political criminals. The United States has been deporting alien criminals for decades. In addition, many counties and municipalities in the United States give some persons accused or convicted of a crime a set number of hours to "get out and stay out" of their jurisdiction.

Death Penalty   The extent to which the death penalty has been used has varied considerably in different societies. The methods used to execute offenders have also varied widely and have included hanging, electrocution, shooting, burning, gas, drowning, boiling in oil,

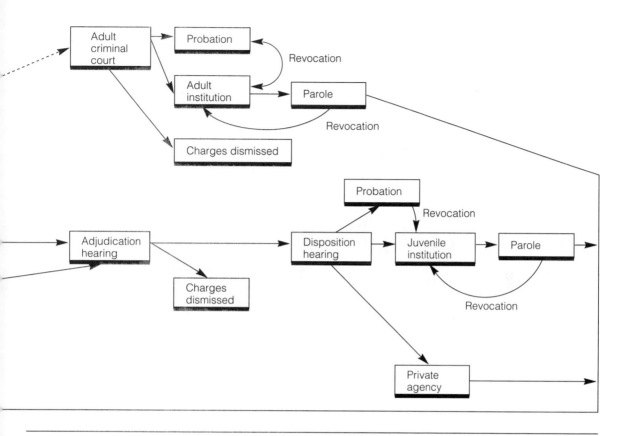

breaking at the wheel, the guillotine, stoning, the iron coffin, piercing with a sharp stake, the sword, and poison. In essence, almost every lethal method has at one time or another been used by some society.

The use of the death penalty in America has had an unusual history. In America "witches" in a few communities were burned at the stake in colonial days. While the West was being developed, those who stole a horse or committed certain other crimes were sometimes shot or hanged (sometimes by a lynch mob or a "kangaroo court"). From the time of the Civil War until the recent past, blacks in the South who were thought to have committed a serious crime against whites (for

example, rape) were sometimes lynched. Gas chambers, firing squads, lethal injections, hangings, and electric chairs are the current methods of execution used in the United States.

From 1967 to 1977, the death penalty was not used in this country, partly due to U.S. Supreme Court decisions that the penalty was unconstitutional. In October 1976, the Supreme Court changed its position on this issue and ruled that states may execute murderers under certain guidelines. On January 17, 1977, Gary Gilmore was the first person in a decade to be executed. The sensational case attracted national attention. Gilmore was convicted of ruthlessly killing several people. The

Throughout our history public reaction to the execution of criminals has ranged from idle curiosity to an almost bloodthirsty desire for revenge. Most of the nearly 10,000 people who witnessed the 1881 execution of two convicted murderers in Leadville, Colorado (above), probably attended the event as much to view Leadville's first legal hanging as to see that justice be done. Over a century later, about 300 people gathered outside the Florida state prison (opposite) where serial killer Ted Bundy was executed. Bundy's electrocution—the "Bundy Barbecue"—was greeted with cheers and champagne toasts. Public executions aren't in vogue today, but it seems that if a criminal's offenses are heinous enough (Bundy raped and murdered some thirty women), many Americans would relish the spectacle.

continued use of the death penalty remains a controversial national issue.

The primary argument for using the death penalty for certain crimes is that it is assumed it will have a deterrence effect. This assumption is questionable, since statistics generally do *not* show that when a country adopts a death penalty, there is a corresponding decrease in serious crime rates.[60] Also, there is no clear-cut evidence that when a country discontinues use of the death penalty, there will be an increase in serious crimes.[61] Additional arguments for use of the death penalty are (*a*) some crimes (such as brutal, premeditated murder) are so abominable that the offender deserves the ultimate punishment, and (*b*) it is less expensive to society to put hardened criminals to death than to incarcerate them for life.

Arguments against use of the death penalty are: (*a*) it constitutes cruel and unusual punishment, as it is the ultimate punishment; (*b*) if the convicted person is later found innocent, the penalty is irreparable; (*c*) the

"eye for an eye" approach is inconsistent with civilized, humanitarian ideals; and (*d*) the "right to life" is a basic right that should not be infringed on.

Imprisonment The penal system currently has enormous importance for our society. A large number of people are incarcerated each year. Nationally, the recidivism rate (return to prison sometime after release) is estimated to be over 50 percent, which raises questions about its effectiveness in curbing future criminal activity.[62] In the past three decades there have been several large-scale prison revolts (for example, Attica Prison, New York in 1971 and New Mexico State Penitentiary in 1980) that have raised the concern of the general public.

Conditions within prisons before this century were deplorable. Frequently, the young were placed with hardened criminals, and women were not separated from men. Only custodial care was provided, frequently with "hard-labor" work projects. There were a number of prison reform studies from 1700 to 1850 that criticized within prisons the use of intoxicating liquors, sexual orgies, gambling, and the personal lewdness of security officers. Some prisons confined inmates in solitary confinement for months at a time, and corporal punishment was also frequently used.

Since 1800 prisons have become more specialized. Jails are used for the shorter sentences and for those awaiting trial. Separate institutions have been built for confining the young, for women, and for those labeled as criminally insane. Prisons also have varying degrees of security: maximum, moderate, and minimum. Special programs have been developed to meet individual needs of inmates: for example, alcohol and drug abuse programs, educational and vocational training, medical and dental programs, and recreational programs.

Prisons are still distasteful and sometimes physically dangerous institutions to be confined in. There is now the danger of AIDS being transmitted by sexual assaults in prison. However, in the past century the horrors of prison life have been somewhat reduced. In addition to rehabilitative programs, improvements have been made in safeguarding civil rights of inmates, in diet, in abandoning long-term solitary confinement, in ventilation, in cleanliness, in physical facilities, in methods of discipline, in promoting contact between

Does imprisonment permanently label individuals as "law breakers"? According to labeling theory, if convicted offenders are treated as "dangerous law violators," the likelihood is great that they will play such a role upon their release.

inmates and the outside world, in providing libraries, and in reducing the monotony of prison life. Gone are such humiliating approaches as shaving the head, chaining inmates, issuing striped clothing, and using the ball and chain. Also, corporal punishment methods, such as whipping, are no longer officially approved. The most severe punishment that remains for many prisoners is that they live in constant fear of being victimized by their fellow prisoners.

The first American institution built specifically for housing juvenile offenders was opened in New York City in 1825. There are now over 300 state and local training schools. From the outset it was contended that such institutions were not prisons, but schools to educate and reform the young. However, until the recent past most were best described as prisons in terms of functions, methods of discipline, and daily routine. Even today a few are still prison oriented. One of the most significant developments in juvenile institutions has been the cottage-type architecture, which provides a more homelike setting. The first were established in Massachusetts and Ohio in 1858. Such settings facilitate, but do not necessarily assure, a treatment orientation.

Objectives of Incarceration   The conflict between the punitive approach and the treatment approach to corrections is strikingly clear in our penal system. Until a few centuries ago the purpose of incarceration was to punish an offender. In the past century there has been an increased emphasis on treatment and a shift away from punishment. There are several reasons for this shift. Practically all prisoners return to society, and it is becoming increasingly recognized that punitive approaches alone do not produce the desired reformation. When an individual's behavior cannot be tolerated in a community, it is indeed a mistake to expect that locking a person in an artificial environment, without providing rehabilitative programs, will sufficiently prepare that person to be a productive citizen on his or her return. Moreover, in this era of accountability, the high recidivism rate (an estimated 50 percent) is unacceptable, especially since the annual cost of incarceration per inmate is more than $16,000.[63]

The most specific objectives for imprisonment are (*a*) to reform offenders so they will no longer commit crimes; (*b*) to incapacitate criminals so they cannot commit crimes for a period of time, thereby protecting society; (*c*) to achieve retribution for the victim and to some extent for the state; and (*d*) to serve as a warning to the general public, thereby having a deterrence effect. A major problem with these objectives is that some components conflict. The infliction of pain and suffering is aimed at meeting the retribution and deterrence objectives, but most punitive approaches are counterproductive in terms of having reformative value.

There are also some dangers with using imprisonment. Association with other offenders may result in prisons serving as "schools for crime," in which inmates learn additional lawbreaking techniques from other inmates. A second danger is that incarceration may label the offender as a "lawbreaker." According to labeling theory, if convicted offenders are related to as if they are "dangerous, second-class citizens who are law-violators," they may begin to perceive themselves as being "law violating."[64] If they perceive themselves in this way they are likely to play such a role upon their release.

In addition, Sutherland and Cressey note: "Hatred of the criminal by society results in hatred of society by the criminal."[65] Relating to criminals as being dangerous, segregating them, and making them keep their distance (both while they are incarcerated and following their release) may force them into a career of criminal activity.

A third danger of long-term imprisonment is "institutionalization." Some prisoners, especially those who have had problems in adjusting to outside society, may eventually prefer prison life over outside society. After several years they may actually feel more comfortable being confined (with their basic needs being met) than having to return to the world outside, which will have undergone substantial change since their entry into prison. They will also have established a circle of friends within the prison from whom they receive respect. If they encounter problems on their return to society (for example, being unemployed and broke), they may yearn at some level to return to prison.

THE TREATMENT APPROACH   There are literally hundreds of treatment programs available in the corrections system. Space limitations prevent an exhaustive coverage of these programs, but a brief summary of major programs will be covered in this section. It is necessary, however, to remember that the punitive approach has the continuous effect of decreasing the efficiency and effectiveness of treatment programs.

The policy of individualized treatment of offenders has been increasingly popular since the 19th century. Individualized treatment developed as a reaction to the classical school, which advocated uniform penalties for criminals. Throughout history, however, there has been a dual standard of justice, with the rich and politically influential being (*a*) much less likely to be charged with a crime; (*b*) much less likely to be found guilty when accused—because of their "character," their position in society, and better legal representation; and (*c*) much less likely to receive a severe sentence if found guilty.

Counseling   Both one-to-one counseling and group counseling have increasingly been used in prisons and by probation and parole officers in this century. The aim is to identify the specific problems of each offender (including the reasons that motivated him or her to become involved in criminal activity) and then to develop specific programs for meeting these needs. The needs may cover a wide array of areas including medical, psychological, financial, family and peer relationships, housing, educational, vocational training, and employment. Attention is also given to the criminal's attitudes, motives, group and peer relationships, and rationalizations regarding criminality. The effectiveness of counselors (social workers, probation and parole officers, psychologists, vocational rehabilitation counselors) is somewhat mitigated by their "dual" role perception by offenders. Some offenders view them as people who will be able to assist with a wide variety of needs, whereas others view them as members of a supervision/discipline system who are authority figures in control of rewards and punishments. With the second conception, offenders are reluctant to discuss socially unacceptable needs and motives and to establish a close relationship for fear that information divulged will be used against them.

Prison Education   Education in prisons has two objectives: (*a*) acquiring formal academic training comparable to schools and (*b*) the broader objective of resocializing inmates' attitudes and behaviors. To accomplish these objectives prisons use TV programs,

These inmates work in the repair shop of a Federal prison in Atlanta. The view that convict labor ought to be difficult or monotonous is still prevalent in many correctional institutions.

movies, libraries, lectures, classroom instruction in academic subjects (covering elementary, secondary, and sometimes even college-level material), religious programs, group discussions, and recreational programs. It should be noted, however, that the bitter attitude that inmates have toward prison and the prison administration is an attitude that continues, even today, to interfere with accomplishing educational objectives.

Vocational Training   The objective of these programs is to train inmates in a job skill suitable to their capacities that will prepare them for employment on release. The quality of such programs in institutions throughout the country varies greatly. In many institutions vocational training is defined as the maintenance work of the institution: laundry, cooking, custodial work, minor repairs, dishwashing. For a period of time vocational training was considered the main component of reha-

bilitation, but now rehabilitation is seen as covering many other areas.

Prison Labor   Throughout the history of prisons the idea that prisoners should be provided work has existed. Unfortunately, idleness and monotony are generally prevalent. When labor was first introduced in prisons, it was seen as a method of punishment. England, for example, for a long period of time had inmates carry a cannonball on treadmills that had a meter that measured the number of units of work produced. For each meal inmates had to produce a certain number of units. Additional units were assigned for misconduct.

Currently, there are two conflicting conceptions of work: (*a*) it should be productive and train inmates for employment on release, and (*b*) it should be hard, unpleasant, or monotonous for retributive purposes. The second view is still rationalized by some authorities as also having a reformative function, as it is said to teach discipline, obedience, and conformity and to develop an appreciation for avoiding criminal activity.

Convict labor has been used for building roads, running agricultural farms, fire fighting, insect control programs, lumber camp work, laundry, making state license plates, and a wide variety of other tasks. Huber Law programs in jails and work-release programs in some prisons now allow inmates to work in employment settings in the community during the daytime, while being locked up in the evening.

Good Time   Good-time legislation permits a prison review board to release a prisoner earlier if the prisoner has maintained good conduct. Most good-time laws specify that for every month of acceptable behavior, a certain number of days will be deducted from the sentence. Good-time laws are designed to make inmates responsible for their conduct, to provide an incentive for good conduct and rehabilitation efforts, and to reduce discipline problems within prisons.

Indeterminate sentences, which were first established in the 1800s, have similar objectives. Many sentences are now indeterminate in length, with a minimum and a maximum limit assigned to the amount of time an inmate can be incarcerated. In recent years, however, a movement to return to determinate sentencing has gained considerable support.

Parole and Probation   Parole is a conditional release of a prisoner serving an indeterminate or unexpired sentence. Parole is granted by an administrative board (parole board) or an executive. While on parole, parolees are considered "in custody" and are required to maintain acceptable conduct and avoid criminal activity. Parole is designed both to punish (certain behavior is restricted and there is a threat of return to prison) and to treat the offender (a parole officer is generally assigned to counsel and help the parolee meet his or her needs).

Probation is granted by the courts and involves the suspension of a prison sentence of a convicted offender and giving him or her freedom during good behavior under the supervision of a probation officer. Probationers are viewed as undergoing treatment. There is, however, the threat of punishment: that is, being sent to prison should the conditions of probation be violated. Similar to parole, probation contains reformation and retribution components.

Probation and parole officers have a "dual" role responsibility, which has the potential of interfering with the rehabilitative process. One of the primary functions of a probation and parole officer is the "police" or authority role of closely monitoring the activities of probationers and parolees to observe whether they are violating laws or violating the conditions of their parole/probation. Those being supervised are continually aware that the probation/parole officer has the authority to initiate procedures to revoke their probation/parole, which will send them to prison. Many probationers and parolees are distrustful of the criminal justice system and therefore are wary of anyone (including probation and parole officers) who is associated with this system. This "police" role conflicts at times with the second primary function of probation and parole officers: the rehabilitative role. For rehabilitation to be most effective, the counselee must trust the counselor, must feel free to reveal socially unacceptable attitudes and activities to the counselor, and must form a close working relationship with the counselor. Obviously, those probationers and parolees who

view their supervising officer as primarily having a "police" role are apt to avoid forming a counseling relationship with their supervising officer.

HOW TO REDUCE CRIME AND DELINQUENCY

The above heading may be inappropriate. Societies have been concerned with reducing crime for centuries. A number of different approaches have been tried, yet the rate of crime seems to fluctuate independently of direct, crime suppression efforts. About twenty-five years ago former President Nixon declared war on crime, and the federal government has since spent billions trying to curb crime, yet the rate continues to increase. The prospects for reducing crime in the future remain uncertain, as we do not as yet know enough about how to prevent people from starting to commit crimes or how to reform them if they choose a criminal career. Even though there is uncertainty about whether crime can be reduced, this section will summarize major approaches that have been advanced to improve the situation. (You will note that some of the proposals are contradictory.) We will consider three general areas:

1. Increasing or decreasing sentences.
2. Reforming the correctional system.
3. Preventing crime in the first place.

Increasing or Decreasing Sentences

There are conflicting opinions concerning the appropriateness of various sentences as related to the crime committed. Suggestions to improve the effects of various sentences include shortening the times between arrest, conviction, and punishment; imposing harsher sentences; permanently imprisoning repeat offenders;

increasing prosecution of white-collar criminals; creating uniform sentences; decriminalizing victimless offenses; and imposing stricter gun control.

INSTITUTING SWIFT AND CERTAIN PUNISHMENT   It is generally agreed that the deterrent value of punishment decreases as the time lag between the crime and the eventual punishment increases. Now, only a fraction of those who commit crimes are arrested, and only a fraction of those arrested are ever found guilty. All too often crime does pay—particularly white-collar crime and organized crime. Criminal court proceedings commonly drag on for months, and even years, with offenders using due process maneuvers in the hope that public anger over their crimes will dissipate so that they will either be found innocent or have the charges reduced. Swifter action in catching, convicting, and punishing a greater percentage of those who violate laws will, it is argued, lead to greater respect for the law and curb crime. The argument against swifter action is that it would conflict with due-process protections and might result in a higher number of innocent people being arrested, convicted, and incarcerated.

IMPOSING HARSHER SENTENCES   This approach is also based on the assumption that punishment has a deterrent effect. Advocates of this approach demand that punishments be more severe, particularly by lengthening prison sentences and by increasing the use of capital punishment. Advocates also assert that lengthier sentences will reduce crime because criminals obviously cannot victimize citizens when they are locked up.

Opponents of this approach claim that lengthier sentences may well increase crime rates rather than reduce them, since practically all people sent to prison return to society, and lengthier sentences may simply increase the bitterness of those serving time, reduce their respect for our laws and criminal justice system, and give them extended training in breaking the law through association with other hardened criminals. Opponents also note that imprisonment is costly to society; it costs more per year to send a person to prison than to send a person to college.

SEPARATING REPEAT OFFENDERS FROM SOCIETY   Crimes of violence (arson, rape, armed robbery, murder) are of particular concern to a society, as are certain other offenses, such as repeated hard-drug trafficking offenses. Some authorities assert that repeated arrests and convictions for these offenses demonstrate that the offenders are so dangerous to our society that protection of society must become the primary concern. It is further asserted that because past efforts at reformation have not been effective, future efforts are not likely to be either. It is argued that the "key should be thrown away" for repeat offenders of serious crimes. Our courts in fact are heading in this direction by locking up "repeaters" for longer periods of time.

A particular problem with this proposal is that serious crimes of violence are often committed by juveniles. As we have seen, juvenile courts use a "child-saving" approach, as their main focus is not on the nature of the crime but on having a treatment or rehabilitative approach. Several states have now made provisions for juveniles arrested for homicide and other violent crimes to be charged and tried as adults. In adult court, convicted juveniles can then be given sentences commensurate with the seriousness of their offenses, rather than receiving the lenient treatment of the juvenile court.

Advocating that repeat lawbreakers who commit serious crimes be locked up for long periods is an admission of rehabilitation failure. On the other hand, it is a proclamation that potential victims have rights too and that their rights take priority over the rights of repeaters.

GETTING TOUGHER ON WHITE-COLLAR CRIME   In the early 1970s, many high-ranking officials in the Nixon administration (which was pledged to "law and order") were accused of committing such offenses as illegal wiretapping, tax fraud, destruction of evidence, misappropriation of campaign funds, extortion, bribery, conspiracy to pervert the course of justice, and conspiracy to violate civil rights. These crimes focused considerable attention on white-collar crime. Many of these officials were convicted but received very light sentences (often in special federal prisons referred to as "resorts") in comparison to harsher sentences given to ordinary burglars and thieves. Former President Nixon was pardoned by President Gerald Ford prior to facing criminal charges. The Watergate scandal aroused a major discussion of the mild way in which white-collar crime is handled in our society. Yet today, white-collar crime still is largely ignored or treated more mildly by the police, the courts, and the correctional system. (It should be noted that organized crime is also increasingly committing white-collar type crimes.) It has been argued that more vigorous arrests, prosecution, and sentencing of white-collar crime and organized crime would lead to increased respect for the law by all citizens and reduce crime. But, in a society in which the white power structure sometimes seems interested only in the vigorous enforcement of laws against such crimes as armed robbery, which are generally committed by members of the powerless groups in our society, some consider it unlikely to expect that the white power structure will urge the police and courts to arrest and prosecute its own members.

CREATING UNIFORM SENTENCES   As noted earlier, there are wide variations in sentences received by different convicted offenders for the same crime. If justice is to be equal for all, then variables such as the economic status, race, and sex of the offender ought not to influence sentencing. Sentencing one murderer to death while putting another on probation undermines respect for the law and the criminal justice system. One way to reduce the disparity in sentences assigned is to make the sentences subject to appeal; currently, the harshness of a sentence cannot be appealed. A second way is to take legislative action to reduce the latitude that is given to judges in assigning sentences for each type of conviction.

DECRIMINALIZING VICTIMLESS OFFENSES   Prohibition is the classic example of creating problems by outlawing a victimless activity. Prohibition made it a crime to manufacture, distribute, or drink alcohol. Police spent substantial time and resources to try to enforce this law but were largely unsuccessful. Prohibition led to the development of bootlegging and fostered the development of organized crime.

Today, victimless crimes are still with us—gambling, smoking marijuana, fornication, and prostitution, to name just a few. If such actions were decriminalized, immense resources of money and time could be diverted to confronting the crimes that do have victims. There is some movement to decriminalize certain offenses; for example, Nevada now allows prostitution in a few counties. In the past decade, police departments have been less vigorous in arresting those smoking marijuana, and there are efforts to decriminalize this activity in a number of states. Gambling laws are beginning to undergo change, as some states have now set up legal gambling activities, such as lotteries, gambling casinos, and betting on horse races and dog races.

IMPOSING STRICTER GUN CONTROL   In the past thirty years, John F. Kennedy, Robert Kennedy, Martin Luther King, Anwar Sadat, and John Lennon have been killed by shootings. In 1981, there were shooting assassination attempts on President Ronald Reagan and on the Pope. There are over 20,000 homicides and over 500,000 robberies annually in the United States.[66] Many homicides and armed robberies involve the use of a handgun.

There are an estimated 60 million handguns in the United States; one handgun for every two homes and one handgun for every four citizens.[67] Over 300,000 people per year are wounded in the United States by the use of handguns.[68] More Americans have been killed by handguns than the number of Americans killed in all the wars fought in the 20th century.[69] States in this country that have a higher proportion of guns have higher rates of homicides, suicides, and deaths during domestic disputes.[70] A number of special interest groups have advocated an end to the sale of handguns except for approved and limited purposes.

Reforming the Correctional System

Perhaps the first step in improving the correctional system is to clarify the present conflicting objectives, some of which are punitive in nature, whereas others are treatment-oriented. When the general public and public officials are confused regarding what the primary objective for incarceration should be, it is obvious prison administration officials and inmates will also become confused, and rehabilitation is unlikely to occur.

If our society decides retribution, deterrence, and vengeance should be the primary goal, then we can expect a continued high rate of recidivism and continued high crime rates, as those being punished are apt to become increasingly bitter and hostile toward society. However, from a society-benefit viewpoint, it would seem the primary objective of a correctional system should be to curb future criminal activity of incarcerated offenders in the least expensive way.

The current prison system is not only ineffectual in preventing recidivism, it is also expensive. The national average per capita cost for institutionalization of adult felons is many times greater than the cost of probation services to adults.

If the correctional system had rehabilitation as its primary objective, there would be a number of changes in the system. For example, sentencing wrongdoers is now primarily based on the nature of their past deeds. If a convicted person has previously committed serious felonies, a long incarceration is the likely sentence. A reformative approach would, instead, focus primarily on how to curb the supervisee's (or criminal's) tendency toward breaking the law. Needed services would be specified, and the responsibilities of the supervisee would be identified—such as maintaining or securing employment, enrolling in an educational or vocational program, receiving counseling or family therapy, undergoing medical or dental treatment, paying debts, and/or making restitution. Removal from society would generally be used only after the supervisee failed to meet requirements of the supervision plan (for example, restitution) or when the supervisee was a definite threat to society.

With this approach, supervisees would become acutely aware that they have the choice and the responsibility to decide which of two avenues to pursue: (*a*) continuation of criminal activity following their release, which will result in continued conflict with the law and probable return to a prison in the future, or (*b*) a more law-abiding, productive, and respectable future. If they choose the latter, they would be informed there are services (for example, counseling and vocational training) available to assist, but they would also be made aware that improving their situation requires being a responsible person and putting forth considerable effort.

The choice facing our society appears to be between a punitive system that enacts retribution but does not deter future crimes and a system that seeks to assist offenders in becoming productive citizens but also may not deter future crimes. The latter approach is not painless to the offenders, since it requires considerable work and effort. With a punitive approach, however, pain itself is the goal and usually does not have a result that is beneficial to the individual or to society. Although rehabilitation makes more theoretical sense than retribution, research results concerning its effectiveness have not been conclusive and have been the subject of intense debate among scholars.

DIVERSION PROGRAMS   Labeling theory suggests that the criminal justice system perpetuates crime by branding and interacting with offenders as if they were delinquents and criminals. Diversion programs have therefore been developed in a number of communities to divert first-time or minor offenders from entering the criminal justice system; instead, they receive services from community agencies.

One such program is "deferred prosecution," which some communities now provide. Adults who are arrested for the first time for a minor offense (such as shoplifting) are referred by either a judge or a prosecuting attorney to deferred prosecution prior to standing trial for the offense for which they are charged. Deferred prosecution programs provide small group sessions over a period of several weeks, which are geared to helping the members refrain from committing additional crimes. The case is dismissed if the defendant (*a*) pays for any damages, (*b*) is not rearrested while participating in the program, and (*c*) attends all the group meetings.

Many diversion programs are focused on keeping juveniles out of juvenile courts and criminal courts by instead referring them to treatment programs handled by community agencies. Juveniles, for example, may be referred for counseling (from social workers, probation officers, or psychologists); they may receive training and help in getting a job; they may receive help for emotional or family problems; or they may receive help with school work.

Many communities have developed "Scared Straight" programs, which seek to discourage delinquents from further crime. "Scared Straight" was first developed at Rahway prison in New Jersey. Juveniles who have committed offenses are taken on a visit to a prison, where inmates harshly describe the realities of prison life. Prison conditions are also observed first-hand. The objective is to expose juveniles to the realities of life in prison so that the threat of going to prison will motivate them to stop breaking the law. It is not yet certain, however, that this exposure has a deterrent effect on juveniles.

TRANSITIONAL PROGRAMS   There are a variety of transitional programs. While in jail or prison, a person may be allowed to work in the community during the daytime. School-release programs allow inmates to attend college or a technical school during the daytime. Halfway houses have been used as an alternative to sending a person to prison; they allow residents to work or go to school in their home community. Halfway houses have also been used to help people who have been in prison to adjust to returning to society. If offenders misbehave while in halfway houses, there is the threat of being sent to jail or prison.

With transitional programs, it is hoped that inmates will maintain and develop stronger ties to the noncriminal elements in their home community. The programs seek to reduce or alleviate the negative effects of incarceration and provide the opportunities and resources for rehabilitation.

Preventing Crime

Theoretically, there are four ways to prevent crime.

1. Make the punishment for violating a law so severe that lawbreakers become so terrorized they no longer commit crimes. Studies on the use of capital punishment, however, suggest that even this severest penalty does not deter crime.

2. Keep the convicted lawbreakers in prison. Such an approach would be very expensive—especially since practically everyone occasionally commits a crime.

3. Change the economic, social, and political conditions that breed crime. A wide number of proposals, beyond the scope of this text, have been advanced: improve family life; improve the educational system to make education an exciting, growth-producing experience for students; end racial discrimination; provide equal opportunities to achieve success for all citizens, including the poor and minority groups; provide full employment with a decent living wage for all able-bodied persons; improve housing conditions and the living conditions in our inner cities; and curb alcohol and drug abuse.

4. Educate the general public on how to avoid becoming a victim of crime. This fourth approach will be discussed in some detail and involves reducing the opportunity for crime to occur. This approach is being highlighted because it is an approach that everyone should be aware of and participate in.

Dae Chang describes this approach, which developed from victimology, a recent area of study in criminology.

Research shows that much crime—and by far the greatest portion of street crime and burglary—is the result of opportunity and luck rather than of careful and professional planning.

Someone sees an "opportunity"—in an open window, an empty house, a person alone in a dark alley—and acts on it. Muggers look for likely victims, not specific individuals; burglars, for a house they can enter, not a particular address. Preselected targets frequently are chosen precisely because they are seen as "easy marks."

Who is the victim of a crime? What causes crime? Who causes crime? There are some startling answers to these questions. In the majority of cases, the victim contributes, and in some cases is a major cause of a criminal act. All of us are potential victims. We frequently present the criminal or an individual with an invitation to commit a crime. We entice him, advertise to him, coax him, give him the opportunity, and even implant the idea into his head. Through our carelessness, open disregard for our personal possessions, forgetfulness, attitudes, vanity, etc., we frequently invite someone to commit a criminal act either directly at ourselves or to our possessions. We also invite bodily harm upon ourselves by our actions in public and private. Our habits, attitudes, dress, etc. all are signals to the people who would be enticed into crime.[71]

In using this approach effectively one must keep asking oneself, "Is what I'm doing, or failing to do, making me vulnerable to becoming a victim of a crime?" Box 8.5 presents a number of specific precautions to prevent becoming a crime victim.

SOCIAL WORK AND CORRECTIONS

The primary role played by social work in the criminal justice system has been confined almost exclusively to the correctional component of the system: a social worker in a prison, a probation and parole officer, or a social worker in a correctional halfway house. There are only a few police departments that employ social workers to provide social services to individuals and families with whom police come in contact.

In treatment programs it should be noted that individual and group counseling is only one of a variety of rehabilitation programs that may be provided. Others include religious programs, vocational training, study release, work release, and educational programs.

Many probation and parole officers are trained in social work. One of the important responsibilities of a probation and parole officer is to prepare a presentence report. A presentence report is a social history of the offender that is prepared to help guide the judge in sentencing. A presentence report is presented in Box 8.6.

In the field of corrections there are certain factors influencing treatment that social workers need to understand.

Factors Influencing Treatment

CUSTODY-TREATMENT CONFLICT In prison settings prison administrators primarily emphasize custody. Over 90 percent of the money spent in such institutions goes for custody.[72] When custody policies clash with treatment programs, treatment almost always comes in second. Prison administrators are primarily concerned with preventing escapes, curbing riots, and calming internal disruptions. New social workers in prison settings soon realize rehabilitation is not the primary focus.

Social workers in prisons, and as probation and parole officers, are often viewed by offenders as part of the larger authoritarian bureaucracy that caught and convicted them. Many offenders are distrustful of social workers because they feel social workers are still "monitoring" or "policing" them.

OFFENDERS' "CON GAME"   Since the 1930s the criminal justice system has promoted both individual and group therapy. Prison administrators and directors of probation and parole programs have required offenders to participate in treatment programs. Social work practice realizes that compelling clients to submit to treatment interventions interferes with establishing the necessary rapport with offenders. Yet, enforced treatment is commonplace in corrections.

Offenders are highly skilled at "conning" professional staff through persuasion and manipulation. Perhaps the majority of convicted offenders disdain corrections. This disdain is strengthened when they see therapy being forced on them. Offenders quickly realize they must participate in such activities as individual and group counseling in order to have a good record. If imprisoned on an indeterminate sentence (as is common in most states), a good record will get them released on parole sooner. If on probation or parole, offenders believe that participation in "treatment"

BOX 8.5

Precautions to Prevent Becoming a Crime Victim

1. Bolt lock doors and windows at home, and use exterior lighting to frustrate burglary techniques.

2. Engrave identification numbers on possessions to curb fencing of stolen property. This reduces the incentives for this type of crime.

3. If you are away from home for part of an evening, make the place look like someone is home. Leave some lights on, and some music as well. Or, leave the television on, keeping it low so that it sounds like muffled voices. To someone outside it will sound as if either people are inside talking or the family is home listening to TV.

4. Double-secure sliding glass doors by placing lengths of metal rod or wooden dowels in the lower tracks to prevent the doors from being opened.

5. Put in exterior lighting over front and back doors of your home. Also, cut back close-in shrubbery around the house where it might be used to provide a hiding place for burglars.

6. If you hear someone breaking in at night, let the person know that you know she or he is there, but don't try to confront the burglar. If the burglar knows that someone is home, chances are the burglar will leave as fast as possible. If you confront the burglar unexpectedly, a fight may occur, and someone could get hurt. Instead yell "Get the shotgun!" even when you are alone, or yell to the neighbors, or get on the phone to the police. One of the best places to have a strong, dead-bolt lock is on the inside of your bedroom door.

7. A small dog that barks a lot is a good deterrent to discourage a burglar from stealing things when you're away for the evening. The yapping of the dog will make the burglar wary that someone else will hear the barking, so the burglar will probably exit in a hurry.

8. Do not leave the key to your home under the door mat, in the mailbox, or on top of the door ledge.

9. Be cautious about inviting door-to-door salesmen into your home. Many communities now require salesmen to carry identification cards.

10. Do not leave possessions on lawns or in your driveway at night. If left, bicycles, barbecue grills, power tools, lawn mowers, and so on are easily removed.

11. Do not leave important papers, expensive jewelry, or large sums of money at home. Rent a bank security deposit box. Security deposit boxes not only protect valuables from burglars but also from fires and natural disasters.

Continued

BOX 8.5 *Continued*

12. When going on an extended vacation make arrangements to have a friend check your home every few days. Do not let newspapers or mail pile up. The post office will hold your mail at no cost while you are away. Inexpensive light timers can be purchased to light a room or two during the evening hours to give the impression you are home.

13. When you are expecting someone to visit, and you are unable to be home, do not leave a note on the outside: "Welcome—will be back at 8 P.M. Walk in and make yourself at home. Door is unlocked." Burglars readily accept such invitations.

14. Do not carry a large sum of money. If forced to carry a large sum, take along a second wallet containing three or four bills and some expired credit cards that you can give a thief if confronted.

15. When in a crowd, place your wallet in a safe place—for example, front pocket or a buttoned back pocket to frustrate pickpocketing efforts.

16. Women should never leave their purses unattended.

17. Do not hitchhike or pick up hitchhikers. Hitchhiking has led to a fair number of robberies and assaults. If you cannot avoid hitchhiking, be very selective about who you accept a ride from.

18. Flashy equipment on autos will invite theft or auto break-ins. If you buy mag wheels, a stereo tape deck, a CB radio, fancy wheel covers, and other expensive gadgets, you will draw attention to your car. The place where you park your car can be an invitation for it to be stolen or broken into. Be sure always to lock your car, put valuables in the trunk, and never leave the key in the ignition.

19. If you are leaving your car someplace for a few days (for example, at an airport) it is nearly theftproof if you pull the center wire out of the distributor—in addition to locking the car and taking the keys. (Before pulling the wire make sure you know how to put it back.)

20. Leave identification off key chains so that if your keys are lost or stolen, no one knows what they open.

21. Women are advised to list only their last name and initials on mailboxes and in phone directories.

22. Avoid going alone to a dark parking lot. It may be cheaper to call a taxi than risk being mugged late at night.

23. There are a variety of approaches to avoid becoming a victim of rape, including physical techniques of self-defense (for example, the martial arts) and distasteful approaches (for example, vomiting or urinating on the rapist, informing the potential rapist you have herpes or the AIDS virus, squeezing the genitals of the rapist, and poking your fingers into the rapist's eyes). Women should become familiar with these approaches, and select a few that they would be comfortable (and prepared) to use should an attack occur.

BOX 8.6

Presentence Report

Walworth County Court
June 23, 1980

Name: James LaMartina

Address: 408 Walnut St.
        Delavan, WI 54987

Legal Residence: Same

Age: 34

Date of Birth: 5-8-46

Sex: Male

Race: Caucasian

Citizenship: U.S.A.

Education: 11th grade

Marital Status: Married

Dependents: Two
           (wife and a 4-year-old
           son)

Soc. Sec. No.: 393-42-9067

FBI No.: 287 1237

Detainers or
Charges Pending: None

Offense: Second-Degree Sexual Assault

Penalty: Imprisoned not more than ten years
        and/or fined not more than $10,000

Plea: Guilty on 6-10-80

Verdict:

Custody: Posted bail of $5,000

Prosecuting Attorney: Richard Jorgenson, assistant
        district attorney

Defense Counsel: Donald Hauser

OFFENSE: OFFICIAL VERSION

Officers Karen Davenport and David Erdmier stated they arrested Mr. LaMartina in Lakeland County Park at 12:30 P.M. on June 5, 1980, while he was having sexual intercourse with a 17-year-old minor. Mr. LaMartina and the minor were in the back seat of the offender's car, and were reported to be unclothed.

    Mr. LaMartina stated he had met the woman in Don's Hillside Tavern earlier in the day. He stated that this was the first time he had met her and did not know her age—he assumed she was an adult. A check with Donald Leesburg, owner of the tavern, indicated that Mr. La-Martina was a frequent patron of the tavern but that the woman was not a regular patron. The owner further stated that the night of June 5, 1980 was busy. He noted that Mr. LaMartina

Continued

BOX 8.6 *Continued*

was there earlier that evening, but the owner was unaware whether Mr. LaMartina had met this woman at the tavern.

The minor appeared intoxicated at the time of the arrest. Her driver's license the night of the arrest revealed her age to be 17 years and 2 months. She was returned home by the police to her parents, who were very angry; Officers Davenport and Erdmier had to restrain the father from physically hitting her.

DEFENDANT'S VERSION OF OFFENSE

Mr. LaMartina stated that he frequently stopped at Don's Hillside Tavern after work with fellow workers of the construction company he has worked with for the past six years. Mr. LaMartina stated this evening was the first time he had met this woman. He mentioned he began buying drinks for her and for the two other women friends she was with. He stated that she had drunk considerably more than he had. He emphasized he assumed she was at least 18 years of age.

Around midnight he asked her if she wanted a ride home, which she accepted. He drove instead to Lakeland County Park, where he emphasized she willingly agreed to go to the backseat with him and willingly became sexually involved. When asked whether he had become sexually involved with other women, Mr. LaMartina became defensive and refused to answer.

PRIOR RECORD

Date	Offense	Disposition
9-7-72	Disorderly conduct	$80 fine
10-11-76	Driving motor vehicle while under the influence	$210 fine and group dynamics course

PERSONAL HISTORY

The defendant was born in Fort Atkinson, Wisconsin, on 5-8-46, the oldest of two children. His parents were dairy farmers. He attended public schools and completed the 11th grade. He received mainly Cs and Ds in school and left school to help on the farm. He had a number of friends in school and was active in several sports, including the high school varsity basketball and baseball teams.

The defendant's father, Leonard, died following a stroke when the defendant was 22 years of age. His mother, Loretta, is still living on the family farm in rural Jefferson County. The defendant ran the farm for six years after his father's death and then sold the cattle in order to work for Johnstone's Road Construction Company. The farm appeared to be only marginally successful when the defendant had dairy cattle. The defendant still plants and harvests crops on the farm.

The defendant's sister, Janine, is 28 years of age and has been married for the past six years to Dennis Richter, a dairy farmer in Dane County.

Mr. LaMartina has been married for the past eight years to Sue Heinz (maiden name). Sue is 32 years of age and graduated from Milton College ten years ago. She taught elementary school for the first four years of their marriage but has not taught school for the past four years—since their son, Tim, was born. She and James LaMartina have lived in the LaMartina's farm house since their marriage.

Sue LaMartina separated from her husband shortly after she heard he was arrested. She and her son are now staying with her parents. She has ambivalent feelings about her husband. She stated he can be a good father and husband, but she is intensely irritated about his drinking and about his staying out late at night with his "cronies." She stated she suspected he may occasionally have been having affairs with other women, but this incident is "the last straw." She stated she is seeing a counselor at the mental health center, has contacted an attorney, and is contemplating a divorce.

Mr. LaMartina stated he does not want a divorce and appears sincerely remorseful about the family problems he has created. He stated if he and his wife can reconcile, he will change his ways: He will not stay out late or become involved with other women. Mr. LaMartina has asked his wife to attend marriage counseling with him, but she indicated she is still too emotionally hurt and embarrassed to be able to discuss the incident and their future with him.

There is some evidence that Mr. LaMartina has been drinking to excess for several years. Mr. LaMartina denies this, but his frequent stops after work at a tavern, and his past arrest record suggest otherwise. The future of his marriage, however, appears to be a more immediate problem needing attention.

EVALUATIVE SUMMARY

The defendant is a 34-year-old male who entered a plea of guilty to second-degree sexual assault. The defendant was arrested while having sexual intercourse with a 17-year-old woman whom he met, apparently for the first time, earlier that evening at a tavern. The defendant apparently did not know the woman was a minor. The defendant's wife has separated from him following this arrest and is contemplating a divorce. The defendant expressed considerable remorse about the embarrassment and domestic strife he has caused.

Mr. LaMartina has a 4-year-old son and has no prior serious arrest record. He may at times drink to excess. He completed eleven years of schooling and has run a dairy farm. For the past six years he has been a road construction worker. His employer reports he is dependable and has been a good worker.

RECOMMENDATION

It is recommended that the defendant be fined and placed on probation. If placed on probation the defendant expresses willingness to seek counseling for his domestic problems. This counseling should also at some future time explore whether he has a drinking problem. The future of his marriage, however, needs first attention.

Respectfully submitted,

Ralph Franzene
Probation and Parole Officer
State of Wisconsin

programs may help in getting the probation and parole officer to do things for them or in getting the officer to overlook minor violations of the rules for probation and parole.

The social worker should be aware that many offenders who request professional assistance are seeking to manipulate the worker rather than having a genuine interest in self-improvement.

SUMMARY

Crime is one of the most serious problems facing our nation. Serious, violent crime has reached alarming proportions. In addition the criminal justice system (the police, the courts, and prisons) are perceived as relatively ineffective in curbing crime.

Everyone, at one time or another, has violated some laws. Those arrested for crimes are disproportionately likely to be male, young, a member of a racial minority, and a city resident. If white-collar crime and organized crime were more vigorously prosecuted, the "typical" criminal would more likely be older, white, and a suburban resident.

Official crime statistics are inaccurate for a variety of reasons. Many crimes are unreported. Police and courts seek to enforce only certain crimes vigorously. Police-reporting practices are affected at times by political considerations, such as reclassifying serious offenses as being less serious to attempt to show that police departments are being effective in curbing serious crimes. In terms of number of people victimized and financial costs to society, it appears that white-collar crime is our most serious type of crime. Yet this type is less vigorously enforced by the police and the courts.

A variety of theories about the causes of crime have been advanced. These theories identify some of the reasons crime occurs. But we do not have a complete explanation identifying all the reasons why crime occurs. With the crime rate continuing to increase, it is also clear that we do not as yet know how to reduce crime effectively.

Current correctional systems throughout the world contain conflicting objectives, with some components being punishment oriented, whereas others are treatment oriented. Generally the two components, when combined, result in a system that is confusing and ineffective in curbing criminal activity. There is a danger that prisons may serve as schools for crime and may have a labeling effect that leads to future criminal activity.

A number of proposals have been advanced for reducing crime, including administering swift and certain punishment, imposing harsher sentences, separating repeat offenders from society, getting tougher on white-collar crime, creating uniform sentencing, decriminalizing victimless offenses, imposing stricter gun control, reforming the correctional system to emphasize the treatment approach, increasing use of diversion and transitional programs, and educating citizens on how to avoid becoming a crime victim. Some of these proposals contradict others. Although each proposal has some research support, no proposal has conclusively been proved valid in reducing crime.

The ways in which societies have punished convicted offenders are as atrocious as the atrocities offenders have inflicted on victims. Do we want the "eye for an eye" retributive approach, which is ineffective in curbing future crime, or do we want something else?

NOTES

1. Ian Robertson and Phillip Whitten, "Sexual Politics in South Africa," in *Society As It Is: A Reader*, eds. Glen Gaviglio and David E. Raye, 2d ed. (New York: Macmillan, 1976).
2. President's Commission on Law Enforcement and Administration of Justice, *The Challenge of Crime in a Free Society* (Washington, D.C.: U.S. Government Printing Office, 1967).
3. Clayton A. Hartjen, *Crime and Criminalization*, 2d ed. (New York: Praeger, 1978), p. 33.
4. *Crime in the United States, 1986, FBI Uniform Crime Reports* (Washington, D.C.: U.S. Government Printing Office, 1987), p. 41.

5. Law Enforcement Assistance Administration, *Sourcebook of Criminal Justice Statistics* (Washington, D.C.: U.S. Government Printing Office, 1977).

6. *Crime in the United States, 1986*, pp. 176–180.

7. Edwin H. Sutherland and Donald R. Cressey, *Criminology*, 8th ed. (Philadelphia: J. B. Lippincott, 1970).

8. *Crime in the United States, 1986*.

9. Ibid., p. 174–175.

10. Ibid., pp. 182–184.

11. Donald Jackson, "Justice for None," *New Times*, January 11, 1974, p. 51.

12. *Crime in the United States, 1986*.

13. Law Enforcement Assistance Administration (LEAA) study reported in UPI Dispatch, April, 15, 1974.

14. "Unreported Crime Twice as High," *LEAA Newsletter* 3 (March 1974), pp. 1–11.

15. Eugene Doleschal and Nora Kapmuts, *Toward a New Criminology* (Hackensack, NJ: National Council on Crime and Delinquency, 1974), p. 4.

16. Charles Goring, *The English Convict* (London: His Majesty's Stationery Office, 1913).

17. Thomas Szasz, *The Myth of Mental Illness* (New York: Hoeber-Harper, 1961).

18. H. J. Eysenck, "The Effects of Psychotherapy," *International Journal of Psychiatry* 1, 1965, pp. 97–144.

19. Charles Zastrow and Ralph Navarre, "Self-Talk: A New Criminological Theory," *International Journal of Comparative and Applied Criminal Justice* (Fall 1979), pp. 167–176.

20. Sutherland and Cressey, *Criminology*.

21. Robert K. Merton, *Social Theory and Social Structure* (New York: Free Press, 1968), p. 232.

22. John M. Johnson and Jack Douglas, eds., *Crime at the Top: Deviance in Business and the Professions* (Philadelphia: J. B. Lippincott, 1978).

23. Walter B. Miller, "Lower Class Culture as a Generating Milieu of Gang Delinquency," *Journal of Social Issues* 14, 1958, pp. 5–19.

24. Albert Cohen, *Delinquent Boys: The Culture of the Gang* (New York: Free Press, 1955).

25. Charles Cooley, *Human Nature and the Social Order* (New York: Charles Scribner's Sons, 1902).

26. "Narcotics: The War Lords," *Newsweek*, October 11, 1976, p. 51.

27. Donald R. Cressey, *Theft of the Nation: The Structure of Organized Crime in America* (New York: Harper & Row, 1969).

28. Marshall B. Clinard and Richard Quinney, *Criminal Behavior Systems: A Typology*, 2d ed. (New York: Holt, Rinehart and Winston, 1973), p. 227.

29. Thomas Sullivan et al., *Social Problems* (New York: John Wiley, 1980), p. 584.

30. Stewart Powell, Steven Emerson, and Orr Kelly, "Busting the Mob," *U.S. News & World Report*, February 3, 1986, pp. 24–31.

31. Ibid.

32. Ibid.

33. Ibid.

34. Ibid.

35. Johnson and Douglas, eds., *Crime at the Top: Deviance in Business and the Professions*.

36. Edwin Sutherland, *White Collar Crime* (New York: Dryden Press, 1949), p. 9.

37. Donald R. Cressey, *Other People's Money* (New York: Free Press, 1953).

38. Thomas Sullivan et al., *Social Problems*, p. 586.

39. *Crime in the United States, 1986*, p. 165.

40. Alexander B. Smith and Harriet Pollack, "Crimes Without Victims," *Saturday Review*, December 4, 1971, pp. 27–29.

41. Janet S. Hyde, *Understanding Human Sexuality* (New York: McGraw-Hill, 1979).

42. Elmer H. Johnson, *Crime, Correction, and Society*, 4th ed. (Homewood, IL: Dorsey Press, 1978).

43. *Crime in the United States, 1986*, p. 155.

44. Edwin H. Sutherland, *The Professional Thief* (Chicago: University of Chicago Press, 1937).

45. M. G. Niethercutt, "Parole Violations and Commitment Offense," *Journal of Research in Crime and Delinquency* 9 (July 1972), p. 87.

46. *Crime in the United States, 1986*, p. 175.

47. Ibid.

48. Eugene Doleschal and Nora Klapmuts, *Toward a New Criminology* (Hackensack, NJ: National Council on Crime and Delinquency, 1972).

49. "Negative Attitudes toward the Criminal Justice System," *New York Times*, April 10, 1978.

50. *Crime in the United States, 1986*.

51. James W. Coleman and Donald R. Cressey, *Social Problems* (New York: Harper & Row, 1980), p. 395.

52. David M. Peterson, "The Police Officer's Conception of Proper Police Work," *The Police Journal* 47 (London: P. Allen & Co., 1974), pp. 102–108.

53. Coleman and Cressey, *Social Problems*, p. 396.

54. John Barbara, June Morrison, and Horace Cunningham, "Plea Bargaining: Bargain Justice?" *Criminology* 14 (May 1976), pp. 55–64.

55. Abraham S. Blumberg, *Criminal Justice* (Chicago: Quadrangle Books, 1967).

56. Coleman and Cressey, *Social Problems*, p. 399.

57. Alan Neigher, "The Gault Decision; Due Process and the Juvenile Court," *Federal Probation* 31, no. 4 (December 1967), pp. 8–18.

58. Sutherland and Cressey, *Criminology.*

59. Ibid., p. 317.

60. Ibid., pp. 331–336.

61. Ibid., p. 333–334.

62. Ibid.

63. Ted Gest, "Bulging Prisons," *U.S. News & World Report*, April 23, 1984, p. 42.

64. Cooley, *Human Nature and the Social Order.*

65. Sutherland and Cressey, *Criminology*, p. 354.

66. *Crime in the United States, 1986*, p. 41.

67. "Guns, Guns, Guns," NBC News Summer Showcase, July 5, 1988.

68. Ibid.

69. Ibid.

70. Ibid.

71. Dae H. Chang, "How to Avoid Becoming a Victim of Crime," in *The Personal Problem Solver*, eds. Charles Zastrow and Dae H. Chang (Englewood Cliffs, NJ: Prentice-Hall, 1977).

72. Sutherland and Cressey, *Criminology*, p. 354.

9

PROBLEMS IN EDUCATION AND SCHOOL SOCIAL WORK

In 1957 the United States and the Soviet Union were involved in an unofficial race to be the first country to place a satellite in orbit. The race became a symbol of international honor and prestige. Russia won when they successfully placed Sputnik I into orbit. Why did the United States lose? There were numerous reasons. However, the general public blamed the American educational system for neglecting subjects that were vital to national survival. For example, one outspoken critic, Max Rafferty, stated, "Instead of offering a four-year program of studies in mathematics, history, foreign languages, and other disciplines (high schools) encourage students to divert themselves with ceramics, stagecraft, table decorating, upholstering, and second-year golf."[1] Following these events, the American educational system was called on to provide greater emphasis on mathematics, natural science courses, and the kind of other courses that would enable our country to successfully compete with Russia.

The educational system has frequently been asked to resolve and alleviate social problems. For example, it is currently being called on to be a means to reduce racism and sexism, by developing new curriculum designed to change the attitudes of school-age children. It is expected to provide students of low-income families with the education and job training skills that will enable them to escape from a life of poverty. It must identify and refer for treatment those children who have emotional or learning problems and those who abuse alcohol and other drugs. It is a mechanism for conveying antidelinquent values. It is required to refer children to protective services who are suspected of being physically abused, neglected, or sexually abused.

Education, which in the past has frequently been called on to solve other social problems, is now recognized as a social problem itself. It can be viewed as a social problem because it is not meeting the expectations of society. Education is in a crisis of controversy and indecision. The self-confidence, morale, and motivation of teachers is low. Some schools have been accused of perpetuating, rather than alleviating, social inequality for the poor and for minorities. Student scores on achievement tests are substantially lower than they were twenty-five years ago.[2] Some inner-city schools are so victimized by vandalism and violence that students and teachers are as concerned with survival as with education. This chapter will:

- Summarize problems that school systems currently face.
- Present proposals for improving education.
- Present proposals for improving educational opportunities for children of low-income families and of minority groups.
- Summarize the functions of school social workers and describe several role models for school social work practice.

PROBLEMATIC AREAS IN EDUCATION

There are a number of crises and problematic areas in education. In this section we will examine the following problems: the question of the quality of education; the issue of equal access to a quality education; confusion about the goals of education; and the shortage of teachers, especially of quality teachers.

The Question of Quality

A number of indicators raise questions about the quality of education in the United States. Mean SAT (Scholastic Aptitude Test) scores on the verbal-reasoning section and on the mathematics-reasoning section are lower than they were twenty-five years ago. The SAT is taken annually by about one million high school students who aspire to attend college. From the mid-1950s to the mid-1960s, SAT scores were fairly constant, ranging from 472 to 478 on the verbal-reasoning section and from 495 to 502 on the mathematical-reasoning section. In the second half of the 1960s, both scores began to decline and continued to do so until around 1980, when the mean verbal score was 424 and the mean mathematical score was 466. Since 1980, there has been a gradual increase, although scores are still significantly below what they were twenty-five years ago.[3]

In an international study of mathematics, twelfth graders in the United States scored much lower than Japanese students and well below the mean score of fifteen industrialized nations.[4] A 1984 National Assessment of Educational Progress study of student writing found a "generally low level of writing proficiency."[5] Although 99 percent of high school seniors have basic reading skills, less than 40 percent are able to comprehend, summarize, and explain what they have read.[6] There have also been studies that indicate many businesses do not believe that recent graduates possess adequate skills for the work place.[7]

In 1983, the National Commission on Excellence in Education summarized the quality of education issue as follows: "For the first time in the history of our country, the educational skills of one generation will not surpass, will not equal, will not even approach, those of their parents.[8]

There have been two primary explanations for the decline in student achievement, neither of which has been proved. One explanation holds the school systems responsible; the other places the cause in societal changes.

The first explanation asserts that school systems responded to the protests of the 1960s by changing their curricula. In the 1960s there were nationwide protests against racial inequality, the Vietnam War, and the role of traditional institutions (such as education) in our society. In response to such protests, many school systems reduced the number of required courses and gave students greater choice in course selections. As a result, for many students there was a decline in the amount of time they spent in courses designed to teach basic skills. Such "softening" of the school curriculum, it has been asserted, has led to the decline in achievement scores.

The second explanation focuses on societal changes since the mid-1960s. Students now spend much more time watching television: In fact, students spend more time watching television than in any other activity except sleeping. It has been argued that because children now watch television more, they spend less time reading books and therefore do not read or write as well. Similarly, with the advent of the computer age, it has been argued that children spend considerable time engaged in computer games and

Doonesbury

A recent study reported that Americans between 18 and 24 scored lower in geographic knowledge than similar age groups in eight other industrialized nations. Less than half could identify Great Britain, France, and Japan on a map; one in seven couldn't locate their own country.

thereby spend even less time in reading and writing. There have also been changes in the family. There is now a much higher proportion of single-parent families. In two-family families, both parents are now more apt to be employed outside of the home, which may result in decreased involvement with the school system and less monitoring of children's homework assignments.

Whatever the reason or reasons, there is considerable pressure on school systems to make changes so that students will better learn the basic skills of reading, writing, and arithmetic.

Equal Access

An egalitarian society has a responsibility to provide equal opportunity for a high-quality education for all its citizens. Our society has generally failed to meet this responsibility, especially with respect to minority groups and the poor.

The Coleman Report and a number of other studies have found social class to be the single most effective predictor of school achievement.[9] Students from the middle and upper classes tend to achieve higher

grades, stay in school longer, and get higher scores on standardized achievement tests. There are two primary explanations for this relationship: One focuses on family background and the other on school systems.

The family background explanation asserts that lower-class children live in a very different environment than middle- and upper-class children. Their homes tend to have fewer magazines, newspapers, and books. Their parents tend to have less education and read less. Thus children in low-income families are less apt to be encouraged to read because their parents are less likely to role model reading. Because lower-class families tend to be larger in size and are more apt to be headed by a single parent, their children are likely to receive less guidance and less educational encouragement. As such, poor children may not view education as a means to achieving in society and may not develop educational goals. Also, poor children are more apt to be hungry and undernourished, which tends to inhibit their motivation to learn. In contrast, middle- and upper-class families tend to place a higher value on education and therefore tend to put more time and effort into helping their children to do homework and into guiding their children to do well in school.

School systems are primarily geared for educating middle- and upper-class students. Several factors are involved in this. Students who live in wealthy tax districts have more money spent on their education than students who live in poorer districts. About 55 percent of the funds for public schools in this country come from local school district taxes. Because most of this money comes from property taxes, school districts containing numerous expensive homes have more revenue for their schools. (Roughly 39 percent of public school revenues come from state taxes and 7 percent from federal taxes.[10])

Amazingly, those who live in poorer school districts generally pay a higher percentage of the assessed value of their property in taxes than people who live in wealthier districts. One study on education concluded:

It is unconscionable that a poor man in a poor district must often pay local taxes at higher rates for the inferior education of his child than the man of means in a rich district pays for the superior education of his child. Yet, incredibly, that is the situation today in most of the 50 states.[11]

Most teachers have middle-class backgrounds, which may mean they are better able to establish relationships with middle- and upper-income children, since they have more in common with them. There is also evidence that teachers expect less of poor children in terms of both academic achievement and behavior than they expect of middle- and upper-class children. Low-income students tend to respond to such expectations by misbehaving and underachieving.[12] The expectation of low achievement and misbehavior thus becomes a self-fulfilling prophecy.

Many school systems place students in one of several different "tracks" or "ability groups." In high school, the "most promising" are placed into college preparatory courses, and others go into "basic" or vocational classes. Lower-class and minority students are more likely to be placed in the basic or vocational track.[13] Those students placed in the latter track are often not exposed to college-oriented math, science, and literature, and some teachers have lower achievement expectations of them. In addition, because such students have little contact with college-bound stu-

dents, they are less apt to aspire to a college education. Without a college education, they have limited opportunities to obtain high-paying jobs.

The small proportion of low-income and minority students who do pursue a college education generally do not have the financial resources to attend prestigious colleges and universities. Also, they have more difficulty competing academically with wealthier students, partly because they generally have to work, at least part time, to offset some of their expenses.

Minority students are particularly apt to have inferior educational opportunities. Until 1954, blacks attended segregated schools in the South that were definitely inferior to those attended by whites. In 1954, the U.S. Supreme Court ruled that racial segregation in public schools was unconstitutional. Although de jure (legal) segregation ended, de facto (actual) segregation has tended to exist in many communities where there are significant proportions of nonwhites. Schools in such communities tend to remain segregated because of a pattern of de facto segregation in housing. To deal with this problem, the Supreme Court ruled that school districts must seek racial balance in schools. In many school districts school busing is used to seek a racial balance. Studies indicate that segregation has been reduced *within* school districts but has increased *between* districts.[14] This increase is largely due to "white flight," that is, whites leaving the inner cities and moving to the suburbs. In some communities, courts have now ordered busing between school districts, and some whites have responded by sending their children to private schools. Chicago's public schools are a classic example of de facto segregation. Some authorities have called this the worst school district in the country: The city's public school system is 88 percent nonwhite, whereas the private school system is primarily white.[15]

Surveys have found that most Americans now favor school integration, but most blacks and whites are opposed to busing programs to achieve school integration.[16] In many large cities (such as Baltimore, Chicago, Cleveland, and Detroit) public schools are approaching 90 percent minority enrollment.[17] In recent years the Supreme Court appears to be less aggressive in mandating that busing be used to achieve desegregation. For instance, the Court has stated there must be proof

BOX 9.1

The Pygmalion Effect

According to Greek mythology, Pygmalion was a king of Cyprus who made a female figure of ivory that was brought to life for him by Aphrodite (the Greek goddess of love and beauty). Robert Rosenthal and Lenore Jacobson performed an intriguing experiment to demonstrate that teachers' expectations of students can increase students' achievement scores. They called this self-fulfilling prophecy the Pygmalion Effect.

These experimenters began by giving a standard achievement test to students in eighteen classrooms of an elementary school. (The teachers were told the test was the Harvard Test of Inflected Acquisition. No such test exists.) The researchers then randomly selected 20 percent of the students and informed their teachers that the test results showed these students would make remarkable progress in the coming school year. When the students were retested eight months later, those who had been predicted to be remarkable achievers showed a significantly greater increase in achievement than the others. The researchers concluded that this increase was due to the fact that teachers had higher expectations for these students and thus worked more intensively with them. If the expectations of teachers do indeed affect student achievement, lower-class and minority students may well be at a disadvantage, since most teachers are white, are from middle-class backgrounds, and have a tendency to expect less from lower-class and minority students.

Source: Robert Rosenthal and Lenore Jacobson, *Pygmalion in the Classroom* (New York: Harper & Row, 1969).

that schools are intentionally discriminating against minority students before busing is ordered. In many inner cities, minority students continue to be segregated in dangerous, crowded, and inferior schools.

Have desegregation programs improved academic performance of nonwhites? The answer is inconclusive. After reviewing 120 studies, Nancy St. John concluded:

In sum, adequate data have not yet been gathered to determine a causal relationship between school racial composition and academic achievement. More than a decade of considerable research effort has produced no definitive positive findings. In view of the political, moral, and technical difficulties of investigation on this question, it is doubtful that all the canons of

scientific method will ever be met or a causal relationship ever established.[18]

Have desegregation programs decreased racial prejudice? Some studies show a decrease in prejudice, whereas others show that prejudice remains the same or even intensifies.[19] In communities where desegregation takes place in an atmosphere of cooperation and good will, prejudice tends to be reduced. However, desegregation programs that are court ordered in an atmosphere of antagonism and misunderstanding are unlikely to reduce prejudice.

Urban Hispanics and blacks are not the only ones who have inferior educational opportunities: Native Americans, Alaskan Eskimos, and migrant workers also

A teacher sounds out a word with a Hispanic boy in a Spanish-English Head Start program. Bilingual education is a topic of intense debate among today's parents and educators.

lack access to high-quality schools. Many Native Americans go to reservation schools, which are inferior in quality.

For Hispanics, bilingual/bicultural education is an issue of intense debate. (There is also controversy about whether black English should be taught in inner-city schools that have high proportions of black students.) With bilingual/bicultural education, students are taught wholly or partly in their native language until they can speak English fairly fluently, and in some cases longer. One side asserts that preserving the culture and language of minorities is a worthwhile (or essential) goal of public education. The opposing side asserts that minority students will be best prepared to compete effectively in American society if they are "immersed" in English language instruction. It is also asserted that black English or Spanish in schools is expensive, and it reinforces separateness, as it is a factor in keeping minorities in the ghettos.

Given all the above factors, it is not surprising that there are significant differences in educational achievement between whites and minorities. Almost twice as many Hispanic and black students drop out of high school as compared to whites.[20] There are wide differences between whites and minorities in the proportions of functional illiteracy (that is, inability to read or write a simple sentence in any language). For whites, the estimated proportion of the adult population (18 years of age and older) that is functionally illiterate is 16 percent. For blacks it is 44 percent, and for Hispanics it is 56 percent.[21] (There are very few jobs for people in our society who are functionally illiterate.) Minorities are also less apt than whites to attend or graduate from college.

Confusion about the Goals of Education

There is agreement that school systems should teach the basic skills of reading, writing, and arithmetic. However, there is considerable controversy over what other values, knowledge, and skills should be taught in schools.

Feminists criticize school systems for teaching and perpetuating sexism: For example, many primary and secondary school textbooks show boys and girls in stereotyped sex roles. Schools have been criticized for helping to perpetuate the class system: As discussed earlier, poor and minority students often receive inferior educations, which greatly limits their chances for attaining high-paying jobs. There is considerable disagreement about the extent to which sex education should be taught in the school system. There is also controversy regarding whether school systems should provide information on safer sex practices to prevent the spread of AIDS. There is disagreement whether prayers should be allowed in public schools, even though the Supreme Court has decided prayers in public schools violate the principle of separation of church and state. There is disagreement about the emphasis that should be placed on teaching such subjects as music, sports, and home economics. There is also disagreement on the extent to which school systems

Low pay, low prestige, inadequate preparation, and poor working conditions are just a few of the reasons many teachers feel disenchanted with their profession.

elective courses and "social services" such as sex education. This movement is calling for the establishment of clear standards of achievement for students, "criteria mastery" as the basis for grade promotion, achievement of certain grade levels before participation in varsity sports is allowed, increased attention to academic subjects and to the teaching of "core values," more testing and homework, longer school hours, and sterner discipline. The movement is also urging that teachers should receive salary increases based on merit rather than on seniority, with the underlying assumption that such a system would motivate teachers to seek to do a better job in the classroom.

Even within the back-to-basics movement, there are controversies. Are principles such as learning to get along with others, and communicating effectively components of a "basic" education? Are "the basics" the same for all students?

There are a variety of other questions that have been raised about education. Should private schooling be financially supported by refunding to those families who send their children to private schools the amounts they spend on public education through taxes? Should public colleges and universities collect more of their funds through higher student tuitions (which makes it more difficult for students of low-income families to attend)? What changes in curriculum need to be made for schools to do a better job in training students for the high-technology jobs that are opening up in our society? Clearly there is a need for increased consensus concerning the priorities and goals in education.

Shortage of Teachers and of Quality Teachers

Our nation is currently facing its greatest shortage of teachers in the past two decades. The Carnegie Forum Task Force on Teaching as a Profession noted in 1986 that:

The many good teachers we have are being driven out of teaching by intolerable conditions, and it will be impossible to attract many new people of real ability to teaching until these conditions are radically altered.[22]

should be used to combat racism, stop drug abuse, prevent unwed pregnancies, help the handicapped, and reduce delinquency. There is controversy whether schools should focus more on developing the creative thinking capacities of students as opposed to emphasizing academic content.

In recent years there has been a conservative trend in our society. In school systems this trend has been expressed in a "back-to-basics" movement. Educational conservatives are opposed to schools being experimental, to schools being custodial institutions for the emotionally disturbed, to schools being recreational facilities, and to schools offering "frill" and

Between 1986 and 1992, public and private schools will need to replace half of the teaching force.[23] This problem is compounded, as colleges are expected to prepare less than 1 million teaching graduates to meet the need for 1.3 million projected vacancies.[24] There is a serious concern that school districts will lower hiring standards (and thereby hire less-qualified teachers) in order to fill teaching vacancies.

In surveys, half of all current teachers say that if they had the opportunity to choose careers again, they would not select teaching.[25] Many factors are contributing to disenchantment with teaching: low pay, low prestige, inadequate preparation, the opening up of other job opportunities for women, and intolerable working conditions. There are many other areas where college graduates can earn substantially more money: accounting, engineering, computer science, sales, and many more.

The quality of students seeking teaching careers has tumbled as well. Since 1978, SAT scores of high school seniors planning to major in teaching have been at least 70 points below the national average.[26] To accommodate such students, some colleges of education have offered less challenging programs, and education at most colleges is often recognized as an "easy major."

Intolerable working conditions in school systems include the following. A federal study of school violence found that 12 percent of secondary school teachers had been threatened by students, and one half of 1 percent had been physically attacked.[27] In some schools, teachers spend as much time trying to keep peace and order as they do on teaching. There are high rates of drug and alcohol abuse among students, which teachers are forced to confront, often without much preparation. Many school districts have insufficient instructional supplies. In 1985 the California Commission on the Teaching Profession reported that one quarter of the state's teachers did not have a textbook for every student, and at least a third reported spending at least $100 of their own money each year to buy supplies that students needed.[28] High student-to-teacher ratios is another concern of teachers: The more students there are, the more difficult it is for teachers to give individualized instruction. There is the additional difficulty of teachers not feeling adequately prepared to teach cer-

tain topics, such as aspects of protective behavior (for example, how to protect oneself against sexual assaults) and alcohol and drug abuse education. Teachers are often not adequately involved in the decision-making processes in education, which contributes to poor morale and lowers motivation to seek positive changes.

STRATEGIES TO IMPROVE EDUCATION

Michael Rutter and his associates evaluated a number of high schools and concluded what most parents already know: "Schools do indeed have important impact on children's development, and it does matter what school a child attends.[29] Rutter found that the best schools required more homework, maintained high academic standards, had well-understood and well-enforced discipline standards, and yet created a comfortable and supportive atmosphere for students.[30] This section will examine two proposals for improving the school system: Increase incentives for teachers, and improve the curriculum.

Increase Incentives for Teachers

Perhaps the only way to encourage more high-quality students to enter the teaching profession and to raise the morale of existing teachers is to increase incentives for teaching. Such incentives include increased pay, expanded inservice training, provision of sufficient school supplies, availability of high-tech equipment (such as computers, films, and videotape equipment) for classroom use, and improved working conditions.

A controversial recommended incentive is the creation of a "master teacher" rank that would recognize and reward ability and dedication to teaching. There now is growing evidence that superior teaching can have immense positive effects on students. Pederson and Faucher found evidence of a high correlation between outstanding first-grade teaching and later adult success of students, all of whom came from an inner-city neighborhood.[31] Master teachers would be paid substantially more and have added professional responsibilities, such as curriculum design and supervision of new teachers.

In 1986 the Carnegie Forum recommended the creation of a "lead teacher" position that is very similar to that of a "master teacher."[32] The title would be awarded to the most experienced and skilled professionals in the classroom. The position would be a twelve-month position and would pay up to $72,000 per year (nearly three times the current median pay for teachers).

The proposal to create a master teacher rank has become highly controversial. Teachers' unions have generally opposed the concept because unions fear that criteria other than ability and dedication will be used in making such selections. Unions also tend to be opposed to higher pay and promotion being based on merit, as the merit concept conflicts with the preferred union concept of basing pay on seniority.

Improve the Curriculum

If few new resources are required, practically everyone is in favor of this proposal. A major question, however, is, In what directions should the curriculum be improved? As noted earlier, there is considerable confusion about the goals of a quality education. In the 1960s and early 1970s there was criticism of the rigidity and authoritarianism in schools, which led to increases in the number of electives in high schools and colleges and a reduction in the number of basic "academic" classes. Other changes were made to respond to concerns that were being expressed. Alternative schools were created for students who found traditional schools to be "stifling." Content began to be included in history and social studies classes about the significant contributions made by Native Americans, blacks, Hispanics, and other minority groups. New courses were developed that attempted to make schoolwork more relevant to the lives of minority students. In the

1980s the concern has shifted to focus on the decline in academic achievement, and school systems are returning to stiffer academic programs. In fact, many of the requirements for basic academic courses that were dropped in the 1960s and early 1970s have been reinstated in the 1980s. In the 1980s there has been a move toward teaching basic skills (such as reading, writing, and arithmetic) and a move away from elective courses such as sociology, psychology, or specialized areas of literature and history. As part of this movement, children are also taught to respect authority, be patriotic, and lead moral lives. Some schools have reestablished strict dress codes and seek to curb unconventional behavior.

At the same time, a critical-thinking movement is taking place that focuses on developing the thinking capacities of students. This approach encourages students to make observations and to analyze issues critically. It stresses class discussions and downplays lectures. It emphasizes critical analysis over rote learning. It asserts that critical thinking is best assessed by analysis of an issue or concept in essay form rather than through the use of objective tests. In some ways the critical-thinking movement conflicts with the back-to-basics movement. The latter places greater emphasis on learning and remembering facts, whereas the former asserts that memorization is much less important than developing one's thinking capacities.

TOWARD EQUAL EDUCATIONAL OPPORTUNITY

As noted earlier, educational opportunities for minorities and the poor are inferior in this country. Nearly everyone agrees that there should be equal educational opportunity for all, but there is considerable disagreement on how this can be achieved. Three proposals for progressing toward equal educational opportunity are (*a*) reform school financing in order to spend an equal amount of money on each student's education, (*b*) establish special compensatory educational programs for

BOX 9.2

Schools Without Failure

I n 1969 William Glasser wrote *Schools Without Failure* (New York: Harper & Row), which
has had considerable impact on improving teaching. The major concepts of Glasser's
approach are summarized as follows.

Glasser asserts that a major problem of school systems is that they are organized in such
a way that most students experience failure. He is critical of schools for a variety of reasons.
Achieving *A*s is considered the paramount goal in schools; since only a few students get a
majority of *A*s, most do not feel successful. Memorization is more valued than developing
thinking capacities. (He believes education is the process of developing thinking capacities.)
He asserts that thinking and creative, artistic, and fun uses of students' brains are drastically
downgraded in schools. Schools do not deal with real-life problems faced by children. Relevance is frequently absent from the curriculum; thereby children do not transfer classroom
learning to problem solving outside of school, and thereby do not gain the motivation to
learn.

Glasser asserts:

*Unless we can provide schools where children, through a reasonable use of their capacities,
can succeed, we will do little to solve the major problems of our country. We will have more
social disturbances, more people who need to be kept in jails, prisons, and mental hospitals,
more people who need social workers to take care of their lives because they feel they cannot
succeed in this society and are no longer willing to try (p. 6).*

Glasser asserts that for a child to succeed in this world, she or he has to develop a
positive identity (sense of self). If a child develops a failure identity, that child is unlikely to
succeed in the world. Instead, such a child is apt to become angry, depressed, alienated,
lonely, or hostile and may express the failure identity through delinquency, withdrawal, or
development of emotional disturbances.

Glasser theorizes that there are two needs that must be met for establishment of a
positive or success identity. Each child has a need for love and a need for self-worth. If these
two needs are unmet, then the child will develop a failure identity. If these two needs are
met, the child will develop a success identity and will pay off society many times over by
being a responsible, contributing citizen.

Because home conditions in many families are less than desirable, many children do not
receive the love or the sense of self-worth that they need. When they cannot fulfill their
needs at home, Glasser asserts they must have the opportunity to do so at school, or they will
develop a failure identity. Schools are in a unique position to identify children who are
starting to develop a failure identity, since every child attends school.

He asserts that teachers need to be better trained in identifying children with failure identities. Colleges of education should seek to provide more content on identifying children with problems and also should put greater emphasis on developing the relationship capacities of education majors.

Glasser asserts that perhaps the greatest strength of a quality teacher is to be able to form positive relationships with students. Teachers need to be able to convey to students that each student has a sense of self-worth. Teachers must also be able to convey that they sincerely care about the well-being of each student. Those students identified as beginning to develop a failure identity need to be referred to Pupil Services for help, or the teacher needs to find a way to make the classroom a success experience for these (and all other) students.

Glasser recommends that more emphasis be placed on the teaching of content that will assist in the personal development of each child: being assertive, learning to problem solve life's problems, improving relationships, handling unwanted emotions, learning responsible sexuality, learning to handle stress better, and so on.

Glasser urges that group problem-solving meetings be held daily in classes. Such group meetings would focus on identifying alternatives for solving the problems that students are encountering at school and in their lives. The topics to be discussed often would be brought up by the students themselves—for example, relationship difficulties they are having with someone. Such discussions should take place in a supportive, positive atmosphere. Blaming and fault finding should be minimized or eliminated entirely. The atmosphere needs to be one in which one person's opinion is valued as being as good as another's opinion.

According to Glasser, students should not be separated into tracts. Students in lower tracts are apt to feel a sense of being a failure. Consistent with the critical-thinking movement, Glasser urges that the focus of education be placed on developing the thinking capacities of students.

Glasser also recommends abolishing the current grading system of A-B-C-D-F. He urges the following replacement system. The school system should establish competence criteria for each course. For example, in a mathematics course, a student would have to be able to perform a predetermined level of mathematical computations in order to pass the course. Students who achieve these standards would receive a P (for pass) on their report card. Students who do superior work and who help other students who are not doing as well may be awarded an S (for superior work). Students who do not achieve the standards would not receive any grade, and no records would be kept of classes that students do not pass. For basic academic courses, students would be required to repeat the classes until they successfully achieve the established competency levels.

*Two music classrooms in New York City reflect current efforts toward achieving equal educational
opportunity. Children with disabilities in a Brooklyn school (above) have the opportunity to participate
in such classes in part because of recent legislation mandating that school districts develop specialized
programs to meet their needs. Members of this budding brass ensemble (opposite) attend a
performing arts magnet school in East Harlem; inner-city magnet schools help foster integration by
offering high-quality programs, often in more intimate academic settings.*

disadvantaged students, and (*c*) integrate students
from different ethnic backgrounds into the same
schools. We will take a closer look at each of these
proposals.

Reform of School Financing

Some schools in wealthy districts receive considerably
more money per student than do schools in poor districts. At present, a majority of the revenues for school
districts comes from local property taxes. Decaying inner cities are especially hard pressed to finance school
systems, and many schools in these areas are inferior
as a result. It has been suggested that the way to eliminate such inequality is for the federal government to

pay for all primary and secondary education, giving the
same amount of money per student to each school.

Critics of this approach assert that schools in this
country have excelled because of local control and
involvement. If the funding would shift to the federal
government, the result would be greater federal control and increased "red tape," as a huge federal bureaucracy would undoubtedly evolve.

Increased federal funding for low-income school
districts appears to be the only viable way that such
districts can progress toward greater revenue equality
with wealthier school districts. The federal government is the only government unit that has the financial
resources to assist low-income school districts. Ideally,
a program of increased federal funding to low-income
school districts should seek to maintain local control.

Compensatory Education

Many authorities believe that special programs and extra assistance would improve achievement levels of the poor and minorities. There are a variety of programs that already exist.

Project Head Start gives preschool instruction to disadvantaged children. Evaluations of the results of Head Start indicate that students who attend are better prepared for starting first grade than are disadvantaged students who do not attend Head Start. Unfortunately, early gains made by those in the program tend to fade as the children reach second and third grade.[33] In the 1980s, funding for Head Start was cut back, and the program now serves only a fraction of the millions of eligible children. Supporters of Head Start programs assert that longer-range efforts are needed to provide assistance to disadvantaged students throughout their school years.

Most school districts have Pupil Services departments that seek to assess the academic, social, and emotional needs of children who are not progressing well in school. Once an assessment of a child is completed, then programs are developed to meet the unique learning needs of the child. A wide variety of services may be provided, depending on the identified needs. There are special classes for the emotionally disturbed and for those with learning disabilities. Counseling is sometimes provided. Some students are referred for drug abuse. Some are referred for visual or hearing difficulties. Pupil Services departments are staffed by a variety of professionals: school psychologists, social workers, and guidance counselors. In 1975, the U.S. Congress passed the Education for All Handicapped Children Act, now known as PL 94-142. This law addresses the numerous physical, developmental, learning, and social-emotional problems that hamper the education of children. In sweeping legislation, the law mandated that all school districts identify students with these problems and then develop specialized programs to meet the needs of these children. Unfortunately, many low-income school districts, because of financial constraints, have not been able to meet the objectives of this bill.

In many states, programs are being developed that seek to prevent children from dropping out of school. Some school districts have drop-out rates approaching 50 percent, and the national average is over 10 percent.[34] Dropping out represents an enormous loss to those individuals and to society because of lost potential productivity. Programs for "at-risk" students are a response to the need to help high school students stay in school while also helping them to develop practical job skills.

Some elementary and secondary school systems now have reading, writing, and arithmetic programs during the summer for students who need assistance in these areas. At the college level a variety of compensatory or educational opportunity programs have been established. These include noncredit courses in English and mathematics, tutoring, and a variety of testing programs. Many colleges have special provisions for the admission of minority students who do not meet standard admission requirements. These colleges encourage such students to use the educational opportunity programs that are available. (Students who attended inferior elementary and secondary school systems in inner cities are often two to four grade levels behind in reading, writing, and arithmetic and therefore need educational opportunity programs in order to have an opportunity to succeed in college.)

Educational opportunity programs have become an accepted part of most colleges and universities. Another question involves special admissions of minority students to graduate and professional schools. Supporters assert that these affirmative action admissions are attempts to compensate for the inferior school systems and other forms of discrimination that minorities have been subjected to in the past. On the other hand, because competition for the limited admissions into these schools is intense, white students complain that they are the victims of reverse discrimination, since they are being rejected even though their scores on

entrance exams are higher than scores of some minority students who are accepted. The legal status of this affirmative action policy has not, as yet, been fully resolved.

Effective Integration

As discussed earlier, school busing has been used to attempt to integrate students within school districts. Many whites in large cities have responded by moving to suburbs or by sending their children to private schools. Some big cities, through court orders, are now experimenting with merging suburban school districts with inner-city school districts and then busing children within each district. The extent to which such merging will occur is questionable. There is a major problem with distance, as some suburban communities are so far from inner cities that students would have to spend a large part of their day on a bus. Most white parents in suburbs would not raise serious objections to a small number of inner-city children being bused to their schools in the suburbs. However, most suburbanites would object to their children being bused to inferior school systems in inner cities because they fear potential violence and a lower quality education. Many white parents, if faced with such a court order, would probably respond by placing their children in private schools.

The ideal way to integrate neighborhood schools is through integration of residential areas, so that neighborhood schools are then automatically integrated. Such integration would provide ongoing opportunities for interracial cooperation and friendships for children and for adults. This proposal seeks to resolve de facto school segregation through the implementation of housing integration. The chances of this proposal working, however, are minute. People of different income, ethnic, and racial groups generally have little desire to live together in the same neighborhood. In addition, many members of minority groups cannot afford to live in affluent neighborhoods, and white residents of such neighborhoods object to low-cost housing being built near them.

Another possibility to move toward integration is

through the use of "magnet" schools in cities. Magnet schools are schools that offer special courses, programs, or equipment. An example would be a fine arts middle school or high school; another would be a school emphasizing curriculum in the area of computer science. Proponents of magnet schools hope that placing such schools in inner-city areas would draw students from suburbs because of the excellent educational opportunities they could offer. President Bush has stated he wants to be remembered as the "Education President" and has proposed increased federal funding to support magnet schools. (He also has proposed federal funding for a "merit schools" program to reward schools that improve education standards.)

The prospects of significant federal help for inner-city schools in the near future are not bright. In this era of trying to reduce the federal deficit through budget cutbacks, the chances of the enactment of a bold new federal program to channel resources to financially distressed school districts are remote.

SCHOOL SOCIAL WORKERS: A RESPONSE TO CRISIS*

School social work is a relatively new role. Before 1960 there were few school social workers, and these were primarily employed by large, urban school systems, for example, New York and Chicago. In fact, one of the earliest books on school social workers was first published in 1955.[35] School social work, then, must be discussed within the context of its evolving role.

Before doing this, however, it will be necessary to have a method of analyzing behavior so that we have an initial base for understanding the nature of children's problems in schools. It is a practical necessity for any school social worker to have a knowledge of

*This section was especially written for this text by Don Nolan, MSSW, school social worker.

the dynamics of behavior, since social workers have been and will continue to be closely involved with problematic behavior in children. In fact, much of the definition of social work services offered in PL-142 regulations specifies (*a*) defining the nature of social or behavioral problems, (*b*) using individual or family counseling skills, and (*c*) using other resources to make an impact on behavioral, emotional, and social problems.

The Nature of Behavior

We will begin with the premise that behavior is purposeful, that we do things for a reason. We may not always know exactly why we are doing things, in that we do not analyze each of our behaviors. But we are always responding to a given situation with a set of beliefs, with a history of past attempts to solve a problem, and within the context of our present environment.[36]

In *Rational-Emotive Therapy*, Albert Ellis looks at behavior within the context of what he calls the ABCs of behavior. In essence, he says that B—a belief system composed of attitudes, interpretations, and emotions—is always juxtaposed between an activating situation, A, and a consequence, C.[37] This belief system for the person, whether child or adult, is based on opinions the person has about himself or herself and others in relation to his or her perceptions about his or her place in the larger world. The person, then, can decide on a course of action given certain circumstances. Children, like adults, do not act in a random fashion. They act in relation to a decision they have made about the consistency and stability of their relationships with adults and other children. There are antecedents of behavior that often depend on *decisions* they have made about their abilities, and not on their *actual* abilities. Thus, although it may seem that a girl is misbehaving when she approaches new situations, in reality she may have decided from past experience that she will have little success in the task and is thus misbehaving because she does not want to face the fear of another failure. The child has made a decision, although it may be based on what can be termed a *mistaken belief system.*[38] The child wrongly assumes that failure means she is worthless and that trying is not important. To understand how to alter that self-perception, one must look more closely at some primary goals of behavior.

Rudolf Dreikurs postulated that the force behind every human action is a goal. We all know some of what we want, although often we do not consciously act on those goals but rather on unanalyzed means of achieving them. It is possible to understand the psychological motivation of the child if one develops diagnostic skills to analyze four goals of misbehavior: attention getting, power seeking, revenge seeking, and assuming a disability.[39] Some children try to get attention, to always be the focal point for others, since they believe that otherwise they are worthless. Other children attempt to prove their power in the belief that only if they can do what they want and defy adult pressure can they be important. Still others may seek revenge: The only means by which they feel significant is to hurt others, as they feel hurt by them. Others may display actual or imaginary disabilities in order to be left alone so that nothing is demanded of them. The crucial point is that whatever deviant behaviors children display, there are always reasons for these behaviors.

Anyone who has worked extensively with children, in any situation, can readily remember children who were acting out these goals. For example, Ted, who is constantly in front of the teacher interrupting and is always calling attention to himself by "forcing" the teacher to repeatedly reprimand him, is clearly seeking attention. John, who is usually confrontational, who is noncompliant to reasonable requests from the teacher, and who rejects praise and social reinforcers from the teacher, is in a power struggle. Carol, who physically injures others and who usually puts others and herself down, is probably seeking revenge for some perceived wrong. Phil, who is withdrawn, who sinks down in his desk, who is shy with classmates, and who fears new situations, is probably displaying a disability.

We must, of course, be careful not to overgeneralize or analyze too quickly, and we must remember that the child could be displaying these behaviors because of dysfunctional family patterns or because of medical or psychiatric problems. Behavior is complicated and can be deceptive at times. However, if we use the goals of behavior construct with its philosophy of purposeful behavior and actions, we have a starting point to respond to these behaviors. Thus, given a general philosophy of behavior as it applies to the educational system, we can talk about specific ways of intervening to solve problems.

School Social Work Role Models

This section summarizes the following role models for school social work practice: caseworker, group worker, truant officer, counselor, parent liaison, advocate, behavioral specialist, mental health consultant, alcohol and other drug abuse specialist, multidisciplinary team member, and systems change specialist.

CASEWORKER   Intervention has always been the essence of social work. Social workers have responded to the complexity of society and to the problems this complexity has caused with a variety of methods. Casework, traditionally, has been one of the first methods employed in any given area. This has made sense for the practitioner in that casework encompasses the more clinical and best-known aspects of social work. Basically, social workers have had to prove their worth; that is, they have had to prove that they do something different than what is already being done. Because social workers have substantial training in family dynamics, they can analyze and diagnose common problems in the dysfunctional family. This is a skill that others in the typical school system do not have, and thus it is viewed as an area of particular expertise for the school social worker.

An example is the case of Mike, age 10, who had a number of problems. He was physically aggressive toward other children and was prone to act with outbursts of emotion and anger when put in new or different situations. He had virtually no coping skills and came to school after weekends or vacations in an angry, violent mood. The family consisted of five children and his mother. His father was no longer living at home but visited on occasion. Mike's emotional problems, and particularly his violent attitudes, were accentuated after these visits. In addition, Mike had dirty, poorly kept clothing, which always seemed either too small or much too big. One of the problems, of course, was Mike's behavior in class. His goals of misbehavior were a combination of attention seeking and getting power. In an attempt to change this behavior pattern, the social workers, using a casework strategy (*a*) made a referral to the county department of social services to make sure that the family was getting all services that were available, for example, homemaking, medical services, and counseling; (*b*) modified Mike's behavior at school by devising a system of reinforcers that were important to him; (*c*) made sure that Mike found success in academic areas in school by helping the teacher to individualize for Mike's needs; (*d*) tried to help the mother understand that Mike should not be put in situations in which he had to adopt a negative attitude toward adults; and (*e*) contacted the father about his relationship to his son. All of this takes considerable time and energy. This case demonstrates that in casework a consistent, organized, step-by-step approach is used by the social worker. Casework thus becomes a one-to-one involvement with a family in an attempt to solve a problem. Another example may help to clarify this approach further.

Phyllis, age 6, was hearing impaired. She was in a special education program four days a week. There were a number of problems: noncompliant behaviors when Phyllis knew what was wanted of her, a difficulty in communicating in any way, and a number of medical problems. The social worker decided that a home intervention program was needed. Consistency was needed in the sign language program between home and school. Consistency and behavior management were also needed in the home, for Phyllis was not expected to do anything there; the only demands were bathroom skills. The parents needed help in developing reasonable goals and expectations for Phyllis and then following through on a program. Medically, Phyllis needed extensive diagnostic work at a nearby hospital. The social worker made contact with the hospital, arranged for a meeting, and then made sure follow-up came from the hospital. Again, the social worker set specific goals and followed these in an attempt to solve a multitude of problems. Much of the emphasis in the caseworker model is on doing things that teachers are not prepared for and do not have the time to do. The school social worker is striving to achieve other than strictly educational goals, but with the purpose of enabling children to achieve in school.

GROUP WORKER   As casework came to be considered outmoded in some areas of social work practice,[40] school social workers found another method of offering services. Group work became another means of intervening in school problems. Essentially, the rationale was that the social worker could influence the lives and educational success of too few people when using the casework approach. It was also presumed that few cases needed such intensive involvement from a social worker and that there was a point of diminishing returns after a given amount of time and involvement were expended. (Recent studies would say that this assumption may be in error, however.[41]) In effect, another somewhat more hidden premise was that one should be involved with the less severe cases, since one could have more successes and ultimately improve the lives of a larger number of children. A few examples will demonstrate these points.

Ms. Tanner's fifth grade class was a problem for her. Specifically, four boys would not listen regularly, clowned around, and were not getting much done in class. In fact, some of the boys were doing less well academically than in the past year and were starting to go around as a group, often getting into trouble on the playground. An intervention strategy was designed— the creation of groups as a means of solving these problems. Two groups of five boys were created, with two of the "problem" boys in each group. The groups worked in specific high-interest areas; for example, one group worked on a science project that involved creating a metric unit for the third grade, while the other studied the principles of flight and aerodynamics, making kites, paper airplanes, and wooden models. There were a number of planned goals for each group. First, the social worker wanted to create new friendships and show the disruptive children models of more appropriate behavior, behavior that could be as rewarding as attention-getting behavior. Second, co-operation was fostered in conjunction with the principles of peer pressure. All children worked toward step-by-step, cooperative goals; unless all helped none could reach their goal. Finally, the social worker wanted everyone, the children in the group, their peers in the class, and their teacher, to realize that the boys could be productive and successful so that both teacher's and students' perceptions of each other would be altered. The social worker also discussed with Ms. Tanner how individual programming could be used to provide additional successful educational experiences for these four boys.

In another case, group experience involved high school freshmen who were failing in their initial coursework. Study habits, poor motivation, and a negative attitude toward school success were the main concerns. In this case the social worker organized a group of students who took a special course organized around ways of studying. The course was named "Ten Ways to Beat the System" and was structured in a way that allowed the student to learn a new mechanism of studying while not seeming to become part of the high school system. At the same time a number of upper-class students were organized to meet informally with the younger students to discuss some positive aspects of high school that the younger students could look forward to. In addition, these older students offered guidance about which teachers to avoid and which teachers they could expect a fair deal from. Thus, a number of groups were combined to offer an alternative to failure in the school system.

A group worker may occasionally view his or her role as a means of intervening in the area of quality of instruction from teachers. Often, because of issues of seniority and union rights, it is impossible to intervene directly in these areas. Group workers at times seek to compensate for these barriers by offering specialized programs to relatively large groups of students.

TRUANT OFFICER　The social worker in the school has also performed a number of other roles. Truant officer was a fairly prevalent role, especially in large school systems. This is still the case today, as knowing the truancy laws and acting as an advocate for the child may be necessary at times. There are times when acting as an agent of social control (the law, the system) need not be looked at adversely. A case in point is a multi-problem family who had three boys in high school. Although none of the boys had reached the legal age after which school was no longer compulsory, the parents decided to keep the boys at home so that they could help the father in his job as a farmhand. The boys had mentioned to different teachers that they feared this was about to happen but were afraid to tell their father that they wanted to attend school. The social worker was able to intervene in this case by using the truancy laws to inform the parents that they had no choice but to send their children to school. In such a way the undesirable role of truant officer could be transformed into one that was advantageous for the children involved. It was also a means of helping to promote the concept of equal access. Given the high truancy and drop-out rates in larger cities, the approach of combining the services of truant officers with creative or alternative approaches to education can be advantageous to children.

COUNSELOR AND PARENT LIAISON　The social worker as a counselor and/or parent liaison or parent trainer is also a fairly common role in school social work. Often, those in the teaching profession who know little about the potential of social work services will expect the school social worker to be the person who will provide a liaison between parent and teacher. Unfortunately, frequently there is also the assumption that the social worker will defend and justify the actions or educational planning of the teacher. This can cause somewhat strained relations between the social worker and the rest of the teaching staff, especially when a worker agrees with a parent that the school system ought to make changes in its educational programs to serve the parent's child better and perhaps to serve other children better as well. This role requires a lot of tact and prior planning, as well as a relatively assertive view toward expanding social work services.

Because many school systems have never had social workers on their staff, it remains with the new school social worker to describe to them the many roles of social work and the potential values these roles

A mother and caregiver confer outside a day care center in Berkeley, California.

may have for the school system. This will be a long and at times frustrating process, for any fundamental change in basic system services will affect the balance and direction of all services. Consequently, the social worker must be in a position to prove that the change she or he beings will ultimately benefit the system and thus will be worth the uneasiness that the other staff will feel in adjusting to a new person in a different and challenging role. Thus, persistence and what Albert Ellis terms self-awareness (being perceptive and accepting of one's strengths and limitations) will be needed initially.[42]

In the role of counselor, the social worker also brings a number of skills to the situation. However, other professionals (such as guidance counselors and school psychologists) have traditionally held this role in schools. Thus, there has been marginal role development in this area, although there have been some changes in recent years. As school social work services have developed, there has been a trend to look at the social worker as a therapist rather than as a counselor. This distinction has been more than semantic, since advanced professional (master's degree) training has greatly increased the diagnostic and psychological skills of school social workers relative to other school professionals. As such, a school social worker can be seen as a specialist in the diagnosis of emotional difficulties in children, as well as the support staff person with the most extensive psychiatric and medically based training.

In essence, role development and expansion is a critical area of concern for school social workers. When joining a school system, there will be a number of expectations and specific job-related demands placed on them. New workers will necessarily meet these demands with a set of assumptions about their role in a system; that is, the specific, individual, unique things that they do as part of their profession. There are bound to be conflicts, since the older roles encompassing casework, group work, or parent liaison, may not provide enough flexibility to meet the demands of the change effort; that is, school social workers assume they are becoming a part of a system because needs of the system are not being met and aspects of the system need to be changed. To help ascertain how school social workers have attempted to solve this problem, we can discuss five distinct and somewhat newer approaches to their role.

Newer Roles

ADVOCATE   Recently one of the most provocative roles for the social worker has become that of advocate.[43] The assumption made for the adoption of this role is that when facing an educational bureaucracy as a complex system, or when attempting to use other systems for the benefit of the family or child, one needs to employ a person who understands and is not intimidated by large complicated systems.

This can be a particularly useful role when working with families who are newly becoming acquainted with the educational system. For instance, in an early education program that is greared to help prekindergarten children who show some evidence of developmental delay, the social worker can employ this role to help the parents understand their rights under the law, including their rights to appeal program decisions if they feel the programs do not fit the needs of their child. The social worker can explain who is teaching what materials and why this should help the child progress. She or he can be an initial contact person and can be the person who follows the child in the program so that the parents can have a familiar person to contact with whom they can feel comfortable and therefore ask questions they might otherwise consider silly or irrelevant. The social worker can also be the person who makes them aware of applicable medical or social service agencies that are available to give them a better knowledge of their child or offer supportive services when these are needed. Finally, the social worker can be a person to talk to about the complexities, difficulties, fears, or guilt associated with raising a child who in some way is different from other children. A combination of all of the above roles expands the role of home liaison and changes the emphasis to create an advocate role within the school system designed to meet needs that have not previously been met in the school context.

BEHAVIORAL SPECIALIST   There has also been a trend at some major universities to train school social workers in one discrete, highly recognizable skill. Within this context an emphasis is often put on the social worker becoming a behavioral specialist, a person who understands and can systematically apply principles of behavior, specifically behavior modification. Within the schools a knowledge of how to alter behavior has immediate and long-term applicability. Using behavioral skills the social worker can provide guidance in general learning principles as applied to overall teaching and can develop specific programs for children who are having difficulty adjusting to normal classroom routine. The following is a case example.

Phillip, age 9, was having difficulty paying attention and was usually noncompliant to directions. His

teacher was having trouble understanding his beahvior and motivating him to be involved in usual classroom activities: for example, doing independent work in math and reading, participating in small-group activities, and cooperating in play arrangements. A social worker with behavioral training was asked to intervene in the situation. After observing the antecedents of the noncompliant behavior and taking baseline data of on-task or attending behaviors in nonacademic situations,[44] the social worker was able to put together a program. The program included (a) the planned use of social reinforcers (praise from the teacher); (b) a reward system built around the student's interest in science, in which other work had to be done before the work in science could begin; and (c) a system that involved ignoring Phillip's verbal noncompliance while reinforcing compliance from other students with praise and tangible rewards, such as helping with a special project and taking notes to the office. In this way Phillip's behaviors were changed in a relatively short time; another program was developed to help the student continue to achieve academic success.

MENTAL   HEALTH   CONSULTANT   The   school social worker can also function as a mental health consultant to the other staff. Curriculum today is no longer as simple as reading, writing, and arithmetic (if this was ever the case). Although there is currently substantial concern about teaching the "basics" in education, teachers must still seek to improve old curriculum and develop new materials. In this pursuit it is not only the materials that can be questioned, but also the style in which they are taught. Because social workers have training in the social psychology of individual behavior, they can serve as consultants to the human relations aspects of curriculum and to teaching style. With this focus the social worker is in a preventive role, seeking to help teachers motivate students via stimulating materials. She or he can help create a teaching approach that is not threatening but intriguing, questioning, and supportive of the process of learning. Naturally, the social worker would also be involved in helping teachers choose to individualize education—that is, motivating them to devise materials and teaching styles that meet the needs of all children, no matter what their current academic level.

The social worker can help create a systematized approach to monitoring progress and then create new approaches to facilitate remediation when necessary. To accomplish these goals it may be necessary to organize "brainstorming" sessions with all the teachers or to begin an investigation of the materials available on a number of topics.

In this way social workers can help provide guidance in curriculum development, with an overall emphasis on human relations. The inclusion of specific human relations goals in teaching has often been overlooked, even though many of the problems in the schools, trouble on the playground, and problems with special and regular education classes can be seen as directly attributable to a lack of human relations materials. Children need to learn that "different is all right"; that cultural or racial differences need not be feared, but enjoyed; that all people deserve respect as human beings; and that values are learned concepts that can be changed.[45] School social workers, because of their training and unique place in the school, can provide the perspective needed to devise such a curriculum and help create systems for implementation.

ALCOHOL AND OTHER DRUG SPECIALIST   Drug use and abuse continues to be a major problem in our society. From the days of prohibition, various segments of society have addressed the "evils" of alcohol and other drug use. Today, with the tragic loss of lives associated with drunk driving and with the much-publicized drug overdose deaths of sports figures such as Len Bias, there is a growing realization of the need for drug prevention programs. Programs having a punitive interventive focus have not been successful. Thus, there has been a recent emphasis on prevention, and schools have become the mechanism for drug prevention programs.

Because schools generally do not have trained specialists in this area, many school districts have hired school social workers to consult with parents and to refer students who are abusing drugs to appropriate inpatient or outpatient treatment centers. Social workers, because of their knowledge of chemical dependency, their training in interviewing, their skills in interacting with parents, and their knowledge of community resources, have become the logical choice to

spearhead the development of prevention programs. They have also been asked to become curriculum specialists in this area. Thus, as part of their overall responsibilities, many school social workers help develop teaching curriculum on drug use and abuse for use in elementary, middle, and high schools. As such, social workers are responding to changes in society and in the family, as education seeks to accomplish more and more societal goals.

MULTIDISCIPLINARY TEAM MEMBER   Another role that is gaining increasing popularity is that of the social worker using his or her skills in conjunction with other members on a team. Within this role the school social worker might be on a team with other professionals (psychologist, speech therapist, special education teacher, physical therapist, and regular education teacher) who help to determine the special educational needs and particular programming appropriate for certain children. This is an area of implementation of PL-142, with the group of professionals commonly called an M-Team (multidisciplinary team). In this case the social worker might be (*a*) involved with an initial assessment of the child and the family, with special emphasis on family functioning and the child's social and adaptive skills; (*b*) involved with the parents clinically, either through family counseling and role analysis or through training in special techniques, such as behavior modification or crisis intervention; or (*c*) involved in teacher observation, training, and support.

The point here is that the social worker acts as part of a team, a member with certain discrete skills and knowledge, and in conjunction with the team seeks to alleviate problems. Although this may appear to be a somewhat more constricting role, as other methods may seem to offer more independence, it can be a useful way to find gaps in services and to decrease overlap between individual skills. It has its advantages, especially if one is responsible for a school (or a school system) with a large population. One particular advantage is the learning that takes place for the social worker as she or he interacts with other professionals on the team.

Up to now we have been looking at the school social worker as a person who responds to problems, someone who employs whatever methods are at his or her disposal to correct situations. We can also look at the role somewhat differently, with the result that what the school social worker does may not change substantially, but his or her perspective will.

SYSTEMS CHANGE SPECIALIST   Alan Pincus and Anne Minahan postulate that the focus of social work practice should be between people and systems in the social environment.[46] If we then look at schools as a natural access point for families (most families must deal with schools at some point in their existence), social workers should be able to perform a truly unique role in the schools. Given the complex nature of society today, most people need to enhance their problem-solving abilities. Social workers can help in this regard, while they link people to systems and improve existing service and delivery mechanisms. This role model can involve situations of equal access or integration, the development of programs to deal with changing family patterns, or issues relating to the quality of education. Schools are a critical link in the total societal resource system. Indeed, the neighborhood school is often the system with which the average citizen feels most comfortable. Thus, we must examine the school and look for the inadequacies in its educational structure. The questions we need to answer are, What do we really need in order to determine success for the student, and how can we use the materials and personnel in the most efficient way? Through a system of assessing present data, determining goals, and forming active systems for the purpose of exercising influence, one can answer the above questions and ultimately build a better, more accessible, more demand-based school program.

The social worker has a large role to play in this process, for he or she can become an organizer, a leader, a catalyst toward change, a liaison for the needs and wishes of the families, and a specialist in devising systems to meet change-oriented goals. Typical focuses are discovering (*a*) the particular deficiencies in the school and the community, (*b*) the under- or unserved population, and (*c*) the programs that are needed to get children back in school and to curb juvenile delinquency. Another focus might be to analyze the interaction between systems components in the schools, or

between the schools and the county departments of social services to see, for example, if these components are really working together or if they have underlying assumptions that work at cross purposes.

As a systems change specialist, a social worker is an institutional change agent, a person analyzing ongoing programs and proposed new programs. The systems change approach seeks to change the goals of the traditional school social worker. The traditional goals were to help the child adapt to the school, to use the learning opportunities available, and to modify student behavior or parent-child relationships to alleviate problems in the school. With the systems approach these goals are changed to analyze which parts of the system are activating stress in a given situation and then to alter that system so that its equilibrium is again in balance. One must find and prioritize targets for change, acknowledging that different approaches must be used to solve different problems.

This approach should be clearer if we analyze a typical problem, as described in Box 9.3, that could be referred to a school social worker. By reevaluating and refocusing the problem, the goals of a systems change specialist should become clearer and more meaningful.

SUMMARY

Education, which in the past has been called on to resolve a variety of social problems, is now recognized as a social problem itself. Education is currently facing a variety of crises and problematic areas.

There are a number of indicators that raise questions about the quality of education in this country. For example, scores on the Scholastic Aptitude Test, which is taken annually by high school seniors, are significantly lower than they were twenty-five years ago.

A second problematic area is that school systems are providing inferior educational opportunities for the poor and for members of minority groups. Less money is spent per student on education in low-income school districts and in school districts in which

BOX 9.3

A Case Example of the Systems Change Role

John is a 10-year-old boy in a special education class. He is in that class because he is considerably behind the rest of his age group in reading and math. He also demonstrates some behavioral problems, particularly in stressful situations. He has not yet been termed EMR (educable mentally retarded), but as he gets older and does less well academically, he may ultimately be tested and found to have an IQ in the educable range. He is involved in a specialized program called mainstreaming, in which he is placed in a regular education class for physical education, music, art, and social studies. In the beginning of the year there was hope for further mainstreaming into remedial reading and math, but behavioral problems have interfered. A referral has been sent to the school social worker asking that a behavioral program be started and contending that mainstreaming should be stopped until further reassessment can be done. If one wishes only to put a "band-aid" on the problem, it would be relatively easy to start a behavioral program and withdraw the child from the situation. Seemingly, all could accept this "solution," but what would it do for John's learning?

Another way of approaching the problem, in a systems change role, is to form a group composed of the teacher, the support personnel, and the principal to discuss mainstreaming as a general educational goal and to form flexible school policies regarding it. Forming a better mainstreaming program in which John can be successful becomes the main goal, as the assumption is that other students are encountering similar difficulties and will also benefit from any change. At the same time the social worker must provide a support system for the regular education teacher involved with John. This could include (*a*) giving the teacher some general suggestions regarding behavioral management that are applicable to many children, (*b*) helping to find curriculum and materials that are interesting to John and applicable to the rest of the group, (*c*) forming a group of students around John who would display good modeling behaviors, (*d*) writing a contract with John in which he could agree to certain limited goals for himself within the classroom, and (*e*) making sure through classroom discussion in human relations that John has the potential for friendships in the regular education class. One could also support the special education teacher and continue to give reinforcement for mainstreaming students. Finally, one could make John's parents aware of the benefits of mainstreaming so that they could talk about it at home and generally tell John how desirable they thought it was. It is hoped that John's parents would then be more actively involved in his education, which would help to increase John's motivation to learn. Another goal would be to use this (or some other successful) mainstreaming effort to encourage more mainstreaming of additional students with other teachers.

As such, one is designing a planned change approach and recognizing motivations for change and problems resulting from change. John is the focus for a much larger problem and is not *the* problem. He is the *access point* for the interconnection between a number of systems: regular education teachers, special education teachers, children with behavioral problems, and children with learning disabilities. As far as the school social worker is concerned, John is a catalyst for the creation of a system that will better serve many children.

high proportions of minority students live. In our society, academic achievement is highly correlated with socioeconomic status.

A third problematic area is that there is considerable confusion about the desirable goals of education. There is agreement that schools should teach the basic skills of reading, writing, and arithmetic. However, there is controversy among different interest groups concerning the other learning goals that education should strive to attain.

There is currently a shortage of teachers and especially of quality teachers. Many factors are contributing to this shortage: low pay, low prestige, intolerable working conditions, and the availability of other job opportunities for women.

Two proposals for improving education in this country are to increase incentives for teachers and to improve the curriculum. One of the controversial proposed incentives for teaching is the creation of master teacher positions that would reward excellence in teaching. A major problem with seeking to improve the curriculum is a lack of agreement about what the curriculum should teach students.

Three proposals were presented for seeking to work toward equal education opportunities for low-income and minority students: (*a*) to reform school financing in order to spend an equal amount of money on each student's education, (*b*) to establish special compensatory educational programs for disadvantaged students, and (*c*) to integrate students from different ethnic and racial backgrounds into the same schools.

The chapter concluded with a summary of several role models for school social work practice. The role models that were described are caseworker, group worker, truant officer, counselor, parent liaison, advocate, behavioral specialist, mental health consultant, alcohol and other drug specialist, multidisciplinary team member, and systems change specialist.

Social workers, along with other professionals in the schools, can help achieve a real school without failure; that is, not a school system where failure is nonexistent, but a system in which failure is not critical but is only part of the learning process. In this way the dynamic context of the social work role can achieve its fullest potential, for the social worker is able to use combinations of numerous skills or methods to examine and creatively deal with problems.

School social workers cannot solve all of the problems in education. Difficulties with integration, differences over goals, problems with the quality of the teaching staff, and changing roles and expectations in the family are all very complex and demanding problems. However, new ideas and creative approaches, which can be developed within the role of a systems change specialist, can help the educational system address the problems of education and ultimately seek solutions.

NOTES

1. Quoted in Joseph Julian and William Kornblum, *Social Problems*, 5th ed. (Englewood Cliffs, NJ: Prentice-Hall, 1986), p. 368.
2. Lucia Solorzano, "Teaching in Trouble," *U.S. News & World Report*, May 26, 1986, pp. 52–54.
3. Julian and Kornblum, *Social Problems*, 5th ed., pp. 359–361.
4. Solorzano, "Teaching in Trouble," p. 53.
5. Ibid., p. 53.
6. Ibid., p. 53.
7. CNN Cable News Report, July 18, 1988.
8. Quoted in "Can Our Schools Be Saved?" *Newsweek*, p. 50.
9. See Harvey A. Averch et al., *How Effective Is Schooling? A Critical Synthesis and Review of Research Findings* (Englewood Cliffs, NJ: Educational Technology Publications, 1974).
10. James W. Coleman and Donald R. Cressey, *Social Problems*, 2d ed. (New York: Harper & Row, 1984), p. 106.
11. Manley Fleischman et al., *The Fleischman Report on the Quality, Cost, and Financing of Elementary and Secondary Education in New York State* (New York: Viking, 1974), p. 57.
12. Charles E. Silberman, *Crisis in the Classroom: The Remaking of American Education* (New York: Random House, 1970), pp. 79–112.
13. Aaron Cicourel and John Kitsuse, *The Educational Decision-Makers* (Indianapolis: Bobbs-Merrill, 1963), p. 51.
14. Silberman, *Crisis in the Classroom*, p. 128.

15. Coleman and Cressey, *Social Problems*, 2d ed., pp. 106–115.

16. Diane Ravitch, "Busing: The Solution That Has Failed to Solve," *New York Times*, December 21, 1975.

17. David G. Savage, "Mandatory Busing: Era Whose Time Has Passed," *Los Angeles Times*, July 1, 1982, p. 1.

18. Nancy H. St. John, *School Desegregation: Outcomes for Children* (New York: Wiley, 1975), p. 36.

19. Ibid., pp. 64–86.

20. Julian and Kornblum, *Social Problems*, 5th ed., p. 359.

21. "A Nation of Illiterates?" *U.S. News & World Report*, May 17, 1982, pp. 54–55.

22. Quoted in Solorzano, "Teaching in Trouble," p. 52.

23. Ibid., p. 52.

24. Ibid., p. 52.

25. Ibid., p. 52.

26. Ibid., p. 53.

27. Ibid., p. 54.

28. Ibid., p. 54.

29. Michael Rutter and associates quoted in W. William Salgank, "British Study Finds Sharp Differences in Schools," *Los Angeles Times*, November 22, 1979, Part VIII, pp. 1–2.

30. Michael Rutter, *15,000 Hours; Secondary Schools and Their Effects on Children* (Cambridge, MA: Harvard University Press, 1979).

31. Eigil Pederson and Therese Annette Faucher, with William W. Eaton, "A New Perspective on the Effects of First-Grade Teachers on Children's Subsequent Adult Status," *Harvard Educational Review* 48 (1978), pp. 1–31.

32. Solorzano, "Teaching in Trouble," pp. 52–57.

33. Christopher Jencks et al., *Inequality: A Reassessment of the Effects of Family and Schooling in America* (New York: Harper & Row, 1972), p. 222.

34. U.S. Bureau of the Census, *Statistical Abstract of the United States, 1987* (Washington, D.C.: U.S. Government Printing Office, 1987), p. 136.

35. See Mildred Sikkema, "The School Social Worker Serves as a Consultant," *Casework Papers* (New York: Family Service Association of America, 1955), pp. 75–82.

36. Alan Guskin and Samuel Guslan, *A Social Psychology of Education* (Reading, MA: Addison-Wesley, 1970), pp. 1–3.

37. Albert Ellis, *Humanistic Psychotherapy* (New York: McGraw-Hill, 1973), pp. 55–69.

38. Edward Jones and Harold Gerard, *Foundations of Social Psychology* (New York: John Wiley, 1967), pp. 83–92.

39. Rudolf Dreikurs, Bernice Grunwald, and Floy Pepper, *Maintaining Sanity in the Classroom* (New York: Harper & Row, 1971), pp. 17–21.

40. Joel Fisher, "Is Casework Effective?" *Social Work* 18 (January 1973), pp. 5–21.

41. Arthur Michaels, David Cournoyer, and Elizabeth Pinner, "School Social Work and Educational Goals," *Social Work* 24 (March 1979), pp. 138–141.

42. Ellis, *Humanistic Psychotherapy*, pp. 129–133.

43. See Mary J. McCormick, "Social Advocacy: A New Dimension in Social Work," *Social Casework* 51 (January 1970), pp. 3–11.

44. For more detailed discussion of behavior modification, see Beth Sulzer and G. Roy Mayer, *Behavior Modification Procedures for School Personnel* (New York: Holt, Rinehart & Winston, 1972).

45. Sidney Simon, *Values Clarification* (New York: Hart Publishing, 1972), pp. 10–21.

46. Allen Pincus and Anne Minahan, *Social Work Practice: Model and Method* (Itasca, IL: F. E. Peacock, 1973), pp. 3–9.

10

WORK-RELATED PROBLEMS AND SOCIAL WORK IN THE WORKPLACE

W hat do you do for a living?" is a question that is commonly asked when two strangers meet. Work is a central focus of our lives. Work not only enables a person to earn money to pay bills, it can also provide a sense of self-respect, provide a circle of colleagues and friends, and be a source of self-fulfillment. A challenging job can help a person to grow intellectually, psychologically, and socially. Work also largely determines a person's place in the social structure. We have considerable choice in the vocations we select, and vocational choice largely determines our social status. We are largely defined by our work.

In our society we highly value the "work ethic"; that is, we consider work to be honorable, productive, and useful. Unemployed, able-bodied persons are often looked down on. The importance of work is shown in a study by Nancy Morse and Robert Weiss. They asked: "If by some chance you inherited enough money to live comfortably without working, do you think that you would work anyway, or not?" Eighty percent of the respondents stated they would prefer to keep on working.[1]

This chapter will:

- Present a brief history of work.
- Describe three major problems involving work: alienation, unemployment, and occupational health hazards.
- Summarize current efforts and proposed new approaches to combat these problems.
- Describe social work in the workplace, which is an emerging field of social work practice.

A BRIEF HISTORY OF WORK

Work has not always been so esteemed. The ancient Greeks, for example, viewed work as a curse imposed on humanity by the gods. Work was thought to be an unpleasant and burdensome activity that was incompatible with being a citizen. Citizens sought to have extensive leisure time so they could further develop

Transit workers rally in support of striking machinists at Eastern Airlines, whose 1989 walkout led the carrier to bankruptcy and brought to a head one of the most bitter labor-management disputes in years.

their minds. The Greeks therefore used slaves and justified slavery on the basis that it freed citizens to spend their time in philosophic contemplation and cultural enrichment. Aristotle remarked, "No man can practice virtue who is living the life of a mechanic or laborer."[2]

Although the Romans viewed commercial banking as acceptable employment, practically all other occupations were considered vulgar and demeaning.

The ancient Hebrews viewed work ambivalently. On one hand they regarded work as a drudgery and a grim necessity. On the other hand they saw it as a penance for Original Sin, which began with the disobedience of Adam and Eve.

The early Christians took a slightly more positive view of work. Like the ancient Hebrews, they accepted the idea of work as doing penance for Original Sin. But they also believed that people needed to work to make their own living and to be able to help those in need.

They also thought work had spiritual value, and they associated it with purification and self-denial. Interestingly, Christian monks thought it was degrading for them to work; they considered it was morally better for them to beg than to work.

The Protestant Reformation, which began in the 17th century, brought about profound changes in social values concerning work. Work became highly valued for the first time. One of the Protestant reformers, Martin Luther, asserted that labor was a service to God. Since the time of Luther, work has continued to be viewed as honorable and as having religious significance.

Another Protestant reformer, John Calvin, had an even more dramatic effect on changing the views toward work. Calvin preached that work is the will of God. Hard work, good deeds, and success at one's vocation were taken to be signs that one was destined for

BOX 10.1

Job Dissatisfaction

Mary and Robert Buyze met in college and were married shortly after Mary graduated in 1987. Bob had graduated a year earlier. Bob majored in history and Mary in psychology. Both had the American dream of having a home in the suburbs, a motorboat, and two cars. With both having graduated from college, they were optimistic that they were well on their way. They fantasized about taking a yearly trip to such places as Acapulco, Europe, Jamaica, and Hawaii.

It is now six years later. Bob is 29 and Mary is 28. They have yet to take a trip and now have two young children. They are deeply in debt, having tried to buy much of their dream with credit. They did buy a run-down "starter" home with two bedrooms that was advertised as a "fixer's delight." Unexpected repairs to the furnace, the roof, and the plumbing have plunged them even further into debt, as have the medical expenses, food, and clothing for the family.

What is even sadder is they both have jobs they dislike. Bob is a life insurance salesman and has held the job with a small company for the past three and one-half years. Bob states:

I took the job because I couldn't find anything else. There were no job openings for historians when I graduated, so I took a variety of odd jobs, none of which I enjoyed. I was a truck driver, manager of a pizza place, taxicab driver, car salesman—and much of the time I was unemployed.

I hoped when I took this job that I would finally be able to make good money. It just hasn't worked out. I hate selling insurance. Most of the time I go door-to-door and beg people to buy a policy. It's like begging for money for a charity. I absolutely despise having to put myself in a position of peddling policies—and being nice and charming to people who at times end up slamming the door in my face. But I have no choice. I've got so many bills to pay that I can't afford not to work. I also hate to see Mary having to work with the kids being so young. But, again we have no choice. What really hurts is that both of us are slaving away

salvation. Calvin preached that God's will was that people should live frugally (that is, spend very little money) and should use profits from work to invest in new ventures, which in turn would bring in more profits for additional investments, and so on. Hard work and frugality came to have great value. Idleness or laziness came to be viewed as sinful. One religious group that was most influenced by Calvin's teachings was the Puritans. The Puritans also developed a strong ascetic lifestyle: that is, the practice of denying worldly pleasures as a demonstration of religious discipline. Calvin's

teachings were widely accepted and formed a new cultural value system that became known as the Protestant ethic. This ethic has three core values: hard work, frugality, and asceticism.

The values of hard work and saving that were advanced by the Protestant ethic have continued throughout our history. For example, Benjamin Franklin cleverly praised these values with:

A penny saved is a penny earned.

Time is money.

at jobs we don't like. Yet with all the bills we have to pay, we hardly are able to buy Christmas presents.

Mary is a clothing store clerk. She also was unable to get a job in her field (psychology). After graduating she worked as a typist for two years, which paid about the same as her present job—slightly above the minimum wage. She quit being a typist shortly before their first child (Rob) was born; she disliked secretarial work even more than her present job. A few months after Rob was born she began working part time in the job she now holds full time.

Mary states:

When I was in college I guess I was too idealistic. I expected to get a challenging job that would help me grow as a person and also pay well. That just hasn't happened. What I earn now is very little, especially after having to pay the babysitter. This job at times is boring, especially during the months when business is slow. November and December are just the opposite—we're running all the time, and I'm exhausted by the end of the day. It's feast or famine. But my day doesn't end when I leave the store. I've got cooking, washing, and cleaning to do—plus trying to find time to spend with the children. The last four years since the kids were born have been a nightmare—changing diapers, getting up in the middle of the night, taking care of sick kids. Don't get me wrong—I wouldn't trade them in, but some days I really wonder where I went wrong. What really hurts is that we have almost nothing to show for our efforts.

I tell you, some mornings I'm so worn out when I get up and so unhappy with work that tears roll out of my eyes when I drive to work. What's just as bad is that I know that Bob hates his job as much as I do. Increasingly, when he has a bad day, he drinks too much—and that is getting me worried. I'm in a dead-end job with no chance for advancement, and I can't afford to give it up. Is this all there is to life?

After industry and frugality, nothing contributes more to the raising of a young man than punctuality.

He who sits idle . . . throws away money.

Waste neither time nor money; an hour lost is money lost.[3]

Former President Nixon, in a speech on welfare reform, declared that labor had intrinsic value, that it had a strong American tradition, and that it was consistent with religious teachings. Nixon added, "Scrubbing

floors and emptying bedpans have just as much dignity as there is in any work done in this country—including my own. . . . Most of us consider it immoral to be lazy or slothful."[4]

Although we no longer value the frugal, ascetic lifestyle of puritanism, we still believe strongly in the ethic of hard work. An able-bodied person, to gain approval from others, is expected to be employed (or at least receiving job training). People on welfare are often "looked down" on. There still remains a strong link between amount of income and personal worth.

The more people are paid, the more highly they are regarded by others and the more highly they regard themselves.

A government report, *Work in America*, found that people in low-status jobs are generally unable to form a satisfying identity from their jobs. Having an assembly line job, for example, often leads workers to view themselves as being personally insignificant. They routinely perform the same task day in and day out—such as attaching nuts to bolts. Such jobs, *Work in America* noted, leads to a worker having "an overwhelming sense of inferiority: he cannot talk proudly to his children of his job, and feels he must apologize for his status."[5]

Because the status of our work has immense effects on our self-concept, having a degrading, boring, and dehumanizing job can have immense adverse effects on our psychological well-being. We judge ourselves not only by how much our job pays, but also on whether the job is challenging, satisfying, and helps us to grow and develop.

TRENDS IN THE AMERICAN WORK FORCE

Since the turn of the last century unions have generally been growing in power in this country, which has led to significant pay increases and fringe benefits for employees. Since 1980, however, the power balance between unions and management has shifted more toward management. Management in a number of businesses has been requesting that employees take zero wage increases (or even pay cuts), with the threat of moving the business elsewhere or closing the doors permanently. Employees have generally chosen, with considerable reluctance, to accept management's offers rather than to strike and risk losing their jobs.

In the past century the nature of work and the composition of the work force have changed radically in our society. Six changes seem especially prominent:

the increase in white-collar workers, the emergence of an employee society, specialization, changes in the sex and age composition of the work force, emphasis on intrinsic rewards, and emphasis on high technology.

Increase in White-Collar Workers

In colonial times most people made a living working on small farms, either on their own or as farm laborers for someone else. We have since moved from an agricultural economy to a modern industrial economy.

In 1900, 27 percent of the labor force were farm workers, and 18 percent were white-collar workers. In 1987 only 2 percent were farm workers, and approximately 50 percent were white-collar workers.[6] The immense productivity of our industrial system has made it possible for 2 percent of the work force to feed all of us! Farm workers (farmers, farmhands, and farm managers), once the largest occupational group, is now one of the smallest.

White-collar workers (professionals, clerical personnel, sales personnel, managers), once the smallest occupational group, is now the largest. This group surpassed the blue-collar workers in terms of numbers in 1956.

Work in industrial societies can be grouped into three categories: primary, secondary, and tertiary.

Primary industry is the gathering or extracting of undeveloped natural resources, such as farming, mining, or fishing. In the early stages of industrialization most workers are employed in this area.

Secondary industry involves turning raw materials into manufactured goods, such as processed food, steel, and automobiles. In the middle stages of industrialization most workers are employed in this area. Most of these workers are blue-collar workers.

Tertiary industry involves service activities of one kind or another, such as dental care, medical services, automobile maintenance, sales, and pest control. In advanced societies such as ours, most workers are employed in service activities, primarily those considered "white-collar" jobs. Now, over 60 percent of our work force is employed in tertiary industry. Work in this area is generally cleaner and more pleasant than in primary and secondary industries.

Emergence of an Employee Society

No longer are Americans apt to be self-employed, as they generally were in colonial times. Less than 10 percent of the work force now classify themselves as self-employed.[7] A few small-business owners, small family-owned farms, independent shopkeepers, and independent carpenters and artists still remain. But small, owner-operated businesses increasingly are finding it difficult to compete against well-organized corporations and businesses. The vast majority of workers are employed by someone else: large corporations, government, unions, and so forth. Even physicians, who once were largely self-employed as general practitioners, are now generally working for a medical clinic or some other organization.

Specialization

The 1850 census listed a total of only 323 distinct job titles in the United States.[8] There are now over 35,000 job titles—an increase of over 100 times as many different occupations.[9] Some of the unusual jobs one can choose for a career are clock winder, tea taster, and water smeller. With this extensive specialization the producing of products is now fragmented into repetitive and monotonous tasks, with each worker contributing only a small portion of the final product. A worker on an assembly line commented:

The assembly line is no place to work, I can tell you. There is nothing more discouraging than having a barrel beside you with 10,000 bolts in it and using them all up. Then you get a barrel with another 10,000 bolts, and you know every one of those 10,000 bolts has to be picked up and put in exactly the same place as the last 10,000 bolts.[10]

Specialization has contributed substantially to highly sophisticated products and services being developed and provided. But it has also created problems. Workers find it difficult to have much pride in their work when they realize they are merely a replaceable adjunct to a machine or a process, and when they contribute only a small part to the final product. Such specialization often results in job dissatisfaction. Those who are trained for a single, narrowly defined job, which later becomes obsolete, are often without marketable skills for other openings. Specialization has also created problems of worker cooperation and coordination that present difficult problems for managers of organizations. Finally, our society has become highly interdependent because of specialization.

With interdependence, disruption in one work area may gravely affect the whole economy. In 1981, for example, 13,000 air traffic controllers went out on strike, seriously disrupting air travel and the entire U.S. economy, which is heavily dependent on air transportation.

Changes in the Sex and Age of the Labor Force

The labor force consists of people 16 years of age and over who are employed or who are actively seeking work (the unemployed). There are some significant trends in the composition of the labor force that will be briefly summarized.

Older men are less likely to be in the labor force. In 1954, 40 percent of males over age 65 were in the labor force, but by 1987 less than 16 percent of this category were in the labor force.[11] Employers are reluctant to hire older workers when younger workers are available, with more recent training, at lower salaries. Myths about the unproductivity of the older workers and job obsolescence also make it difficult for unemployed older workers to be hired.

Women are increasingly entering the labor force. In 1900 only 20 percent of all adult women were in paid employment, compared to over 50 percent at present.[12] Women, however, still tend to be employed

BOX 10.2

Max Weber and the Protestant Ethic

In 1904 the German sociologist Max Weber published what has become one of the most provocative theories in sociology. In *The Protestant Ethic and the Spirit of Capitalism* Weber asserted that the Protestant ethic encouraged and made possible the emergence of capitalism. Weber theorized that the ideas of puritanism (advocated by Martin Luther and John Calvin) provided the value system that led to the transformation from traditional society to the Industrial Revolution.

Weber noted that puritan Protestantism embraced the doctrine that people were divinely selected for either salvation or damnation. There was nothing people could do to alter their fate. No one knew for sure whether she or he was destined for eternal salvation or eternal damnation. However, people looked for signs from God to suggest their fate. Because they also believed that work was a form of service to God, they concluded that success at work (making profits) was a sign of God's favor. They therefore worked very hard to accumulate as much wealth as possible.

Because the Protestant ethic viewed luxury and self-gratification as sinful, the profits acquired were not spent on luxuries or spent extravagantly. Instead, profits were reinvested into new ventures to increase incomes.

Such new ventures included building factories and developing new machines. Thus, according to Weber, the Industrial Revolution began, and capitalism was born.

Source: Max Weber, *The Protestant Ethic and the Spirit of Capitalism*, rereleased (New York: Charles Scribner's Sons, 1958).

---

in the less prestigious, lower-paying positions, as indicated in Chapter 12.

Two groups that have historically had high rates of unemployment and received low pay if employed have been minority group workers and teenage workers. Unemployment rates are particularly high for nonwhite, teenager workers: In some cities more than 50 percent of persons in this category are unemployed. As noted in Chapter 12, women who work full time are paid, on the average, only about 65 percent of what men who work full time are paid. Nonwhite women, subjected to double discrimination, earn even less.

Emphasis on Intrinsic Rewards

Intrinsic rewards are rewards that come from the nature of the work itself. Such rewards include having work that is fulfilling and challenging, helps one grow socially and emotionally, contributes to physical fitness, promotes a sense of accomplishment through the use of one's talents, gives a person a feeling of self-respect, provides interest and enjoyment, provides an opportunity to meet new friends, and so on. In the past, people primarily took a job for its extrinsic rewards—usually to receive a paycheck that would enable them to pay their bills. In the last thirty years William Glasser has noted that workers are increasingly concerned about the intrinsic rewards prospective job opportunities will provide.[13]

Emphasis on High Technology

Our society is increasingly developing an economy that emphasizes high technology, such as computers and communication. Automation and robots are now doing more of the work that was previously done by blue-collar workers.

Technology is a double-edged sword. Every major technological innovation has both freed humans from previous hardships and created new, unanticipated problems. For example, the development of nuclear power is an important source of energy, but a nuclear mishap has the potential to kill thousands (and even millions) of people. Technology can be defined as the totality of means employed to provide objects necessary for human comfort and sustenance. Daniel Bell defines technological change as "the combination of all methods (apparatus, skills, organization) for increasing the productivity of labor and capital."[14]

Technological innovations are causing major changes in the types of work available to Americans. Blue collar and agricultural jobs are declining, and jobs in high-technology fields (such as computers and communications) are increasing. For example, between 1975 and 1982, employment in the production of scientific instruments and engineering increased by about 23 percent, whereas employment in textile mill products decreased by 15 percent.[15] People who are laid off or discharged in industries (such as the steel industry) in which jobs are declining face immense obstacles in obtaining employment that pays comparable wages. On the other hand, people who are trained for high-tech positions have excellent career opportunities. In the employment market technological advances are a boon for some and a disaster for others. Automobile executives welcome the coming of robots to the assembly line, since robots will cut production costs. Unemployed assembly line workers with house mortgages will probably curse the use of robots.

There is a growing concern among many educational, political, and civil rights leaders that as our society comes to depend increasingly on computers and other technological innovations, only a select portion of the population will have the skills needed to function well in our society. Those who lack such skills may find themselves trapped in lower social-class positions.

PROBLEMS IN THE WORK SETTING

Alienation

Alienation has a specific sociological meaning. *It is the sense of meaninglessness and powerlessness that people experience when interacting with social institutions they consider oppressive and beyond their control.*

The term *worker alienation* was originally developed by Karl Marx. (Perhaps because Marx has been associated with communism, the subject of alienation has tended to be neglected in our country.) Marx suggested that worker alienation occurs largely because workers are separated from ownership of the means of production and from any control over the final product of their labor. They feel powerless and view their work as meaningless. Marx described alienation as follows:

In what does this alienation consist? First, that work is external to the worker, that it is not part of his nature, that consequently he does not fulfill himself in his work but denies himself, has a feeling of misery, not well-being, does not develop freely a physical and mental energy, but is physically exhausted and mentally debased. . . . His work is not voluntary but imposed, forced labor. . . . Finally, the alienated character of work for the worker appears in the fact that it is not his work but work for someone else, that in work he does not belong to himself but to another person.[16]

Marx thought that specialization was a major cause of alienation. With specialization workers are forced to perform an unfulfilling task repeatedly. People use only a fraction of their talents. Work becomes an enforced, impersonalized activity rather than a creative venture.

Marx argued that worker alienation would eventually lead to such discontent that the workers would band together and revolt against owners. Marx thought another reason workers would revolt is because they would realize they were being exploited by the dominant class. They produce more than they get, with the dominant class prospering from their toil.

Marx's prediction of a class revolution has not occurred in the United States. Marx did not foresee the effectiveness of collective bargaining and new technology in improving the conditions of workers during this century. Interestingly, even workers in such socialist countries as Russia and Poland experience considerable alienation. (Marx had predicted that alienation would be less in socialist countries.)

It may well be that much of the alienation that Marx attributed to capitalistic societies was really caused by industrialism. Workers in this country, contrary to what Marx predicted, continue to have basic trust and faith in the American capitalistic system. Many workers have made financial investments in stocks, bonds, real estate, savings, and so forth. To a significant extent, they are also part of the dominant class. Marx only saw a struggle between two classes—owners and workers. He did not foresee considerable overlap occurring between these classes, nor did he foresee the development of a large middle class that tends to include both investors and workers. Because of Americans' faith in our system and their disdain of Communism, it is highly unlikely that there will be a class revolution in our country in the foreseeable future.

It might be further noted that the working class has not successfully staged a socialist revolution in any industrialized country. The socialist revolutions that have occurred—Russia, China, Cuba, and so forth—have all occurred in developing or preindustrial countries. It is important to note that even China and Russia are increasingly using the profit motive (a key component of capitalism) as an incentive to work and as a method to stimulate their economies.

PRESENT SOURCES OF ALIENATION   There are many sources of alienation. Specialization has led workers to feel that they have a meaningless job and that they are contributing only a minor part to the business. It is difficult, for example, for assembly-line workers to take pride in producing an automobile when they only attach an ignition wire.

Working for a large business or corporation and knowing you can readily be replaced leads to a sense of feeling powerless and having a meaningless job. Not being involved in the decision-making process and being aware that supervisors do not want workers "to make waves" also lead to a feeling of powerlessness and meaninglessness.

In some businesses machines have been developed to do most of the work. This "automation" (for example, assembly lines in the auto industry) has led workers to feel they are insignificant cogs in the production process. Even the pace at which they work is controlled by the assembly-line machinery. Having a job in which one has little opportunity to be creative but instead repetitively does the same task has also contributed to alienation. Such jobs include being a typist, receptionist, janitor, garbage collector, assembly line worker, or telephone operator.

Jobs that do not provide opportunities to learn, that do not provide a sense of accomplishment, and that do not provide an opportunity to work with interesting or congenial people also lead to alienation. Many authorities believe that alienation leads to acts of disruption in the production process—work of poor quality, high rates of absenteeism, and vandalism or theft of company property.

JOB SATISFACTION AND DISSATISFACTION   Dissatisfaction with one's job is a useful indicator of alienation at work. Studies on job satisfaction show wide differences, according to vocation, in worker satisfaction with their job (see Table 10.1).

Table 10.1 suggests that many people, if given a choice, would select a different career. Yet it is noteworthy that when public opinion polls (Gallup and

TABLE 10.1

Percent of People in Occupational Groups Who Would Choose Similar Work Again

Professional and Lower White-Collar Occupations	Percent	Working-Class Occupations	Percent
Urban university professors	93	Skilled printers	52
Mathematicians	91	Paper workers	42
Physicists	89	Skilled autoworkers	41
Biologists	89	Skilled steelworkers	41
Chemists	86	Textile workers	31
Firm lawyers	85	Blue-collar workers, cross section	24
Lawyers	83		
Journalists, Washington correspondents	82	Unskilled steelworkers	21
		Unskilled autoworkers	16
Church university professors	77		
Solo lawyers	75		
White-collar workers, cross section	43		

Source: *Work in America: Report of a Special Task Force to the Secretary of Health, Education, and Welfare* (Cambridge, MA: M.I.T. Press, 1973), p. 16.

other polls) ask people if they are satisfied with their job, over 80 percent consistently answer yes.[17] At present it is unclear why some approaches to measuring job satisfaction show high levels of satisfaction, whereas other approaches suggest that large numbers of workers are sufficiently dissatisfied that they would choose another occupation if given a choice.

Although the amount of pay received is an important factor in worker satisfaction, it appears it is not the most important factor. The *Work in America* report asked workers to rank various aspects in order of importance. Respondents gave the following ranking:

1. Interesting work.
2. Enough help and equipment to get the job done.
3. Enough information to get the job done.
4. Enough authority to get the job done.
5. Good pay.
6. Opportunity to develop special abilities.
7. Job security.
8. Seeing the results of one's work.[18]

Morton reviewed a number of studies on job satisfaction and identified the following factors as the sources of job satisfaction.

Psychological satisfaction: A satisfactory job provides a sense of accomplishment, provides an opportunity to learn, is closely matched to a worker's

Jobs that call for little creativity are apt to be alienating.

interests and abilities, and provides an opportunity to work with congenial or interesting people.

Monetary compensation: Workers tend to be satisfied when they feel they are paid fairly.

Physical factors: Job satisfaction is increased when the setting is pleasant, when the setting is viewed as free from hazards, when commuting time to work is short, and when transportation to work is readily available.

Control: Workers are more satisfied in jobs in which they feel they have some decision-making responsibilities and some control over their work schedules. Punching a time clock is disliked, whereas flexitime is appealing. Flexitime seeks to reduce alienation from work by making work schedules more flexible. The idea is to have most

workers present during the busiest time of the day but to leave the remaining hours and days per week up to the discretion of the workers. Those who want to start earlier, so they can leave earlier, can do so. Those who want to start later and work later can do so. In some places it is possible with flexitime to work four days a week (ten hours per day) and thereby have an extra day off.

Institutional aspects: Workers are more satisfied with jobs that have promotion from within policies, training programs, personnel policies that assure equal opportunity for advancement and education, and good physical facilities and conveniences—lounges, cafeterias, gyms, and the like.

Economic, political, and social aspects: The national mood affects job satisfaction. In the late

1960s and 1970s there was severe discontent and controversy about the Vietnam War, which lowered job satisfaction. On the other hand, a feeling of national prosperity increases job satisfaction.[19]

Daniel Yankelovich has noted that in the last thirty years there have been changes in the factors that contribute to worker satisfaction.[20] The affluence of the late 1950s, the 1960s, and the 1970s has led to a "New Breed" of workers. Also better educated, they not only are concerned about the traditional rewards of salary and fringe benefits, but also place a greater value on individuality, independence, and the intrinsic rewards the job will provide. They identify less with their jobs than did their parents and are less loyal to employers. They are also more concerned about leisure time and whether they will have enough leisure time to devote to their personal growth and individual interests. New Breed workers seek jobs that will provide opportunities to use and develop their job talents. Flexitime and staggered hours are very appealing to these workers. One study found that many workers are willing to remain in a job they dislike if the job has flexible work schedules.[21]

CONFRONTING ALIENATION AND JOB DISSATISFACTION
One of the best known efforts to increase worker satisfaction and productivity was that of Hawthorne Works, a division of Western Electric Company in Chicago. The results were surprising, as described in Box 10.3.

Many employers have become aware that job dissatisfaction often reduces efficiency and productivity. There are a number of ways to increase job satisfaction. The first step is to find out precisely what the workers are dissatisfied about and then seek to make changes. In one job setting workers may be most concerned about safety conditions (as in coal mining); in another they may be most concerned about boring, repetitive work (as on an assembly line); in another it may be wages (as for jobs that only pay at or above the minimum wage); in another it may be lack of recognition (as for clerical workers who make their supervisors look good).

There are a wide variety of changes that can be made to improve job satisfaction. The following list is far from exhaustive.

Find ways to make the work challenging and interesting.

Provide opportunities for career advancement.

Provide inservice training on aspects related to the work—for example, stress-management programs for stressful jobs.

Increase wages, salaries, and fringe benefits.

Involve workers in the decision-making process.

Have social get-togethers to help increase group morale.

Improve the physical facilities to make the work experience more pleasant and enjoyable.

Give workers a share of the profits through a profit-sharing program.

Have a reward system to recognize significant contributions made by workers.

Have employee policies that generate a sense of job security.

Have policies that allow workers to have some control over the hours they work—for example, flexitime.

Make the work setting as free of hazards as possible.

Some of the more successful efforts to increase worker satisfaction will be described.

Control Data Institute, Metropolitan Life Insurance, many government agencies, and many other private companies are now on flexitime.[22] Although supervisors have found it is more difficult to coordinate work schedules when using flexitime, it has also been found that absenteeism declines and productivity increases.

Many European and Japanese companies are using plans that involve workers in decision making. Giving workers decision-making input can be done in a variety of ways. One way is for workers to become members of workers' councils that meet regularly with management officials. In such meetings workers can air their gripes—which in itself has a ventilating effect in reducing job dissatisfaction. In such meetings workers not only identify problems that reduce productivity, they also often have valuable suggestions for alleviating these concerns. Some firms have gone a step further by appointing worker representatives to their boards

BOX 10.3

The Hawthorne Effect

T he Hawthorne Works of the Western Electric Company in Chicago in 1927 began a series of experiments designed to discover ways to increase worker satisfaction and worker productivity. Hawthorne Works primarily manufactured telephones, with the plant operating on an assembly-line basis. Workers needed no special skills in this production process and performed simple, repetitive tasks. The workers were not unionized, and management sought to find ways to increase productivity. It was thought if they found ways to increase job satisfaction, the employees would work more efficiently, and productivity would increase.

The company tested a number of factors to examine the effects on productivity. These factors included rest breaks, better lighting, changes in the number of work hours during the day, changes in the wages paid, improved food facilities, and so on.

The results were surprising. Productivity increased, as expected, with improved working conditions; but it also increased when working conditions worsened. This latter finding was unexpected and led to additional study to find an explanation.

The investigators discovered that participation in the experiments was extremely attractive to the workers. They felt they had been selected by the management for their individual abilities, and so they worked harder, even when working conditions became less favorable. There were additional reasons. The workers' morale and general attitude toward work improved, as they felt they were receiving special attention from management. By participating in this study they were able to work in smaller groups, and they also became involved in making decisions. Working in smaller groups allowed them to develop a stronger sense of solidarity with their fellow workers. Being involved in making decisions decreased feelings of meaninglessness and powerlessness about their work.

The results of this study have become known as the "Hawthorne effect" in sociological and psychological research. The Hawthorne effect holds that when subjects know they are participants in a study, this awareness may lead them to behave differently and substantially influence the results of the study.

Source: Fritz J. Roethlisberger and William J. Dickson, *Management and the Worker* (Cambridge, MA: Harvard University Press, 1939).

of directors. Chrysler Corporation in this country in 1980 took this approach by appointing to its board a representative from the United Auto Workers (the union for auto workers). It is expected that worker participation in the decision-making process will not only lead to suggestions for improving productivity but will also reduce feelings of alienation and job dissatisfaction.

General Foods redesigned its work assignments to reduce alienation. Extensive efforts were made to make the work challenging and to eliminate the dull, routine jobs. The repetitive jobs that could not be eliminated were shared among several workers so that no one was permanently stuck with a tedious task. In addition, General Foods abolished status symbols (for example, assigned parking stalls, types of office furniture, separate cafeterias) for different ranks of workers. Productivity was found to increase sharply.[23]

Corning Glass improved productivity in the hot plate division by allowing each worker to assemble hot plates fully and also to add his or her initial to the finished product. Before this change each worker assembled only a small part of the hot plate. Workers were also encouraged to form their own small group of workers to conduct quality checks. A six-month review of these changes found that productivity had increased by 47 percent, that absenteeism had declined, and that hot plate rejects had dropped from 23 percent to 1 percent of output.[24]

Several American companies have increased productivity through conducting "climate surveys," in which workers are asked to vent their concerns and to criticize their jobs. Sometimes such surveys identify problematic situations that can be improved through relatively minor changes. Even when the problems cannot be resolved, work tensions are often temporarily reduced by allowing workers to let off steam.[25]

Unemployment

THE COSTS OF UNEMPLOYMENT   As illustrated in Box 10.4, unemployment can have devastating effects. Most obvious, it reduces (sometimes to below poverty lev-els) the amount of income that a family or single person receives. Short-term unemployment, especially when receiving unemployment compensation (described in Chapter 3), may have only minor effects. But long-term unemployment may have numerous adverse effects.

Harold Wilensky found that long-term unemployment often leads to extreme personal isolation. Work is a central part of many people's lives. When unemployment occurs, work ties are cut, and many of the unemployed see friends less, cut their participation in community life, and increasingly became isolated.[26]

D. D. Braginsky and B. M. Braginsky found that long-term unemployment causes attitude changes that persist even after reemployment.[27] Being laid off (or let go) is often interpreted by the unemployed as a sign of being incompetent and worthless. Self-esteem is lowered, they are apt to experience depression, and they feel alienated from society. Many suffer deep shame and avoid their friends. They feel dehumanized, insignificant, and that they are an easily replaced statistic. They also tend to lose faith in our political and economic system, with some blaming our political system for their problems. Even when they find new jobs, they do not fully recover their self-esteem.

Harvey Brenner found a strong association between unemployment and emotional problems. During an economic recession he found that mental hospital admissions increase. The suicide rate also increases, indicating an increase in depression. Also higher during times of high unemployment are the divorce rate, the incidence of child abuse, and the number of peptic ulcers (a stress-related disease).[28]

The National Advisory Commission on Civil Disorders noted in 1967 that unemployment and underemployment are key factors in leading to civil disorder.

Employment problems have drastic social impact in the ghetto. Men who are chronically unemployed or employed in the lowest status jobs are often unable or unwilling to remain with their families. The handicap imposed on children growing up without fathers in an atmosphere of poverty and deprivation is increased as mothers are forced to work to provide support.

BOX 10.4

American Dream Becomes Economic Nightmare through Unemployment

Lorraine and Jim Dedrick thought they had it made. They had a five-bedroom, stone-foundation home on a lake, a landscaped yard, two well-behaved children, a car, a van, a motor-powered boat, and a sailboat. The home, the vehicles, and the boats were bought on time payments. Because both were working they were confident they could easily make the monthly payments. Mrs. Dedrick describes what happened.

My husband worked at Dana Corporation in Edgerton (Wisconsin). (Dana Corporation was a car and truck-axle manufacturing plant.) He was a crew supervisor and was making over $23,000 a year. I was, and still am, a legal secretary for a firm in Madison.

When the layoffs started in spring 1979, we didn't think it would touch Jim. He had six years of seniority. But by March of 1980 we knew a layoff was inevitable. Neither Dana nor the whole American auto industry was doing well. When the layoff came in June of 1980, we weren't surprised.

At first we weren't worried. Jim thought it would be nice to have a summer off and looked forward to doing some fishing and some fixing up around the house. Because he was 39 years old and had worked steadily since he was 18, I also thought a few months break would do him good. He was of course able to draw unemployment benefits, and with my salary I was certain we could get by. Surely the auto industry would recover, and he would be called back in the fall.

In late summer, however, a rumor started and quickly spread throughout the plant that Dana was going to close its plant in Edgerton. In September they announced the plant was going to close.

Both of us immediately became alarmed. Jim started looking for other work in earnest. Unfortunately, there were no comparable jobs in the area—and for that matter the whole auto industry was suffering.

Jim applied at many different jobs, but had no luck. I know of nothing worse than to see a once proud, secure person come home each evening with the look on his face that he has once again been rejected. Jim began developing stomach problems from the rejections, and I started having, and still have, tension headaches. We used to go out a lot, laugh, and have a good time. Now, we not only cannot afford it, we no longer have an interest.

The culture of poverty that results from unemployment and family breakup generates a system of ruthless exploitative relationships within the ghetto. . . . Children growing up under such conditions are likely participants in civil disorder.[29]

In many cases the long-term unemployed are forced to exhaust their savings, sell their homes, and become public assistance recipients. A few turn to crime, particularly the young. The unemployed no longer enjoy the companionship of their fellow workers. They are apt to experience feelings of embarrassment, anger, despair, depression, anxiety, boredom, hopelessness, and apathy. Such feelings may lead to

Jim grabbed at every straw. He even went to apply for jobs in Milwaukee and Chicago. In the last year he appears to have aged ten years.

In February of 1981 his unemployment benefits ended. Bill collectors began hounding us. We soon depleted all our savings. We got so many calls from bill collectors that we took out an unlisted telephone number. Never before were we unable to pay our bills.

The months since February have been hell. Increasingly we have gotten into arguments. Whenever I bring my check home, Jim has a pained look on his face, as he feels he's not doing his share. I try to tell him that it's not his fault, but whenever we talk about it he gets hurt and angry.

At the end of February he began to advertise by word of mouth that he was an independent carpenter. He's good with his hands. Unfortunately, the few jobs he got have as yet not even paid for the extra tools he's had to buy. It has only gotten us deeper into debt.

When I drive to work, the tears often fall. It's my only time alone. Driving home I often cry as I think about our situation and know I'll have to face Jim's sad look.

We don't associate much with friends now. They either pity us or have that arrogant "I told you so" look in response to our optimism when Jim was first laid off.

It just doesn't look like Jim is going to be able to get a job in this area. Next week he's going to go to Houston, Texas—we've heard there are a lot of job openings there. (It was August 1981 when Mrs. Dedrick discussed her family's plight.)

Dennis, our 12-year-old son, is alternately sad and angry about the possibility of leaving this area. He's got a lot of friends and loves to go boating, fishing, and sailing. Having to take your son away from something he really loves is one of the most difficult things I'll probably ever have to do.

Karen, our daughter who's 15, really had a bad year at school. Her grades fell, and when we asked why, she said, "What's the use in studying—won't help in getting a job." That remark hurt deeply, probably because it may have a ring of truth in it.

It looks like we're going to have to give up our dream house on this lake. (Tears came to Mrs. Dedrick as she spoke.) We've lived here for the past five years and really loved it. This is our first real home. We've added on a patio, a bedroom, and enlarged the living room. We also spent a lot of time in painting and fixing it up. It's really become a part of us. If Jim gets a job in Texas, we'll be forced to sell. We checked what market prices are, and there's no way we're going to get what we put into this house.

A few years ago we thought we were starting to live the American dream. This past year and a half has been hell. Here we are broke, unhappy, and about to lose our home. At our age starting life over is almost more than we can take.

alcoholism, drug abuse, insomnia, psychosomatic illnesses, marital unhappiness, and even violence within the family. The work ethic is still prominent in our society: When people lose their jobs they devalue themselves and also miss the sense of self-worth that comes from doing a job well.

Widespread unemployment can have devastating effects on society. Those still working are apt to fear they may lose their jobs. Severe unemployment leads to disenchantment with (and sometimes even rebellion against) political and social institutions. Widespread unemployment also cuts sharply government tax revenues. When tax revenues are reduced, governmental units are then forced to cut services at a time when services are most needed. Such cuts further add to alienation and despair.

High unemployment also leads to high rates of underemployment. Underemployment is where people are working at jobs below their level of skill. A sizable number of people who are unemployed during periods of high unemployment are forced to take whatever jobs are available. College graduates, for example, may be forced to take unskilled road construction work or become clerical workers.

WHO ARE THE UNEMPLOYED?   In the past several years the unemployment rate nationally has ranged from 4 percent to 11 percent. Official statistics on the rate of unemployment are compiled by the Bureau of Labor Statistics. The Bureau, usually monthly, makes a survey of households randomly selected from the total population.

Practically every worker risks being unemployed, and most are unemployed sometime during their working years. There is some variation from time to time in the groups that are subjected to unemployment. In the late 1970s and early 1980s unemployment was particularly high among steel workers and automobile workers. In the late 1970s schoolteachers had high unemployment rates. In the middle 1970s PhDs in the liberal arts and social sciences had high unemployment rates. In the early 1980s the housing industry was in a slump, and there were high unemployment rates among carpenters and construction workers. In the middle and late 1980s there were high rates of unemployment among workers in the petroleum production industry.

There are groups, however, that have chronically high unemployment rates. These groups include minorities, teenagers, women, older workers, the unskilled, and the semiskilled.

High unemployment among racial minorities is partly due to discrimination, which makes it more difficult to obtain employment. Unfortunately, there is truth in the cliche that minorities are "last to be hired, first to be fired." Another reason for high unemployment is due to their lower average level of educational achievement, which leaves them unqualified for many of the available jobs. (Lower educational achievement levels and lack of marketable job skills are largely due to *past* discrimination.)

High unemployment among women is also partly due to discrimination. Many employers (most of them men) are still inclined to hire a man before a woman, and many jobs are still erroneously thought to be "a man's job." Women have also been socialized to seek lower-paying jobs, to not be competitive with men, and to believe their place is in the home and not in the work force. (See Chapter 12 for a fuller discussion.)

There are many myths about older workers—age 40 and over—that make it more difficult to obtain a new job if they become unemployed. They are *erroneously* thought to be less productive, more difficult to get along with, more difficult to train, clumsier, more accident prone, less healthy, and more prone to absenteeism (see Chapter 13 for a further discussion of these myths, along with a review of research studies that refute these stereotypes). An additional problem for unemployed older workers is that younger workers are often available at salaries far below what the older applicants were paid at their last job.

Unemployment is high for teenagers and young people, partly because they have not received job-skill training that would provide them with marketable skills.

Employers are willing to hire unskilled workers when they have simple, repetitive tasks to be performed. But unskilled workers are the first to be laid off when there is a business slump. These workers can readily be replaced if business picks up. Highly skilled workers are more difficult to replace, and employers often have much more invested in skilled workers, as they have spent more time in training such workers.

Blue-collar workers are more affected by economic slumps than white-collar workers. Industries that employ large numbers of blue-collar workers— housing, road construction, manufacturers of heavy equipment such as tractors, the auto industry—are the ones that are most quickly and deeply affected and are often forced to lay off workers. As noted earlier the number of blue-collar jobs is decreasing, whereas white-collar jobs are increasing. A major reason for this decline is automation. *Automation* is the production technique in which the system of production is increasingly controlled by means of self-operating machinery.

Planting and harvesting machines have drastically reduced the number of people needed in producing food.

Examples of automation include the automobile assembly line and direct dialing of the telephone (which displaced thousands of telephone operators). Robots are now replacing workers in a number of industries—particularly in doing the simple, repetitive tasks.

REASONS FOR THE HIGH UNEMPLOYMENT RATE   The reasons for the high unemployment rate in this country are numerous and complex. First, it should be noted that even when a society has "full employment" there will always be some people capable of working who are temporarily unemployed. There will be some people who are changing jobs. There will be some recent graduates (and recent high school or college dropouts)

who have not yet found a job. And, there will be some people who have had a prolonged illness who are now starting to look for a job. It is for these reasons that most countries generally consider that they have full employment when the unemployment rate does not exceed 2 or 3 percent of the work force. Unfortunately, the unemployment rate in America in recent years has been considerably higher than 2 or 3 percent.

In many areas of the country there are more people in the work force than there are available jobs. Automation in many industries has reduced the number of workers needed and made certain job skills (such as blacksmith) obsolete. Planting and harvesting machines in agriculture, for example, have reduced

During World War II, British and American women entered the work force at record levels. The defense industries—shipbuilding, aircraft, and munitions—attracted the greatest number of new women workers. This crew cleans and paints England's "Whitely" bomber in 1942.

drastically the number of people needed in producing food. Picking beans, digging potatoes, and picking cotton and corn once required large numbers of workers, but such work is now done by machines.

From the end of World War II until around 1965 there was a "baby boom," when large numbers of children were born. For the past twenty-five years these baby-boom children have grown up and are entering the labor force in large numbers. The last few decades have also seen a dramatic change in women being liberated from the cultural expectation that they should remain at home. Millions of women are now employed or seeking full- or part-time work.

In the 1970s the oil-producing countries sharply increased the cost of a barrel of oil. Because practically all companies are dependent on oil for energy and in other ways, the price of most products increased. Because consumers were able to buy less, the demand for

products slackened. Companies had to reduce production, and layoffs occurred.

A decrease in orders of American products by foreign countries forces American companies to cut back their production and often to lay off workers.

Excessively dry summers in our country sharply reduce the amount of food produced. The law of supply and demand therefore drives up the price of available food. Consumers are less able to buy other products, and companies are then forced to cut back production and lay off workers.

High interest rates make it too costly for consumers to purchase homes, automobiles, and other expensive items that are normally purchased with a loan. The demand for such items goes down, and again businesses have to cut back production and lay off workers.

A major reason for the high unemployment rate in this country is that we have a structural unemployment problem, as large numbers of unemployed people are not trained for the positions that are open. In recent years a large number of blue-collar jobs have closed (as in the steel industry), while at the same time a number of high-skill jobs have opened in other areas (such as in the high-technology field of computers). As people become trained for current positions, the employment needs of our economy will continue to shift so that there will continue to be disharmony between skills needed for vacant positions and skills held by unemployed people.

FACTORS THAT REDUCE UNEMPLOYMENT   There are also many factors that increase the number of jobs and thereby reduce the unemployment rate. Lower interest rates encourage consumers to purchase more items through loans and by credit. Consumers buy more, stimulating companies to produce more to meet the demand and thereby to hire more people. Lower interest rates also have a direct effect on businesses. Businesses often borrow money to purchase capital items (for example, additional machines to produce their goods or buildings to expand the business) in order to increase the production. If interest rates are lower, businesses are more apt to borrow money to increase production—and when expansion in production occurs, additional jobs are usually created.

A war almost always reduces the unemployment rate. Some workers are drafted to fight as soldiers. Their former jobs are then available for those who are unemployed. In addition, it takes many additional jobs to provide the military with the products needed to fight a war—bullets, bombs, tanks, fighter planes, food, medicine, and so on.

Businesses and governments in many other countries take a much more paternalistic approach to employees and to assuring there will be jobs available for those who are unemployed. In the United States when an economic slump occurs, businesses usually lay off workers. By contrast, in Japan businesses are much less likely to lay off workers; they paternalistically seek to have their employees spend their entire working lives with the same company. Governments in many other countries attempt, when there is an economic slump, to create jobs for those who are unemployed. West Germany, for example, pays the unemployed to receive

work training. Russia and other countries in Eastern Europe have successfully controlled unemployment by creating government jobs—although some departments are at times considerably overstaffed.

The development of new products, widely wanted and used by the public, opens up many new jobs. The invention of the automobile, airplane, television set, hair dryer, and refrigerator have opened up many new jobs, not only for factory workers but also for managers, repair personnel, sales personnel, insurance personnel, and so on.

In the early 1960s the economy was in a slump, and the unemployment rate was fairly high. President Kennedy stimulated the economy through a tax cut to individuals and to businesses. With the tax cut individuals were able to buy more and businesses had additional money to reinvest so they could increase production. Kennedy's plan worked: The economy was stimulated, production increased, more jobs were created, and the unemployment rate went down. In the early 1980s we were again in an economic slump, with both a high inflation rate and a high unemployment rate. President Reagan's administration developed and implemented a plan to revitalize the economy. The plan involved giving tax cuts to individuals and to businesses, which were designed to stimulate production and create more jobs. The plan also involved immense cuts in federal spending for social welfare programs and for educational programs. Such cuts were made partly to reduce the inflation rate. (Big spending by the federal government has often been blamed for being a major contributor to inflation.) Reagan's plan largely worked. The economy was again stimulated, and the rates of unemployment and inflation were nearly cut in half. Unfortunately, massive tax cuts (along with sharp increases in military spending) have led to the emergence of other problems: a huge federal deficit that threatens to increase the inflation rate in the future and cuts in social programs that have increased the rates of poverty, homelessness, people going hungry, and a variety of other social problems. George Bush, who was elected president in 1988, has stated that one major focus of his economic program will be to seek to reduce the size of the federal deficit.

Economics is a complicated and complex area. Certainly it is a mistake to assume that tax cuts will always stimulate the economy, and lead to reductions in the rates of unemployment and inflation. For example, a case can be made that high rates of inflation and unemployment in the 1970s were due to rising oil prices and that drops in these rates in the 1980s were not due to tax cuts but to declining oil prices. Petroleum is the major source of energy in manufacturing practically all products. When the price of petroleum goes up, the costs of manufacturing products increases, which raises prices and results in inflation. When inflation occurs, the public cannot afford to buy as much, which results in an oversupply of goods. Industries then lay off workers, which increases the unemployment rate. When the price of petroleum goes down, the costs of manufacturing products goes down, which reduces the price and thereby reduces the rate of inflation. Also, the public is able to purchase more goods (because prices are lower), which reduces the supply of available goods. Industries are then stimulated to produce more goods, and they do so by hiring more employees, which reduces the unemployment rate.

CONFRONTING UNEMPLOYMENT   Economists agree that the ideal way to cure unemployment is through increased economic growth. Economists disagree, however, about the causes of a sluggish economy and about the best ways to stimulate such an economy.

It should be noted that rapid economic growth will probably reduce substantially the rate of unemployment. But it is a mixed blessing. Rapid economic growth has historically had adverse effects on the natural environment and has always led to more rapid consumption of scarce resources (see Chapter 16). These adverse effects of rapid economic growth illustrate again the principle that a solution to one problem often creates or aggravates another problem; that is, in sociological terms, the solution has both functional and dysfunctional aspects.

We will now briefly describe some of the proposals that have been advanced for reducing unemployment. As mentioned previously, both President Kennedy and President Reagan used a tax-cut plan to stimulate the economy and create more jobs in the private sector.

Another proposal is for the government to be a "last resort" employer. Those who are unemployed and are unable to find employment in the private sector would be hired by the government. The work to be performed would ideally be useful to society—for example, building and repairing highways, planting trees for use in future years, and providing services in social service agencies (such as recreational services to youths in high delinquency areas). Ideally, working for the government in such capacities would also provide workers with job skills that would increase their opportunities to be hired in the private sector.

Another proposal is for the government to subsidize private companies to maintain their payrolls during economic recessions. A number of foreign governments do this.

Throughout our history, there have been both geographical areas of high unemployment and areas that are booming and wanting more workers. It has been suggested the government could take a more active role in identifying those areas that want more workers, publicizing what jobs are available in such areas and providing assistance in paying relocation expenses for unemployed workers who are willing to move from areas of high unemployment.

Another proposal is for the government to expand its role in providing job training to the unskilled and semiskilled and to those workers whose skills have become obsolete. West Germany, for example, not only provides such work training to a greater extent than in this country, but also usually pays such workers during the weeks or months they are learning new skills for available jobs.

Critics of the last four proposals argue that extensive government efforts in any of these areas would sharply increase government spending and thereby increase the rate of inflation. They also maintain that government-supplied jobs would merely be a stop-gap measure that would not solve the overall problem of joblessness and that government should not be in the business of creating "make-work" jobs.

Occupational Health Hazards

There are a number of occupational health hazards that affect many workers. These health hazards include (*a*) on-the-job accidents and work-related illnesses and (*b*) job stress.

ON-THE-JOB AND WORK-RELATED HEALTH HAZARDS   Every year there are more than two million persons injured in the United States through on-the-job accidents; 100,000 are permanently disabled, and approximately 15,000 are fatally injured.[30]

Although industrial accidents are serious, an even more serious occupational hazard appears to be work-related diseases. The U.S. Public Health Service estimates that 100,000 Americans die of job-related diseases each year, with nearly 400,000 new cases of job-related diseases occurring annually. Cancer and respiratory diseases are two of the illnesses that are often job related.[31]

Two of the most dangerous workplaces are mines and farms. Coal miners are, in particular, exposed to a variety of dangers: underground floods, cave-ins, explosions, and respiratory diseases. Every year, it seems, we hear about cave-ins in coal mines that trap and kill a number of miners. Statistically, for coal miners, incurable lung ailments affect and kill many more workers than cave-ins. Unless a mine is properly ventilated, the air is filled with coal dust. Years of breathing such dust can lead to respiratory diseases. The most publicized miner's disease is "black lung," which is a fatal, pneumonconiosis disease. It is estimated that nearly 10 percent of American miners have it.[32] An even more common respiratory disease among coal miners is silicosis, which the World Health Organization has called "the major cause of disability and mortality" among occupational diseases.[33] The 1969 Coal Mine and Safety Act set standards for allowable dust levels, and technology is now available to clean the air. Unfortunately, these standards have not as yet been strictly enforced.

Farming also has a number of occupational hazards. Farmers, their families, and the workers they employ operate a wide range of equipment. Often, the workers are not carefully trained in being aware of the dangers. Newspapers frequently note that a 13- or 14-year-old youth is fatally injured when a tractor overturns. On-the-job accidents are common on farms. An even graver danger for farm workers comes from pesticides and herbicides that are misused or overused. More farm workers are poisoned by chemicals than are injured in other farm accidents.[34]

Other industries also have serious health hazards. Cotton dust levels are a threat in the textile and cotton-seed oil industries. Continued inhalation of cotton dust in the air of mills causes the respiratory disease called "brown lung" or byssinosis. The disease is irreversible and fatal. It is estimated that 150,000 of the 800,000 textile workers in this country have brown-lung disease, with 35,000 workers being disabled from it.[35] Although brown lung was recognized as a disease in the 18th century, it was not until 1968 that it was officially recognized as an occupational illness. (Plant owners did not want official recognition because they did not want to pay compensation for those workers who became ill.) Even after the disease was officially recognized, it took another eight years of pressure from such labor groups as the Amalgamated Clothing and Textile Workers Union to force the government to set standards for allowable levels of cotton dust. (Plant owners informed the government that they were reluctant to have standards set, because it would cost sizable sums of money to remodel the plants and purchase the equipment necessary to meet the standards. Plant owners argued that it might be more profitable for them to close the plants and relocate in foreign countries that are less safety conscious. They also noted they could hire workers at much lower wages in foreign countries.)

At present, one of the most controversial occupational hazards is the use of nuclear power for energy purposes. A number of nuclear power plants have already been built. In 1979 there was an accident at the nuclear power plant located at Three Mile Island in Pennsylvania. Small amounts of radioactive particles were released into the air, and thousands of people in the surrounding area were evacuated. Some authorities feared there was a serious threat of substantial amounts of radioactivity being released. This accident demonstrated to the American public that nuclear energy is a potential hazard for plant workers and also for people living in the surrounding area. In 1986 there was an accident at the nuclear power plant in Chernobyl, Russia, which released massive amounts of radioactivity into the atmosphere. Over twenty people were killed, and thousands of people now face the possibility of an early death due to exposure to radiation. This accident has raised a worldwide concern about the dangers of using nuclear power plants to produce electricity.

This worker sprays water to bring down asbestos dust during a clean-up operation at the National Cathedral in Washington, D.C.

One of the most serious problems involving occupational hazards is that some substances take years before their deadly effects appear. Asbestos is a prime example. Asbestos is a mineral that has multiple uses—from construction to brewing beer—and has been handled by workers in a wide range of industries. Only a few years ago it was discovered that asbestos, after a lengthy exposure period, often causes cancer. It is not only the worker who is in danger, but also spouses and children, who are exposed to clinging asbestos particles on the worker's clothes when she or he returns home. The government is now advising persons who have been exposed to asbestos to receive periodic medical examinations for early detection and treatment of cancer.

People who work with or around asbestos die from lung cancer at a rate more than seven times that of the general public.[36] Mesothelioma was once a rare form of cancer. It attacks the abdominal organs and the lining of the lungs and is usually fatal. This type of cancer has become relatively common among asbestos workers. Asbestos may only be the tip of the iceberg. In 1977 Dorothy McGhee reported there are 2,400 suspected carcinogens (cancer-causing substances), but only 16 of these have been so designated and regulated by the government.[37]

Rubber workers are exposed to a variety of carcinogens and are dying of cancer of the prostate, cancer of the stomach, leukemia, and other cancers of the blood and the lymph-forming tissues. These cancer rates for rubber workers range from 50 percent to 300 percent higher than for the general population.[38]

Steelworkers, especially those handling coal, are becoming victims of lung cancer at excessive rates. Workers exposed to benzidine and other aromatic amines (often used in producing dyestuffs) have excessively high rates of bladder cancer. Dry cleaners, painters, printers, and petroleum workers are exposed to benzene, which is a known leukemia-producing agent. Miners of iron ore, uranium, chromium, nickel, and other industrial metals fall victim to a variety of occupationally related cancers. Insecticide workers, farm workers, and copper- and lead-smelter workers are exposed to inorganic arsenic, a carcinogen that results in high rates of lymphatic cancer and lung cancer.

The gravest health danger comes from the relatively young chemical industry. The modern-day chemical industry was born in the technological innovations during World War II and has been growing rapidly ever since. Chemicals are now involved in manufacturing practically every product we use—our clothing, the processed food we eat, the soaps we wash with, and our televisions and automobiles. A fair number of these chemicals have been found to cause certain diseases, such as cancer, birth defects, heart problems, nervous disorders, weight loss, and sterility. Kepone is described in Chapter 8, and DDT is described in Chapter 16; both of these chemicals have been found to be carcinogens.

It is extremely difficult to prove that a substance causes cancer. Scientists disagree about how much evidence is needed to document a causal relationship. In

BOX 10.5

A Question of Jobs versus Health

T he world's largest smokestack is located in Anaconda, Montana. The red brick stack is owned by Anaconda Company, and rises 585 feet above the ground in this section of the picturesque Rocky Mountains. The smokestack is part of Anaconda's giant copper-smelting plant. The smokestack sends thick clouds of white smoke high up into the air all day and all night long.

One of the problem emissions being spread across the land is arsenic. Until 1976 company officials denied the emissions were a problem. The director of Montana's Environment Sciences Division had seriously questioned whether the emissions were a health hazard as far back as 1967.

Then, in 1976 cancer researchers found that the county's annual death rate from cancer was 65.2 deaths for every 100,000 persons. (This figure is nearly twice the national average, and more than three times as high as the expected rate for a rural county of this size.)

Surprisingly, the reactions of workers and residents in the area to the study results were that they were much more concerned about the plant closing than the health hazards. If the plant closed, people would immediately lose their jobs and their means of support. They were less concerned about the air pollution that could cause cancer 10 or 20 years in the future.

Matt Strizich, president of the union local and a truck driver at the smelter, summed up the community's feelings:

What bothers me is not what happens 20 years from now, but how I feed my kids tomorrow.

So the studies are right, what are my options? I'm 42 years old, I've got six kids and a high school education. If the plant closes, what do I do?

Source: Bill Richards, "A Question of Jobs versus Health," *Washington Post*, February 8, 1976.

addition, certain diseases (such as cancer and respiratory disorders) first appear several years after exposure. When a segment of the population has a high incidence of cancer it is often difficult to identify the cancer-causing substances they were exposed to several years earlier.

Because new chemicals are being introduced at the rate of one every twenty minutes,[39] it is extremely difficult to study carefully the hazards of all the chemicals currently in use, as well as the hazards of chemicals that will be discovered and used in the future.

The National Institute for Occupational Safety and Health (NIOSH) estimates 2.35 million workers are exposed to a dozen highly toxic substances. These substances includes asbestos, arsenic, benzene, silica dust, mercury, and vinyl chloride.[40]

Simply documenting that certain chemicals are hazardous does not automatically mean they will be taken off the market. For example, there is considerable evidence that tobacco is a health hazard, yet many Americans continue to smoke and chew tobacco in spite of the hazards.

Workers, when given the choice of being unemployed or working in an industry that is a recognized health hazard (such as coal mining or the textile industry), often elect to work. Because of the high cost of meeting safety standards, businesses commonly drag their feet in complying with the standards and often threaten to relocate in other countries when the government applies pressure on them to meet safety standards. In many occupational areas, such as in textile mills, there is considerable controversy regarding what should be considered "safe" levels of exposure to substances.

The federal government has become increasingly concerned about occupational illnesses. In 1970 it passed the Occupational Safety and Health Act, which established two new organizations to combat occupational hazards. The Occupational Safety and Health Administration (OSHA) was created in the Department of Labor to establish health standards for industry. The National Institute for Occupational Safety and Health (NIOSH) was created in the Department of Health and Human Services to research occupational hazards.

In 1976 the federal government enacted the Toxic Substances Control Act, which established systems and guidelines for screening and controlling dangerous substances. With the rapid development of chemicals and other substances, OSHA and NIOSH face formidable tasks in testing the effects of all of these substances and in setting and enforcing safety limits for substances found to be health hazards.

JOB STRESS   Most standard textbooks in medicine attribute anywhere from 50 percent to 80 percent of all diseases to stress-related or psychosomatic origins.[41] One of the main sources of stress is job pressures. Practically any job has stresses. Some of the more stressful jobs are air traffic controller, police officer, surgeon, fire fighter, coach in professional sports, labor arbitrator, prison warden, and administrator of a large agency. (Stress is further described in Chapter 14.) The list of stress-related illnesses includes bronchial asthma, peptic ulcer, ulcerative colitis, mucous colitis,

hay fever, arthritis, hyperthyroidism, enuresis, hypertension, alcoholism, insomnia, cancer, migraine headache, impotence, atopic dermatitis, amenorrhea, and chronic constipation. As described in Chapter 14, stress is also one of the causes of emotional disorders.

Employers are increasingly becoming aware of the costs of stress to employees and to their businesses: absenteeism, low productivity, short- and long-term psychosomatic illnesses, job alienation and job dissatisfaction, marital difficulties, and emotional disorders. Therefore, many companies are sponsoring stress management programs to help their employees learn to reduce stress through such techniques as meditation, relaxation approaches, hypnosis, exercise programs (such as jogging), time management, biofeedback, and hobbies.[42]

SOCIAL WORK IN THE WORKPLACE

Social work in the workplace has had a variety of other titles in recent years, including industrial social work, occupational social work, and employee assistance. No term has yet emerged as the "preferred" term. In this section we will primarily use the terms *social work in the workplace* and *industrial social work*.

Industrial social work is generally viewed as a new and emerging specialization. Social workers in the past decade have been employed in industry in increasing numbers and in a variety of settings and roles. However, the roots of industrial social work go back in time much farther than most people realize.

A Brief History

In the late 1800s, there was a welfare movement in American businesses. Programs and services were developed by businesses to help employees in work-related areas, as well as with personal or domestic problems such as marital conflicts. From the late 1800s, the welfare movement grew steadily into the 1920s. By 1926, 80 percent of the 1,500 largest companies in the United States had at least one type of welfare program.[43]

The welfare movement emerged at this time for several reasons. Businesses were growing to such a size that personal contact between management personnel and labor personnel was practically nonexistent. In addition, an increasing percentage of the labor force was made up of women and immigrants whom management did not seem to understand. Employee turnover, employee sabotage, and the development of labor organizations also stimulated management's interest in the welfare movement. The threat of government regulation in the area of employee welfare also influenced businesses to take action.

The programs that were developed during this welfare movement needed staff to provide the services. The staff positions that emerged became known as social secretaries, welfare secretaries, or social welfare secretaries. With little previous knowledge on which to draw, the methods and techniques used by these secretaries evolved from experimentation. One popular approach was that of group work. It was soon discovered that formation of groups benefited employees in both work- and nonwork-related areas. For example, groups that formed for socialization or recreation fostered employee morale, which was reflected in work production and attitude. In addition to working directly with the employees, many of the duties of these secretaries were administrative, such as handling pension and insurance programs.

The number of positions of welfare secretaries declined sharply in the 1930s for several reasons.[44] Labor leaders tended to oppose such positions because they felt the secretaries were antiunion. (All too often management urged welfare secretaries to mold employees into loyal workers and to fight unionization.) Laborers tended to react negatively to the paternalistic character of the position. With the Great Depression in the 1930s many businesses were forced to cut back on welfare programs.

Aspects of the welfare secretary's role still exist today. Many of these aspects are now included in what is being called personnel management, such as the handling of grievances, linking employees who need help with available resources, and handling health insurance and pensions.

In the 1960s and early 1970s, large corporations developed training programs designed to hire and train inexperienced, long-term unemployed persons, including members of minority groups. Directors of these training programs soon concluded that a fair number of these trainees needed help in a variety of areas—such as day care, interpersonal skills, family problems, personal problems, and obtaining adequate housing and transportation. In the past two decades industries have increasingly been employing social workers to provide services in these areas.

The development of Employee Assistance Programs (EAPs) has also been a major factor in the emergence of industrial social work. The EAP movement had its roots in the development of alcoholism programs in the 1930s and 1940s. These programs were originally operated by industrial physicians or were informal programs staffed by recovering alcoholics. Employee Assistance Programs have emerged to focus primarily on the restoration of employees' job performance when alcohol or other drug abuse, emotional or personal problems, or changes in the nature of a job have interfered. Industrial social work is now sometimes erroneously considered as synonymous with EAP. However, EAP is essentially a specific, performance-focused program, whereas (as we will see) industrial social work is much broader in scope.

There are now thousands of EAPs across the United States. They are staffed by people with a variety of backgrounds: social work, psychology, counseling, medicine, nursing, alcohol and drug abuse counseling, business administration, economics, and management.[45] The professional staff members of EAPs have generally completed some specialized training in alcohol and drug abuse counseling, mental health, and/or employee assistance programming.

The Present Status of Social Work in the Workplace

In the past several years businesses and industries have been proclaiming that industrial social work is an emerging area for social work practice. Schools of social work have begun to modify their curriculums for social work students who want a career in industry. Industrial social work has the potential to become one of the higher-paying areas for social work practice because most businesses and industries have the financial resources.

In a newly emerging field there is always considerable confusion over what the specific tasks and functions of the professionals should be. This is particularly true in industrial social work.

Social workers might help employees meet problems in the following areas: day care, financial problems, family problems, retirement problems, alienation, legal problems, health problems, mental health problems, alcohol and substance abuse, and recreation problems. Social workers might become involved in providing training and staff development programs. They might serve as advocates to develop programs to combat hazardous working conditions. They might provide consultation regarding the physical or social environment within the company. They might help strikers meet basic needs. Another possibility is to become involved in community relations—for example, acting as a representative of the business in fund-raising and/or planning for community services. They might become involved in proposing new job designs to replace boring, tedious, assembly-line work. Thus, industrial social workers may have many more functions than simply being involved in operating direct service programs. Paul Kurzman and Sheila Akabas note:

Social workers may . . . be called on to consult with management on its human resource policy, donations to tax-exempt activities, collective bargaining demands, or other dimensions of emerging corporate efforts at social responsibility. Professionals may be expected to analyze legislation, administer health and welfare benefit systems, or assist in developing programs designed to attract unorganized workers to trade union membership.[46]

Leo Perlis, longtime community relations director of the American Federation of Labor–Congress of Industrial Organizations, cautions that an industrial social worker needs knowledge of labor-management relations to help avoid direct involvement in the adversary relationship between labor and management.[47]

(Industrial social workers should not make the mistake made by many welfare secretaries of becoming identified as being on the side of management.)

There are already a number of other professionals in industry providing services similar to industrial social work, so questions of turf are arising. Such other professionals include psychiatrists, psychologists, drug and alcohol counselors, nurses, and experts in personnel management. It would seem that the profession of social work needs to develop models of industrial social work that will clarify to management, labor, and other helping professionals what it can realistically provide.

Businesses and industries do not provide social services for humanitarian reasons. Social workers in the workplace are expected to be accountable by demonstrating that their services promote improved productivity and reduced tardiness and absenteeism and make it easier to retain members of the company's work force, many of whom have received expensive training.

At present over 12 percent of workers have access to EAPs, and the number of these programs is growing.[48] It is essential that EAPs operate outside the disciplinary system of an organization. Donald Brieland, Lela Costin and Charles Atherton describe the importance of employees feeling free to use EAP services without adverse reactions from management:

Employees ideally should come for help in the early stages of difficulties but are understandably reluctant to share information that management could use against them. Therefore, we have seen that employees tend to conceal problems from both management and fellow workers. After they are referred by management or by a supervisor or union steward for help, the employee may feel labeled as a problem. If they are confronted by management, they fear loss of their job or discrimination in promotion. Managers have similar fears about revealing their own personal problems. Sometimes getting help is specified as a condition for retaining a job. Workers have to be convinced of the ultimate value of getting help.[49]

It is also essential that employees are aware that what they say to EAP staff will remain confidential, otherwise they will be reluctant to discuss their personal concerns and circumstances openly. Sometimes management finds confidentiality a difficult concession to make because it is paying the bill, but there is no other way to establish trust with employees. Brieland, Costin and Atherton note:

Social workers in industry need a written agreement to guarantee that the services they provide will be confidential and also to spell out the guidelines for referral to other community resources. . . .

Management or supervisors who refer the employee should be concerned with job performance but not with diagnosis. If they detect problems they expect some response. One way to handle the issue is to submit a statement indicating that the employee was in contact with the EAP and to provide a brief statement of general progress later.[50]

There are at least five ways in which social services may be sponsored in industry.

1. Sponsorship by management in companies with or without a union.

2. Sponsorship by the union.

3. Sponsorship by both management and labor, with management employing social workers, and dual monitoring responsibility by management and labor.

4. Private consultantship by social worker under contract to union or management to provide services to workers and/or the organization.

5. Sponsorship by a community mental health center or family service agency having a specific contractual arrangement with the company.[51]

Research is needed to identify the merits and shortcomings of each of these approaches to sponsorship.

Current Uses of Social Services in the Workplace

ALCOHOL AND DRUG ABUSE COUNSELING   Most social services in the workplace are currently provided by EAPs. As noted earlier, other professionals (such as psychologists and guidance counselors) may also be employed by EAPs.

The major focus of EAPs has been to deal with alcohol and drug abuse. It is well recognized that alcohol and drug abuse costs businesses and industries millions of dollars in productivity each year, through lower-quality work, absenteeism, tardiness, and deterioration of well-trained employees who have serious drinking problems. EAP programs tend to view alcoholism and other drug use as a disease and to emphasize total sobriety or total abstinence rather than a reduction in use. Alcoholics Anonymous or Narcotics Anonymous are also emphasized in the treatment process. Inpatient hospital treatment is sometimes used, but outpatient efforts are preferred because they cost less and because they do not involve loss of work time. Some EAPs provide treatment to those who are chemically dependent, whereas other EAPs serve as brokers by arranging for treatment with other resources.

Students seeking a career in social work in the workplace are advised to become knowledgeable about the abuse and treatment of alcohol and other drugs, through courses and probably a field internship in the treatment of chemical dependency. Employees who have a chemical dependency that is affecting their work are generally offered treatment by EAP staff, which is paid by the employer (generally through health insurance programs). Employees who refuse treatment encounter the risk of their employment being terminated.

EAPs also provide services to employees who have emotional problems, such as depression. Similar to alcohol and drug abuse treatment, EAP staff either provide treatment services for emotional difficulties or serve as brokers by arranging for treatment with other resources.

FAMILY COUNSELING   Brieland, Costin, and Atherton summarize the primary family problems that EAPs become involved in:

Stresses involving the spouse and other family members are an important concern. Not only does the employee take family problems to the workplace but he or she brings workplace problems home and displaces them on family members. Marriage counseling and child care are the most common needs. Separation and divorce take their toll in stress on the job. Child abuse and family violence increasingly come to the attention of the assistance program. These behaviors may lead to criminal prosecution. If publicity results, assault may lead to rejection in the workplace, even though no sentence results.[52]

EAPs either provide counseling in these areas or refer employees and their families to other therapists. If the family dispute involves court action, as in the case of spouse abuse, the court may ask the employer to provide an evaluation, which is then often conducted by staff of the EAP.

Financial problems for families are sometimes created when the employer lays off employees. EAP staff may help employees to obtain unemployment benefits. Because layoffs are a contributing cause to increased drinking and to child and spouse abuse, EAPs may provide counseling and referral services for such difficulties during layoffs. For employees who need child care, EAPs may serve a broker role in helping to link such employees with child-care services.

CAREER COUNSELING AND EDUCATION   EAPs have become involved in two areas of career counseling: helping employees to set and work on specific career goals and assisting employees in learning and using stress management techniques. In helping employees to set career goals, EAPs may administer, or arrange for, aptitude tests. They may also help employees to understand the promotion and advancement opportunities within the company. EAPs also help employees to enroll in educational efforts that enhance their physical and mental health and increase their skills on the job. Many companies provide or pay for training that will facilitate promotion. Some companies will also pay for courses that increase employees' assertiveness, personal adjustment, self-understanding, and problem-solving capacities. (Many EAPs are reluctant to provide assistance to those employees seeking a job outside the company.)

EAPs also provide, or arrange for, workshops and seminars on stress management techniques. A wide range of techniques are available: using relaxation techniques, hypnosis, time management, or positive thinking; developing hobbies and exercise programs; improving interpersonal relationships; learning to problem solve; and establishing a positive sense of self. Those employees who are experiencing burnout or severe job stress may receive counseling by EAP staff or be referred elsewhere for therapy.

CREDIT COUNSELING   Many EAPs have become involved in providing assistance to employees who are having financial difficulties. Usually employees with financial problems need credit counseling. One aspect of this involves debt counseling, in which they receive assistance in renegotiating their payments to creditors over a longer period of time. They are also encouraged to make a commitment to defer further credit purchases until the financial burden is reduced. Often they also receive financial counseling on developing a budget to meet their financial needs.

In some states creditors can claim part of the debtor's wages through legal garnishment. In such cases the employer must deduct a portion of the employee's wages, which is then paid to the creditor to pay off the debt. This process reveals the credit problems to the employer. (Some employers may view an employee with bad credit as being a bad employee and may then discharge the employee.) EAP staff members may get involved in cases of legal garnishment to help employees in trouble to straighten out their financial circumstances.

Some EAPs also provide financial planning assistance to employees who are burdened with alimony and child-support payments.

RETIREMENT PLANNING   In recent years employees have shown increased interest in retirement planning. EAPs can arrange for retirement-planning workshops and seminars to be offered to employees. A wide variety of programs can be explained to employees, including social security benefits, IRA plans, pension plans, profit-sharing plans, stock option plans, and tax-sheltered annuity plans.

EAP staff should be knowledgeable about the retirement plans available from the firm in order to help interested employees individually in making intelligent decisions. EAP staff may also provide assistance to employees nearing retirement. Such employees need to make plans not only for their financial needs but also for what they will do to maintain a high level of positive mental and physical activity.

Industrial social work appears to be a challenging new growth area for social work. But careful planning is needed to avoid the mistakes that led to the demise of welfare secretaries. Because there are over 100 million workers in the United States, workers and their families constitute a massive target population. Business and industry could hire every graduating social worker and hardly dent their payrolls.[53]

SUMMARY

The major social problems involving work are alienation, unemployment, and occupational health hazards. Alienation is the sense of meaninglessness and powerlessness that many people feel about their jobs.

Work is highly esteemed in our society. Under the influence of the Protestant ethic, work has become a moral obligation. It is also a source of self-respect, an opportunity to form friendships, and may be a source of self-fulfillment and an opportunity to use one's talents. To a large extent our work determines our social status and also defines who we are. Before the Protestant Reformation work was denigrated and even considered a curse by some societies.

There have been significant changes or trends in the nature of work and the composition of the work force in the past few decades. There is an increase in white-collar workers and a decrease in farmers and blue-collar workers. Most workers are now employees rather than being self-employed. Work is increasingly becoming specialized, and considerable automation is occurring. More women are entering the labor force, and older male workers are increasingly becoming unemployed. Workers are increasingly seeking intrinsic rewards (rewards that come from the nature of the work itself). Our society is increasingly developing an economy that emphasizes high technology. Those who

are well-educated in high-technology areas have a promising future, whereas the unskilled in our society face increased prospects of being trapped in the lower socioeconomic class.

Alienation appears to be a serious problem for many workers. Sources of alienation include specialization, automation, lack of involvement in the decision-making process, performance of routine and repetitive tasks, and lack of opportunity to be creative or to use one's talents fully. Alienation may lead to poor-quality work, absenteeism, job turnover, and low productivity. Job dissatisfaction is one measure of alienation. Available studies indicate conflicting results about how satisfied American workers are with their jobs. Sources of workers' satisfaction and dissatisfaction with their jobs were presented, and suggestions were reviewed on how to reduce worker alienation and job dissatisfaction.

In recent years the unemployment rate has ranged between 4 percent and 11 percent, which is considered high. Long-term unemployment has serious adverse effects: depletion of savings; loss of self-respect; loss of friends; isolation; and feelings of embarrassment, anger, despair, depression, anxiety, boredom, hopelessness, and apathy. It may be a factor in leading to emotional problems, suicide, alcoholism, and pscyhosomatic illnesses.

Groups that have chronically high rates of unemployment are minorities, teenagers, women, older workers, the unskilled, and the semiskilled. The reasons for high unemployment among these groups were discussed. The reasons for the high unemployment rate among the total work force were also discussed. These reasons are numerous and complex.

Economists agree that the ideal way to cure unemployment is through rapid economic growth. Economists, disagree, however, about the causes of a sluggish economy and about the best ways to stimulate it. Some of the proposals that have been advanced were described.

There are three main occupational health hazards: on-the-job accidents, working conditions that lead to work-related physical diseases (for example, breathing coal dust leads to black-lung disease), and job stress that leads to psychosomatic illnesses. The wide number of untested chemicals that are increasingly being used poses perhaps the greatest health danger in the future. Many chemical substances have a delayed reaction in which an illness (such as cancer) first occurs several years after exposure.

Social work in the workplace is an emerging field for social work practice. Most social services in the workplace are currently provided by Employee Assistance Programs (EAPs). EAP services include alcohol and drug abuse counseling, family counseling, career counseling and education, credit counseling, and retirement planning.

NOTES

1. Nancy C. Morse and Robert S. Weiss, "The Function and Meaning of Work," *American Sociological Review*, April 1955, pp. 191–98.
2. Aristotle, *Politics*, Book 3, sec. V, trans. Benjamin Jowett (Oxford: Clarendon Press, 1945).
3. Quoted in Thomas Sullivan et al., *Social Problems* (New York: John Wiley, 1980), p. 300.
4. Quoted in Ian Robertson, *Social Problems*, 2d ed. (New York: Random House, 1980), p. 87.
5. *Work in America: Report of a Special Task Force to the Secretary of Health, Education, and Welfare* (Cambridge, MA: M.I.T. Press, 1973), p. 45.
6. United States Bureau of the Census, *Statistical Abstract of the United States, 1987* (Washington, D.C.: U.S. Government Printing Office, 1987), p. 619.
7. Ibid., p. 415.
8. Seymour Wolfbein, *Work in American Society* (Glenview, IL: Scott, Foresman, 1971), p. 45.
9. Robertson, *Social Problems*, p. 89.
10. Charles R. Walker and Robert Guest, *Man on the Assembly Line* (Cambridge, MA: Harvard University Press, 1952), p. 54–55.
11. U.S. Bureau of the Census, *Statistical Abstract of the United States, 1987*, p. 376.
12. Ibid., p. 376.
13. William Glasser, *The Identity Society* (New York: Harper & Row, 1972).
14. Daniel Bell, *The Coming of Post-Industrial Society: A Venture in Social Forecasting* (New York: Basic Books, 1973), pp. 188–195.
15. Joseph Julian and William Kornblum, *Social Problems*, 5th ed. (Englewood Cliffs, NJ: Prentice-Hall, 1986), p. 380.
16. Karl Marx, *Selected Writings in Sociology and Social Philosophy*, trans. T. B. Bottomore (New York: McGraw-Hill, 1964).
17. Robertson, *Social Problems*, p. 108.
18. *Work in America*, p. 16.
19. Herbert C. Morton, "A Look at Factors Affecting the Quality of Working Life," *Monthly Labor Review*, October 1977, p. 64.
20. Daniel Yankelovich, "The New Psychological Contracts at Work," *Psychology Today*, May 1978, p. 46.
21. Patricia A. Renwick and Edward E. Lawler, "What You Really Want from Your Job," *Psychology Today*, July 1978, p. 79.
22. "The Flexitime Concept Gets a Wider Test," *Business Week*, May 24, 1976, p. 38.
23. Richard E. Walton, "How to Counter Alienation in the Plant," *Harvard Business Review* 50 (November–December 1972), pp. 70–82.
24. Robertson, *Social Problems*, p. 115.
25. "A Productive Way to Vent Employee Gripes," *Business Week*, October 16, 1978, pp. 168–171.
26. Harold L. Wilensky, "Work as a Social Problem," in *Social Problems*, ed. Howard Becker (New York: John Wiley, 1966), p. 129.
27. D. D. Braginsky and B. M. Braginsky, "Surplus People: Their Lost Faith in Self and System," *Psychology Today*, August 1975, p. 70.
28. Harvey Brenner, *Mental Illness and the Economy* (Cambridge, MA: Harvard University Press, 1973).
29. *Report of the National Advisory Commission on Civil Disorders* (New York: Bantam Books, 1968), pp. 13–14.
30. Joseph A. Califano, "Occupational Safety and Health: A Healthier Working Environment," *Vital Speeches of the Day* 44, no. 24 (October 1, 1978), p. 738.
31. Erik Eckholm, "Unhealthy Jobs," *Environment* 19, no. 6 (August/September 1977), p. 29.
32. Ibid., p. 34.
33. Ibid., p. 34.
34. Joel Schwartz, "Poisoning Farmworkers," *Environment* 17, no. 5 (June 1975), pp. 26–33.
35. Jerry DeMuth, "Brown Lung in the Cotton Mill," *America*, March 18, 1978, p. 108.
36. Larry Agran, "Getting Cancer on the Job," *The Nation*, April 12, 1975.
37. Dorothy McGhee, "The Secret Killers," *The Progressive*, August 1977, p. 26.
38. Agran, "Getting Cancer on the Job."

39. Joseph Julian, *Social Problems*, 3d ed. (Englewood Cliffs, NJ: Prentice-Hall, 1980), p. 468.

40. Clemens P. Work and Ronald A. Taylor, "Toxic Chemicals: Just How Real a Danger," *U.S. News & World Report*, May 21, 1984, p. 67.

41. K. R. Pelletier, *Mind as Healer, Mind as Slayer* (New York: Delta, 1977).

42. Ibid.

43. Philip R. Popple, "Social Work Practice in Business and Industry, 1875–1930," *Social Service Review* 55 (June 1981), pp. 257–269.

44. Norman L. Wyers and Malina Kaulukukui, "Social Services in the Workplace: Rhetoric vs. Reality," *Social Work* 29 (March–April 1984), pp. 167–172.

45. Ibid., p. 168.

46. Paul A. Kurzman and Sheila H. Akabas, "Industrial Social Work as an Arena for Practice," *Social Work* 26 (January 1981), p. 53.

47. Leo Perlis, "The Human Contract in the Organized Workplace," *Social Thought* 3 (Winter 1977), p. 49.

48. Donald Brieland, Lela B. Costin, and Charles R. Atherton, *Contemporary Social Work*, 3d ed. (New York: McGraw-Hill, 1985), p. 334.

49. Ibid., pp. 342–343.

50. Ibid., p. 343.

51. "Industrial Social Work Movement Expanding," *NASW News* 23 (February 1978), p. 7.

52. Brieland, Costin, and Atherton, *Contemporary Social Work*, p. 339.

53. Kurzman and Akabas, "Industrial Social Work as an Arena for Practice," p. 52.

11

RACISM, ETHNOCENTRISM, AND STRATEGIES FOR ACHIEVING EQUAL RIGHTS

We see ethnic and racial conflict—riots, beatings, murders, and civil wars—nearly every time we turn on the evening news on television. In recent years there have been clashes resulting in bloodshed from Northern Ireland to South Africa, from Lebanon to Israel, and from the United States to South America. Practically every nation with more than one ethnic group has had to deal with ethnic conflict. The oppression and exploitation of one ethnic group by another is particularly ironic in democratic nations, since these societies claim to cherish freedom, equality, and justice. In reality, the dominant group in all societies that controls the political and economic institutions rarely agrees to share (equally) its power and wealth with other ethnic groups.

Our country was supposedly founded on the principle of human equality. The Declaration of Independence and the Constitution assert equality, justice, and liberty for all. Yet, in practice, our society has always been racist: Inequality and racial prejudice and discrimination have always existed.

From its earliest days, our society has singled out certain minorities to treat unequally. A *minority* can be defined as a group who has a subordinate status and is being subjected to discrimination.

The categories of people who have been singled out for unequal treatment in our society have changed somewhat over the years. In the late 1800s and early 1900s, people of Irish, Italian, and Polish descent were discriminated against, but that discrimination has been substantially reduced. In the first half of the 19th century, Americans of Chinese and Japanese descent were severely discriminated against, but this has also been declining for many decades.

As time passes, new minorities are occasionally recognized as being the victims of discrimination. For example, women, the handicapped, and homosexuals have always been discriminated against, but only in the past twenty years has there been extensive national recognition of this discrimination. This chapter will:

- Define and describe ethnic groups, ethnocentrism, racial groups, racism, prejudice, discrimination, and institutional discrimination.

- Outline the sources of prejudice and discrimination.

- Summarize the effects and costs of discrimination.

- Present background material on racial groups—blacks, Hispanic Americans, Native Americans, and Asian Americans.

- Outline strategies to combat discrimination.

- Describe social work's commitment to work toward ending racial discrimination.

- Forecast the pattern of race and ethnic relations in the United States in the future.

ETHNIC GROUPS AND ETHNOCENTRISM

An ethnic group has a sense of togetherness, a conviction that its members form a special group, and a sense of common identity or "peoplehood." Milton Gordon defines an ethnic group as

any group which is defined or set off by race, religion, or national origin, or some combination of these categories . . . all of these categories have a common social-psychological referent, in that all of them serve to create, through historical circumstances, a sense of peoplehood.[1]

Practically every ethnic group has a strong feeling of *ethnocentrism*. Ethnocentrism is "the tendency to view the norms and values of one's own culture as absolute and to use them as a standard against which to judge and measure all other cultures."[2] Ethnocentrism leads members of ethnic groups to view their culture as the best, as superior, as the one that other cultures should emulate. Ethnocentrism also leads to prejudice against foreigners, who may be viewed as barbarians, heathens, uncultured people, or savages.

Feelings of ethnic superiority within a nation are usually accompanied by the belief that political and economic domination by one's own group is natural, is morally right, is in the best interest of the nation, and perhaps also is "God's will." Ethnocentrism has led to some of the worst human atrocities in history, such as the American colonists' nearly successful attempt to exterminate Native Americans and Adolph Hitler's mass

executions of over 6 million European Jews, gypsies, people with disabilities, and other minority group members.

In interactions between nations, ethnocentric beliefs sometimes lead to wars and serve as justifications for foreign conquests. At practically any point in the last several centuries there have been at least a few wars occurring between nations in which one society has been seeking to force its culture on another. In the past few decades, the United States and Russia have been engaged in a struggle to extend their influence on other cultures. We hold a number of negative stereotypes about the Russian culture, and their citizens have a number of negative stereotypes about our culture. Also, in the last few decades, Israel and the Arab countries have been involved in a bitter struggle in the Middle East. China and Taiwan are in conflict, as are countries in Southeast Asia (such as Cambodia and Vietnam).

RACE AND RACISM

Although a racial group is often also an ethnic group, the two groups are not necessarily the same. A *race* is believed to have a common set of physical characteristics. But the members of a racial group may or may not share the sense of togetherness or identity that holds an ethnic group together. A group that is both a racial group and an ethnic group is Japanese Americans, as they are thought to have some common physical characteristics and also have a sense of "peoplehood." On the other hand, white Americans and white Russians are of the same race, but they hardly have a sense of togetherness. In addition, there are ethnic groups that are composed of a variety of races. For example, a religious group (such as Roman Catholic) is sometimes considered an ethnic group and is composed of members from diverse racial groups.

In contrast to ethnocentrism, racism is more apt to be based on physical differences than on cultural differences. Racism is ". . . a belief in racial superiority that leads to discrimination and prejudice toward those races considered inferior."[3] However, similar to ethnocentric ideologies, most racist ideologies assert that members of other racial groups are inferior.

PREJUDICE AND DISCRIMINATION

Prejudice means to prejudge, to make a judgment in advance of due examination. The judgment may be unduly favorable or negative. In terms of race and ethnic relations, however, prejudice refers to negative prejudgments. Gordon Allport defines prejudice as thinking negatively of others without sufficient justification.[4] His definition has two elements: an unfounded judgment and a feeling tone of scorn, dislike, fear, and aversion. In regard to race, prejudiced people apply racial stereotypes to all or nearly all members of the group according to preconceived notions of what they believe the group to be like and how they think the group will behave. Racial prejudice results from the belief that people who have different skin color and other physical characteristics also have differences in behaviors, values, intellectual functioning, and attitudes.

The term *to discriminate* has two very different meanings. It may have the positive meaning "to be discerning and perceptive." However, in minority group relations, it refers to making categoric differentiations based on a social group ranked as inferior, rather than judging an individual on his or her own merits. Racial discrimination involves denying to members of minority groups equal access to opportunities, certain residential housing areas, membership in certain religious and social organizations, certain political activities, access to community services, and so on.

Prejudice is a combination of stereotyped beliefs and negative attitudes, so that prejudiced individuals think about people in a predetermined, usually negative, categorical way. Discrimination involves physical actions—unequal treatment of people because they belong to a category. Discriminatory behavior often derives from prejudiced attitudes. Robert Merton, however, notes that prejudice and discrimination can occur

independently of each other. Merton describes four different "types" of people:

1. *The unprejudiced nondiscriminator*, in both belief and practice, upholds American ideals of freedom and equality. This person is not prejudiced against other groups and, on principle, will not discriminate against them.

2. *The unprejudiced discriminator* is not personally prejudiced but may sometimes, reluctantly, discriminate against other groups because it seems socially or financially convenient to do so.

3. *The prejudiced nondiscriminator* feels hostile to other groups but recognizes that law and social pressures are opposed to overt discrimination. Reluctantly, this person does not translate prejudice into action.

4. *The prejudiced discriminator* does not believe in the values of freedom and equality and consistently discriminates against other groups in both word and deed.[5]

An example of an unprejudiced discriminator is the unprejudiced owner of a condominium complex in an all-white middle-class suburb who refuses to sell a condominium complex to a black family because of fear (founded or unfounded) that the sale would reduce the sale value of the remaining units. An example of a prejudiced nondiscriminator is a personnel director of a fire department who believes Chicanos are unreliable and poor fire fighters but complies with affirmative action efforts to hire and train Chicano fire fighters.

It should be noted it is very difficult to keep personal prejudices from eventually leading to some form of discrimination. Strong laws and firm informal social norms are necessary to break the causal relationship between prejudice and discrimination.

Discrimination is of two types: de jure and de facto. *De jure* discrimination is legal discrimination. The so-called Jim Crow laws in the South gave force of law to many discriminatory practices against blacks, including denial of the right to trial, prohibition against voting, and prohibition against interracial marriage. Today, in the United States, there is practically no de jure discrimination, since such laws have been declared unconstitutional and removed.

De facto discrimination refers to discrimination that actually exists, whether legal or not. Acts of de facto discrimination are against the law but abide by powerful informal norms that are discriminatory. Marlene Cummings gives an example of this type of discrimination and urges victims to confront assertively such discrimination:

Scene: department store. Incident: Several people are waiting their turn at a counter. The person next to be served is a black woman; however, the clerk waits on several white customers who arrived later. The black woman finally demands service, after several polite gestures to call the clerk's attention to her. The clerk proceeds to wait on her after stating, "I did not see you." The clerk is very discourteous to the black customer; and the lack of courtesy is apparent, because the black customer had the opportunity to observe treatment of the other customers. De facto discrimination is most frustrating . . . ; the customer was served. Most people would rather just forget the whole incident, but it is important to challenge the practice even though it will possibly put you through more agony. One of the best ways to deal with this type of discrimination is to report it to the manager of the business. If it is at all possible, it is important to involve the clerk in the discussion.[6]

RACIAL AND ETHNIC STEREOTYPES

Racial and ethnic stereotypes involve attributing a fixed and usually inaccurate or unfavorable conception to a racial or ethnic group. Stereotypes may contain some truth but generally are exaggerated, taken out of context, or distorted. Stereotypes are closely related to the way we think, as we seek to perceive and understand things in categories. We need categories to group things that are similar in order to study them and to communicate about them. We have stereotypes about many categories, including mothers, fathers, teenagers, Communists, Republicans, school teachers, farmers, construction workers, miners, politicians, Mormons, and Italians. These stereotypes may contain some useful and accurate information about a member in any category. Yet, each member of any category will have many characteristics that are not suggested by the stereotypes and may even have some characteristics that run counter to some of the stereotypes.

Racial stereotypes involve differentiating people in terms of color or other physical characteristics. In our history, for example, there was the erroneous stereotype that Native Americans would rapidly become intoxicated and irrational when using alcohol. This belief was then translated into laws that existed for a number of years that prohibited Native Americans from buying and consuming alcohol. A more recent stereotype is that blacks have "natural rhythm" and therefore have greater natural ability to play basketball and certain other sports. Although such a stereotype appears complimentary to blacks, it has broader, negative implications. The danger with this stereotype is that if people believe the stereotype, it may well suggest to them that other abilities and capacities (such as intelligence, morals, and work productivity) are also determined by race. In other words, believing this "positive" stereotype increases the probability that people will also believe negative stereotypes.

RACIAL AND ETHNIC DISCRIMINATION

Gunnar Myrdal points out that minority problems are actually majority problems.[7] The white majority determines the "place" of nonwhites and other ethnic groups in our society. The status of different minority groups varies in our society because whites apply different stereotypes to various groups; for example, blacks are viewed and treated differently from Japanese. Elmer Johnson notes, "Minority relationships become recognized by the majority as a social problem when the members of the majority disagree as to

Overt expressions of racism seem out of context in democratic societies that champion such ideals as freedom, equality, and justice. But the reality of race relations in America has yet to match those ideals: Our history is one of discrimination, inequality, and racial prejudice.

whether the subjugation of the minority is socially desirable or in the ultimate interest of the majority."[8] Concern about discrimination and segregation has also received increasing national attention because of a rising level of aspiration among minority groups who demand (sometimes militantly) equal opportunities and equal rights.

Race Is a Social Concept

Ashley Montague considers "race" to be one of the most dangerous and tragic myths in our society.[9] Race is erroneously believed by many to be a biological classification of people. Yet, there are no clearly delineating characteristics of any "race." Throughout history, the genes of different societies and "racial" groups have occasionally been intermingled. No "racial"

group has any unique or distinctive genes. In addition, biological differentiations of racial groups have gradually been diluted through such sociocultural factors as changes in preferences of desirable characteristics in mates, effects of different diets on those who reproduce, and such variables as wars and diseases in selecting those who will live and reproduce.[10]

In spite of definitional problems, it is necessary to use racial categories in the social sciences, as race has important (though not necessarily consistent) social meanings for people. In order to have a basis for racial classifications, a number of social scientists have used a social, rather than a biological, definition. A social definition is based on the way in which members of a society classify each other by physical characteristics. For example, a frequently used social definition of a black person in America is anyone who either displays overt black physical characteristics or is known to have a black ancestor.[11] The sociological classification of races is indicated by different definitions of a race among various societies. For example, in the United States, anyone who is not "pure white" and is known to have a black ancestor is considered to be black, whereas in Brazil, anyone who is not "pure black" is classified as white.[12]

Race, according to Montague, becomes a very dangerous myth when it is assumed that physical traits are linked with mental traits and cultural achievements.[13] Every few years, it seems, some noted scientist stirs the country by making this erroneous assumption. For example, Arthur Jensen[14] asserted several years ago that whites on the average are more intelligent, since IQ tests show whites average scores of ten to fifteen points higher than blacks. Jensen's findings have been sharply criticized by other authorities as falsely assuming that IQ is largely genetically determined.[15] These authorities contend that IQ is substantially influenced by environmental factors, and it is likely that the average achievement of blacks, if given similar opportunities to realize their potentialities, would be about the same as whites. Also, it has been charged that IQ tests are racially slanted, as the tests ask the kinds of questions that whites are more familiar with and thereby more apt to answer correctly. These authorities also assert that the assumption that blacks are biologically inferior in intelligence is disastrous because it serves to rationalize oppression and rigidly assign black people to a second-class, low-income status.

Elmer Johnson summarizes the need for an impartial, objective view of the capacity of different racial groups to achieve:

Race bigots contend that, the cultural achievements of different races being so obviously unlike, it follows that their genetic capacities for achievement must be just as different. Nobody can discover the cultural capacities of any population or race ... until there is equality of opportunities to demonstrate the capacities.[16]

Most scientists, both physical and social, now believe that, in biological inheritance, all races are alike in everything that really makes any difference. With the exception of several very small, inbred, isolated, primitive tribes, all racial groups appear to show a wide distribution of every kind of ability. All important race differences that have been noted in personality, behavior, and achievement (for example, a higher percentage of white students graduate from high school as compared to black students) appear to be due to environmental factors.

Causes of Racial Discrimination

No single theory provides a complete picture of why racial discrimination occurs. By presenting a variety of theories, the reader should at least be better sensitized to the nature and sources of discrimination. The sources of discrimination are both internal and external to those who are prejudiced.

PROJECTION   Projection is a psychological defense mechanism in which one attributes to others characteristics that one is unwilling to recognize in oneself. Many people have personal traits they dislike in themselves. They have an understandable desire to get rid of such traits, but this is not always possible. Such people may "project" some of these traits onto others (often to some other group in society), thus displacing the negative feelings they would otherwise direct at themselves. In the process, they then reject and condemn those onto whom they have projected the traits.

For example, a minority group may serve as a projection of a prejudiced person's fears and lusts. People who view blacks as lazy and preoccupied with sex may be projecting their own internal concerns about their industriousness and their sexual fantasies onto another group. It is interesting to note that, although some whites view blacks as being promiscuous, sexually indiscreet, and immoral, historically it has generally been white men who pressured black women (particularly slaves) into sexual encounters. Perhaps historically, many white males felt guilty about these sexual desires and adventures and dealt with their guilt by projecting their own lusts and sexual conduct onto black males.

FRUSTRATION-AGGRESSION   Another psychic need satisfied by discrimination is the release of tension and frustration. All of us at times become frustrated when we are unable to achieve or obtain something we desire. Sometimes we strike back at the source of frustration, but many times direct retaliation is not possible— for example, we are apt to be reluctant to tell our employers what we think of them when we feel we are being treated unfairly, as we fear repercussions.

Some frustrated people displace their anger and aggression onto a scapegoat. The scapegoat may not be limited to a particular person but may include a group of people, such as a minority group. Similar to people who take out their job frustrations at home on their spouses or family pets, some prejudiced people vent their frustrations on minority groups. (The term *scapegoat* derives from an ancient Hebrew ritual in which a goat was symbolically laden with the sins of the entire community and then chased into the wilderness. It "escaped"; hence the term *scapegoat*. The term was gradually broadened to apply to anyone who bears the blame for others.)

INSECURITY AND INFERIORITY   Still another psychic need that may be satisfied by discrimination is the desire to counter feelings of insecurity or inferiority. Some insecure people seek to feel better about themselves by putting down another group, as they thus then can tell themselves that they are "better than" these people.

AUTHORITARIANISM   One of the classic works on the causes of prejudice is *The Authoritarian Personality* by T. W. Adorno et al.[17] Shortly after World War II, these researchers studied the psychological causes of the development of European fascism and concluded there was a distinct type of personality associated with prejudice and intolerance. The *authoritarian personality* is inflexible and rigid and has a low tolerance for uncertainty. This type of personality has a great respect for authority figures and quickly submits to their will. Such a person highly values conventional behavior and feels threatened by unconventional behavior of others. In order to reduce this threat, such a personality labels unconventional people as being "immature," "inferior," or "degenerate," and thereby avoids any need to question his or her own beliefs and values. The authoritarian personality views members of minority groups

as being unconventional, degrades them, and tends to express authoritarianism through prejudice and discrimination.

HISTORY   There are also historical explanations for prejudice. Charles F. Marden and Gladys Meyer note that the racial groups now viewed by white prejudiced persons as being second class are groups that have been either conquered, enslaved, or admitted into our society on a subordinate basis.[18] For example, blacks were imported as slaves during our colonial period and stripped of human dignity. Native Americans were conquered, and their culture was viewed as inferior. Mexican Americans were allowed to enter this country primarily to do seasonal, low-paid farm work.

COMPETITION AND EXPLOITATION   Our society is highly competitive and materialistic. Individuals and groups are competing daily with one another to acquire more of the available goods. These attempts to secure economic goods usually result in a struggle for power. In our society, whites have historically sought to exploit nonwhites. As previously mentioned, they have either conquered, enslaved, or admitted nonwhites into our society on a subordinate basis. Once the white group achieved dominance, they then used, and are still using, their powers to exploit nonwhites through cheap labor—for example, as sweatshop factory laborers, migrant farm hands, maids, janitors, and bellhops.

Members of the dominant group know they are treating the subordinate group as inferior and unequal. To justify such discrimination, they develop an ideology (set of beliefs) that their group is superior and that it is right and proper that they have more rights, goods, and so on. Often, they assert that God divinely selected their group to be dominant. Furthermore, they assign inferior traits to the subordinate group (lazy, heathen, immoral, dirty, stupid) and conclude that the minority need and deserve less because they are biologically inferior.

SOCIALIZATION PATTERNS   Prejudice is also a learned phenomenon and is transmitted from generation to generation through socialization processes. Our culture has stereotypes of what different racial group members "ought to be" and the ways racial group members "ought to behave" in relationships with members of certain outgroups. These stereotypes provide norms against which a child learns to judge persons, things, and ideas. Prejudice, to some extent, is developed through the same processes by which we learn to be religious and patriotic, or to appreciate and to enjoy art, or to develop our value system. Racial prejudice, at least in certain segments in our society, is thus a facet of the normative system of our culture.

IN THE EYE OF THE BEHOLDER   No one of the above theories explains all the causes of prejudices, as prejudices have many origins. Taken together, however, they identify a number of causative factors. It should be noted that all these theories assert that the causative factors of prejudice are in the personality and experiences of the person holding the prejudice and not in the character of the group against whom the prejudice is directed.

A novel experiment documenting that prejudice does not stem from contact with the people toward whom prejudice is directed was conducted by Eugene Hartley. Hartley gave his subjects a list of prejudiced responses to Jews and blacks and to three groups that did not even exist: Wallonians, Pireneans, and Danireans. Prejudiced responses included such statements as all Wallonians living here should be expelled. The respondents were asked to state their agreement or disagreement with these prejudiced statements. The experiment showed that most of those who were prejudiced against Jews and blacks were also prejudiced against people whom they had never met or heard anything about.[19]

Institutionalized Racism

In the last two decades, institutionalized racism has become recognized as a major problem. Institutionalized racism refers to discriminatory acts and policies that pervade the major institutions of society, such as the legal system, politics, the economy, and education. Some of these discriminatory acts and policies are illegal; others are not.

Stokely Carmichael and Charles Hamilton make the following distinction between individual racism and institutional racism:

When white terrorists bomb a black church and kill five black children, that is an act of individual racism, widely deplored by most segments of society. But when in the same city . . . five hundred black babies die each year because of the lack of proper food, shelter, and medical facilities, and thousands more are destroyed and maimed physically, emotionally, and intellectually because of conditions of poverty and discrimination in the black community, that is a function of institutional racism.[20]

Discrimination is built, often unwittingly, into the very structure and form of our society. The following examples reflect institutional racism. A family counseling agency with branch offices assigns less skilled counselors and provides lower-quality services in an office located in a minority neighborhood. A public welfare department encourages white applicants to request funds for special needs (for example, clothing) or to use certain services (for example, day-care and homemaker services with the costs charged to the agency), whereas nonwhite clients are not informed or are less enthusiastically informed of such services. A public welfare department takes longer to process the requests of nonwhites for funds and services. A police department discriminates against nonwhite staff in terms of work assignments, hiring practices, promotion practices, and pay increases. A probation and parole agency tends to ignore minor violations of the rules for parole of white clients but seeks to return to prison nonwhite parolees having minor violations of parole rules. A mental health agency tends to assign "psychotic" labels to nonwhite clients but assigns labels indicating a less serious disorder to white clients. White staff at a family counseling center are encouraged to provide intensive services to clients with whom they have a good relationship (often white clients) and are told to give less attention to those clients "they aren't hitting it off well with" (and they may be disproportionately nonwhite). The unemployment rate for nonwhites has consistently been over twice that for whites. The infant mortality rate for nonwhites is nearly twice as high as for whites. The life expectancy age for nonwhites is several years less than for whites. The average number of years of educational achievement for nonwhites is considerably less than for whites.[21]

There are many examples of institutional racism in school systems. Schools in white suburbs generally have better facilities and more highly trained teachers than in minority neighborhoods. Minority families are, on the average, less able to provide the hidden costs of "free" education (higher property taxes, transportation, class trips, clothing, and supplies), and therefore their children become less involved in the educational process. Textbooks generally glorify the white race and give scant attention to minorities. Jeannette Henry writes about the effects of history textbooks on Native American children:

What is the effect upon the student, when he learns from his textbooks that one race, and one alone, is the most, the best, the greatest; when he learns that Indians* were mere parts of the landscape and wilderness which had to be cleared out, to make way for the great "movement" of white population across the land; and when he learns that Indians were killed and forcibly removed from their ancient homelands to make way for adventurers (usually called "pioneering goldminers"), for land grabbers (usually called "settlers"), and for illegal squatters on Indian-owned land (usually called "frontiersmen")? What is the effect upon the young Indian child himself, who is also a student in the school system, when he is told that Columbus discovered America, that Coronado "brought civilization" to the Indian people, and that the Spanish missionaries provided havens of refuge for the Indians? Is it reasonable to assume that the student, of whatever race, will not discover at some time in his life that Indians discovered America thousands of years before Columbus set out upon his voyage; that Coronado brought death and destruction to the native peoples; and that the Spanish missionaries, in all too many cases, forcibly dragged Indians to the missions?[22]

---

*The term *Indian* was originally used by early European settlers to describe the native populations of North America. Because of its non-native derivation and the context of cultural domination surrounding its use, many people, particularly Native Americans, object to the use of the word. The term *Native American* is now generally preferred.

Our criminal justice system also has elements of institutional racism. Our justice system is supposed to be fair and nondiscriminatory. The very name of the system, *justice*, implies fairness and equality. Yet, in practice, there is evidence of racism. Although blacks compose only about 12 percent of the population, they make up 42 percent of the jail population. (There is considerable debate about what extent this is due to racism as opposed to differential crime rates by race.) The average prison sentence for murder and kidnapping is longer for blacks than for whites. Half of those sentenced to death are black.[23] Police departments and district attorney's offices are more likely to enforce vigorously the kinds of crimes committed by lower-income groups and minority groups than by middle- and upper-class white groups. Poor people (a disproportionate number of nonwhites are poor) are substantially less likely to be able to post bail. As a result, they are forced to remain in jail until their trial, which often takes months or sometimes more than a year to come up. Unable to post bail, they are more apt to be found guilty, as Paul Wice notes:

Numerous studies clearly show that detained defendants are far more likely to be found guilty and receive more severe sentences than those released prior to trial. Limited visiting hours, locations remote from the counsel's office, inadequate conference facilities, and censored mail all serve to impede an effective lawyer-client relationship.[24]

The Effects and Costs of Discrimination

Grace Halsell is a white woman who, through chemical treatments, changed the color of her skin to look like a black person for a brief period of time in order to determine what it means to "live black" in a white world. She reports on her experiences in working one day as a maid for a white woman in the South:

Long before I have one job completed, there are new orders: "Now sweep off the front porch, the side porch, the back porch, and mop the back porch."

The tone is unmistakably that of the mistress-slave relationship. . . .

I feel sorry for her. We are two women in a house all day long, and I sense that she desperately wants to talk to me, but it can never be as an equal. She looks on me as less than a wholly dignified and developed person. . . .

My eight hours are up. She asks if I know where to catch the bus. No, I say, should I turn left or right "when I go out the front door?" The front door *comes out inadvertently, because I am only trying to get an idea of directions. She hands me five dollars and ushers me to the back door, quite pointedly.*

Two bus transfers and an hour later, I am back in "nigger-town." Near the Summers Hotel, young, bright-eyed Negro* children I've come to know wave, smile, and say "hi!"

I want to tell each one of them because I feel so degraded, so morally and spiritually depressed, "Don't do what I did! Don't ever sell yourself that cheap! Don't let it happen to you."

And I want to add, ". . . whatever you do, don't do what I did." The assault upon an individual's dignity and self-respect has intolerable limits, and I believe at this moment my limits have been reached.[25]

Racial discrimination is an extra handicap. Everyone in our competitive society seeks to obtain the necessary resources to lead a contented and comfortable life. Being a victim of discrimination is another obstacle that has to be overcome. Being discriminated against because of race makes it more difficult to obtain adequate housing, financial resources, a quality education, employment, adequate health care and other services, equal justice in civil and criminal cases, and so on.

Discrimination also has heavy psychological costs. All of us have to develop a sense of identity—who we are and how we fit into a complex, swiftly changing world. Ideally, it is important that we form a positive

self-concept and strive to obtain worthy goals. Yet, as we have noted before, according to C. H. Cooley's "looking-glass self," our idea of who we are and what we are is largely determined by the way others relate to us.[26] When members of a minority group are treated by the majority group as if they are inferior, second-class citizens, it is substantially more difficult for such members to develop a positive identity. Thus, people who are the objects of discrimination encounter barriers to developing their full potentials as human beings.

In 1965, prior to most "black pride" movements, Kenneth Clark described the devastating effects of discrimination on blacks:

Human beings who are forced to live under ghetto conditions and whose daily experience tells them that almost nowhere in society are they respected and granted the ordinary dignity and courtesy accorded to others will, as a matter of course, begin to doubt their own worth. Since every human being depends upon his cumulative experiences with others for clues as to how he should view and value himself, children who are consistently rejected understandably begin to question and doubt whether they, their family, and their group really deserve no more respect from the larger society than they receive. These doubts become the seeds of pernicious self- and group-hatred, the Negro's complex and debilitating prejudice against himself. . . . Negroes have come to believe in their own inferiority.[27]

Young children of groups who are the victims of discrimination are apt to develop low self-esteem at an early age. Studies have found that black children who have been subjected to discrimination have a preference for white dolls and white playmates over black[28] (although no comparison was made to those not subjected to discrimination).

Discrimination also has high costs for the majority group. It impairs intergroup cooperation and communication. It has resulted in race riots, particularly in our inner cities, which have caused a number of deaths and cost billions of dollars. Discrimination also is a factor in contributing to social problems among minorities—for example, higher rates of crime, emo-

---

*When this was written in 1969, the term *Negro* was still used widely; but, in the 1970s, the preferred term changed to *black*, and the term *Negro* now is sometimes used to suggest a black person who interacts submissively with whites.

tional problems, alcoholism, drug abuse, all of which have cost billions of dollars in social programs. Albert Szymanski argues that discrimination is a barrier to collective action (for example, unionization) among whites and nonwhites (particularly people in the lower-income classes) and therefore is a factor in perpetuating low-paying jobs and poverty.[29] Of course, this increases profits for the owners of businesses; but it hurts less affluent whites, who could benefit from collective action.

Finally, discrimination in the United States undermines some of our nation's political goals. Many other nations view us as hypocritical when we advocate human rights and equality. In order to make an effective argument for human rights on a worldwide scale, we must first put our own house in order by eliminating racial and ethnic discrimination. Few Americans realize the extent to which racial discrimination damages our international reputation. Nonwhite foreign diplomats to the United States often complain about being victims of discrimination, as they are mistaken for being members of American minority groups. With most of the nations of the world being nonwhite, our racist practices severely damage our influence and prestige.

BACKGROUND OF RACIAL GROUPS

The largest racial group in America is the white race, which is the majority group, both in numbers (nearly 80 percent of the population)[30] and in power. Blacks compose about 12 percent of the population,[31] and Hispanics compose about 8 percent of the population.[32] The other nonwhite groups compose about 2 percent of our population and primarily include Native Americans, Japanese, Chinese, and Filipinos. There are also small numbers of the following nonwhite groups: Aleuts, Asian Indians, Eskimos, Hawaiians, Indonesians, Koreans, and Polynesians. In educational attainment, occupational status, and average income, most of these nonwhite groups are clearly at a disadvantage as

compared with the white groups. (The two major nonwhite groups that now approach whites in terms of socioeconomic status are the Japanese and Chinese.)

Blacks

The United States has always been a racist country. Although our forefathers talked about freedom, dignity, equality, and human rights, our economy prior to the civil war depended heavily on slavery.

Many slaves came from cultures that had well-developed art forms, political systems, family patterns, religious beliefs, and economic systems. However, their home culture was not European, and therefore slave owners viewed it as being of "no consequence" and prohibited slaves from practicing and developing their art, their language, their religion, and their family life. For want of practice, their former culture soon died in America.

The life of a slave was harsh. Slaves were not viewed as human beings but as chattel to be bought and sold. Long, hard days were spent working in the field, with the profits of their labor going to their white owners. Whippings, mutilations, and hangings were commonly accepted white control practices. The impetus to enslave blacks was not simply racism, as many whites believed that it was to their economic advantage to have a cheap supply of labor. Cotton-growing, in particular, was thought to require a large labor force that was also cheap and docile. Marriages among slaves were not recognized by the law, and slaves were often sold with little regard to effects on marital and family ties. Throughout the slavery period and even after it, blacks were discouraged from demonstrating intelligence, initiative, or ambition. For a period of time, it was even illegal to teach blacks to read or write.

Some authorities have noted that the opposition to the spread of slavery preceding the Civil War was primarily due to the North's fears of competition from slave labor and the rapidly increasing migration of blacks to the North and West rather than to moral concern for human rights and equality.[33] Few whites at that time understood or believed in the principle of racial equality—not even Abraham Lincoln, who believed blacks were inferior to whites. In 1858 in a speech in Charleston, Illinois Lincoln asserted:

I will say, then, that I am not, nor ever have been in favor of bringing about in any way the social and political equality of the white and black races; that I am not, nor ever have been, in favor of making voters or jurors of Negroes, nor of qualifying them to hold office, nor to inter-marry with White people . . . and inasmuch as they cannot so live, while they do remain together there must be the position of superior and inferior, and I as much as any other man am in favor of having the superior position assigned to the White race.[34]

Following the Civil War, the federal government failed to develop a comprehensive program of economic and educational aid to blacks. As a result, most blacks returned to being economically dependent on the same planters in the South who had held them in bondage. Within a few years, laws were passed in the southern states prohibiting interracial marriages and requiring racial segregation in schools and public places.

A rigid caste system in the South hardened into a system of oppression known as "Jim Crow." The system prescribed how blacks were supposed to act in the presence of whites, asserted white supremacy, embraced racial segregation, and denied political and legal rights to blacks. Blacks who opposed Jim Crow were subjected to burnings, beatings, and lynchings. Jim Crow was used to "teach" blacks to view themselves as inferior and to be servile and passive in interactions with whites.

World War II opened up new employment opportunities for blacks. A large migration of blacks from the South began. Greater mobility afforded by wartime conditions led to upheavals in the traditional caste system. Awareness of disparity between the ideal and reality led many people to try to improve race relations, not only for domestic peace and justice, but to answer criticism from abroad. With each gain in race relations, more blacks were encouraged to press for their rights.

A major turning point in black history was the U.S.

Supreme Court decision in *Brown vs. Board of Education* in 1954, which ruled that racial segregation in public schools was unconstitutional. Since 1954, there have been a number of organized efforts by both blacks and certain segments of the white population to secure equal rights and opportunities for blacks. Attempts to change deeply entrenched racist attitudes and practices have produced much turmoil: for example, the burning of our inner cities in the late 1960s;* the assassination of Martin Luther King, Jr.; and clashes between black militant groups and the police. There have also been significant advances. Wide-ranging civil rights legislation has been passed, protecting rights in areas such as housing, voting, employment, and use of public transportation and facilities. During the riots in 1968 the National Advisory Commission on Civil Disorders warned that our society was careening "toward two societies, one black, one white—separate and unequal."[35] David Gelman summarizes the current atmosphere of black-white relations in our society:

Twenty years and a social eon have passed. Mercifully, America today is not the bitterly sundered dual society that the riot commission grimly foresaw. Nor is it King's promised land of racial amity. Rather, it is something uneasily between the two: a society less unequal but also less caring than it was in the '60s. . . .

Blacks and whites now more often work together, lunch together, even live side by side, yet few really count each other as friends.[36]

Four out of five blacks now live in metropolitan areas, over half of them in our central cities.[37] American cities are still largely segregated, with blacks living primarily in black neighborhoods. In recent years, the main thrust of the civil rights movement among blacks has been economic equality. The economic gap between blacks and whites continues to be immense. Black families are three times as likely as white families to fall below the poverty line.[38]

---

*On April 4, 1968 Martin Luther King, Jr. was killed by a white assassin's bullet. His death helped trigger extensive rioting in forty cities; in many cities whole blocks were burned down.

Occupational status in our society is crucially related to self-esteem and lifestyle, as demonstrated in the following statement by a 39-year-old black male:

How can you have any pride? I'm a part-time worker—a part-time husband. I guess I'm really a part-time man. I can't find enough to do to keep food on the table. Guess some people would think that I'm the sorriest man that ever wore out shoe leather. It ain't that I don't have no get-up, it's just that I can't find nothing to do. I had to leave home so the children could eat. While I'm sitting here with you, they're out looking for me. That ain't so bad—what really hurts is that my wife is going to tell them people down at the welfare that some other man is the baby's daddy, or else she thinks she can't get no aid. If they take her off the welfare, she'll starve. So every time she has another baby, she gives a different guy's name— excuse me for bawling, man, I just can't help it—but it sure ain't no justice when a man's got to make his own children bastards in order to feed them.[39]

We, as a nation, have come a long way since the Supreme Court's decision in 1954. But we still have a long way to go before we eliminate black poverty and respond to the deep frustrations of the black masses in our ghettos. Living conditions in black ghettos remain as bleak as they were when our inner cities erupted in the late 1960s. Dissatisfaction with living conditions in the 1960s led blacks in many inner-city areas to torch and burn down numerous buildings. These buildings were owned largely by white absentee landlords.

Two developments have characterized the socioeconomic circumstances of blacks in the past twenty-five years, as Gelman notes:

Two striking developments mark the black situation since the '60s. One is the emergence of an authentic black middle class, better educated, better paid, better housed than any group of blacks that has gone before it. As measured sometimes by white-collar occupation—anything from bank clerk to engineer—sometimes by incomes of $20,000 a year and up, the middle class grew to near 56 percent of black wage earners by 1980. . . .

The second development is, in a way, the reverse side of the first. As comparatively well off blacks move to better neighborhoods, they have left behind a stripped-down, socially disabled nucleus of poor people who have come to be called (somewhat pejoratively) the "underclass." With a population estimated at 2.5 million—roughly three times what it was in the '70s—this group generates a disproportionate share of the social pathology usually associated with the ghetto, including high crime rates.[40]

People in this underclass tend to be chronically on welfare, to drop out of high school, to have families headed by single parents, and males in this underclass tend not to participate in the work force. Statistics on the black population illustrate this underclass. Around 55 percent of all black families are headed by a single female parent.[41] The rate of pregnancy among 15- to 19-year-old black women is more than twice that of whites in that age group.[42] Blacks account for about half of all crimes of violence.[43] The rate of unemployment for black youths is more than double that of white youths.[44] Median black income is still only 57 percent of whites.[45]

In a study of pregnant teenagers on Chicago's West Side, Orfield indicated that the data, "showed that most of these girls didn't know anyone who had a job, anyone who went to college, anyone who was married. Within their society, it looks rational to have a baby when you're a teenage girl."[46]

Hispanic Americans

Hispanic Americans are Americans of Spanish origin. Hispanics are diverse groups bound somewhat together by their language, culture, and ties to Roman Catholicism. This broad categorization includes Mexican Americans (Chicanos), Puerto Ricans, Cubans, people from Central and South America and the West Indies, and others of Spanish origin (Figure 11.1). The Hispanic population is growing at a rate five times faster than the rest of the population.[47] There are three main reasons for this large growth: a trend to have

FIGURE 11.1

Percentage Distribution of Hispanic Americans by Land of Spanish Origin

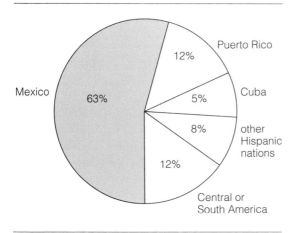

Source: *Parade Magazine*, November 29, 1987, p. 13.

large families, a continual inflow of immigrants (particularly from Mexico), and a high proportion of Hispanics in this country being of child-bearing age.

MEXICAN AMERICANS   The largest Hispanic group in the United States is Mexican Americans. Although many Americans are unaware of the fact, Mexican Americans have had a long history of settlement and land ownership in what is now the United States. In the 1700s and 1800s, there were a number of small Spanish communities in what later became the American Southwest—in areas that have since gained statehood (including Texas, Arizona, New Mexico, and California). These early Hispanics were generally small landholders. In the 1800s, Anglos moved into these regions, and competition for good land became fierce. Many Mexican Americans had their land taken away by large Anglo-owned cattle and agricultural interests. Texas was once part of Mexico. In 1836, the settlers (including many of Spanish descent) staged a successful insurrection

against the Mexican government, and in 1845 Texas was annexed to the United States. As a consequence, many of the Spanish settlers became U.S. citizens.

Since the 1850s, there has been a steady migration of Mexicans to the United States, with a number of the immigrants entering this country illegally. The average income in Mexico is much lower than it is in the United States, so the quest for higher wages and a better life has lured many Mexicans to this country.

Relations between Anglos and Mexican Americans have on occasion become vicious and ugly. Similar to black-white confrontations, there have been many riots between whites and Mexican Americans.

Many Mexican Americans now live in barrios (Spanish-speaking sections of U.S. cities that have become ghettos) in such cities as Los Angeles, Denver, and Chicago. Although some are moving up in socioeconomic status, most are employed in low-paid occupations.

A smaller number of Mexican Americans are employed in temporary, seasonal work, largely on farms. Some migrate north in the summer to be farm laborers and return to the Southwest in the fall. In rate of acculturation and assimilation, these migrant workers are among the least "Americanized" of all ethnic groups.[48] They are reluctant to seek help from social agencies, partly because of their pride and partly because of language and cultural barriers.

An increasingly large segment of this ethnic group is becoming involved in the "Chicano" movement. Chicanos are Americans of Mexican origin who resent the stereotypes that demean Mexican Americans—particularly the image of laziness, since they are employed to do some of the hardest physical labor in our society. The origin of the word *Chicano* is not clear, but until the last generation it was a derogatory term Anglos used for Mexican Americans. Now the word and the people have come full circle, and Chicano has taken on a new, positive meaning. The Chicano movement asserts that institutional change is needed to be more responsive to the needs of Chicanos. There now is a Chicano-oriented college in San Jose, California, and Chicano studies programs have been developed at a number of other universities.

Cesar Chavez formed the first successful union to represent migrant workers nearly twenty-five years ago. His nationwide boycotts of table grapes that are picked by underpaid workers and contaminated with pesticides have inspired other collective action by Chicanos.

The civil rights activities of blacks have provided encouragement for the Chicano's more militant stance. In addition, second- and third-generation Mexican Americans have fewer ties to Mexico than did their elders, and they are oriented more toward the majority American culture in terms of aspirations and goals. Yet, similarly to blacks, Mexican Americans generally have low-paying jobs, high rates of unemployment, and high levels of poverty. They also have high rates of infant mortality, low levels of educational attainment, and high levels of substandard housing. Their standard of living is no better, and possibly slightly worse, than that faced by blacks.

Studies have found that many employers in the Southwest consistently hire Chicano workers at or below minimum wage rates—yet another example of institutional racism.[49] One study in the garment industry in California found that only 8 percent of nearly 1,000 companies were paying at or above the minimum wage.[50] Some of these workers are illegal aliens who are unable to file a complaint with our government for fear of being deported.

Over the past two decades, Cesar Chavez has unionized migrant workers in California, organized several strikes, and led successful nationwide boycotts of fruit and vegetables picked by underpaid workers. Powerful white economic interests made several violent attempts to break these strikes. Chavez's campaigns have provided an example and incentive for other collective action by Chicanos. The future is likely to see Chicanos becoming an increasingly powerful political force with which to be reckoned.

PUERTO RICANS   After World War II, large numbers of Puerto Ricans migrated to the mainland United States, largely because of population pressure and insufficient job opportunities on the island. Although found in all the states, they have settled mainly in New York City where they are heavily employed in the garment industry and as service workers. Those migrating from Puerto Rico were from the higher socioeconomic classes in their home society. Although their earnings in the mainland are higher than in Puerto Rico, they have experienced lower job status than other whites in New York and are housed primarily in slum ghettos.

For Puerto Ricans, the Spanish culture has been dominant; but they have also been influenced by the Taino, American, African, and European cultures. In Puerto Rico, status is based on culture or class, not skin color. Interracial marriages have been extensive in Puerto Rico. On entering the mainland United States, many Puerto Ricans, understandably, become puzzled by the higher priority given to skin color here.

J. Julian Rivera summarizes the unique factors facing Puerto Rican migrants to New York City:

As United States citizens, Puerto Ricans can move freely between the island and the continent. The migration tends to follow economic trends in both the United States and Puerto Rico. The heaviest migrant waves from Puerto Rico came in the early 1950's, encouraged by faster and cheaper air transportation as well as by the demand for semiskilled and unskilled labor.

The average Puerto Rican migrant is young, has little formal education, and comes from the rural areas, in some cases an urban slum. His move to the United States is not seen as permanent; he intends to go back to the island after making some money. Consequently, he does not see the need to become assimilated and grow roots in this land, nor to give up his language and his culture. In many cases, this fact constitutes a problem in his adjustment to this society, particularly in the establishment of community and political organizations. Some Puerto Ricans are able to save some money and fulfill their dream of returning to Puerto Rico to start a small business or buy a house and retire. Many others return, poor and frustrated, only to find that there is no place for them in Puerto Rico either. Some families are caught in a pattern of traveling between the United States and Puerto Rico without making a satisfactory adjustment in either place. Ironically, many never make it back to the island, and their children prefer to stay here.[51]

CUBANS   Most Cuban Americans are recent migrants to the United States. Many are political refugees, having fled Cuba following the takeover of the government by Fidel Castro in 1959. In 1980, Castro opened the doors of his socialist island, and over 100,000 more Cubans fled to this country. Cuban Americans tend to differ from other Hispanics in that they are generally well-educated and often have a managerial or professional background. Large numbers have settled in southern Florida, particularly in the Miami area.

Many of the latest arrivals in 1980, however, were from the lower class, some of whom had been imprisoned in Cuba for a variety of crimes. (Castro apparently sent them to the United States to reduce the costs of the correctional system in Cuba.) Many of these most recent arrivals have settled in southern Florida, with there being some confrontations with whites, increased crime, and other adjustment problems.

HISPANOS   After the Mexican-American War in 1848, Mexico ceded a large territory to the United States, thus making U.S. citizens of a number of Spanish-speaking people. Many of their descendants call themselves "Hispano" to distinguish themselves from the Mexican Americans who migrated later from Mexico. Still residing primarily in the Southwest, Hispanos are predominantly a rural people and have had limited contact with the outside world. Their standard of living is low. They are living in a 17th-century culture and are using agricultural techniques from that period. Approximately half of New Mexico's population is composed of Hispanos.[52]

Native Americans

When Columbus first came to America in 1492, there were about a million Native Americans grouped into more than 600 distinct societies.[53] Tribal wars between the groups were common, and there were wide variations among tribes in customs, culture, lifestyles, languages, and religious ceremonies. The whites gradually expanded settlements, moving westward and slowly taking native land. Colonists and pioneers adopted a policy that amounted to deliberate extermination of Native Americans. The saying "The only good Indian is a dead Indian" became popular. Whites took their lands away, depleted the buffalo herds on which many tribes depended for survival, slaughtered tribes, and indirectly killed many others through leading forced marches in freezing weather and bringing diseases and famine.[54] Unable to mobilize a common defense, all native tribes were defeated in 1892.

In 1887, Congress passed the General Allotment Act, which empowered Congress unilaterally to revise treaties made with Native Americans. This action opened the way for land-hungry whites to take productive native land. From 1887 to 1928, the land held by Native Americans decreased from 137 million acres to 50 million acres, with most of the remaining property being

*Native American groups organized dramatic protests that drew national attention in the 1960s and
1970s. One of the most famous occurred in February 1973, when members of the militant American
Indian Movement (AIM) began a seventy-one-day occupation of the town of Wounded Knee, South
Dakota, at the site of the U.S. Cavalry's 1890 massacre of three hundred Sioux. Oscar Running Bear
(above) and other protesters demanded government attention to their grievances. AIM took eleven
hostages and occupied several buildings; the siege collapsed following a gun battle that left one
protester dead and another wounded.*

some of the least productive real estate in the country.[55]

Contact with the white culture has undermined
Native Americans' traditional living patterns. It has
been said that "the buffalo are gone"—meaning that
Native Americans can no longer sustain themselves
through hunting and fishing. Segregation to reservations has further served to damage their pride and
sense of self-worth. Government programs now attempt to meet subsistence needs, but they also have
served to pauperize Native Americans. Being disillu-
sioned, Native Americans on reservations have high
rates of suicide, alcoholism, illiteracy, poverty, homicide, child neglect, and infant mortality.

Earlier in this century, the plight of Native Americans was largely ignored because of their isolation on
remote reservations. Through the Bureau of Indian Affairs, they received the most paternalistic treatment by
the government of all minorities. For many years, the
BIA had programs designed to destroy Native American
culture, religion, and language. Today, the BIA has become a symbol of frustration and despair.[56]

In the 1960s and 1970s, the plight of the Native
Americans received national concern, and many whites
became actively involved in their problems. Films de-
picting the "glorious" victories of the whites over "savages" have been replaced by the realization that early

white settlers exploited the Native Americans by taking away their land and destroying their way of life.

During most of this century, Native Americans have been passive. However, in the 1960s and 1970s there were some organized efforts to make changes. Similarly to blacks and Chicanos, Native Americans had some widely publicized demonstrations, such as at Wounded Knee, South Dakota in the 1970s. In the 1980s our country became more conservative, and political action efforts among Native Americans have subsided. High rates of poverty and other social problems continue among Native Americans.

Some tribes are taking legal action to recover land that was illegally taken from them. The Nonintercourse Act of 1870 stated that any land transaction between Indians and others must be approved by Congress or it is null and void. Many such transactions were not ratified by Congress. Now, some tribes have brought legal claims for land and for rights to minerals and rivers. Some of these claims have already been upheld. Two tribes in Maine have won their claim to half the land in the state, and the state has been ordered to negotiate a financial settlement with the tribes. In Alaska, Native Americans have been awarded $1 billion and 40 million acres of land in compensation for illegal seizures of their territory in the past.[57]

Asian Americans

Asian Americans in the United States include the Japanese, Chinese, Filipinos, Koreans, Burmese, Indonesians, Guamanians, Samoans, South Vietnamese, and Thais. A large number of South Vietnamese immigrated to this country in the early 1970s following the end of the Vietnam War. Contrary to a popular stereotype, Asians are not homogeneous. Each ethnic group has its own history, religion, language, and culture. These Asian American groups also differ in terms of group cohesion, levels of education, and socioeconomic status. Comparable to the mistake of viewing all Europeans as being the same, it is an error to view all Asians as a single entity.

Like other disenfranchised groups, Asian Americans are victimized by discrimination. Immediate problems include housing, education, income maintenance, unemployment and underemployment, health care, and vocational training and retraining. Because of language and cultural barriers, many needy Asians (particularly new immigrants and the aged) do not seek out services to which they are entitled. The two prominent Asian groups in this country are the Japanese and the Chinese.

JAPANESE   Until 1900, few Japanese migrants came to America, partly because of legal restrictions against their migration and partly because of the unfriendly reception they received in this country. Japanese Americans refused to accept discrimination, which aroused the antagonism of white Americans.

After the turn of the century, Japanese migration increased. Japanese settled primarily on the West Coast. By 1941 (when Pearl Harbor was attacked), there were few distinctive Japanese-American settlements outside the West Coast other than in New York and Chicago. During World War II, the loyalty of Japanese Americans was viewed with intense suspicion, and they severely felt the impact of prejudice, war hysteria, and the denial of certain civil rights. On March 2, 1942, the commander of the Western Theater of Operations established "relocation centers" (concentration camps) to which Japanese Americans who lived on the West Coast were sent. The confused policies of our nation during this war are indicated by the fact that 33,000 Japanese Americans served in the armed forces for the United States while 110,000 Japanese Americans were confined in concentration camps.[58] Not only were their civil rights violated, but they also were forced to sell their property. (In comparison, Americans who were of German or Italian descent were not similarly persecuted, although the war was fought against Germany and Italy as well as Japan.) Following the war, their return to the West Coast met with some initial opposition, but a counterreaction soon developed among whites that emphasized fair play and acceptance. Since 1946, Japanese Americans have settled in other parts of the country, and their socioeconomic status is now approaching that of whites.

These Japanese-Americans, among 110,000 others, were deemed a national security risk and interned in "relocation centers" during World War II. The War Relocation Authority, which forced families to sell their property on extremely short notice, allowed them to bring only what they could carry to ten crowded, hastily built camps in remote areas of several Western states. Forty-five years passed before Congress offered financial restitution and a formal apology to the survivors of an ignoble exercise in wartime prejudice and paranoia.

CHINESE   In the 1800s, Chinese were encouraged to immigrate in search of jobs in U.S. mines, on railroad construction, and for farm work. These immigrants soon encountered hostility from some whites, particularly in western states, because of their willingness to work for low wages. Their racial and cultural distinctiveness also made them targets for scapegoating, particularly during periods of high unemployment. Charles Henderson et al. describe the extent to which

Chinese Americans were subjected to racism during this time period.

Racism against Asians is shown in the 1854 decision of the California Supreme Court in The People vs. Hall. *The appellant, a white Anglo-American, had been convicted of murder upon the testimony of Chinese witnesses. Was such evidence admissible? The judge ruled that Asians should be ineligible to testify for or against a white man. This ruling opened the floodgate for anti-Chinese abuse, violence, and exploitation. Group murders, lynchings, property damage, and robbery of the Chinese were reported up and down the West Coast. Because of the harsh treatment of the Chinese, any luckless person was described as not having a "Chinaman's chance."*[59]

In the early 1900s, Chinese Americans were concentrated largely on the West Coast; but since the 1920s, they have tended to disperse throughout the nation. They tend to settle in large cities, and many live in Chinatowns in such cities as Los Angeles, San Francisco, New York, Boston, and Chicago.

The struggles of China against Japan before and during World War II brought about a more favorable image of Chinese Americans. Some discrimination continues. They have been subjected to less discrimination in Hawaii than on the mainland. Their cultural distinctiveness is being preserved by the frequency of intraracial marriages and by little contact with the white culture. Chinese Americans continue to have a large lower class, although they have experienced recent social and economic progress.

STRATEGIES AGAINST DISCRIMINATION

A wide range of strategies have been developed to reduce racial discrimination. These strategies include the following, which will be summarized here: mass media appeals, strategies to increase interaction among the races, civil rights laws, activism, school busing, affirmative action programs, human relations programs, confrontation of racist remarks and actions, and confrontation of the problems in inner-city ghettos.

Mass Media Appeals

Newspapers, radio, and television at times present programs that are designed to explain the nature and harmful effects of prejudice and to promote the "har-

mony" of humanity. Mass media is able to reach large numbers of people simultaneously. By expanding public awareness of the existence of discrimination and its consequences, the media may strengthen control over racial extremists. But mass media has limitations in changing prejudiced attitudes and behaviors; it is primarily a provider of information and seldom has a lasting effect in changing deep-seated prejudices through propaganda. Broadcasting such platitudes as "all people are brothers and sisters" and "prejudice is un-American" is not very effective. Highly prejudiced persons are often unaware of their own prejudices. Even if they are aware of their prejudices, they generally ignore mass media appeals as irrelevant to them or dismiss the appeals as propaganda. It should be noted, however, that the mass media probably has had a significant impact in reducing discrimination through showing nonwhites and whites harmoniously working in commercials, on news teams, and on TV shows.

Greater Interaction among the Races

Increased contact among races is not in itself sufficient to alleviate racial prejudice. In fact, increased contact may, in some instances, highlight the differences between groups and increase suspicions and fear. George Simpson and J. Milton Yinger reviewed a number of studies and concluded that prejudice is likely to be increased when contacts are tension-laden or involuntary.[60] Prejudice is apt to subside when individuals are placed in situations where they share characteristics in nonracial matters: for example, as coworkers, fellow soldiers, or classmates. Equal status contacts, rather than inferior-superior status contacts, are also more apt to reduce prejudices.[61]

Civil Rights Laws

In the past twenty-five years, equal rights have been legislated in areas of employment, voting, housing, public accommodation, and education. A key question is, "How effective are laws in changing prejudice?"

Proponents of civil rights legislation make certain assumptions. The first is that new laws will reduce discriminatory behavioral patterns. The laws define what was once "normal" behavior (discrimination) as now being "deviant" behavior. Through time, it is expected that attitudes will change and become more consistent with the forced nondiscriminatory behavior patterns.

A second assumption is that the laws will be used. Civil rights laws were enacted after the Civil War but were seldom enforced and gradually were eroded. It is also unfortunately true that some officials will find ways of evading the intent of the law by eliminating only the extreme, overt symbols of discrimination, without changing other practices. Thus, the enactment of a law is only the first step in the process of changing prejudiced attitudes and practices. However, as Martin Luther King, Jr. noted, "The law may not make a man love me, but it can restrain him from lynching me, and I think that's pretty important."

Activism

The strategy of "activism" attempts to change the structure of race relations through direct confrontations of discrimination and segregation policies. Activism has three types of politics: the politics of creative disorder, the politics of disorder, and the politics of escape.[62]

The *politics of creative disorder* operates on the edge of the dominant social system and includes school boycotts, rent strikes, job blockades, sit-ins (for example, at segregated restaurants), public marches, and product boycotts. This type of activism is based on the concept of nonviolent resistance. A dramatic illustration of nonviolent resistance began on December 1, 1955, when Rosa Parks of Montgomery, Alabama refused to give up her seat on a bus to a white person. Alabama and many other southern states at that time had Jim Crow laws that were designed to enforce segregation. One such law required blacks to sit in the back seats of buses. Mrs. Parks refused to get up and move to the back because her feet were hurting. She was arrested and unintentionally began the famous Montgomery Bus Boycott. The Boycott lasted for a year

and resulted in a U.S. Supreme Court ruling that declared ordinances that required segregated seating on public conveyances to be unconstitutional. The boycott had an even more important psychological impact, as it suggested that minority citizens had rights equal to those of whites and that united nonviolent resistance could overturn discriminatory laws.[63]

The *politics of disorder* reflects alienation from the dominant culture and disillusionment with the political system. In this type, those being discriminated against resort to mob uprising, riots, and other forms of violence.

In 1969, the National Commission on Causes and Prevention of Violence reported that 200 riots had occurred in the previous five years, when our inner cities erupted.[64] In the early 1980s, there were again some riots in Miami and in some of our other inner cities. The focus of most of these riots has been minority group aggression against white-owned property.

The *politics of escape* engages in passionate rhetoric about how minorities are being victimized. But, because the focus is not on arriving at solutions, the rhetoric is not productive, except perhaps for providing an emotional release.

The principal value of activism or social protest seems to be the stimulation of public awareness of certain problems. The civil rights protests in the 1960s made practically all Americans aware of the discrimination to which nonwhite groups were being subjected. With this awareness, at least some of the discrimination has ceased, and race relations have improved. Continued protest beyond a certain (although indeterminate) point, however, appears to have little additional value.[65]

School Busing

Housing patterns in many large metropolitan centers have led to "de facto" segregation; that is, blacks and certain other nonwhite groups live in one area, and whites live in another. This segregation has affected educational opportunities for nonwhites. Nonwhite areas have fewer financial resources, and, as a result, the educational quality is often substantially lower than in white areas. In the past two decades courts in a number of metropolitan areas have ordered that a certain proportion of nonwhites must be bused to schools in white areas, and that a certain proportion of whites must be bused to schools in nonwhite areas. The objectives are twofold: to provide equal educational opportunities and to reduce racial prejudice through interaction. In some areas, school busing has become accepted and appears to be meeting the stated objectives. In other areas, however, the approach is highly controversial and has exacerbated racial tensions. Busing in these areas is claimed (*a*) to be highly expensive; (*b*) to destroy the concept of the "neighborhood school" in which the facility serves as a recreational, social, and educational center of the community; and (*c*) to result in lower-quality education. A number of parents in these areas feel so strongly about busing that they are sending their children to private schools. In addition, some have argued that busing increases "white flight" from neighborhoods where busing has been ordered.[66] In 1970, William Raspberry, a columnist for the *Washington Post*, commented about the effects of busing in Washington, D.C.: "We find ourselves busing children from all-black neighborhoods all the way across town to schools that are rapidly becoming all-black."[67]

There have been additional concerns expressed about busing. It is argued that busing children a long distance is very costly and uses funds that could otherwise be used to improve the quality of education. Busing lessens local control and interest in schools; and it makes it less practical for parents to become involved in school affairs because the school is less accessible.

In certain communities, busing may also intensify racial tensions. For example, in Boston in 1975, a federal judge ordered school busing in order to counter housing segregation patterns. The Irish and Polish descendants of South Boston (who saw themselves as oppressed ethnic minorities) violently opposed the busing, and racial tensions intensified for several years. Sociologists also voice concern that school busing in an atmosphere of hostility may reduce the quality of education and increase racial prejudices and tensions.

School busing to achieve integration was vigorously pursued by the court system and the federal Justice Department in the 1970s. In 1981, the Reagan administration stated it would be much less active in advocating that busing be used as a vehicle to achieve integration. In recent years there has been less of an emphasis in many communities in using school busing to achieve integration.

Affirmative Action

Affirmative action programs provide for preferential hiring and admission requirements (for example, admission to medical schools) for minority applicants. Affirmative action programs cover minority groups, including women. These programs also require that employers must (*a*) make active efforts to locate and recruit qualified minority applicants and (*b*) in certain circumstances, have hard quotas under which specific numbers of minority members, regardless of their qualifications, must be accepted to fill vacant positions (for example, a university with a high proportion of white, male faculty may be required to fill half of its faculty vacancies with women and members of other minority groups). Affirmative action programs require that employers must demonstrate, according to a checklist of positive measures, that they are not guilty of discrimination.

A major dilemma with affirmative action programs is that preferential hiring and quota programs involve reverse discrimination, where qualified majority-group members are sometimes arbitrarily excluded. There have been several successful lawsuits claiming reverse discrimination. The best-known case to date has been that of Alan Bakke, who was initially denied admission to the medical school at the University of California at Davis in 1973. He alleged reverse discrimination, since he had higher grades and higher scores on the Medical College Admissions Test than several minority applicants who were admitted under the university's minorities quota policy. In 1978, his claim was upheld by the U.S. Supreme Court in a precedent-setting decision.[68] The Court ruled that strict racial

Many public schools hold activities that promote multicultural understanding. Each year Shorewood Hills Elementary School in Madison, Wisconsin, presents International Day—a festival of songs and dances that helps students learn about and appreciate cultural differences around the world. These Balinese dancers offer friendship to welcome guests in the traditional Pendet dance.

quotas were unconstitutional, but the Court did not rule out that race might be used as one among many criteria in making admissions decisions. There will undoubtedly be more court cases before a coherent policy emerges in this area.

Charles Henderson et al. summarize some of the views of whites and minority groups about affirmative action:

The minority worker in white agencies often asks himself: "Why have I been hired?"... The worker may meet resistance from white colleagues if he or she is a product of "affirmative action," seen by some white people as simply "reverse discrimination." Whites may be quick to say that competence is what counts. Blacks perceive this as saying that they are not competent. Considering the many ways in which whites have acquired jobs, blacks wonder why competence is now suggested as the only criterion for employment. For every white professional who may dislike affirmative

action to compensate for past exclusions and injustices, there is a black professional who feels that it is tragic that organizations have had to be forced to hire minorities.[69]

Supporters of affirmative action programs also note that the dominant group expressed little concern about discrimination when its members were the beneficiaries instead of the victims of discrimination. They also assert there is no other way to make up rapidly for past discrimination against minorities, many of whom may presently score slightly lower on qualification tests simply because they did not have the opportunities and the quality of training that the dominant group members have had.

Affirmative action programs raise delicate and complex questions about achieving equality through giving preferences in hiring and admissions to minorities. Yet, no other means has been found to end subtle discrimination in hiring and admissions.

Admission to educational programs and securing well-paying jobs are crucial elements in working toward integration. The history of immigrant groups who "have made it" (such as the Irish, the Japanese, and the Italians) suggests equality will only be achieved when minority group members gain middle- and upper-class status. Once such status is achieved, the minority group members become an economic and political force with which to be reckoned. The dominant groups then are pressured into modifying their norms, values, and stereotypes. For this reason, a number of authorities have noted that the elimination of economic discrimination is a prerequisite for achieving equality and harmonious race relations.[70] Achieving educational equality between races is also crucial, since lower educational attainments lead to poorer jobs, lower incomes, lower living standards, and the perpetuation of racial inequalities from one generation to the next.

Human Relations Programs

A number of school systems are developing human relations programs, which are designed to alleviate prejudice and discrimination. The program developed by the public school system in Madison, Wisconsin will be briefly described for illustrative purposes.[71] The goal is to help children gain a better awareness of themselves as individuals and a better understanding of, and respect for, individual differences in others.[72]

The program has several steps, along with some suggested activities, books, and other helpful hints for parents and teachers to use with their children. Some of the key concepts are:

- Each person is unique, with all people having common needs.
- Each person can do some things better than other things. It is a serious mistake to use yourself as a yardstick to measure others' abilities or to use others as a yardstick to measure yours. Words such as "stupid" or "dumb" hurt deeply, especially when one is doing one's best.

- Each person has different attitudes, ideas, beliefs, and values. Although the beliefs of others may differ from one's own, they are no less important.
- Prejudice differs from a dislike. Prejudice is defined broadly as "when you are against someone you do not know because of some/one of their differences."[73]

The program assists children in learning some of the differences found in people and how a lack of understanding about these differences can be related to prejudice. The program explains that melanin is the pigment responsible for light and dark skin color differences. The more melanin you have, the darker you are; but melanin, of course, in no way governs the personality or behavior of a person. Suntanning occurs because the skin produces more melanin to protect it from the hot sun; yet tanning does not change the inner "self," only the outside wrapping. Besides skin color differences, students are given an understanding of other individual differences (such as retardation, religious differences, epilepsy, hearing impairments, and so on) so they can be more respectful of such differences. The program also assists students in learning about and appreciating cultural and ethnic differences.

Such human relation programs offer considerable promise of being a highly effective strategy in alleviating discrimination in the following areas: race, sex, ethnic or cultural differences, religious or political differences, and physical or mental handicaps.

Confrontation of Racist and Ethnic Remarks and Actions

Jokes and sarcastic remarks related to race help shape and perpetuate racist stereotypes and prejudices. It is important that both whites and nonwhites tactfully but assertively indicate they do not view such remarks as being humorous or appropriate. It is also important that people also tactfully and assertively point out the inappropriateness of racist actions by others. Such confrontations make explicit that subtle racist remarks and actions are discriminatory and harmful, which has a consciousness-raising effect. Gradually, it is expected that such confrontations will reduce racial prejudices and actions.

Noted author, lecturer, and abolitionist Frederick Douglass stated:

Power concedes nothing without a demand—it never did, and it never will. Find out just what people will submit to, and you've found out the exact amount of injustice and wrong which will be imposed upon them. This will continue until they resist, either with words, blows, or both. The limits of tyrants are prescribed by the endurance of those whom they oppress.[74]

Confrontation of the Problems in Inner-City Ghettos

It is difficult to find the right adjectives to describe the dismal living conditions in inner-city ghettos. The following apply: decaying, inhuman, dreadful, distasteful, shocking, and degrading. Ghettos are primarily inhabited by the poor, by the elderly, and by members of minority groups, particularly blacks and Hispanics. Many ghettos have an ethnic concentration, such as black, Mexican American, Cuban, or Puerto Rican.

Ghettos have high rates of crime, illiteracy, births out of marriage, single-parent households, mental illness, suicide, drug and alcohol abuse, unemployment, infant mortality, rape, aggravated assault, and delinquency. High proportions of the residents are on welfare. Many city services are inferior in ghettos. Schools are inferior, and streets are narrow and often filled with potholes. Police and fire protection services are inadequate to meet the needs.

The housing is crowded and decaying, and much of it is substandard. Heat in winter is often inadequate. Many units lack adequate plumbing. Broken windows, peeling paint, and doors hanging off their hinges are common sights. Minority group members inhabit much of this substandard housing because most cannot

afford an alternative and because discrimination makes it difficult to relocate even for those whose incomes would enable them to relocate.

One of the factors that is leading to the decline of inner cities is the sharp decline of blue-collar jobs in our society. Many blue-collar jobs are unskilled or semiskilled jobs that require less training and education than white-collar and service jobs. The employable in inner cities have in the past largely held blue-collar jobs. For a neighborhood to resist deterioration, a minimal economic base must be maintained. As blue-collar jobs decline and as the quality of municipal services (such as transportation and public schools) deteriorates, faith in community restoration and revitalization fades.

Ghettos are a national disgrace. The United States is the richest and most powerful country in the world, yet we have been unable to improve living conditions in our inner cities.

Our country has tried a variety of approaches to improve ghetto living conditions. Programs and services provided include work training, job placement, financial assistance through public welfare, low-interest mortgages to start businesses, Head Start, drug and alcohol treatment, crime prevention, housing, rehabilitation, day-care services, health care services, and public health services.

One of the most comprehensive undertakings to assist inner cities was the Model Cities Program, which was part of the War on Poverty in the 1960s. Several inner cities were targeted for this massive intervention. The program involved tearing down dilapidated housing and constructing comfortable living quarters. Salvageable buildings were renovated. In addition, these Model City projects had a variety of programs that provided job training and placement, health care services, social services, and educational opportunities. The results were more than depressing. The communities have again become slums, and living conditions are as bleak, or bleaker, than at the start of the Model City interventions.[75]

To date, all programs that have been tried have had, at best, only short-term success. No other conclusion can be made. Ghettos continue to have abysmal living conditions. In the 1980s and early 1990s the federal government, at least for the time being, appears to have given up trying to improve living conditions; federal programs for inner cities have either been eliminated or sharply cut back.

Ghetto living is becoming a way of life. Poverty and dependency on welfare are becoming a lifestyle in ghettos, and this lifestyle is being passed on from one generation to another.

On January 25, 1986 CBS aired a program entitled "CBS Reports: The Vanishing Black Family." The program presented alarming information that the single-parent family headed by a mother is becoming the typical family in inner cities. The program suggested that unless dramatic changes are made, by the year 2000 seventy percent of black families will have a female head of household. This program also indicated that many young black mothers (and the unwed fathers) are using Aid to Families with Dependent Children (AFDC) payments to support their families. For example, one 25-year-old male who had been unemployed for the past two and one-half years was interviewed. He was proud that he had fathered six children by four different women and took it for granted that welfare programs would pay the bills for raising his children. The program suggested that AFDC mothers in inner cities are resigned to raising their children on welfare and that such values are being passed on from generation to generation.

Our society, for better or worse, is a materialistic society. The two main legitimate avenues for acquiring material goods are by getting a good education and obtaining a high-paying job. It appears that many ghetto residents realize the prospects are bleak for them to get a good education (when only inferior schools exist in their areas) or to obtain a high-paying job (when they have few marketable job skills). As a result, many are turning to illegitimate ways to get material goods (shoplifting, drug trafficking, robbery, and con games). Many have also turned to immediate gratifications (including sex and drug highs). A value system is developing of being resigned to being dependent on the government through welfare for a substandard lifestyle.

One approach that has been suggested to try to combat the problems of inner cities is to use birth control technology to seek to stabilize (and perhaps even slightly reduce) the population size in inner cities. Residents of large cities could be encouraged to have only one child. Sex education programs in schools could be expanded to teach responsible sex. Birth control information and services could be provided by the government at no cost to recipients. Increased taxes might be levied for those who had more than one or two children. Health clinics (which provide free birth control information and services) could be located in every inner-city high school. Mothers and their teenage daughters who are receiving AFDC benefits might be given higher monthly grants for voluntarily using effective birth control methods. If effective contraceptives are developed for males, teenage males who are receiving AFDC benefits could also be given higher monthly grants for using effective contraceptives.

Such a proposal is designed to reduce the number of children on AFDC gradually, to reduce poverty being passed from one generation to another, and to seek to strengthen inner-city families. With smaller-sized families on AFDC, the AFDC parents should be better able to provide higher-quality care to the children they presently have.

There are a number of criticisms of this proposal. There is a strong value in our country that holds that every person has a right to be a natural parent to as many children as he or she desires. Some religions, such as the Roman Catholic Church, strongly object to birth control. Encouraging AFDC recipients to use birth control is viewed by many as being "nonwhite genocide"; a higher percentage of nonwhites receive AFDC assistance, and a policy of encouraging AFDC recipients to receive birth control would thereby have the greatest impact on the birth rates of nonwhites.

Our society has tried a variety of programs in the past to combat the problems faced by inner-city residents. All past programs have largely failed to improve our inner cities. At present, our federal government has a laissez-faire approach, and conditions are deteriorating in many of our inner cities. Will our country try an unpopular program such as using birth control

To be effective in a culturally diverse environment, social workers must first evaluate their own attitudes and beliefs and learn to challenge whatever ethnic stereotypes they may hold.

technology to stabilize population size in inner cities? Or, are there other workable alternatives that have not as yet been thought of or implemented? (The author strongly hopes other workable alternatives can be found and implemented.)

DISCRIMINATION AND SOCIAL WORK

Social work has an obligation to work vigorously toward ending racial discrimination. Charles Henderson and Bok-Lim Kim summarize seven recommendations that are consistently advocated in the literature of each racial group.

1. Clients are entitled to a general understanding of their culture so they are not served inappropriately out of ignorance.

2. All clients should be served without discrimination or prejudice.

3. Minority clients should have a voice in planning and managing services provided for them.

4. Minority staff members are generally best qualified to serve members of their own group and should be hired to do so.

5. Opportunities for promotion and advancement should be available to minority employees on an equitable basis.

6. Minorities should be accorded special opportunities for professional training. This may mean modifications in educational programs.

7. Minority faculty members are essential. Credentials of experience and skill are more important than academic degrees.[76]

Ione Dugger Vargus reports that the following problems arose when black graduate social work students worked in white-dominated social agencies.

1. Some were given all-black caseloads.

2. Students were expected to be authorities on blacks and were frequently consulted by other workers.

3. Some white workers considered themselves the experts on black people and accepted no suggestions or ideas.

4. When black workers were permitted to develop their own ways of making contact and channeling services, white workers were upset by the departure from the rules.[77]

Most students remarked that although they would prefer to work with blacks, an all-black caseload implied that both the clients and the worker were inferior.

The students did not like to be perceived as authorities on blacks because they recognized that individual differences make pat answers impossible. They felt some conflicts in giving advice to white practitioners, unless the practitioner had already tried several approaches before seeking advice. They felt that practitioners should work on their own cases. If they had tried several ideas already, the request was just like any other consultation.

The social work professional needs to recognize the reality of practice in a culturally diverse environment. Social workers do have many of the prejudices and misperceptions of the general society. The tendency to use one's own prejudices and stereotypes poses dangers for the well-meaning practitioner. For example, a social worker assigned to a Native American client might assume that the quietness of the client suggests either that the client is being uncooperative or that the client is fully agreeing with the worker. Unfortunately, it is possible that neither assumption is accurate. As a general rule a Native American will not challenge or correct a worker who is off the track because to do so would violate "noninterference." Non-

interference is a basic value of Native American culture that asserts that Native Americans should handle unwanted attempts at intervention with withdrawal—emotional, physical, or both.[78]

Another response pattern of white social workers that is counterproductive with Native Americans is the attempt to maintain direct eye contact. Such face-to-face eye contact is considered rude and intimidating by many Native Americans.[79]

A bilingual practitioner working in a Chicano community may not possess the necessary knowledge to understand all aspects of the language. For example, the special language of the barrio often contains words that have a variety of connotations that differ from formal Spanish.[80] As a consequence the worker who does speak Spanish must be acutely alert to the possibility that the words may have very different meanings for clients living in a barrio.

Thus, a worker dealing with diverse cultural groups must (*a*) acquire a knowledge of self, including one's stereotypes, values, feelings, attitudes, and beliefs; (*b*) acquire a knowledge of the culture and characteristics with whom one is working; (*c*) acquire an understanding of the unique effects that standard counseling and intervention approaches will have on the client group; and (*d*) learn to challenge and change the stereotypic perceptions that one has of the client group.

The reader should not get the impression that working effectively with a different cultural group presents insurmountable barriers and obstacles. In actuality, the similarities between worker and clients almost always outweigh the dissimilarities.[81]

The major professional social work organizations have in the past few decades taken strong positions to work toward ending racial discrimination. The National Association of Social Workers, for example, has lobbied for the passage of civil rights legislation. The Code of Ethics of NASW (see Appendix) has an explicit statement that every "social worker should act to prevent and eliminate discrimination against any person or group on the basis of race, color . . ." The Council on Social Work Education (CSWE) has required in accreditation standards for baccalaureate and master's programs that content on racism must be included throughout the social work curriculum. CSWE also has an accreditation standard that prohibits racial discrimination and mandates affirmative action programs in social work educational programs.

THE FUTURE OF AMERICAN RACE AND ETHNIC RELATIONS

The 1980s turned into a decade of struggle for minorities as they tried to hold onto past gains in the face of reactions against minority rights. Vowing to take "big government" off the back of the American people and to strengthen the economy by giving businesses the incentive to grow and produce, President Reagan and his administration largely removed the federal government from its traditional role as initiator and enforcer of programs to guarantee minority rights. The government is now looking to businesses and to local community groups to correct the problems of poverty and discrimination. (Because many businesses profit from paying low wages, it is questionable whether they will aggressively seek to improve the financial circumstances and living conditions of minorities.) Perhaps because of the federal government's shift in policies, minorities were less active in the 1980s in using the strategy of activism. In these times of shrinking federal budgets, minority groups are finding it difficult to maintain the gains they achieved in the 1960s and 1970s in the job market through affirmative action and equal employment opportunity programs.

However, it is clear that minorities (such as blacks, Hispanics, Asian Americans, and Native Americans) will assertively, and sometimes aggressively, pursue a variety of strategies to change racist prejudices and actions. Counteractions by certain segments of the white dominant group are also likely to occur. (Even in the social sciences, every action elicits a reaction.) For example, in recent years, there have been increased member-

ship in organizations that advocate white supremacy, such as the Ku Klux Klan and the John Birch Society.

In 1988 a report released by the Commission on Minority Participation in Education and American Life asserted:

America is moving backward—not forward—in its efforts to achieve the full participation of minority citizens in the life and prosperity of the nation. . . .

In education, employment, income, health, longevity, and other basic measures of individual and social well-being, gaps persist—and in some cases are widening—between members of minority groups and the majority population.

If we allow these disparities to continue, the United States inevitably will suffer a compromised quality of life and a lower standard of living.

In brief, we will find ourselves unable to fulfill the promise of the American dream.[82]

Minorities have been given hope of achieving equality of opportunity and justice. Their hope has been kindled, and it is clear they will no longer submit to a subordinate status. It is obvious there will be continued struggles to achieve racial equality.

What will be the pattern of race relations in the future? Milton Gordon has outlined three possible patterns of intergroup relations: Anglo-conformity, the melting pot, and cultural pluralism:

Anglo-conformity *assumes the desirability of maintaining modified English institutions, language, and culture as the dominant standard in American life. In practice, "assimilation" in America has always meant Anglo-conformity, and the groups that have been most readily assimilated have been those that are ethnically and culturally most similar to the Anglo-Saxon group.*

The melting pot *is, strictly speaking, a rather different concept, which views the future American society not as a modified England but rather as a totally new blend, both culturally and biologically, of all the various groups that inhabit the United States. In practice, the melting pot has been of only limited significance in the American experience.*

Cultural pluralism *implies a series of coexisting*

For many, Jesse Jackson's last two presidential bids embodied much of the struggle for minority rights in the 1980s. In 1988 in particular, Jackson became more than a "minority candidate"—he successfully forged a coalition that led him to victory in several state primaries and caucuses. Some political observers felt his presence at the Democratic Convention in Atlanta virtually upstaged that of the party's nominee, Michael Dukakis.

groups, each preserving its own tradition and culture, but each loyal to an overarching American nation. Although the cultural enclaves of some immigrant groups, such as the Germans, have declined in importance in the past, many other groups, such as the Italians, have retained a strong sense of ethnic identity and have resisted both Anglo-conformity and inclusion in the melting pot.[83]

Members of some European ethnic groups (such as the British, French, and Germans) have assimilated the dominant culture of the United States and are now integrated. Other European ethnic groups (such as the Irish, Italian, Polish, and Hungarian) are now nearly fully assimilated and integrated.

Cultural pluralism appears to be the form that race and ethnic relations are presently taking. There has been a renewed interest on the part of a number of ethnic European Americans in expressing their pride in their own customs, religions, and linguistic and cultural traditions. Slogans are appearing such as "Kiss me, I'm Italian," "Irish Power," and "Polish and Proud." Blacks, Native Americans, Hispanics, and Asian Americans are demanding entry into mainstream America, but not assimilation. They are demanding coexistence in a plural society, while seeking to preserve their own traditions and cultures. This pride is indicated by such slogans as "black is beautiful" and "red power." They are finding a source of identity and pride in their own cultural backgrounds and histories.

Some progress has been made toward ending discrimination since the *Brown vs. Board of Education* Supreme Court decision in 1954. Yet, equal opportunity for all people in America is still only a dream, as Martin Luther King, Jr. noted in his famous speech in 1963:

I say to you today, my friends, though, even though we face the difficulties of today and tomorrow, I still have a dream. It is a dream deeply rooted in the American dream. I have a dream that one day this nation will rise up, live out the true meaning of its creed: "We hold these truths to be self-evident, that all men are created equal."

I have a dream that one day on the red hills of Georgia sons of former slaves and the sons of former slave-owners will be able to sit down together at the table of brotherhood. I have a dream that one day even the state of Mississippi, a state sweltering with the heat of injustice, sweltering with the heat of oppression, will be transformed into an oasis of freedom and justice.

I have a dream that my four little children will one day live in a nation where they will not be judged by the color of their skin, but by the content of their character.

When we allow freedom to ring—when we let it ring from every city and every hamlet, from every state and every city, we will be able to speed up that day when all of God's children, black men and white men, Jews and Gentiles, Protestants and Catholics, will be able to join hands and sing in the words of the old Negro spiritual, "Free at last, Free at last, Great God Almighty, We are free at last."[84]

SUMMARY

Our country has always been racist and ethnocentric, but there has been progress in the past three decades in alleviating prejudice and discrimination. Yet, we cannot relax. Discrimination continues to have tragic consequences for those who are victims. Individuals who

are targets of discrimination are excluded from certain types of employment, educational and recreational opportunities, certain residential housing areas, membership in certain religious and social organizations, certain political activities, access to some community services, and so on. Discrimination is also a serious obstacle to developing a positive self-concept and has heavy psychological and financial costs. Internationally, racism and ethnocentrism severely damages our credibility in promoting human rights.

Race is primarily a social concept, rather than a biological concept. No "racial" group has any unique or distinctive genes. A social definition is based on the way in which members of a society classify each other by physical characteristics.

Prejudice is an attitude, whereas discrimination involves actions. Discrimination is often based on prejudice, although either may occur independently of the other.

Racial and ethnic discrimination is largely a social problem of whites, as whites tend to be the primary discriminators in power. (This does not mean, however, that only whites must work to end discrimination; discrimination by any group must be ended, and achieving this result must be an interracial effort.)

Theories of the sources of discrimination include projection, frustration-aggression, insecurity and inferiority, authoritarianism, historical explanations, competition and exploitation, and socialization processes. Institutionalized racism is pervasive in our society and involves discrimination being built into the institutions of our society, such as the legal system, politics, employment practices, health care, and education.

There are numerous white and nonwhite groups in our nation, each with a unique culture, language, and history and with special needs. This uniqueness needs to be understood and appreciated if we are to achieve progress toward racial and ethnic equality.

Strategies against discrimination include mass media appeals, increased interaction among races, civil rights legislation, protests and activism, school busing, affirmative action, human relations programs in school systems, confrontation of racist and ethnic remarks and actions, and confrontation of the problems in inner-city ghettos.

Three possible patterns of intergroup race and ethnic relations in the future are Anglo-conformity, the melting pot, and cultural pluralism. Cultural pluralism is the form that race and ethnic relations are presently taking and may well take in the future. As a profession, social work has an obligation to work vigorously toward ending racial and ethnic discrimination.

NOTES

1. Milton Gordon, *Assimilation in American Life: The Role of Race, Religion, and National Origins* (New York: Oxford University Press, 1964), pp. 27–28.
2. *Encyclopedia of Sociology* (Guilford, CN: Duskin Publishing Group, 1974), p. 101.
3. Ibid., p. 236.
4. Gordon W. Allport, *The Nature of Prejudice* (Reading, MA: Addison-Wesley, 1954), p. 7.
5. Robert Merton, "Discrimination and the American Creed," in *Discrimination and National Welfare*, ed. Robert M. MacIver (New York: Harper, 1949).
6. Marlene Cummings, "How to Handle Incidents of Racial Discrimination," in *The Personal Problem Solver*, eds. Charles Zastrow and Dae H. Chang (Englewood Cliffs, NJ: Prentice-Hall, 1977), p. 200.
7. Gunnar Myrdal, *An American Dilemma* (New York: Harper, 144).
8. Elmer H. Johnson, *Social Problems of Urban Man* (Homewood, IL: Dorsey Press, 1973), p. 344.
9. Ashley Montague, *Man's Most Dangerous Myth: The Fallacy of Race*, 4th ed. (Cleveland: World, 1964).
10. Johnson, *Social Problems*, p. 350.
11. Arnold Rose, *The Negro in America* (New York: Harper & Row, 1964).
12. Paul Ehrlich and Richard Holm, "A Biological View of Race," in *The Concept of Race*, ed. Ashley Montague (New York: The Free Press, 1964).
13. Montague, *Man's Most Dangerous Myth*.
14. Arthur Jensen, "How Much Can We Boost I.Q. and Scholastic Achievement?" *Harvard Educational Review* 39 (1969), pp. 1–123.
15. Ashley Montague, ed., *Race & I.Q.* (London: Oxford University Press, 1975).
16. Johnson, *Social Problems*, p. 50.
17. T. W. Adorno, E. Frenkel-Brunswik, D. J. Devinson, and R. N. Sandord, *The Authoritarian Personality* (New York: Harper & Row, 1950).
18. Charles F. Marden and Gladys Meyer, *Minorities in American Society* (New York: American Book, 1962).
19. Eugene Hartley, *Problems in Prejudice* (New York: King's Crown Press, 1946).
20. Stokely Carmichael and Charles V. Hamilton, *Black Power: The Politics of Liberation in America* (New York: Vintage Books, 1967), p. 4.
21. Joseph Julian and William Kornblum, *Social Problems*, 5th ed. (Englewood Cliffs, NJ: Prentice-Hall, 1986), pp. 240–251.
22. Jeannette Henry, *The Indian Historian* 1 (December 1967), p. 22.
23. U.S. Bureau of the Census, *Statistical Abstract of the United States, 1987* (Washington, D.C.: U.S. Government Printing Office, 1987), p. 176.
24. Paul Bernard Wice, *Bail and Its Reform: A National Survey* (Washington, D.C.: U.S. Government Printing Office, 1973), p. 23.
25. Grace Halsell, *Soul Sister* (New York: Fawcett Crest, 1969), pp. 156–157.
26. C. H. Cooley, *Human Nature and the Social Order* (New York: Scribner's, 1902).
27. Kenneth B. Clark, *Dark Ghetto* (New York: Harper & Row, 1965).
28. Judith Porter, *Black Child, White Child: The Development of Racial Attitudes* (Cambridge, MA: Harvard University Press, 1971).
29. Albert Szymanski, "Racial Discrimination and White Gain," *American Sociological Review* 41 (June 1976), pp. 403–414.
30. *Statistical Abstract of the United States, 1987*, p. 17.
31. Ibid., p. 17.
32. "Hispanics Rise," *Parade Magazine*, November 29, 1987, p. 13.
33. Charles H. Henderson and Bok-Lim Kim, "Racism," in *Contemporary Social Work*, eds. Donald Brieland, Lela Costin, and Charles Atherton (New York: McGraw-Hill, 1975), p. 180.
34. Excerpted from a speech by Abraham Lincoln in Charleston, Illinois, in 1858, as reported in Richard Hofstader, *The American Political Tradition* (New York: Alfred A. Knopf, 1948), p. 116.
35. Quoted in David Gelman, "Black and White in America," *Newsweek*, March 7, 1988, p. 19.
36. Ibid., p. 19.

37. Thomas Sullivan et al., *Social Problems* (New York: John Wiley, 1980), p. 422.
38. Gelman, "Black and White in America," p. 21.
39. William Moore, Jr., *The Vertical Ghetto* (New York: Random House, 1969), p. 71.
40. Gelman, "Black and White in America," pp. 19–20.
41. Ibid.
42. Ibid.
43. Ibid.
44. Ibid.
45. Ibid.
46. Cited in Gelman, "Black and White in America," p. 20.
47. "Hispanics Rise," *Parade Magazine*, p. 13.
48. Robert Lindsey, "U.S. Hispanic Populace Growing Faster Than Any Other Minority," *New York Times*, February 18, 1979, pp. 1, 16.
49. Ibid.
50. Ibid.
51. J. Julian Rivera, "Growth of a Puerto Rican Awareness," *Social Casework* 55 (February 1974), p. 84.
52. Helen M. Crampton and Kenneth K. Keiser, *Social Welfare: Institution and Process* (New York: Random House, 1970), p. 109.
53. Johnson, *Social Problems*, p. 349.
54. Dee Brown, *Bury My Heart at Wounded Knee* (New York: Holt, Rinehart and Winston, 1971).
55. Crampton and Keiser, *Social Welfare*, p. 104.
56. Brown, *Bury My Heart at Wounded Knee*.
57. Robertson, *Social Problems*, p. 218.
58. Johnson, *Social Problems*, p. 349.
59. Charles Henderson, Bok-Lim Kim, and Ione D. Vargus, "Racism," in *Contemporary Social Work*, 2d ed., eds. Donald Brieland, Lela Costin and Charles Atherton (New York: McGraw-Hill, 1980), p. 403.
60. George E. Simpson and J. Milton Yinger, *Racial and Cultural Minorities*, 3d ed. (New York: Harper & Row, 1965), p. 510.
61. Sullivan et al., *Social Problems*, p. 437.
62. Johnson, *Social Problems*, pp. 374–379.
63. Cummings, "How to Handle Incidents," p. 197.
64. Johnson, *Social Problems*, p. 376.
65. Sullivan et al., *Social Problems*, p. 438.
66. Ibid., p. 439.
67. *Washington Post*, February 20, 1970.
68. Allan P. Sindler, *Bakke, DeFunis and Minority Admissions: The Quest for Equal Opportunity* (New York: Longmans, Green, 1978).
69. Henderson, Kim, and Vargus, "Racism," p. 403.
70. David L. Featherman and Robert M. Hauser, "Changes in the Socioeconomic Stratification of the Races, 1962–73," *American Journal of Sociology* 82 (November 1976), pp. 621–651.
71. Roland L. Buchanan, Jr. and Marlene A. Cummings, *Individual Differences: An Experience in Human Relations for Children* (Madison, WI: Madison Public Schools, 1975).
72. Ibid., p. 1.
73. Ibid., p. 13.
74. Quoted in Cummings, "How to Handle Incidents," p. 201.
75. Charles Weltner, "The Model Cities Program: A Sobering Scorecard," *Policy Review*, Fall 1977, pp. 73–87.
76. Henderson and Kim, "Racism," p. 193.
77. Ione Dugger Vargus, "The Minority Practitioner," in *Contemporary Social Work*, eds. Donald Brieland, Lela Costin, and Charles Atherton (New York: McGraw-Hill, 1975), p. 421.
78. Jimm G. Good Tracks, "Native American Noninterference," *Social Work* 18 (November 1973), pp. 30–34.
79. Ronald G. Lewis and Man Keung Ho, "Social Work with Native Americans," *Social Work* 20 (September 1975), pp. 378–382.
80. Dolores G. Morton, "Incorporating Content on Minority Groups into Social Work Practice Courses," in *The Dual Perspective* (New York: Council on Social Work Education, 1978).
81. Grafton H. Hull, Jr., "Social Work Practice with Diverse Groups," in *The Practice of Social Work*, 2d ed., ed. Charles Zastrow (Homewood, IL: Dorsey Press, 1985).
82. Quoted in Michele Collison, "Neglect of Minorities Seen Jeopardizing Future Prosperity," *The Chronicle of Higher Education*, 34, no. 37 (May 25, 1988), p. 1.
83. Milton Gordon, "Assimiliation in America: Theory and Reality," *Daedalus* 90 (Spring 1961), pp. 363–365.
84. Jim Bishop, *The Days of Martin Luther King, Jr.* (New York: G. P. Putnam, 1971), pp. 327–328.

12

SEXISM AND EFFORTS FOR ACHIEVING EQUALITY

Women who work full time are paid about 65 percent of what men who work full time are paid.[1] The average woman college graduate is paid less than the average male high school dropout.[2] The average working white woman is paid less than the average working black man, and the average working black woman (subjected to double discrimination) earns least of all.[3] Thirty-four percent of families headed by women are below the poverty line, compared to 9 percent of families headed by men.[4]

This chapter will:

- Present a history of sex roles, sexism, and sexual harassment.

- Describe traditional sex-role expectations.

- Examine whether there is a biological basis for sexism.

- Describe traditional sex-role socialization practices.

- Examine the consequences of sexism on males and females.

- Describe the sex-role revolution in our society.

- Present strategies for achieving sexual equality.

- Summarize social work's commitment to combat sexism.

HISTORY OF SEX ROLES AND SEXISM

In almost every known society women have had a lower status than men.[5] Women have been bound by more social restrictions and have consistently received less recognition for their work than men. Women have been regarded differently than men, not only biologically, but also emotionally, intellectually, and psychologically. Double standards have often existed for dating, for marriage, and for social and sexual conduct.

Most religions (including Judeo-Christian, Hindu, and Islam) in their traditional doctrines ascribe an inferior status to women. This tradition continues to exist today in most countries, even though women attend

413

BOX 12.1

Examples of Erroneous Sexist Stereotypes

HOW TO TELL A BUSINESS MAN FROM A BUSINESS WOMAN

He's aggressive; she's pushy.

He's good at details; she's picky.

He loses his temper because he's so involved in his job; she's bitchy.

When he's depressed (or hung over) everyone tiptoes past his office; she's moody so it must be her time of the month.

He follows through; she doesn't know when to quit.

He's confident; she's conceited.

He stands firm; she's hard.

He has judgments; she's prejudiced.

He's a man of the world; she's been around.

He drinks because of excessive job pressure; she's a lush.

He isn't afraid to say what he thinks; she's mouthy.

He exercises authority diligently; she's power mad.

He's close-mouthed; she's secretive.

He's a stern taskmaster; she's hard to work for.

He climbed the ladder to success; she slept her way to the top!

Source: Author unknown.

church more often, hold firmer religious beliefs, pray more often, and are more active in church programs.[6] Many societies have concluded that it is divinely ordained that women shall play a secondary and supportive role to men. In many Christian religions, women cannot become ministers or priests. Some orthodox Jewish men offer a daily prayer of thanks to God for not having made them a woman. In almost all churches God is referred to as "He."

Primitive hunting and gathering societies provide insight into the processes that have resulted in women being assigned a lower status. Hunting and gathering societies usually lived in small tribes consisting of several married couples and their dependents. Men generally were the hunters, and women were the gatherers of nuts, plants, and other foods. There are several explanations for this differentiation. Males, it has been suggested, were better suited to hunting because they were physically stronger and could run faster. It has also been noted that the infant mortality rate was very high in these tribes, so it was necessary for the women to be pregnant or nursing throughout most of their childbearing years in order to maintain the size of the tribe. The need to tend to children largely prevented women from leaving the camp for days at a time in order to hunt large game. Even though women often gathered more food than men were able to obtain through hunting, the male's hunting activities were viewed as more prestigious.

Women spent much of their adult lives being pregnant, nursing infants, and raising children. Women, because they were forced to remain around the home, were also assigned the less prestigious "domestic tasks" of cooking, serving, and washing. Once these sex roles became part of tradition, these distinctions were not only recognized as practical means of doing the necessary work, but also came to be seen as "natural" ways for men and women to behave.

Gradually, more behavior patterns were added to these sex-role distinctions. Because men were trained at hunting, these skills led them to be recognized as the defenders of their tribe in case of attack from other tribes. Childrearing patterns were developed to teach boys to be aggressive and to be leaders. Women, on the other hand, were assigned supportive roles to men and were taught to be more passive and dependent and to provide emotional support to their men.

Before the Industrial Revolution, practically all societies had come to assign distinct roles to men and to women. Women were generally involved in domestic and childrearing activities, whereas men were involved in what were then considered to be the productive* (such as hunting and economic support) and protective functions for the family. It should be noted that women in preindustrial societies were also often involved in food producing and economic support, such as making clothes, growing and harvesting garden crops, and helping on the farm. But their specific responsibilities

*The use of the term *productive* indicates the higher status that was assigned to the role of men. In actuality, the roles of women were often as or more "productive" in completing the essential tasks that needed to be performed.

were often viewed as inferior and requiring fewer skills.

The 19th-century Industrial Revolution brought about dramatic changes in sex roles. Men, instead of working on a small farm, went outside of the home to work in a factory or other setting to provide economic support. The economic role of women declined, since they were less likely to be performing economically productive tasks. The roles of women became increasingly defined as childrearing and housework. But the amount of time required to perform these roles declined for several reasons. Families had fewer children. With mass education older children went to school. Gradually, labor-saving devices reduced the need for women to perform time-consuming domestic tasks (for example, baking bread, canning vegetables, and washing). As the traditional roles of women began to change, some women began to pursue activities (for example, outside employment) that had traditionally been limited to men. With these changes sex roles began to blur and to become less clear-cut.

The struggle for women's rights in America has been going on for nearly two centuries. In the early part of the 19th century women who were working for the abolition of slavery became aware that they too were denied such rights as voting. (An 1840 antislavery conference even refused seats for women while the male delegates gave impassioned speeches about the moral right of ending slavery.)

In 1848 two feminists, Susan B. Anthony and Elizabeth Stanton, organized the first women's rights caucus, which was held in the state of New York.[7] These early leaders demanded suffrage (the vote for women) and the reform of many laws that were openly discriminatory toward women. It took over seventy years, until 1920, to pass the 19th Amendment to the Constitution, which gave the vote to women. The suffrage movement was marked by jailings of feminist militants and fierce controversy. The huge struggles and number of years spent in getting this amendment passed led many women leaders to believe that the right to vote went hand in hand with sexual equality. After the 1920 passage the "women's movement" was nearly dormant for the next forty years.

In the early 1900s some modern birth control

When feminists marched down the streets of New York in 1971 (bottom photo), the primary goal of their grandmothers—equal voting rights in national and state elections—had been a reality for some fifty years. But in spite of affirmative action programs and other important gains of the last two decades, full political and economic parity between men and women is yet to come.

techniques became available. Through this advance women gained greater freedom from the traditional roles of childrearing and housework.

During World War II large numbers of women were employed outside the home for the first time to take the places of men who had been drafted into the military. At this time over 38 percent of all women 16 years of age and over were employed, causing a further blurring of traditional sex roles.[8]

In the 1960s, there was a resurgence of interest in sex-role inequality for a variety of reasons. The civil rights movement had a consciousness-raising effect in that people became more aware of and concerned about inequalities. The civil rights movement to curb racial discrimination also served as a model, suggesting to a number of concerned women that sexual discrimination could also be alleviated through social action. More women attended college and thereby became more informed about inequalities. As women moved into new occupational positions, they became increasingly aware of discriminatory practices. Finally, there was an explosion of research suggesting that sex-role differences were not innately determined but were in fact the result of socialization patterns and that the effects of such sex roles were often discriminatory toward women.

One such study was conducted in 1955 by John Money, J. G. Hampson, and J. L. Hampson on hermaphrodites.[9] A hermaphrodite is a person who is born with both male and female sexual characteristics but is labeled either a male or a female at birth and is then related to according to the gender on the birth certificate. These researchers did *not* find a significant correlation between physical characteristics and the hermaphrodites' own feelings about their sexual identities. These people were fulfilling the sex-role expectations of their labeled gender, although their observable anatomical characteristics would often tend to place them in the other category. This research raised questions about the biological determination of sex roles.

Other studies have found dramatic differences in socialization patterns between males and females. Boys are given more sports equipment and task-oriented toys (like construction sets) to play with,

whereas girls are given more dolls and toys relating to marriage and parenthood.[10] During the first few months of life girls receive more distal stimulation (like looking and talking) from their parents, whereas boys receive more proximal stimulation (like rocking and handling).[11] Fathers tend to play more aggressively with sons than with daughters.[12] But American sex-role socialization practices are not universal. In some Middle Eastern societies, males are reared, and turn out to be, more emotional and sensitive than females; females tend to be more impassive and practical.[13] In Sweden, most heavy machinery operators are women.[14] In the Soviet Union most physicians are women.[15]

Betty Friedan, in her 1963 book *The Feminine Mystique*, provided the ideological base for the resurgence of the women's movement.[16] With the term *feminine mystique*, Friedan referred to the negative self-concept, lack of direction, and low sense of self-worth among women. The book served as a rallying point for women and led Friedan to form the National Organization for Women (NOW) in 1966. Today NOW has over 60,000 members, making it the largest women's rights group in the country and an influential political force.[17] NOW and other women's groups have been working to end sexual discrimination, to achieve sexual equality, to end sexual double standards, and to improve the self-identity of women.

The Civil Rights Act of 1964, primarily intended to end racial discrimination, also prohibited discrimination on the basis of sex. Yet, local businesses in some states are as yet not covered by sex discrimination laws.[18]

In 1972 the Equal Rights Amendment (ERA) received congressional approval but required ratification by three fourths (38) of the states to become the 27th Amendment to the Constitution. ERA stated: "Equality of rights under the law shall not be denied or abridged by the United States or any state on account of sex." Time ran out on ERA in 1982, when after ten years of extensive political action, it narrowly failed to gain the support of enough states to be ratified.

Emotions ran high on both sides of the question of ERA ratification. Proponents asserted that ERA would eliminate numerous state laws that are discriminatory toward women.[19] Opponents argued that passage of

ERA would mean women could be drafted into the armed forces. Opponents further argued that women would lose preferential treatment in divorce actions and that the amendment would make parents equally liable for alimony, child support, and spouse support. They asserted that certain labor laws that give preferential treatment to women would have to be revised, such as the amount of weight women may lift on the job. They also asserted that "maternity leaves" would have to be made available to husbands who want to stay home with a newborn child.[20] A number of women concluded that ERA would be more detrimental than beneficial to women, and they actively opposed its passage.

Even though ERA failed to be ratified, there have been a variety of statutes passed that are designed to prevent sex discrimination. The federal Equal Pay Act of 1963 and a number of similar state laws require equal pay for equal work. As mentioned earlier, the Civil Rights Act of 1964 outlaws discrimination on the basis of race, color, sex or religion. Executive Order 11246, as amended by Executive Order 11375 on October 13, 1967, forbids sex discrimination by federal suppliers and contractors and provides procedures for enforcement. In addition, numerous court decisions have set precedents establishing the illegality of sex discrimination in hiring, promotions, and rates of pay.[21] Several landmark decisions have required employers to pay female employees millions of dollars to compensate for past wage discriminations.[22] In 1973, for example, American Telephone and Telegraph was required to pay $15 million in back wages to its female employees because the company had paid them less than males who were doing the same work. The Equal Credit Act of 1974 bars discrimination on the basis of marital status or sex in credit operations. A number of states have passed laws prohibiting discrimination against pregnant women in hiring, training, and promotion.[23]

Affirmative action programs apply to women as well as to certain racial minorities. Women are considered a minority group because for generations they have been subjected to discrimination and have been denied equal opportunities.

The following employers are required to have affirmative action programs: government contractors and suppliers, recipients of government funds, and businesses engaged in interstate commerce. Affirmative action primarily applies to job vacancies. Employers must demonstrate active efforts to locate and recruit minority applicants (defined to include women); demonstrate positive efforts to increase the pool of qualified applicants (for example, special training programs for minorities); give preference to hiring minority applicants; and in some cases set hard quotas that specify numbers of minority members that must be accepted (regardless of qualifications) to fill vacant positions. The clout of affirmative action programs is the threat of loss of government funds if employers do not have such programs effectively in place. (As noted in Chapter 11, there is an active backlash movement against affirmative action programs. This backlash threatens to curtail affirmative action programs.)

SEXUAL HARASSMENT

Sexual harassment may be defined as repeated and unwanted sexual advances. Sexual harassment has recently become recognized as a form of sex discrimination. Most of the victims are women; men are rarely the object of unwanted sexual advances.

Paul Horton et al. identify some of the victims of sexual harassment:

Sexual harassment is an ancient practice. Attractive female slaves were routinely bought as sex playthings, and domestic servants were often exploited. If the Victorian housemaid denied her bed to a lecherous master, he dismissed her; if she admitted him, she soon became pregnant and disgraced, and his wife dismissed her. Either way, she lost!

Sexual harassment can be found anywhere, but is likely to be a problem only where men have supervisory or gatekeeper power over women. The "casting couch" is a well-known feature of show business, and women in many occupations can escape unwelcome attentions only by quitting their jobs, often at a sacrifice. Sexual harassment on the campus has also surfaced, with many female graduate students' claiming that senior professors

BOX 12.2

Two Examples of Sexual Harassment

M olly works in a factory and wears an apron filled with bolts for the assembly line. Her supervisor "checks" the bolts by reaching into the apron and feeling around. He does not "check" the aprons of the male workers. He also waits until Molly is alone in the cloakroom and backs her up against the wall. When Molly protests, he says he's being "friendly," and she shouldn't be "uncooperative" or she'll lose her job.

Susan works in an insurance office and has to travel to other cities with her boss. He wants to share a hotel room "to save some money." When Susan refuses he tells her to "smarten up" or he'll give her a poor rating on her next job review and demote her back to a clerical job. In the meantime, he doubles Susan's workload and complains that she "can't keep up."

Source: From leaflet, *Sexual Harassment on the Job*, distributed by Michigan Task Force on Sexual Harassment in the Workplace, in cooperation with WJBK-TV2, Detroit.

claimed sexual privileges as the price for grades, degrees, and recommendations.[24]

The definition of what is and what is not sexual harassment is somewhat vague. Repeated, unwanted touching is certainly harassment. But some definitions also include telling sexual "stories" after victims indicate they are not interested in hearing such stories. A few years ago the University of Minnesota included in its definition faculty having consenting sexual relationships with adult students, since students are in a low power position and may suffer adverse consequences if they refuse.

Those found guilty of sexual harassment are subject to reprimand and other consequences at their place of employment. Unfortunately, even a successful protest sometimes further victimizes the victim. She must endure the unpleasantness of pursuing the complaint, and she may be viewed by some as having invited the advances. Some women who protest eventually are forced to seek a new job because of the discomfort they feel in the old workplace.

TRADITIONAL SEX-ROLE EXPECTATIONS

Sex roles are learned patterns of behavior that are expected of the sexes in a given society. Sex-role expectations define how men and women are to behave and how they are to be treated by others. Sex-role expectations are largely based on stereotypes. Stereotyping is the attributing of a fixed and usually inaccurate and unfavorable conception to a category of people. Stereotyping makes it easier for discrimination (unequal treatment) to occur.

American women traditionally are expected to be affectionate, passive, conforming, sensitive, intuitive, dependent, and "sugar and spice and everything nice." They are supposed to be primarily concerned with domestic life, to be nurturing, to love to care for babies and young children instinctively, to be deeply concerned about their personal appearance, and to be self-sacrificing for their family. They should not appear to

Nebraska's "first couple" defies old notions of proper male and female roles. Kay Orr is not only her state's first female governor, she is also the first Republican woman in the nation elected to the office. Her husband, Bill Orr—Nebraska's "First Gentleman"—is an insurance executive and author of the recently published First Gentlemen's Cookbook. *Mr. Orr says he found himself spending more time in the kitchen as his wife became more involved in politics.*

be ambitious, aggressive, competitive, or more intelligent than men. They are expected to be ignorant about and uninterested in sports, economics, or politics. They are not supposed to initiate relationships with men and are expected to be tender, feminine, emotional, and appreciative in these relationships.

There are also a number of traditional sex-role expectations for males in our society. A male is expected to be tough, fearless, logical, self-reliant, independent, and aggressive. He should have definite opinions on the major issues of the day and is expected to make authoritative decisions at work and at home. He is ex-

pected to be strong, to be a sturdy oak, and never to be depressed, vulnerable, or anxious. He is not supposed to be a "sissy." He is not expected to cry or openly display "feminine" emotions. He is expected to be the provider, the breadwinner, and competent in all situations. He is supposed to be physically strong, self-reliant, and athletic; to have a manly air of confidence and toughness; to be daring and aggressive; to be brave and forceful; to always be in a position to dominate any situation—to be a "Rambo" or a "Clint Eastwood."[25] He is supposed to initiate relationships with women and is expected to be dominant in these relationships.

Men who are supported by their wives, or who earn less than their wives, are apt to be criticized and to experience feelings of shame and inadequacy.

Even when young, boys are expected to be masculine. Parents and relatives are far more concerned when a boy is a "sissy" than when a girl is a "tomboy." A tomboy is expected to outgrow her "masculine" tendencies, but it is feared that a sissy will never fare well in our competitive society and may even become homosexual. (The right of a boy to wear his hair long had to be won in many court battles in this country, whereas hardly anyone is concerned when a girl wears her hair short or long.)

IS THERE A BIOLOGICAL BASIS FOR SEXISM?

Let us examine this sexist ideology, which assumes that the differences between men and women are the result of biology—that anatomy equips men to play an active and dominant role in the world and women to play a passive and secondary role.

There are certain biological differences between men and women. Of course, there are the obvious anatomical, sexual, and reproductive differences between the sexes. There are also hormone-level differences. Each sex has both male and female hormones, but women have higher levels of female hormones, and males have higher levels of male hormones. Research on some animal species (which may or may not be applicable to humans) has shown that if male hormones are injected into females, the females have a heightened sex drive and become more aggressive.[26] Scientists, however, believe this hormone difference plays only a minor role in humans, since human behavior patterns are almost entirely learned, whereas behavior patterns of lower animals are more influenced by hormonal factors.[27]

Men, on the average, are taller and heavier than women and have greater physical strength. Women can tolerate pain better and have greater physical endurance (except in short-term feats of strength).[28] In most respects women are physically healthier.[29] Women are less susceptible to most diseases and on the average live longer. Males have higher rates of fetal and infant mortality. Male fetuses can inherit a greater number of sex-linked weaknesses: Over thirty disorders have been found exclusively among males, including hemophilia, certain types of color blindness, and webbing of the toes.

Soon after birth female babies tend to be more content and less physically active.[30] As children develop there are other differences, but it has not yet been determined whether the identified differences are due to inherited or learned factors. Girls learn to talk and read at an earlier age. Girls become more docile, dependent, and seem more intellectually mature (most remedial education classes have a large majority of boys). Boys are superior in elementary school in tasks based on spatial, mechanical, and analytic ability, whereas girls are superior at tasks involving verbal capacities and numerical computation.[31] Whether these differences are learned or innate is uncertain. Girls, for example, may be better at reading and language because they are encouraged to spend more time with adults and to read more rather than becoming involved in competitive sports or other activities.

There is considerable research supporting the position that sex-role differences are primarily due to socialization patterns. John Money et al. examined cases in which a baby's sex had been incorrectly classified—for example, where parents raised a boy to be a girl or vice versa.[32] The study found that children will learn to play the role that they are socialized to learn rather than the genital role outlined by traditional sex-role expectations. Money concluded that children are "psychosexually neuter at birth," and that sex role is independent of physiological sex.

The fact that there are wide variations in sex-role expectations between cultures also suggests that sex roles are learned rather than biologically determined. (If all cultures defined sex-role expectations similarly, this would suggest a biological basis for sex-role distinctions.) A few examples follow. Most cultures expect that women will do most of the carrying of heavy objects, whereas in this country and in most European countries men are expected to do most of the lifting and carrying of heavy objects. In some societies, unlike ours, the men do most of the cooking. Not so long ago in Europe it was the males who wore stockings, perfume, and silks. Men in Scotland still wear kilts (skirts). In the societies of the Maoris and the Trobrianders it is the women who are expected to take the initiative in sexual activity.[33]

Margaret Mead in a classic study examined sex-role expectations in three tribes in New Guinea. She found that one tribe required both males and females to behave in a way we would define as "masculine"; a second required both to behave in a "feminine" fashion; and a third had the females act "masculine" and the males act "feminine." Mead concluded that sex-role expectations are primarily determined by cultural learning experiences (see Box 12.3).

SEX-ROLE SOCIALIZATION

In the United States, sex-role socialization starts shortly after birth. Baby girls are dressed in pink, and baby boys are dressed in blue. Babies are given sex-related toys. Boys are bounced on the knee and handled roughly, whereas girls are cooed over. At a very early age children become aware that they are a "girl" or a "boy," long before they become aware of the anatomical differences between the sexes.[34] Lawrence Kohlberg notes that children make basic decisions (based on what others tell them) that they are boys or girls and then select those activities that significant others (that is, people that they view as important to them) say conform to this self-concept.[35]

During the childhood years parents go to great lengths to socialize their children according to sex-role expectations. Little boys are given toy trucks to play with, and girls are given dolls. Boys are encouraged to play ball, and girls are urged to play house. Ruth Hartley notes: "Girls gain approval . . . by doing the rather undemanding things that are expected of them. . . . A girl need not be bright as long as she is

docile and attractive. . . . This kind of treatment is likely to produce rather timid, unventuresome, unoriginal, conformist types."[36] According to Hartley the early socialization of boys is quite different.

Almost from birth the boy has more problems to solve autonomously. In addition, he is required to limit his interest at a very early age to sex-appropriate objects and activities, while girls are permitted to amble their way to a similar status at a more gradual and natural pace. . . . He is challenged to discover what he should do by being told what he should not *do, as in the most frequently employed negative sanction, "Don't be a sissy!". . . . Interest in girlish things is generally forbidden and anxiety-provoking in American boyhood. . . . The boy is constantly open to a challenge to prove his masculinity. He must perform, adequately and publicly, a variety of physical feats that will have very little utility in most cases in adulthood. He is constantly under pressure to demonstrate mastery over the environment, and, concomitantly, to suppress expression of emotion.*[37]

Young girls in many families are still raised by their parents to be mothers and homemakers and/or are encouraged to seek employment of a lower status and lower pay.

Boys are encouraged to play more competitive games than girls and to be outgoing and aggressive, whereas young girls are encouraged to be passive and reserved.[38] Young children are impressionable. Such sex-role stereotyping often becomes a self-fulfilling prophecy. According to Charles Cooley's "looking-glass self" people will come to view themselves as others relate to them.[39] Boys are discouraged from showing overt affection and are taught to seek material rewards, to be dominant in dating and marital relationships, and to seek respect, power, and prestige. Boys are socialized not to cry, to keep their concerns within themselves, to be "macho."

In contrast, girls are taught to be more passive, nurturing, and maternal. Research shows that some females are taught to fear success and achievement and to "play dumb" in order to "boost the male ego."[40] To be feminine, females are expected to display softness, helplessness, tenderness, and understanding and to be generally nonassertive.

BOX 12.3

Sex-Role Expectations Are Culturally Determined

I n the classic study *Sex and Temperament in Three Primitive Societies* Margaret Mead refuted the notion that sex-role expectations are biologically determined. The study was conducted in three tribes in the early 1930s in New Guinea. Mead demonstrated that many characteristics Americans classify as typically female or male are classified differently in these tribes.

Both sexes among the Arapesh would seem feminine to us. Both men and women are gentle, nurturant, and compliant. The personalities of males and females in this society are not sharply differentiated by sex. Both girls and boys learn to be unaggressive, cooperative, and responsive to the needs and wants of others. Relations between husband and wife parallel the traditional mother-child relations in our society, with the Arapesh husband often seeing his role as providing training to his much younger wife.

In contrast, among the Mundugamors, both sexes would seem masculine to us. Both are headhunters and cannibals and are nonnurturant, aggressive, and actively initiate sexual involvement.

The most interesting society studied was the Tchambuli. This society virtually reverses our traditional sex-role expectations and stereotypes. The men spend much more time than the women in grooming and decorating themselves. Also, the men spend much of their time in painting, carving, and practicing dance steps. In contrast, the women are efficient, impersonal, unadorned, managerial, and brisk. The women are the traders and have most of the economic power.

Mead concludes:

We no longer have any basis for regarding such aspects of behavior as sex linked. . . . Standardized personality differences between the sexes are . . . cultural creations to which each generation, male or female, is trained to conform.

Source: Margaret Mead, *Sex and Temperament in Three Primitive Societies* (New York: Morrow, 1935).

A significant part of the socialization process occurs in school. Girls are often channeled into sewing, typing, and cooking classes, whereas boys are channeled into such classes as woodworking, printing, and mechanics. Nearly 90 percent of grade-school teachers are female, whereas close to 90 percent of principals are male.[41] Thus, children see men in superior, decision-making positions and women in subordinate positions. One study found that grade-school teachers generally hold traditional sex-role stereotypes—that teachers erroneously believe that males are innately more aggressive and more capable of abstract reasoning than females.[42]

Textbooks in preschool, elementary, junior high, and high school portray female characters as being more passive and dependent and less creative than

Children learn to engage in sex-appropriate activities at a very early age.

males.[43] Florence Howe, for example, analyzed textbooks in the first three grades and concluded:

Primers used in the first three grades offer children a view of a "typical" American family: a mother who does not work, a father who does, two children—a brother who is always older than a sister—and two pets—a dog and sometimes a cat—whose ages and sexes mirror those of the brother and sister. In these books, boys build or paint things; they also pull girls in wagons and push merry-go-rounds. Girls carry purses when they go shopping; they help mother cook or pretend they are cooking; and they play with their dolls. . . . Plots in which girls are involved usually depend on their inability to do something—to manage their own roller skates or to ride a pony.[44]

School counselors generally advise students to pursue careers, not just on the basis of their abilities,

but also on the basis of traditional sex-role expectations. For example, a young girl who excels at math may be encouraged to be a teacher, whereas a young boy with equal skills may be urged to consider engineering. Janet Chafetz comments on such advising practices.

Counselors defend such practices on the basis of what youngsters may "realistically" expect to face in the future: marriage, child care, and a lack of opportunity in a number of career fields for females, and the need to support a family at the highest income and status levels possible for males. "Realism," however, has always been an excuse for maintaining the status quo, and it is no different in the case of sex role stereotypes. If, for instance, females do not prepare to enter previously masculine fields, such fields will remain male-dominated, allowing another generation of counselors to assure girls that females can't work in them. In addition, it is questionable whether counselors' notions of "reality" in fact keep pace with reality. There is undoubtedly a lag between expanding opportunities and changing sex role definitions on the one hand, and counselors' awareness of these phenomena on the other.[45]

Even contemporary theories in psychology describe women as being more passive and emotional, lacking in abstract interests, and having an instinctive tenderness for babies.[46] Even though masculinity and femininity are largely learned roles, contemporary psychological theories subtly imply (erroneously) that sex-role differences are largely genetically determined. Sigmund Freud's theory of the development of the female personality is probably the most sexist and outrageous. Freud theorized that young girls discover their genitals differ from boys', which leads them to have "penis envy." He alleges that because of this difference, girls conclude that they are biologically inferior to males and then develop a passive, submissive personality as a way to adjust to interactions with males, whom they view as superior.[47]

There are many sexist implications built into the English language. Until a few years ago male pronouns (like *he*) were employed when speaking of human beings. Additional commonly used words and phrases that subtly (and erroneously) imply the superiority of males include *manmade, mankind, manned, man-power, chairman, congressman, businessman, mail-man, salesman, foreman, policeman, the best man for the job,* and *man and wife*. It is customary for women, on marriage, to take their husbands' last name, again subtly suggesting the dominance of males.

The mass media, particularly advertisements, also play an important role in sex-role socialization. Women have been more frequently portrayed in commercials as being wives, mothers, or sex objects or as being primarily interested in becoming more attractive in order to entice men into asking them for a date. They used to be portrayed invariably as less intelligent and more dependent than men. Women were practically never shown in executive positions. Some TV ads still foster traditional sex-role stereotypes by portraying women in traditional roles, such as delighting in wax-ing their floors or in ecstasy over discovering a new detergent to get their families' white clothes whiter. Fortunately, changes are occurring in the mass media's portrayal of women, reflecting changes in our nation. Women are increasingly portrayed in nontraditional roles. For example, many commercials are now revers-ing traditional roles to make the point. Because the mass media is an important socialization factor, it can serve to change attitudes about "proper" sex roles in the future.

CONSEQUENCES OF SEXISM

Sexism is prejudice or discrimination against women. Although women are a numerical majority in our soci-ety, they are considered a minority group because they are victims of discrimination on many fronts and have unequal access to valued resources.

Effects on Occupation and Income

The jobs held by women tend to be concentrated at the bottom of the occupational status hierarchy, as indi-cated in Table 12.1.

Women tend to be concentrated in the lower-pay-ing, lower-status positions: secretaries, child-care workers, receptionists, typists, nurses, hairdressers, bank tellers, cashiers, and file clerks. Men tend to be concentrated in higher-paying positions: lawyers, judges, engineers, accountants, college teachers, phy-sicians, dentists, and sales managers. As noted earlier, full-time working women are paid only about 65 per-cent of what full-time working men are paid.[48] Of fam-ilies headed by women, 34 percent are below the poverty line, compared with 9 percent of families headed by men.[49] Even with a number of sex discrimi-nation laws being passed, job discrimination has been found in a number of studies.[50]

Women hold fewer than 10 percent of the nation's elective offices. There has never been a woman presi-dent or vice president in the United States. Of the thou-sands of people who have been U.S. senators, less than twenty have been women.[51] It is a rarity when a woman is elected governor in a state. Nebraska in 1986 was the first state in our country's history in which both the Democratic and the Republican nominees for governor were women. Men are still in control of the political processes to nominate candidates and to campaign for their election. The potential political clout of women, however, is immense, as they compose a majority of the nation's voters.[52]

Women hold fewer than 1 percent of the top-management positions in American corporations, fewer than 2 percent of the directorships of top cor-porations, and about 5 or 6 percent of all middle-man-agement positions in this country.[53] Women today account for a smaller percentage of college faculties than they did 100 years ago and a smaller proportion of graduate students than in 1930.[54] About 75 percent of the working women in America are employed in the "girls' ghetto" positions of housekeepers, secretaries, receptionists, telephone operators, clerks, and so on.[55]

Overall, women earn less income than men in practically every job category, according to the Census Bureau.[56] Even in the armed forces, where pay levels are standardized, it is less likely that women will re-ceive additional income as "flight pay," "combat pay," or "hazardous duty" pay.[57] It is true that differences in income between men and women by job category are partly due to seniority pay from men having worked

TABLE 12.1

Employment Positions Held by Women

Position	Percentage Held by Women	Position	Percentage Held by Women
Dental assistants	99.0	Cashiers	83.1
Secretaries	97.7	File clerks	81.0
Receptionists	97.6	General office clerks	80.1
Child-care workers	96.1	Social workers	66.7
Cleaners, servants	95.8	Food-service workers	62.5
Typists	95.6	Psychologists	50.4
Registered nurses	95.1	Writers, artists, entertainers, athletes	44.5
Teachers' aides	93.6	Financial managers	40.7
Bank tellers	93.0	College teachers	35.2
Bookkeepers	91.5	Natural scientists	20.8
Health service workers	89.9	Lawyers and judges	18.2
Hairdressers, cosmetologists	89.9	Physicians	17.2
Telephone operators	88.8	Architects	11.3
Librarians	87.0	Police officers	10.8
Waiters, waitresses	84.0	Engineers	6.7
Elementary school teachers	84.0	Dentists	6.5
Maids, housemen	83.5	Firefighters	1.4

Source: U.S. Bureau of the Census, *Statistical Abstract of the United States, 1987* (Washington, D.C.: U.S. Government Printing Office, 1987, pp. 386–387.

longer, but studies taking seniority into account have found that women tend to receive less pay for doing the same job.[58]

There are probably many reasons for these occupational and income differences between men and women. Female children are socialized to seek lower-paying occupations and careers. For example, boys are more apt to be encouraged to be lawyers and doctors, whereas girls are encouraged to be teachers and secretaries. Men and women are also "sex typed" for various jobs. For example, males looking for employment are encouraged by prospective employers to apply for higher-status positions, whereas women are encouraged to apply for lower-level positions.[59] Then there is the tendency for our society to assign lower pay to job categories where women are concentrated: for example, receptionists, secretaries, and typists. Nonetheless, lower pay for women holding the same jobs as men suggests there are discriminatory practices occurring even after women are hired.

Paul Horton and Gerald Leslie provide additional reasons, stemming from sex-role socialization, for the job and income disparity between men and women:

Motivation for career advancement is difficult to measure, and rash generalization is dangerous. Yet there are good reasons to suspect that intense career ambitions have been less common among women than among men. Beginning in early socialization, most girls are trained to please and to charm others; most boys are trained to impress and outdistance others. Boys are trained to dominate and lead; girls, to submit and follow. Boys are taught to make demands upon others; girls learn to serve others' needs. Boys are praised for their strength: girls, for their prettiness and graciousness. As adults, men in our society are evaluated primarily according to their career success ("Meet my son, the doctor"), while women have been evaluated primarily according to their skill in human relationships ("She has a handsome husband and three darling children"). Husbands who knowingly neglected their families to pursue career advancement (moonlighting, night school, weekends working at the office) were praised for their ambition, while wives who allowed their careers to interfere with family life were scolded and scorned. A woman's spectacular success might alienate men, and much has been written about the avoidance-of-success syndrome in women.[60] In sum, it is reasonable to believe that some part of the different career successes of men and women is caused by women's lesser feeling of need for career achievement and a lesser willingness to sacrifice other values to its attainment.[61]

Effects on Human Interactions

The effects of sexism on human interactions are immense. Some examples will be briefly described.

Parents place more social restrictions on teenage daughters than on teenage sons. Daughters cannot stay out as late, their friends are more closely monitored, they are less likely to obtain the family car for going out, and they are discouraged from getting involved in athletic activity.

There are extensive pressures on women to have the "Miss America" look—to have well-developed busts, shapely figures, and attractive features. Practically all women find it difficult to maintain (even if they once had) such features. Unfortunately, women who are judged to be less attractive, according to current American stereotypes, receive less attention from males, find it more difficult to obtain dates, and may find it more difficult to obtain higher-status employment. The psychological costs are particularly severe when a woman reaches middle age. Socialized into believing her main function is the rearing of her family and that her main asset is her physical attractiveness, she often watches with despair as both her children and her youth leave her.

There are many double standards for male and female social interactions. If teenage males are sexually active, they are viewed as being "studs," whereas sexually active teenage females may be called derogatory names. To a greater extent, males are allowed to be aggressive and to use vulgar language. There are social restrictions that discourage women from entering certain nightclubs and other places of entertainment. Married women who have an affair are usually subjected to more disapproval than are married men who do.

In interactions between males and females, there is a tendency for the male to seek to be dominant and for the female either to seek an equalitarian relationship or to be manipulated into being submissive. For example, in dating, the male usually is expected to ask the female for a date and to select what they will do on a date. Also, males often try to be "macho"; some females find that, in order to receive positive reinforcement and social acceptability, they must play along by being submissive, passive, or "feminine." When both husband and wife are working, there is a tendency for the wife to follow her husband to a new geographical area when the location of the husband's job changes.[62]

Often, there are power struggles between males

and females related to sex-role expectations. Males may seek to be dominant, whereas females are more likely to seek equalitarian relationships. Marriage counselors are now seeing many couples in which the husband wants his wife to play a traditional role—stay at home, raise the children, and do the housework. If a wife does work, the husband often demands that the job not interfere with her doing the domestic tasks and wants the job to be viewed as a "second income" in contrast to a "career." Wives who want equalitarian relationships and who are becoming increasingly aware of the negative effects of sex-role stereotyping are apt to have power struggles with husbands who seek to have them fulfill the traditional wife role.

Jessie Bernard has noted that women experience more depression and greater dissatisfaction in marriage than men.[63] Women are expected to make most of the adjustments necessary to keep the marriage intact. Middle-aged women frequently suffer severe depression when many of their tasks as mothers and homemakers are phased out—especially if they do not have outside jobs.[64] Research demonstrates that employed wives are happier than full-time homemakers.[65] Women who are extensively battered by their husbands, yet continue to live in these circumstances for years, sadly document the extent to which some women are trapped by social arrangements that perpetuate their dependence and submission.

Matina Horner found that many women are motivated to avoid success because they fear that the more ambitious and successful they appear, the less feminine they will appear in their interactions with men.[66]

Sex-role stereotypes probably also play a role in women being treated only as sex objects by some men and in women being sexually harassed at work, at school, and in other settings.

It is not only female stereotypes that cause human interaction difficulties. Males also experience problems in living up to the image of a "model man." This "Clint Eastwood" image was described earlier. It is almost impossible for any male to live up to this image. Yet, there are considerable pressures on males to try—or to suffer the consequences. Take the example of Senator Edmund Muskie in the Democratic presiden-

tial primary campaign in 1968. Senator Muskie was the leading candidate for the nomination. Then a newspaper in New England made some derogatory accusations about his wife, and Muskie reacted by "breaking down and crying" in public. Very quickly, the American public concluded that Muskie did not have the emotional stability to be president, and his popularity plummeted in the polls. Deborah David and Robert Brannon describe another example:

A friend explained to me that he broke down and cried in front of a colleague at the office after some personal tragedies and office frustrations. He explained, "The news of my crying was all over the office in an hour. At first, no one said anything. They just sort of looked. They couldn't handle the situation by talking about it. Before this, only girls had cried. One of the guys did joke, 'Hear you and Sally been crying lately, eh?' I guess that was a jibe at my masculinity, but the 'knowing silence' of the others indicated the same doubts. What really hurt was that two years later, when I was doing very well and being considered for a promotion, it was brought up again. My manager was looking over my evaluations, read a paragraph to himself, and said, 'What do you think about that crying incident?' You can bet that was the last time I let myself cry."[67]

Ruth Hartley notes that sex-role socialization of boys inevitably leads to personal conflicts in later years:

The boy is not adequately socialized for adulthood. . . . The boy is conditioned to live in an all-masculine society, defining his own self-image by rejecting whatever smacks of femininity. In adulthood, he will have to adjust to a heterosexual work world, perhaps even take orders from a female, a species he has been taught to despise as inferior. Finally, the emphasis on repression of the emotions, the high value of stoicism, leaves the boy wholly unprepared for the emotional closeness and intimate personal interaction now more and more expected of a lover and a spouse.[68]

Men frequently feel they must put their careers first and thereby sharply limit the interactions and satisfactions received in being husbands or fathers. In contrast, women are urged by traditional expectations to put their roles as wives and mothers first and thereby limit their growth, capacities, and satisfactions in other areas.

Men in this country are disadvantaged before the law in several areas. For one, they can be drafted. If a war occurs, only men in the armed services can be required to fight in combat. In some jurisdictions, husbands are legally required to provide financial support for their families, and failure to do so is grounds for divorce by the wife. If a marriage breaks up, there is a tendency for the court to grant custody of the children to the wife. Alimony is much more frequently awarded to wives, even when both spouses can support themselves. Will we see a men's liberation movement in the future?

Sex-role stereotyping probably also plays a key role in the following statistics.[69] Men are three times more likely than women to commit suicide, three times more likely to have a severe emotional disorder, substantially more likely to be involved in violence, and commit most crimes. Alcoholics and drug addicts are primarily men. Males also have higher rates of stress-related illnesses, such as heart disease, ulcers, and hypertension. The life expectancy for men in our society is several years less than for women. Could this shorter life expectancy for men be partially explained by the pressures on men to succeed financially and by the fact that they are socialized not to ventilate their emotions? Men may experience more psychological stress, which leads to higher rates of stress-related illnesses; some of those illnesses then result in a shorter life span for men.

Because of male stereotypes, many men view themselves as failures when they cannot meet the financial needs of their families. Some men are badly beaten in fights they felt they could not walk away from and still be "real men." Many women find it frustrating to interact with men who are unable to be honest and open about their feelings. Not being able to live up to the "model man" image makes many men unhappy, depressed, and unfulfilled. Thus, sex-role stereotyping has huge costs (financial, social, and personal) not only for women, but also for men.

RECENT DEVELOPMENTS AND THE FUTURE

There is currently a sex-role revolution occurring in our society. Men as well as women are becoming aware of the negative effects of sex-role distinctions. Increasingly, there are courses on this topic in high schools, vocational schools, and colleges. More and more women are entering the labor force. The proportion of employed females to employed males is about 46 to 54.[70]

Women are becoming more involved in athletics than they were in the past, and they are entering certain types of competition previously confined to males. Women are now playing basketball, football, softball, and volleyball. There are increasing numbers of women in track and field events, swimming, boxing, wrestling, weight lifting, golf, tennis, and stock-car racing.

In 1983 Sandra Day O'Connor was the first woman appointed to be a justice on the United States Supreme Court. In 1984 Geraldine Ferraro was the first woman selected to be a vice-presidential candidate for a major political party.

Women are also pursuing a number of professions and careers that previously were nearly all male: the military, engineers, lawyers, judges, firefighters, physicians, dentists, accountants, administrators, police officers, managers. Entering such new careers often has obstacles. Carl Glassman, for example, reports that women who have become police officers receive stares from other citizens and are often viewed with suspicion by male partners.[71] (Male police partners fear that women may break under pressure, that women may not be able to subdue and handcuff a resisting offender, and that women may not be able to handle disorderly males and several other types of violent situations. Male officers tend to feel both hostile and protective toward patrolwomen, and one woman's failing is often held up as an indictment against all the rest.)

There are also changes in human interactions, with

more women being assertive and seeking out equalitarian relationships with males. To some extent, men
are also (more slowly) beginning to realize the negative effects of sex-role distinctions. Men are gradually
realizing that the stereotyped "model man" role limits
the opportunities open to them in terms of emotional
expression, interpersonal relationships, occupations,
and domestic activities. Jack Sawyer has noted:

If men cannot play freely, neither can they freely cry,
be gentle, nor show weakness—because these are
"feminine," not "masculine." But a fuller concept
of humanity recognizes that all men and women
are potentially both strong and weak, both active
and passive, and that these and other human
characteristics are not the province of one sex.

The acceptance of sex-role stereotypes not only
limits the individual, but also has bad effects on
society generally.[72]

Sex-role stereotypes have been costly to society.
Such stereotypes have prevented a number of people
from entering more productive roles and have resulted
in society expending substantial resources on emotional and physical problems generated by these
stereotypes.

Men are also taking on new roles and entering new
careers. It is increasingly becoming more common for
men to accept equal responsibility for domestic tasks
and many childrearing tasks; and there are now more
male nurses, secretaries, child-care workers, nurs-
ery school teachers, telephone operators, and flight
attendants.[73]

In the past two decades, millions of Americans
have begun to change their ideas about the "naturalness" of making sex-role discriminations. Such traditional discriminations are now beginning to be seen as
an irrational system that threatens women with lifelong
inferiority and wasted potential and restricts men into
the "unnatural" role of always being competitive, aggressive, and emotionally insensitive.

What will the future be like in terms of sex roles?
Sex-role stereotypes are now undergoing change. Predicting the precise direction that sex-role stereotypes
will take is difficult. Thomas Sullivan et al. note that:

Women are advancing in areas where their presence was
all but unthinkable just a few years ago. Barbara Harris
blesses her congregation after recently being ordained as
the first female bishop in the history of the Episcopal
Church.

It seems likely that any meaningful change in our sex-
role structure will involve some degree of redefinition
of both masculinity and femininity. In the years to
come, it is likely that we will see significant shifts in the
way children are socialized and revisions of our legal
system that affect both men and women. The extent of

the change that will occur is something that cannot yet be determined. . . . We are in the midst of a very exciting era of experimentation. We have an opportunity to shape our destiny in this area. If people decide that sexual differences are important, this need not entail a return to the inequality, discrimination, and oppression that were common in the past and still linger today.[74]

Some feminists and social scientists have urged that men and women be socialized to be flexible in their role playing and to seek to express themselves as human beings rather than in traditional feminine or masculine ways.[75] This idea is called "androgyny," from *andro* (male) and *gyne* (female). The notion is to have people explore a broad range of role-playing possibilities and to choose to express emotions and behaviors without regard to sex-role stereotypes. People thus are encouraged to pursue tasks and careers at which they are most competent and with which they are most comfortable and to express attitudes and emotions they really feel. If a male wants to be a cook or an elementary school teacher and a female wants to be a soldier or an athlete—and they're good at it—then it is functional for society if both develop their talents and are allowed to achieve everything of which they are capable.

SEXISM AND SOCIAL WORK

Because 67 percent of social workers are female, there is the notion that social work is a female-dominated profession.[76] Some other statistics suggest otherwise. David Fanshel, in a study of NASW members, found that the proportion of men in leadership positions (for example, in administration) was twice that of women.[77] In addition, about half of social work faculty members in the United States are men.[78] Juliana Szakacs compiled statistics on leadership positions by sex in feder-

ally funded, private, nonprofit organizations and found that over 80 percent were headed by men.[79]

In 1982 the median salary of male members of the National Association of Social Workers was $7,500 higher than for female members.[80] One major reason for the salary difference is that men were more likely to hold administrative positions, which are higher paying, whereas women worked predominately in clinical, direct-practice positions. In 1988 Anne Fortune and Lou Hanks conducted a study of 520 recently graduated master's level social workers.[81] Other relevant factors affecting salary (such as age, experience, and marital status) were controlled. Initial salaries were comparable between men and women at the point of hiring, but the researchers found that men moved into non-clinical positions (such as supervision and administration) earlier in their careers and within a few years earned more than women. The authors conclude, "There is little evidence that social work has improved the inequities between men and women in its own ranks."[82] Taken together, these statistics indicate that males tend to predominate in occupying leadership positions in social work.

There is, however, some evidence that the profession is responding to women's issues. In 1973 the Delegate Assembly of NASW responded to the women's movement by adding the elimination of sexism to poverty and racism as basic concerns and priorities for the profession. The Council on Social Work Education (CSWE) has required in accreditation standards for baccalaureate and master's programs that content on women's issues must be included throughout the curriculum. CSWE also has an accreditation standard that prohibits sexual discrimination in social work educational programs and mandates affirmative action programs for women administrators, faculty, students, and staff in social work educational programs.

NASW Legal Defense Fund has provided financial support in sex discrimination cases. In addition, NASW supported the Equal Rights Amendment, has voiced opposition to the Hyde Amendment (which prohibits the use of federal funds for abortions), and is working on other issues related to sexism.

On a practice level there is some truth that social

BOX 12.4

Strategies for Achieving Sexual Equality

S exual equality does not mean achieving a "unisex" approach. Advocates of sexual equality are not urging using the same bathroom in public facilities, nor are they urging dressing the same or playing professional football and hockey together. What they *are* advocating is the equal treatment of the sexes (for example, in employment) and the end to traditional sex-role stereotyping. They are advocating that no role, behavior, aptitude, or attitude should be limited to one sex alone. True sexual equality simply means that people would be free to be themselves.

To achieve sexual equality will require action in many areas, some of which are summarized as follows:

- An end must be put to the motherhood myth, which holds that women are most fulfilled as mothers.

- Fathers must share equally in the process of childrearing and in domestic tasks. This guideline does not mean men should do exactly half of each domestic task, but involves husband and wife communicating with each other about how best to allocate family responsibilities. Women cannot compete equally with men in the work world if they also are required to assume all of the traditional childrearing and homemaker responsibilities.

- Additional day-care provisions are needed for working mothers and fathers, particularly for one-parent families. Unless quality day-care arrangements are available, many mothers who want to work are prevented from working.

- Laws preventing sex discrimination need to be enforced, and laws in areas where legal discrimination still exists need to be enacted. (For example, sometimes women have a more difficult time obtaining a bank loan.) Sex discrimination laws are also needed for men in certain areas (such as in alimony and child custody).

work is a women's profession, as a majority of social work clients are women. About three fourths of all persons receiving public assistance and welfare payments are women.[83] Because women still primarily care for children, they are the main users of child welfare services. Women are more apt to seek and receive counseling, and they are the major consumers of services for the aged. Women are also the primary consumers of family planning, pregnancy counseling, abortion services, rape crisis services, services from shelters for battered wives, and displaced homemaker services.

There are a number of reasons why more women than men are social work clients. For one thing, women outnumber men in the United States. Julia B. Rauch identifies another reason: "Most women in this country

- Dysfunctional sex-role socialization practices should be ended. Children should be reared to take on the roles, attitudes, and behaviors they desire and in which they have capacities, rather than boys being raised to be "masculine" and girls to be "feminine." Parents and teachers should learn to relate to each child as an *individual*, rather than as a *male* or a *female*.

- Assertiveness training programs should be used more widely, to help both men and women effectively express themselves and gain skills in countering sex-role stereotypes.

- Advertisers who still portray women only as homemakers or as sex objects should start giving equal treatment to men and women.

- Consciousness groups need to be expanded to reach more men and women. Such groups are now being held largely with women, to help them become more aware of sex-role stereotypes, to help them establish a better self-concept, and to foster contact with others who are working to end sexism.

- Continued development of such services as shelters for battered women, rape-crisis centers, abortion counseling, family planning services, and marriage and sexual counseling is needed if people are to develop their capacities fully.

- School counselors and teachers should help students to make career decisions based on their abilities, not on their gender.

- Girls and boys should be encouraged to take vocational courses they desire (cooking, shop, typing, printing) without regard to gender.

- Publishers should continue to put an end to sex-role stereotyping and portray females and males in a variety of roles—such as males performing domestic tasks and women being pilots and medical doctors.

---

are socialized to accept weakness and dependence with more ease than men. The role of client is compatible with behaviors expected of women but is not congruent with men's expectations of themselves."[84] Women tend to need more services because poverty is a problem that disproportionately affects women, as women who work full time are paid substantially less than men who work full time. Women have higher rates

of unemployment and are much more likely to be single heads of households.

Rauch summarizes a number of additional reasons why women are more apt to be social work clients:

. . . teenage and unwanted pregnancies, postpartum depression, and sexual dysfunction; the need, resulting from the concentration of parenting

Shared domestic tasks and child-rearing responsibilities are fundamental to achieving equality between the sexes.

functions in women's hands, for services for mothers who abuse or neglect their children and for the mothers of emotionally disturbed, learning disabled, mentally retarded, blind, or otherwise handicapped children; women's vulnerability to wife abuse and rape; the limitations of the wife-mother role and the "empty nest" syndrome; the practical and emotional stresses for women of separation or divorce and the difficulties of raising children alone; and the norm that women marry older men, which, in combination with women's longer life expectancy leads to widowhood and the stresses of bereavement, loss of the role of wife, and loneliness.[85]

On a practice level it is important for social workers to understand that the traditional socialization process and the sex-role stereotypes in our society account for many of the problems that confront female, as well as male, clients. Workers should be skilled in helping clients to actualize themselves and to stop being negatively influenced by rigid sex-role stereotypes. As noted earlier, many interaction problems between males and females in our society are consequences of sex-role stereotyping. One therapy approach that is widely being used to help both men and women more effectively express themselves and gain skills in countering sex-role stereotypes is assertiveness training (described in Chapter 17). Consciousness-raising groups are being held, largely with women, to help them become more aware of sex-role stereotypes, to establish a better self-concept, and to foster contact with others who are also working to end sexism.

The growing awareness of sexism and women's issues has led to the provision of improved services to groups that were largely ignored—victims of rape, battered wives, women seeking abortions, husbands and wives with marital concerns, people with sexual dysfunctions, single-parent households headed by women, and displaced homemakers.[86]

THE FUTURE DIRECTION OF THE WOMEN'S MOVEMENT

Within the women's movement there is currently much debate over policy directions.[87] The conservative trend in the 1980s jeopardized the progress that feminists made in some areas during the 1960s and 1970s. Both President and Mrs. Reagan, as well as most members of the Reagan cabinet, opposed the Equal Rights Amendment, and it eventually failed to be ratified. The conservative movement and the Reagan administration put less emphasis on enforcing affirmative action programs and actively opposed the concept of setting "quotas" for the percent of minorities that must be hired by employers. Cuts were made in a number of social programs that the women's movement has vigorously supported, such as cuts in funding for public day care, sex education, and contraception. George Bush was elected president in 1988 and has stated that his administration will seek to continue the Reagan program agenda. Bush opposes the Equal Rights Amendment.

The National Organization for Women (NOW) has been united in its determination to fight efforts to prohibit abortions. The women's movement views access to abortions as a basic right that women have in deciding what happens to their body and to their life.

Women burdened by unwanted children often become dependent on their husbands or on welfare and are unable to compete competitively with men in the job market. In the 1980s the Reagan administration and various prolife groups sought to pass a constitutional amendment that would make practically all abortions illegal. President Bush has stated he also supports passage of such an amendment, which would allow abortions only in cases of rape or incest or to save a woman's life.

Thus, in some areas, the 1980s has been a time of setbacks for the women's movement. There is a debate in the women's movement about whether the movement should devalue the traditional roles held by women. When the movement advocates for modern roles that emphasize equality and careers, some authorities assert that it appears the traditional role of homemaker is being devalued—yet, some leaders of NOW assert that traditional roles should not be devalued.

One of the future directions that the women's movement appears to be taking is to seek help for single-parent families, particularly low-income, female-headed families. There has been a feminization of poverty in this country, since an increasing proportion of poor people are women. It is almost impossible for single mothers to be "financially equal" to males in the job market when day care is highly expensive and when women who work full time are paid considerably less than men who work full time. It is certain that the women's movement will continue to advocate for child care and children's aid.

Another area that the women's movement has been

advocating for is "comparable worth." Comparable worth involves the concept of "equal pay for comparable work," rather than "equal pay for equal work." Comparable worth asserts that the intrinsic value of different jobs, such as that of a secretary or a plumber, can be measured. Those jobs that are evaluated to be of comparable value should receive comparable pay. If implemented, it is believed that the concept will reduce the disparities in pay between women and men who work full time. Some states (such as Wisconsin and Washington) have initiated efforts to develop comparable worth programs for state employees.

Another direction that the women's movement is taking is to encourage and support more women running for public offices at federal, state, and local levels. The women's movement recognizes that achieving equality partially depends on moving toward political equality.

Although the women's movement has had some setbacks in the 1980s, it is clear the general thrust of the movement toward equality will continue.

SUMMARY

In almost every known society women have had a lower status than men. Women have traditionally been assigned housework and childrearing responsibilities and have been socialized to be passive, submissive, and feminine. The socialization process and sex-role stereotyping have led to a number of problems. There is sex discrimination in employment, with men who work full time being paid substantially more than women who work full time. There are double standards of conduct for males and females. There are power struggles between males and females because men are socialized to be dominant in interactions with women, whereas women often seek equalitarian relationships. Sex-role stereotyping and the traditional female role have led women to be unhappier in marriages and to be more depressed.

Sex-role stereotyping is pervasive in our society, with aspects being found in childrearing practices, the educational system, religion, contemporary psychological theories, our language, the mass media, the business world, marriage and family patterns, and our political system.

The women's movement, which had a resurgence in the 1960s, is revolutionizing sex-role stereotypes and the socialization process. A number of laws forbidding sex discrimination have been enacted. Women as well as men are now pursuing new careers and are taking on roles and tasks that run counter to traditional sex stereotypes. The androgyny notion is gaining strength. It involves people exploring a broad range of role-playing possibilities and choosing to express emotions and behaviors without regard to sex-role stereotypes.

Interestingly, the women's movement also has many payoffs for males. Males find it extremely difficult and encounter many problems in trying to fulfill the stereotypes of the model-man role—to always be dominant, strong, never depressed or anxious; to hide emotions; to be the provider; to be self-reliant, aggressive, brave; and to never cry. Men are gradually realizing that the stereotypical model-man role limits the opportunities open to them in terms of interpersonal relationships, occupations, emotional expression, and domestic activities. Sex-role stereotyping has huge costs for women, for men, and for society. True sexual equality simply means that people would be free to be themselves.

The social work profession has made commitments to eliminate sexism, both within its own ranks and in the broader society. Although 67 percent of practicing social workers are female, more males are concentrated in administrative and other leadership positions in social work. Most social work clients are women. Social workers need to become skilled in helping clients to actualize themselves and to stop being negatively influenced by sex-role stereotypes.

NOTES

1. U.S. Bureau of the Census, *Statistical Abstract of the United States, 1987* (Washington, D.C.: U.S. Government Printing Office, 1987), p. 403.

2. Scott Lautenschlager, "Hurdles Block Female Workers," *Wisconsin State Journal*, June 25, 1987, p. 3.

3. Jean Stockard and Miriam M. Johnson, *Sex Roles* (Englewood Cliffs, NJ: Prentice-Hall, 1980), p. 31.

4. U.S. Bureau of the Census, *Statistical Abstract of the United States, 1987*, p. 445.

5. Stockard and Johnson, *Sex Roles*.

6. Joseph H. Fichter and Virginia K. Mills, "The Status of Women in American Churches," *Church and Society* (September–October 1972).

7. Thomas Sullivan et al., *Social Problems* (New York: John Wiley, 1980), p. 452.

8. Francine D. Blair, "Women in the Labor Force: An Overview," in *Women: A Feminist Perspective*, ed. Jo Freeman (Palo Alto, CA: Mayfield Publishing, 1979), p. 272.

9. John Money, J. G. Hampson, and J. L. Hampson, "An Examination of Some Basic Sexual Concepts: The Evidence of Human Hermaphroditism," *Bulletin of the John Hopkins Hospital*, 1955, pp. 301–309.

10. H. L. Rheingold and K. V. Cook, "The Contents of Boys' and Girls' Rooms as an Index of Parents' Behavior," *Child Development* 46 (June 1975), p. 461.

11. Eleanor Maccoby and Carol Jacklin, *The Psychology of Sex Differences* (Stanford, CA: Stanford University Press, 1974).

12. Ibid.

13. Clarice Stasz Stoll, ed., *Sexism: Scientific Debates* (Reading, MA: Addison-Wesley, 1973).

14. Warren Farrell, *The Liberated Man* (New York: Random House, 1975).

15. Sullivan et al., *Social Problems*, p. 455.

16. Betty Friedan, *The Feminine Mystique* (New York: Dell Books, 1963).

17. Sullivan et al., *Social Problems*, p. 475.

18. Paul B. Horton, Gerald R. Leslie, and Richard F. Larson, *The Sociology of Social Problems*, 8th ed. (Englewood Cliffs, NJ: Prentice-Hall, 1985), pp. 261–264.

19. Ibid., p. 260.

20. Sullivan et al., *Social Problems*, pp. 475–476.

21. Horton, Leslie, and Larson, *The Sociology of Social Problems*, pp. 256–264.

22. "$2 Million Settlement is Reported in Women's Bias Suit Against NBC," *New York Times*, February 13, 1977.

23. "ERA Stalled, but Women Make Piecemeal Gains," *U.S. News & World Report*, August, 20, 1979, p. 56.

24. Horton, Leslie, and Larson, *The Sociology of Social Problems*, p. 266.

25. Deborah S. David and Robert Brannon, eds., *The Forty-*

Nine Percent Majority: The Male Sex Role (Reading, MA: Addison-Wesley, 1976).

26. Stockard and Johnson, *Sex Roles*, pp. 133–147.

27. Richard C. Friedman, Ralph M. Richart, and Raymond L. Vande Wiehe, eds., *Sex Differences in Behavior* (New York: John Wiley, 1974).

28. See Shirly Weitz, *Sex Roles: Biological, Psychological, and Social Foundations* (New York: Oxford University Press, 1977); Betty Yorburg, *Sexual Identity: Sex Roles and Social Change* (New York: John Wiley, 1974); Michael Teitelbaum, ed., *Sex Roles: Social and Biological Perspectives* (New York: Doubleday Anchor Books, 1976).

29. Ibid.

30. Maccoby and Jacklin, *The Psychology of Sex Differences*.

31. Ibid.

32. John Money, Joan Hampson, and John Hampson, "Imprinting and the Establishment of Gender Role," *Archives of Neurology and Psychiatry* 77 (March 1967), 333–336; see also John Money and Anke A. Ehrhardt, *Man and Woman, Boy and Girl* (New York: New American Library, 1974); and Richard Green, *Sexual Identity Conflict in Children and Adults* (Baltimore: Penguin Books, 1975).

33. Clellan S. Ford and Frank Beach, *Patterns of Sexual Behavior* (New York: Harper & Row, 1951).

34. Allan Katcher, "The Discrimination of Sex Differences by Young Children," *Journal of Genetic Psychology* 87 (September 1955), pp. 131–143.

35. Lawrence Kohlberg, "A Cognitive-Developmental Analysis of Children's Sex-Role Concepts and Attitudes," in *The Psychology of Sex Differences*, eds. Maccoby and Jacklin, pp. 82–173.

36. Ruth E. Hartley, "American Core Culture: Changes and Continuities," in *Sex Roles in Changing Society*, eds. Georgene H. Seward and Robert C. Williamson (New York: Random House, 1970), pp. 140–141.

37. Ibid., p. 141.

38. Sullivan et al., *Social Problems*, pp. 460–465.

39. Charles H. Cooley, *Social Organization* (New York: Charles Scribner's Sons, 1909).

40. Matina Horner, "Fail: Bright Women," *Psychology Today*, November 1969, pp. 36–38; Vivian Gornick, "Why Women Fear Success," *Ms. Magazine*, Spring 1972, pp. 50–53.

41. Marcia Guttentag and Helen Bray, "Teachers as Mediators of Sex Role Standards," in *Beyond Sex Roles*, ed. Alice Sargent (St. Paul, MN: West Publishing, 1977), pp. 395–411.

42. Pam Maye and Sara McMillan, "Student Project," in *Masculine, Feminine or Human?* ed. Janet Saltzman Chafetz (Itasca, IL: F. E. Peacock, 1974).

43. Lenore Weitzman et al., "Sex Role Socialization in Picture Books for Preschool Children," *American Journal of Sociology* 72 (May 1972), pp. 1125–1150; Sullivan et al., *Social Problems*, p. 463.

44. Florence Howe, "Sexual Stereotypes Start Early," *Saturday Review*, October 16, 1971, p. 82.

45. Janet S. Chafetz, *Masculine, Feminine, or Human? An Overview of the Sociology of Sex Roles* (Itasca, IL: F. E. Peacock, 1974), p. 69.

46. Viola Klein, *The Feminine Character: History of an Ideology* (Urbana, IL: University of Illinois Press, 1975).

47. See Judd Marmor, "Changing Patterns of Femininity," in *Family in Transition*, eds. Arlene S. Skolnick and Jerome H. Skolnick (Boston: Little, Brown, 1971), pp. 210–221.

48. U.S. Bureau of the Census, *Statistical Abstract of the United States, 1987*, p. 403.

49. Ibid., p. 445.

50. Sullivan et al., *Social Problems*, p. 466.

51. James Coleman and Donald Cressey, *Social Problems*, 2d ed. (New York: Harper & Row, 1984), p. 292.

52. Ibid., p. 292.

53. "Women and Power–A Status Report," *New York Times*, May 1, 1977, sec. 3, pp. 1, 4.

54. Warren Farrell, *The Liberated Man* (New York: Random House, 1975), p. 150.

55. "Working Women: Joys and Sorrows," *U.S. News & World Report*, January 15, 1979, p. 64.

56. U.S. Bureau of the Census, "Money Income in 1976 of Families and Persons in the United States," *Current Population Reports*, series P-60, no. 114 (Washington, D.C.: U.S. Government Printing Office, July 1978).

57. Sullivan et al., *Social Problems*, p. 468.

58. Ibid., p. 468.

59. Richard M. Levinson, "Sex Discrimination and Employment Practices: An Experiment with Unconventional Job Enquiries," *Social Problems* 22 (April 1975), pp. 533–543.

60. Peter J. Weston and Martha T. Shuch Mednick, "Race, Social Class, and the Motive to Avoid Success in Women," *Journal of Cross-Cultural Psychology* 1 (September 1970), pp. 283–291; Matina S. Horner, "Toward an Understanding of Achievement-related Conflicts in Women," *Journal of Social Issues* 28, no. 2 (1972), pp. 157–175; Lois Wladis Hoffman, "Fear of Success in Males and Females," *Journal of Consulting and Clinical Psychology* 42 (April 1974), pp. 353–358.

61. Paul B. Horton and Gerald R. Leslie, *The Sociology of*

Social Problems, 6th ed. (Englewood Cliffs, NJ: Prentice-Hall, 1978), p. 424.

62. Ibid., p. 420.

63. Jessie Bernard, "The Paradox of the Happy Marriage," in *Women in Sexist Society*, eds. Vivian Gonick and Barbara K. Moran (New York: Basic Books, 1971), pp. 145–162.

64. Pauline B. Bart, "Depression in Middle-Aged Women," in *Women in Sexist Society*, eds. Vivian Gornick and Barbara K. Moran, pp. 163–186.

65. Carol Tavris and Carole Offir, *The Longest War: Sex Differences in Perspective* (New York: Harcourt Brace Jovanovich, 1976), p. 223.

66. Matina S. Horner, "Femininity and Successful Achievement: A Basic Inconsistency," in *Feminine Personality and Conflict*, ed. Judith M. Bardwick (Belmont, CA: Brooks/Cole, 1970).

67. David and Brannon, *Forty-Nine Percent Majority*, pp. 53–54.

68. Hartley, "American Core Culture," p. 142.

69. U.S. Bureau of the Census, *Statistical Abstract of the United States, 1987*.

70. Ibid., p. 376.

71. Carl Glassman, "How Lady Cops Are Doing," *Parade*, July 27, 1980, pp. 4–5.

72. Jack Sawyer, "On Male Liberation," in *Men and Masculinity*, eds. Joseph H. Pleck and Jack Sawyer (Englewood Cliffs, NJ: Prentice-Hall, 1974), p. 172.

73. "Now, Men are Going for 'Women's Jobs,'" *U.S. News & World Report*, October 16, 1978, pp. 97–98.

74. Sullivan et al., *Social Problems*, p. 474.

75. Horton and Leslie, *Sociology of Social Problems*, pp. 425–426.

76. U.S. Bureau of the Census, *Statistical Abstract of the United States, 1987*, pp. 386–387.

77. David Fanshel, "Status Differentials: Men and Women in Social Work," *Social Work* 21 (November 1976), pp. 450–451.

78. Allen Rubin and G. Robert Whitcomb, eds., *Statistics on Social Work Education in the United States, 1978* (New York: Council on Social Work Education, 1979), p. 10.

79. Juliana Szakacs, "Is Social Work a Woman's Profession?" *Womanpower: A Quarterly Newsletter of the Committee on Women in Social Welfare*, February 1977, p. 3.

80. "Membership Survey Shows Practice Shifts," *NASW News* 28 (November 1983), pp. 6–7.

81. Anne Fortune and Lou Hanks, "Gender Inequities in Early Social Worker Careers," *Social Work* 33, no. 3 (May-June 1988), pp. 221–225.

82. Ibid., p. 225.

83. Julia B. Rauch, "Gender as a Factor in Practice," *Social Work* 23, no. 5 (September 1978), pp. 388–395.

84. Ibid., p. 391.

85. Ibid., p. 392.

86. Ketayun H. Gould, "Sexism," in *Contemporary Social Work*, 2d ed., eds. Donald Brieland, Lela Costin, and Charles Atherton (New York: McGraw-Hill, 1980), pp. 427–428.

87. Joseph Julian and William Kornblum, *Social Problems*, 5th ed. (Englewood Cliffs, NJ: Prentice-Hall, 1986), pp. 288–289.

13

AGING AND GERONTOLOGICAL SERVICES

The plight of the elderly (for so long overlooked) has now become recognized as a major social problem in the United States. The elderly face a number of social and personal problems: high rates of physical illness and emotional difficulties, poverty, malnutrition, lack of access to transportation, low status, lack of a meaningful role in our society, and inadequate housing. To a large extent the elderly are a "recently discovered" minority group. Similar to other minority groups the elderly are victims of job discrimination, are excluded from the mainstream of American life on the basis of supposed group characteristics, and are subjected to prejudice that is based on erroneous stereotypes.

This chapter will describe:

- The specific problems faced by the elderly.
- The causes of these problems.
- Current services to meet these problems.
- Gaps in current services.
- The role of social work in providing services to the elderly.
- Needed social and political changes to improve the status of the elderly.

AN OVERVIEW

Tom Townsend (see Box 13.1) has no serious financial concerns, at least at present. Gordon and Walter Moss describe the plight of someone who is old and poor.

An old woman turned quickly away from the dismal scene outside her Florida hotel room window. Listlessly, she mixed her own breakfast: a cup of Sanka and a small glass of Tang. After finishing her breakfast, she looked at her wardrobe. It contained a few unwanted dresses given to her by a relative, and one she had bought herself seven years ago. After choosing one, she made her bed and dusted her dresser, two small tables, and their lamps. She then turned on a small fan in anticipation of a hot muggy day, wound her clock, straightened her small pile of old books, blew dust from the artificial flowers in a

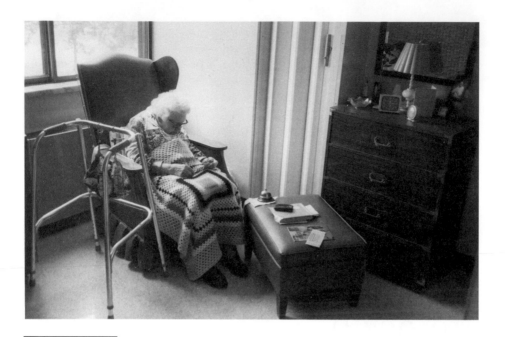

Some traditional societies abandoned their elderly because of scarce resources. We can take comfort in the fact that our society is more enlightened, but our abandonment of the elderly is no less real. In some ways it is more unethical—most of us don't face such serious survival issues.

cheap vase, and sat down in her only chair to watch television. Finally, it was noon, time for her to go down to the church for a hot lunch. In the afternoon, she would watch television soap operas, or perhaps spend an hour or two visiting with the many other widows in the hotel.

All the while, uncertainty gnawed at her. Already she was paying over half of her small retirement and welfare income for rent; and if the rent went up anymore she would be unable to stay. The hot lunch, sponsored by the federal government, cost her only 50 cents and helped a little. Nevertheless, due especially to medical bills, she frequently ran out of money before the end of the month.

Her ulcer was her biggest worry. A few weeks earlier, it had started to bleed, and she had passed out.

She had lain helpless for some time before finally managing to crawl to the phone. The desk clerk and some friends had then helped her get to the hospital. She had been more fortunate than some others in the hotel. Their lives had ended in their rooms because they had been too weak from malnutrition to crawl for help.[1]

Do these two stories sound like sentimental fiction? We wish! Sadly, however, these accounts are typical retirements turned into nightmares.[2]

Throughout time some tribal societies have abandoned their enfeebled old. The Crow, Creek, and Hopi Indians, for example, built special huts away from the tribe where the old were left to die. The Eskimos left the incapacitated elderly in snowbanks or forced them

BOX 13.1

The Best Years of Your Life

This is Tom Townsend. He had been with the iron works plant forty-two years. Being promoted to foreman sixteen years ago had fulfilled his dreams, and there was nothing he desired more than to be on the job and managing his crew. He had been married to Laura for the past thirty-seven years. At first, their marriage had some rough moments, but Laura and Tom had long since grown accustomed to and comfortable with each other. She was a fine woman, and her main job was managing the home. They had had two children who had grown up and moved away and now had homes of their own.

Life was at the factory for Tom. He didn't have time to develop other hobbies and interests, nor was he interested in picnics or socials. When he had time off from work, he used it to repair things around home and to "tool up" for getting back to work. Television replaced talk in his home, and Tom usually spent weekends watching a variety of sports programs.

One day, it was May 18, and Tom was 70. The company marked the occasion with a dinner that was well attended. Tom and Laura were there along with their children and families, the members of Tom's crew and their wives, and the company managers and their wives. At first, everyone was a little anxious, as these people did not often get together with each other socially. The dinner, however, went fairly well. Tom was congratulated by everyone, received a gold watch, and made appropriate remarks about his positive feelings about the company. After a few more cocktails, everyone went home. Tom was feeling sentimental but also good about himself because everyone was acknowledging his contributions.

Tom awoke at 7 o'clock the next morning, the usual time for him to get ready for work. Then it hit him. He was retired, with nowhere to go and no reason for rising. His life at the plant was over. What should he do now? He didn't know.

He spent the next week following Laura around the house, getting on her nerves. At times, he complained about feeling useless. Twice, he commented he wished he were dead. He went back to the plant to see his men, but they were too busy to talk. Besides, there was Bill, who had been promoted to foreman and who enjoyed showing Tom how the department's productivity had increased and bored Tom with his plans for making changes to increase production further.

Long walks didn't help much, either. As he walked, he thought about his plight and became more depressed. What was he going to do? What could he find to occupy his time meaningfully? He looked into a mirror and saw his receding hairline and numerous wrinkles. More and more, he started to feel a variety of aches and pains. He thought to himself, "I guess I'm just a useless old man." He wondered what the future would hold. Would his company pension keep pace with increasing bills? Would he eventually be placed in a nursing home? What was he going to do with the remainder of his life? He just didn't know.

to paddle away in a kayak. The Siriono of the Bolivian forest simply left them behind when they moved on in search of food.[3] Even today the Ik of Uganda leave the elderly and disabled to starve to death.[4] (Generally, the primary reason tribal societies have been forced to abandon the elderly is scarce resources.)

Although we might consider such customs shocking and barbaric, have we not also abandoned the old? We force them to retire when many are still productive. All too often, when a person is forced to retire, his or her status, power, and self-esteem are lost. Also, in a physical sense we seldom have a place for large numbers of older people. Community facilities—parks, subways, libraries—are oriented to serving children and young people. Most housing is designed and priced for the young couple with one or two children and an annual income in excess of $25,000. If the elderly are not able to care for themselves (and if their families are unable to care for them), we "store" them away from society in nursing homes. Our abandonment of the elderly is further indicated by our taking little action to relieve financial problems of the elderly, as nearly a quarter of the elderly have incomes close to or below the poverty line.[5] (In one sense our abandonment of the elderly is more unethical than that of tribal societies who are forced by survival pressures to abandon the elderly—we do not have such serious survival problems.)

A "RECENTLY DISCOVERED" MINORITY GROUP

Our treatment of the elderly has only recently come to be viewed as a major social problem. Earlier, the plight of the aged was overlooked. The elderly are also a recently discovered minority group. It is now recognized that, similar to other minority groups, they are subjected to job discrimination. The most striking example of age discrimination has been the practice of mandatory retirement, under which people were forced to leave their jobs once they reached a certain age.

The retirement age used to be 65. In 1978 Congress enacted legislation that raised the age to 70 for most jobs. In 1986, Congress (recognizing that mandatory retirement was overtly discriminatory against the elderly) outlawed most mandatory retirement policies.

The elderly are discriminated against in many ways. Older workers are erroneously believed to be less productive. Unemployed workers in their 50s and 60s have greater difficulty finding new jobs and remain unemployed much longer than younger unemployed workers. The elderly are given no meaningful role in our society.

Ours is a youth-oriented society that devalues growing old. Our society glorifies the body beautiful and physical attractiveness and thereby shortchanges the elderly. The elderly are viewed as "out of touch with what's happening," and therefore their knowledge (which is acquired over the years) is seldom valued or sought. It is also erroneously believed that intellectual ability declines with age, even though research shows that intellectual capacity, barring organic problems, remains essentially unchanged until very late in life.[6]

The elderly are erroneously thought to be senile, conservative, resistant to change, inflexible, incompetent workers and a burden on the young. Given opportunities, elderly individuals usually prove such prejudicial concepts wrong.

The aged generally react to prejudice against them in the same way that racial and ethnic minorities react—by displaying self-hatred and by being self-conscious, sensitive, and defensive about their social and cultural status.[7] (If individuals frequently receive negative responses from others, Cooley's looking-glass-self theory suggests that they will eventually come to view themselves negatively.)

WHAT IS OLD AGE?

Elizabeth Ferguson describes some of our myths and stereotypes about the elderly.

BOX 13.2

Age Need Not Be a Barrier to Making Major Contributions

At age 80 George Burns received his first academy award for his role in *The Sunshine Boys*.

At 81 Benjamin Franklin mediated the compromise that led to the adoption of the U.S. Constitution.

At 82 Winston Churchill finished his four-volume text, *A History of the English-Speaking Peoples*.

At 88 Konrad Adenauer was chancellor of Germany.

At 88 Michelangelo designed the Church of Santa Maria degli Angeli.

At 89 Arthur Rubinstein gave a critically acclaimed recital in Carnegie Hall, New York City.

At 89 Albert Schweitzer was directing a hospital in Africa.

At 90 Pablo Picasso was producing engravings and drawings.

At 91 Eamon de Valera was president of Ireland.

At 93 George Bernard Shaw wrote a play entitled *Farfetched Fables*.

At 100 Grandma Moses was still painting.

Source: *U.S. News & World Report,* September 1, 1980, pp. 52–53.

Stereotyped notions about aging and the elderly exist in all segments of the population. Many of them are myths, but they are held tenaciously, and sound data to rebut them are scarce. The aging are generally thought to be less intelligent, less able to learn, more rigid, riskier as employees, less ambitious, and therefore more easily satisfied, less able to adapt and cope. How often these stereotypes turn into self-fulfilling prophecies is not known, but the existence of those who refute all the myths should be more widely publicized.[8]

On the other hand, the mass media portray some retired people as being able to travel and play golf, as being in good health, as sunning themselves in warm climates in the winter, and as being free of money worries. For the "young aging," particularly those in upper-income groups, there is some validity to this stereotype. But this is not the experience of most of the elderly in our society.

Attention to the social and physical needs of the elderly is a relatively recent phenomenon. In prior societies few persons survived to advanced ages. Life expectancy has increased dramatically in America since the turn of the century—up from 49 years in 1900 to 75 years at present.[9] Also, in most other societies, in

BOX 13.3

Age Need Not Be a Barrier to Staying Physically Active

Jodi Durkee celebrated her 70th birthday last week by swimming across Lake George. She said she was thinking of swimming over and back for next year's birthday. "I feel great," Mrs. Durkee, a great grandmother, said after completing the mile and a half swim in an hour and 20 minutes. "I just want to prove that just because you get old, you don't have to put yourself on a shelf somewhere." Mrs. Durkee, aquatic director at the Glen Falls, N.Y., YMCA, said before churning across the lake.

Source: *Wisconsin State Journal,* August 8, 1977.

contrast to ours, the elderly had some meaningful role to perform—as arbitrators and advisers, as landowners and leaders, as repositories of the wisdom of the tribe, as performers of tasks within their capabilities.

Members of primitive tribes often do not know how old they are. In contrast, chronological age is very important to us. Our passage through life is partially governed by our age. Chronological age controls when we are old enough to go to school, to drive a car, to marry, or to vote. Our society has also generally selected 65 as the beginning of old age.

In primitive societies old age is generally determined by physical and mental conditions rather than by chronological age. Primitive societies' definition of old age is more accurate than ours. Everyone is not in the same mental and physical condition at age 65. Aging is an individual process that occurs at differing rates in different people, and social-psychological factors may retard or accelerate the physiological changes.

The process of aging is called *senescence.* Senescence is the normal process of change in the body that accompanies aging. Senescence affects different persons at different rates. Also, the rates of change in various body processes affected by aging vary among

persons. Visible signs of aging include the appearance of wrinkled skin, graying and thinning of hair, and stooped or shortened posture from compressed spinal discs.

As a person ages blood vessels, tendons, the skin, and connective tissue lose their elasticity. Hardening of blood vessels and stiffening of joints occur; bones become brittle and thin; hormonal activity slows; and reflexes become slower. Many of the health problems faced by the aged result from a general decline of the circulatory system. Reduced blood supply impairs mental sharpness, interferes with balance, and reduces the effectiveness of the muscles and body organs. The probability of strokes and heart attacks also increases.

As a person ages the muscles lose some of their strength, and coordination and endurance become more difficult. There is also a decline in the functioning of such body organs as the lungs, the kidneys, and to a lesser extent the brain. As senescence proceeds, hearing and vision capacities decline, food may not taste the same, the sense of touch may become less acute, and there may be a loss of memory of recent and past events. Fortunately, the degree to which one's body loses its vitality can be influenced by one's lifestyle.

TABLE 13.1

Composition of U.S. Population Age 65 and Older

	Year				
	1900	1950	1970	1980	1986
Number of older persons (in millions)	3	12	20	25	29
Percent of total population	4	8	9.5	11	12

Source: United States Bureau of the Census, *Statistical Abstract of the United States, 1987* (Washington, D.C.: U.S. Government Printing Office, 1987).

People who are mentally and physically active throughout their younger years remain more alert and vigorous in their later years.

A key notion to remember about senescence is that no dramatic decline need take place at one's 65th birthday or at any other age. We are all slowly aging throughout our lives. The rate at which we age depends on many factors. A large number of elderly people are physically active and mentally alert. Unfortunately, in describing the process of aging, there is a tendency to give the impression that both the physical functioning and the mental functioning of the elderly person are reduced to a minimal level. Although functioning may slow somewhat, it remains at a high enough level to enable a large number of elderly to be physically active and mentally alert.

There is growing evidence demonstrating that many of the effects of aging are neither irreversible nor inevitable. Many of the supposed effects of aging are largely due to the inactivity that is often associated with aging. Learning to reduce stress along with exercising and maintaining a healthful diet can reverse, or at least hold in abeyance, many of the effects thought to be caused by aging. In one study a group of 70-year-old, inactive men participated in a daily exercise program, and at the end of a year they had regained the physical fitness levels of 40 year olds.[10]

In defining "old age" the federal government generally uses a chronological cutoff point—age 65—to separate elderly adults from others. There is nothing magical or particularly scientific about 65. In 1883 the Germans set age 65 as the criterion of aging for the world's first modern social security system for the elderly.[11] When the Social Security Act was passed in 1935, the United States also selected 65 as the eligibility age for retirement benefits, based on the German model. It should be noted that the elderly are an extremely diverse group, spanning a 30- to 35-year age range. This large age range, by itself, leads to considerable diversity. Just as there are generally substantial differences between people age 20 and those age 50, there are generally substantial differences between those age 65 and those age 95.

An Increasing Aged Population

There are now about ten times as many people age 65 and older than there were at the turn of the century.[12] Table 13.1 shows that the number of older people has steadily been increasing.

There are several reasons for the phenomenal growth of the older population. The improved care of expectant mothers and newborn infants has reduced

Most senior citizens are physically active and mentally alert. The scribe at right repairs Torah scrolls using pens he has carved from quills and ink he has mixed from scratch.

the infant mortality rate, and vaccinations have prevented many life-threatening childhood illnesses, allowing an increased proportion of those born to live to old age. New drugs, better sanitation, and other medical advances have increased the life expectancy of Americans. Another reason for the increasing proportion of the aged is that the birthrate is declining; fewer babies are being born.

After World War II there was a baby boom that lasted roughly from 1947 to 1960. The most rapid rise in birthrates ever recorded in our society occurred during this period. Children born during these years flooded our schools in the 1950s and 1960s. Today these young adults are crowding the labor market. At the turn of the century this generation will reach retirement. After 1960 there was a "baby bust," a sharp de-

cline in birthrates. (The average number of children per woman went down from a high of 3.8 in 1957 to a low of 1.8 in 1976.[13])

The increased life expectancy, with the baby boom being followed by the baby bust, will significantly increase the median age of Americans in future years (see Table 13.2, p. 448).

The "Old Old" — The Fastest-Growing Age Group

As our society is having more success in treating and preventing heart disease, cancer, strokes and other killers, an increasing percentage of the elderly are living

into their 80s, 90s, and beyond. People age 85 and over constitute the fastest-growing age group in the United States.

In 1940, only 365,000 Americans were 85 or over, a mere 0.3% of the total population. By 1982, the number had zoomed to 2.5 million, or 1.1% of the population. By the year 2000 the Census Bureau predicts this oldest old group will top 5.1 million, almost 2% of all Americans. By the year 2000, more than 100,000 Americans will be age 100 or over, three times the present number.[14]

We are witnessing "the graying of America," also called "the aging of the aged." This population revolution is rather quietly occurring in our society.

Those who are age 85 and over will create a number of problems and difficult decisions for our society. Alan Otten notes:

It is these "oldest old"—often mentally or physically impaired, alone, depressed—who pose the major problems for the coming decades. It is they who will strain their families with demands for personal care and financial support. It is they who will need more of such community help as Meals on Wheels, homemaker services, special housing. It is they who will require the extra hospital and nursing-home beds that will further burden federal and state budgets.

And it is they whose mounting needs and numbers already spark talk of some sort of rationing of health care. "Can we afford the very old?" is becoming a favorite conference topic for doctors, bioethicists and other specialists.[15]

Elaine Brody briefly summarizes the number of old old who need extensive health care:

From the population of very old people come most of the million and more who are so disabled that they require round the-clock care in nursing homes, the two million who are equally disabled but who are not in institutions, and many of the six million more who require less intensive services.[16]

TABLE 13.2

━━━━━━

Median Age of Americans: 1970–2030

Year	Median Age
1970	28.1
1980	30.2
1990	32.8
2000	35.5
2010	36.6
2020	37.0
2030	38.0

Source: Beth J. Soldo, *America's Elderly in the 1980s* (Washington, D.C.: Population Reference Bureau, 1980), p. 9.

━━━━━━

Many of the old old suffer from a multiplicity of chronic illnesses. Common medical problems of the old old include arthritis, heart conditions, hypertension, osteoporosis (brittleness of the bones), Alzheimer's disease, incontinency, hearing and vision problems, and depression.

Although only 6.4 percent of the 75 to 84 year olds are in nursing homes, 21.6 percent of those 85 or over are in nursing homes.[17] The cost to society for such care is expensive, as it costs around $22,000 per year per person to provide nursing home care.[18] Despite the widespread image of families dumping aged parents into nursing homes, most frail elderly are still outside institutional walls, with a spouse, a child, or a relative still the chief caretaker. Some middle-aged people are now simultaneously encountering demands to put children through college and to support an aging parent in a nursing home.

With people retiring at age 65 or 70 and then living to age 85 or 90, the number of years spent in retirement is considerable. To maintain the same standard of living after retiring will require immense assets.

Rising health care costs and superlongevity have ignited controversy of whether to ration health care to the very old: For example, should people over age 75 be prohibited from receiving liver transplants or kidney dialysis? Discussion of euthanasia (the practice of killing individuals that are hopelessly sick or injured) has also been increasing. In 1984 Governor Richard Lamm of Colorado stirred a controversy when he asserted the terminally ill have a duty to die. Dr. Eisdor Fer stated:

The problem is age-old and across cultures. Whenever society has had marginal economic resources, the oldest went first, and the old people bought that approach. The old Eskimo wasn't put on the ice floe; he just left of his own accord and never came back.[19]

PROBLEMS FACED BY THE ELDERLY

━━━━━━

We have a personal stake in improving the status and life circumstances of the elderly. The elderly are what we are becoming—someday we will be elderly too. If we do not face and solve the problems of the elderly *now,* we will be in dire straits in the future. Some of these problems are as follows.

Low Status

The aged suffer because we have generally been unsuccessful in finding something important or satisfying for them to do. In most primitive and earlier societies, the old were respected and viewed as useful to their people to a much greater degree than is the case in our society. Industrialization and the growth of modern society have robbed the old of a high status in our society. Prior to industrialization, older people were the primary owners of property. Land was the most important source of power; therefore, the elderly controlled much of the economic and political power. Now, people primarily earn their living in the job market, and the vast majority of the aged own little land and are viewed as having no salable labor.

In earlier societies, the elderly were also valued because of the knowledge they possessed. Their experiences enabled them to supervise planting and harvesting and to pass on knowledge about hunting, housing, and craft making. The elderly also played key roles in preserving and transmitting the culture. But the rapid advances of science and technology have tended to limit the value of technological knowledge of the elderly, and books and other "memory-storing" devices have made old people less valuable as storehouses of culture and records.

The low status of the elderly is closely associated with "ageism." The term *ageism* refers to having negative images of and attitudes toward people simply because they are old. Today, the reaction to the elderly by many people is a negative one. Ageism is like sexism or racism because it involves discrimination and prejudice against all members of a particular social category.

Two hundred years ago, the elderly had a high status in our society. The status of the elderly has declined since then for several reasons. The elderly no longer hold positions of economic power. Children no longer learn their future profession or trade from their parents: Instead, such skills are learned through institutions, such as the school system. In addition, the children of the elderly are no longer dependent on their parents for their livelihood, since they generally are capable of making a living through a trade or profession that is independent of their parents. Finally, the elderly no longer perform tasks that are viewed as essential by society: Often the older workers' skills are viewed as outmoded even before they retire.

The prejudice against the elderly is shown in everyday language, by the use of terms that no racial or ethnic group would ever accept—"old buzzard," "old biddy," "old fogey." From a rational view, ageism makes no sense: those who delight in discriminating against the elderly will one day be old themselves.

Early Retirement

The maintenance of a high rate of employment in our society is a major goal. In many occupations the supply of labor is exceeding the demand. An often-used remedy for the oversupply of available employees is the encouragement of ever earlier retirement. Forced retirements often create financial and psychological burdens that retirees usually face without much assistance or preparation.

Our massive social security program supports early retirement, as retirement can come as early as 62. Pension plans of some companies and craft unions make it financially attractive to retire as early as 55. Perhaps the extreme case is the armed forces, which permits retirement on full benefits after 20 years' service as early as age 38.

Many workers who retire early supplement their pension by obtaining another job, usually of a lower status. Nearly 90 percent of Americans 65 years of age and older are retired even though many are intellectually and physically capable of working.[20]

Early retirement has some advantages to society, such as reducing the labor supply and allowing younger employees to advance faster. But there are also some serious disadvantages. For society the total bill for retirement pensions is already huge and still growing. For the retiree it means facing a new life and status without much preparation or assistance. Although our society has developed educational and other institutions to prepare the young for the work world, it has not developed comparable institutions to prepare the elderly for retirement. Being without a job in our work-oriented society is often a reality shock for older people.

In our society we still view a person's worth partly in terms of his or her work. People often develop their self-image (their sense of who they are) in terms of their occupation—"I am a teacher," "I am a barber," "I am a doctor." Because the later years generally provide no exciting new roles to replace the occupational roles lost on retirement, a retiree cannot proudly say "I am a ..." Instead, she or he must say, "I *was* a good ... " The more a person's life revolves around work, the more difficult retirement is apt to be.

There are several myths about the older worker that have been widely believed by employers and the general public. Older workers are thought to be less healthy, clumsier, more prone to absenteeism, more

BOX 13.4

Disengagement Theory: Response of Individuals and Society to Aging

In 1961, Elaine Cumming and William E. Henry coined the term *disengagement* to refer to a process whereby people respond to aging by gradually withdrawing from the various roles and social relationships they occupied in middle age.[a] Such disengagement is claimed to be functional for the individual, since he or she is thought to gradually lose the energy and vitality to sustain all the roles and social relationships held in younger years.

The term *societal disengagement* has been coined to refer to the process whereby society withdraws from the aging person.[b] It is claimed it is functional for our society—which values efficiency, competition, and individual achievement—to disengage from the elderly, who have the least physical stamina and the highest death rate. Societal disengagement occurs in a variety of ways: Older people may not be sought out for leadership positions in organizations, their employers may seek to force them to retire, their children may no longer want them involved in making family decisions, and the government may be more responsive to meeting the needs of people who are younger. To be fair, societal disengagement is often unintended and unrecognized by society. A number of the elderly do not handle forced role losses well. Some even try to escape with alcohol, drugs, or suicide.

With reference to the two terms just explained, *disengagement theory* thereby hypothesizes a mutual disengagement or withdrawal between the individual and society. Disengagement theory has stimulated considerable interest and research. There is considerable controversy regarding whether disengagement is functional for the elderly and for our soci-

---

accident-prone, more forgetful, and slower in task performance.[21] Research has shown that these myths are erroneous. Older workers have lower turnover rates, produce at a steadier rate, make fewer mistakes, have lower absenteeism rates, have a more positive attitude toward their work, exceed younger employees in health, and have low on-the-job injury rates.[22] However, if the older worker does become ill, she or he usually takes a somewhat longer time to recover.[23]

It would seem far better if workers who are still productive could stay on the job longer on a part- or full-time basis rather than being unemployed on a pension plan or being forced to take another job of a lower

status. (This perspective will be expanded on later in this chapter.)

Societal Emphasis on Youth

Our society fears aging and old age more than do most other societies. Our emphasis on youth is indicated by our dread of getting gray hair and wrinkles or becoming bald. The youth emphasis is also indicated by the pleasure we experience when someone guesses our age to be younger than it actually is. More than other societies, we place a high value on change and new

ety. Research has found that some people undeniably do voluntarily disengage as they grow older. Yet, disengagement is neither a universal nor an inevitable response to aging. Contrary to disengagement theory, most older persons maintain extensive associations with friends. Most also maintain active involvements in voluntary organizations (such as church groups, fraternal organizations, and unions). Some of the elderly, after retiring, develop new interests, expand their circle of friends, do volunteer work, and join clubs. Others *rebel* against society's stereotypes and refuse to be treated as if they had little to offer to society. Many of these people are marshaling political resources to force society to adapt to their needs and skills.

A severe criticism of societal disengagement theory is that the theory may be used to justify society's failure to help the elderly maintain meaningful roles and that it may be used to justify ageism. Disengagement theory may, at best, be merely a description of the age/youth relationships (and reactions to them) that we should combat as we try to combat ageism.

In contrast to the disengagement theory of aging is the activity theory. It asserts that the more physically and mentally active the elderly are, the more successfully they will age. There is considerable evidence that being physically and mentally active will help to maintain the physiological and psychological functions of the elderly. In contrast to the disengagement theory, which expects the elderly to "slow down," the activity theory urges the elderly to remain physically and mentally active.

---

[a]Elaine Cumming and W. E. Henry, *Growing Old: The Process of Disengagement* (New York: Basic Books, 1961), p. 6.

[b]Robert C. Atchley, *Aging: Continuity and Change* (Belmont, CA: Wadsworth, 1983), p. 97.

---

programs. European societies, on the other hand, place a higher value on tradition and preserving customs and lifestyles from the past.

Our society places a high value on mobility, action, and energy. We like to think we are doers. But why this emphasis on youth in our society? The reasons are not fully clear. There appear to be several factors. Industrialization has resulted in a demand for laborers that are energetic and agile and have considerable strength. Rapid advances in technology and science have made past knowledge and certain specialized work skills (for example, that of a blacksmith) obsolescent. Pioneer living and the gradual expansion of our nation to the West required "brute" strength, energy, and stamina. Competition has always been emphasized and has been reinforced by Darwin's notions on evolution, which highlighted survival of the fittest and the need of a struggle for existence.

Health Problems and Costs of Care

Old age is partly a social problem because of the high costs of health care. Most older persons have at least one chronic condition, and many have multiple conditions. In 1986 the most frequently occurring conditions for the elderly were arthritis (48 percent), hypertension (39 percent), hearing impairments (29 percent), and orthopedic impairments and sinusitis (17 percent each).[24]

Almost one in ten is bedridden.[25] Four out of ten have physical impairments that interfere with performing major self-care tasks.[26] Older people see their doctor more often, spend a higher proportion of their income on prescribed drugs, and once in the hospital, they stay longer. Although the elderly constitute only 12 percent of the population, they consume a quarter of the drugs prescribed each year and compose a third of those hospitalized.[27] The health status of the "old" old (75 and older) is worse than that of the "young" old (65 to 74).[28]

The medical expenses of each elderly person average six times more than those faced by young adults.[29] The medical costs are high partly because the elderly suffer much more from chronic (long-term) illnesses, such as diabetes, heart problems, cancer, and glaucoma.

The physical process of aging (senescence) is one reason why the elderly have a higher rate of health problems. However, research in recent years has demonstrated that social and personal stresses also play a major role in causing diseases. The elderly face a wide range of stressful situations: loneliness, death of friends and family members, retirement, changes in living arrangements, loss of social status, reduced income, and a decline in physical energy and physical capacities. Medical conditions may also result from substandard diets, inadequate exercise, cigarette smoking, and excessive drinking of alcoholic beverages.

Marilyn Flynn notes:

Studies of long-living peoples of the world show that neither heredity nor low prevalence of disease is a significant determinant of longevity. Four other factors are much more likely to predict long-term survival: (1) a clearly defined and valued role in society; (2) a positive self-perception; (3) sustained, moderate physical activity; and (4) abstinence from cigarette smoking. Studies in this country indicate

that secure financial status, social relationships, and high education are also important.[30]

(Health care for the elderly is further discussed in Chapter 14.)

Inadequate Income

Many of the elderly live in poverty. A fair number lack adequate food, essential clothes and drugs, and perhaps a telephone in the house to make emergency calls.

Nearly one fourth of the elderly have incomes close to or below the poverty line.[31] The median income of older persons in 1986 was $11,544 for males and $6,425 for females.[32] The major source of income for older families and individuals in 1985 was social security (35 percent), followed by asset income (25 percent), earnings (23 percent), public and private pensions (14 percent), and "transfer" payments such as supplemental security, unemployment, and veterans' payments (2 percent).[33]

The financial problems of the elderly are compounded by additional factors. One factor is the high cost of health care as previously discussed. A second factor is inflation. Inflation is especially devastating to those on fixed incomes. Most private pension benefits do not increase in size after a worker retires. For example, if living costs rise annually at 7 percent, a person on a fixed pension would in twenty years be able to buy only one fourth as many goods and services as she or he could at retirement.[34] Fortunately, in 1974, Congress enacted an "automatic escalator" clause in social security benefits, providing a 3 percent increase in payments when the Consumer Price Index increased a like amount. However, it should be remembered that social security benefits were never intended to make a person financially independent: It is nearly impossible to live comfortably on monthly social security checks.

Among the elderly, those living in poverty include (*a*) a higher proportion of blacks, Hispanics and women as compared to men and (*b*) those living alone or with nonrelatives as compared to persons living with members of their family.[35]

The importance of financial security for the elderly is emphasized by Thomas Sullivan et al. as follows:

Financial security affects one's entire lifestyle. It determines one's diet, ability to seek good health care, to visit relatives and friends, to maintain a suitable wardrobe, and to find or maintain adequate housing. One's financial resources, or lack of them, play a great part in finding recreation (going to movies, plays, playing bridge or bingo, etc.) and maintaining morale, feelings of independence, and a sense of self-esteem. In other words, if an older person has the financial resources to remain socially independent (having her own household and access to transportation and medical services), to continue contact with friends and relatives, and to maintain her preferred forms of recreation, she is going to feel a great deal better about herself and others than if she is deprived of her former style of life.[36]

THE SOCIAL SECURITY SYSTEM   The social security system was never designed to be the main source of income for the elderly. It was originally intended as a form of insurance that would *partially supplement* other assets when retirement, disability, or death of a wage-earning spouse occurred. Yet, many of the elderly do not have investments, pensions, or savings to support them in retirement, and therefore social security has become the major source of income for the elderly.

The social security system was developed in the United States in 1935. Financially, the system has been fairly solvent until recently. For the first few decades after the social security system was enacted in 1935 more money was paid into the system from social security taxes on employers and employees than was paid out. This was largely due to the fact that the life expectancy rate was only somewhat over 60 years of age. The life expectancy rate, however, has gradually increased to age 75.[37] The system is now paying out more than it is taking in. Social security taxes have been sharply increased in recent years, but with the old old being the fastest growing age group in our society and with the proportion of the elderly increasing in our society, the system is going bankrupt.

The *dependency ratio* is the ratio between the number of working people and the number of non-working people in the population. With the increasing proportion of the population who is elderly, the non-workers will represent a greater and greater burden on the workers. Authorities predict that by the year 2020 the dependency ratio will decline from the 1983 level of 3.3 workers for every nonworking person to a ratio of about 2 to 1.[38]

Some serious problems now exist with the system. First, the benefits are too small to be the major source of income for the elderly. With the payments from social security, an estimated 80 percent of retirees are now living on less than half of their preretirement annual income. And, the monthly payments from social security are generally below the poverty line.[39] Second, it is unlikely that the monthly benefits will be raised much, since the system is already losing money. Our society faces some hard choices about keeping the social security system solvent in future years. Benefits might be lowered, but this would even further impoverish the recipients. Social security taxes might be raised, but there is little public support for this. Table 13.3 shows that social security taxes are already increasing dramatically. The maximum tax that is paid will increase from $405.60 in 1971 to $5,117.85 in 1990.

The future of the social security system is unclear. The system is likely to continue to exist, but reduced benefits is a distinct possibility. Young people are well-advised to plan financially for retirement through savings, investment, and pension plans that are autonomous of the social security system.

Loss of Family and Friends

The single elderly are generally less well off than married elderly. The longer life span of women has unfortunately left nearly two thirds of those over age 65 without a spouse.[40] Gordon and Walter Moss comment about the value of marriage for older persons:

They now have much more time for and are more dependent upon each other. Some marriages cannot handle this increased togetherness, but those that can

TABLE 13.3

Taxable Wage Base and Maximum Social Security Payroll Tax as Set by Legislation

Year	Maximum Tax Rate	Maximum Taxable Earnings	Tax
1971	5.2 %	$ 7,800	$ 405.60
1972	5.2	9,000	468.00
1973	5.85	10,800	631.80
1974	5.85	13,200	772.20
1975	5.85	14,100	824.85
1976	5.85	15,300	895.05
1977	5.85	16,500	965.25
1978	6.05	17,700	1070.85
1979	6.13	22,900	1403.77
1980	6.13	25,900	1587.67
1981	6.65	29,700	1975.05
1982	6.7	32,700	2190.90
1985	7.05	43,500	3066.75
1986	7.15	47,700	3410.55
1990	7.65	66,900	5117.85

Source: Social Security Administration, Department of Health and Human Services, *Income and Resources of the Aged* (Washington, D.C.: U.S. Government Printing Office, 1980).

become the major source of contentment to both partners. The understanding wife can be enormously important in helping her husband adjust to retirement. The understanding husband can help his wife adjust to a new role when all the children have left home. A good marriage, or a remarriage, provides the elderly person with companionship and emotional support, sex, the promise of care if he is sick, a focus for daily activities, and frequently greater

financial independence. Sex roles often blur, and the husband actively helps in household chores.[41]

The elderly person's life is made more isolated and lonely when close friends and relatives move away or die. Old age is a time when close friends are most apt to die; naturally, the longer a person lives, the more likely close friends will die.

The needs of aging parents can present some painful dilemmas for their children, especially if the parents are poor or in ill health. The children may have families of their own requiring heavy responsibilities on their time and finances. For those on tight budgets, deciding how to divide their resources among their parents, their own children, and themselves can be agonizing. Some face the difficult question of whether to maintain a parent within their home, to leave the parent living alone, or to seek to place the parent in a nursing home.

Substandard Housing

We have heard so much about nursing homes in recent years that few people realize that 95 percent of the elderly do not live in nursing homes or in any other kind of institution.[42] About 70 percent of all elderly males are married and live with their wives.[43] Because females tend to outlive their spouses, nearly two thirds of women over age 65 live alone.[44] Nearly 80 percent of older married couples maintain their own households—in apartments, mobile homes, condominiums, or their own houses.[45] In addition, nearly half of the single elderly (widows, widowers, divorced, never married) live in their own homes.[46] When the aged do not maintain their own households, they most often live in the homes of relatives, primarily one of their children.

Old people who live in rural areas generally have a higher status than those living in urban areas. People living on farms can retire gradually. People whose income is in land, rather than in a job, can retain importance and esteem to an advanced age.

However, almost three quarters of our population live in urban areas, and the elderly often live in poor-quality housing. At least 30 percent of the elderly live

Retirement communities are growing in number, particularly in Sun Belt states.

in substandard, deteriorating or dilapidated housing.[47] Many of the elderly in urban areas are trapped in decaying, low-value houses needing considerable maintenance and often surrounded by racial and ethnic groups different from their own. Many of the urban elderly live in hotels or apartments in the inner cities with inadequate living conditions. Their neighborhoods may be decaying and crime-ridden, and such elderly are easy prey for thieves and muggers.

Fortunately, many mobile-home parks, retirement villages, and apartment complexes geared to the needs of the elderly are being built throughout the country. Many such communities for the elderly provide a social

center, security protection, sometimes a daily hot meal, and perhaps a little help with maintenance.

When the aged do not maintain their own households, they most often live in the homes of relatives, primarily with one of their children.

Transportation

Owning and driving a car is a luxury only the more affluent and physically vigorous elderly can afford. The lack of convenient, inexpensive transportation is a problem faced by most elderly.

Crime Victimization

Having reduced energy, strength, and agility, the elderly are most easily victimized by crime, particularly robbery, aggravated assault, burglary, larceny, vandalism, and fraud. Many of the elderly live in constant fear of being victimized, although reported victimization rates for the elderly are lower than rates for younger people. The actual victimization rates for the elderly may be considerably higher than official crime statistics indicate, because many of the elderly feel uneasy about becoming involved with the legal and criminal justice systems. Therefore, they may not report some of the crimes they are victims of. Some of the elderly are afraid of retaliation from the offenders if they report the crimes, and some of the elderly dislike the legal processes they have to go through if they press charges.

Some of the elderly are hesitant to leave their homes for fear they will be mugged or for fear their homes will be burglarized while they are away. A Louis Harris poll among the elderly showed that fear of becoming a crime victim was their major concern: it was ranked higher than poverty, isolation, sickness, loneliness, and other problems associated with old age.[48]

Sexuality in Old Age

There is a common misconception that older people lose their sexual drive. If an older male displays sexual interest he is labeled a "dirty old man." When two older people exhibit normal heterosexual behavior, someone is apt to comment "Aren't they cute?" Yet many older people have a strong sexual interest and a satisfying sex life.[49] Sexual capacities, particularly in women, show little evidence of declining with age, and a large percentage of elderly males are capable of sexual relations.[50]

William Masters and Virginia Johnson see no reason why sexual activity cannot be enjoyed by the elderly.[51] If sexual behavior does decline, it probably is due more to social reasons than to physical reasons. According to Masters and Johnson, the most important deterrents to sexual activity when one is older are the lack of a partner, overindulgence in drinking or eating, boredom with one's partner, attitudes toward sex (such as the erroneous belief that sex is inappropriate for the elderly), poor physical or mental health, attitudes toward menopause, and fear of poor performance.[52]

The attitudes of the "younger generation" frequently create problems for the elderly. A widow or widower at times faces strong opposition to remarrying from other family members. Negative attitudes are often strongest when an elderly person becomes interested in someone younger who will become an heir if the older person dies. Old people are sometimes informed that they should not be interested in members of the opposite sex, and that they should not establish new sexual relationships when they have lost a mate.

Fortunately, the attitudes toward sexuality in old age are changing. Merlin Taber notes:

With the changing attitudes of younger people to alternatives to the traditional family, some older people are finding informal arrangements for living together attractive. The couple who do not have a marriage ceremony can share all the companionship and sexual satisfactions without upsetting inheritance rights and retirement benefits. When they become aware of it, their children may accept such a pattern because they find it preferable to remarriage. We have no idea of the numbers that are involved, but the old as well as the young have new options as societal norms change. The popularity of living together without marriage will probably increase.[53]

Malnutrition

The elderly are the most uniformly undernourished segment of our population.[54] There are a number of reasons for chronic malnutrition among the elderly: transportation difficulties in getting to grocery stores; lack of knowledge about proper nutrition; lack of money to purchase a well-balanced diet; poor teeth and lack of good dentures, which greatly limit one's diet; lack of incentives to prepare an appetizing meal when one is living alone; and inadequate cooking and storage facilities.

Emotional Problems

Depression is the most common emotional problem. The suicide rate of white men in their 80s is four times as high as that of men in general.[55] Although the elderly comprise about 12 percent of the population, about 25 percent of reported suicides occur among the elderly.[56] Given the problems of the elderly (many created by our society by making old age a largely "useless" role), the high rate of depression is understandable.

Those who have emotional problems in earlier life, unless resolved, will continue to have them when older. Often these problems will be intensified by the added stresses of aging.

The National Institute of Mental Health, after an eleven-year study, identified two major barriers to good mental health in the later years: (*a*) failure to bounce back from psychosocial losses and (*b*) failure to have "meaningful" life goals.[57] Old age is a time when there are drastic changes thrust on the elderly that may create emotional problems: loss of a job and its accompanying status, loss of a spouse, loss of friends and relatives through death or moving, poorer health, loss of accustomed income, and changing relationships with one's children and grandchildren.

Unfortunately, there is an erroneous assumption that "senility" and "mental illness" are inevitable and untreatable. Robert Butler has found, on the contrary, that old people respond well to both individual and group counseling.[58] In addition, many 90 year olds show no sign of senility. Senility is by no means a necessary part of old age.

Death

Preoccupation with dying, particularly with the circumstances surrounding it, is an ongoing concern of the elderly. They see their friends and relatives dying. The elderly's concern about dying is most often focused on dreading the disability, pain, and long periods of suffering that may precede death.[59] They generally would like a death with dignity, where they can die in their own homes, with little suffering, with mental faculties intact, and with families and friends nearby. Old people are also concerned about the costs of their final illness, the difficulties they may cause others by the manner of their death, and whether their resources will permit a dignified funeral.

In our society we tend to wall the dying off with silence. Apparently, we try to do this in order not to have to confront our own mortality. We often force people to die alone. In hospitals great efforts are made to separate the dying from the living. Dying patients are moved into separate rooms. Often the medical staff attempts to shield the dying person from becoming aware of his or her impending death. Families, too, begin to treat the patient differently when they know the end is near. (Being treated differently by medical staff and family often subtly informs the dying that death is imminent.)

A number of authorities have urged our society to treat death more openly.[60] Such openness would enable the dying person to prepare for death better, perhaps by having additional time to reassess his or her life and to come to some conclusions about what has been accomplished and what life has meant. It would also give the dying person more time to become accepting of death and time to make financial arrangements, such as making a will. It would give family members time to make necessary arrangements (including financial) and time to redress old wrongs and heal misunderstandings. For all members of society, it would better enable them to face, and psychologically

come to terms with, their eventual death. The recent popularity of courses in death and dying on college campuses shows that people feel a need to become more comfortable psychologically with facing death.

People in primitive societies were generally better prepared for death than people in our society. Margaret Mead notes:

In peasant communities where things didn't change and where people died in the beds they were born in, grandparents taught the young what the end of life was going to be. So you looked at your mother, if you were a girl, and you learned what it was like to be a bride, a young mother. Then you looked at your grandmother and knew what it was like to be old. Children learned what it was to age and die while they were very small. They were prepared for the end of life at the beginning.[61]

(Unfortunately, in our society many of us seek to deny our own deaths, even though we are all "terminal" from birth.)

In the modern United States more than two thirds of all deaths occur in nursing homes or hospitals, surrounded by medical staff.[62] Such deaths often occur without dignity.

Fortunately, the hospice movement has been developing in recent years to attempt to counter death without dignity. Hospices allow the terminally ill to die with dignity—to live their final weeks in the way they want to. Hospices originated in the Middle Ages among European religious groups who welcomed travelers who were sick, tired, or hungry.[63] Hospices today are located in a variety of settings—in a separate unit of a hospital, in a building independent of a hospital, or in the dying person's home. Medical services and social services are provided in hospices, and extensive efforts are made to allow the terminally ill to spend their remaining days as they choose. Hospices sometimes have educational and entertainment programs, and visitors are common. Pain relievers are used extensively so that the patient is able to live out his or her final days in relative comfort. Hospices view the disease as terminal, not the patient. The emphasis in hospices is on helping patients to use the time that is left, rather than on trying to keep people alive as long as possible. Many hospice programs are set up to assist patients to live their remaining days in the home of their family. In addition to medical and visiting nurse services, hospices have volunteers to help the patient and family members with such services as counseling, transportation, filling out insurance forms and other paperwork, and respite care for family members.

Parent Abuse

Parent abuse refers to elderly parents who are abused by their children with whom they live or on whom they depend. This problem is described in more depth in Chapter 5.

CURRENT SERVICES

Present services and programs for the elderly are principally "maintenance" in nature, as they are primarily designed to meet basic physical needs. Nonetheless, there are a number of programs, often federally funded, that provide services needed by the elderly.

Older Americans Act of 1965

This federal law created an operating agency (Administration on Aging) within the Department of Health, Education, and Welfare.* This law and its amendments are the bases for financial aid by the federal government to assist states and local communities to meet the needs of the elderly. Ten objectives of the act are to secure for the elderly:

1. An adequate income.
2. Best possible physical and mental health.

3. Suitable housing.
4. Restorative services for those who require institutional care.
5. Opportunity for employment.
6. Retirement in health, honor, dignity.
7. Pursuit of meaningful activity.
8. Efficient community services.
9. Immediate benefit from research knowledge to sustain and improve health and happiness.
10. Freedom, independence, and the free exercise of individual initiative in planning and managing their own lives.[64]

Although these objectives are commendable, the reality is that these goals have not been realized for many of the elderly.

White House Conferences on Aging

The problems of the elderly have now been focused on by the public spotlight and have become a popular cause. There have been three White House Conferences on Aging—in 1961, in 1971, and in 1981. Many states now have a state office on aging, and some municipalities and counties have established community councils on aging. A number of universities have established centers for the study of gerontology; and nursing, medicine, sociology, social work, architecture, and other disciplines and professions are establishing fields of study on gerontology. (Gerontology is the scientific study of aging and the problems of the aged.) Government research grants are being given to encourage the study of the elderly by academicians. Publishers are now producing books and pamphlets to inform the public about the elderly, and a few high schools are beginning to offer courses to help teenagers understand the elderly and their circumstances.

There are a number of programs, often federally funded and administered at state or local levels, to provide funds and services needed by the elderly. A few of these are briefly described in Box 13.5.

---

*This Department was renamed the Department of Health and Human Services in 1980.

Day care centers for the elderly can prevent or postpone institutional care. Iona House in Washington, D.C., provides meals and activities for people with Alzheimer's disease.

Nursing Homes

Nursing homes were created as an alternative to expensive hospital care and are substantially supported by the federal government through Medicaid and Medicare. Over 1.5 million older people now live in extended-care facilities, making nursing homes a billion-dollar industry.[65] There are more patient beds in nursing homes than in hospitals, and over 40 cents of each medicaid dollar goes to nursing homes.[66]

Nursing homes are classified according to the kind of care they provide. At one end of the scale there are residential homes that provide primarily room and board, with some nonmedical care (such as help in dressing). At the other end of the scale are nursing-care centers that provide skilled nursing and medical atten-

tion twenty-four hours a day. The more skilled and extensive the medical care given, the more expensive the home. The costs vary from a few hundred dollars to more than $2,000 per month. Although only a small percentage of the elderly live permanently in homes (about 5 percent), many spend some time convalescing in them.

The quality of nursing-home care ranges from excellent to awful. Nursing homes are definitely needed, particularly for those needing round-the-clock health care for an extended time.

Some years ago Ralph Nader released a report highly critical of nursing-home care. The report cited instances of patients heavily tranquilized in a stuporous state so that they were easier to manage, use of patients as guinea pigs in drug experiments, abysmal

BOX 13.5

Some Programs for the Elderly

Medicare: Helps pay the medical and hospital expenses of the elderly (described in Chapter 14).

Old Age, Survivors, and Disability Insurance: Provides monthly payments to eligible retired workers (described in Chapter 3).

Supplemental Security Income: Provides a minimum income for the indigent elderly (described in Chapter 3).

Medicaid: Pays most medical expenses for low-income people (described in Chapter 14).

Food stamps: Offset some of the food expenses for low-income people who qualify (described in Chapter 3).

Nursing Home Ombudsman Program: Investigates and acts on concerns expressed by residents in nursing homes.

Meals on Wheels: Provides hot and cold meals to housebound recipients who are incapable of obtaining or preparing their own meals but who can feed themselves.

Retired Senior Volunteer Program (RSVP): Seeks to match work and service opportunities with the elderly volunteers seeking them.

Foster Grandparent Program: Pays the elderly for part-time work in which they provide individual care and attention to ill and needy children and youths.

Service Corps of Retired Executives (SCORE): Provides consulting services to small businesses.

Senior-citizen centers, golden age clubs, and similar groups: Provide leisure time and recreational activities for the elderly.

Special bus rates: Reduce bus transportation costs for the elderly.

---

neglect and dehumanization, and kickbacks to nursing home administrators from druggists.[67]

One scandal after another characterizes care in nursing homes. Several years ago in Houston an elderly woman was so neglected in a nursing home that her death was not discovered until rigor mortis had set in, and another woman was hospitalized from rat bites.[68] It has been charged that some doctors are giving needless repeated injections to nursing home patients in order to make high profits.[69] In 1980 a nursing home in Madison, Wisconsin strapped a 37-year-old

stroke patient into her wheelchair for over forty minutes at a time, when the patient had no bladder or bowel control, and she was not assisted to the toilet despite her repeated cries for help.[70]

Robert Butler visited a number of nursing homes and found patients lying in their own feces or urine.[71] He also found that the food was so unappetizing that residents at times refused to eat it, that many homes had serious safety hazards, and that boredom and apathy were common among staff as well as residents.

In 1987 investigators for the U.S. Senate Special

Property tax relief: Available to the elderly in many states.

Special federal income tax deduction: For people over 65.

Housing projects for the elderly: Built by local sponsors with financing assistance by the Department of Housing and Urban Development.

Reduced rates at movie theaters and other places of entertainment: Often offered voluntarily by individual owners.

Home health services: Provide visiting nurse services, physical therapy, drugs, laboratory services, and sickroom equipment.

Nutrition programs: Provide meals for the elderly at group "eating sites." (These meals are generally provided four or five times a week and usually are luncheon meals. These programs improve the nutrition of elderly persons and offer opportunities for socialization.)

Homemaker services: Provided in some communities to take care of household tasks that the elderly are no longer able to do for themselves.

Day-care centers for the elderly: Provide activities that are determined by the needs of the group. (This service gives the family some relief from twenty-four-hour-a-day care. Programs such as home health services, homemaker services, and day-care centers prevent or postpone institutional care.)

Telephone reassurance: Provided by volunteers, often older persons, who telephone elderly people who live alone. (Such calls are a meaningful form of social contact for both parties and also ascertain whether any accidents or other serious problems have arisen that require emergency attention.)

Nursing homes: Provide residential care and skilled nursing care when independence is no longer practical for the elderly who cannot take care of themselves or for the elderly whose families can no longer take care of them.

Committee on Aging found that one third of nursing homes did not comply with federal regulations and that conditions in 800—almost one in ten—were "shockingly, dangerously bad."[72] The study found neglect, medical maltreatment, and in a few isolated cases even beatings and rape. The study also found evidence of unnecessary deaths of nursing home residents; for example, the study found in California that seventy-nine patients died between 1985 and 1986 as a direct result of neglect.[73]

Although only 5 percent of the elderly population

are currently residing in nursing homes, it is estimated that one out of every five persons who lives beyond age 65 will spend part of his or her life in a nursing home.[74]

Donald Robinson conducted a nationwide investigation of nursing homes in 1988 and concluded:

I learned that the majority of nursing homes are safe, well-run institutions that take good care of the sick people entrusted to them. Some are superb.[75]

Robinson also noted a number of horrors and abuses

The majority of nursing homes are safe and well run. When homes are properly administered, residents can expand rather than restrict their life experiences.

in some of the homes. The abuses included giving new and unapproved drugs to patients without their consent, giving patients heavy doses of tranquilizers to keep them docile, stealing funds from patients, submitting phony cost reports to Medicare, sexual abuse by staff of some patients, and charging patients thousands of dollars to gain admission to a home.[76]

In spite of the criticism, nursing homes are needed, particularly for the elderly who require medical and nursing care. If nursing homes were abolished, some other institution (such as a hospital) would have to serve the elderly who can no longer live independently or with their families. Life in nursing homes need not be bad. Where homes are properly administered, residents can expand rather than restrict their life experiences.

At present, people of all ages tend to be prejudiced against nursing homes, even those that are well run. Frank Moss describes the elderly person's view of nursing homes: "The average senior citizen looks at a nursing home as a human junkyard, as a prison—a kind of purgatory, halfway between society and the cemetery—or as the first step of an inevitable slide into

oblivion."[77] To some degree there is reality to the notion that nursing homes are places where the elderly wait to die.

The most common complaint against nursing homes appears to be the lack of well-trained, professional staff.[78] Nurses trained in the special needs of the aged are in short supply. Nursing home administrators in some states need only be 18 years old and have taken a six-month training course in nursing home administration. Few homes have social workers, occupational therapists, physical therapists, or other rehabilitative services.

Because of limits on reimbursement in nursing homes funded primarily by government sources, a number of other problems may arise. There is an effort to keep salaries down and to have a minimum number of staff. A home may postpone repairs and improvements on the facilities. Food is apt to be inexpensive—such as macaroni, which is high in fats and carbohydrates. Congress has provided that every nursing home patient on Medicaid is entitled to a monthly personal spending allowance. The homes have control over these funds, and some homes keep this money.[79]

Gordon and Walter Moss present additional complaints.

The quality of care from both particular staff members and from the institution as a whole is another major source of problems and complaints. There may be much delayed or no response to calls for help. Patients may be left sitting for a long time on bedpans. The staff may harass patients they dislike or consider to be insufficiently docile by doing these things, or by withholding services, isolating them in separate rooms in little-used parts of the building, or forcing them to remain bedridden.[80]

There are many complaints about the physical facilities. There may not be enough floor space, or there may be too many people in a room. The call light by the bed may be difficult to reach, or the toilets and showers may not be conveniently located. The building may be decaying. Nursing home patients may also have complaints about some of the other patients who cause problems by being noisy, by stealing, and by disrupting others' privacy.

BOX 13.6

Community Options Program: Providing Alternatives to Nursing Home Placement

C ommunity Options Program (COP) is an innovative program in Wisconsin to provide alternatives to nursing home placement. COP is funded by the state and by the federal government and is administered by county social services departments.

To qualify for the program a person must have a long-term or irreversible illness or disability and be a potential or current resident of a nursing home or of a facility for the developmentally disabled. The person must also have income and assets that are below the poverty line. If these eligibility guidelines are met, a social worker and a nurse assess applicants for their social and physical abilities and disabilities to determine the types of services needed.

If an alternative to nursing home placement is available, is financially feasible, and, most important, is preferred by an applicant, a plan for services is drawn up, and a start date for in-home or in-community services is determined.

A wide variety of services may be provided that are designed to be alternatives to placement in nursing homes. Typical services that are provided include homemaker services, visiting nurse services, home-delivered meals, adult foster care, group home care, and case management. COP is a coordinated program that makes use of a number of resources from a variety of agencies. Wisconsin is finding that the program is not only cost effective in comparison to the high cost of nursing home care but is also preferred over nursing home care by service recipients.

A senate committee on aging reported in 1977 after eight years of investigation that "the evidence is overwhelming that many pharmacists are required to pay kickbacks to nursing home operators as a precondition of obtaining a nursing home's business."[81]

Frank Moss, along with a number of other authorities, is critical of our society's response to the problems of the elderly: "The phenomenon of large numbers of ill elderly is a comparatively recent problem in the United States, as is our solution—nursing homes. The solution reflects today's society: the sick and the aged are an embarrassment; they remind us of our own mortality and therefore should be removed from view."[82]

SOCIAL WORK AND THE ELDERLY*

Social work education is taking a leading role in identifying the problems of the aged and is developing gerontological specializations within their curricula. Although in the past, social workers have not been a significant part of the staff of most agencies serving the aging, this is changing. Some states, for example, are

---

*For a fuller discussion see Louis Lowy, *Social Work with the Aging: The Challenge and Promise of the Latter Years* (New York: Harper & Row, 1979).

now requiring that each nursing home must employ a social worker.

Social work has a number of skills to help meet the special needs and concerns of the aged. Social workers are needed as brokers to link the elderly with available services. In any community there are a wide range of services available, but few people are knowledgeable about the array of services and about various eligibility requirements. The social worker's knowledge of community resources prepares him or her for this broker role. The elderly are in special need of this "broker" service as some have difficulty with transportation and communication, and others may have outmoded prejudices against seeking assistance.

Counseling is another function social workers can provide to the elderly or to the families of the elderly. Areas involved include counseling on emotional problems, employment counseling, counseling to find new "meaning" in living, counseling on coping with health problems, counseling on death and dying, and counseling on whether to enter a nursing home.

Outreach is another role for social workers, including identifying and offering services to those aged who need financial assistance, better housing, health care services, recreational and leisure-time services, transportation, companionship, consumer protection services, sex education, and hot-meal programs. Communities are now finding it is more cost efficient—and better for most of the elderly—to provide services to the elderly in their home than to use the alternative of a nursing home. Social workers are increasingly becoming involved in providing and coordinating services to the elderly in their home.

There are other roles that are opening up for social workers in the field of aging: consultants, community planners, researchers, and administrators of services. The role of advocate may also become crucial. Jordan Kosberg makes the following comments about this role.

Some time in the not-too-distant future there may well be a thundering outcry against the conditions in which the aged live. Call it an eruption of social conscience. Such a phenomenon has occurred in regard to racial prejudice, poverty, the status of women, pollution, and overpopulation. Social

workers have the motivation and responsibility to care for the disadvantaged; this care is the raison d'etre of their profession. If they are not in the vanguard of such a movement on behalf of the aged—making sure that it is a long-range effective effort—they will be denying their commitment to their profession and to society.[83]

Because the size of the elderly population is the most rapidly growing age group in our society, it is anticipated that services to the elderly will significantly expand in the next few decades. This expansion will generate a number of additional employment opportunities for social workers.

THE EMERGENCE OF THE ELDERLY AS A POWERFUL POLITICAL FORCE

In spite of all the maintenance programs that are now available for the elderly, the key problems of the elderly remain to be solved. A high proportion of the elderly do not have "meaningful" lives, respectful status, adequate income, adequate transportation, good living arrangements, adequate diet, or adequate health care.

Currently, we hear a great deal about various kinds of discrimination: racism, sexism, anti-Semitism, ethnocentrism. There is another kind that we are starting to hear about and that many of us (perhaps unknowingly) are guilty of: namely, ageism—prejudice against the elderly. How can we defend urging people to retire when they are still productive? How can we defend the living conditions within some of our nursing homes? How can we defend our restrictive attitudes toward sexuality among the elderly? How can we defend providing services to the elderly that are limited to maintenance and subsistence, while a wide range of services are being provided to help younger people

The best age
is the age you are.

GRAY PANTHERS   3635 Chestnut Street   Philadelphia PA 19104

*The Gray Panthers promote the quality of life for people
of all ages. "We have got to effect change, and we have
nothing to lose," says the group's founder, Maggie Kuhn
(above).*

live gratifying and fulfilling lives? Gordon and Walter
Moss comment, "Just as we are learning that black can
be beautiful, so we must learn that gray can be beautiful, too. In so learning, we may brighten the prospects
of our own age."[84]

In the past, prejudice has been most effectively
combated when those being discriminated against join
together for political action. It therefore seems apparent that if major changes in the elderly's role in our
society are to take place, it will have to be done through
political action.

Older people are, in fact, becoming increasingly
involved in political activism and, in some cases, even
radical militancy. Two prominent organizations are the
American Association of Retired Persons and, its affili-
ated group, the National Retired Teachers Association.

These groups, among other projects, are lobbying for
the interests of the elderly at local, state, and federal
levels of government.

An action-oriented group that has caught the public's attention is the "Gray Panthers." The organization
argues that a fundamental flaw in our society is the
emphasis on materialism and on the consumption of
goods and services rather than on improving the quality of life for all citizens (including the elderly). The
Gray Panthers seek to end ageism and to advance the
goals of human freedom, human dignity, and self-
development. This organization emphasizes using social action techniques, including getting the elderly
to vote as a bloc for their concerns. The founder of the
group, Maggie Kuhn, states, "We are not mellow,
sweet old people. We have got to effect change, and
we have nothing to lose."[85]

There are clear indications that the politics of age
have arrived. The elderly are likely to have a say in the
future on many social and political issues. The election
of Ronald Reagan (who was widely supported by the
elderly) as president at age 69 in 1980 (and age 73 in
1984) is a sign that the elderly are already having a
stronger political voice.[86] The elderly are rapidly becoming one of the most politically organized and influential groups in the United States. Another reason the
elderly are becoming a powerful political group is that
they tend to be more likely to vote than the young.[87]

One reason that the elderly will be more politically
active in the future is that the composition of the elderly population is changing. At present, most of the
elderly are poorly educated—only 49 percent have
completed high school and only 10 percent are college
graduates—and thereby are often less familiar with
American laws and political processes.[88] The coming
generation of elderly will be better-educated, better-
informed, and more politically conscious.[89]

Significant steps toward securing a better life for
the elderly have been made in the last twenty-five
years: increased social security payments, enactment of
the Medicare and Medicaid programs, the emergence
of hospices, and the expansion of a variety of other
programs for the elderly. With the elderly becoming a
powerful political bloc, we are apt to see a number of
changes in future years to improve the status of the
elderly in our society.

DEVELOPMENT OF SOCIAL ROLES FOR THE ELDERLY

The elderly face a variety of problems. Following retirement, their income drops, often to below poverty levels. Health care expenses rise considerably, as the elderly are more susceptible to chronic illnesses. With reduced income, their living standard drops dramatically. With less money, the elderly often reduce their physical and mental activities, which accelerates the aging process. The life expectancy of the elderly is increasing, with the old old being the fastest-growing age group in our society. The elderly depend on the social security system for a large amount of their income; yet the monthly payments are inadequate, and with the increasing number of recipients, the system is going bankrupt. Young people today can no longer count on the social security system being their primary source of income when they grow old and retire. The elderly have a roleless role in our society and are the victims of ageism. How can these problems be combated?

In a nutshell, it would seem essential to find a meaningful productive role for the elderly. At present, early retirement programs and the stereotypic expectations of the elderly often result in the elderly being unproductive, inactive, dependent, and unfulfilled. To develop a meaningful role for the elderly in our society, it appears that the productive elderly should be encouraged to continue to work and the stereotypic expectations of the elderly should be changed.

The elderly who want to work and are still performing well should be encouraged to continue working well past age 65 or 70. Also, it is suggested here that if an elderly person wants to work half time or part time, this should be encouraged. For example, two elderly persons working half time could fill a full-time position. New roles might also be created for the elderly to be consultants after they retire in the areas where they possess special knowledge and expertise. For those that do retire, there should be educational and training programs to help the elderly develop their interests and hobbies (such as photography) into new sources of income.

Working longer in our society would have a number of payoffs for the elderly and for society. The elderly would continue to be productive, contributing citizens. They would have a meaningful role. They would continue to be physically and mentally active. They would have higher self-esteem. They would begin to break down the stereotypes of the elderly being unproductive and a financial burden on society. They would be paying into the social security system rather than drawing from it.

What is being proposed here is a system for the elderly to have a productive role, either as paid workers or as volunteers.

In our materialistic society perhaps the only way for the elderly to have a meaningful role is to be productive. The elderly face the choice (as do younger people) between having adequate financial resources through productive work or inadequate financial resources by not working.

Objections to such a system may be raised by those who maintain that some of the elderly are no longer productive. This may be true, but some younger people are also unproductive. What is needed to make the proposed system work is jobs having realistic, objective, and behaviorally measurable levels of performance. Those at any age who do not meet the performance levels would be informed about the deficiencies and would be given training to meet the deficiencies. If the performance levels still were not met, discharge processes should be used as a last resort. (For example, if a tenured faculty member was deficient in levels of performance—as measured by student-course evaluations, peer faculty evaluations of teaching, record of public service, record of service to the department and to the campus, and record of publications—that faculty member should be informed of the deficiencies. Training and other resources to meet the deficiencies should be offered. If the performance did not improve to acceptable standards, then dismissal proceedings would be initiated. Some colleges and universities are now moving in this direction.)

In the productivity system that is being suggested, the elderly would have an important part to play. They

Volunteer activities are highly satisfying for many senior citizens.

would be expected to continue to be productive within their capacities. By being productive, they would serve as examples to counter the current negative stereotypes of the elderly.

Another objection that has been voiced about this new system is that the elderly have worked most of their lives and therefore deserve to retire and live in leisure with a high standard of living. It would be nice if the elderly really had this option. It would be nice if no one had to work, yet had a high standard of living. However, that is not realistic. Most of the elderly do not have the financial resources, after retiring, to maintain a high standard of living. The fact is that when most of the elderly retire, their income and their standard of living are both sharply reduced. The choice in our society is really between working and thereby maintaining a high standard of living or retiring and having a lower standard of living.

It should be noted we are already seeing a number of the elderly heading in this productive direction. Most members of the U.S. Supreme Court and many members of Congress are over age 70. In addition, a number of organizations have been formed to promote the productivity of the elderly. Three examples of these organizations are Retired Senior Volunteer Program, Service Corps of Retired Executives, and Foster Grandparent Program.

The *Retired Senior Volunteer Program (RSVP)* offers people over age 60 the opportunity of doing volunteer service to meet community needs. RSVP agencies place volunteers in hospitals, schools, libraries, day-care centers, courts, nursing homes, and a variety of other organizations.

The *Service Corps of Retired Executives (SCORE)* offers retired businessmen and businesswomen an opportunity to help owners of small businesses and managers of community organizations who are having management problems. Volunteers receive no pay but are reimbursed for out-of-pocket expenses.

The *Foster Grandparent Program* employs low-income older people to help provide personal, individual care to children who live in institutions. (Such children include the mentally retarded, the developmentally disabled, and the emotionally disturbed.) Foster grandparents are given special assignments in child care, speech therapy, physical therapy, or as teacher's aides. This program has been shown to be of considerable benefit to both the children and the foster grandparents.[90] The children served become more outgoing and have improved relationships with peers and staff. They have increased self-confidence, improved language skills, and decreased fear and insecurity. The foster grandparents have an additional (although small) source of income, increased feelings of vigor and youthfulness, an increased sense of personal worth, a feeling of being productive, and a renewed sense of personal growth and development. For society, foster grandparents provide a vast pool of relatively inexpensive labor that can be used to do needed work in the community.

The success of these programs illustrates that the elderly can be productive in both paid and volunteer positions. In regard to using elderly volunteers in agencies, Robert Atchley makes the following recommendations to increase the opportunities for successful outcomes:

First, agencies must be flexible in matching the volunteer's background to assigned tasks. If the agency takes a broad perspective, useful work can be found for almost anyone. Second, volunteers must be trained. All too often agency personnel place unprepared volunteers in an unfamiliar setting. Then the volunteer's difficulty confirms the myth that you cannot expect good work from volunteers. Third, a variety of placement options should be offered to the volunteer. Some volunteers prefer to do familiar things; others want to do anything but *familiar things. Fourth, training of volunteers should not make them feel that they are being tested. This point is particularly sensitive among working-class volunteers. Fifth, volunteers should get personal attention from the*

placement agency. There should be people (perhaps volunteers) who follow up on absences and who are willing to listen to the compliments, complaints, or experiences of the volunteers. Public recognition from the community is an important reward for voluntary service. Finally, transportation to and from the placement should be provided.[91]

PREPARATION FOR OLD AGE

Growing old is a lifelong process. Becoming 65 does not destroy the continuities between what a person has been, presently is, and will be. Recognition of this fact should lessen the fear of growing old. For those of modest means who have prepared thoughtfully, old age can be a period, if not of luxury, then at least of reasonable comfort and pleasure.

Our lives largely depend on our goals and our motivations to achieve those goals. How we live prior to retiring will largely determine whether old age will be a nightmare or will be fulfilling and gratifying. There are a number of areas we should attend to in our younger years:

Health: A sound exercise plan and periodic health examinations are critical to the prevention of chronic health problems. Also critically important in maintaining health is learning and using approaches to reduce psychological stress.

Finances: Saving money for later years is important, as is learning to manage or budget money wisely.

Interests and hobbies: Psychologically, people who are traumatized most by retirement are those whose self-image and life interests center around their work. People who have meaningful hobbies and interests look forward to retirement in order to have sufficient time for their hobbies and interests.

Self-identity: People who are comfortable and realistic about who they are and what they want out of life are better prepared, including in later years, to deal with stresses and crises that arise.

Looking toward the future: A person who dwells in the past or rests on past achievements is apt to find the older years depressing. On the other hand, a person who looks to the future generally has interests that are alive and growing and is thereby able to find new challenges and new satisfactions in later years. Looking toward the future involves planning for retirement, including deciding where you would like to live, in what type of housing and community, and what you look forward to doing with your free time.

Coping with crises: If a person learns to cope effectively with crises in younger years, these coping skills will remain when a person is older. Involved in effective coping is learning to approach problems realistically and constructively.

SUMMARY

Aging is an individual process that occurs at differing rates in different people. Chronological age is not an accurate measure of how physically fit and mentally alert an elderly person is.

People 65 and older now compose over one tenth of our population. The old old are now the fastest growing age group in our society. The elderly encounter a number of problems in our society: low status, lack of a meaningful role, the emphasis on youth in our society, health problems, inadequate income, loss of family and friends, inadequate housing, transportation problems, restrictive attitudes about expressing their sexuality, malnutrition, crime victimization, and emotional problems, such as depression and concern with circumstances surrounding dying. A majority of the elderly depend on the social security system as their major source of income. Yet monthly payments are inadequate, and the system is no longer financially sound, as it is paying out more money than it is taking in.

A wide array of services are available to the elderly, but these are primarily geared to maintaining the el-
derly, often at or only slightly above a subsistence level of existence. Services provided in many of our nursing homes are inadequate, and the level of care provided in some of these homes has been sharply criticized. Nursing homes have also been criticized as being "storage centers" for the elderly so that members of our society can avoid coming face to face with their own mortality.

Although the level of care needs to be substantially improved in some of them, nursing homes are needed for the elderly who cannot take care of themselves and/or for those whose families can no longer provide care. Most of the elderly, however, do not need nursing homes for permanent care or shelter. (It is generally unknown that 95 percent of the elderly live independently or with relatives, and not in nursing homes.)

In order to provide the elderly with a productive, meaningful role in our society it is suggested that the elderly should be encouraged to work (either in paid work or as volunteers) as long as they are productive and have an interest in working to maintain their standard of living. Enabling the elderly to be productive in their lives is predicted to have a number of personal payoffs for them and to be highly beneficial to society.

In many ways the elderly are victims of ageism. Social workers have numerous skills and roles in serving the elderly, including that of an advocate to secure system changes that will better serve the elderly. Increasingly, the elderly are becoming politically active and organized to work toward improving their status. Gradually, the composition of the elderly population will change; aging people will become better educated and a more powerful political bloc. In the future there are apt to be a number of social, economic, and political changes that will improve the status of the elderly.

NOTES

1. Gordon Moss and Walter Moss, *Growing Old* (New York: Pocket Books, 1975), pp. 17–18.
2. Eric Sharp, "The 'Retirement in Florida' Dream Can Become a Nightmare for Some," *Detroit Free Press,* September 9, 1973.
3. Moss and Moss, *Growing Old,* p. 18.

4. Colin M. Turnbull, *The Mountain People* (New York: Simon and Schuster, 1972).

5. U.S. Census Bureau, *Statistical Abstract of the United States, 1987* Washington, D.C.: U.S. Government Printing Office, 1987).

6. James E. Birren, "Psychological Aspects of Aging and Intellectual Functioning," *The Gerontologist* 8, no. 1, part 2 (1968), p. 19.

7. Milton L. Barron, "The Aged as a Quasi-Minority Group," in *The Other Minorities,* ed. Edward Sagarin (Lexington, MA: Ginn, 1971), p. 149.

8. Elizabeth Ferguson, *Social Work: An Introduction,* 3d ed. (Philadelphia: J. B. Lippincott, 1975), p. 238.

9. U.S. Census Bureau, *Statistical Abstract of the United States, 1987,* p. 68.

10. Joan Arehart-Triechel, "It's Never Too Late to Start Living Longer," *New York Magazine* (April 11, 1977), p. 38.

11. Thomas J. Sullivan et al., *Social Problems* (New York: John Wiley, 1980), pp. 335–370.

12. U.S. Census Bureau, *Statistical Abstract of the United States, 1987.*

13. Ibid.

14. Alan S. Otten, "Ever More Americans Live into 80s and 90s, Causing Big Problems," *The Wall Street Journal,* July 30, 1984, p. 1.

15. Ibid., p. 1.

16. Elaine Brody, quoted in Otten, "Ever More Americans Live into 80s and 90s, Causing Big Problems," p. 10.

17. Otten, "Ever More Americans Live into 80s and 90s, Causing Big Problems," p. 10.

18. "Where Time Stands Still," *U.S. News & World Report,* July 20, 1987, p. 59.

19. Eisdor Fer, quoted in Otten, "Ever More Americans Live into 80s and 90s, Causing Big Problems," p. 10.

20. *A Profile of Older Americans: 1987* (Long Beach, CA: American Association of Retired Persons, 1987), p. 11.

21. Robert N. Butler and Myrna I. Lewis, *Aging and Mental Health: Positive Psychosocial Approaches,* 2d ed. (St. Louis: Mosby, 1977).

22. Ibid.

23. Ibid.

24. *A Profile of Older Americans: 1987,* p. 13.

25. Marilyn L. Flynn, "Aging," in *Contemporary Social Work,* 2d ed., eds. Donald Brieland, Lela Costin, and Charles Atherton (New York: McGraw-Hill, 1980), p. 352.

26. Ibid.

27. Ian Robertson, *Social Problems,* 2d ed. (New York: Random House, 1980), p. 307.

28. Flynn, "Aging," p. 352.

29. Robertson, *Social Problems,* p. 307.

30. Flynn, "Aging," p. 353.

31. U.S. Census Bureau, *Statistical Abstract of the United States, 1987.*

32. *A Profile of Older Americans: 1987,* p. 9.

33. Ibid., p. 10.

34. "Will Inflation Tarnish Your Golden Years?" *U.S. News & World Report,* February 26, 1979, p. 57.

35. *A Profile of Older Americans: 1987,* pp. 10–11.

36. Sullivan et al., *Social Problems,* pp. 357–358.

37. U.S. Census Bureau, *Statistical Abstract of the United States, 1987,* p. 69.

38. Joseph Julian and William Kornblum, *Social Problems,* 4th ed. (Englewood Cliffs, NJ: Prentice-Hall, 1983), p. 388.

39. B. Koeppel, "The Big Social Security Ripoff," *Progressive* 39, no. 7 (1975), pp. 13–18.

40. *A Profile of Older Persons: 1987,* p. 3.

41. Moss and Moss, *Growing Old,* p. 47.

42. *A Profile of Older Persons: 1987,* p. 4.

43. Ibid., p. 3.

44. Ibid., pp. 3–4.

45. Ibid., pp. 3–4.

46. Ibid., pp. 3–4.

47. Beth J. Soldo, *America's Elderly in the 1980s* (Washington, D.C.: Population Reference Bureau, 1980), p. 24.

48. Steven Schack and Robert S. Frank, "Police Service Delivery to the Elderly," *The Annals of the American Academy of Political and Social Science,* no. 438 (July 1978), p. 83.

49. Merlin Taber, "The Aged," in *Contemporary Social Work,* eds. Donald Brieland, Lela Costin, and Charles Atherton (New York: McGraw-Hill, 1975), p. 359.

50. Bert K. Smith, *Aging in America* (Boston: Beacon Press, 1973), pp. 31–32.

51. William H. Masters and Virginia E. Johnson, "The Human Sexual Response: The Aging Female and the Aging Male," in *Middle Age and Aging,* ed. L. Neugarten (Chicago: University of Chicago Press, 1968).

52. Ibid., p. 269.

53. Taber, "The Aged," p. 359.

54. Ferguson, *Social Work,* p. 238.

55. U.S. Census Bureau, *Statistical Abstract of the United States, 1987,* p. 76.

56. Ibid., pp. 77–80.

57. Rex A. Skidmore and Milton Thackeray, *Introduction to Social Work,* 2d ed. (Englewood Cliffs, NJ: Prentice-Hall, 1976), p. 225.

58. Robert N. Butler, "Myths and Realities of Aging," address presented at the Governor's Conference on Aging, Columbia, MD, May 28, 1970.

59. Moss and Moss, *Growing Old,* p. 72.

60. See, for example, Elisabeth Kübler-Ross, *On Death and Dying* (New York: Macmillan, 1969); and R. E. Kavanaugh, *Facing Death* (Los Angeles: Nash Publishers, 1972).

61. Margaret Mead, "Dealing with the Aged: A New Style of Aging," *Current,* no. 136 (January 1972), p. 44.

62. Elisabeth Kübler-Ross, *On Death and Dying* (New York: Macmillan, 1969).

63. Sullivan, *Social Problems,* p. 363.

64. *Older Americans Act of 1965, as Amended, Text and History* (Washington, D.C.: U.S. Department of Health, Education and Welfare), November 1970.

65. Donald Robinson, "The Crisis in Our Nursing Homes," *Parade Magazine,* August 16, 1987, p. 13.

66. Abigail Trafford, "The Tragedy of Care for America's Elderly," *U.S. News & World Report,* April 24, 1978, p. 56.

67. Claire Tounsend, *Old Age: The Last Segregation* (New York: Grossman, 1971).

68. Trafford, "America's Elderly," p. 56.

69. Robert N. Butler, *Why Survive? Being Old in America* (New York: Harper & Row, 1975), p. 264.

70. Dianne Paley, "Nursing Home Is Cited Again," *Wisconsin State Journal,* May 23, 1980, sec. 4, p. 1.

71. Butler, *Why Survive? Being Old in America,* p. 264.

72. Robinson, "The Crisis in Our Nursing Homes," p. 13.

73. Ibid., p. 13.

74. Ibid., p. 13.

75. Ibid., p. 13.

76. Ibid., pp. 13–14.

77. Frank Moss, "It's Hell to Be Old in the U.S.A.," *Parade Magazine* (New York: Parade Publications) July 17, 1977, p. 9.

78. Moss and Moss, *Growing Old,* p. 61.

79. Ibid., p. 66.

80. Ibid., p. 64.

81. Ibid., p. 65.

82. Moss, "It's Hell to Be Old in the U.S.A.," p. 9.

83. Jordan J. Kosberg, "The Nursing Home: A Social Work Paradox," *Social Work* 18, no. 2 (March 1973), p. 109.

84. Moss and Moss, *Growing Old,* p. 79.

85. Quoted in Butler, *Why Survive? Being Old in America,* p. 341.

86. John W. Mashek, "Massive Shift to Right: Story of '80 Elections," *U.S. News & World Report,* November 17, 1980, p. 29.

87. John R. Barry and C. Ray Wingrove, eds., *Let's Learn About Aging* (New York: John Wiley, 1977).

88. *A Profile of Older Americans: 1987,* p. 12.

89. Barry and Wingrove, *Let's Learn About Aging,* p. 97.

90. Robert C. Atchley, *The Social Forces in Later Life: An Introduction to Social Gerontology,* 2d ed. (Belmont, CA: Wadsworth, 1977), p. 267.

91. Ibid., p. 81.

14

MEDICAL PROBLEMS AND MEDICAL SOCIAL SERVICES

Health and happiness are perhaps the highest values in our society. Wealthy people who develop a chronic illness are often heard to say they would, if given a choice, relinquish their wealth for a return to health. Most Americans now consider proper medical care a basic human right that society should pay for if an individual is unable to. The view that health is a basic right rather than a privilege is of relatively recent origin. For example, in 1967 the president of the American Medical Association still asserted that health care should be available only to those who could afford it.[1] The view of health care as a right was expressed by former President Richard Nixon in his Health Message of 1971.

Just as our National Government has moved to provide equal opportunity in areas such as education, employment, and voting, so we must now work to expand the opportunity for all citizens to obtain a decent standard of medical care. We must do all we can to remove any racial, economic, social, or geographic barriers that now prevent any of our citizens from obtaining adequate health protection. For without good health, no man can fully utilize his other opportunities.[2]

This chapter will:

- Briefly describe the health care system in America.

- Summarize problems in health care: profit orientation, limited attention to preventive medicine, unequal access to health services, health care for the elderly, AIDS, unnecessary and harmful medical services, use of life-sustaining equipment, and high cost of medical care.

- Discuss current efforts to resolve these problems.

- Outline a number of proposed policies and programs to combat these problems.

- Describe medical social work.

PHYSICAL ILLNESSES AND THE HEALTH CARE SYSTEM

There are hundreds of thousands of different medical conditions, ranging in severity from a minor scratch to a terminal illness. The causes are also nearly infinite: accidents, infections, birth defects, viruses, bacteria, the aging process, stress, diet inadequacies, and so on.

Medical services in this country are organized into four basic components: physicians in solo practice, group outpatient settings, hospital settings, and public health services.[3]

Physicians in individual or solo practice are, proportionately, more often found in rural than in urban areas. Such a physician is usually a general practitioner who is trained to provide treatment for the more common medical ailments. Supervision of general practitioners is minimal or nil; they are primarily accountable only to patients. Except through referrals for consultation and occasional use of laboratories and hospitals, a physician in solo practice works in relative isolation from colleagues.

Group outpatient settings can be organized in several ways. A group of general practitioners may share facilities, such as a waiting room, examining rooms, and a laboratory. Or, each physician within a group may have a different specialty and complement the skills of the others. Because medical knowledge and treatment techniques have become so vast and diverse, it is now impossible for a physician to have in-depth knowledge in all areas. Another type of outpatient setting is one in which a third party (a university, union, business, or factory) employs a group of physicians to provide medical care for its constituency. Still another type is one in which a group of doctors with the same specialty (for example, neurological surgery) provides services in the same facility.

A third subsystem of health care is the hospital setting, which has a wide range of laboratory facilities, specialized treatment equipment, inpatient care facilities, and highly skilled technicians. Hospitals employ diverse and numerous medical personnel. A hospital is generally the center of the medical care system in com-

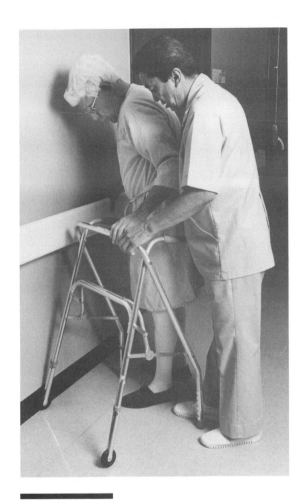

Hospitals, at the center of the health care system in most communities, employ a wide variety of medical personnel. This technician assists patients who need post-operative physical therapy.

munities. Because of the spiraling cost of hospital care and the lack of sufficient beds, many communities are now building nursing homes and convalescent homes for those needing fairly extensive medical care but not inpatient hospital attention.

Public health services are organized on five levels: local (city or county), regional, state, national, and international. The majority of public health services to a community are provided through local health programs. The priorities in public health keep changing; as success is achieved in dealing with one problem, other problems emerge that demand attention. Public health services have virtually eliminated a number of communicable diseases in this country, such as tuberculosis, polio, and smallpox. The focus of public health services is primarily preventive in nature. Services provided through local health departments include (*a*) health counseling to families regarding family planning, prenatal and postpartum care, child growth and development, nutrition, and medical care; (*b*) skilled nursing care and treatment to the acute and chronically ill; (*c*) physical rehabilitation to patients with strokes, arthritis, and similar medical conditions; (*d*) school health services to public and parochial schools and liaison between home, school, and community; (*e*) disease prevention and control; (*f*) immunization services; (*g*) referral of families and individuals in order to make maximum use of available community resources; (*h*) environmental sanitation, which involves developing and enforcing codes, rules, and regulations designed to maintain and/or improve conditions in the environment that affect health. This activity covers a broad area including air and water pollution, food protection, waste material disposal, and sanitation of recreation facilities; (*i*) maintenance of an index of all area births, deaths, marriages, and current communicable diseases; and (*j*) health education and information services to stimulate the public to recognize existing health problems. In the United States the vast majority of health care services are private rather than public (that is, administered by the government).

PROBLEMS IN HEALTH CARE

Service Orientation versus Profit Orientation

Most Americans believe that the only focus of health care is to keep people healthy, that is, to prevent diseases, illnesses, and impairments from occurring and to restore to health as rapidly as possible those who do become ill. If this were the only objective, the health care system would not receive very high grades. Our infant mortality rate of 11 per 1,000 live births is higher than that of seven other countries.[4] Six other countries have higher life expectancy rates than ours.[5] The death rate from heart disease in the United States is the highest in the world, and the incidence of and death rate from cancer rank among the highest.[6]

Nearly all the money spent on health care in this country goes to treating medical conditions once they arise, with very little being spent on prevention. Many people in this country have considerable difficulty in obtaining access to medical care. Access is particularly difficult in urban ghettos, low-income neighborhoods, and smaller rural communities, since health care facilities tend to be located in affluent urban and suburban neighborhoods. The late Robert Kennedy described the health care system in America as being "a national failure," that is "providing poor quality care at high costs."[7]

The objectives of health care providers in the United States are not only to restore and maintain health but also to make a profit. There are numerous statistics documenting that the system is prospering. Many of our more than 7,000 hospitals are among the most modern in the world. Physicians have the highest median income of any occupational group. They earn several times more than the average wage earner. In 1987 the mean income of American doctors was $120,000, and their incomes are rising at a faster rate than those of any other occupational group.[8] The average daily cost for a hospital bed has gone from $74 in 1970 to $411 in 1984.[9] One of the most profitable small businesses in this country is private medical practice. One of the most profitable intermediate-sized businesses is operating a nursing home. Nursing home stocks have gone up dramatically in the past two decades on Wall Street. The drug industry, involving the manufacture and sale of drugs, has been one of the most profitable large-sized industries in the country. The United States spends more money on health care (in both absolute and proportionate terms) than any other country. Medical costs constitute over 10 percent of this country's total production of goods and services. The medical system is the third largest industry in the country in terms of money spent, surpassed only by agriculture and construction. Total expenditures on health care have gone from $3.8 billion in 1940 to over $400 billion in 1985.[10]

Consumers seeking rapid and inexpensive health care in our country are often frustrated and angered over the high costs and delays in getting access to care. But, as noted, health care is both service oriented and profit oriented. Other industrialized nations regard medical care as a social service, a philosophy based on the premise that the kind of care you receive depends on the kind of illness you have. In contrast, in the United States the kind of medical care you receive depends not only on your illness but also on how much money you are able and willing to spend.

In summary, the United States is spending substantially more on health care per capita than other industrialized nations. Yet certain statistics (such as infant mortality rates) suggest that other countries provide health services that are as good (or better) than ours at a lower cost.

Emphasis on Treatment Rather than on Prevention

The major causes of death today in America are chronic diseases: cancer, heart disease, cerebrovascular disease (such as strokes), cirrhosis of the liver, diabetes, bronchitis, and the like (Table 14.1). Chronic diseases progress and persist over a considerable part of a person's life. Chronic diseases frequently exist long before we are aware of them because there are often no symptoms in the early stages and because we tend to ignore early symptoms. Social, psychological, and environmental factors are important influences in the progression of these diseases. Heart disease, for example, is known to be associated with a diet of highly saturated animal fats (beef, butter, and cheese), lack of consistent and vigorous exercise, heavy smoking, and stress.

A major problem is that modern medicine is oriented toward crisis medicine, which is geared to treating people *after they become ill*. The crisis approach is effective in coping with some types of medical conditions, such as acute problems (for example, accident victims and patients having influenza or pneumonia). Unfortunately, with chronic diseases, once the symp-

TABLE 14.1
■■■■■■■

Ten Leading Causes of Death in the United States

Rank	Percent of Total Deaths
1. Heart disease	38.2
2. Cancer	21.9
3. Stroke	7.7
4. All accidents	4.6
5. Chronic obstructive pulmonary disease	3.3
6. Pneumonia and influenza	2.8
7. Diabetes	1.8
8. Suicide	1.4
9. Homicide	1.4
10. Atherosclerosis	1.3

Source: U.S. Bureau of the Census, *Statistical Abstract of the United States, 1987* (Washington, D.C.: U.S. Government Printing Office, 1987), p. 75.
■■■■■■■

toms manifest themselves, much of the damage has already been done, and it is often too late to effect a complete recovery. In order to curb the incapacitating effects of chronic diseases more effectively, the health care delivery system needs to emphasize the prevention of illness before extensive damage occurs. To date, preventive medicine has had a lower priority than crisis-oriented medicine in terms of research funding, the allocation of health care personnel, and the construction of medical facilities. (There are more profits to be made in treatment programs than in prevention programs.) The emphasis on treatment violates the commonsense notion that "an ounce of prevention is worth a pound of cure."

The kinds of health problems that we have in this country are largely due to our lifestyles. Millions of

BOX 14.1

Health and Longevity

Nedra Belloc and Lester Breslow in a study of 6,928 adults found that the following seven health practices are positively related to good health and longevity:

Eating breakfast.

Exercising regularly.

Staying within 10 percent of your proper weight.

Not smoking cigarettes.

Not drinking to excess.

Not eating between meals.

Sleeping seven to eight hours a night.

At age 45 a person who follows these practices has a life expectancy that is 11 years longer than a person who follows fewer than four. A 70 year old who practices all seven is apt to be as healthy as a 40 year old who follows only one or two.

Source: A. F. Ehrbar, "A Radical Prescription for Medical Care," *Fortune,* February 1977, p. 169.

Americans smoke, drink, or eat to excess. Our diet is high in starches, sugars, and animal fats, all of which are factors in a wide variety of illnesses, including heart disease and sugar diabetes. A Harris poll found that only 15 percent of adults are sufficiently active to be physically fit.[11] Environmental factors also pose health risks. The air and water are filled with thousands of toxic chemicals (caused by emissions from autos and factories) that pose many health hazards, such as cancer and emphysema. The fatality rate from automobile crashes is staggeringly high. Many such accidents occur from driving while intoxicated.

Physicians often treat the symptoms of chronic illnesses rather than the underlying causes. Patients who are tense or anxious are prescribed tranquilizers rather than receiving therapy to reduce the psychological stress that is causing the tension. Patients who are depressed are prescribed antidepressant medication rather than being counseled to determine the underlying reasons for the depression. Patients with psychosomatic disorders (for example, ulcers, migraine headaches, insomnia, diarrhea, digestive problems, hypertension) are often prescribed medication rather than receiving therapy for changing certain aspects of their lifestyles that would reduce the underlying psychological stress, which is a major factor in producing such problems. Psychosomatic disorders are partially caused by mental processes such as psychological stress.

In recent years a wide variety of holistic programs, which are preventive in nature, are beginning to be established in industry, in hospitals, in school settings, in medical clinics, and elsewhere. Holistic medicine recognizes that our thinking processes function together with our body as in integrated unit, and it gives attention to both the physical and the psychological functions of a person. K. R. Pelletier documents that the major determinants of most illnesses are our life-styles (including exercise, diet, sleep patterns, and particularly stress reaction patterns).[12] Holistic medicine instructs people in proper exercises, proper diets, and ways to reduce psychological stress in order to maintain health and curb the development of chronic disorders.

Thomas McKeown emphasizes the responsibility that each person has (although it is often not recognized) in maintaining good health.

The role of individual medical care in preventing sickness and premature death is secondary to that of other influences, yet society's investment in health care is based on the premise that it is the major determinant. It is assumed that we are ill and are made well, but it is nearer the truth to say that we are well and are made ill. Few people think of themselves as having the major responsibility for their own health. . . .

The public believes that health depends primarily on intervention by the doctor and that the essential requirement for health is the early discovery of disease. This concept should be replaced by recognition that disease often cannot be treated effectively, and that health is determined predominately by the way of life individuals choose to follow. Among the important influences on health are the use of tobacco, the misuse of alcohol and drugs, excessive or unbalanced diets, and lack of exercise. With research, the list of significant behavioral influences will undoubtedly increase.[13]

Unequal Access to Health Services

Aaron Antonovsky has noted that class and race "influence one's chances of staying alive."[14] He has found that the lack of medical care among the poor and racial minorities leads to higher rates of serious illnesses that result in shortened life expectancies.

The life expectancy age for whites is six years longer than for nonwhites.[15] In addition, the infant mortality rate for nonwhites is nearly twice that of whites (19 per 1,000 live births for nonwhites and 11 for whites).[16] Nonwhites have higher rates of practically every illness than whites. Income differences play a part. But even when income is the same, death rates are still higher for nonwhites.[17]

Membership in a lower social class is also correlated with higher rates of illnesses. The poor are disabled more frequently and for longer periods of time. They have higher rates of untreated illnesses and higher mortality rates for almost all illnesses. Contrary to popular belief, the highest rates of heart disease occur among the lowest salaried and not among top-level executives and managers.[18] (Stress levels may in fact be higher among the poor who continually face psychological stress from financial crises. Differences in diet, exercise, and lifestyle patterns may also be factors.)

The poor have higher rates of illnesses and higher rates of untreated illnesses partly because they cannot afford private, high-quality medical care. Max Seham has noted: "For the most part, delivery of health care services is geared to the upper- and middle-class culture because these services take on all the qualities of a commodity for sale and the affluent are the preferred and often the only market. This is especially true in the preventive areas."[19] In addition, because of the profit motive, health care services are primarily located in affluent urban areas and in suburbs. The poor who live in small rural areas or in urban, low-income areas therefore have much more difficulty in obtaining access to medical care, especially if they have transportation barriers. In the United States, health care services are provided on a *fee-for-service* basis. As a result, the wealthy receive excellent care, whereas the poor receive indifferent and decidedly inferior care.

When poor people do decide to seek treatment (often they wait until they are seriously ill), they tend to visit a clinic rather than a private or family physician. At the clinic they often feel self-conscious about their appearance. They frequently have to wait hours in

BOX 14.2

Understanding and Reducing Stress

P elletier in *Mind as Healer, Mind as Slayer* documents that rational and positive thinking have a major impact in promoting healing and maintaining health and that irrational and negative thinking are major determinants of psychosomatic illnesses. (Thinking is irrational if it does one or more of the following: (*a*) is inconsistent with objective facts, (*b*) hampers you in protecting your life, (*c*) hampers you in achieving your short- and long-term goals, (*d*) causes significant trouble with other people, and (*e*) leads you to feel unwanted emotions.) Stress-related physiological and psychological disorders have now become our leading health problem.[a]

A simplified description of the effects of our thinking processes in determining psychosomatic illnesses is outlined as follows:

Stressor ⎰ Events or experiences
            ⎱ Certain kind of self-talk: (for example, "This is a very dangerous situation.")

Stress ⎧ Emotions: (such as tenseness, anxiety, worry, alarm)
          ⎪
          ⎪ Psychological reactions (A general stress reaction will occur. The physiological changes of a general stress reaction have been described by Hans Selye.[b] The symptoms include an accelerated heart and pulse rate, shallow respiration, perspiring hands, tenseness of the neck and upper back, a rise in red blood count for fighting infection, increased metabolism, and secretion of pro-inflammatory hormones. The physiological reactions that most students experience prior to giving a speech before a group are aspects of the general stress reaction.)

If the emotional and physiological reactions are intensive and long term, a psychosomatic disease is apt to develop, such as an ulcer, migraine headache, diarrhea, heart problems, digestive problems, cancer, hypertension, bronchial asthma, hay fever, arthritis, enuresis, certain skin problems, constipation.

According to the above formula, there are two components of a "stressor": (*a*) the event and (*b*) the self-talk that we give ourselves about that event. "Stress" is the emotional and physiological reactions to a "stressor." Self-talk plays a key role in producing stress. The self-talk approach enables us to understand how positive events (as well as negative events) can lead to a stress reaction:

Positive event: Receiving a promotion.

Self-talk: "I now will have additional responsibilities that I may not be able to handle."

"If I fail at these new responsibilities, I will be fired and will be a failure. My career plans will never be realized."

"This promotion will make others in the office jealous."

"I'm in big trouble."

Emotion: Worry, tension, anxiety.

Physiological   The general stress reaction will occur. If intensive and prolonged, conditions
reaction: exist for a psychosomatic illness to develop.

Stress can be reduced in three primary ways. One way is to identify the irrational and negative self-talk and then give yourself rational self-challenges (see Chapter 4 for examples of this approach). A second way is to be become involved in activities that you enjoy, which will lead you to stop your irrational thinking and instead have you focus your thinking on events you view more positively. For example, if you enjoy golf, playing golf will lead you to stop thinking about your day-to-day problems and instead lead you to think about the enjoyable experiences associated with golfing. Activities that are apt to stop your irrational thinking include hobbies, attending entertainment events, jogging and other exercise programs, biofeedback programs, muscle relaxation exercises, and meditation.[c] A third way to reduce stress is to change the event that is involved in producing stress: for example, take a job that you view as having less pressure.

---

[a]K. R. Pelletier, *Mind as Healer, Mind as Slayer* (New York: Delta, 1977).

[b]Hans Selye, *The Stress of Life* (New York: McGraw-Hill, 1956).

[c]These stress-reducing techniques are described in Charles Zastrow, *The Practice of Social Work*, 3d ed. (Belmont, CA: Wadsworth, 1989).

crowded waiting rooms and generally receive imper-sonal care. A trusting relationship with a physician is seldom developed. Doctors generally come from the middle and upper classes and therefore may face barriers in being able to establish rapport with low-income and nonwhite people. Seham notes:

In general, health professionals have little —if any— understanding of the lifestyle of the poor. For a doctor to advise a patient who is living in poverty to increase his intake of protein, without helping him to work out how to do it, is useless. Similarly, to suggest to a working mother that she come to the clinic for weekly treatments, when the clinic hours coincide with her working hours, is tantamount to not providing treatment at all.[20]

Lee Rainwater has noted that being poor promotes poor health. The poor cannot afford to eat properly, so inadequate diet makes them more susceptible to ill-nesses. They are more apt to live in the most polluted areas, so they are more susceptible to cancer, emphy-sema, and other respiratory diseases. They cannot af-ford proper housing, have less heat in the wintertime, and are more exposed to disease-carrying rodents and garbage. Their lives are more stress-filled, particularly surrounding financial concerns. They are less likely to know about and use preventive health approaches. They are less likely to seek early treatment that would prevent a serious disorder from developing. Because they are often treated with hostility and contempt by physicians and other medical personnel, they are apt to avoid seeking medical help.[21]

Low-Quality Health Care for the Elderly

As noted in Chapter 13, the proportion of the elderly in our society is increasing dramatically, and the old old (age 75 and over) is the most rapidly growing age group in our society. Today, there is a crisis in health care for the elderly. There are a variety of reasons for this crisis.

As described in Chapter 13, the elderly are much more apt to have long-term illnesses. In the 1960s the Medicare and Medicaid programs were created to pay

for much of their medical costs. Because of the high costs of these programs, the Reagan administration in the 1980s made cuts in eligibility for payments and set limits for what the government would pay for a variety of medical procedures.[22]

Physicians are primarily trained in treating the young and generally are less interested in serving the elderly. As a result, when the elderly become ill, they often do not receive quality medical care. For example, Hugh Downs, in an ABC news report, described the case of an 82-year-old woman who was shuffled from one hospital to another over a three-month period and finally dumped in a county hospital, where she even-tually died of a single grossly neglected bedsore. Downs notes:

The revolution of longer life has produced a new complex of critical medical needs, needs this nation does not yet seem prepared to meet. For example, there seems little prospect that there will be anything like the numbers of geriatricians needed to care for the elderly. It's a field still avoided by young doctors. Because of the complicated problems of the aging, there is a need for more health evaluation services and more psychiatric and rehabilitation assistance. Even for the limited efforts we now make, funding has always been meager.

The new era of the longevity revolution is already bringing with it multiplying health problems to which our society remains largely blind. . . . and within this nation's vast medical complex, many old who could be helped are left adrift, trapped, their needs unrecognized.[23]

Medical conditions of the elderly are often misdi-agnosed because physicians receive little specialized training in the unique medical conditions of the el-derly. Many of the elderly who are seriously ill do not get medical attention. One of the reasons physicians are uninterested in treating the elderly is that the Medicare program sets reimbursement limits on a va-riety of procedures that are provided to the elderly. Thus, most physicians prefer to work with younger patients because the fee-for-service system is much more profitable.

There have also been restrictions put on hospital payments under Medicare. In the past, the payment

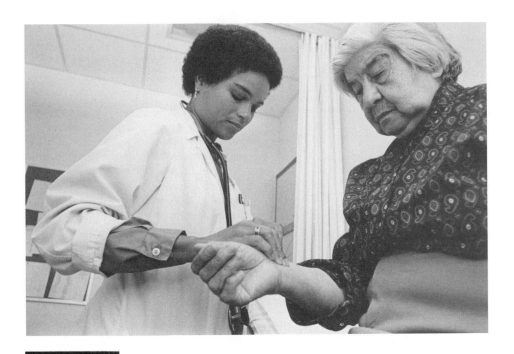

Physicians today are primarily trained in treating the young. The scarcity of doctors trained in geriatrics has compounded the crisis in health care for the elderly.

system covered the full cost of the medical expenses. To curtail rampant costs, the federal government in the 1980s set flat payments for each category of illness. These categories are called "diagnostic related groups" (DRGs). With this system, instead of reimbursing hospitals for the actual cost of treating Medicare patients, the government now pays a set fee for each medical condition. If a hospital spends less on a patient than the fixed amount, it makes money; if it spends more, it must absorb the loss. A perverse, unintended consequence of DRGs is that many seriously ill elderly patients are being discharged prematurely.[24] Hospitals that have a social conscience and continue to treat the elderly beyond the length of time allowed by the DRG regulations must cover the expenses themselves and thereby face bankruptcy.

The elderly who live in the community often have transportation difficulties in getting medical care. Those living in nursing homes sometimes receive inadequate care because some health professionals are not interested in providing high-quality medical care for patients who no longer have much time to live. Medical care for the elderly is becoming a national embarrassment.[25]

Spread of AIDS

Acquired immune deficiency syndrome (AIDS) is a contagious, presently incurable disease that destroys the body's immune system. AIDS is caused by the human immunodeficiency virus (HIV), which can be transmitted from one person to another primarily during sexual contact or through the sharing of intravenous drug needles and syringes.

AIDS made national headlines in 1985 when it was revealed that Rock Hudson (a prominent male actor) had contracted AIDS. (Hudson died from AIDS a few months after public release of the story.) A public hysteria has arisen about AIDS: For example, many parents

EXTENDING HELP TO AIDS PATIENTS

The tragedy of AIDS is unparalleled in our time. Few of us are lucky enough not to have lost fathers, sisters, lovers, or friends.

Despite the growing toll, we have more reason for hope today than at any other time in the epidemic's ten-year history. New treatments are prolonging lives both for people with AIDS and for those who test positive for the HIV virus. Health care professionals, including nurses, counselors, and hospice workers, are working daily to improve the quality of life for those who are ill.

Almost from the beginning, volunteers have been the lifeblood of AIDS caregiving. In one community in particular, the depth and extent of that care are unmatched. The photographs on these pages tell a story of San Francisco's response to AIDS—a response that continues to draw upon unending reserves of compassion, concern, and love.

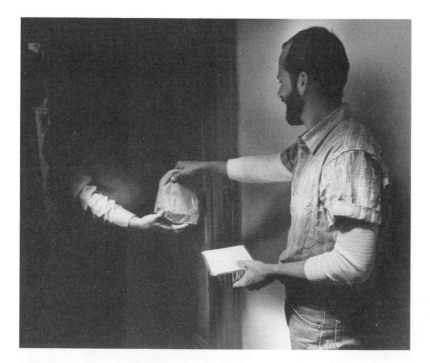

Project Open Hand delivers over 1,000 meals a day to people shut in by AIDS. "I sincerely believe that people who have AIDS are dying first of malnutrition, not AIDS," says Open Hand founder Ruth Brinker.

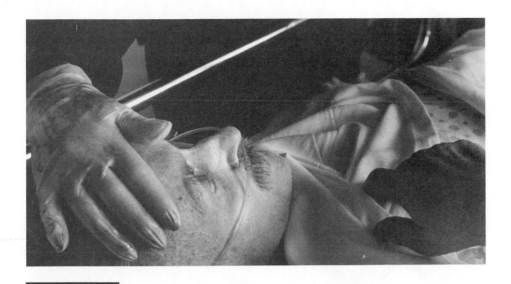

A hospice volunteer shares a dying friend's final hours. She wears protective gloves not for herself but for other patients she visits.

"My work is one on one, talking about feelings," says Maria, a nurse and case manager who coordinates social and medical services for patients who live at home. "People open up and see that AIDS isn't this mean, awful, terrible thing."

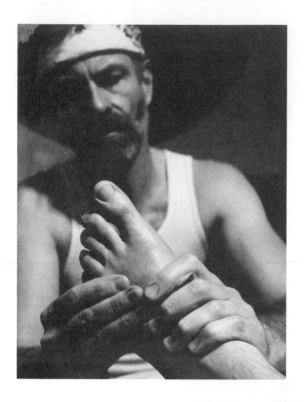

Ray, a volunteer massage therapist, sees touch as a basic healing technique. Warm, human contact is badly needed in an often impersonal hospital setting. As one man with AIDS admits, "It's so civilized compared to the brutality of tests and treatments. His touch says, 'You're okay, you're not just a number, you're going to be all right.'"

Members of a gay and lesbian softball team extend an Easter greeting to a friend in San Francisco General Hospital's AIDS ward.

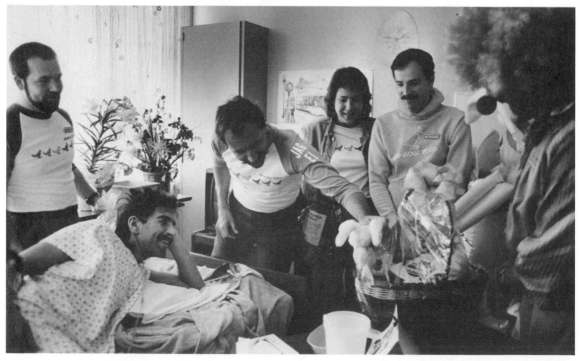

are hesitant to send their children to a school in which an identified child affected by HIV is attending. Box 14.3 describes how people who have AIDS are further victimized by discrimination.

HIV attacks a person's immune system and damages his or her ability to fight other diseases. Without a functioning immune system to combat germs, the affected person is vulnerable to becoming infected by bacteria, fungi, malignancies, and other viruses that may cause life-threatening illnesses such as cancer, pneumonia, and meningitis.

As far as scientists know, HIV can live in only a very limited environment. It prefers one type of cell—the T-helper cell in human blood. It may also be able to live in brain cells. Outside these environments, the virus apparently dies. It cannot live in food. It dies shortly after contact with a toilet seat. In all other environments—such as air or water—it dies rapidly. AIDS is not transmitted by casual social contact, such as hugging, shaking hands, social kissing, coughing, sneezing, or crying. AIDS has not been contracted from swimming in pools or from eating in restaurants, even when a restaurant worker carries HIV. It is not possible to get AIDS from doorknobs, toilets, or telephones, and it does not appear to be transmitted by mosquito bites.

Once a person is infected with HIV, there are several outcomes. Some people remain well but have the capacity to transmit the virus to others. Others may develop AIDS Related Complex (ARC). The symptoms of ARC patients are less severe than symptoms of persons who have AIDS. Symptoms of ARC include loss of appetite, fever, night sweats, weight loss, diarrhea, skin rashes, tiredness, swollen lymph nodes, and lack of resistance to infection. Some people develop AIDS, the disease in which the immune system is unable to fight off "opportunistic" diseases. Two of the most common opportunistic diseases are pneumocystis carinii pneumonia and Kaposi's sarcoma (a rare form of cancer).

Since AIDS was first identified in the late 1970s, a sufficient amount of time has not elapsed to determine what proportion of the population affected with HIV will eventually develop AIDS. (In some cases it may take ten to twenty years or more before AIDS develops in a person who has HIV.) Some authorities are projecting that nearly everyone with HIV will eventually develop AIDS.

In some patients HIV may also attack the nervous system and cause damage to the brain. The deterioration gradually occurs over a period of time (sometimes a few years). Symptoms of brain deterioration include memory loss, indifference, partial paralysis, mental disorder, and loss of coordination.

Although many people believe any contact with HIV guarantees illness and death, such fears are not justified. Body fluids (such as fresh blood, semen, urine, and vaginal secretions) infected with the virus must enter the bloodstream in order for the virus to be transmitted from one person to another. Male homosexuals account for many AIDS cases because they are apt to engage in anal intercourse. Anal intercourse often results in a tearing of the lining of the rectum, which allows infected semen to get into the bloodstream. Interestingly, there are no known cases where AIDS has been transmitted sexually among lesbians.

Sharing a needle during drug mainlining with someone who is carrying the virus is dangerous because there is transmission of blood. A small amount of the previous user's blood is often drawn into the needle and then injected directly into the bloodstream of the next user.

At present, there is no evidence to suggest that the scant amounts of virus in saliva is sufficient to transmit the virus. Nevertheless, the announcement that saliva can contain the virus has led the Screen Actors Guild to inform their members that they have the right to refuse to do kissing scenes if they are afraid of acquiring AIDS. In studies of families of people with AIDS, there has not been a single reported case as of 1988 of the virus being passed by close family contact (eating together, hugging, sharing food and toothbrushes, sharing towels and cups, and any other kind of nonsexual contact).

A test has been developed to determine if a person has been exposed to the virus. The test is called ELISA (for enzyme-linked immunosorbent assay). This test does not directly detect the virus; it detects the antibodies a person's immune system develops to fight the virus. A positive ELISA doesn't mean a person has AIDS, but only that he or she has had contact with the virus. For a person who has been infected with HIV it generally takes two to three months before enough antibodies are produced to be detected by ELISA.

BOX 14.3

AIDS Discrimination

P eople who test positive to HIV or who have AIDS often are additionally victimized by discrimination. Dr. Robert Huse was a pediatrician who was earning $100,000 annually from his medical practice in Dallas, Texas. In 1985 he went to the public health department for an anonymous HIV antibody test and discovered he tested positive. Physicians informed him he was not a danger to his patients. Two years later, in October 1987, he became involved in a complex civil lawsuit involving his former roommate, and the newspapers in Dallas were allowed by the courts to publish a notice of his positive HIV test. Within a week, his patient load dropped from 100 to fewer than 40 a week. Within a few weeks he was forced to close his practice. Dr. Huse experienced, "utter frustration, bitterness, hurt and mind-numbing depression."[a]

Many Americans have a "them and us" mentality about those who test positive to HIV or who have AIDS. Many Americans want to have no contact with anyone who has HIV. They erroneously think casual social contact may put them at risk. As a result, those having the AIDS virus are apt to be shunned, risk losing their jobs, and often are abandoned by family, spouse, lovers, and friends. In some communities where it becomes public knowledge that a child has the virus, parents of other children have reacted by not allowing their children to attend the same school and by prohibiting their children from having any contact with the child who has HIV.

Patrick Haney, a social worker who has been diagnosed as having ARC, describes one of the negative aspects of being diagnosed as having the AIDS virus:

Like no other illness since the advent of modern medicine, AIDS carries with it a stigma of shame and pointed finger of blame, suggesting those of us who are sick are at fault for being infected. This is a very negative impact of AIDS, yet it is also illogical. Do we blame Legionnaires for Legionnaires' disease, children for mumps, measles or chicken pox; the elderly for Alzheimer's disease or death, or epileptics for seizures? It makes no sense to blame anyone for AIDS. AIDS is caused by a virus, not by behavior or identity.

Moreover, shame and blame can lead persons with AIDS into denial and hiding, which may cause potential avoidance of medical care, involvement in unsafe sexual activity, and a lack of support from a support system that doesn't know the person is HIV infected. This further isolates the person with AIDS and exacerbates feelings of aloneness and despair.[b]

Social work has traditionally supported and advocated for oppressed and disenfranchised groups in our country—blacks, Hispanics, the poor, the elderly, gays, and women. Social workers have an ethical obligation to combat the numerous injustices connected with AIDS. AIDS is not a gay disease or an intravenous drug users' disease. It is a human disease.

---

[a]Linda Little, "HIV Disclosure Ruins Pediatrician's Practice," *Wisconsin State Journal,* sec. 3, p. 1.

[b]Patrick Haney, "Providing Empowerment to the Person with AIDS," *Social Work* 33, no. 3 (May–June 1988), p. 251.

If a person is exposed to the virus, the virus usually becomes inactive. Certain factors help the virus to stay active once it is in the body: a history of infections with certain other viruses, general poor health, the abuse of certain recreational drugs (such as butyl nitrite), malnutrition, and genetic predisposition. For those who do develop AIDS, the mortality rate is nearly 100 percent. In the early 1980s AIDS was transmitted in some cases through blood transfusions. Because blood that is used in blood transfusions is now tested for AIDS, it is unlikely that AIDS will be transmitted by blood transfusions. Because antibodies do not form immediately after exposure to the virus, a newly infected person may unknowingly donate blood after becoming infected but before his or her antibody test becomes positive. It is estimated that this might occur less than once in 100,000 donations.[26]

At present, there is no cure for AIDS, nor is there a vaccine to prevent the transmission of AIDS. Unless a cure for AIDS is found in the near future, AIDS has the potential to kill more people than any other disease. Presently, the best way to stop the spread of AIDS is through educating people to avoid known risks. The following are high-risk factors:

- Having anal intercourse, especially men with other men.

- Having multiple sex partners without using safe sex practices (such as using condoms). The risk of infection increases according to the number of sexual partners, male or female.

- Sharing intravenous needles. HIV may be transmitted by reusing contaminated needles and syringes.

- Having sex with prostitutes. Prostitutes are at high risk because they have multiple sex partners and are more apt to be intravenous drug users.

To avoid getting the AIDS virus, Surgeon General C. Everett Koop recommends:

The most certain way to avoid getting the AIDS virus and to control the AIDS epidemic in the United States is for individuals to avoid promiscuous sexual practices, to maintain mutually faithful

monogamous sexual relationships and to avoid injecting illicit drugs.[27]

It is advisable to use a condom when having sexual intercourse with a new partner until you are certain the person does not test positive to HIV. You cannot acquire AIDS from someone who is not infected by HIV.

Unnecessary or Harmful Care

As indicated earlier, one of the objectives of the health care system is to make a profit. Profits can be, and often are, made by using unnecessary diagnostic and treatment approaches—by using diagnostic tests that are unnecessary, by prescribing drugs and other medication that are unnecessary, and by performing unneeded operations. It is estimated that over 2 million unnecessary operations are performed each year, with most of these operations being for hysterectomies and tonsillectomies.[28]

Nonwhites and women are more apt to be victimized by inferior care. Barbara and John Ehrenreich note:

Since blacks are assumed to be less sensitive than white patients, they get less privacy. Since blacks are assumed to be more ignorant than whites, they get less by way of explanation of what is happening to them. And since they are assumed to be irresponsible and forgetful, they are more likely to be given a drastic, one-shot treatment, instead of a prolonged regimen of drugs, or a restricted diet. . . . Women are assumed to be incapable of understanding complex technological explanations, so they are not given any. Women are assumed to be emotional and "difficult," so they are often classified as neurotic well before physical illness has been ruled out. (Note how many tranquilizer ads in medical journals depict women, rather than men, as likely customers.) And women are assumed to be vain, so they are the special prey of the paramedical dieting, cosmetics, and plastic surgery businesses.[29]

A more serious problem than unnecessary or inferior care is harmful care. About 30,000 deaths occur annually from reactions to antibiotics and other prescribed drugs. Adverse reactions to medication result in 300,000 people being hospitalized each year. A large number of people each year are becoming addicted to tranquilizers and to pain-killing drugs prescribed by physicians. Over 11,000 people die each year from complications after undergoing unnecessary surgery. No surgery is without its risks. Even with such a simple operation as a tonsillectomy, 2 out of every 1,000 patients die.[30]

Why does harmful treatment occur? One reason is that physicians make a profit from prescribing unnecessary treatment, and such treatment sometimes leads to complications. Another reason is that it is conservatively estimated that about 10 percent of the nation's physicians are incompetent and should have their licenses revoked.[31] Unfortunately, most patients are unable to judge the professional competence of their physicians.

Suing has become a national pastime, particularly malpractice suits in the medical field. The large number of successful suits documents the common existence of harmful treatment. At the same time the possibility of a malpractice suit arising from failure to make a correct diagnosis because an unlikely diagnostic procedure was *not* used leads many physicians to order routinely more diagnostic tests than are likely to be needed. Such tests are costly.

Controversy over Use of Life-Sustaining Equipment

Medical technology has made dramatic advances this century. Technology is able to keep people alive for months, and in many cases years, who in the past would have died.

Even after a person's brain has stopped functioning, technology can keep the respiratory processes, the heart, the liver, and other vital organs functioning for months. The lives of those who are terminally ill can be prolonged for substantial periods of time, but they will experience considerable pain and be in a deteriorated condition. Many controversial issues have arisen about the use of life-sustaining technology. How should death now be defined, since vital functions can be kept going even when the brain is dead? Some law suits have already arisen in organ donor cases where it is charged that organs have been removed before the donor was deceased. Should the lives of the terminally ill be prolonged when there is practically no hope for recovery and the patients are in severe pain? Should society seek to keep alive people who are so severely and profoundly retarded that they cannot (and will never be able to) walk or sit up? Should abortion be mandatory if genetic defects are diagnosed in the fetus? When should life-prolonging efforts be used, and when should the patient be allowed to die? Because of the adverse consequences of being kept alive indefinitely when there is no hope of recovery, an increasing number of people are signing "living wills." In a living will a person states that if a situation arises in which there is no reasonable expectation of recovery from physical or mental disability involving a life-threatening illness, she or he requests to be allowed to die and not be kept alive by artificial means. A living will is not binding, but it conveys a patient's wishes to those (such as relatives and attending physicians) who have to make a decision about whether to use life-sustaining equipment.

The President's Commission for the Study of Ethical Problems in Medicine and Biomedical and Behavioral Research recommended in 1981 that all states define death as occurring when either of the following are judged to have taken place: (*a*) the irreversible cessation of circulatory and respiratory functions (this is essentially the definition used in the past) or (*b*) irreversible cessation of all functions of the entire brain, including the brain stem (this is a new definition). In adopting the "whole brain concept," the commission rejected a more controversial argument that death should be deemed to occur when "higher-brain functions" (those controlling consciousness, thought, and emotions) are lost. Patients who have lost higher-brain functions but retain the brain-stem functions can persist for years in a chronic vegetative state. Many states have now incorporated this definition of death into their statutes.

BOX 14.4

How Should Financial Resources Be Allocated?

F iscal conservatives argue that our economy cannot afford to use medical technology widely to prolong the lives of those who will not be productive in the future. They point to cases such as that of Geri D., which they say document the fact that too much money is already being spent in some areas.

At 5 months of age, Geri D. is residing in a residential facility for the retarded at an annual cost of $40,000 per year. She has severe medical problems, including cardiovascular dysfunctions. She is so profoundly retarded that she will never be able to sit up, a developmental milestone that children of average intelligence achieve at 6 months of age. Geri was born prematurely, with multiple medical problems. Lifesaving technology kept her alive. Already, over $250,000 has been spent in keeping her alive. By the time she becomes a young adult, more than $1 million will have been spent on keeping her alive.

With medical advances our society will face increasingly difficult issues regarding where financial resources should be used.

The High Cost of Medical Care

Statistics presented earlier document that medical care is highly expensive in this country. The high cost is recognized as a matter of national concern. There are many reasons why the cost is so high and why the costs continue to increase more rapidly than the rate of inflation.

A major reason is that one of the objectives of the health care system is to make a profit. There are few controls designed to keep fees and prices down. Although the United States uses a marketplace approach to health care, consumers when ill are not in a position to shop around for medical treatment. They are often suffering so much that in order to feel better they are willing to pay whatever a physician chooses to charge. Most patients are not even informed before receiving treatment what the physician will charge. Prices for doctors' services are not advertised and therefore are not subjected to the competition that exists elsewhere in marketplace systems. Physicians have successfully established a public image where they are so revered that most patients will sit for hours in waiting rooms without complaining and are reluctant to ask questions about charges before receiving treatment. (The same patients will voice their frustrations about having to stand in line for five minutes at a checkout counter in a store.)

A significant amount of the high cost of health care is due to dramatic technological advances in developing a wide range of life-saving treatment interventions. This equipment, along with the cost of highly skilled personnel to operate it, is expensive. Twenty-five years ago we did not have expensive medical equipment such as cobalt machines, heart pacemakers, artificial heart valves, and microsurgical instruments with which we could perform surgery under a microscope.

Another reason is the increased life span of Americans. Now, a larger proportion of our population is old, and the elderly require more health care than younger people. An additional reason is because many technically and professionally trained groups (such as nurses and physical therapists) are demanding salaries consistent with their training and responsibilities.

Another reason for the high cost of health care is that third-party financing is increasingly paying medical bills. Historically, medical bills were primarily charged to and paid by consumers. Now, most bills are charged to and paid by third parties, including private insurance companies and the public Medicare and Medicaid programs. Physicians are more likely to recommend expensive diagnostic and treatment procedures if they feel such procedures will not be a financial burden to the patient. In addition, the rise in the rate of malpractice suits encourages physicians to "play it safe" by using extensive diagnostic procedures. Third-party payments also tempt some physicians to perform surgeries that may be unnecessary. Spencer Klaw has concluded that "At least one out of every five or six operations in the United States is medically unjustified."[32]

Walter Friedlander and Robert Apte (along with many other authorities) blame the high cost partially on inadequate planning.

Our health system is a hodge-podge that has grown out of a variety of historical trends rather than out of conscious planning. Care is often fragmented, and is oriented toward treating episodic illnesses rather than toward maintaining the health of the whole person or family. . . . Some of the current high cost of care, in fact, can be attributed to the inefficiency, overlap of effort, and gaps in the system. Consumer groups are beginning to press for a better-organized, comprehensive health system which would give quality care at lower cost. As yet, however, their voice is not strong enough to overcome the opposition of *the medical profession and other forces resisting change in the medical care system.*[33]

The increase in malpractice suits is also a contributing factor. Juries in many cases have awarded large settlements where malpractice is judged to have occurred. Physicians are required by law to carry malpractice insurance, with annual premiums ranging from $3,000 to over $40,000 depending on the area of practice. (Anesthesiologists pay the highest amount, since their field is considered to carry the greatest risk.[34]) These premium costs are, of course, passed on to consumers through fee increases.

The tendency toward increased specialization by doctors is another factor. At present 88 percent of physicians have a specialty.[35] The growth of medical knowledge has encouraged specialization, as it is impossible for a physician to be an expert in all medical areas. Specialization, however, has also raised costs, since specialists charge more than general practitioners in order to receive compensation for their additional training and expertise. Specialization also raises costs because patients are often required to consult with (and pay) two or more physicians for each illness that they have. (A serious additional problem caused by specialization is that medical care becomes impersonal, dehumanized, and fragmented, since patients now rarely establish a trusting, long-term relationship with one physician.)

Similar to physicians, there are few incentives for hospitals to keep prices down. It is estimated that one third of all hospital procedures could be performed as safely—and much more economically—on an outpatient basis.[36] Hospitals also compete with one another in a community to see who can have the most prestigious and expensive equipment, which often leads to a duplication of expensive and seldom-used equipment. And hospitals, similar to physicians, are not subjected to fees being set by consumers on a supply and demand basis. Patients are generally not able to shop around for the hospital they want to go to.

Hospitals, physicians, nursing home operators, and drug companies are politically powerful. Health care providers are represented by such influential organizations as the American Medical Association, the Phar-

BOX 14.5

Financial Disaster for a Family that Earned Too Much

$10.80 PREVENTS CANCER VICTIM
FROM RECEIVING FEDERAL AID

Mrs. G. is dying of cancer. Her medical bills could reach $60,000, but she is ineligible for Medicaid. She once worked in a textile mill in Georgia, and is now receiving $239 a month in disability benefits. This amount is $10.80 more per month than a person can collect in unearned income and remain eligible for Medicaid. Had she not worked, Medicaid would be paying her medical bills.

Both Mrs. G. and her husband are described as hard-working, honest people. A social security office staff member in the community commented:

We see more of these cases than we would like to. We have had cases that are $1 over the limit. But Congress sets the budget and draws the line, and right now the cut-off for Medicaid is $228.20 a month.

Source: *Wisconsin State Journal,* June 23, 1980, sec. 1, p. 11.

maceutical Manufacturers Association, the American Hospital Association, and the American Association of Medical Schools. Health care providers appear, at least at present, to have the political power to prevent changes in health care that would sharply restrict their profits.

FINANCING MEDICAL CARE

Medical expenses are paid for by private insurance, through governmental programs, and by direct payments from the individual to the health care provider.

In 1985 private insurance paid 32 percent of the total cost for health care, the consumer paid 28 percent, and the government paid 40 percent.[37]

Most of the 40 percent of the federal government's health care bill is paid through Medicaid and Medicare. (The government also participates in the health insurance of federal employees, provides medical programs for families of members of the armed forces, and provides payments for those who have had military service through Veterans Administration hospitals.)

Medicaid

This program was established in 1965 by an amendment (Title XIX) to the Social Security Act. Medicaid primarily provides medical care for recipients of public assistance. It enables states to pay directly to hospitals, doctors, medical societies, and insurance agencies for services provided to recipients of public assistance. The federal government shares the expense with states, on a 55 to 45 percent basis, for recipients of Aid to Families with Dependent Children and Supplemental Security Income (formerly recipients of Old-Age Assistance, Blind Aid, and Disabled Aid). Medical expenses that are covered include diagnosis and therapy performed by a surgeon, physician, and dentist; nursing services in the home or elsewhere; medical supplies, drugs, and laboratory fees.

Under the Medicaid program, benefits vary from state to state. The original legislation encouraged states to include coverage of all self-supporting persons whose marginal incomes made them unable to pay for medical care. However, this inclusion was not mandatory, and "medical indigence" has generally been defined by states to provide insurance coverage primarily to recipients of public assistance.

Although the stated purpose of Medicaid was to assure adequate health care to the nation's poor and near poor, the program covers less than half of all poor families.[38] Part of the reason less than half are covered is that the federal government has restricted eligibility in order to cut costs. In the past, hospitals supported the uninsured by charging paying patients more. But after years of soaring costs, government and private insurers have rebelled against "cost-shifting" by setting limits on what they will pay for services provided in hospitals. Unable to support the cost of indigent care, many hospitals are turning these patients away. *A two-tiered system of health care is emerging in this country, based on ability to pay.*[39]

Medicare

The elderly are more afflicted with illnesses, yet have less income to pay for medical care. People over age 65 now make up 12 percent of the population, and the percentage is increasing each year. Six times as many dollars are spent per capita for the health care of aged persons than for younger persons, mostly for hospital

or nursing care.[40] Therefore, in 1965 Congress enacted Medicare (Title XVIII of the Social Security Act). Medicare helps the elderly pay the high cost of health care. It has two parts—hospital insurance (Part A) and medical insurance (Part B). Everyone age 65 or older who is entitled to monthly benefits under the Old Age, Survivors, and Disability Insurance program gets Part A automatically, without paying a monthly premium. Practically everyone in the United States age 65 or older is eligible for Part B. Part B is voluntary, and beneficiaries are charged a monthly premium. Disabled people under age 65 who have been getting social security benefits for twenty-four consecutive months or more are also eligible for both Part A and Part B, effective with the twenty-fifth month of disability.

Part A—hospital insurance—helps pay for time-limited care in a hospital, in a skilled nursing facility (home), and for home health visits (such as visiting nurses). Coverage is limited to 90 days in a hospital, and to 100 days in a nursing facility. If patients are able to be out of a hospital or nursing facility for sixty consecutive days following confinement, they are again eligible for coverage. Covered services in a hospital or skilled nursing facility include the cost of meals and a semiprivate room, regular nursing services, drugs, supplies, and appliances.

Part B—supplementary medical services—helps pay for physicians' services, outpatient hospital services in an emergency room, outpatient physical and speech therapy, and a number of other medical and health services prescribed by a doctor such as diagnostic services, X-ray or other radiation treatments, and some ambulance services.

The costs of health care are rapidly rising, as are the costs of health insurance, Medicaid, and Medicare. Those that are not covered through group plans at their place of employment are increasingly finding it difficult to purchase private health insurance programs. Ehrenreich and Ehrenreich have noted: "In the face of rising health care costs, the cost of . . . health insurance has soared, too. As a result, an increasing number of people fall into no man's land—too rich for Medicaid, too young for Medicare, too poor to buy private health insurance, and certainly too poor to pay hospital bills.[41]

IMPROVING THE CURRENT SYSTEM

Practically everyone agrees that the rising costs of medical care are a threat to a family's financial security and, on a broader scale, are a threat to the economic stability of our society. Yet there is no general consensus on the specific measures that should be taken to hold down costs and to resolve the other problems that have been identified in this chapter. Some of the specific suggestions that are being advocated by authorities in the field will be briefly summarized.

Holding Down Costs

A number of proposals to hold down health care costs have been suggested:

- Increase the number of admissions to medical schools in order to train more doctors. Increasing the number of doctors may reduce difficulties in gaining access to health care and also lead to competition between physicians to attract patients and thereby lead to reductions in fee charges.

- Expand outpatient facilities (such as emergency care facilities that are open not only during the day but also during evening hours and on weekends) so that illnesses can be detected and treated early, thereby preventing the development of more serious and costly medical conditions.

- Permit doctors to advertise their services and fees. Other professionals, such as attorneys and dentists, are increasingly doing this. Such competition may result in fee reductions.

- Encourage (through fellowships and scholarships) medical students to become general practitioners rather than specialists.

- Expand outpatient treatment facilities so that more illnesses could be treated without hospitalization.

- Train more physician assistants and paramedics to handle treatment for common routine illnesses (for example, flu and colds), to provide preventive

services, and to service geographical areas without physicians. China, for example, makes extensive use of lay persons with some training to provide basic health care. They administer simple diagnostic tests, treat routine illnesses, refer patients with serious symptoms to physicians, and teach nutrition and birth control. This system is considered to be working very successfully.[42]

- Encourage patients to seek a second opinion before consenting to an operation, in order to reduce unnecessary surgeries. Many insurance programs are now paying for the costs of a second opinion.

- Expand and encourage the use of generic drugs. Generic drugs are nonpatent drugs that have the same chemical composition as patent drugs. The only differences between generic and patent drugs are that the latter carry a trade name and cost considerably more.

Practicing Preventive Medicine

Prevention programs might also be cost saving in the long run. Note:

- Most Americans unfortunately believe that physicians have nearly magical powers to treat medical conditions that arise. Patients generally rely on a physician to cure them. Educational programs are needed in schools and to inform the general public that it is our lifestyles (diet, handling of stress, exercise patterns, amount of sleep, hygiene habits) that primarily determine when we will become ill and what illnesses we will develop. Educational programs are also needed to help people recognize that when they become ill, they are important participants in the treatment process, as their attitudes, emotions, diet, and hygiene patterns will greatly influence treatment results.

- The present health care system is primarily curative in focus, as it concentrates on illness and injury rather than on prevention. At present, most private health insurance policies do not cover periodic

BOX 14.6

The British System: A Comparison

About four decades ago Britain created a health care system that has become known as "socialized medicine." This system will be briefly described, not because the author is advocating that such a system be developed here but because the description will show that there are other ways of providing health care than our marketplace, for-profit system.

The British system, in contrast to ours, is a system in which medical care is provided as a public service, similar to the way in which elementary and secondary education is provided here. Most physicians are employed by the British government, and the government owns and operates the clinics, hospitals, and other facilities.

In the British system every individual selects and registers with a physician. Most physicians are general practitioners who see patients at their office and who when needed will make house calls. Each physician receives a basic salary paid by the government and an additional small annual fee based on the number of patients on his or her register. (This fee is the same whether a person sees a physician fifty times a year or not at all.) Doctors' incomes, then, depend on the number of people that register with them and not on the amount or kind of treatment they provide. There are some specialists in Britain to whom general practitioners may refer cases for consultation and treatment.

General practitioners earn on the average less than half of what physicians earn in this country.

Physicians are allowed to take private, fee-paying patients if they desire. A few physicians choose to serve only private patients. In addition, some individuals (generally the wealthy) choose to receive private physician and hospital care, which, of course, they pay for. The quality of public care is generally about the same as private care, although in private care patients generally obtain an appointment sooner for nonemergency medical care, and private hospital rooms are generally more spacious and pleasant in appearance.

---

screening examinations but only provide coverage when a person is actually sick or injured. Such a model rewards providers of health services for treating illnesses but not for preventing illnesses.

■ Health-Maintenance Organizations (HMOs), in contrast, are prepaid health care insurance plans that emphasize prevention. Subscribers pay a fixed annual sum, usually in installments, and, in return, receive comprehensive care. HMOs vary in size and structure but generally include physicians (both general practitioners and specialists) who provide a wide range of services—diagnostic, treatment, and hospital and home care. The program operates similarly to an insurance program. Subscribers pay a fee (the fee is often paid by the subscriber's employer), and the HMO pays for all of the medical expenses that occur.

The federal government is encouraging HMOs as an

The British system provides free medical care to any person in the country—including visitors who have a medical emergency. Practically all costs (for physician visits, surgery, hospital rooms and meals, ambulance services, diagnostic tests, and essential medical supplies such as eyeglasses and wheelchairs) are paid by the government. There is a small charge for any drug prescription, even though the actual cost may be many times higher. There also is a small charge for each dental visit. (Those over age 65 and under age 16 are excused from these fees.) Individuals do have to pay for purely cosmetic services such as face lifts or gold fillings.

This health care system is financed through taxes.

British opinion polls show that around 80 percent of the public approves of the National Health Service. Health care in Britain is the most highly rated government service. The service is also supported by the medical profession and both political parties. Costwise, the system appears to be more efficient than ours. The per person cost of health care in Britain is less than half of what it is in the United States. Britains also appear to be healthier than Americans on a number of indicators: They live longer, have a lower infant mortality rate, and spend less time in hospitals.

The main complaint that Britains have about this public health care system is that there are long waiting lists for treatment of nonemergency medical problems, such as minor illnesses. Patients sometimes have to wait days, and in some cases even months, for treatment. Emergency problems such as heart attacks or broken arms receive immediate attention.

Britain's historical tradition in health care is different from ours. The primary focus of their system is service, whereas ours has both a service and a profit orientation. It is uncertain whether their system would work in our country. The medical profession has considerable vested interest in maintaining its high profits and perhaps would be successful in sabotaging efforts to establish a similar system in this country.

Source: Judith Randa, "Health Service Is 30 and British Still Love It," *Daily News* (New York), July 5, 1978, p. 36.

---

alternative to other private insurance programs. The following is a description of the advantages of HMOs:

Because HMO revenues are fixed, their incentives are to keep patients well, for they benefit from patient well-days, not sickness. Their entire cost structure is geared to preventing illness and, failing that, to promoting prompt recovery through the least costly services consistent with maintaining quality. In contrast with prevailing cost-plus insurance plans, the *HMO's financial incentives tend to encourage the least utilization of high cost forms of care and also tend to limit unnecessary procedures. . . .*

In contrast with more traditional and alternative modes of care, HMOs show lower utilization rates for the most expensive types of care (measured by hospital days in particular); they tend to reduce the consumer's total health-care outlay; and—the ultimate test—they appear to deliver services of high quality. Available research studies show that HMO members are more

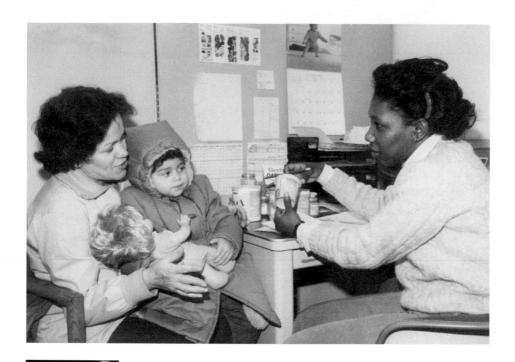

Prevention programs, including health and nutrition counseling, can be cost saving in the long run.

likely than other population groups to receive such preventive measures as general checkups and prenatal care and to seek care within one day of the onset of symptoms of illness or injuries.[43]

It is crucial that incentives are found throughout the health care system to focus on prevention and cost reduction. HMOs compose a system that emphasizes prevention and cost reduction. Numerous public and private employers have chosen to provide HMO programs for their employees. HMOs have been successful in reducing overall health care costs per patient, partly because they emphasize prevention. They also have been successful in reducing rates of hospitalization and in limiting the length of hospital stays by alternative forms of care and by greater use of out-of-hospital surgery.[44] HMOs are rapidly growing in popularity.

Over 10 percent of the U.S. population now belongs to HMOs.[45]

Taking Action to Resolve Problems

Suggestions for taking action to resolve some of the other problems that were identified follow:

- Incentives need to be developed to encourage physicians to practice in rural areas and in low-income areas in the cities and to specialize in working with the elderly. One approach is to give stipends that would help pay the school expenses of medical students in exchange for a requirement that stipend recipients practice for a few years in areas currently underserved by physicians.

■ More nonwhite students should be admitted to medical schools, as such students on graduation tend to serve nonwhite communities.

■ Further guidelines need to be established concerning when prolonged life-sustaining measures should be used and when the patient should be allowed to die. The definition of what constitutes death has to be defined more precisely. (In the not-too-distant future, the high cost of keeping people alive who will never again be productive may raise some national concerns about euthanasia—so-called "mercy killing.")

■ Colleges and universities need to expand existing programs and develop new programs to meet the emerging health care needs of the elderly. Physicians and other health care professionals (nurses, social workers, physical therapists, and so on) need to receive training in diagnosing and treating the medical conditions of the elderly. Health care for the elderly is a national crisis. Incentives need to be developed for health care professionals to work with the elderly.

■ Many state and local jurisdictions where AIDS has afflicted large numbers of people have appointed AIDS task forces. These task forces have heavy representation from the field of public health. Such task forces are needed in every community to develop programs to serve those who have HIV and to develop public information programs to inform the community about how AIDS is spread and how it can be prevented and to dispel myths that have led to discrimination against those known to have HIV.

■ Sex education and education concerning AIDS must start at the lowest grade possible as part of any health and hygiene program. People need to be informed of the importance of practicing safe sex activities (such as using condoms).

■ Offices, factories, and other work sites should develop a plan for educating the work force and ac-commodating ARC or AIDS patients before the first case appears at the work site. Employees with AIDS or ARC should not be discriminated against but should be dealt with as are any other workers with a chronic illness.

Establishing a U.S. National Health Insurance Program

This country does not as yet have a national health insurance program. Great Britain and many other European countries have such a plan (see Box 14.6), in which public tax dollars are used to pay for medical care for all citizens. In the past two decades, a number of congressmen and organizations have pressed for a public health insurance program. Now, many families receive partial coverage of costs through subscribing to private insurance plans, which are primarily available to employed persons and their families. Those who are either marginally employed or unemployed are generally not covered by health insurance.

There are multiple reasons why a national health insurance plan is needed. The rapid rise in health and insurance costs makes it impossible for the poor, those of marginal income, and even middle-class families to pay for insurance or extensive medical bills. The poor who are not covered by Medicaid are unable to pay for even moderate medical expenses; thereby, they often forego early treatment and develop more serious medical conditions. Medicare covers short-term hospitalization expenses for the elderly but not long-term expenses. Extensive medical treatment can wipe out substantial savings and force a family deeply into debt, thereby changing dramatically its standard of living and lifestyle.

Hospitals cannot survive without assured income when services are provided. Physicians, as well, need to be paid for their services. Alarmingly, 33 million Americans are without private or government-sponsored health insurance.[46]

Starting with Franklin Roosevelt, every president except Ronald Reagan and George Bush has proposed a national health insurance program, without any being passed. The result is that the United States is the only industrialized nation lacking a comprehensive national medical insurance system.[47] A variety of national health insurance programs have in the past been advanced by Democratic and Republican legislators, administration officials, organized labor, representatives of private insurance companies, and the American Medical Association.

The proposals for national health insurance involve three major types. In the public approach, governmental agencies would collect funds (for example from employers and employees) and pay the claims. In the mixed public-private approach, health insurance funds would be collected by the federal government and disbursed by private insurance companies. In the private approach, tax credits would be given to individuals for the purchase of private health insurance.

The main objection to a national health insurance program has been the cost to taxpayers and the effect such an expensive new program would have on the economy. There is concern that such a program would escalate the costs of health care, similarly to what has happened with Medicare and Medicaid.

MEDICAL SOCIAL WORK

Many public and private social welfare agencies (such as public welfare departments, adoption agencies, family service agencies, neighborhood centers, and probation and parole departments) are perceived as the specialty of social workers. Because such agencies are often managed by social workers, and because social work is the primary service, such agencies are considered *primary* settings. Hospitals, medical clinics, and schools are, on the other hand, *secondary* settings, since the primary service is not social work. But this secondary focus does not reduce their importance for social work, as health care and education serve a vital function and spend a substantial proportion of our national resources. Because social workers are not administratively in charge of secondary settings, prob-

lems related to status and influence sometimes arise. In such settings it is important for social workers to learn to work with those in control. American doctors are the highest paid professional group in our society, and they tend to expect a status consistent with their salary. Some allied health professionals who work with physicians state that many doctors expect "Godlike" respect.

The main setting for medical social work is the hospital. Dr. Richard C. Cabot first introduced social services into the Massachusetts General Hospital in 1905 in Boston. Now, almost every hospital has a social services department. Having a social services department is required by the American Hospital Association as a condition for accreditation.[48] Social workers provide not only direct casework with patients and their families but also group work with certain patients, consultation, and training of other professionals. They also are involved in planning and policy development within the hospital and with various health agencies. At times medical social workers teach medical school courses in which they convey their professional knowledge of the sociopsychological components of illnesses and of the treatment process.

Increasingly, it is becoming recognized that psychological processes are causative factors in nearly every illness: for example, in psychosomatic illnesses; alcoholism; depression; drug addiction; heart conditions; hypertension; and susceptibility to viruses, bacteria, and infections. The patient's emotions and motivation for recovery also substantially affect the treatment process. Venereal disease, AIDS, and cirrhosis of the liver, for instance, may evoke feelings of shame and guilt because of the stigma attached to these illnesses. People with heart conditions need to learn how to relax, avoid continued stressful conditions, and have the motivation to follow a prescribed diet. A miscarriage may result in a wide variety of emotional reactions that need to be dealt with. Adjusting to a chronic or permanent disability also evokes a variety of negative psychological reactions. A medical treatment team is increasingly dependent on social workers to attend to social and psychological factors that are either contributing causes of medical ailments or are side effects of a medical condition that must be dealt with to facilitate recovery and prevent the occurrence of nonfunctional dependency.

Physicians consider social work an allied medical discipline, and in medical settings social workers become an integral part of the medical team. Along with doctors, nurses, and other therapists, social workers take part in the study, diagnosis, and treatment-planning processes for patients. A medical social worker frequently obtains important diagnostic information on the living conditions, environment, habits, personality, and income of patients. Because physicians are no longer as well acquainted with patients, such information is often vital in arriving at a diagnosis and a treatment plan. Through interviews with the patient and members of his or her family, the worker gains a perspective on the social and emotional components of the illness and how such components may affect treatment.

In medical social work (now often referred to as social work in the health field) a wide variety of problems and situations are encountered, examples of which are:

Helping terminally ill patients and their families adjust.

Counseling women who have had a mastectomy.

Helping a low-income wife from a distant area find lodging in the community while her husband undergoes heart surgery.

Counseling people who are so depressed they are contemplating suicide.

Helping an unwed mother plan for the future.

Providing genetic counseling for a young couple who gave birth to a mentally retarded child.

Helping an executive of a large company to make plans for the future following a severe heart attack.

Counseling a woman about her emotional reactions following a miscarriage or a stillbirth.

Being a support person to a hospitalized person with AIDS and to his or her friends and relatives.

Finding living arrangements that will provide some medical attention for people who no longer need to be hospitalized.

Counseling alcoholics and drug addicts or making appropriate referrals to other agencies.

Counseling patients about their apprehensions of undergoing surgery.

Helping someone suddenly struck with a permanent disability adjust and make plans for the future.

Meeting with relatives and friends of patients to help interpret the nature of the medical condition and perhaps solicit their help in a treatment plan to facilitate recovery.

Counseling someone with emphysema on how to stop smoking.

Counseling a rape victim on her psychological reactions.

Informing relatives about the medical condition of someone who has just had a severe automobile accident.

While dealing with such problems and situations, a social worker is almost always a member of a medical team that is headed by a physician.

The job of a social worker in the health field is a dynamic one that requires continued study and knowledge expansion. With the dramatic expansion of new therapy approaches for medical conditions (for example, organ transplants, new prescription drugs, extensive new surgery techniques), it is essential that medical social workers keep informed about new technological approaches.

Social work in hospitals tends to be short term and crisis oriented because there is generally a fairly rapid turnover of patients. Social workers are often involved in discharge planning (for example, making arrangements for patients to return to their families or to a convalescent home). Sometimes the social worker must act as an advocate to assure that the patient's rights are secured and that his or her needs are best served.

Although social workers in medical settings are involved primarily in direct services to patients and their families, there are occasions when they are involved in activity planning, administration of programs (for example, directing a hospice program so that terminal patients can live their final months in dignity), research, and education of other professionals.

BOX 14.7

A Case Illustration of Medical Social Work

J anet Ely was hospitalized to have a hysterectomy because she had a tumor in her uterus. Janet was an attractive, single, 22-year-old woman.

Before the surgery, the nursing staff noted she was apprehensive, depressed, and anxious. Following the surgery Janet became even more agitated and withdrawn. Her physician, Dr. Connors, again fully answered her questions related to her hysterectomy. Janet, however, appeared very concerned and confused about her future, making statements such as, "No one will ever marry me now," "Life isn't worth living," "My family doesn't care about me; no one does," "Oh well, I'm going to die soon anyway." At this point, Dr. Connors asked Janet if she would be willing to discuss such concerns with the social worker at the hospital, Miss Vicki Vogel, and she indicated she would.

Miss Vogel met with Janet five of the remaining seven days that she was hospitalized. Janet had a number of problems, primarily involving planning for her future. She had alienated nearly all her relatives when at age 17 she quit school in her senior year and began living with her 20-year-old boyfriend. A year and one half later her boyfriend discovered she was having an affair with another man and angrily requested that she leave. She went to live with the other man and became rather heavily involved in drinking and experimenting with drugs. A year ago Janet left this man and moved to this area. She is now living with a divorcé.

Janet continued to have a number of questions related to her hysterectomy—"Would her sex life be changed?"; "Might the cancer reoccur?"; "Would the hysterectomy affect her future as a woman?"; "Can a person be orgasmic following a hysterectomy?" Miss Vogel attempted to provide some answers and also arranged for Debra Nass (a 32-year-old woman who had had a hysterectomy three and one half years ago) to talk with Janet. Although some uncertainty remained (for example, the possible recurrence of a malignancy), Janet became more comfortable about having undergone a hysterectomy after talking to Mrs. Nass.

Janet, however, had a number of questions that she felt she needed to look at. She wondered why when people were nice to her, she sometimes was "rotten" to them. For instance, she mentioned she had lived with two different men, and each time she continued to have sexual relationships with other men. She also wondered what the future held for her. She was not skilled at a trade or a profession and did not know what kind of a career, if any, she desired. She was very confused about what she wanted out of life and also admitted that she had occasional blackouts from heavy drinking.

These problems were briefly discussed with Miss Vogel. The focus of social services at this hospital, however, was limited to short-term, "crisis" counseling. Because these complicated problems indicated longer-term counseling was needed, Miss Vogel suggested, and Janet Ely agreed to, a referral to the mental health center in the area.

Several months later Miss Vogel heard from a friend of hers that Miss Ely had gotten engaged but had recently "on the spur of the moment" moved with another man to live on the West Coast.

In summary, the immediate psychological "crisis" situations surrounding the hysterectomy appear to have been resolved. However, problems still appear to remain in Janet's relationships with others.

Specialized clinics that focus on family planning, eating disorders, and alcohol and drug dependency have created new opportunities for social workers in the medical field.

The development of specialized clinics and programs for providing genetics counseling, providing abortion counseling, treating alcoholics, providing family planning, treating drug abusers, serving the terminally ill, treating those with eating disorders, providing services to persons with AIDS and to those who test positive to HIV, and providing services to rape victims have created new opportunities for social workers in the health field. Sometimes these programs are located in offices away from hospitals. Nursing homes for the elderly and for the physically impaired are also increasingly employing social workers.

One of the emerging fields of practice for social workers is combating AIDS. Social workers are getting involved in advocating to end AIDS discrimination; in providing counseling to those who are tested for HIV; and in providing services in hospitals, nursing homes, and hospices to those who have AIDS. Social workers have become case managers for many persons with AIDS. The case manager works with the person with AIDS, loved ones, providers of care, and payers to supply necessary health care; to make certain that pressing

medical, financial, social, and other needs are being met; and to ensure that the most cost-effective care possible is provided. In providing services to persons with AIDS the trend is to have more and more of the medical care being delivered outside the hospital or nursing home, often at home or in an outpatient clinic.[49]

There is also a trend for group medical clinics, individual practitioners, family practice clinics, and prepaid health clinics to employ social workers to be part of a team in diagnosing and treating patients. Increasingly, social workers in such settings are working with high-risk groups where they play a preventive as well as a therapeutic role. High-risk groups include teenage mothers, women requesting abortions, drug and alcohol abusers, persons undergoing organ transplants, severely depressed or highly anxious persons, persons under stress, persons attempting suicide, and amputees.

COUNSELING
THE TERMINALLY ILL

One of the most difficult tasks of doctors, nurses, social workers, and other allied professionals in the health field is to help a terminally ill patient deal with dying. Death is often a frightening event, and the fear of death is felt universally in all cultures. Material on counseling the terminally ill will briefly be presented to give the reader an experiential "feeling" of one of the most difficult counseling areas for health professionals.

Most people in our society die in a hospital. This setting, in itself, is one of the primary reasons that dying is so hard. Health professionals are committed to recovery, to healing. When someone is found to have a terminal illness, health professionals experience a sense of failure. In some cases health professionals may feel guilty that they cannot do more or that they might have made a mistake that contributed to the terminal illness. A fair number of health professionals are not comfortable in counseling the terminally ill. They feel

BOX 14.8

Five Stages of Dying that Terminally Ill People Typically Proceed Through

T he following stages have been found to be a valuable paradigm in understanding a terminally ill person's behavior:

Stage 1: Denial—"It can't be." "No, not me." "There must be a mistake." This is generally the first reaction when a person learns she or he has a terminal illness. Dr. Ross believes such a reaction is functional, since it helps cushion the impact that death will soon be inevitable.

Stage 2: Rage and anger—"Why me?" "Look at the good things I've done and still need to do for the members of my family." "This just isn't fair !" Patients resent the fact that they will soon die while others remain healthy and alive. God is frequently a special target of the anger during this stage, as He is viewed as unfairly imposing a death sentence. Dr. Ross believes such anger is permissible and inevitable, and she adds, "God can take it."

During this stage family and hospital staff frequently experience difficulty in coping with the anger that is displaced in many directions and onto the surroundings. The patient may charge that the doctor is incompetent, that the hospital surroundings are inhumane, that the nurses are unconcerned about people, that there is too much noise, and so on. The underlying reasons generating the patient's anger need to be remembered during this stage. Reacting personally or angrily to the patient's anger will only feed into the patient's hostile behavior. During this stage conveying to the patient that she or he is an important person who is worthy of respect, time, and understanding, will usually lead to a reduction of the angry demands.

Stage 3: Bargaining—"I realize my death is inevitable, but if I could just live six months more I could. . . ." During this stage patients come to accept their terminal illness but try to strike bargains (frequently with God) for more time. They promise to do something worthwhile or to be good in exchange for another month or year of life. Dr. Ross indicates that even agnostics and atheists sometimes attempt to bargain with God during this stage.

Psychologically, such promises may be associated with some underlying guilt. Frequently

---

insecure and do not know what to say or do. Often, they have not come to terms with their own mortality; that is, they have not come to see death as an integral part of their lives. If a professional person views death as a frightening, horrible, taboo topic, she or he will never be able to face it calmly and helpfully with a patient.

Dr. Elisabeth Kübler-Ross (perhaps the foremost authority on death and dying in our era) has identified five stages that terminally ill patients may go through.[50] These stages are not absolute; not everyone goes through every stage according to the sequence described in Box 14.8. (Some patients never advance beyond the first or second stage, and some patients vacillate back and forth from stage to stage.)

when such guilt exists it involves guilt for not attending church more regularly. It is helpful to have an interdisciplinary approach to counseling the terminally ill; in this stage it is often helpful to have a chaplain discuss such religious guilt with the patient.

Stage 4: Depression—"Yes, it will soon be over." "It's really sad, but true." The first phase of this stage is where the patient mourns things not done, past losses, and wrongs committed. This type of depression is frequently exacerbated by guilt or shame about acts of omission or commission. Counseling during this phase generally focuses on helping the patient to resolve feelings of guilt and shame; in some cases this may involve helping family members to make realistic plans for their future and to help the patient realize that other vital unfinished situations are being taken care of.

The second phase of this stage is where the patient enters a state of "preparatory grief," in which she or he is getting ready for the inevitable by taking into account impending losses. During this stage the patient should not be encouraged to look at the sunny side of things, as this would interfere with the necessity for the patient to contemplate his or her impending death. During this phase the patient generally becomes quiet and does not want to see visitors. The patient is in the process of losing everything and everybody she or he loves. If allowed to express this sorrow, the patient will find final acceptance of death much easier and will be grateful to those who are able to sit quietly with him or her, without telling him or her not to be sad. According to Dr. Ross, when a dying patient no longer continues to request to see someone to discuss his or her situation, it is a sign she or he has finished his or her unfinished business and has reached the final stage.

Stage 5: Acceptance—"I will soon pass on, and it's all right." Dr. Ross describes this final stage as "not a happy stage, but neither is it unhappy. It's devoid of feelings but it's not resignation, it's really a victory." During this stage visitors are often not desired because the patient no longer is in a talkative mood. Communications with a counselor may become more nonverbal than verbal. Patients may just want to hold the counselor's hand—to sit together in silence with someone who is comfortable in the presence of a dying person.

Sources: Elisabeth Kübler-Ross, *On Death and Dying* (New York: Macmillan, 1969), and Elisabeth Kübler-Ross, ed., *Death: The Final Stage of Growth* (Englewood Cliffs, NJ: Prentice-Hall, 1975).

The one thing that usually persists through all five stages is hope—hope for the discovery of an immediate "miracle" cure. Terminally ill patients all seem to have a little bit of it and are supported and nourished by it, especially during the most difficult times. With respect to hope, the desired direction in counseling is to be honest with the patient about the probable outcome, while allowing the patient to hope for the million-to-one chance of a miracle recovery.

To work with the terminally ill requires maturity, which comes only from experience. The most important communication is the "door-opening interview," in which the counselor conveys verbally and nonverbally to the dying patient that she or he is ready and willing to share the dying person's concerns without fear and anxiety. A prerequisite is that the counselor has an attitude toward his or her own death with which she or he is comfortable.

Mwalimu Imara views dying as having the potential for being the final stage of growth and gives a number of suggestions on how to come to terms with one's own dying.[51] Having a well-developed sense of identity (that is, sense of who you are) is an important step. (Chapter 2 in this text elaborates on how to develop a positive identity.) Involved in developing a sense of identity is arriving at realistic life goals that one will have pride in achieving. Without a blueprint of what will give meaning and direction to our lives, we will experience our lives as fragmented and aimless.

Imara indicates that the fifth stage of acceptance for a dying patient corresponds to a person with a healthy identity. A person who comes to accept a terminal illness has also arrived at a fairly well-thought-out, unified sense of himself or herself. Death is the final stage of growth for a terminally ill person: The patient finally develops a unified sense of self and accepts imminent death. It is hoped that people will develop a healthy identity long before the final crisis and thus be fairly prepared before the final crisis arises.

Imara adds that all of us experience separations and pains throughout life that lead to personal growth, for example, leaving family to attend kindergarten, leaving high school to seek work or attend college, leaving work and friends to seek a better position in a different geographical area, experiencing romantic and perhaps marital separations that it is hoped lead to personal growth. Imara indicates that "Abandoning old ways and breaking old patterns is like dying, at least dying to old ways of life for an unknown new life of meaning and relationships. But living without change is not living at all, not growing at all."[52] Imara adds that making changes in our lives also creates fears and anxieties in us. But if such changes lead to personal growth we will be prepared to face new challenges and new changes. Through a willingness to risk the unknown, we are undertaking the search of ourselves. Such separations and new challenges raise fears and anxieties that are analogous to those that will arise when we become aware our death is near. Overcoming fears and anxieties that arise from current challenges (and learning more about ourself through these experiences) prepares us for the fears and anxieties that will arise when we learn that our death is near.

SUMMARY

There are a number of problems with our health care system. In contrast to other industrialized countries in which health care is viewed as having a service orientation, the health care system in the United States has the dual (and sometimes conflicting) objectives of providing service and of making a profit. The system is indeed prospering. The United States is now spending substantially more on health care per capita than are other industrialized nations. Yet, a number of other countries have lower infant mortality rates and longer life expectancies than ours. Such statistics suggest that other countries are providing health care that is as good as (or better than) ours at a lower cost.

There are other problems in the health care system. The system is focused on treating people *after* they become ill, with little attention being given to preventing illnesses from occurring. It is increasingly being recognized that the lifestyles of people (including exercise, diet, sleep patterns, and stress-reaction patterns) largely determine whether illness will occur and also influence the recovery process when an illness does occur. People need to realize that they, and not their physicians, have the major responsibility for their own health.

The poor and racial minorities have higher rates of illnesses and shorter life expectancies for a variety of reasons. Largely because of the profit motive, low-income areas in cities and rural areas are generally underserved by health care services.

The profit motive has also led to unnecessary diagnostic and treatment approaches being used, including diagnostic tests, medication and drugs, and surgical operations. A more devastating problem is receiving harmful care. It is estimated that 10 percent of practicing physicians are incompetent.

Health care for the elderly is becoming a national disgrace. Many of the elderly lack access to quality care. Medical conditions of the elderly are often misdiagnosed, and treatment is often inadequate.

AIDS has emerged as a major health problem. The two primary ways in which it is transmitted from one person to another is through sexual contact and through sharing of intravenous needles. There are many misconceptions about AIDS that have led those who are identified as having HIV and those who have AIDS to be shunned and discriminated against.

The use of life-sustaining equipment has raised a number of questions. Should such equipment be used to prolong the life of someone who is terminally ill and in considerable pain? How should death be defined? Should society seek to keep alive people who are so severely and profoundly retarded that they will never be able to walk or even sit? Can society afford to continue to expand the use of such costly life-sustaining equipment?

The high costs of medical care, which are still rapidly increasing, have become an issue of national concern. Illnesses now can threaten a family's financial stability. The high costs are also a threat to the economic stability of our country. There are a variety of reasons why medical expenses are so high, including the profit-making focus, high costs of technological advances, increased life span of people, third-party financing, inadequate health care planning, increase in malpractice suits, and increased specialization by doctors.

A number of possibilities are available to resolve each of these problems. Some suggestions include increasing admissions to medical schools, permitting doctors to advertise their services and fees, training more physician assistants and paramedics, expanding use of generic drugs, encouraging patients to seek a second opinion before consenting to an operation, developing more preventive medical programs, expanding the use of health maintenance organizations, and developing a national health insurance program.

Health care is a secondary setting for social work. In such a setting social workers are generally a member of a team, and need to learn to work with those in charge. A medical treatment team is increasingly dependent on social workers to attend to sociopsychological factors that are either contributing causes of illnesses or side effects of a medical condition that must be dealt with to facilitate recovery. As a member of a medical team social workers have an important role in diagnosing and treating medical conditions.

A social worker in the health field needs skills and knowledge on how to counsel people with a wide variety of medical conditions. Some, such as counseling the terminally ill, require a high level of emotional maturity, a well-thought-out identity, and a high level of competence in counseling.

NOTES

1. Joseph Julian, *Social Problems,* 3d ed. (Englewood Cliffs, NJ: Prentice-Hall, 1980), p. 25.
2. Richard Nixon, "Health Message of 1971," February 18, 1971, White House.
3. Julian, *Social Problems,* pp. 23–38.
4. U.S. Bureau of the Census, *Statistical Abstract of the United States, 1987* (Washington, D.C.: U.S. Government Printing Office, 1987), p. 822.
5. Ibid., p. 820.
6. Joseph Julian and William Kornblum, *Social Problems,* 5th ed. (Englewood Cliffs, NJ: Prentice-Hall, 1986), pp. 28–39.
7. Quoted in John A. Denton, *Medical Sociology* (Boston: Houghton-Mifflin, 1978), p. 65.
8. "Doctors' Income Nears $120,000, says AMA," *Wisconsin State Journal,* November 21, 1987, sec. 2, p. 8.
9. U.S. Bureau of the Census, *Statistical Abstract of the United States, 1987,* p. 96.
10. Ibid., p. 85.
11. Ian Robertson, *Social Problems,* 2d ed. (New York: Random House, 1980), p. 318.
12. K. R. Pelletier, *Mind As Healer, Mind as Slayer* (New York: Delta, 1977).
13. Thomas McKeown, "Determinants of Health," *Human Nature* 1 (April 1978), p. 66.
14. Aaron Antonovsky, "Class and the Chance for Life," in *Inequality and Justice,* ed. Lee Rainwater (Chicago: Aldine Publishing, 1974), p. 177.
15. U.S. Bureau of the Census, *Statistical Abstract of the United States, 1987,* p. 69.

16. Ibid., p. 74.

17. Max Seham, *Blacks and American Medical Care* (Minneapolis: University of Minnesota Press, 1973), p. 10.

18. *Source Book of Health Insurance Data, 1977–1978* (Washington, D.C.: Health Insurance Institute); and S. Leonard Syme and Lisa Berkman, "Social Class, Susceptibility, and Sickness," *American Journal of Epidemiology* 104 (July 1976), pp. 1–8.

19. Seham, *Blacks and American Medical Care,* p. 20.

20. Ibid., pp. 22–23.

21. Lee Rainwater, ed., *Social Problems and Public Policy: Inequality and Justice* (Chicago: Aldine Publishing, 1974).

22. "Growing Old in America," ABC News Program Transcript (New York: Journal Graphics Inc., December 28, 1985).

23. Ibid., p. 11.

24. Ibid.

25. Ibid.

26. C. Everett Koop, *Surgeon General's Report on Acquired Immune Deficiency Syndrome* (Washington, D.C.: U.S. Department of Health and Human Services, 1987), p. 22.

27. Ibid., p. 27.

28. "Incompetent Surgery is Found Not Isolated," *New York Times,* January 27, 1976, p. 1.

29. Barbara Ehrenreich and John Ehrenreich, *The American Health Empire: Power Profits and Politics* (New York: Vintage Books, 1971), pp. 14–16.

30. Julian and Kornblum, *Social Problems,* p. 36.

31. Paul B. Horton, Gerald R. Leslie, and Richard F. Larson, *The Sociology of Social Problems,* 8th ed. (Englewood Cliffs, NJ: Prentice-Hall, 1985), p. 373.

32. Spencer Klaw, *The Great American Medicine Show* (New York: Viking Press, 1975).

33. Walter A. Friedlander and Robert Z. Apte, *Introduction to Social Welfare,* 4th ed. (Englewood Cliffs, NJ: Prentice-Hall, 1974), p. 414.

34. Robertson, *Social Problems,* p. 32.

35. U.S. Bureau of the Census, *Statistical Abstract of the United States, 1987,* p. 91.

36. Julian and Kornblum, *Social Problems,* p. 32.

37. U.S. Bureau of the Census, *Statistical Abstract of the United States, 1987,* p. 86.

38. Jennifer B. Hull, "Growing Number in U.S. Lack Health Insurance as Companies, Public Agencies Seek to Cut Costs," *The Wall Street Journal,* June 3, 1986, p. 54.

39. Ibid.

40. Robertson, *Social Problems,* p. 307.

41. Ehrenreich and Ehrenreich, *The American Health Empire,* pp. 130–132.

42. Victor W. Sidel, "Medical Care in the People's Republic of China: An Example of Rationality," in Howard D. Schwartz and Cary S. Kart, *Dominant Issues in Medical Sociology* (Reading, MA: Addison-Wesley, 1978), p. 385.

43. *Towards a Comprehensive Health Policy for the 1970's: A White Paper* (Washington, D.C.: U.S. Department of Health, Education and Welfare, May, 1971), pp. 31–32.

44. Julian and Kornblum, *Social Problems,* p. 45.

45. Clemens P. Work, "Health, Wealth, and Competition," *U.S. News & World Report,* November 10, 1986, p. 59.

46. Ibid., pp. 59–60.

47. Julian and Kornblum, *Social Problems,* p. 45.

48. Donald Brieland, Lela B. Costin, and Charles R. Atherton, *Contemporary Social Work* (New York: McGraw-Hill, 1975), p. 123.

49. Susan Dentzer, "Why AIDS Won't Bankrupt Us," *U.S. News & World Report,* January 18, 1988, pp. 20–21.

50. Elisabeth Kübler-Ross, *On Death and Dying* (New York: Macmillan, 1969).

51. Mwalimu Imara, "Dying as the Last Stage of Growth," in *Death: The Final Stage of Growth,* ed. Elisabeth Kübler-Ross (Englewood Cliffs, NJ: Prentice-Hall, 1975), pp. 147–163.

52. Ibid., p. 148.

15

PHYSICAL AND MENTAL DISABILITIES AND REHABILITATION

There are over 50 million people with disabilities in the United States—nearly one out of four persons.[1] People with disabilities include:

- Those who are temporarily injured (severe burns, injuries to back or spine, broken limbs).

- Those who have a chronic physical disability (including people who use canes, crutches, walkers, braces, or wheelchairs; the mobility-impaired elderly; and people with illnesses such as severe cardiovascular disorder, cerebral palsy, chronic arthritis, and AIDS).

- Those who are hearing impaired or deaf.

- Those who are visually impaired or blind.

- Those who have a mental disability (including those who have an emotional disorder, are retarded, or have a severe learning disability).[2]

This chapter will:

- Provide a brief history of rehabilitation practices and of how different cultures have treated the disabled.

- Describe different levels of mental retardation and summarize the causes.

- Discuss our society's reactions to disabilities.

- Identify current services for the disabled.

- Summarize the roles of social workers in working with disabled clients and their families.

HISTORY OF REHABILITATION PRACTICES

Society's willingness to tend to the needs of those impaired has been determined largely by the perceived causes of the impairments, the existing medical knowledge, and the general economic conditions. Ancient and modern religious faiths (including Christians) have at times been an aid and at other times a detriment to viewing those with disabilities as "people." Attitudes have ranged from viewing those with disabilities as being possessed by demons to viewing them as being saint-like, with the community having a responsibility to care for them.

When the early Greek civilization prospered a few thousand years ago, the Greeks had the philosophy of the unity of body and soul, with a blemish on one signifying a blemish on the other.[3] This philosophy led to a negative attitude toward those with disabilities, with the extreme implication of this doctrine being found in Sparta, where "the immature, the weak, and the damaged were eliminated purposefully."[4] Centuries later in Rome, the Romans also put to death some people with disabilities who were considered "unproductive."[5] In ancient history there were almost no organized efforts to meet the needs of the mentally retarded. In early Greece and during the reign of the Roman Empire, mental illness was seen as being due to demons entering the body, with exorcism being the primary treatment.[6]

During the Middle Ages, disabilities were either seen as the result of demonic possession or as God's punishment.[7] Modern Christian values of charity and humanitarian treatment were generally absent during this period, partly as a result of poor economic conditions. About the only employment for those with disabilities provided by feudal lords was that of court jester, a position considered suitable for the mentally retarded and for the physically disabled.[8] The mentally ill continued to be viewed as being possessed by demons, and cruelty was advocated and used to punish and drive out the demons.

The Elizabethan English Poor Laws of 1601 provided financial support for the involuntary unemployed (including the handicapped). These Poor Laws were the first major secular-based relief effort for the poor and the handicapped.[9]

In early colonial America, conditions were not yet suitable for the development of rehabilitation programs, as the colonists were barely able to earn a living from the soil and because disability was viewed as the result of God's punishment.[10]

In the 19th century gradual recognition was given to the needs of the disabled in the United States. A few of the efforts to develop programs will be mentioned.

Thomas Gallaudet opened the first school for educating the deaf in this country in 1817 in Hartford, Connecticut.[11] Gallaudet demonstrated that the deaf could be taught to read and speak, which led to the opening of other schools for the deaf. The first school for the blind was opened in 1832 in Massachusetts.[12] The first sheltered-type work situation for the employment of the blind was established in 1850 in Massachusetts.[13]

Mental retardation, before and during the early part of the 19th century, was thought to be inherited and therefore incurable.[14] In the first half of the 19th century most of the mentally retarded "were relegated to lunatic asylums, poorhouses, almshouses, or local jails."[15] Interest in providing services to the retarded began in France, especially after the physician Jean Itard made considerable progress over a five-year period in the early 1800s in educating a 12-year-old "wolf child" found in a forest, who was diagnosed as severely retarded. When found, the child was unsocialized and walked on all fours.[16] The philosophy of providing services to the retarded gradually spread to this country. In 1848 the first residential school for the retarded was opened in Barge, Massachusetts.[17] Unfortunately, the orientation toward the retarded during the latter half of the 19th century switched from one of education and training to one of custodial care. A major reason for this change was the popularity of social Darwinism, which asserted that it was far better for society to allow the poor and the weak to perish rather than to sustain their existence and encourage their multiplication through government-supported programs.[18] The mentally retarded were viewed as having defective genetic strains, and as a result sterilization was extensively used at the end of the 19th century.[19]

The first mental hospitals for the mentally ill were built in this country in the 1850s and 1860s.[20] Before this time Dorothea Dix had visited many locations documenting that the mentally ill were either kept "out of sight" in the homes of their families or confined in almshouses and local jails.[21] It should be noted that the living conditions of almshouses and mental hospitals were deplorable and would make even our worst present-day prisons and jails look like country clubs in comparison.

One of the earliest attempts to meet the needs of the disabled occurred in 1817 when Thomas Hopkins Gallaudet founded the first school for deaf children in the United States. Today hearing-impaired students from around the world attend Gallaudet University in Washington, D.C. (above). In 1988 the board of trustees elected the first deaf president in the college's history.

The physically disabled, until the latter half of the 19th century, were either taken care of by their family or placed in almshouses. Toward the end of the 19th century the disabled first began to benefit from medical advances–antiseptic surgery, orthopedic surgery, heat and water therapy, use of braces, and exercise programs.[22] Near the end of the 19th century public funds began to be used for the education and training of children with handicaps.[23]

The charity organization movement during the latter part of the 19th century created a structure not only for future social work practices but also for vocational rehabilitation casework.[24] These early organizations had a rehabilitation rather than a maintenance focus. The movement also advocated extensive investigation of each case and the use of individualized treatment determined by the needs of each client. Unfortunately, the volunteers who provided the services of the charity organization movement operated from the premise that the causes of poverty and having a handicap had

moral roots, and that the primary way to be helped was through spiritual means.[25]

During the late 19th and early 20th centuries, few precautions were taken by industries to improve worker safety. As a result a large number of people suffered impairments from poor working conditions and industrial accidents. To meet the tolls being taken by the Industrial Revolution, the first worker's compensation law was passed in 1910 in New York.[26]

In the early 20th century large numbers of unskilled rural youths began flocking to cities seeking employment. There were also increasing numbers of dislocated industrial workers who needed retraining. Therefore, the federal government, in 1917, passed the Smith-Hughes Act, which made federal monies available for vocational education programs and also created the Federal Board of Vocational Education.[27] The next year (1918) the Soldier's Rehabilitation Act was passed, which was a program designed to rehabilitate veterans who had a disability.[28]

The federal Social Security Act of 1935 established the permanency of rehabilitation programs and established public assistance programs for the blind and for the disabled. The Barden-LaFollette Act of 1943 extended rehabilitation services to the mentally ill and to the mentally retarded.[29]

During World War II there was a severe labor shortage, which provided work opportunities to people with disabilities. In these positions people with disabilities demonstrated to thousands of employers that if placed in an appropriate job, they could perform well. This growing realization led in 1945 to the establishment of the President's Committee on Employment of the Handicapped.[30]

After World War II there were a number of federal programs passed that underscored society's growing belief that those with impairments could be productive workers and should be given the opportunities and training to demonstrate their work capacities.[31]

Spurred by the civil rights movement in the 1950s and 1960s, a new minority group began to be heard in the late 1960s and in the 1970s. Persons with physical disabilities began speaking out, marching forth, and demanding equal rights. They have been seeking

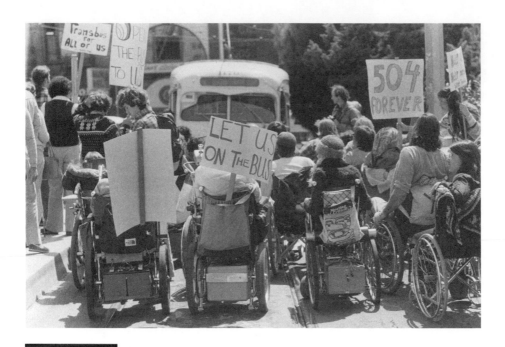

In the last two decades, the physically disabled have been actively demanding equal rights. These demonstrators, fighting for equal access to mass transit, block buses during rush hour in San Francisco.

(including through legislation and lawsuits) an end to job discrimination, limited educational opportunities, architectural barriers, and societal discrimination. In 1973 Congress passed the Vocational Rehabilitation Act, one section of which prohibits discrimination against the handicapped by any program or organization receiving federal funds. Included in this nondiscriminatory policy is an affirmative action policy (described in Chapter 11) in which employers who receive federal funds must demonstrate extensive efforts to hire those with impairments.

The 20th century has seen the development of numerous programs and technological advances to help the physically impaired, the temporarily injured, the deaf and the hearing impaired, the blind and the visually impaired, the mentally impaired, and those with chronic health disorders. Yet, as will be discussed, much remains to be done in changing society's atti-

tudes toward the impaired and in helping them to live satisfying and productive lives. Increasingly, people with impairments are receiving improved services that facilitate the development of their capacities.

OVERVIEW OF MENTAL RETARDATION*

There is considerable public misunderstanding about the nature and causes of mental retardation. Because

---

*This section was written by Maureen O'Gorman Foster, who was a social worker at Central Wisconsin Center for the Developmentally Disabled, a residential treatment center for the retarded. Ms. Foster is currently the director of a hospice program.

BOX 15.1

Impaired People Are Now Making It to the Top in Many Careers

Criss Cole is a judge in Houston, Texas and is blind.

Dana Wakefield is a juvenile-court judge in Denver and is blind.

W. Mitchell is mayor of Crested Butte, Colorado and is a paraplegic.

Phyllis Frelich won the Tony Award as the best Broadway actress in 1980 and is deaf.

S. Craig Kiser is chief counsel for Florida's Department of Banking and Finance and is blind.

Shirley K. Price is an employment executive at the Johnson Space Center in Houston and is a dwarf with no arms.

Max Cleland heads the U.S. Veterans Administration Department and lost his legs and one arm in Vietnam. Similar to a growing number of other people who are impaired, he drives his car to work, travels widely, and participates in sports.

Source: "For Disabled, Jobs Few—But Many Make It," *U.S. News & World Report*, September 8, 1980, p. 45.

social workers are highly involved in providing services to those who are retarded, this section will summarize material on the nature and causes of retardation.

Definition of Terms

There is no single area of human services and human service delivery systems that has taken such giant steps during the past thirty years as that of mental retardation. Within the memory of many of us in the field, words like *imbecile, moron,* and *idiot* were used to describe those individuals who were generally classified as "feeble-minded." These terms perpetuated elements of fear and mystery among the general public because of their connotations.

For the past century the American Association on Mental Deficiency (AAMD) has been active in diminishing public ignorance and establishing a system of classification of the retarded for use by professionals.

Terms have been adopted to describe the approximate level of intellectual and adaptive behavior. AAMD defines *mental retardation* as referring to "significantly subaverage general intellectual functioning existing concurrently with deficits in adaptive behavior and manifested during the developmental period."[32] Roughly, the terms now used give an idea of the intellectual and adaptive functioning of the individuals as determined by use of the standardized IQ tests and an assessment of the appropriateness of behavior according to age level. The terms and the scores used to make this determination on the basis of the Stanford-Binet and Cattell IQ tests are as follows:

Mild: 68 to 52

Moderate: 51 to 36

Severe: 35 to 20

Profound: 19 and below

Before 1973 the term *borderline retarded* was used to describe those individuals whose IQs were one to two standard deviations (IQ from 70 to 80) from the

Special Olympics games foster pride and self-worth for developmentally disabled children.

to determine intellectual and adaptive functioning. These determinations are limiting insofar as they say nothing about the etiology or prognosis of the individual tested, yet they do serve as a general guideline to social workers and other professionals in programming and planning.

Another term recently adapted for use is *developmental disability*. This term is more inclusive than mental retardation because it includes disabilities attributable to cerebral palsy, epilepsy, or other neurological conditions closely related to mental retardation or requiring treatment similar to mental retardation. As in the definition of mental retardation, these disbilities are limited to those that occur in the developmental period (below age 18), and that can be expected to continue to constitute a substantial handicap to the individual. The use of this broader term in recent legislation has made it possible to have this group considered eligible for services provided for in legislation for the retarded.[33]

Nature and Etiology of Retardation

An entire volume would be needed to describe the various causes of retardation adequately. Time and place necessitate a brief summary of the causes under the general categories suggested by AAMD. Examples will be given to assist the reader in placing those disorders such as Down's syndrome (mongolism) and phenylketonuria (PKU) with which most of the general public are familiar. The discussion will include new services and tests that have reduced the risks of mental retardation and that all social workers should be aware of in dealing with clients in every area of social service.

MENTAL RETARDATION AND GESTATIONAL DISORDERS Many infants born prematurely (before 37 weeks' gestation) or during what is considered the postmaturity period (generally more than seven days after the normal pregnancy period) are considered to be at increased risk for being mentally retarded. Specialized clinics for mothers who are known to be at increased

normal. This group has been dropped from the definition of mental retardation by including the words "substantially subaverage." The current thinking is that these individuals should be referred to as persons with "borderline intelligence."

The determination of the intellectual functioning of the retarded is made by a professional person trained in the administration of the tests necessary

risk for premature or postmature delivery are now available in many large metropolitan areas and are complemented by neonatal intensive care units for the infant. These reduce the risk of neurological damage as a result of gestational problems by providing teams of highly trained specialists and advanced equipment and testing devices.

TRAUMA OR PHYSICAL AGENT   Injury to the brain can occur at any time in the prenatal, perinatal, or postnatal development. If the brain is deprived of oxygen (anoxia) or receives an amount of oxygen insufficient to maintain functioning of the brain tissue (hypoxia), then brain cells will be destroyed and mental retardation may result. In the prenatal and perinatal period this can occur for a number of reasons, including premature separation of the placenta, knotted umbilical cord, or difficult birth as a result of breech position, to name a few. Postnatal damage from trauma can occur from so many causes that to dwell on them would make most parents tremble with fear. In my experience alone, I have seen children severely damaged as a result of battering by a parent or caretaker; child victims of near drowning in everything from a pail to a pond; and children who suffered trauma from football accidents, car and bicycle accidents, and accidents involving sleds, go-carts, horses, and motorbikes.

INFECTIONS AND INTOXICATIONS   Mental retardation following prenatal infection and intoxication is the result of such diseases and conditions as:

Rubella   Pregnant women who have a clinical or subclinical case of German measles during their first trimester of pregnancy have a substantially increased risk of having a child who is retarded and who has other congenital abnormalities such as blindness, deafness, microcephaly, and heart anomalies. Mass immunization programs during the last ten years protect the generation of childbearing women of the future and provide some protection to women now in their childbearing years by reducing the source of infection. Blood tests are available to determine the level of protection a woman has against the virus so that she can become immunized before pregnancy. Public

awareness and immunization may possibly make this cause a matter for historical consideration in the next twenty years.

Syphilis   This condition occurs from the infection of the fetus through the placenta. The results can be devastating and include many physical and behavioral problems in addition to mental retardation. To the extent that the services and treatment for venereal diseases are used, this cause of mental retardation might also be eradicated.

Other viral infections are known to be contributing causes of retardation. For example, in the 1980s our society recognized that HIV, the AIDS virus, can cause mental retardation in children born to infected mothers and that it may lead to brain deterioration in infected older children and adults.

Toxemia and Other Prenatal Influences   Although strides have been made in determining the conditions under which an unborn child might be affected by the mother's general health, there are far too many unanswered questions about the cause-effect relationship.

Toxemia is a condition associated with the presence of toxic (that is, poisonous) substances in the blood. In addition to posing a risk for the pregnant woman, this condition can pose a risk for the unborn infant if prolonged and untreated. Any woman getting early, regular, and specialized care during pregnancy can avoid the effects of toxic poisoning; screening for toxemia is a regular part of all prenatal care.

Drug Intoxication   Use of drugs during pregnancy should be limited to those prescribed by a physician. Many of the medications used in medical practice are harmful to the fetus.

Alcohol   The most serious risk to the developing fetus is the fetal alcohol syndrome (FAS). This syndrome is associated with heavy drinking, generally considered to be five or six drinks on occasion. FAS is characterized by cranial and facial abnormalities, joint and limb anomalies, possible cardiac defects, and delayed physical and mental development. Binge drinking and regular social drinking have been associated with decreased weight of the fetus, increased risk of still-birth, and increased risk of anomalies and behavioral deficits in the newborn.[34]

Maternal Conditions Other than Above   Generally, any mother who is a diabetic or has other metabolic conditions has an increased risk of having a retarded child.

Postnatal Cerebral Infection   Bacterial and viral infections such as meningitis and encephalitis can cause severe and irreversible brain damage, especially if not treated in the early stages of illness.

DISORDERS RELATED TO METABOLISM OR NUTRITION Included in this category are disorders of amino acid metabolism, such as phenylketonuria, and many disorders of lipids and carbohydrates. Retardation due to phenylketonuria has been greatly reduced because of mandatory infant screening through blood tests in the neonatal period. Careful dietary programs have prevented or diminished the severe effects of this condition. The lipid storage disorders are less well known but include Tay-Sachs disease, and Hunter's and Hurler's syndromes. These involve a progressive degenerative process because of the accumulation of fatty substances in the cells, that is, "storage" eventually leading to the death of the affected individual. These conditions are inherited, and although little is known about effective treatment, the incidence can be greatly reduced through genetic counseling programs and prenatal diagnosis. Also included in this general category are the disorders of endocrine function such as cretinism and the carbohydrate disorders.

DISORDERS OF UNKNOWN PRENATAL INFLUENCE   Conditions such as hydrocephalus and microcephalus fall under this category. Microcephalus refers to the reduced circumference of the head. As a primary condition this disorder might be inherited as a recessive characteristic or might be secondary to fetal or neonatal brain damage. Hydrocephalus refers to a condition in which there is an increased amount of cerebrospinal fluid within the skull, usually causing an enlargement of the skull. Great strides have been made in diminishing the retardation resulting from hydrocephalus

through neurosurgical techniques that prevent brain damage by decreasing the pressure that causes brain damage. Spina bifida means an incomplete formation of the spinal column. This condition may or may not be accompanied by hydrocephalus; if nervous tissue herniates through the defect it is called meningomyelocele and can cause paralysis in varying degrees.

MENTAL RETARDATION ASSOCIATED WITH CHROMOSOME ABNORMALITIES   Down's syndrome is the most common and best known of the disorders in this category. This condition, in which there exists an extra chromosome in the pair of number 21 chromosome, occurs in children born to mothers of all ages. The incidence, however, in mothers over age 35 is substantially higher than in the general population (1 in 150 births for mothers over 35). Ordinarily, diagnosis is made in the immediate neonatal period. These children bear a striking resemblance to one another. Intelligence range is from moderate to severe. Other chromosomal abnormalities can occur in either structure or number of many other chromosomes. Through a test called amniocentesis, prenatal detection of Down's syndrome and other conditions that involve chromosome defects and some metabolic disorders is possible. Although some small risk of miscarriage is involved, amniocentesis is a fairly simple procedure. A needle is inserted through the uterus, and amniotic fluid is extracted for chromosome or chemical studies. The procedure should be performed in the first trimester of pregnancy if the mother is known to be at risk for having a child with a specific chromosome or metabolic condition. This same test may be used to detect anencephaly and meningomyelocele and later in pregnancy, usually the last trimester, to determine maturation of the fetus. This is indicated if the mother has a complicated medical or gestational history.

A new test called chorionic villi sampling (CVS) has recently been developed to help determine if fetuses are normal. The test can be performed in a physician's office as early as the fifth week of gestation (which is several weeks earlier than the time in which amniocentesis can first be used). CVS is painless, is relatively simple to perform, and is a viable alternative to amniocentesis.

ENVIRONMENTAL INFLUENCES   There are a number of individuals whose functioning is impaired by adverse environmental factors and a lack of sufficient stimuli. In the past these cases were referred to as the cultural-familial type. They are likely to occur in economically deprived families or in families where either or both parents are themselves impaired in their intellectual and adaptive development. The cause is probably multiple—a combination of genetic, inherited factors compounded by environmental influences such as poor prenatal care, malnutrition, frequent accidents, infections, lack of discipline, poor health habits, and lack of stimulation.

After reading the above survey of causes the temptation is to think that with all the possibilities of having a retarded child, it is impossible to believe that one could have a baby who is normal and healthy and stays that way through the entire developmental period. The risk of having a retarded child is low, and every prospective parent should approach parenthood with optimism. In fact, each parent does just that. Each person reading this chapter is assuming either consciously or subconsciously that the percentage of retarded children born in this generation will be born to someone other than themselves. Most likely each of the parents of retarded children I have dealt with thought the same thing. Other than retardation of the cultural-familial origin, the problems we have discussed have no respect for educational level, social status, or good intentions of the parents. Although precautions can be taken to decrease the chances of retardation, it can and does occur every day in families in which early and excellent prenatal care was sought, in which the mother stayed away from all agents known or suspected to be toxic, in which no illness occurred during the gestational period, and in which the birth was uncomplicated.

SOCIETY'S REACTIONS TO DISABILITIES

Our culture places a high value on having a beautiful body. There are a number of physical fitness health clubs, and Americans spend large proportions of their budgets on clothes, cosmetics, exercise programs, and special diets to look more attractive. Beauty is identified with goodness and physical ugliness with evil. Movies, television, and books portray heroes and heroines as being physically attractive and villains as being ugly. Snow White, for example, was beautiful, whereas the evil witch was ugly. Children are erroneously taught that being physically attractive will lead to the good life, whereas having unattractive features is a sign of being inferior. Richardson found that young children rated people with disabilities as being "less desirable" than people without impairments.[35]

Unfortunately, this emphasis on the body beautiful has caused those with impairments to be the object of cruel jokes and has occasionally led to the disabled either being shunned or treated as inferior. According to C. H. Cooley, if the impaired are related to as if they are inferior, second-class citizens, they are apt to come to view themselves as inferior and to have a negative self-concept.[36] Our society needs to reassess its values about the perfect physique. It would seem that other traits ought to weight more—honesty, integrity, pleasant personalty, responsibleness, kindness, and helpfulness.

Wright has noted that the emphasis on the body beautiful has also led society to believe that the impaired "ought" to feel inferior.[37] Wright has coined the term *the requirement of mourning* for this expectation of society. An able-bodied person who spends a great deal of time, money, and effort to be physically attractive psychologically wants an impaired person to mourn the impairment because the able-bodied person needs feedback that it is worthwhile and important to strive to have an attractive physique.

Another consequence of the "body beautiful" cult is that disabled persons are sometimes pitied as being less fortunate and given sympathy. Many of the impaired decry receiving pity and being patronized. They seek to be treated as equals.

There is also a tendency in our society to conclude that because a person is handicapped in one area, they are also handicapped in other areas. Nancy Weinberg has noted that people talk louder in the presence of someone who is blind, as it is erroneously assumed that people who cannot see also have hearing problems.[38] People with physical impairments are also erroneously assumed at times to be mentally and socially retarded. A 22-year-old college student in a wheelchair describes one example of this tendency.

I'm in church with my father and my father is standing beside me and I'm in a wheelchair. I'm relatively intelligent, but I'm disabled. I'm sitting there like anyone else. And somebody comes up to my father and they're about as far away from me as from him and they say to my father, "How's he doing?" "Well he's looking pretty good." And I just want to kick him in the stomach.[39]

Unfortunately, relating to the impaired as if they are socially and mentally retarded may lead the impaired to believe they are less intelligent and less effective in social interactions.

Studies have found that people end interactions sooner with impaired people than with nonimpaired people.[40] Many people are uncomfortable when an impaired person is near because they are uncertain about what is appropriate and inappropriate to say. They fear saying something that may offend the impaired person. They do not want to make any direct remarks about the disabling condition. Yet if they try to ignore the disability they may make impossible demands on the impaired person (for example, conversing while moving along a hallway with a person in a wheelchair and then being confronted by a flight of stairs). People show their discomfort in a variety of ways—abrupt and superficial conversations, fixed stares away from the impaired person, compulsive talking, or an artificial seriousness. Impaired people are sensitive to such artificial interactions. Fred David describes a set of encounters about these interactional strains.

I get suspicious when somebody says, "Let's go for a uh, ah [imitates confused and halting speech] push with me down the hall," or something like that. This to me is suspicious because it means that they're aware, really aware, that there's a wheelchair here, and that this is probably uppermost with them. . . . A lot of people in trying to show you that they don't care that you're in a chair will do crazy things. Oh, there's one

person I know who constantly kicks my chair, as if to say "I don't care that you're in a wheelchair. I don't even know that it's there." But that is just an indication that he really knows it's there.[41]

Impaired people detest being treated as socially different simply because they have a physical impairment.

CURRENT SERVICES

There are a number of programs (some of which are federally funded and administered at state or local levels) that provide funds and services to the disabled. A few of these programs will be briefly described.

Sheltered Workshops

These workshops provide a variety of services that generally include vocational evaluation, sheltered employment, work adjustment, counseling services, and placement services. Each of these services will be briefly described.

VOCATIONAL EVALUATION   Clients are assessed on the basis of work behavior, physical capacities, social interaction, psychological functioning, and vocational goals and interests. Emphasis is placed on identifying the client's vocational assets and limitations.

SHELTERED EMPLOYMENT   A work environment is provided for individuals unable to secure immediately or maintain jobs in the community. Clients are paid (often below the minimum wage level) for work produced. Work tasks consist of various subcontract jobs from industries in the community that allow for long-term vocational development and possible placement into competitive employment. There is periodic evaluation of clients' progress in meeting rehabilitation objectives to ensure maximum vocational and personal development.

WORK ADJUSTMENT TRAINING   Vocational training experiences are provided to clients who are not yet ready for competitive employment following their initial vocational evaluation. The program is conducted in a work setting, using various types of subcontract jobs secured from industries in the community. The work is used to train individuals in developing good work skills and appropriate behavior on the job. Counselors are available to discuss problems, to assist in learning new tasks, and to help develop better work habits.

COUNSELING SERVICES   Counseling services include individual, group, parent, and vocational guidance. Individual counseling stresses treatment goals applied to mutually determined problem areas. Group counseling focuses on the stimulation of peer interaction and development of social skills. Parent counseling acquaints parents with treatment objectives, thus providing support for the total rehabilitation objectives in the home. Exposure to the work world, development of job-seeking skills, and identification of realistic goals are the major emphases of vocational counseling.

PLACEMENT SERVICES   This program assists clients in securing competitive employment. Clients' work habits and skills are first assessed. Then clients receive training in the proper skills for job seeking, applying for a job, and holding a job. Counselors then seek, together with clients, to place the clients with local employers. After placement, contact is maintained for a period of time to handle work adjustment problems that may arise.

Educational Programs

Historically, many public schools either refused to serve the severely impaired or segregated them in special programs. In 1975 Congress enacted the Education for All Handicapped Children Act. This statute mandates that all local school districts must provide full and appropriate educational opportunities to all impaired children. An individualized educational program designed to meet the unique needs of each impaired child must be developed to provide instruc-

tion in the least restrictive environment that is feasible. The intent is to "mainstream" each impaired child so that each can participate as much as possible in regular educational programs. Most school districts now have "special education programs" designed to meet the educational needs of the retarded, the emotionally disturbed, those with learning disabilities, and the physically handicapped. Most states have schools for the hearing impaired, and schools for the visually impaired. Often these specialized schools also provide statewide consultation for young children.

Residential Programs

GROUP HOMES, HALFWAY HOUSES, AND NURSING HOMES There are a number of these facilities that provide living arrangements for the mentally retarded, emotionally disturbed, and physically impaired who for a variety of reasons are unable to live with their parents.

RESIDENTIAL TREATMENT CENTERS   There are a variety of treatment centers that provide residential care and treatment, such as mental hospitals, residential treatment centers for the emotionally disturbed, and developmental training centers for the mentally retarded. Average length of stay varies between facilities and may range from several days to permanent care. Some of these residential facilities also serve clients on an outpatient basis, providing diagnostic, evaluative, and planning services.

DAY-CARE CENTERS   These centers provide day-care services to the retarded, emotionally disturbed, or physically impaired. The centers not only serve to give the parents some free time but also provide training in the areas of self-help, socialization, homemaking, communication, and leisure-time activities.

HOSPITAL SERVICES   Hospitals provide a variety of rehabilitation services for the impaired, such as medical services, physical therapy, and speech therapy. For those who are severely injured or have a serious chronic illness, hospitals are often the entry point into the rehabilitation system.

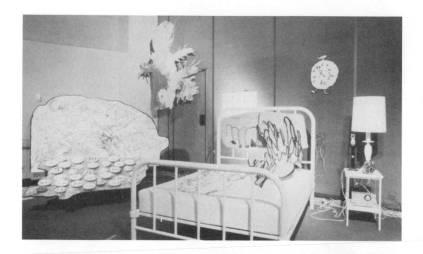

We assume too quickly that one kind of disability necessarily signals others. Artists Unlimited, a Seattle-based arts organization that offers professional development opportunities for physically disabled adults, proves otherwise. At a recent arts festival it mounted "A Home Is not Always a House," a collaborative exhibition representing the work of twenty-nine disabled artists. Highlights from the show included Call Light Lottery *and* The Bed *(top) and* Flying Wheelchair *and* Marionettes *(center). At bottom, artist John Norman works in Artists Unlimited's studios.*

Home Services

MEALS ON WHEELS   This program provides hot and cold meals to housebound recipients who are incapable of obtaining or preparing their own meals but who can feed themselves.

HOME HEALTH SERVICES   Services provided under such programs include visiting nurse services, drugs, physical therapy, laboratory services, and sickroom equipment.

HOMEMAKER SERVICES   In some communities homemakers are available to take care of household tasks that the impaired are unable to do for themselves.

Federal Assistance Programs

VOCATIONAL REHABILITATION FUNDING   Federal funding for rehabilitation programs has gradually evolved in this country. Two of the key statutes were the Vocational Rehabilitation Act Amendments of 1954 and the Rehabilitation Act of 1973.[42] At present, there are federal matching funds available to states for basic rehabilitation programs at the matching rate of 80 percent federal and 20 percent state. Individuals are eligible for vocational rehabilitation services if they have a mental or physical disability that substantially interferes with their ability to obtain employment and if there is a reasonable expectation that services will enable them to obtain employment. Potential clients receive medical testing free of charge to assess the extent of their disability and to check their overall health. Rehabilitation counselors employed by the state review these results. Applicants found eligible may then receive, at state and federal expense, a variety of services.

- Special equipment, such as hearing aids, guide dogs, wheelchairs, canes, or prosthetics.
- Special training in such areas as sign language, vocational training, reading, or social adjustment. This training may take place at a sheltered workshop, vocational school, public or private college, or on the job.
- Money for transportation and living expenses during the period of training.
- Medical, surgical, and other services that will lessen the extent of the client's impairment.
- Individual counseling and guidance.
- Assistance in finding a suitable job and essential equipment, licenses, tools, or stock for a small business.
- Follow-up to smooth the client's entrance into employment.

Under this program states are able to set priorities for categories of eligible clients who will be served when financial resources are limited: For example, states may assign a higher priority to clients who need medical restoration over those who need psychological counseling. Each state also has the option of whether an economic means test should be used to determine the applicant's entitlement for certain services.

MEDICAID   This program (described in Chapter 14) covers medical expenses for low-income people.

OLD-AGE, SURVIVORS, AND DISABILITY INSURANCE   This is a social insurance program (described in Chapter 3) for those who are no longer able to work, following several years of covered employment.

SUPPLEMENTAL SECURITY INCOME   This is a public assistance program (described in Chapter 3) for the visually impaired and disabled.

FOOD STAMPS   This program (described in Chapter 3) offsets some of the food expenses for low-income people who qualify.

WORKER'S COMPENSATION PROGRAM   Workers injured or disabled on the job, as well as the surviving dependents of workers who die as a result of such injury, are provided financial assistance to compensate for lost wages and to pay for the cost of any required medical or rehabilitative care.

ROLES OF SOCIAL WORKERS

Social workers encounter the impaired in two general ways. First, the impaired are encountered in settings where the primary service focus is other than rehabilitation. For example, workers at family counseling agencies usually see families with marital and interpersonal problems. Yet, at times, one or more of the family members may have an impairment. The impairment may be unrelated to the family problems or may be an important contributing factor. When the latter occurs, the social worker's role is to help the family assess and understand the nature and impact of the impairment and then help the family develop effective strategies for handling the difficulties associated with the impairment.

Second, social workers are employed in settings that serve primarily people with disabilities, such as sheltered workshops, nursing homes, general hospitals, day-care centers for the impaired, rehabilitation hospitals, and specialized schools (such as schools for the visually impaired).

Rehabilitation of the impaired can be defined as restoration of people with disabilities to the fullest physical, mental, social, vocational, and economic usefulness of which they are capable.[43] Rehabilitation involves several focuses: vocational training, vocational counseling, psychological adjustment, medical and physical restoration, and job placement. Clients, of course, differ in which of these service focuses are needed. Some clients require services in all of these areas.

There are a wide range of professionals providing rehabilitation services: physicians, nurses, clinical psychologists, physical therapists, psychiatrists, occupational therapists, recreational therapists, vocational counselors, speech therapists, hearing therapists, industrial arts teachers, social workers, special education

Situational counseling can take place in community settings as well as in sheltered workshops. The counselor at left helps a developmentally disabled man learn appropriate behavior in a fast food restaurant.

teachers, and prosthetists. Most of these therapists focus on the physical functioning of clients, whereas social workers focus primarily on the social functioning of clients. In most rehabilitation settings a team approach is used.

The major functions of social workers in rehabilitation settings are discussed below.

Counseling Clients

Such counseling involves helping clients adjust to the impairment and to the rehabilitation programs at the agency. A wide range of problems may be covered: personal, interpersonal, family, financial, vocational adjustment, and educational adjustment.

Counseling Families

In some rehabilitation settings a worker is involved primarily in working with the family and not with the client, especially if the client is a young child. Counseling with the family involves helping the family to understand the nature of the impairment and the prognosis, helping the family members to make the essential adjustments to help the client, and providing counseling on personal and interpersonal concerns associated with the disability. In such a role a worker provides information, comfort, understanding, counseling on specific concerns, and sometimes referral services.

Taking Social Histories

A social history contains information about the client's family background and present status. The history contains information about what the client's family life was like before contact with the agency, what it is like now, and what it will probably be like in the future. A social history contains a history of the disability, positive and negative reactions of family members to the disability, significant family relationships, summary of strengths and weaknesses within the family for handling the impairment, information on social skills of the client, a history of the client's functioning at school and at work, a history of services provided in the past, and a summary of the problems and concerns of family members associated with the disability. Information for the social history is gathered from the client, from family members, and from case records of other social and medical agencies that the client has had contact with.

Serving as Liaison between the Family and the Agency

Keeping the lines of communication open is essential in any human service setting. In a rehabilitation setting social workers generally have the responsibility to serve as liaison between the agency staff and the family. At times a worker arranges meetings between the staff and the family to discuss the client's impairment and factors affecting rehabilitation and to discuss future plans and services. In a hospital setting it is the physician's responsibility to explain the particular medical condition to the client, but a social worker often has the responsibility to discuss the implications of the medical condition with the client and the family. Implications covered include the likely effect the impairment will have in the future on the capacity of the impaired person to function at work, at school, in social situations, and within the family. To be an effective liaison a social worker in a rehabilitative setting needs a basic knowledge of a variety of medical conditions and of medical terminology, and an awareness of the implications of these medical conditions for emotional, physical, and social functioning.

Being a Broker

Often a social worker serves a linkage function in helping families to make use of other community resources. To be an effective broker a worker needs a knowledge of other community services, including the programs provided, eligibility requirements, and admission procedures. Clients may need a variety of services from other community agencies, such as financial assistance, wheelchairs, prosthetic services, day-care services, special job training, visiting nurse services, and transportation.

Doing Discharge Planning

In some rehabilitation settings, such as hospitals, social workers have major responsibility for discharge planning. If a client is unable to return home, arrangements have to be made for placement in some other setting, such as a nursing home or a group home. Social workers often help clients and their families to prepare for returning home or to some other facility. Involved in

BOX 15.2

Social History of a Client at a Vocational Testing Division of a Sheltered Workshop

Hillside Vocational Training Center
Columbus, Ohio

Name: Jim Frey   Marital Status: Single

Date of Birth: 6-30-64   Height: 5'10"

Address: 550 S. Adams, Columbus   Weight: 180

Telephone: 478-2346

Religion: Lutheran

Occupation: Unemployed

Race: Black

REASON FOR TESTING

Three years ago on April 30, 1981, Jim Frey was involved in an automobile accident with his older brother, Bob. Bob was killed in the accident, and Jim's spine was severed. Mr. Frey was hospitalized for three months, spent five more months convalescing in a nursing home, and since that time has been living with his parents. Mr. Frey is paralyzed from the waist down. Following the accident he was also severely depressed. He was referred to this agency by Lakeland Counseling Center, an agency that Mr. Frey and his parents have been receiving counseling from. Mr. Frey's depression has gradually decreased, and he is now seeking testing and vocational counseling to explore career opportunities.

Family Background and Early History. Mr. Frey's father, Donald Frey, has been an insurance salesman for the past twenty-seven years. His mother, Joan Frey, has been a real estate broker for the past fourteen years. Both Mr. and Mrs. Donald Frey appear to be very concerned about their son's future, and both stated they are willing to do whatever they can to help. The Freys live in a middle-class neighborhood and have a home that is clean and well kept. The Freys appeared to have considerable respect for each other and a good relationship.

The only children that the Donald Frey's had were Jim and Bob, with Bob being two years older. The Freys reported that both their children did well academically in school, and each had a number of friends. The boys were both active in intramural sports, with Bob being a second-string player on the basketball team in his junior and senior years. The most serious trouble that either of the boys had gotten into prior to the accident was Bob being arrested for setting off firecrackers around the 4th of July five years ago.

The automobile accident occurred late one evening after Jim and Bob had left a party in which alcoholic beverages were served. Their car hit a bridge abutment. Bob was killed instantly. The parents reported they were extremely distraught following this accident and felt their whole world had shattered. They indicated they had few friends they socialized with, as they spent most of their time prior to the accident with their work and their children. They received counseling for grief and depression for eighteen months from Lakeland Counseling Center. They indicated they discontinued counseling when the person they were seeing made a job transfer to the West Coast.

For nearly the past two years Mr. and Mrs. Frey have been caring for Jim at home. Mrs. Frey indicated she has taken a leave of absence from her real estate position in order to care for her son. They acknowledged that caring for Jim has been "taxing," as he has been quite depressed and has required considerable physical attention. Only recently has he been able to get into and out of a wheelchair without assistance. The parents still mourn the loss of Bob but are increasingly becoming optimistic with the progress that Jim has been making, including a decrease in his depression, increased physical agility, and now a motivation to receive training for a career.

School Performance. Jim Frey attended Franklin Elementary School, Stevens Junior High, and Randal High School. At the time of his accident, Jim was a senior. He was near graduation but as yet has not completed the course work. School records show that Jim generally received *A*s and *B*s, with a few *C*s. Jim had an intelligence test in his sophomore year in which he achieved a score of 122. Before the accident Jim was planning to attend college. He reportedly had a number of friends, and most continued to visit him for the first several months following the accident. But as time passed, and as Jim's depression continued, his friends gradually stopped coming by to see him. At present he has no close friends.

General Health. Until the accident his health was generally good. He had a hernia operation at age 10 and a broken collar bone at age 12. During the accident Mr. Frey suffered a severed spine and is now partially paralyzed. He also had a variety of cuts from glass that required over 80 stitches. Since the accident he at times has experienced considerable pain connected with his injury and has been prone to catch flus and colds. Medical reports indicate Mr. Frey received intensive physical therapy while at the hospital and while convalescing in the nursing home. On returning to his home, Mr. Frey's parents were instructed on giving him a variety of exercises.

Dating History. Mr. Frey indicated he dated a number of young women before the accident. At the time of the accident he was dating someone steadily (during his senior year). At first this person showed considerable interest in Mr. Frey and his circumstances. However, Mr. Frey stated that after a few months she started dating others, and her interest in continuing their relationship rapidly declined.

Employment History. Mr. Frey was a paperboy for a few years. Before the accident he worked part-time as a busboy at a restaurant. He has not worked since the accident.

Continued

BOX 15.2   *Continued*

Prior Contact with Social Agencies. Mr. Frey was hospitalized in 1981 for three months at St. Mary's hospital. Records show he received extensive physical therapy and counseling for depression from the social work staff. Following this hospitalization he was transferred to Countryside Nursing Home, where he continued to receive physical therapy and counseling. Mr. Frey had fallen asleep on the fateful night when his brother was killed. For months after that, Mr. Frey was depressed and continued to feel guilty because he felt if he had stayed awake he might have kept his brother awake. (The police concluded that the accident occurred after Bob Frey had fallen asleep.) Jim Frey also has been depressed over the breakup with his girl friend, over the loss of other friends, and particularly over the shattered hopes and expectations for his future. After Jim Frey returned home, his parents made arrangements with the referring agency (Lakeland Counseling Center) for Jim to receive counseling associated with his depression and also focused on his future. Reports received from Lakeland Counseling Center also indicated that Mr. Frey's parents have expressed concerns in the past year that Jim may be drinking beer and other alcoholic beverages to excess.

General Impressions. Mr. Frey has made gradual progress in putting his life back together since his auto accident three years ago. At times he is still somewhat depressed, but he now is making efforts to stop brooding about his past and is motivated to make efforts to improve his situation. He is looking forward to the test results at this center, since he wants to receive training for a career. At the present time he is uncertain which career he desires to pursue and is uncertain which vocations or professions he is qualified to pursue. He is articulate, personable, and appears to possess a high intellect. He has expressed a strong interest in graduating from high school and wonders whether he might have the capacities

---

such arrangements are making plans for financial aid and for such specialized care as visiting nurse services, day care, physical therapy, and job training.

REACTIONS TO HAVING AN IMPAIRMENT

To work effectively with the impaired and their families requires that the social worker understand and deal effectively with the emotional reactions to having an impairment. Clients and their families have a variety of reactions on being informed that an impairment exists. The effectiveness of counseling frequently depends on the social worker understanding such reactions in order to assist clients and their families in acknowledging the impairment so that they can be helped with available services.

The reactions that a person has on becoming aware that she or he (or a member of the family) has a disability are centered around the realization that a loss has occurred. For example, when parents become aware their young daughter is retarded they are apt to mourn the loss of not having a "normal" child. When a loss occurs a person goes through a grieving process.

Nearly all of us are currently grieving about some loss that we have had. It might be the end of a romantic

and financial resources to attend college. His parents appear supportive of his desires to seek a higher education and stated they would be willing and able to provide some financial support.

Mr. Frey stated he is also interested in learning to drive and hopes to be able to secure a driver's license and an auto with assistive devices that would enable him to drive.

Mr. Frey's drinking was discussed with him. He stated he may at times drink to excess, but he said this only happens when he is bored, depressed, or has nothing to do. It would seem that Mr. Frey's drinking is a potential difficulty that should be monitored.

Mr. Frey, after three years of brooding about the accident and his problems, is now enthusiastically looking forward to the testing results at this center and is highly optimistic about the future. This enthusiasm is indeed a positive sign. However, it is important for Mr. Frey to realize that testing is only the first step. Mr. Frey hopes to acquire the necessary training, employment, and financial resources to live independently of his parents. Although his parents are supportive, there are occasional conflicts between Mr. Frey and his parents, such as over his drinking. Mr. Frey may occasionally get discouraged when obstacles are encountered in arriving at the goals that he has set. It is at these times that Mr. Frey may need continued counseling to prevent the return of a long-term depression.

Respectfully submitted,

Frank Lia
Social Worker

relationship, or a move away from friends and parents, or the death of a pet, or failure to get a grade we wanted, or the death of someone close. The reactions that a person has when a disability occurs are analogous to the grieving all of us go through when a loss occurs. Examples of losses in the area of disabilities include the following: a couple is informed their 1-year-old daughter is mentally retarded; a 20-year-old male is informed he will be paralyzed for the rest of his life as the result of an auto accident; a couple is informed their 6-month-old son has cerebral palsy; a 33-year-old business executive has a massive heart attack and is informed he will have to make major changes in his lifestyle; a husband is informed his wife will be severely visually impaired following an accident at work; a 26-year-old woman is informed she has multiple sclerosis; a 28-year-old farmer is informed his leg must be amputated following an accident; a couple is informed their 2-year-old son has a severe hearing impairment; a 17-year-old girl is informed she has rheumatoid arthritis; a 27-year-old actor is informed he has tested positive to having the HIV, the AIDS virus. This list could perhaps be indefinitely expanded.

The Grieving Process

It is a mistake to believe that grieving over a loss should end in a set amount of time, such as six months, a year, or three years. The "normal" grieving process is often the life span of the griever. When we first become aware of a loss of very high value, we are apt to grieve

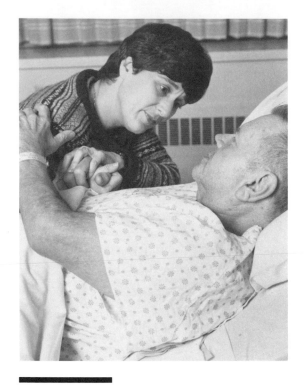

Acceptance is the final phase in Elizabeth Kübler-Ross's model of the grieving process.

intensively—to cry, be depressed, be in a state of shock, and so on. Gradually we will have hours, then days, then weeks, then months when we will not dwell on the loss and will not grieve. However, there will always be something that reminds us of the loss (such as anniversaries of when the disability occurred), and we will again grieve. The intense grieving periods will, however, gradually become shorter in duration, occur less frequently, and gradually decrease in intensity.

Two models of the grieving process will be presented: the Kübler-Ross model and the Westberg model. Some people who are grieving believe the Kübler-Ross model better describes the grieving process, whereas others assert that the Westberg model more accurately describes their grieving. These models help us to understand the grief we feel from *any* loss we experience.

KÜBLER-ROSS MODEL   In *On Death and Dying*, Kübler-Ross presents five stages of dying that terminally ill people typically proceed through.[44] These five stages are summarized in Chapter 14 and include denial, rage and anger, bargaining, depression, and acceptance. These stages are not absolute, as not everyone goes through each stage. Some people waver back and forth from one stage to another. It appears to this writer that Kübler-Ross's five stages are reactions that *all* clients typically display when confronted with evidence that they have a personal problem—including being informed they have an impairment. These five stages will be more fully described.

Stage 1: Denial ("No, not me.")   During this stage clients tell themselves, "No, this can't be," "There must be a mistake," "This just isn't happening." For clients (or the families of clients) to admit they have an impairment is difficult, as they may often (erroneously) perceive themselves as sinful, weak, or irresponsible. In our society, which glorifies "the body beautiful," acknowledging that an impairment exists is often erroneously interpreted by clients as indicating they are less important or worthy. Also, recognizing that an impairment exists means a client has to acknowledge that his or her life will have to change. When such change is inevitable clients often mourn the loss of that which must be changed. For example, a young, successful businesswoman may have to change her whole life following a heart attack, including pursuing some other career with fewer pressures. Denial is often important and necessary, as it helps cushion the impact of the client's awareness that change is inevitable.

Stage 2: Rage and Anger ("Why me?")   Clients (or their families) resent the fact that others remain the same while they are afflicted with an impairment. Clients feel it is "unfair" that they are afflicted. Also, clients may resent the fact that relatives, old friends, and others are doing the things that they can no longer do. Anyone may be the target of the anger. At times the anger may be directed at the social worker for confronting them with the reality of their handicap.

Stage 3: Bargaining ("Yes, me, but . . .")   During this

stage clients begin to accept the existence of the impairment but will bargain for a wide variety of things: getting a second opinion, substituting cigar smoking for cigarette smoking for someone who has emphysema, working two more weeks to organize things at the office before taking an extended period of relaxed recovery for someone who has had a heart attack, and so on. Clients promise to be good or to do something in exchange for another week or month before they use the alternatives presented to them to change. Or, they hope that there will be scientific breakthroughs that will fully cure the impairment.

During the bargaining stage clients will usually try to change a few circumstances in their lives, and they then hope that these changes will miraculously eliminate the impairment. Parents of a severely retarded child may hope, for example, that increased training and education will enable their child, in several years' time, to be of "normal" intelligence.

Stage 4: Depression ("Yes, me.")   Clients (and their families) at this stage have stopped denying the existence of their impairment. Their anger has subsided, and they no longer try to bargain. They understand the nature of their impairment and realize they will need to make changes in their lives. However, they as yet are not ready to put forth the efforts to improve their circumstances. They tend to brood about having an impairment and convey an attitude of "Woe is me," "How awful this is," and "Poor me." Often, they blame themselves for having the impairment. Frequently, they mourn about how the impairment will affect their future, and they mourn the loss of what they will have to change in their lives.

Stage 5: Acceptance ("I have a problem, but it's all right; I can.")   Clients now, for the first time, make a concerted effort at this stage to minimize the effects of the impairment and to put their lives back together. They have the attitude now of "I can do it." There is hope. A plan for rehabilitation can be presented at this stage if one was lacking or dismissed in earlier stages. Fear and apprehension are still present but very much reduced. Clients now have the motivation to do what they can to put their lives back together. Only when clients reach this stage are they ready to work on a rehabilitation program.

WESTBERG MODEL   The Westberg Model[45] of the grieving process is diagramed in Figure 15.1.

Shock and Denial   Many people when informed about a tragic loss are so numb and in such a state of shock that they are practically void of feeling. It could well be that when emotional pain is unusually intense, the system temporarily "blows out" so that the person hardly feels anything and thus acts as if nothing has happened. Denial is a way of avoiding the impact of a tragic loss.

Emotions Erupt   As the realization of the loss becomes evident, the person expresses the painful loss by crying, by screaming, or through gentle tears or deep sighs.

Anger   At some point a person usually experiences anger. The anger may be directed at God for causing the loss. The anger may be partly due to the unfairness of the loss. If a child is born with a disability, or later develops a disability, it is not uncommon for the parents to become angry at the child at times for having a disability and for causing huge hassles.

Illness   Because grief is stress producing, stress-related illnesses are apt to develop, such as colds, flus, an ulcer, tension headaches, diarrhea, rashes, insomnia, and so on.

Panic   Because the grieving person realizes she or he does not feel like the "old self," the person may panic and may even worry about going insane. Nightmares, unwanted emotions that appear uncontrollable, and physical illnesses contribute to the panic. Also contributing to panic may be a variety of fears. Those with a disability may fear the reactions of others. Parents may fear their other siblings will suffer from having a brother or sister who has a disability. They may also fear the burdens of caring for a child with a disability. They may also fear that both their child and themselves will be the target of ridicule.

FIGURE 15.1

Westberg Model of the Grieving Process

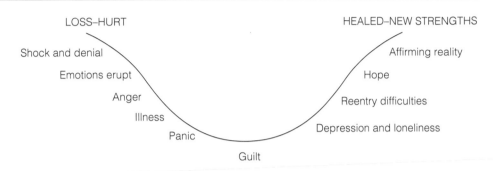

Guilt   The grieving person may blame himself or herself for having done something that contributed to the loss or disability or may feel guilty for not having done something that might have prevented the loss. If a child is born with a disability the mother may wonder, "Could this have been caused by my smoking or drinking during pregnancy?" This tendency to blame oneself is reinforced by the questions asked by professionals. For example, if a child is born with a disability, the mother is asked "Did you smoke during the pregnancy? Did you have a serious fall or illness? Did you drink? What pills did you take?" (Although these questions need to be asked, professionals should be careful about how they are phrased because they can have devastating effects.)

Depression and Loneliness   At times the grieving person is apt to feel very sad about the disability or loss and also to have feeings of isolation and loneliness. The grieving person may withdraw from others who are viewed as not being supportive or understanding.

Reentry Difficulties   At this point the grieving person makes efforts to put his or her life back together. Reentry problems are apt to arise: The person may resist letting go of attachments to the past, and loyalties to memories may hamper reentry.

Hope   Gradually, hope of putting one's life back together returns and begins to grow.

Affirming Reality   The grieving person puts his or her life back together again, and the old feeling of having control of one's life returns. The reconstructed life is not the same as the old, and memories of the loss remain, but the reconstructed life is "OK."

In both of these models Kübler-Ross and Westberg note the following. Some people continue to grieve and never reach the final stage (acceptance in the Kübler-Ross model and affirming reality in the Westberg model). Kübler-Ross and Westberg also caution that it is a mistake to believe rigidly that everyone will progress through these stages as diagramed. There is often considerable movement back and forth in these stages. For example, in the Kübler-Ross model a person may go from denial to depression, to anger and rage, back to denial, then to bargaining, then to depression, back to anger and rage, and so on.

ADDITIONAL CONSIDERATIONS IN APPLYING THE KÜBLER-ROSS AND WESTBERG MODELS   With an understanding of the Kübler-Ross and Westberg paradigms, social workers are better able to understand why clients are reacting in various ways to their impairments. In helping clients handle these various reactions it is important that workers help clients identify those emotions that are interfering with a habilitative or rehabilitative program. Strategies can then be developed to counter those emotions that are interfering. For example, if a mother of a child born with Down's syndrome feels guilty because she thinks she caused this impairment during the pregnancy by lifting too much, arrangements can be made with a physician or a genetics counselor to explain the etiology of the disorder and to assure her that her concerns over lifting something heavy had nothing to do with causing the disorder.

It should also be noted that Kübler-Ross's and Westberg's paradigms may not always apply to young children. Children born with an impairment are generally not initially aware of their disability. Awareness gradually comes through interacting with others over a lengthy period of time. Children with disabilities gradually learn they are different and that others often place negative values on their impairment. In the following excerpt from an autobiography, Christy Brown, born with cerebral palsy, describes some of his feelings. Christy Brown used to ride in a wagon that was pulled by his brothers and sisters, but when it broke he was unable to get around.

I was now just ten, a boy who couldn't walk, speak, feed, or dress himself. I was helpless, but only now did I begin to realize how helpless I really was. I still didn't know anything about myself: I knew nothing beyond the fact that I was different from others. I didn't understand what made me different or why it should be I. . . .

I couldn't reason this out. I couldn't even think clearly about it. I could only feel it, feel it deep down in the very core of me, like a thin sharp needle. . . .

Up to then I had never thought about myself. True, there had come sometimes a vague feeling that I wasn't like the others, an uneasy sort of stirring in my mind that came and went. But it was just one dark spot in the brightness of things; and I used to soon forget it. . . .

Now it was different. Now I saw everything, not through the eyes of a little boy eager for fun and brimming with curiosity, but through those of a cripple, a cripple who had only just discovered his own affliction.

I looked at Peter's hands. They were brown, steady hands with strong, square fingers, hands that could clasp a hurley firmly or swing a chestnut high into the air. Then I looked down at my own. They were queer, twisted hands, with bent, crooked fingers, hands that were never still, but twitched and shook continually

so that they looked more like two wriggling snakes than a pair of human hands.

I began to hate the sight of those hands, the sight of my wobbly head and lopsided mouth.[46]

Christy's awareness of his impairment involved four steps: (*a*) an avoidance of thinking about himself and his handicap; (*b*) a vague sense that he was different from others; (*c*) a critical incident—not being able to go out—that forced Christy to acknowledge that he had an impairment; and (*d*) self-depreciation because of his impairment.

There is a tendency for parents to overindulge and overprotect a handicapped child. The child is given less responsibility, fewer limits are placed on unwanted behaviors, personal whims of the child are indulged more, and the child is often punished less, partly because there is sympathy for the suffering the child is undergoing. Children become aware of this special status and sometimes use this sympathy to manipulate those they come in contact with. Louise Baker describes how she manipulated others at age 8, shortly after a leg was amputated following an automobile accident.

Even before I left the hospital my sudden power over people was showing itself. First of all, with completely unconscious brilliance, I chose rather inspired subjects to discuss during my five days of postoperative delirium. I rambled on feverishly but with moving feeling about a doll with real golden hair and blue eyes that opened and closed. I even conveniently mentioned the awesome price and just where such a doll might be purchased, and I sighed over my father's attested poverty which prevented him from buying this coveted treasure. . . . The news spread: "The poor little crippled child in the hospital . . . wants a doll. . . ." When I left the hospital it took two cars to transport my loot.

Very soon after I came home from the hospital I realized that all I had to do was mumble the magic words . . . "I'll never be able to run again, will I?" This sad little speech—then the moment was ripe to make almost any demand. . . .

Three months before, I was a reasonably well-mannered child . . . now I was a precocious golddigger, and anyone was fair game.[47]

BOX 15.3

How to Cope with Grief

T he following suggestions are given. If you are grieving, you are urged to try those suggestions that you believe will be most useful.

Crying is an acceptable and valuable expression of grief. Cry as you feel the need. Crying releases tension that is part of grieving.

Talking about your loss and your plans for the present and the future is very constructive. Sharing your grief with friends, family, the clergy, or a professional counselor is advisable. You may seek to become involved with a group of others having similar experiences. Talking about your grief eases loneliness, allows you to ventilate your feelings, and helps you in accepting your loss and making constructive plans for the present and the future. Talking with close friends gives you a sense of security and brings you closer to others you love. Talking with others who have similar losses helps put your problems into perspective, as you will see that you are not the only one with problems, and you will feel good about yourself when you assist others in handling their losses.

Disabilities often cause us to examine and question our faith or philosophy of life. Do not become concerned if you begin questioning your beliefs. Talk about them. For many, a religious faith provides help in accepting the loss.

Writing out a rational self-analysis of your grief will help you to identify irrational thinking that is contributing to your grief. (See Chapter 4 for how to write a rational self-analysis). Once your irrational thinking is identified you can relieve much of your grief through rational challenges to your irrational thinking.

Try not to dwell on how unhappy you feel. Become involved and active in life around you. Do not waste your time and energy on self-pity.

If there are certain days of the year when you tend to grieve deeply (such as an anniversary of a disabling automobile accident), seek to spend these days with family and friends who will give you support.

You may feel that you have nothing to live for and may even think about suicide.

When clients or members of their family are reacting (emotionally or behaviorally) in ways that substantially interfere with the rehabilitation process, social workers have a responsibility to confront the clients or their families about this tactfully. Sometimes a considerable amount of evidence will have to be presented, perhaps over a period of time, to clients and family members before they will acknowledge that certain reactions are intensifying the negative effects of the impairment. Once the acknowledgment occurs, then strategies for changing the reaction patterns can be discussed, and one or more approaches may be selected and implemented in order to change the destructive reaction patterns.

Understand that many people who encounter severe losses feel this way. Seek to find assurance in the fact that a sense of purpose and meaning will return.

Intense grief is very stressful. Stress is a factor in leading to a variety of illnesses, such as headaches, colitis, ulcers, colds, and flus. If you become ill, seek a physician's help, and tell the physician you believe your illness may be related to grief you are experiencing.

Intense grief may also lead to sleeplessness, sexual difficulties, loss of appetite, or overeating. You may find you have little energy and cannot concentrate. All of these reactions are "normal." Do not become worried that you are going crazy or losing your mind. Seek to take a positive view that you will get your life back together—just as practically everyone else does who suffers a similar loss. Seek during your grief to eat a balanced diet, to get ample rest, and to exercise moderately. Every person's grief is unique: If you are experiencing unusual physical reactions (such as nightmares) try not to become overly alarmed.

Medication should be taken sparingly and only under the supervision of a physician. Avoid trying to relieve your grief with alcohol or other drugs. Many drugs are addictive and may stop or delay the necessary grieving process.

Recognize that guilt, real or imagined, is a normal part of grief. Parents who have a child with a disability often feel guilty about things they have done or about things they think they should have done. If you are experiencing intense guilt, it is helpful to share it with friends or with a professional counselor. It might also be helpful to write a rational self-analysis on the guilt (see Chapter 4). Learn to forgive yourself. All humans make mistakes. If you didn't make mistakes you wouldn't be human.

You may find that friends and relatives appear to be shunning you. If this is happening they are probably uncomfortable around you because they do not know what to say or do. Take the initiative and talk with them about your loss. Tell them about ways in which you would like them to be supportive to you.

If possible put off making major decisions (changing jobs, moving elsewhere, and so on) until you become more emotionally relaxed. When you're highly emotional, you're more apt to make undesirable decisions.

SUMMARY

Those who have disabilities include the temporarily injured, the physically impaired, the deaf and hearing impaired, the blind and visually impaired, the mentally retarded and emotionally disturbed, and those with degenerative illnesses and chronic health disorders. There are hundreds of illnesses and medical conditions that have been identified as contributing causes of mental retardation.

Throughout history the willingness of societies to care for the needs of those impaired has always been largely determined by the perceived causes of the impairment, the existing medical knowledge, and the general economic conditions. Throughout much of history disability was often viewed as the result of demonic possession or as God's punishment.

In this century our society has made progress in better understanding the needs of the impaired and in designing services to meet these needs. Yet there is still a general lack of acceptance of people with disabilities, which is often related to the emphasis on the "body beautiful" in our society. The impaired are still frequently pitied, shunned, or made the brunt of jokes. Our society has yet to learn that people with disabilities are people, who want to be treated as peers. (All of us are only an accident away from being disabled.) Until the impaired are given an opportunity, not only legally, but socially, to be treated as peers, social services will only be partially effective. Ideally, the impaired should only be limited by the physical restrictions of their impairment. Sadly, the psychological and social obstacles faced by people with disabilities are often greater than their actual physical limitations. Our society has yet to learn that an impaired person is a person—a person who happens to have an impairment.

Social workers are only one of numerous professionals that provide services to the impaired. The roles of social workers in providing rehabilitative services include counseling the impaired, counseling family members of the impaired, gathering information through social histories, serving as liaison between the family and the agency, being a broker, and doing discharge planning.

Another role of a social worker is to help the impaired and their family members change emotional and behavioral reactions that are interfering with the rehabilitative process. Two useful paradigms were described that summarize emotional, behavioral, and physiological reactions to having an impairment: the Kübler-Ross model and the Westberg model. Both of these models conceptualize the reactions in terms of the disability being a loss.

NOTES

1. Donald Brieland, Lela B. Costin, Charles R. Atherton, *Contemporary Social Work*, 3d ed. (New York: McGraw-Hill, 1985), p. 294.
2. Ibid., p. 294.
3. G. L. Dickinson, *Greek View of Life* (New York: Collier Books, 1961), p. 95.
4. S. Nichtern, *Helping the Retarded Child* (New York: Grosset & Dunlap, 1974), p. 14.
5. J. F. Garrett, "Historical Background," in *Vocational Rehabilitation of the Disabled*, eds. D. Malikin and H. Rusalem (New York: New York University Press, 1969), pp. 29–38.
6. J. C. Coleman, *Abnormal Psychology and Modern Life*, 3d ed. (Glenview, IL: Scott, Foresman, 1964).
7. C. E. Obermann, *A History of Vocational Rehabilitation in America* (Minneapolis: The Dennison Co., 1964).
8. L. Kanner, *A History of the Care and Study of the Mentally Retarded* (Springfield, IL: Charles C. Thomas, 1964), p. 6.
9. M. Judge, "A Brief History of Social Services," part I, *Social and Rehabilitation Record* 3, no. 5 (September 1976), pp. 2–8.
10. Stanford Rubin and Richard Roessler, *Foundations of the Vocational Rehabilitation Process* (Baltimore: University Park Press, 1978), p. 4.
11. A. F. Tyler, *Freedom's Ferment* (New York: Harper & Row, 1962), pp. 294–296.
12. J. Lenihan, "Disabled Americans: A History," *Performance* 27, Bicentennial issue (Washington, D.C.: The President's Committee on Employment of the Handicapped).
13. Obermann, *A History of Vocational Rehabilitation in America*, p. 333.
14. L. M. Dunn, "A Historical Review of the Retarded," in *Mental Retardation*, ed. J. Rothstein (New York: Holt, Rinehart & Winston, 1961), pp. 13–17.
15. Obermann, *A History of Vocational Rehabilitation in America*, p. 80.
16. Kanner, *A History of the Care and Study of the Mentally Retarded*, pp. 36–38.
17. Ibid., p. 39.
18. Rubin and Roessler, *Foundations of the Vocational Rehabilitation Process*, pp. 12–13.
19. Ibid., pp. 13–14.
20. Lenihan, "Disabled Americans: A History."
21. Tyler, *Freedom's Ferment*, p. 306.
22. Rubin and Roessler, *Foundations of the Vocational Rehabilitation Process*, pp. 8–9.

23. Ibid., pp. 10–11.

24. R. Lubove, *The Professional Altruist* (Cambridge, MA: Harvard University Press, 1965).

25. Ibid.

26. Obermann, *A History of Vocational Rehabilitation in America*, p. 121.

27. Rubin and Roessler, *Foundations of the Vocational Rehabilitation Process*, pp. 22–23.

28. Obermann, *A History of Vocational Rehabilitation in America*, pp. 155–157.

29. R. Thomas, "The Expanding Scope of Services," *Journal of Rehabilitation* 36, no. 5, pp. 37–40.

30. Rubin and Roessler, *Foundations of the Vocational Rehabilitation Process*, pp. 30–32.

31. Ibid., pp. 32–45.

32. Herbert Grossman, M.D., ed., *Manual on Terminology and Classification in Mental Retardation*, rev. ed. (Washington, D.C.: American Association on Mental Deficiency, 1975), p. 11.

33. U.S. Public Law 91–517, *United States Statutes at Large*, 91st Congress, vol. 84, part 1 (Washington, D.C.: U.S. Government Printing Office, 1971), pp. 1316–1317.

34. Ruth E. Little, "Drinking During Pregnancy: Implications for Public Health," *Alcohol Health and Research World* 4, no. 1 (1979), pp. 21–29.

35. S. Richardson et al., "Cultural Uniformity in Reaction to Physical Disabilities," *American Sociological Review* 26 (April 1961), pp. 241–247.

36. C. H. Cooley, *Human Nature and the Social Order* (New York: Charles Scribner's Sons, 1902).

37. Beatrice A. Wright, *Physical Disability: A Psychological Approach* (New York: Harper & Row, 1960), p. 259.

38. Nancy Weinberg, "Rehabilitation," in *Contemporary Social Work*, 2d ed., eds. Donald Brieland, Lela Costin, and Charles Atherton (New York: McGraw-Hill, 1980), p. 310.

39. Ibid., p. 310.

40. R. Kleck, H. Ono, and A. H. Hastorf, "The Effects of Physical Deviance upon Face-to-Face Interaction," *Human Relations* 19 (1966), pp. 425–436.

41. Fred David, "Deviance Disavowal: The Management of Strained Interaction by the Visibly Handicapped," in *The Other Side: Perspectives on Deviance*, ed. Howard S. Becker (New York: The Free Press, 1964), p. 123.

42. Rubin and Roessler, *Foundations of the Vocational Rehabilitation Process*, pp. 32–44.

43. *Symposium on the Process of Rehabilitation* (Cleveland: National Council on Rehabilitation, 1944), p. 6.

44. Elisabeth Kübler-Ross, *On Death and Dying* (New York: Macmillan, 1969).

45. Granger Westberg, *Good Grief* (Philadelphia: Fortress Press, 1962).

46. Christy Brown, *The Story of Christy Brown* (New York: Pocket Books, 1971).

47. Louise Baker, *Out on a Limb* (New York: Whittlesly House, 1946), pp. 4–5.

16

OVERPOPULATION, MISUSE OF THE ENVIRONMENT, AND FAMILY PLANNING

Problems associated with overpopulation and despoiling the environment seriously threaten to reduce the quality of human life throughout the world. The seriousness of these problems is illustrated by the fact that some nations are contemplating the enactment of compulsory sterilization laws. This chapter will:

- Describe the problems associated with rapid population growth throughout the world.
- Discuss pollution and misuse of the environment.
- Summarize current efforts to curtail the growth of the world's population and to preserve the environment.
- Outline proposals that have been advanced for population control and for environmental protection in the future.
- Describe the role of social work in family planning.

THE POPULATION CRISIS

There are now over 5 billion people living on earth.[1] In 1930 there were 2 billion. The world's population is increasing at the rate of 350,000 people per day[2] (see Table 16.1).

Assuming a continued doubling rate of forty years, by 2025 there will be 10 billion people. If this growth continued for 900 years, there would be 60 *million billion* people! This would mean there would be about 100 persons for each square yard of the earth's surface, both land and water.[3]

Doubling time is based on the extent to which the birthrate exceeds the death rate. Doubling times have a compound effect. Just as interest dollars earn interest, people added to the population produce more people. Table 16.2 shows the relationship between the annual population growth rate and the doubling time of the population.

Thus, what seems a small population growth rate of 1.9 percent per year (the current rate in the world) leads to a dramatic doubling time of forty years. With

TABLE 16.1

Doubling Times of the World's Population

Date	Estimated World Population	Time Required for Population to Double
8000 B.C.	5 million	
1650 A.D.	500 million	1,500 years
1850	1 billion	200
1930	2 billion	80
1975	4 billion	45
2015	8 billion	40

Sources: Paul Ehrlich, *The Population Bomb* (New York: Ballantine Books, 1971), p. 21; Werner Fornos, *Gaining People, Losing Ground* (Washington, D.C.: The Population Institute, 1987), p. 4.

TABLE 16.2

Rate of Population Growth and Doubling Time

Annual Percent Increase	Doubling Time
1.0	70 years
2.0	35 years
3.0	24 years
4.0	17 years

Source: Paul Ehrlich, *The Population Bomb* (New York: Ballantine Books, 1971), p. 10.

an annual growth rate of 1.9 percent, 90 million people are being added to the world's population annually.[4]

The countries experiencing the most severe doubling-time problems are the "developing countries" (also called the Third World nations). These countries are beginning to industrialize. Sadly, population growth is greatest in the countries that can least afford increases—that is, the countries that need to spend their resources on improving their economic conditions. Developing countries have over two thirds of the world's population, and doubling times of about twenty to thirty-five years.[5] People are "hungry"; many are starving in these countries. Developing countries tend to have primitive and inefficient agriculture, small gross national products, and high illiteracy rates. The bulk of the population in such countries spend most of their time in trying to meet basic subsistence needs.

Developing countries are characterized by high birthrates and declining death rates. The trend in the past has been that when a country begins to industrialize, the death rate drops (people live longer), whereas the birthrate tends to remain high for a substantial

period of time. The result is a rapid population growth rate. Unfortunately, developing countries, where people's living conditions most need improvement, are precisely the countries whose populations are increasing so rapidly that most people are scarcely better off than they were a generation ago. Nine out of every ten people added to the world's population are born in the poorer, developing countries.[6] Figure 16.1 shows that developing countries are much more likely to have a population explosion than industrial countries.

The population crisis in the world today is not due to families having more children than they did in the past, as families are no larger than they were in the past. However, more people are living to the age of fertility and beyond. In effect, more babies are growing to maturity to produce babies themselves. This change is due to several factors: (*a*) advances in medicine, sanitation, and public health and (*b*) increased capacity to reduce the effects of famines, floods, droughts, and other natural disasters.

Lee Rainwater has noted that "the poor get children."[7] There is a vicious circle involving rapid population growth and poverty. Rapid population growth places an increasing strain on a nation's ability to feed

BOX 16.1

Compulsory Sterilization Laws

O verpopulation is now recognized as one of the most severe problems affecting the survival of the quality of human life. Some countries are now seriously considering enacting compulsory sterilization laws to control rapid population growth. One such country is India. In 1976 Maharashtra (a state in India) passed a compulsory sterilization law to limit family size. The law required that any male under age 55, and any female under age 45, would have to be sterilized within 180 days of the birth of their third living child. Prison terms of up to two years could be assigned to those who failed to comply, although offenders were generally sterilized and then paroled. From April 1976 through December 1976, more than seven million sterilizations were reportedly performed. This law was rescinded with the fall of Prime Minister Indira Gandhi's government in 1976—a few years later she returned to power. Although rescinded, the law illustrates the extent to which some countries are seriously considering drastic measures to alleviate the pressures of unwanted population growth.

Source: "Maharashtra Passes Family Size Limitation Measure," *Intercom* 9 (September 1976), p. 5; Lynn C. Landman, "Birth Control in India: The Carrot and the Rod?" *Family Planning Perspectives* 9 (May–June 1977), p. 102.

and clothe its growing masses. Thus, rapid population growth strains resources, which leads to poverty. Poverty, in turn, leads to a high birthrate, which leads to further population growth. Former World Bank President Robert S. McNamara warns: "Short of thermonuclear war itself, rampant population growth is the gravest issue the world faces over the decades ahead."[8]

Developed or industrialized countries have doubling times in the 50- to 200-year range.[9] In the United States the birthrate has in recent years steadily decreased and is nearing a zero population growth rate (an average of two children per family). The basic reason the doubling time in developed countries is longer is because people decide to have fewer children (for financial and other reasons). It now costs $140,000 to raise a child from birth to age 18 in this country.[10] Developed nations are characterized by low birthrates and low death rates.

The slower doubling times in industrialized countries in no way means such nations are not part of the problem. If one looks at consumption rates of raw materials, they are the major culprit. The United States, for example, uses about one third of all the raw materials consumed each year but has less than one-fifteenth of the world's population.[11] The United States is therefore using five times its "fair share" of raw materials. People in the United States also consume, on the average, four times as much food per person as inhabitants of developing countries.[12]

Werner Fornos noted in 1987 that most of the population growth in the future will occur in the urban centers of the developing (Third World) countries:

The population of the Third World as a whole is increasing by a significant 2.1 percent each year, but the population of the Third World's cities is growing by a swift 3.5 percent annually—fully three times as fast as the industrialized world's urban centers. Africa's

FIGURE 16.1

Age-Sex Population Pyramids: Industrial and Developing Country Models

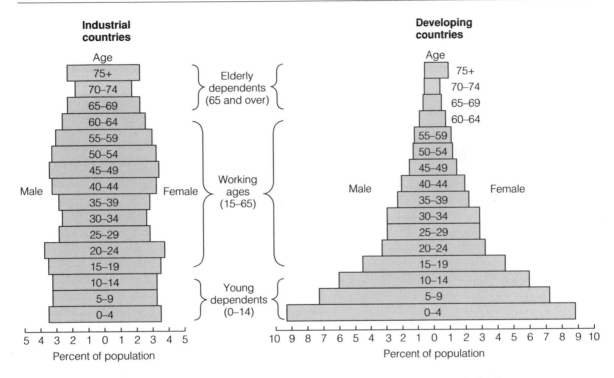

Industrial countries have 3 or 4 adults of economically productive ages for each dependent child. When an industrial country's children grow up and reproduce, the population structure will change only a little.

Developing countries have one (or less) adult of economically productive age for each dependent child. When the developing country's children grow up and reproduce, a population explosion will occur.

---

cities are growing fastest, at a runaway 5 percent each year. The slum squatter settlements associated with these centers are growing at twice the rate of the cities themselves.[13]

In many developing countries, families average seven or eight children.[14] As a result, these developing countries are increasingly populated by the young. In Latin America and Asia, nearly 40 percent of the population is under 15 years old.[15] Figure 16.1 indicates one result of this younger age population is that developing countries are much more apt to have a population explosion.

An Optimal Population Size

A frequent question is, "What is the capacity of the world to support people?" Asserting that a country's population is too large or too small implies there is an optimal size. Such a conception may be in error;

Ethiopian children are fed at a relief camp. Up to twenty million people, mostly children in developing countries, die of starvation each year.

probably no exact figure can be precisely determined for the optimum population for the world.

Many variables and values would enter into specifying an optimal world population size, including preservation of a certain standard or quality of life, rate of consumption of nonrenewable raw materials, future technological breakthroughs in finding new energy sources and new food sources, maintenance of "safe" levels of clean air and water, and public acceptance of the government's role (perhaps compulsory) in population control. The industrialized nations, with their high consumption and high waste economies, are using up more of the earth's raw materials and generating more pollution than developing countries. Because of

consumption rates, adding 1 million people to industrialized countries is comparable to adding 30 million people to developing countries.[16]

Problems of Overpopulation

A wide range of problems are associated with overpopulation. We will examine a number of these problems, including too little food, too little water, economic problems, international terrorism, crowding, too little energy, and shortages of nonrenewable resources.

TOO LITTLE FOOD   An estimated half-billion people today are undernourished—that is, slowly starving—and another billion are malnourished.[17] Paul Ehrlich, Anne Ehrlich, and John Holdren estimate that 10 to 20 million people, mostly children in developing countries, are dying of starvation each year.[18] Even in the United States, a number of people are undernourished, with some dying of starvation.[19] In approximately the time it takes to read this sentence, four people will die (three of them children) from malnutrition.[20] Incredible as it may seem, 43 percent of all deaths in India are of children under the age of 4.[21]

In a poor country, overpopulation leads to malnutrition for many, and often most, of the inhabitants. Malnutrition has severe effects on the body and the mind. It causes brain damage and mental retardation, stunts physical growth, directly causes a number of diseases, lowers resistance to other diseases, and reduces the life span. The brain of an infant grows to 80 percent of its adult size within the first three years of life. If supplies of protein are inadequate during this period, the brain stops growing, and the damage is irreversible; such children are permanently mentally retarded.[22]

Nearly 200 years ago (in 1798), Thomas Malthus theorized that population growth, if left unchecked, would outstrip the food supply.[23] Malthus theorized that unchecked population growth increases in powers of two: 1, 2, 4, 8, 16, 32, 64—that is, in a geometric ratio. In contrast, the food supply cannot possibly increase that fast. At best, the food supply increases in a steady

BOX 16.2

Super Livestock: A Likely Breakthrough in Food Production

U sing genetic-engineering techniques, scientists have successfully incorporated genes in fertilized mouse eggs that control the production of growth hormones in rats and humans. As a result they have produced "super mice" that have grown more than twice as large as their litter mates without these genes. Within the next few years scientists are predicting that this same technique will produce super livestock. The hope is a breakthrough that will allow farmers to produce livestock that grow faster and bigger, and that more efficiently convert feed into meat.

Kim McDonald speculates on the possibilities:

Giant sheep, cattle, and poultry that eat normal amounts of feed but grow faster and put less fat and more protein on their bodies than do ordinary livestock.

Pigs that produce mammoth porkchops at no extra charge to the farmer.

Dairy cows that can, at the farmer's command, increase their milk production 30 percent over normal amounts with the simple addition of a harmless chemical to their feed.

Source: Kim McDonald, "Rapid-Growth Genes Could Yield 'Super Livestock,'" *Chronicle of Higher Education*, February 8, 1984, p. 1.

---

additive fashion: 1, 2, 3, 4, 5, 6, 7—that is, in an arithmetic ratio. Inevitably, according to Malthus, population growth overtakes the growth in food supplies. Therefore, either population would have to be controlled by society or starvation, hunger, and poverty would be the unavoidable fate of most of the world's people. The fact that widespread starvation and poverty is fairly common in many countries today provides some evidence of the validity of the Malthus theory.

There has been an ongoing, heated controversy among scientists whether technology will be able to increase substantially the world's food supply. Some scientists are claiming at present that we have already reached the limit where technology will no longer be able to increase the food supply to meet the food needs of even a slowly growing world population. Others are predicting that future technology can probably provide food for a population ten times as large as our current population.[24]

Can technology meet increasing food needs? The verdict is not yet in. For example, several years ago, a technological breakthrough led to a dramatic improvement in the yield of new strains of wheat and rice. This so-called "green revolution," however, requires increased use of fertilizers and water. Fertilizers are becoming scarce and increasingly expensive, and many of the developing countries cannot afford expensive irrigation systems. Because of such variables, the beneficial effect of the green revolution is not as yet precisely known.

Research on increasing the food supply is also taking other approaches. One effort is to investigate the feasibility of cultivating the tropical rain forests of Africa, South America, and Indonesia. Such areas have large amounts of sunshine and water but poor soil (requiring large quantities of fertilizer) and severe insect infestations. Another effort is geared to finding new ways to harvest increased amounts of fish and plant life from the sea. The sea contains huge quantities of food, much of which is currently not palatable. Not only does more food need to be produced but food distribution systems have to be improved. In the United States it is more than ironic that farmers are producing more food than Americans can eat, yet an estimated 20 million people in the country do not have enough food to eat.[25]

TOO LITTLE WATER   Somewhat surprisingly, fresh water is also in short supply in the world. Ninety-seven percent of the world's water is salt water; only 3 percent is fresh water.[26]

Developed nations are using substantially more water per person than developing nations. It has been estimated that an African uses 0.8 gallons of water a day compared to 270 gallons for a New Yorker.[27]

Water is also needed in large quantities to produce food. A pound of wheat requires about 60 gallons of water; a pound of meat requires from 2,500 to 6,000 gallons.[28] If irrigation efforts are expanded in the world to grow food, fresh water resources will obviously be depleted at a faster rate. Removing salt from water (desalinization) is now being done on a small scale, but it is so expensive that it is currently only being used for drinking purposes.

ECONOMIC PROBLEMS   In industrialized countries, rapid population growth reduces the standard of living and the quality of life because rapid growth reduces the average per capita income.[29] Because birthrates are consistently higher among the lower-income groups, there are additional social and economic strains. Some authorities openly express alarm that high birth rates among the lower-income groups may lead to a reduction in average educational achievements among the population and may provide a threat to the values held

and espoused by the middle and upper classes. Rapid population growth also leads to other problems: not enough jobs, air and water pollution, traffic jams, inadequate and insufficient housing, and so on.

Economic problems are even more serious in developing nations. Economic progress tends to be canceled out by the increased population. For poor countries to industrialize requires that the inhabitants invest (either through public or private funds) in capital items such as factories, tractors, and industrial equipment. Many developing nations simply do not have the funds even to provide adequate food for their people. Being unable to invest in capital items practically guarantees they will be unable to improve their people's standard of living.

Lack of funds also creates educational and political problems. Developing countries have a high proportion of school-age children. Generally, such countries do not have the resources to provide enough schools. For example, Dr. Benson Morah describes the situation in Nigeria: "You have schools with 70 children in the classrooms, there are children sitting in the windows, children carrying their chairs to school."[30]

As a result, in many countries, a majority of children do not attend school. Being illiterate and poorly trained further locks the inhabitants into poverty.

In addition, people who are poorly housed, hungry, and miserably clothed are apt to view the government as being the protectors of the rich and the oppressors of the poor. Such conditions often lead to political unrest, political revolutions, and civil wars—as have been common in Africa, Asia, and South America.

The gap between the living standards of the industrialized and developing countries is wide and growing wider. In 1985, for example, the average per capita gross income was $16,700 in the United States, and in some developing nations it was less than $500.[31]

INTERNATIONAL TERRORISM   Rapid population growth is a factor that contributes to civil unrest, violence, and international strife. Rapid population growth intensifies poverty and feelings of hopelessness. Overpopulation leads to unemployment, rapid urbanization, declining public health, environmental degradation, economic stagnation, and a large youthful population. Young people in Third World countries are in destitute poverty and have little hope for a better future; yet, at the same time they have a gnawing awareness that people in industrialized nations are much more affluent. Such conditions and awareness create an "Aspiration Bomb." Many such young people see violence and terrorism as the only avenue for themselves and others in their country to achieve a better life.

In a 1980 report on population, the U.S. National Security Council noted:

Recent experience, in Iran and other countries, shows that this younger age group, frequently unemployed and crowded into urban slums, is particularly susceptible to extremism, terrorism, and violence as outlets for frustration. On balance, these factors add up to a growing potential for social unrest, political stability, mass migrations, and possible conflicts over control of land and resources.[32]

Werner Fornos makes the following comments about the perils of the Aspiration Bomb:

Fully 60 percent of the Third World is under 20 years of age; half are 15 years or less. These population pressures create a volatile mixture of youthful aspirations that when coupled with economic and political frustrations help form a large pool of potential terrorists.

The "Aspiration Bomb" may well present a greater threat to U.S. security than the atomic bomb. This is because while there is always the hope that mutual deterrence or common sense will preclude the use of nuclear weapons, there is no such counterveiling influence against the violence and frustration embodied in the Aspiration Bomb.[33]

CROWDING   Crowding is a person's subjective judgment that he or she has insufficient space. There have been a number of studies investigating the effects of crowding on animals. John Calhoun placed rats in laboratory pens and allowed them to breed until their number rose far beyond that found in their natural environment. A number of behavioral changes took place. Many females became infertile, others began to

abort, and some to whom offspring were born did not adequately care for their young.[34]

In other studies, overcrowding among animals has led them to become irritable, overly aggressive, nervous, inattentive to grooming, and messy, with some even resorting to cannibalism. In many cases, such negative behaviors continued to occur when the animals were returned to a normal environment.[35]

Although animal research is suggestive, it is not necessarily applicable to humans. The effects of crowding on humans have not been sufficiently researched. Some authorities believe it is a factor in leading to crime, emotional problems, incest, child abuse, suicide, violence, dirty streets, and polluted air. Other authorities believe increases in these behaviors are not due to overcrowding but to poverty and to the breakdown in traditional values. Nonetheless, we should remember that *a delicate balance often exists between a population and an environment, which can be drastically changed by a slight increase in population.* For example, adding one or two fish to a fully populated aquarium may result in a shortage of oxygen and kill most of the fish.[36]

TOO LITTLE ENERGY   The consumption of energy has doubled every twelve years in our recent history.[37] Over nine tenths of the world's energy consumption is provided by fossil fuel sources: oil, coal, and natural gas. Natural gas sources are rapidly being depleted. The domestic supply of oil in the United States is incapable of meeting our needs, and therefore this country is heavily dependent on foreign sources.

It has been estimated that world petroleum and natural gas reserves will be substantially depleted within a century from now.[38] The problem is particularly serious for the United States, which has nearly half the passenger cars in the world and consumes more than half of the world's gasoline.[39] New sources of energy that work as well as fossil fuel sources will have to be found.

SHORTAGES OF OTHER NONRENEWABLE RESOURCES   Mineral resources other than fuels have become essential elements for industrial production. Essential elements include copper, lead, zinc, tin, nickel, tungsten, mercury, chromium, manganese, cobalt, molyodenum, aluminum, platinum, iron, and helium. Consumption of such minerals is proceeding so rapidly that reserve sources will eventually be depleted, expensive mining of low-quality ores will have to be undertaken, and substitutes will have to be found. As the developing countries continue to industrialize, the demand for these nonrenewable minerals will far exceed the supply.

The Theory of Demographic Transition

The rate of population growth is highest in developing countries. Researchers on population growth have observed that growth rates tend to decrease and then stabilize after a fairly high level of industrialization has been achieved. This observation is assumed to be true about population growth in general, and the assumption is called the *theory of demographic transition.* This transition is thought to take place in three stages:

1. *Preindustrial, agricultural societies.* In this stage, there is a fairly stable population size, as the societies have both high birthrates and high death rates.

2. *Developing societies that are beginning to industrialize.* In such societies, the birthrates remain high, but the death rates drop, leading to a rapid increase in the population growth rate. The death rates drop because these societies have the medical capacities to keep people alive for a substantially longer average life span.

3. *Developed industrial societies.* Such societies have both low birthrates and low death rates, resulting in a stable population once again. The low birthrates are thought to be due to people voluntarily limiting the number of children they have. Parents decide to have fewer children in order to maintain a higher standard of living for themselves and their children.

The theory of demographic transition gives hope that as developing countries continue to industrialize, their high population growth rates will eventually decrease and then stabilize. It should be noted, however, that the concept of demographic transition is merely a theoretical model. It is a summary statement of what happened in the United States and in many other industrialized nations. Because some past societies have had this demographic history does not necessarily mean that current developing nations will repeat the same process.

Different factors, such as religious and cultural values, can greatly affect the rate of population growth. In Japan, for example, certain values rapidly accelerated the passage of the second stage in the demographic transition. At the end of World War II, Japan was a developing nation and had a high birthrate. Two variables rapidly speeded Japan into the third stage of demographic transition. First, there was a general consensus that population control was needed. Second, abortion was not considered immoral (as it was in Western societies). As a result, in the decade from 1947 to 1957, the birthrate in Japan dropped from thirty-four children per thousand to fourteen per thousand, one of the sharpest declines on record. During this decade, half the conceptions were terminated by abortion.[40] It is doubtful that such a rapid transition could be achieved in countries having cultural traditions encouraging large families.

In regard to stabilizing population growth, Ian Robertson notes:

The question is not whether population will stabilize—it will. If the global population exceeds the carrying capacity of the earth, death rates will rise and halt population growth. The issues are whether stability will result from a decrease in birth rates or an increase in death rates, how long it will take before stability occurs, and how many people will be here when this finally happens. The prospect of a demographic transition offers the hope that if certain preconditions are met, population growth rates in the developing world will be reduced by a decline in birth rates rather than the grim alternative.[41]

At present, tragically, most developing countries have become lodged in a "holding pattern" in the middle stage of demographic transition, with high birthrates and lowered death rates.[42] The longer these

Afternoon traffic jams the streets in Calcutta. At its current annual growth rate of about two percent, India will have a population of over one billion by the end of the century.

countries remain in this stage, the more the size of their populations will swell, and the more difficult it becomes for them to industrialize and to complete the "demographic transition."

Problem Attitudes and Values

The Roman Catholic Church still objects to using any birth-control approach except the rhythm method. In many countries, widely accepted values encourage parents to have large families. Abortions are still a controversial issue in our society, with efforts now being made to pass a constitutional amendment to prohibit abortions. Until recent years, laws in many states prohibited selling birth-control devices to unmarried people. A Gallup Poll showed that most Americans still believe population growth is *not* a major issue requir-

ing immediate attention.[43] With such attitudes and values, it is clear that Americans as yet do not recognize that overpopulation is one of our most serious problems.

Two Countries with Severe Population Problems

India and China are two countries having immense problems associated with overpopulation. We will briefly look at these problems. If the population growth rate in the world is not curbed, most countries will in the future be facing similar problems.

INDIA   With an area about one third the size of the United States, India has a population three times as

BOX 16.3

Humorous, True, and Sad

One of the reasons for India's overpopulation problem is that it is often difficult to convey to poorly educated persons how to use birth control methods properly. In one rural village a family-planning worker showed residents how to use condoms by unrolling one over a broomstick handle. Returning to the village a year later, the worker found a large number of new babies. The natives were as puzzled as he. Before intercourse, they had dutifully put condoms on their broomsticks.

Source: "Facts," *National Lampoon*, November 1976, p. 34.

large as this country—over 800 million people. It is also one of the world's poorest nations, with a per capita income of $250 per year.[44] Many of its citizens are malnourished and starving. The average Indian has a daily food intake of about 2,000 calories. (The minimum requirement for staying healthy is about 2,300 to 2,500 calories.) With the current annual growth of around 2 percent, India will have a population of over a billion by the end of this century.[45]

In 1952, India became the first country in the world to adopt a public family-planning program to reduce the birthrate. At first, the program was poorly funded: In 1956, for example, total expenditures amounted to 1 cent per year for every twenty persons. The principal contraceptive method that was promoted was the "rhythm" method—one of the least effective methods. In the 1960s, vasectomies and the intrauterine device (IUD) were added to the techniques used. At the end of the 1960s, oral contraceptives were also added, although vasectomies and IUDs remain the preferred methods.

Although the birthrate has declined somewhat in India, birth-control devices have not reduced the rate to the zero-growth level. A major reason is because most people using birth-control techniques only decide to do so after they already have a large family.[46]

In 1976, the Indian government under Mrs. Indira Gandhi decided to promote a more aggressive population-control strategy. Public educational programs were developed to try to persuade Indians that their main problem was not too little food but too many people. The federal government threatened to dismiss civil service employees who had more than three children. Individual states were asked to pass bills requiring compulsory sterilization of parents after the birth of their third child. As mentioned in the beginning of this chapter, one state, Maharashtra, passed such a law and began compulsory sterilization.

However, in 1977, Mrs. Gandhi received a crushing electoral defeat, partly because of her government's record on civil liberties and partly because of the unpopularity of the population control programs. A few years later Mrs. Gandhi returned to power and shortly afterward was assassinated. Her son, Rajiv Gandhi, became prime minister and appears committed to curbing population growth—primarily through promoting voluntary family-planning policies.

At present, India's population has a growth rate of over 2 percent per year and a doubling time of thirty-one years.[47] Prior to the year 2000, at this rate India will have a population of over 1 billion! Is India continuing to race toward starvation and famine, or will it find politically acceptable approaches to control its population growth and begin to raise the standard of living for its citizens? This question is of vital significance to all developing countries (and will also have substantial consequences for the rest of the world).

CHINA   In terms of sheer size, China's population dwarfs that of India. China's population is over 1 billion: It has over one fifth of the world's entire population.[48]

China's attitude to population growth has varied over the years. For many years, the government stated that its huge population was an important military resource in any military conflict with the Soviet Union or the United States. Furthermore, it urged other developing nations to take the same view. As is common with many developing nations, the standard of living of its people is low, and much of the farming and factory work is done by hand.

Poor harvests and resulting food shortages (along with changes in the top leadership of the Chinese government and a closer relationship with the United States) have convinced Chinese leaders that population control is essential. The government is now promoting the view that limiting family size will improve the health and living conditions of all of its citizens and will also liberate women from traditional restrictions. Propaganda posters advertise that an education and a good career are more easily attained with a small family.

Prior to the present policies on family size Chinese women averaged three children each.[49] In 1980 China's government established a one-child-per-family policy. It raised the minimum legal age of marriage by two years to 22 years of age for men and 20 years for women. In some higher-density areas, this minimum age is even higher; in Beijing it is 28 years for men and 25 years for women.[50] (A higher minimum age for marriage is correlated with a smaller average family size.[51]) To have a large family is now regarded as disrespectful to the Communist party and to the country.

Women who become pregnant after the birth of their first child are sometimes pressured to have an abortion. China has also established a number of economic and social incentives for couples to have no more than one child, including income bonuses, priority consideration in urban housing assignments, subsidies in health care, promises of higher pensions, and private vegetable gardens for city residents. For cou-

ples who have more than two children, there are also disincentives, such as a possible wage deduction to fund welfare programs.

China has greatly slowed its growth rate with these policies. Its doubling time is now fifty-three years.[52] The pace of childbearing in China has decelerated faster than in any other large developing country.[53] Yet, amazingly, new problems have emerged. The government has begun to reevaluate its policy of the one-child family. Some fears have surfaced about the possibility of an emerging generation of spoiled and self-centered only children. Also, if the one-child family policy were fully achieved, China would become a society without brothers, sisters, uncles, or aunts.[54]

In recent years, China has opened its doors to the West, inviting tourists and Western technology and investments. Undoubtedly, there will be rapid technological, social, cultural, and lifestyle changes. History suggests such changes will be accompanied by political turmoil. (For example, in the 1970s, the Shah of Iran developed programs to facilitate industrialization, using funds from the sale of its crude oil to foreign countries. These rapid changes led to political turmoil, civil war, and the eventual ouster of the Shah.) The future changes in China will have immense implications for the Soviet Union, the United States, and the rest of the world.

ENVIRONMENTAL PROBLEMS

Higher concentrations of people in an area usually intensify environmental problems. In this section, we will examine the following problems: despoilment of the land, radioactive wastes, solid waste disposal, air pollution, radioactive leaks, nuclear war, water pollution, acid rain, and general pollutants.

Despoilment of the Land

The scenic beauty of our land and often its long-term economic value are being spoiled by a variety of

Monument Valley, Arizona, meets the "throw-away" society.

struction. Dinosaurs once ruled the earth, but all died from some as yet unknown environmental change. The Sahara Desert, less than 2,000 years ago, was a luxuriant forest. Overgrazing by domesticated sheep and goats and clearing of the forests were major factors in destroying the area.[55]

Paul and Anne Ehrlich describe what happens when forests are cleared:

Numerous animals that depend on the trees for food and shelter disappear. Many of the smaller forest plants depend on the trees for shade; they and the animals they support also disappear. With the removal of trees and plants, the soil is directly exposed to the elements, and it tends to erode faster. Loss of topsoil reduces the water-retaining capacity of an area, diminishes the supply of fresh water, causes silting of dams, and ... flooding.... Deforestation ... reduces the amount of water transferred from ground to air by the trees in the process known as "transpiration." This modifies the weather downwind of the area, usually making it more arid and subject to greater extremes of temperature.[56]

Some areas of the world are losing several inches of topsoil each year because of poor management that exposes the land to water and wind erosion. This is particularly alarming when one considers that it takes 300 to 1,000 years to produce one inch of topsoil under favorable conditions.[57] Each year 25 billion tons of topsoil is lost, primarily by erosion and by being washed into the sea.[58]

Forests, water, and soil are renewable resource systems that have "carrying capacities" that is, a level at which they can provide maximum yields without injuring their capacity to repeat that yield. We can only chop down a certain number of trees in a forest each year without injuring the forest's capacity to replace those trees. Populations in many parts of the world have grown so large that they are beginning to exceed the "carrying capacities" of their environments.[59]

Waste Disposal

As yet our country does not have a safe way of disposing of radioactive waste material. We will look at

short-term human efforts: strip mining of coal, oil drilling, clearing of trees and forests, building of highways, construction of oil pipelines, overgrazing by cattle and sheep, dumping of garbage, littering, and erection of highway billboards. In nature, there is often a delicate balance between the elements: Some fertile land needs trees and grass to retain moisture and fertility; grass-eating animals need grass to survive; carnivorous animals need the grass-eating animals; some birds need seeds and insects; other birds feed on small animals or larger animals that have died; all are in need of water. Upsetting this balance often leads to devastating de-this problem, and also examine solid waste disposal problems.

RADIOACTIVE WASTES   America now has over 100 nuclear power plants, with plans to build more in the future.[60] A danger is that nuclear power plants generate radioactive nuclear wastes, and disposing of radioactive wastes is a major problem. In large doses, radiation from these wastes can cause death; small doses may lead to cancer or birth deformities. These wastes are particularly hazardous because they remain radioactive for many years—as long as 300,000 years. The Nuclear Regulatory Commission has considered various proposals for disposing of these wastes: firing them into space by rockets, burying them at sea, burying them in solid rock formations, and burying them in the deepest abandoned mines that can be found. An ultimate solution has not as yet been found. Such wastes are now generally put in concrete tanks and buried. A serious danger is that these tanks are built to last for a couple of hundred years, even though thousands of years are needed.

Radioactive wastes are a serious problem partly because the wastes remain boiling hot for years. Leakage from some of these waste tanks has already occurred. In 1974, one leak continued for fifty-one days and raised the radiation count substantially above the minimum acceptable levels.[61] A crucial question is, with our current ways of disposing of nuclear wastes, are we creating a lethal problem for the future?

SOLID WASTE DISPOSAL   So much public concern is focused on radioactive waste disposal that we sometimes overlook another serious disposal problem: good old-fashioned junk. Each year, Americans junk billions of tons of wastes: food, glass, paper, plastics, cans, paints, dead animals, abandoned cars, old machinery, and a host of other things. We are often referred to as a "consumer society." More accurately, we are a throw-away society.

Solid wastes are ugly, unpleasant, and odorous. They pollute water that circulates through them and provide breeding grounds for rats and other noxious pests.

The two principal methods of solid waste disposal are so-called landfill (supposedly burying in the

Even on cloudless days, Los Angeles is frequently blanketed with dense smog.

ground) and incineration. Many of the garbage dumping areas, particularly in small towns, do not meet the sanitary standards set by the federal government.[62] In addition, improperly designed municipal incinerators are major contributors to urban air pollution.

Air Pollution

Air pollution is most severe in large, densely populated industrial centers. Some cities (such as Los Angeles) occasionally have such dense smog that even on some clear days there is a haze over the city. Moreover, it is not only city air that is polluted, but the entire atmosphere of the earth is affected to some degree.

Air pollution rots windshield wiper blades and nylon stockings, blackens skies and clothes, damages crops, corrodes paint and steel, and kills people. Death rates are higher when and where smog occurs, especially for the very old, the very young, and those with respiratory ailments. Pollution contributes to a higher incidence of pneumonia, emphysema, lung cancer, and bronchitis. A 1952 London smog disaster was directly linked to some 4,000 deaths. And such disasters are of substantially less significance than the far-reaching effects of day-to-day living in seriously polluted cities. Every day, New York City residents inhale enough cancer-producing substances to equal two packs of cigarettes.[63] Also, poor visibility caused by smog is recognized as a major factor in both airplane and automobile accidents.

In the United States, the National Public Health Service estimates that 90 million tons of carbon monoxide are being added annually to the atmosphere— nearly one half of a ton per person annually![64] Cars emit much of these pollutants; industrial centers (particularly pulp and paper mills, petroleum refineries, chemical plants, and iron and steel mills) add a large share, as does burning trash and burning fuel for heating homes and offices. Carbon monoxide is not the only pollutant being released into the air; others include nitrogen oxides, sulfur oxides, and hydrocarbons.

AIR POLLUTION AND ENVIRONMENTAL CHANGES   Air pollution may also be breaking down the earth's protective ozone layer. The ozone layer surrounds the earth from an altitude of 8 to 30 miles above sea level and screens out many of the harmful rays from the sun. Some studies suggest that fluorocarbon gases (commonly used in refrigerating systems and spray cans) may be destroying this ozone layer.[65] If the ozone layer is breaking down, it is predicted there will be sharp increases in skin cancer, crop failure, and also changes in the world's climate. When these studies became public knowledge, the use of fluorocarbon spray cans by American consumers dropped sharply (demonstrating that individuals acting in the same direction can and do make a difference). Manufacturers responded to this drop in sales by developing spray cans that do not use fluorocarbons. However, fluorocarbons are still being

Firemen in West Germany clean automobiles contaminated with radioactive dirt following the nuclear power plant explosion at Chernobyl.

used in coolants in refrigerators and air conditioners, for making plastic foams, and as cleaning solvents for microelectronic circuitry. Under certain conditions these compounds escape into the atmosphere, rise high into the stratosphere, and set off chemical reactions that rapidly destroy ozone.

Air pollutants have the potential to alter the earth's atmosphere and climate in other ways as well. For example, some scientists are concerned that a build up of carbon dioxide in the atmosphere could produce a "greenhouse" effect; that is, the carbon dioxide could trap heat near the earth's surface, raising the average temperature. Such overheating, even just a few degrees, could melt much of the polar icecaps and lead

Nuclear Power Plant Explosion in Chernobyl, Russia

In spring 1986, there was an explosion and fire at a nuclear power plant in Chernobyl, Russia. The explosion blew the top off the reactor and sent a radioactive plume across large parts of the Soviet Union and much of Eastern and Western Europe. The 4,000-degree Fahrenheit fire burned in the reactor's graphite core for over a week before it was extinguished. Within a few weeks after the disaster, over twenty people had died from massive doses of radiation. It is feared that exposure to lesser amounts of radiation will result in early deaths for tens of thousands of people from cancers of the bone marrow, breast, and thyroid.

The disaster happened at a highly vulnerable place. Eighty miles from the site is the city of Kiev, which has a population of over 2 million people. Chernobyl is also near the breadbasket area of the Soviet Union; nearly half of the country's winter wheat is grown in this area. Much of the grass and animal feed in the area was contaminated with radioactive particles.

Such accidents have informed the public of the dangers of nuclear power plants and have slowed the growth of nuclear energy use. Whether to expand or curtail the development of nuclear power plants is an international issue. This issue illustrates the complexity of trying to make a decision between energy needs and physical safety, especially when experts are in sharp disagreement about the technological risks. Those exposed to radioactivity in Cherynobyl, Russia would, if given a choice, undoubtedly choose less energy than the reality that they are now more apt to have birth defects when they have children and are more apt to an early death from cancer.

to incredible flooding around the world. Other scientists predict the opposite may occur; that is, air pollutants may reflect sun rays away from the earth. The earth would then become cooler and perhaps enter into a new ice age.[66] The greenhouse effect is largely due to the burning of fossil fuels (such as coal and petroleum), which emits carbon dioxide into the atmosphere.

Radioactive Leaks from Nuclear Power Plants

We already mentioned one of the problems associated with nuclear energy: radioactive wastes. Another nuclear energy problem is the potential for radioactive

leaks into the air. In the United States there have been numerous malfunctions at nuclear power plants that have resulted in the release of minor amounts of radioactivity into the air.[67] In 1979, over 200,000 residents had to be evacuated from the area surrounding the power plant at Three Mile Island, Pennsylvania. Radioactive leakage from a damaged reactor caused fear that an explosion might occur. In 1986 an explosion did occur at a nuclear power plant in Chernobyl, Russia (see Box 16.4).

Nuclear War

On the morning of August 6, 1945, adults in Hiroshima were preparing to go to work. An American bomber was spotted overhead. Seconds later, an atomic bomb was dropped, which exploded 2,000 feet above the center of the city. The destruction was devastating. The heat and force of the blast killed tens of thousands of people almost instantly. It also released radiation, which eventually killed more than 100,000 more people.[68] Numerous bombs have since been built that are 1,600 times more powerful than the one that destroyed Hiroshima.[69]

One of the greatest dangers to the survival of civilization is a nuclear war. A nuclear war would have devastating effects on the environment. Many authorities believe a nuclear war could end human civilization. The Soviet Union and the United States have the nuclear capacity to destroy each other several times over. Many other nations in the world now possess nuclear bombs or are seeking to develop nuclear warheads or purchase them from other countries.[70]

If a nuclear war occurred, those located near where the bombs struck would be killed instantly. Those who initially survived would face death from a variety of sources. (Exposure to radiation may cause cancer and a variety of other fatal medical conditions.) Some scientists predict that survivors would face a "nuclear winter," in which a cloud of soot would block the sun over much of the earth, which would push temperatures far below freezing and prevent the growth of most foods. Another worry is that the ozone layer would break down. This layer protects the earth from the full power of the sun's rays. Clearing of the cloud of soot would cause intense sunrays to penetrate humans and animals, resulting in skin cancer and other disorders. Another danger is that crops would be affected by radioactivity and would be potentially dangerous as food sources. It could well be that the initial survivors would face a slow, painful death. Their quailty of life could slip into a new age in which they would grub out a brutelike, barely human existence. The quality of life for survivors would decline drastically because the social infrastructure would unravel; that is, the industrial, educational, agricultural, transportation, health care, political, and communication systems would cease to function. Those who did survive would also face intense psychological stress from grief, despair, disorientation, hopelessness, and anger.[71]

How can a nuclear war be averted? This is perhaps the most important question facing civilization today. Dr. William Langer Ury, director of the Nuclear Negotiation Project at Harvard University, suggests the following. He indicates that the greatest danger is not the weapons but people making mistakes. Dr. Ury states:

Too many paths exist by which an unexpected nuclear crisis could erupt—and they are gradually multiplying. The superpowers could become embroiled in their friend's wars, as in the Middle East. Missiles might be fired by accident or without authorization. A "mad" leader with a few atomic bombs believing that his nation or terrorist group would be better off without the superpowers, might detonate a bomb in an American city, hoping thereby to trigger a Soviet-American exchange.[72]

If one side starts to send nuclear missiles at the other, the other side only has ten or fifteen minutes to respond, as it only takes fifteen or twenty minutes for nuclear missiles to reach their objectives once they are launched. Therefore, it is extremely important for both sides to have accurate information and flawless communication with each other. Ury suggests that three crisis control measures be used.[73] The first has already been put in place—a crisis hot line where the leaders of the United States and the Soviet Union can immediately communicate with each other.

His second recommendation is the establishment of a U.S.–Soviet crisis control center in Moscow and Washington, D.C. It would be staffed around the clock with American and Soviet experts. These people would be highly trained military and diplomatic experts who know each other and who have prepared intensively together for a nuclear war crisis. The staff of such a center would simultaneously inform both the United States and the Soviet Union of available information about which country or terrorist group launched a missile that was headed for either country.

His third suggestion is that the crisis center might take on the additional function of being the mechanism in which the United States and the Soviet Union share intelligence and act jointly to prevent nuclear terrorism or a nuclear attack from a third nation.

The unwritten policy with regard to armament has

been "peace through strength." Both the United States and the Soviet Union seek to intimidate the other with superior military force so that the other does not dare to attack. The United States has committed itself to an expensive program of research and large-scale experimentation in the use of satellites and laser weaponry that is designed to destroy nuclear weapons before they reach their targets. This effort, commonly known as "Star Wars," has the objective of developing a space-based defensive shield that would protect the United States from nuclear missile attack.[74]

The concept is currently in the realm of science fiction and may or may not be attainable. Former President Reagan argued that a Star Wars system could end the arms race because it would make offensive nuclear weapons obsolete, and President Bush strongly supports research and development for such a program. Critics argue that even if the project were feasible, it would result in the Soviet Union eventually developing a similar system. If both countries were then successful, each country would probably seek to develop a whole new offensive system that would be designed to destroy the other. The history of international conflict has been that as an offensive system is made obsolete by a defensive system, a new offensive system is developed. One hundred years ago, rifles and cannons were considered the ultimate weapons. We have since developed tanks, fighter planes, bombers, nuclear missiles, germ warfare, laser beams, submarines, battleships, aircraft carriers, and many other weapons. Even if Star Wars is successful, new offensive systems are apt to be developed unless effective nonviolent mechanisms are established for resolving international conflicts.

One way for our country to alleviate Soviet fears about U.S. development of Star Wars is for our country to propose and work out an arrangement with the Soviet Union for a cooperative effort in developing Star Wars technology. Such a cooperative effort would have a number of advantages. It would be less expensive for the United States, since the Soviet Union would bear some of the expense. The two superpowers would be working together on an immensely important project, which may lead to increased cooperation and trust in the future. If the project is successful, the two superpowers would have a defense against nuclear attack from terrorist groups and from other hostile countries.

Water Pollution

The water supply of many American cities is rated by the U.S. Public Health Service as being a "potential health hazard" or as "unsatisfactory."[75] Reasons include tap impurities, infrequent testing for bacteria, and impure water sources. A 1982 study found that 28 percent of the U.S. population was not served by sewage treatment facilities, with another 21 percent being served by treatment plants that released a significant portion of the raw sewage directly into some body of water.[76] The bacteria in such untreated sewage makes the water unfit for swimming, drinking, and many industrial uses.

As the population grows in an industrial center, so does industry, which pours into the water a vast array of contaminants: detergents, sulfuric acid, lead, hydrofluoric acid, ammonia, and so on. Increased agricultural production also pollutes water via insecticides, herbicides, and nitrates (from fertilizers). The result is the spread of pollution in creeks, streams, and lakes; along coastlines; and—most seriously—in groundwater, where purification is almost impossible. Water pollution poses the threat of epidemics of diseases such as hepatitis and dysentery, as well as poisoning by exotic chemicals. Some rivers and lakes are now so polluted they cannot support fish and other organisms that require relatively clean, oxygen-rich water. Such lakes and rivers are accurately described as "dead."

The United States has the dubious distinction of being the only country in the world having a river that has been called a fire hazard. So many industrial chemicals, oils, and other combustible pollutants have been dumped into the Cuyahoga River in Ohio that it has twice caught on fire.

Acid Rain

There is a growing concern over acid rain. Formed from emissions from automobiles and industrial plants, acid rain has become a serious problem in eastern Canada and the northeastern United States. Acid rain is killing fish in lakes and streams and is reducing the number of plant nutrients in the ground, thereby making soil less fertile. It has also damaged timber and may eventually start damaging synthetic structures,

On March 24, 1989, the Exxon Valdez *ran aground off Alaska, dumping a quarter of a million barrels of crude oil into Prince William Sound. Clumsy clean-up efforts by Exxon and the Coast Guard failed to keep the slick from spreading and turning into the worst oil spill in U.S. history. This animal recovery crew picks up dead sea otters from the sound—now little more than a marine graveyard.*

including classic architecture and sculptures. Scientists estimate that 50,000 lakes in the United States and Canada are now so polluted by acid rain that fish populations have either been destroyed or severely damaged.[77]

Canada Environment Minister John Fraser has called acid rain his country's "worst environment problem."[78] Acid rain is created when sulfur and nitrogen oxides emitted from automobiles and industrial plants combine with moisture in the air to form sulfuric and nitric acids.

General Pollutants

Some substances—such as chlorinated hydrocarbons, lead, mercury, and fluorides—reach us in so many ways that they are considered *general pollutants*. Of the chlorinated hydrocarbons, DDT has been used the longest but now is banned. DDT is a synthetic insecticide. DDT as a chemical breaks down slowly; it will last for decades in soil. Unhappily, the way DDT circulates in ecosystems leads to a concentration in carnivores (including humans); that is, it becomes increasingly concentrated as it is passed along a food chain. Following World War II, DDT was widely used as an insecticide until research involving laboratory animals showed that DDT affects fertility, causes changes in brain functioning, and increases the incidence of cancer.[79]

The long-term effects of DDT (and of many other general pollutants) are still unknown. DDT has a poisoning effect that may (or may not) lead to subtle physiological changes. Some mother's milk in the United

BOX 16.5

Tragedy at Love Canal

L ove Canal was once a pleasant neighborhood of tree-lined streets in the city of Niagara Falls, New York. Up until the late 1970s, hardly anyone was concerned that the area had once been a chemical dumping ground. Over a twenty-five-year period, ending in 1953, Hooker Chemicals and Plastic Corporation had buried 20,000 tons of toxic substances in leaky drums. Among the chemicals dumped was highly lethal dioxin. In the late 1970s, it was noted that the residents of Love Canal had substantially higher rates of birth defects, cancer, miscarriages, chromosome damage, kidney failure, and deaths.

The neighborhood—homes, schools, and parks—had been built above this dump site. Families noted that bluish-black substances would ooze through the ground. These substances were discovered to be toxic. Dumped pesticides and other poisons had polluted the ground water, seeping up through the ground and into basements, creating hazardous vapors. Tests in certain basements found 80 different toxic chemicals to be present. It was also thought contamination was occurring from eating home-grown garden vegetables.

In 1980, the Environmental Protection Agency conducted tests in the area and found it to have dangerously high levels of toxic substances. Love Canal has since been evacuated, and the area is now a ghost town.

Environmental experts acknowledge that the Love Canal disaster is not an isolated problem. Of the nearly 50,000 toxic-chemical dumps in America, more than 1,000 are considered potential health hazards.

Source: "Living with Uncertainty: Saga of Love Canal Families," *U.S. News & World Report*, June 2, 1980, p. 32.

States now contains a high enough level of DDT that it would be declared illegal in interstate commerce.[80] DDT was used extensively before research indicated it had dangerous long-term effects. An important question is, among the thousands of chemicals currently being used, which ones have unknown toxic side effects?

Radioactive wastes and certain poisons such as DDT pose serious problems because of the process of biological magnification. With this process (mentioned above), the concentration of the substance increases as it ascends in the food chain. For example, Richard Curtis and Elizabeth Hogan found in a study of the Colum-

bia River in the western United States that although the radioactivity of the water was at such low levels it was nonhazardous, the radioactivity of river-related biological forms was much higher and potentially hazardous.

. . . the radioactivity of the river plankton was 2,000 times greater; the radioactivity of the fish and ducks feeding on the plankton was 15,000 and 40,000 times greater, respectively; the radioactivity of young swallows fed on insects caught by their parents in the river was 500,000 times greater; the radioactivity of the egg yolks of water birds was more than a million times greater.[81]

The radioactivity was thought to be due to isotopes released into the river from the nuclear power plant at Hanford, Washington.

DDT, many other pesticides, and radioactive material are cumulative poisons; that is, they are retained in the tissues of the organisms that consume them rather than being excreted back into the environment. Thus, one never loses the poison of previous exposure, with future exposures compounding the potential dangerous effects of the poison to the individual. In 1984 the National Academy of Sciences released a report stating that little or nothing is known about the effects on humans of 80 percent of the 48,500 different chemicals in use, as very little research has been conducted on the effects of these chemicals.[82]

Chronic lead poisoning is also serious; it leads to loss of appetite, weakness, and apathy. It causes lesions of the neuromuscular system, the circulatory system, the gastrointestinal tract, and the brain. Exposure to lead comes from a variety of sources: combustion of leaded gasoline, pesticides, lead pipes, lead-contaminated food and water. It perhaps is most hazardous when children eat paint containing lead. It should be noted that most household paints today do not contain lead, but the problem still exists with older buildings and furniture that were painted with a lead-based paint. Many of these buildings have been painted over with lead-free paint, but peeling of the lead-free paint may expose the original lead-based ones.

Exposure to high concentrations of mercury may cause blindness, deafness, loss of coordination, severe mental disorders, or even death. Mercury is added to the environment in many ways. It may leak into the water from industrial processes that produce chlorine. It is emitted by the pulp and paper industry. It is a primary ingredient of agricultural fungicides. Small amounts are released when fossil fuels are burned.

WHAT NEEDS
TO BE DONE

This chapter highlights several national and international problems: overpopulation, food and water short-

ages, economic problems, international terrorism, crowding, energy shortages, shortages of nonrenewable resources, despoilment of the land, radioactive and solid waste disposal, air pollution, radioactive leaks from nuclear power plants, nuclear war, water pollution, acid rain, and general pollutants. This section will briefly summarize a number of recommendations for confronting overpopulation and environmental problems.

Confronting Overpopulation

Limiting population growth will have a major positive impact on all of the problems discussed in this chapter. If the world's population growth rate is reversed to head toward a zero growth rate, and even to go negative, it may give us the necessary time to find solutions to the other problems that have been discussed. Limiting population growth is a key factor in maintaining our current quality of life.

How can the size of the population be limited? Dr. Paul Ehrlich provides the following suggestions. Being the most affluent and influential superpower, the United States should become a model for population control by (*a*) setting a goal of a stable optimum population size for our country and displaying our determination to achieve this goal rapidly and (*b*) reversing our government's current "reward" system for having children. Specific measures include:

- No longer allowing income tax deductions for children.

- Placing a luxury tax on layettes, diapers, cribs, expensive toys, and diaper services.

- Rewarding small families by such measures as giving "responsibility prizes" to each man who has a vasectomy after having two children.

- Subsidizing adoptions and simplifying adoption procedures.

- Guaranteeing the right of any woman to have an abortion.

- Enacting a federal law requiring sex education in schools—sex education that includes material on the need for regulating the birthrate and the techniques of birth control.

- Developing new contraceptives that are reliable and easy to use and do not have harmful side effects.[83]

Bernard Berelson compiled a list of other proposals to control population, including:

- Adding temporary sterilants to water or food supplies, with doses of an antidote being carefully rationed by the government to produce the desired population size (such sterilants are not as yet in existence).

- Compulsory sterilization of men with three or more living children.

- Raising the minimum age of marriage.

- Providing benefits (money, goods, or services) to couples not bearing children for extended time periods.

- Requiring that foreign countries must establish effective population control programs before *any* foreign aid will be provided.[84]

Some of these proposals appear "too radical" for most Americans to accept, and they conflict with moral and ethical values of many U.S. citizens. But will we reach such an overpopulation crisis that they may be necessary in the future? Many developing nations are now providing sex education and family-planning programs to their people, which (at least temporarily) are showing evidence of lowering birth rates. It is hoped that the population control measures recommended by Berelson can be avoided.

One of the developing countries that has had success in reducing the rate of population growth is Mexico. Its government has made progress by a comprehensive "social marketing" campaign to promote the values of smaller-sized families and of delaying pregnancy.[85] Mexico has spread these messages through advertisements on radio, television, and billboards. It has also produced a popular love song in which a teenage duet agrees to delay having sex. Mexico has also produced a television series that promotes the value of smaller-sized families and the view that true "machismo" is proved by a male fathering only as many children as he can support, rather than by prolific

reproduction. This "soap opera" has had considerable success in promoting family planning among young males and females. For use in other countries, Mexico's program must be adapted to each nation's unique culture and values so that viewers can more readily identify with the characters, situations, and dilemmas.[86]

Ehrlich, Ehrlich, and Holdren provide an elegant summary of the need to establish a worldwide vision of the future of the human race:

Perhaps the major necessary ingredient that has been missing from a solution to the problems of both the United States and the rest of the world is a goal, a vision of the kind of Spaceship Earth that ought to be and the kind of crew that should man her. Society has always had its visionaries who talked of love, beauty, peace, and plenty. But somehow the "practical" men have always been there to praise smog as a sign of progress, to preach "just" wars, and to restrict love while giving hate free rein. It must be one of the greatest ironies of the history of the human species that the only salvation for the practical man now lies in what they think of as the dreams of idealists. The question now is: can the self-proclaimed "realists" be persuaded to face reality in time?[87]

THE ABORTION CONTROVERSY   If the world's population continued to grow at or near its present rate, the current controversy over voluntary abortions may look "pale" compared to controversies that will be generated if compulsory population control measures are needed.

The abortion controversy has now been going on for nearly two decades, but it was heightened when, in January 1973, the U.S. Supreme Court, in a 7 to 2 decision, overruled state laws that prohibited or restricted a woman's right to obtain an abortion during the first three months of pregnancy. States still have the authority to impose restrictions after the third month. States may prohibit abortions in the last ten weeks of pregnancy (a time when there is a good chance that the fetus will live) if they desire, except where the life or health of the mother is endangered.

In 1977, Congress passed, and President Carter signed into law, the so-called Hyde Amendment (named for its original sponsor, Representative Henry

Pro-life or pro-choice? Abortion is probably the single most divisive public issue today.

Hyde from Illinois). This amendment bars Medicaid spending for abortions except when a woman's life would be endangered by childbirth or in cases of promptly reported rape or incest. In June 1980, this amendment was upheld on a 5 to 4 vote by the U.S. Supreme Court as constitutional. The ruling means that the federal government and individual states do not have to pay for most abortions wanted by women on welfare.

The Hyde Amendment is significant because more than one third of the legal abortions performed in the United States between 1973 and 1977 were for women on welfare.[88] The passage of the Hyde Amendment shows the strength of the antiabortion forces in this country. Is it fair for middle- and upper-class women to

have greater access to obtaining an abortion than do lower-income women?

In the 1980s there was a move toward conservatism in our society. Certain groups, such as the Roman Catholic Church and the "Moral Majority" (headed by Jerry Falwell) have been strongly urging that a constitutional amendment be passed to prohibit abortions, except in cases where the woman's life is endangered.

The major objection to permitting abortions is based on moral principles. The Catholic Church views the abortion issue as one of the most important current moral issues. This church and "right to life" groups condemn abortions as being synonymous to murder. They assert that life begins at conception and point out that there is no phase during pregnancy in which there is a distinct, qualitative difference in the development of the fetus. The Catholic Church views abortion as acceptable only when it is done to save the physical life of the mother. This type of abortion is justified on the principle of "double effect," which holds that a morally evil action (an abortion) is allowable when it is the side effect of a morally good act (saving the life of the mother).

There are numerous arguments that have been advanced for permitting abortions:

- If abortions were prohibited again, women would seek illegal abortions as they did in the past. Performed in a medical clinic or hospital, an abortion is a relatively safe operation; but performed under unsanitary conditions, perhaps by an inexperienced or unskilled abortionist, the operation is extremely dangerous and may even imperil the life of the woman. If abortions were again prohibited, some women would attempt to self-induce abortions. Attempts at self-induced abortions can be extremely dangerous. Women have tried such techniques as severe exercise, hot baths, and pelvic and intestinal irritants and have even attempted to lacerate the uterus with such sharp objects as hatpins, nail files, and knives.

- Recognizing abortions as being legal helps prevent the birth of unwanted babies; such babies have a higher probability of being abused or neglected.

- Permitting women to obtain an abortion allows women to have greater freedom, as they would not be forced to raise a child at a time when they had other plans and commitments.

Opponents of abortion argue that the "right to life" is the basic right that everyone has and should in no way be infringed on. Proponents of abortion seek to counter this view by arguing that there may be a more basic right than the right to life, that is, the preservation of the quality of life. Given the overpopulation problem and given the fact that abortion appears to be a necessary population-control technique (in some countries the number of abortions is approaching the number of live births), some authorities are asserting that abortion is a necessary measure (although less desirable than contraceptives) to preserve the quality of life.[89] Unless life has quality, the right to life is meaning-less. Table 16.3 presents arguments both for and against legal abortion.

Providing Family-Planning Services

Family-planning services are obviously essential programs for preventing unwanted pregnancies. Such services include providing birth-control information and contraceptives, pregnancy testing, infertility counseling, counseling about AIDS and other venereal diseases, sex education, abortion counseling and abortions, counseling on child spacing, sterilization information and operations, and infertility counseling. Family planning includes helping couples who desire children to have children. It also helps couples to prepare for parenthood.

GOVERNMENTAL PROGRAMS   National family-planning programs are governmental efforts to lower birth rates by funding programs that provide birth-control information and services. With family-planning programs, families voluntarily decide whether to limit the number of children they have. Most countries, including developing and developed nations, now have official family-planning programs. This is a remarkable achievement, since forty years ago no developing country had a governmental family-planning program. (In fact, forty years ago, several countries had programs with the opposite objective—to increase the birthrate and the rate of immigration.) This indicates that concern about world population growth is a recent phenomenon.

In spite of these advances, only a few countries have established population-control policies. Two countries that have are India and China, as described earlier in this chapter. (Population control is the deliberate regulation of the size of the population by society. Family planning, in contrast, is the regulation of births by individual families.) As we noted, India's population-control program launched in 1976 included a sterilization policy that was soon retracted after the party that passed the legislation failed to be reelected.

TABLE 16.3

Legal Abortion: Arguments Pro and Con

Against Legal Abortion	In Favor of Legal Abortion
Human life begins at conception; therefore, abortion is murder of a person. Even scientists have not reached a consensus on any other point in fetal development that can be considered the moment the fetus becomes a person. Life is a matter of fact, not religion or values.	The belief in personhood at conception is a religious belief held by the Roman Catholic Church. Most Protestant and Jewish denominations regard the fetus as a potential human being, not a full-fledged person and have position statements in support of legal abortion. When the unborn becomes a person is a matter of religion and values, not absolute fact.
We must pass a constitutional amendment to protect unborn babies from abortion. To say the law will not be followed and should not be made is like saying people still get murdered so laws against murder should be repealed.	No law has ever stopped abortion and no law ever will. The issue is not whether abortions will be done, but whether they will be done safely, by doctors, or dangerously, by back-alley butchers, or by the women themselves. History has shown that antiabortion laws are uniquely unenforceable, as they do not prevent abortions.
Medicaid should not pay for abortion. It is wrong to try to eliminate poverty by killing the unborn children of the poor. Tax money should not be used for the controversial practice of aborting unwanted children. The decision not to have children should be made before getting pregnant.	The original intent of Medicaid was to equalize medical services between the rich and the poor and to help the poor become independent and self-sufficient. To make them ineligible for abortion defies justice, common sense, and rational policy. Women burdened by unwanted children cannot get job training or go to work and are trapped in the poverty/welfare cycle. Neither abortion nor childbirth should be forced on poor women.
If you believe abortion is morally wrong, you are obligated to work for the passage of a "human life" amendment to the Constitution.	Many people who are personally opposed to abortion, including most Roman Catholics, believe it is wrong to impose their religious or moral beliefs on others.
The right of the unborn to live supersedes any right of a woman to "control her own body."	The Supreme Court has affirmed that the constitutional right to privacy includes the right to terminate a pregnancy and that fetuses are not persons with constitutional rights.
The "abortion mentality" leads to infanticide, euthanasia, and killing of retarded and elderly persons.	In countries where abortion has been legal for years, there is no evidence that respect for life has diminished or that legal abortion leads to killing of any persons. Infanticide, however, is prevalent in countries where the overburdened poor cannot control their childbearing and was prevalent in Japan before abortion was legalized.
Abortion causes psychological damage to women.	The Institute of Medicine of the National Academy of Sciences has concluded that abortion is not associated with a detectable increase in the incidence of mental illness. The depression and guilt feelings reported by some women are usually mild, temporary, and outweighed by feelings of relief. Such negative feelings would be substantially lessened if

TABLE 16.3

(Continued)

Against Legal Abortion	In Favor of Legal Abortion
	antiabortion advocates were less vehement in expressing their beliefs. Women choosing abortion should be informed of the risks and benefits of the procedure and should decide for themselves what to do.
Women have abortions for their own convenience or on "whim."	Right-to-life dismisses unwanted pregnancy as a mere annoyance. The urgency of women's need to end unwanted pregnancy is measured by their willingness to risk death and mutilation, to spend huge sums of money, and to endure the indignities of illegal abortion. Women only have abortions when the alternative is unendurable. Women take both abortion and motherhood very seriously.
In a society where contraceptives are so readily available, there should be no unwanted pregnancies and therefore no need for abortion.	No birth control method is perfectly reliable, and for medical reasons many women cannot, or will not, use the most effective methods. Contraceptive information and services are not available to all women, particularly teenagers, the poor, and rural women.
Abortion is not the safe and simple procedure we're told it is.	Before the 1973 Supreme Court rulings, illegal abortion was the leading cause of maternal death and mutilation. Having a legal abortion is medically less dangerous than childbirth.
Doctors make large profits from legal abortions.	Legal abortion is less costly and less profitable than illegal abortion was. Many legal abortions are done in nonprofit facilities. If it's not improper to "make money" on childbirth, it is not wrong to earn money by performing legal abortions.
Parents have the right and responsibility to guide their children in important decisions. A law requiring parental notification of a daughter's abortion would strengthen the family unit.	Many teenagers voluntarily consult their parents, but some simply will not. Forcing the involvement of unsympathetic, authoritarian, or very moralistic parents in a teen's pregnancy (and sexuality) can damage the family unit beyond repair. Some family units are already under so much stress that knowledge of an unwed pregnancy could be disastrous.
Proabortionists are antifamily. Abortion destroys the American family.	The unwanted child of a teenaged mother has little chance to grow up in a normal, happy American home. Instead, a new family is created: a child and her child, both destined for a life of poverty and hopelessness. Legal abortion helps women limit their families to the number of children they want and can afford, both emotionally and financially, and reduces the number of children born unwanted. Prochoice is definitely profamily.

Planned Parenthood, the largest family planning organization in the country, offers medical, counseling, and educational services. The agency actively promotes condom use as a birth control measure.

Whether India will attempt to enact another population-control policy is unclear; future population growth may be a decisive factor in India's determining whether population control is necessary.

Until President Lyndon Johnson's 1965 State of the Union Address, family planning was not considered a proper concern for our government. In his address, President Johnson stated that $5 spent on family planning was worth $100 invested in some other area of world economic development. In 1966, the federal government developed regulations that, for the first time, allowed federal funds to provide family-planning services to welfare clients on a voluntary basis. The avowed purpose of this policy (which was widely criticized) was not phrased in terms of family-planning goals but instead had the objectives of reducing the welfare burden by lowering the illegitimacy rate and of breaking the poverty cycle by decreasing the transmission of poverty from one generation to another.

The National Center for Family Planning Services was established by the passage of the Family Planning Services and Population Research Act of 1970. This act recognized that family planning was part of the delivery of comprehensive health services for all. In 1972, Congress mandated that family-planning services must be provided to all welfare recipients who desired them. At that time, contraceptive policy changes were also made, lifting restrictions on marital status and age for receiving birth-control information and devices.

PRIVATE AGENCIES   In the United States, most family-planning services have in the past been provided by private agencies and organizations. The largest and best-known organization is Planned Parenthood: This organization was founded in 1916 by Margaret Sanger, with the opening of the first birth-control clinic in Brooklyn. The organization now has clinics located throughout the nation. Planned Parenthood now offers (*a*) medical services—physical examinations, pap-smear tests, urine and blood tests, venereal disease screening, all medically approved methods of contraception, and pregnancy testing; (*b*) counseling services—infertility, premarital, contraceptive, pregnancy, and sterilization for males and for females; and (*c*) educational services—sex education, contraceptive information including effectiveness and side effects of the varied approaches, and breast self-examinations. (Table 16.4 shows a ranking of the effectiveness of various contraceptives in preventing pregnancies.)

Family-planning services are now available in practically all areas in the United States from a variety of public and private organizations, including health departments, hospitals, physicians in private practice, Planned Parenthood affiliates, and other agencies such as community action groups and free clinics.

TABLE 16.4

Ranking of Effectiveness of Contraceptives in Preventing Pregnancies

Method	Number of Pregnancies per 100 Women during One Year of Use
1. Sterilization	.1
2. Pill	2
3. Intrauterine devices	5
3. (tie) Condom and foam	5
5. Condom alone	10
6. Sponge	15–18
7. Foam	18
8. Diaphragm with spermicide	19
9. Withdrawal	23
10. Fertility awareness (rhythm)	24

Source: *Methods of Contraception* (Milwaukee, WI: Planned Parenthood, 1986), p. 15.

Note: After the first five listed contraceptives, the risk of pregnancy for sexually active users is sharply increased.

THE FUTURE   A national policy of family planning is needed. Currently, there is considerable controversy about a number of issues associated with family planning: sex education in schools, abortions, provision of birth-control information and devices for teenagers, and the issue of whether the federal government should pay for abortions for those who cannot afford them.

In the United States, public family-planning centers have been concentrated in poor communities and in nonwhite communities. Middle-class families primarily receive family-planning services from private agencies and from private physicians. Some leaders of nonwhite communities have charged that public family-planning centers have a "genocide" objective— that is, the objective of reducing the size of the nonwhite community.[90] Increased public education programs are needed to understand that family planning is not an antipoverty measure. Our citizens also need to understand that our country's historical treatment of nonwhite groups justifiably makes nonwhites suspicious of outside efforts to limit their number of births. Family planning should not simply seek to limit births but should be part of a comprehensive approach to health care.

If problems associated with overpopulation continue to intensify, a national policy of population control may also need to be developed. A number of authorities are predicting dire consequences for the future of the world unless population-control measures are implemented immediately. Other authorities discount overpopulation concerns and predict that technological advancements will prevent cataclysmic effects from rapid population growth. If the latter authorities are mistaken, we may be forced in a few years to apply population control measures that now seem unethical and "inhumane."

Werner Fornos strongly urges that the United States fund international programs that are designed to slow population growth in developing countries:

If Americans now feel anguish over witnessing the recent human suffering and needless deaths in Ethiopia, just imagine a world in which virtually the entire Third World will be wracked by vast poverty and human misery. . . .

And if Americans are now troubled by the specter of instability, revolution, and authoritarianism in the Third World, they have only to imagine the consequences of inaction, because the fragile seed of democracy cannot survive long in societies with escalating misery, crippled economies, and dying environments.

In shaping the federal budget, the U.S. Congress

BOX 16.6

New Contraceptive Breakthrough

N orplant contraceptive implants have been hailed as a major breakthrough in birth
control in this decade. The Norplant method consists of small silicone rubber capsules
containing levonorgestrel, a progestin widely used in oral contraceptives for many years. The
implants are inserted under the skin of a woman's arm and continuously release small
amounts of the contraceptive drug into the bloodstream. The contraceptive effect is achieved
within twenty-four hours and lasts for five years.

The implants were developed by the Population Council, an international nonprofit organization in New York. The implants have already been approved for sale and distribution
in many parts of Europe, Asia, Africa, and Latin America. The method has been found to be a
highly effective birth control measure and to have few health side effects. The method also
appears to be usable by a broad range of cultures and among various social and demographic groups, which suggests Norplant implants will make a substantial contribution to
international family-planning programs.

Sources: Finland Approves Implants," *Popline* 5, no. 11 (December 1983), pp. 1–4; Werner Fornos, *Gaining People,
Losing Ground* (Washington, D.C.: The Population Institute, 1987), pp. 84–85.

---

*must ask not only how much it will cost to fund
population programs, but also what will be the cost of
not funding them.*[91]

Confronting Environmental Problems

Although environmental problems are very serious, it
would be a mistake to assume that the environment is
heading for catastrophe. It was not until the late 1960s
that the public began to realize the seriousness of the
environmental problems we face. Dozens of organizations have since been formed (many of them with international memberships) that are now working on
everything from saving wild animals to recycling aluminum cans to developing new sources of energy.

Since the 1960s there has been progress in a number of areas. Air quality has improved. Less sewage is

being dumped into water. Most automobiles have
emission control devices. Life expectancy in the United
States has been rising, which is an indirect measure
that environmental living conditions may be improving. Relationships between the United States and
the Soviet Union have improved, which reduces the
chances for a nuclear war. However, obviously much
more needs to be done.

Energy development, preservation of the environment, and economic growth are interdependent
problems. Programs that advance one of these often
aggravate the others. For example, the development of
nuclear power plants led to an explosion in a nuclear
reactor in Chernobyl, Russia in 1986 that released radioactivity into the air, which may shorten the lives of
tens of thousands of people who were exposed. There
are other examples. Devices that clean exhaust from
automobiles reduce air pollution but also decrease
fuel economy and thereby more rapidly deplete oil

reserves. Strip mining of coal increases available energy supplies but despoils the scenery. Effective environmental programs in the future need to strike a balance between the competing objectives of preserving the environment, developing energy sources, and fostering economic growth.

Since the late 1960s, environmentalists have been waging a political and educational campaign that has not only increased public awareness of environmental concerns but has also won passage of significant legislation to protect the nation's air, land, and water. For example, the Clean Air Act of 1970 established the Environmental Protection Agency (EPA) and empowered it to set and enforce standards of environmental quality. However, in the 1980s political opposition to environmental concerns intensified. For example, some of the largest corporations in the world have sought to drill oil wells and dig mines in fragile wilderness areas, or have sought to get "the government off their back" when they spew pollutants into the air and water.[92] Such corporations have spent millions of dollars to persuade the government to let them pursue such activities. In the 1980s environmentalists struggled to preserve the gains made in the 1970s. Environmentalists do not have the financial resources that large corporations do. Therefore, it is crucial for those who are concerned about preserving our environment to be aware of political issues in this area and express their views to political leaders.

In the future it is clear that our environmental problems are not going to disappear on their own. In fact, left alone, existing problems are likely to increase, and new ones will come to the fore. What can be done? Actions needed include changing values from consumption to conservation and developing new sources of energy.

Changing Values

We have to realize that "bigger is not necessarily better." We need to focus on preserving and conserving our resources rather than consuming them. George Ritzer notes:

We need a reorientation of American culture, a reorientation that may already be underway.

Learning to live more harmoniously with the environment means changing our attitudes and behavior, usually in simple ways. Recycling is an effective means of putting these new values to a very practical use.

Basically, we need to move away from a system that values things growing constantly bigger and better. We are no longer able to master and subdue all that surrounds us. Rather, we must learn to live more harmoniously with our environment. We need to learn to value and protect our environment rather than seeing it as something to be exploited, raped and despoiled. Most importantly, we need to accept the idea that we are approaching the limits of what the environment can yield to us. At best, we can expect a steady state, at worst a marked decline in our style of life. . . . We need, in other words, to focus on, and invest in, resources that we can renew rather than the

*current propensity to exploit such nonrenewable
resources as coal and oil.*[93]

The move toward conserving resources can be put
into action in a variety of ways, a few of which will be
mentioned here. Garbage can be used as fuel to run
mills to make recycled paper. Water in communities
can be purified again and again, so it can continually
be reused without being discharged into a river, lake,
or ocean. Homes can be better insulated to conserve
heat. Smaller cars can be driven at more energy-effi-
cient speeds. People can ride trains and buses instead
of cars. People in our society need to use the conservation measures that are already available.

Finding New Sources of Energy

Reduction of pollution, population, and energy consumption will not alter the fact that much of our current energy comes from nonrenewable fuel sources.
Sooner or later, we will have to find new sources of
energy.

NUCLEAR ENERGY   Nuclear energy has been one attempt to solve the energy shortage, but concerns over
controlling the safety of nuclear power plants have
slowed construction of them. In March of 1979, the
near disaster at the nuclear power plant at Three Mile
Island in Pennsylvania increased these concerns. Radioactive steam escaped, and there was a danger of a
meltdown that probably would have killed many in the
area from lethal overdoses of radiation. In April 1986
there was an explosion in a nuclear reactor in Chernobyl, Russia that was a much more serious accident. Tens
of thousand of inhabitants were exposed to radioactivity, which threatens to shorten their lives.

Such accidents emphasize that the safety in any
nuclear power plant cannot be taken for granted. Nuclear energy out of control has the potential for a large-
scale disaster. A major question is whether future
development of the use of nuclear energy is worth
the risks.

SYNTHETIC FUEL   In 1980, the federal government
passed legislation to finance and create a synthetic-fuel
industry. The raw materials for synthetic fuel are in oil
shale formations, coal deposits, and gooey-tar sands.
The term "synthetic fuel" is a misnomer, since its components have the same carbon base as crude oil. Coal,
for example, will become gas if it is pulverized and
then mixed with oxygen and steam under extreme
heat. Shale is a dark-brown, fine-grained rock that contains carbon. Production problems are considerable, as
it is estimated that it takes 1.7 tons of shale to produce
a barrel of oil and that it takes a ton of coal to produce
two barrels of oil.[94] Whether synthetic fuel is cost effective remains a major question. A few years after the
initiation of the synthetic-fuel program, a temporary
glut of crude oil occurred worldwide. Partly as a result
of this glut, synthetic fuel efforts have been postponed
or discontinued. When another shortage of crude oil
occurs, it remains to be seen whether programs to
develop synthetic fuel will again be initiated.

On a positive note, it is estimated that the United
States has a 600-year supply of the raw materials for
synthetic fuel.[95]

SOLAR ENERGY   Solar energy is another hope. Thousands of U.S. homes and offices are getting all or part
of their heating and cooling from the sun.[96] Even the
White House has a solar water-heating system on its
roof. Another potential use of sunlight is direct conversion to electricity. Sunlight can be converted directly
into electricity with photovoltaic cells, but the process
is as yet too expensive to be used widely at present. A
growing number of scientists and concerned citizens
are coming to see solar power as one answer to the
world's energy problems. Such technology is really an
imitation of nature, since all energy ultimately comes
from the sun.

SOCIAL WORK AND FAMILY PLANNING

Social workers tend to be concerned about overpopulation and the problems it is creating now and the

The earth covering this Vermont home keeps its temperature constant. A wood-burning stove provides the only additional heat this household will need.

even greater problems it may create in the future. In almost every social service agency, social workers come in contact with clients who want and need family-planning information. In their work, social workers also must respond to controversial issues: for example, possible racist implications when family-planning services are directed at serving the poor, providing abortion information and making referrals, providing contraceptive information to teenagers, responding to those who advocate involuntary sterilization of people who are seriously handicapped with hereditary conditions, and locating family-planning clinics in high schools so that contraceptive information and devices are more readily accessible to teenagers.

Few social workers are now employed in settings where the primary service is family planning. Yet, many roles in family planning are well suited for social workers: premarital counseling; pregnancy counseling; provision of contraceptive information including effectiveness and side effects of the varied approaches; sex education services; venereal disease counseling;

AIDS education and counseling; abortion counseling; infertility counseling, and community organization efforts to develop family-planning services in the area and create a community atmosphere that is accepting of family planning as a legitimate service. Now, family-planning counseling is fragmented in many communities, with a wide variety of agencies providing counseling on a few of the above areas: public health departments provide venereal disease counseling, adoption agencies provide infertility counseling, medical clinics that perform abortions provide abortion counseling, public welfare departments provide contraceptive information for clients, family service agencies provide premarital counseling, and so on.

There are several reasons for anticipating that family-planning services will be expanded in future years, thereby creating new career opportunities for social workers. The general public is increasingly becoming aware of the dangers of overpopulation. There has been a growing acceptance and use in our society of contraceptives, sex education, and abortions. The specter of the perils of AIDS has led to greater awareness that AIDS education and sex education are widely needed.

Increasingly, social workers are being hired in specialized agencies that deal with family planning—Planned Parenthood, maternal and child health clinics, and agencies providing abortions and abortion counseling.

School social workers have become increasingly involved in family-planning activities in connection with sex education for sexually active teenagers. Social workers in single-parent units of social services departments (also called public welfare or human services departments) are heavily involved in providing family-planning services. Social workers in many other settings are also heavily involved in providing family-planning services, for example, in pediatrics and gynecology departments in hospitals and clinics, child welfare agencies, and residential treatment facilities for teenagers.

Unfortunately very few undergraduate and graduate social work programs have family-planning courses. A number of programs do provide some family-planning instructional units in other courses. In reviewing the extent of family-planning education in social work, Ketayun H. Gould concludes, "If social work is to play a significant role in family planning and in social policy related to population problems, the schools of social work have to provide effective educational programs."[97]

SUMMARY

Problems associated with overpopulation and misuse of the environment are very serious and may have an adverse, dramatic effect on the quality of life in the future. The world's population has more than doubled in size since 1930. At current growth rates, the population will again double in size in the next forty years. Already we are experiencing resource crises. Some of the problems associated with overpopulation and misuse of the environment are:

- Too little food. At present, a large proportion of the people in the world are undernourished, and many are starving.

- Too little water. Fresh water is in short supply.

- Economic problems. Overpopulation lowers the average per capita income, reduces the standard of living, and often leads to political turmoil.

- International terrorism. Rapid population growth is a factor that contributes to civil unrest, violence, and international strife.

- Crowding. There is some evidence that the subjective feeling of insufficient space may be a factor in leading to such problems as crime, emotional problems, suicide, violence, incest, and child abuse.

- Too little energy. We currently have an energy crisis. Fossil fuel resources (oil, coal, and natural gas), which provide over nine tenths of the world's energy consumption, are rapidly being depleted.

- Depleted mineral resources. Essential elements such as copper, zinc, iron, and manganese are increasingly becoming in short supply.

- Despoiling the land. Coal strip mining, oil drilling, destroying trees and forests, and overgrazing by cattle and sheep are not only unsightly but also have devastating environmental damage when the delicate balance between nature's elements is interrupted.

- Radioactive wastes. As yet, we have not found a safe approach to disposal of nuclear wastes, which may create lethal problems in the future.

- Garbage. Increased consumption has increased throw-aways, the disposal of which often leads to air pollution, water pollution, and other undesirable environmental effects.

- Air pollution. In large industrial centers, air pollution is a health hazard.

- Water pollution. Water pollution is also a serious health hazard; some rivers and lakes are now so polluted they cannot support fish and other organisms.

- Acid rain. Acid rain has damaged timber and is killing fish in lakes and streams.

- Radioactive leaks from nuclear power plants. Leaks and accidents at nuclear power plants in Russia and the United States raise the question whether nuclear energy is worth the risks.

- Nuclear war. The number of countries having nuclear warheads is increasing, which increases the chances of nuclear warheads being used in international conflicts.

- General pollutants. Increasingly, we are becoming aware of the harmful effects of such pollutants as lead, mercury, DDT, and other chlorinated hydrocarbons.

Unless the size of the world's population is brought under control, the above problems are apt to intensify. A number of proposals have been advanced to curtail the growth of the world's population, some of which, if implemented, would radically change current lifestyles. Proposals include subsidizing adoptions, expanding sex education in schools, developing safer contraceptives, enforcing compulsory sterilization, raising the minimum age of marriage, no longer allowing tax deductions for children, making birth-control information and devices more available, and making abortions more accessible. If nations are not successful in controlling the birth rate with voluntary family-planning programs, pressure will mount for countries to adopt population-control programs.

In order to confront environmental problems, actions are needed on a variety of concerns. Two primary actions that are essential are to change values toward conserving resources and to develop new sources of energy, such as solar energy.

Family-planning services are essential programs for population control. Social workers are increasingly being employed in settings that offer family-planning services. Family planning appears to be an emerging career field for social work, as many roles are well suited for social workers: premarital counseling, pregnancy counseling, provision of contraceptive information, sex education services, abortion counseling, venereal disease counseling, and community organi-

zation efforts to develop family-planning services further.

NOTES

1. Werner Fornos, *Gaining People, Losing Ground* (Washington, DC: The Population Institute, 1987), p. 57.
2. Ibid., p. 1.
3. Paul Ehrlich, *The Population Bomb* (New York: Ballantine Books, 1971), p. 4.
4. Fornos, *Gaining People, Losing Ground*, p. 1.
5. Ibid.
6. Ibid., p. 7.
7. Lee Rainwater, *And the Poor Get Children* (Chicago: Quadrangle Books, 1960).
8. Quoted in Donald C. Bacon "Poor vs. Rich: A Global Struggle," *U.S. News & World Report*, July 31, 1978, p. 57.
9. Fornos, *Gaining People, Losing Ground*, pp. 38–61.
10. Beth Brophy, "Children Under Stress," *U.S. News & World Report*, October 27, 1986, p. 59.
11. Ehrlich, *The Population Bomb*, p. 129.
12. Joseph Julian and William Kornblum, *Social Problems*, 5th ed. (Englewood Cliffs, NJ: Prentice-Hall, 1986), p. 457.
13. Fornos, *Gaining People, Losing Ground*, p. 7.
14. Ibid.
15. Ibid., pp. 19–22.
16. Rufus E. Miles, Jr., statement made at the hearings of the President's Commission on Population Growth and the American Future, April 15, 1971, *Population Bulletin* 27 (June 1971), p. 13.
17. Bacon, "Poor vs. Rich: A Global Struggle," p. 58.
18. Paul R. Ehrlich, Anne H. Ehrlich, and John P. Holdren, *Human Ecology: Problems and Solutions* (San Francisco: W. H. Freeman, 1973), p. 227.
19. "Study Cites Hunger in U.S.," *Wisconsin State Journal*, February 27, 1985, sec. 1, p. 8.
20. Ian Robertson, *Social Problems*, 2d ed. (New York: Random House, 1980), p. 31.
21. Fornos, *Gaining People, Losing Ground*, p. 12.
22. Robertson, *Social Problems*, p. 41.
23. Thomas R. Malthus, *On Population*, ed. Gertrude Himmelfarb (New York: Modern Library, 1960), pp. 13–14. (Original edition in 1798)
24. Roger Revelle, "Food and Population," in *The Human*

Population, ed. *Scientific American* (San Francisco: W. H. Freeman, 1974), pp. 119–130.

25. "Study Cites Hunger in U.S.," *Wisconsin State Journal*, p. 8.

26. Paul R. Ehrlich and Anne H. Ehrlich, *Population, Resources, Environment* (San Francisco: W. H. Freeman, 1970), p. 65.

27. "Warning: Water Shortages Ahead," *Time Magazine*, April 4, 1977, p. 48.

28. Ketayun H. Gould, "Population and Family Planning," in *Contemporary Social Work*, eds. Donald Brieland, Lela Costin, and Charles Atherton (New York: McGraw-Hill, 1975), p. 130.

29. Fornos, *Gaining People, Losing Ground*, pp. 7–23.

30. Quoted in Fornos, *Gaining People, Losing Ground*, p. 10.

31. U.S. Bureau of the Census, *Statistical Abstract of the United States, 1987* (Washington, DC: U.S. Government Printing Office, 1987), pp. 419, 824.

32. Quoted in Fornos, *Gaining People, Losing Ground*, pp. 20–21.

33. Fornos, *Gaining People, Losing Ground*, p. 21.

34. John B. Calhoun, "Population Density and Social Pathology," *Scientific American* 206 (February 1962), pp. 139–148.

35. Joseph Julian, *Social Problems*, 3d ed. (Englewood Cliffs, NJ: Prentice-Hall, 1980), p. 502.

36. Ibid., p. 502.

37. Gould, "Population and Family Planning," p. 130.

38. M. King Hubbert, "Energy Resources," in *Resources and Man*, ed. Preston E. Cloud, Jr. (San Francisco: W. H. Freeman, 1969).

39. Steward L. Udall, "The Last Traffic Jam," *Atlantic Monthly* 320 (October 1972), p. 72.

40. Irene B. Taeuber, "Japan's Demographic Transition Re-examined," *Population Studies* 14 (July 1960), p. 39.

41. Robertson, *Social Problems*, p. 43.

42. Fornos, *Gaining People, Losing Ground*, p. 5.

43. Gallup Organization, Inc., "News Release," Research Department, April 1971.

44. U.S. Census Bureau, *Statistical Abstract of the United States, 1987*, p. 824.

45. Fornos, *Gaining People, Losing Ground*, p. 45.

46. Ibid., pp. 45–46.

47. Ibid., pp. 45–46.

48. Ibid., pp. 41–42.

49. "Monster Problem," *Parade Magazine*, April 19, 1981, p. 14.

50. Fornos, *Gaining People, Losing Ground*, pp. 41–42.

51. Ibid.

52. Ibid., p. 41.

53. Ibid., pp. 41–42.

54. Ibid., p. 42.

55. Ehrlich, Ehrlich, and Holdren, *Human Ecology*, pp. 159–160.

56. Ehrlich and Ehrlich, *Population, Resources, Environment*, p. 202.

57. Ehrlich, Ehrlich, and Holdren, *Human Ecology*, pp. 80–89.

58. Fornos, *Gaining People, Losing Ground*, p. 14.

59. Ibid., p. 13.

60. U.S. Bureau of the Census, *Statistical Abstract of the United States, 1987*, p. 558.

61. Robertson, *Social Problems*, p. 71.

62. Ehrlich, Ehrlich, and Holdren, *Human Ecology*, pp. 180–182.

63. Julian, *Social Problems*, p. 528.

64. Julian and Kornblum, *Social Problems*, 5th ed., p. 457.

65. Philip H. Howard and Arnold Hanchett, "Chlorofluoro-carbon Sources of Environmental Contamination," *Science*, July 1974, pp. 217–219.

66. Robertson, *Social Problems*, p. 72.

67. *Village Voice*, July 4, 1974.

68. Julian and Kornblum, *Social Problems*, p. 488–489.

69. Ibid., p. 489.

70. Orr Kelly, "Nuclear War's Horrors: Reality vs. Fiction," *U.S. News & World Report*, November 28, 1983, pp. 85–86.

71. Ibid.

72. William L. Ury, "What We Can Do to Avert Nuclear War," *Parade Magazine*, March 25, 1984, p. 15.

73. Ibid., pp. 15–16.

74. Robert Kittle, "Space-War Era," *U.S. News & World Report*, December 17, 1984, pp. 28–32.

75. Ehrlich and Ehrlich, *Population, Resources, Environment*, p. 126.

76. Julian and Kornblum, *Social Problems*, p. 469.

77. "The Growing Furor Over Acid Rain," *U.S. News & World Report*, November 19, 1979, p. 66.

78. Ibid.

79. Ehrlich, *Population Bomb*, pp. 31–35.

80. Ehrlich, Ehrlich, and Holdren, *Human Ecology*, p. 132.

81. Richard Curtis and Elizabeth Hogan, *Perils of the Peaceful Atom* (New York: Ballantine Books, 1969), p. 194.

82. "Chemical Dangers May Be Unknown," *Wisconsin State Journal*, March 3, 1984, p. 1.

83. Ehrlich, *Population Bomb*, pp. 127–145.

84. Bernard Berelson, "The Present State of Family Planning

Programs," *Studies in Family Planning* 57 (September 1970), p. 2.

85. Fornos, *Gaining People, Losing Ground*, pp. 29–30.

86. Ibid., p. 30.

87. Ehrlich, Ehrlich, and Holdren, *Human Ecology*, p. 279.

88. "Abortion Foes Gain Victory," *Wisconsin State Journal*, July 1, 1980, sec. 1, p. 1.

89. Fornos, *Gaining People, Losing Ground*, pp. 78–85.

90. Gould, "Population and Family Planning," p. 138.

91. Fornos, *Gaining People, Losing Ground*, pp. 106–107.

92. Julian and Kornblum, *Social Problems*, pp. 480–482.

93. George Ritzer, *Social Problems*, 2d ed. (New York: Random House, 1986), p. 556.

94. "Fuels for America's Future," *U.S. News & World Report*, August 13, 1979, p. 33.

95. Ibid., p. 33.

96. Ibid., p. 33.

97. Gould, "Population and Family Planning," p. 138.

III

SOCIAL

WORK

PRACTICE

The preceding chapters have focused on describing prominent social problems and discussing current social services to meet these problems. The focus of this chapter will be on generalist social work practice. This chapter will discuss social casework with individuals, group work, and social work community practice. This chapter will:

- Define generalist social work practice.
- Describe the casework process.
- Summarize essential skills needed by caseworkers.
- Identify the various types of groups that social workers lead and participate in.
- Present material on how to start and lead groups.
- Describe roles of community practice and present three models of community practice.
- Summarize skills and knowledge needed by community practitioners.

17

GENERALIST SOCIAL WORK PRACTICE

GENERALIST SOCIAL WORK PRACTICE

There used to be an erroneous belief that a social worker was either a caseworker, a group worker, or a community organizer. Practicing social workers know that such a belief is faulty because every social worker is involved as a change agent in working with individuals, groups, and community groups. The amount of time spent at these levels varies from worker to worker, but every worker will, at times, be assigned and expected to work at these three levels and therefore needs training in all of them.

The Council on Social Work Education (the national accrediting entity for baccalaureate and master's programs in social work) requires all bachelor's level and master's level programs to train their students in generalist social work practice. (MSW programs, in addition, usually require their students to select and study in an area of specialization. MSW programs generally offer several specializations, such as family therapy, administration, corrections, and clinical social work.)

Generalist social work practice requires training in working with individuals, groups, and communities.

In working as a generalist, it is essential that a social worker be trained to work with individuals, with groups (including families), and in community practice. In the following definition of generalist practice, Louise Johnson notes the importance of a generalist social worker having the knowledge and skills to work effectively with individuals, groups, families, and communities:

Generalist practice. Practice in which the client and worker together assess the need in all its complexity and develop a plan for responding to that need. A strategy is chosen from a repertoire of responses appropriate for work with individuals, groups, agencies, and communities. . . . The plan is carried out and evaluated.[2]

The remainder of this chapter will present material on working with individuals, groups, and communities.

A generalist social worker is trained to assess and treat people (who have a variety of social and personal problems) with a large number of assessment and intervention techniques. Anderson has identified three characteristics of a generalist social worker: (*a*) The generalist is often the first professional to see clients as they enter the social welfare system; (*b*) the worker must therefore be competent to assess their needs and to identify their stress points and problems; and (*c*) the worker must draw on a variety of skills and methods in serving clients.[1] A generalist social worker has the following four goals, which are described in further detail in Chapter 2:

1. Enhance the problem-solving, coping, and developmental capacities of people.

2. Link people with systems that provide them with resources, services, and opportunities.

3. Promote the effectiveness and humane operation of systems that provide people with resources and services.

4. Develop and improve social policy.

CASEWORK

A majority of social workers spend most of their time working with individuals in public or private agencies or in private practice. Social casework is aimed at helping individuals, on a one-to-one basis, to resolve personal and social problems. Social casework services are provided by nearly every social welfare agency that provides direct services to people. Social casework encompasses a wide variety of activities, such as counseling runaway youths, helping unemployed people secure training or employment, counseling someone who is suicidal, placing a homeless child in an adoptive or foster home, providing protective services to abused children and their families, finding nursing homes for stroke victims who no longer need to be confined in a hospital, counseling individuals with sexual dysfunctions, helping alcoholics to acknowledge they have a drinking problem, counseling those with a terminal illness, being a probation and parole officer, providing services to single parents, and being a catalyst for the development of services in a community for those who test positive to HIV and to those who have AIDS.

All of us at times face personal problems that we cannot resolve by ourselves. Sometimes, other family members, relatives, friends, or acquaintances can help. At other times, we need more skilled help to handle emotional problems, to obtain resources in times of crises, to handle marital or family conflicts, to deal with problems at work or school, or to cope with a medical emergency. Furnishing skilled, personal help is what social casework is all about.

Caseworkers provide a number of different services. At times they are "brokers" when they help link an individual who needs help with community services. Another role is "public education," in which they seek to inform other individuals or groups about current problems and services. Another role is that of an "advocate" for clients to secure needed services when such services are not readily available. Other roles are "outreach," "teacher" of new information and skills, "behavioral specialist," "consultant," and "case manager." But the primary skill and role of a caseworker is that of counseling. As previous examples in this book indicate, social workers counsel people with a wide variety of personal and social problems.

The author dislikes some of the negative connotations associated with the term *caseworker. Webster's New Collegiate Dictionary* (1983) defines a case as "a set of circumstances or conditions"; "a situation requiring investigation or action, as by the police"; "the object of investigation or consideration." With such definitions the term *caseworker* connotes someone who performs primarily an investigative function. Thus, the term does not convey the respect that should be given to clients, nor does it convey the importance of building a working relationship with clients. The author believes a term such as *counselor* conveys a more realistic image of the skills, functions, and approach of social work with individuals.

The Counseling Process

Accountability is increasingly becoming an important emphasis in social welfare. Social service programs that are unable to demonstrate their effectiveness are gradually being phased out. In January 1973, Joel Fischer raised the question of whether casework is effective.[3] He reviewed outcome studies on casework services and concluded that such services failed to demonstrate that they are effective. Critics of Fischer's review have criticized his methodology. But the question has been raised—is casework effective? As yet, research has *not* demonstrated that casework is effective!

Counseling is the core of casework practice. Chapter 4 in this text has conceptualized the counseling process from the counselor's perspective. The process was conceptualized as involving three phases: (*a*) building a relationship, (*b*) exploring problems in depth, and (*c*) exploring alternative solutions.

The counseling process can also be conceptualized from the client's point of view. In order for counseling to be successful, clients must give themselves a progressive series of "self-talk" statements (that is, clients must arrive at having certain thoughts and beliefs that will then facilitate their capacities to resolve their problems). These self-talk stages will be presented briefly.

STAGE I—PROBLEM AWARENESS   At this initial stage clients must say to themselves, "I have a problem"; "I need to do something about my situation." If people with problems refuse to acknowledge they have a problem they will, of course, not be motivated to make the efforts needed to change. In certain areas of social work—for example working with problem drinkers—it is sometimes difficult to have people acknowledge they have a problem. For people who deny that a problem exists, constructive changes are not apt to occur, unless the counselor finds a way to convince them that they *do* have a problem. When a person denies a problem exists, counseling needs to focus on this denial by exploring why the client believes a problem does not exist and by gathering evidence to document the existence of the problem to the client. The client then needs to be confronted, in a tactful manner, with this evidence by the counselor. If after such a confrontation the client still denies a problem exists, the counselor should be aware that the client *owns* the problem, and

A counselor comforts a child at Covenant House, a New York shelter for runaway youths. Skilled, personal help is what social casework is all about.

there is little more that the counselor can constructively do at this time, except perhaps to indicate that he or she will be available in the future if the client wants to talk.

STAGE II—RELATIONSHIP TO COUNSELOR　The next stage of the counseling process is one in which the client arrives at the point where his or her self-talk is, "I think this counselor will be of help to me." If the client instead has the self-talk, "This counselor can't help me; I don't need a head shrinker; I just don't trust this counselor," then counseling is apt to fail. Chapter 4 in this text discusses in some detail helpful guidelines for how to establish a working relationship with clients.

STAGE III—MOTIVATION　Clients must come to say to themselves, "I think I can improve my situation"; "I want to better myself." Unless a client becomes moti-

vated to change, constructive changes are not apt to occur. Helping a person become motivated to improve his or her situation is a key to effective counseling. Chapter 3 in this text provides a number of guidelines and suggestions on how to motivate discouraged or apathetic people.

STAGE IV—CONCEPTUALIZATION OF THE PROBLEM　In order for counseling to be effective, a client needs to recognize, "My problem is not overwhelming but has specific components that can be changed." Many clients initially tend to view their situation as being so complex that they become highly anxious or emotional. They tend to "awfulize" about how bleak or bad their situation is. They are unable to see that their problem has a number of components that they can change in a step-by-step fashion. Several years ago, for example, one of the authors of this chapter counseled a teenager who had missed her menstrual period for the past three months and was so overwhelmingly afraid of being pregnant that she was unable to figure out on her own that the first step was to have a pregnancy test. (After counseling, she had a pregnancy test, which turned out to be negative.) In order to help clients conceptualize their problems, the counselor needs to explore the problems together, in depth, with the client. Guidelines on how to explore problems in depth with clients are presented in Chapter 4.

STAGE V—EXPLORATION OF RESOLUTION STRATEGIES
One of the steps of the counseling process is for the client and counselor to explore resolution strategies jointly. Each client is unique and so are his or her problems. What works for one client may not be in the best interest of another. An abortion, for example, may be compatible with one client's values and circumstances but may well be undesirable for another unmarried pregnant woman who has a different set of values and goals. If counseling is going to be effective the client needs to say to himself or herself, "I see there are several courses of action that I might try to do something about my situation." Unless a client comes to realize there are some resolution strategies, counseling is apt to fail.

STAGE VI—SELECTION OF A STRATEGY   As indicated in Chapter 4, the counselor and client need to discuss the probable effects and consequences of possible resolution strategies. If counseling is going to be successful the client must conclude, "I think this approach might help me and I am willing to try it." If a client is indecisive or refuses to make an honest commitment to trying a course of action, constructive change will not occur. For example, if a client says to himself or herself, "I know I have a drinking problem but am unwilling to take any action to cut down on my drinking," counseling probably will not be successful.

STAGE VII—IMPLEMENTATION OF THE STRATEGY   Counseling will only be successful if the client follows through on his or her commitment and then concludes, "This approach is beginning to help me." If the client follows through on the commitment but then

concludes, "I don't believe this approach is helping me," counseling again is failing. If this occurs the reasons for no gain need to be examined, and perhaps another resolution strategy needs to be tried.

STAGE VIII—EVALUATION   If constructive change is to be long-lasting or permanent, the client must conclude, "Although this approach takes a lot of my time and effort, it's worth it." On the other hand, if she or her concludes, "This approach has helped a little, but it's really not worth what I'm sacrificing for it," then counseling will be ineffective, and an alternative course of action needs to be developed and implemented.

The advantage of this conceptualization of the counseling process is that it presents a framework for improving the effectiveness of counseling. When counseling is not helping, this framework indicates that by examining the self-talk of clients about the counseling they are receiving, the reasons for no progress can be identified and then needed changes made in the counseling process. (It should be noted that there is some overlap between these stages; for example, Stage II involving the relationship between client and counselor needs to be given attention throughout the counseling process.)

Essential Skills Needed by Caseworkers

CAPACITY TO BUILD A WORKING RELATIONSHIP   Counselors need to establish a nonthreatening atmosphere in which the client feels safe to communicate his or her troubles. In initial meetings the counselor needs to "sell" himself or herself as an understanding, knowledgeable person who might be able to help. The counselor needs to show respect and genuine interest in the client and convey that the client (in spite of perhaps shocking behavior) is a worthwhile person. Generally, a counselor is nonjudgmental; respect is shown for the client's values without the counselor trying to sell his or her own value system.

CAPACITY TO EXPLORE PROBLEMS IN DEPTH   A counselor needs to have interviewing skills to help a client tell his or her story; to have a positive attitude; and to be able to identify hidden meanings between verbal and nonverbal messages. To be a competent interviewer requires the capacity to listen and view what the client is saying from the client's perspective. One of the reasons it is difficult to develop good listening skills is because we can think much faster than the rate at which people can speak. The average rate of spoken speech is about 125 words per minute, whereas we can read and understand an average of about 300 to 500 words per minute. With this "dead" time, there is a tendency for the listener to become lost in his or her personal thoughts and concerns. A counselor also needs to have empathy, which is the capacity to convey that the counselor is understanding and cares about what the client is thinking and feeling. Finally, a knowledge of human behavior (how people think and feel about events that happen to them) is needed.

CAPACITY TO EXPLORE ALTERNATIVE SOLUTIONS   Once the client's set of problems is explored in depth, resolution approaches must be discussed jointly. It is the counselor's responsibility to have a knowledge of numerous treatment approaches and community resources so that appropriate courses of action can be shared and discussed with the client. The probable effects and consequences of various courses of action need to be explored carefully with the client. The client generally has the right of self-determination, that is, the right to choose the course of action among possible alternatives.

A Variety of Treatment Approaches

To be an effective counselor a social worker must have a working knowledge of (*a*) interviewing principles and (*b*) a variety of treatment approaches. Casework is not a single method. In fact, numerous treatment approaches are used. Table 17.1 provides a partial list of comprehensive counseling approaches. (Comprehen-

sive treatment approaches are designed to treat a wide range of emotional and behavioral problems.)

In addition to these large-scale or comprehensive approaches to casework, there are a growing number of specialized approaches for specific problems: for example, sexual therapies for sexual problems, assertiveness training for aggressive or shy people, parent effectiveness training to improve effective parenting, specialized drug counseling approaches, Alcoholics Anonymous, Parents Anonymous, and so on. Table 17.2 contains a partial listing of a variety of specialized treatment approaches.

It is impossible for any social worker to have an effective working knowledge of all of these comprehensive and specialized treatment approaches. A social worker should, however, continue throughout his or her career to learn additional approaches and to continue to learn to apply more effectively those approaches he or she is already acquainted with. Social work agencies encourage this continual learning by offering inservice training and workshops, by sending workers to conferences, and by encouraging workers to take additional college courses in the helping professions.

A worker should continue to learn a wide variety of intervention approaches so that he or she can select which intervention approach—given each client's unique set of problems and circumstances—is apt to be most effective. It should be noted that the selection of an intervention approach is also based on a worker's personality. Counselors soon become aware that their personality partially determines which therapy approaches they are more comfortable in applying.

At first glance Tables 17.1 and 17.2 present such a long "shopping list" of intervention approaches that the reader is apt to be bewildered about which treatment approaches she or he should attempt to learn. Practice or methods courses in social work programs provide an overview of many of these approaches, so the reader will begin to become aware which approaches she or he will be comfortable in applying.

Furthermore, the employment area that one seeks in social work will also be a factor in focusing the reader's attention on which treatment approaches to learn about. If you're working with shy or aggressive

TABLE 17.1

Comprehensive Theoretical Approaches to Doing Casework

Casework or Counseling Approach	Name of Primary Developer	Casework or Counseling Approach	Name of Primary Developer
Psychosocial model	Gordon Hamilton	Behavior modification	Numerous theoreticians
Functional model	Jessie Taft	Provocative therapy	Frank Farrelly
Problem-solving model	Helen H. Perlman	Radical therapy	Numerous theoreticians
Task-centered model	William J. Reid	Adlerian therapy	Alfred Adler
Family therapy	Numerous theoreticians	Analytical therapy	C. G. Jung
Psychoanalysis	Sigmund Freud	Existential therapy	Numerous theoreticians
Client-centered therapy	Carl Rogers	Encounter therapies	Numerous theoreticians
Transactional analysis	Eric Berne	Ego psychology approaches	Numerous theoreticians
Gestalt therapy	Frederick Perls	Cognitive approaches	Numerous theoreticians
Rational-emotive therapy	Albert Ellis	General systems approaches	Numerous theoreticians
Reality therapy	William Glasser	Role theory approaches	Numerous theoreticians
Crisis intervention	Numerous theoreticians	Neuro-linguistic programming	Numerous theoreticians

Note: A summary of each of these approaches is well beyond the scope of this text. These therapies are summarized in *Social Work Treatment*, ed. Francis J. Turner (New York: The Free Press, 1979); in *Current Psychotherapies*, ed. Raymond Corsini (Itasca, IL: F. E. Peacock, 1979); and in Charles Zastrow, *The Practice of Social Work*, 3d ed. (Belmont, CA: Wadsworth, 1989).

people, assertiveness training is recommended. Alcoholics Anonymous is recommended for people with drinking problems, rational therapy for people who are depressed, systematic desensitization for people who have phobias, and so on.

A useful guideline in deciding which intervention approach to use when you have a client in front of you is to place yourself in "the client's shoes" and ask yourself, "Given this client's unique set of problems and circumstances, which intervention approach is apt to be most helpful?"

At present, the needed research has *not* yet been conducted to determine the effectiveness of most of the approaches listed in Tables 17.1 and 17.2.[4] Obviously, with this wide array of approaches to casework

or counseling, some approaches are going to be found to be more effective than others. For example, from 1920 to 1950 casework practice was heavily influenced by psychoanalytic theory. Since 1950 a number of studies have found psychoanalytic approaches to be generally ineffective,[5] and counselors are increasingly using approaches other than those suggested by psychoanalytic theory.*

Increasingly, federal and state governmental units

---

*It should be noted that psychoanalytic theories on personality development are still fairly widely taught at undergraduate and graduate schools of social work. These theories are useful in helping to understand human behavior and personality dynamics. However, psychoanalytic treatment techniques are now taught in only a few social work programs.

TABLE 17.2

Specialized Treatment Approaches

Treatment Approaches

Psychodrama	Parent effectiveness training
Assertiveness training	Muscle relaxation
Token economies	Deep-breathing relaxation
Contingency contracting	Imagery relaxation
Systematic desensitization	Meditation
In vivo desensitization	Hypnosis
Implosive therapy	Self-hypnosis
Covert sensitization	Biofeedback
Aversive techniques	Encounter groups
Thought stopping	Marathon groups
Sex therapy	Sensitivity groups
Milieu therapy	Parents Anonymous
Play therapy	Weight Watchers

Note: These therapies are summarized in *Social Work Treatment*, ed. Francis J. Turner (New York: The Free Press, 1979); and in Charles Zastrow, *The Practice of Social Work*, 3d ed. (Belmont, CA: Wadsworth, 1989).

are requiring that the effectiveness of treatment approaches be measured. Gradually, programs found to be ineffective are being phased out.

The trend for the future seems clear. Increasingly, social workers will have to document the quantity of services they provide, as well as the effectiveness (quality) of their services. Extensive paperwork is involved in this accountability process. An effective social worker generally has a working knowledge of a variety of treatment approaches. In working with clients, the worker should focus on selecting the most effective treatment approaches to help the client solve the problem(s) rather than trying to redefine the client's problem so as to be able to use the worker's favorite treatment approach.

GROUP WORK

A group may be defined as

. . . a plurality of individuals who are in contact with one another, who take one another into account, and who are aware of some significant commonality—an essential feature of a group is that its members have something in common and that they believe that what they have in common makes a difference.[6]

Social group work's historical roots were in the informal recreational organizations—the YWCA and YMCA, scouting, Jewish centers, settlement houses and 4-H clubs.

George Williams established the Young Men's Christian Association in London in 1844 for the purpose of converting young men to Christian values.[7] Recreational group activities and socialization activities were a large part of the early YMCA's programs. In 1851 YMCAs were first founded in this country in Baltimore and Boston. The Young Women's Christian Association began in Boston in 1866.[8]

Settlement houses, which were established in many large cities of this country in the late 1800s, are generally given a major share of the credit for being the roots of social group work.[9] Settlement houses sought to use the power of group associations to educate, reform, and organize neighborhoods; to preserve religious and cultural identities; and to give emotional support and assistance to newcomers from both the farm and abroad.

Now, almost every social service agency provides one or more of the following types of groups: recreation-skill, education, socialization, and therapy. Most undergraduate and graduate social work programs provide methods courses to train students to lead groups, particularly socialization and therapy groups.

Types of Groups in Social Work

The following summary identifies a variety of groups in social work: social conversation, recreation, recrea-

BOX 17.1

Assertiveness Training—An Example of a Specialized Treatment Approach

D o you handle put-down comments well? Are you reluctant to express your feelings and opinions openly and honestly in a group? Are you frequently timid in interacting with people in authority? Do you react well to criticism? Do you sometimes explode in anger when things go wrong, or are you able to keep your cool? Do you find it difficult to maintain eye contact when talking? If you are uncomfortable with someone smoking near you, do you express your feelings? Are you timid in arranging a date or social event? If you have trouble in any of these situations, there is, fortunately, a useful technique—assertiveness training—that enables people to become more effective in such interpersonal interactions.

Assertiveness problems range from extreme shyness, introversion, and withdrawal to inappropriately flying into a rage that results in alienating others. A nonassertive person is often acquiescent, fearful, and afraid of expressing his or her real, spontaneous feelings in a variety of situations. Frequently, resentment and anxiety build up, which may result in general discomfort, feelings of low self-esteem, tension headaches, fatigue, and perhaps a destructive explosion of temper, anger, and aggression. Some people are overly shy and timid in nearly all interactions. Most of us, however, encounter occasional problems in isolated areas where it would be to our benefit to be more assertive. For example, a bachelor may be quite effective and assertive in his job as a store manager but still be awkward and timid while attempting to arrange a date.

There are three basic styles of interacting with others: nonassertive, aggressive, and assertive. Characteristics of these styles have been summarized by Robert Alberti and Michael Emmons.

In the non-assertive *style, you are likely to hesitate, speak softly, look away, avoid the issue, agree regardless of your own feelings, not express opinions, value yourself "below" others, and hurt yourself to avoid any chance of hurting others.*

In the aggressive *style, you typically answer before the other person is through talking, speak loudly and abusively, glare at the other person, speak "past" the issue (accusing, blaming, demeaning), vehemently expound your feelings and opinions, value yourself "above" others, and hurt others to avoid hurting yourself.*

In the assertive *style, you will answer spontaneously, speak with a conversational tone and volume, look at the other person, speak to the issue, openly express your personal feelings and opinions (anger, love, disagreement, sorrow), value yourself equal to others, and hurt neither yourself nor others.[a]*

EXAMPLES OF BEHAVIOR

You are flying with a business associate to Los Angeles for a conference. The associate lights up a pipe; you soon find the smoke irritating, and the odor somewhat stifling. What are your choices?

1. Nonassertive response—you attempt to carry on a "cheery" conversation for the three-hour trip without commenting about the smoke.

2. Aggressive response—you increasingly become irritated, until exploding, "Either you put out that pipe, or I'll put it out for you—the odor is sickening."

3. Assertive response—in a firm, conversational tone you look directly at the associate and state, "The smoke from your pipe is irritating me. I'd appreciate it if you put it away."

At a party with friends, during small-talk conversation, your husband gives you a subtle "put-down" by stating, "Wives always talk too much." What do you do?

1. Nonassertive response—you don't say anything but feel hurt and become quiet.

2. Aggressive response—you glare at him and angrily ask, "John, why are you always criticizing me?"

3. Assertive response—you carry on as usual, waiting until driving home, then calmly look at him and say, "When we were at the party tonight, you said that wives always talk too much. I felt you were putting me down when you said that. What did you mean by that comment?"

BEING ASSERTIVE

Simply stated, assertive behavior is being able to express yourself without hurting or stepping on others.

Assertiveness training is designed to lead a person to realize, feel, and act on the assumption that she or he has the right to be himself or herself and to express his or her feelings freely. Assertive responses generally are not aggressive responses. The distinction between these two types of interactions is important. If, for example, a wife has an overly critical mother-in-law, aggressive responses by the wife would include ridiculing the mother-in-law, intentionally doing things that she knows will upset the mother-in-law (not visiting, serving the type of food the mother-in-law dislikes, not cleaning the house), urging the husband to tell his mother to "shut up," and getting into loud verbal arguments with the mother-in-law. On the other hand, an effective assertive response would be to counter criticism by saying: "Jane, your criticism of me deeply hurts me. I know you're trying to help me when you give advice, but I feel when you do that you're criticizing me. I know you don't want me to make mistakes; but to grow, I need to make my own errors and learn from them. If you want to help me the most, let me do it myself and be responsible for the consequences. The type of relationship that I'd like to have with you is a close, adult relationship and not a mother-child relationship."

The steps for learning to become more assertive are presented in the following material:[b]

1. Examine your interactions. Are there situations that you need to handle more assertively? Do you at times hold opinions and feelings within you for fear of what would happen if you expressed them? Do you occasionally blow your cool and lash out angrily at others?

Continued

BOX 17.1 *Continued*

Studying your interactions is facilitated by keeping a diary for a week or longer, recording the situations in which you acted timidly, those in which you were aggressive, and those that you handled assertively.

2. Select those interactions in which it would be to your benefit to be more assertive. They may include situations in which you were overpolite, overly apologetic, or timid and allowed others to take advantage of you, at the same time harboring feelings of resentment, anger, embarrassment, fear of others, or self-criticism for not having the courage to express yourself. Overly aggressive interactions in which you exploded in anger or walked over others also need to be dealt with. For *each* set of nonassertive or aggressive interactions, you can become more assertive, as shown in the next steps.

3. Concentrate on a specific incident in the past in which you were either nonassertive or aggressive. Close your eyes for a few minutes and vividly imagine the details, including what you and the other person said and how you felt at the time and afterward.

4. Write down and review your responses. Ask yourself the following questions to determine how you presented yourself:

    a. Eye contact—Did you look directly at the other person with a relaxed, steady gaze? Looking down or away suggests a lack of self-confidence. Glaring is an aggressive response.

    b. Gestures—Were your gestures appropriate, free-flowing, relaxed, and used to emphasize your messages effectively? Awkward stiffness suggests nervousness; other gestures (such as an angry fist) signal an aggressive reaction.

    c. Body posture—Did you show the importance of your message by directly facing the other person, by leaning toward that person, by holding your head erect, and by sitting or standing appropriately close?

    d. Facial expressions—Did your facial expressions show a stern, firm pose consistent with an assertive response?

    e. Voice tone and volume—Was your response stated in a firm, conversational tone? Shouting may suggest anger. Speaking softly suggests shyness, and a cracking voice suggests nervousness. Tape recording and listening to one's voice is a way to practice increasing or decreasing the volume.

    f. Speech fluency—Did your speech flow smoothly, clearly, and slowly? Rapid speech or hesitation in speaking suggests nervousness. Tape recording assertive responses that you try out to problem situations is a way to improve fluency.

    g. Timing—Were your verbal reactions to a problem situation stated at a time closest to the incident that would appropriately permit you and the other person time to review the incident? Generally, spontaneous expressions are the best, but certain situations should be handled at a later time—for example, challenging some of your boss's erroneous statements in private rather than in front of a group she or he is making a presentation to.

    h. Message content—For a problem situation, which of your responses were nonassertive or aggressive, and which were assertive? Study the content and consider why you responded in a nonassertive or aggressive style.

5. Observe one or more effective models. Watch the verbal and nonverbal approaches that are assertively used to handle the type of interactions with which you are having problems. Compare the consequences between their approach and yours. If possible, discuss their approach and their feelings about using it.

6. Make a list of various alternative approaches for being more assertive.

7. Close your eyes and visualize yourself using each of the above alternative approaches. For each approach, think through what the full set of interactions would be, along with the consequences. Select an approach, or combination of approaches, that you believe will be most effective for you to use. Through imagery, practice this approach until you feel comfortable that it will work for you.

8. Role play the approach with someone else, perhaps a friend or counselor. If certain segments of your approach appear clumsy, awkward, timid or aggressive, practice modifications until you become comfortable with the approach. Obtain feedback from the other person about the strengths and shortcomings of your approach. Compare your interactions to the verbal/nonverbal guidelines for assertive behavior in step 4. It may be useful for the other person to model through role playing one or more assertive strategies, which you would then, by reversing roles, practice using.

9. Repeat steps 7 and 8 until you develop an assertive approach that you believe will work best for you and that you are comfortable with and believe will work.

10. Use your approach in a real-life situation. The previous steps are designed to prepare you for the real event. Expect to be somewhat anxious when first trying to be assertive. If you are still too fearful of attempting to be assertive, repeat steps 5 through 8. For those few individuals who fail to develop the needed confidence to try out being assertive, seeking professional counseling is advised, as expressing yourself effectively in interactions with others is essential for personal happiness.

11. Reflect on the effectiveness of your effort. Did you "keep your cool?" Getting angry at times is a normal human emotion, and it needs to be expressed. However, the anger should be expressed in a constructive, assertive fashion. When expressed in a destructive, lashing-out fashion, you are "blowing your cool." Considering the nonverbal/verbal guidelines for assertive behavior discussed in step 4, what components of your responses were assertive, aggressive, and nonassertive? What were the consequences of your effort? How did you feel after trying out this new set of interactions? If possible, discuss how you did in regard to these questions with a friend who may have observed the interactions.

12. Expect some success but not complete personal satisfaction with your initial efforts. Experiencing personal growth and interacting more effectively with others is a continual learning process. Quite appropriately "pat yourself on the back" for the strengths of your approach—you earned it. But also note the areas where you need to improve, and use the above steps for improving your assertiveness efforts.

Continued

BOX 17.1   *Continued*

These steps systematically make sense but are not to be followed rigidly. Each person has to develop a process that works best for himself or herself.

A concluding remark about assertiveness training is that the structure of the technique is relatively simple to understand. Considerable skill (common sense and ingenuity), however, is needed to determine what an effective assertive strategy will be when a "real-life" situation arises. The joy and pride obtained from being able to express oneself assertively is nearly unequaled.

Source: This material is excerpted from Charles Zastrow, "How to Become More Assertive," in *The Personal Problem Solver,* eds. Charles Zastrow and Dae Chang (Englewood Cliffs, NJ: Spectrum Books, 1977), pp. 236–240. © 1977 Reprinted by permission of Prentice-Hall, Englewood Cliffs, New Jersey.

[a] Robert E. Alberti and Michael L. Emmons, *Stand Up, Speak Out, Talk Back!* (New York: Pocket Books, 1975), p. 24.

[b] These self-training steps are a modification of assertiveness training programs developed by Robert E. Alberti and Michael L. Emmons, *Your Perfect Right* (San Luis Obispo, CA: Impact, 1970); and by Herbert Fensterheim and Jean Baer, *Don't Say Yes When You Want to Say No* (New York: Dell, 1975).

---

tion-skill, education, problem solving and decision making, self-help, socialization, therapy, and sensitivity.

SOCIAL CONVERSATION   Such conversation is often loose and tends to drift aimlessly. There is no formal agenda of topics. If the topic is dull, the subject is apt to change. Individuals may have some goal, perhaps only to establish an acquaintanceship, but such individual goals may not become the agenda for the entire group. Social conversation is often employed for "testing" purposes, to determine how deep a relationship might develop with people we do not know very well. In social work, social conversation with other professionals is frequent, but groups involving clients generally have objectives other than conversation.

RECREATION   The objective is to provide activities for enjoyment and exercise. Often such activities are spontaneous, and the groups are practically leaderless. The group service agency (such as YMCA, YWCA, or neighborhood center) may offer little more than physical space and the use of some equipment. Spontaneous playground activities, informal athletic games, and an open game room are examples. Some group agencies providing such physical space claim that recreation and interaction with others help to build "character" and help prevent delinquency among youth by providing an alternative to the street.

RECREATION-SKILL   The objective is to improve a set of skills while at the same time providing enjoyment. In contrast to recreational groups, an adviser, coach, or instructor is generally present and there is more of a task orientation. Examples of activities include golf, basketball, needlework, arts or crafts, and swimming. Competitive team sports and leagues may emerge. Frequently, such groups are led by professionals with recreational training rather than social work training. Social service agencies providing such services include YMCA, YWCA, Boy Scouts, Girl Scouts, neighborhood centers, and school recreational departments.

EDUCATION   The focus of such groups is to acquire knowledge and learn more complex skills. The leader generally is a professional person with considerable training and expertise in the topic area. Examples of

Social group work grew out of the 4-H Club and other informal youth organizations. These two photographs suggest some early 4 H activities: outdoor games and boys' corn-growing clubs.

topics include childrearing practices, training in becoming a more effective parent, preparing for becoming an adoptive parent, and training volunteers to perform a specialized task for a social service agency. Educational group leaders often function in a didactic manner and frequently are social workers. These groups may resemble a class, with considerable group interaction and discussion being encouraged.

PROBLEM SOLVING AND DECISION MAKING   Both providers and consumers of social services may become involved in this type of group. Providers of services use group meetings for such objectives as developing a treatment plan for a client or a group of clients, deciding how best to allocate scarce resources, deciding how to improve the delivery of services to clients, arriving at policy decisions for the agency, deciding how to improve coordination efforts with other agencies, and so on.

Potential consumers of services may form a group to seek to find approaches to meet some current community need. Data on the need may be gathered, and the group may be used as a vehicle either to develop a program or to influence existing agencies to provide services. Social workers may function as stimulators and organizers of such group efforts.

In problem-solving and decision-making groups each participant normally has some interest or stake in the process and stands to gain or lose personally by the outcome. Usually, there is a formal leader of some sort, and other leaders sometimes emerge during the process.

SELF-HELP   Self-help groups are becoming increasingly popular and are often successful in helping individuals with certain social or personal problems. Alfred Katz and Eugene Bender provide a comprehensive definition of self-help groups.

Self-help groups are voluntary, small group structures for mutual aid, and the accomplishment of a special purpose. They are usually formed by peers who have come together for mutual assistance in satisfying a common need, overcoming a common handicap or life-disrupting problem, and bringing about desired social, and/or personal change. The initiators and

members of such groups perceive that their needs are not, or cannot be, met by or through existing social institutions. Self-help groups emphasize face-to-face social interactions and the assumption of personal responsibility by members. They often provide material assistance, as well as emotional support. They are frequently "cause"-oriented, and promulgate an ideology or values through which members may attain an enhanced sense of personal identity. [10]

Alcoholics Anonymous, developed by two former alcoholics, was the first to demonstrate substantial success. A number of other self-help groups have since been formed. Alan Gartner and Frank Riessman in a text entitled *Help: A Working Guide to Self-Help Groups* describe over 200 self-help groups that are now active,[11] some of which are presented in Table 17.3.

Many self-help groups stress (*a*) a confession to the group by each member that she or he has a problem, (*b*) a testimony to the group recounting past experiences with the problem and plans for handling the problem in the future, (*c*) when a member feels a crisis (for example, an abusive parent having an urge to abuse a child), that member is encouraged to call another member of the group who comes over to stay with the person until the crisis subsides.

There appear to be several other reasons why such self-help groups are successful. The members have an internal understanding of the problem, which helps them to help others. Having experienced the misery and consequences of the problem, they are highly motivated and dedicated to find ways to help themselves and others who are fellow sufferers. The participants also benefit from the "helper therapy principle," that is, the helper gains psychological rewards by helping others.[12] Helping others makes a person feel "good" and worthwhile and also enables the helper to put his or her own problems into perspective as he or she sees that others have problems that may be as serious, or even more serious.

Some self-help groups, such as the National Organization of Women, focus on social advocacy and attempt to make legislative and policy changes in public and private institutions. Some self-help groups (such as associations of parents of the mentally retarded) raise

TABLE 17.3

587

Self-Help Groups

Organization	Service Focus
Abused Women's Aid in Crisis	For battered wives and other abused women
Adoptee's Liberty Movement Association	For adoptees searching for their natural parents
Alcoholics Anonymous	For adult alcoholics
American Diabetes Association	Clubs for diabetics, their families, and friends
Brain Tumor Support Group	For persons with brain tumors or their loved ones
Burns Recovered	For burn victims
Caesarian Birth Association	For those expecting a caesarian birth
Candlelighters	For parents of young children with cancer
Checks Anonymous	For persons in debt
Concerned United Birthparents	For parents who have surrendered children for adoption
Depressives Anonymous	For depressed persons
Divorce Anonymous	For divorced persons
Emotions Anonymous	For persons with emotional problems
Emphysema Anonymous	For those with emphysema
Fly without Fear	For people who are afraid of flying
Fortune Society	For ex-offenders and their families
Gam-Anon	For families of gamblers
Gray Panthers	An intergenerational group
Make Today Count	For persons with cancer and their families
Mensa	For persons of high IQs
Naim Conference	For widowed persons
The National Council of Stutterers	For adult stutterers
National Organization for Women	For women's equal rights
Overeaters Anonymous	For overweight persons
Parents Anonymous	For parents of abused children
Phobia Self-Help Groups	For persons with phobias
Prison Families Anonymous	For family members of prisoners
Resolve	A support group for infertile people
Stroke Clubs	For those who have had strokes and their families
Survivors of Suicide Victims	For the relatives and friends of suicide victims
We Care	Support group for divorced and separated persons

BOX 17.2

Example of a Socialization Group— a Rap Group at a Runaway Shelter

New Horizons is a private, temporary shelter care facility for runaways in a large midwestern city. It is located in a large house that was built eighty-four years ago. Youth on the run can stay for up to two weeks. State law requires that parents must be contacted and parental permission received for New Horizons to provide shelter overnight. Services provided include temporary shelter care, individual and family counseling, and a twenty-four-hour hot line for youths in crisis. The facility is licensed to house up to eight youths. Because the average stay is nine days, the population is continually changing. During the stay intensive counseling is provided the youths (and often their parents), focusing on reducing conflicts between the youths and their parents and on making future living plans, since the maximum stay at New Horizons is two weeks. This fourteen-day limit is partially used to convey to youths and their families, beginning with day one, that they must work on the reasons for leaving home.

Every evening at 7 P.M. a rap group meeting is held. All the residents and the two or three staff members on duty are expected to attend. The meetings are convened and led by the staff. This rap group has four main objectives. One is a vehicle for residents to express their satisfactions and dissatisfactions with the facilities and program at New Horizons. Sometimes the rap group appears to be primarily a "gripe" session, but the staff make conscientious efforts to improve those aspects where the youths' concerns are legitimate. For example, the

funds and operate community programs. Many people with a personal problem use self-help groups in the same way that others use social agencies. An additional advantage of self-help groups is that they are generally able to operate with a minimal budget. (See Table 17.3 for a partial listing of self-help groups and their service focus.)

SOCIALIZATION   Some authorities consider this type as being the primary focus of group work.[13] The objective generally is to develop or change attitudes and behaviors of group members to become more socially acceptable. Developing social skills, increasing self-confidence, and planning for the future are other focuses. Illustrations include working with a group of predelinquent youth in group activities to curb delinquency trends; working with a youth group of diverse racial backgrounds to reduce racial tensions; working with a group of "at-risk" young children in an elementary school to improve their interpersonal and problem-solving skills and to motivate them to succeed in a school setting; working with a group of elderly residents at a nursing home to remotivate them and get them involved in various activities; and working with a group of boys at a correctional school to help them make plans for returning to their home community. Leadership of such groups requires considerable skill and knowledge in using the group to foster individual growth and change. Leadership roles of socialization groups are frequently filled by social workers.

youth may indicate that the past few days have been "boring," and staff and residents then jointly plan activities for the next few days.

A second objective is to handle interaction problems that arise between residents and between staff and residents. A wide range of problems may arise: A resident may be preventing others from sleeping, some residents may refuse to do their "fair share" of domestic tasks, there may be squabbles about which TV program to watch, some residents may be overly aggressive, and so forth. Because most of the youths face a variety of crises associated with being on the run, many tend to be anxious and under stress. In such an emotional climate, interaction problems are apt to arise. Staff are sometimes intensely questioned about their actions, decisions, and policies. For example, one of the policies at New Horizons is that each resident must agree not to use alcohol or narcotic drugs while staying at this shelter, with the penalty being expulsion. Occasionally, a few youths use some drugs and are caught and expelled. Removing a youth from this facility has an immense impact on the other residents, and at the following rap meetings staff are expected to clarify and explain such decisions.

A third objective of rap meetings is for staff to present material on topics requested by residents. Examples of topics include sex, drugs, homosexuality, physical and sexual abuse (a fair number of residents are abused by family members), how to avoid being raped, how to handle depression and other unwanted emotions, legal rights of youths on the run, how to be more assertive, how to explain running away to relatives and friends, and what other human services are available to youths in the community. During such presentations, considerable discussion with residents is encouraged and generally occurs.

The final objective of rap groups is to convey information about planned daily activities and changes in the overall program at New Horizons.

THERAPY   Therapy groups are generally composed of members with rather severe emotional or personal problems. Leadership of such groups generally requires considerable skill in being perceptive, in having a knowledge of human behavior and group dynamics, in having group counseling capacities, and in being able to use the group to bring about behavioral changes. Among other skills, the group leader needs to be highly perceptive regarding how each member is being affected by what is being communicated. Considerable competence is needed in being able to develop and maintain a constructive atmosphere within the group. Similar to one-to-one counseling, the goal of therapy groups is generally to have members explore their problems in depth and to then develop one or more strategies for resolving such problems. The group therapist generally uses one or more psychotherapy approaches as a guide for changing attitudes and behaviors; examples of such therapy approaches include Gestalt therapy, reality therapy, learning theory, rational therapy, transactional analysis, client-centered therapy, and psychodrama.

Group therapy is increasingly being used in counseling. It has several advantages over one-to-one therapy. The "helper" therapy principle generally is operative, where members at times interchange roles and sometimes become the "helper" for someone else's problems. In such roles members receive psychological rewards for helping others. Groups also help members to put their problems into perspective,

BOX 17.3

An Example of a Therapy Group

S everal years ago when I was employed as a social worker at a maximum security hospital for the criminally insane, my supervisor requested that I develop and be a leader for a therapy group. When I asked such questions as "What should be the objectives of such a group?" and "Who shall be selected to join?" my supervisor indicated those decisions would be mine. He added that no one else was doing any group therapy at this hospital, and the hospital administration thought it would be desirable, for accountability reasons, for group therapy programs to be developed.

Being newly employed at the hospital and wary because I had never been a leader for a group before, I asked myself "Who is in the greatest need of group therapy?" and "If the group members do not improve, or even deteriorate, how will I be able to explain this; that is, cover my tracks?" I concluded that I should select those identified as being the "sickest" (those labeled chronic schizophrenic) to invite as members of the group. Those labeled chronic schizophrenic are generally expected to show little improvement. With such an expectation, if they did not improve, I felt I would not be blamed. However, if they did improve, I thought it would be viewed as a substantial accomplishment.

My next step was to invite those labeled chronic schizophrenic to join the group. I met with each individually and explained the purpose of the group and the probable topics that would be covered. I then invited them to join. Eight of the eleven who were contacted decided to join. Some of the eight frankly stated they would join primarily because it would look good on their record and increase their chances for an early release. In counseling these group members, the therapy approach used was based on reality therapy,[a] as described in the following material.

At the first meeting the purpose and the focus of the group was again presented and described. It was explained that the purpose was not to review their past but to help them make their present life more enjoyable and meaningful and to help them to make plans for the future. Various topics, it was explained, would be covered, including how to convince the hospital staff they no longer needed to be hospitalized, how to prepare themselves for returning to their home community (for example, learning an employable skill while at the institution), what to do when they felt depressed or had some other unwanted emotion, and following their release what they should do if and when they had an urge to do something that would get them into trouble again. It was further explained that occasional films covering some of these topics would be shown and then discussed, and it was indicated that the group would meet for about an hour each week for the next twelve weeks (until the fall when I had to return to school).

This focus on improving their current circumstances stimulated their interest, but soon they found it uncomfortable and anxiety producing to examine what the future might hold for them. The fact that they were informed they had some responsibility and some control of that future also created anxiety. They reacted to this discomfort by stating they were labeled mentally ill and therefore had some internal condition that was causing their strange behavior. Because they were aware that a cure for schizophrenia had not yet been found, they concluded that they could do little to improve their situation.

They were informed their excuses were "garbage" (stronger terms were used), and we spent a few sessions on getting them to understand that the label "chronic schizophrenic" was meaningless. I spent considerable time explaining (as discussed in Chapter 4) that mental illness is a myth; that is, people do not have a "disease of the mind," even though they may have emotional problems. I went on to explain that what had gotten them locked up was their deviant behavior and that the only way for them to get out was to stop exhibiting their strange behavior and to convince the other staff that they would not be apt to exhibit deviant behavior if released; in essence, they needed to "act sane" in order to convince the staff they had improved sufficiently to warrant being released.

The next set of excuses they tried was that their broken homes, or ghetto schools, or broken romances, or something else in their past had "messed them up" and therefore they could do little about their situation. They were informed such excuses were also "garbage." True, their past experiences were important in their being here. But it was emphasized that what they wanted out of the future, along with their motivation to do something about achieving their goals, were more important than their past experiences in determining what the future would hold for them.

Finally, after we had worked through a number of excuses we were able to focus on how they could better handle specific problems: how to handle being depressed, how to stop exhibiting behavior considered "strange," how to present themselves as being "sane" to increase their chances of an early release, how they would feel and adjust to returning to their home communities, what kind of work or career they desired on their release, how they could prepare themselves by learning a skill or trade while at this institution, helping them to examine what they wanted out of the future and the specific steps they would have to take to achieve their goals, why it was important that they should continue to take the psychoactive medication that had been prescribed, and so on.

The results of this approach were very encouraging. Instead of idly spending much of the time brooding about their situation, they became motivated to improve their situation. At the end of the twelve weeks the eight members of the group spontaneously stated that the meetings were making a positive change in their lives and requested that another social worker from the hospital be assigned to continue the group after I left to return to school. This was arranged. Three years later on a return visit to the hospital I was informed that five of the eight group members had been released to their home community and two of the others were considered to have shown improvement. The final group member's condition was described as "unchanged."

---

[a]William Glasser, *Reality Therapy* (New York: Harper & Row, 1965).

as they realize others have problems as serious as theirs. Groups help members who are having interaction problems to test out new interaction approaches. Research has also shown that it is generally easier to change the attitudes of an individual while in a group than to change a person's attitudes individually.[14] Research has demonstrated that group pressure can have a substantial effect on changing attitudes and beliefs.[15] Furthermore, group therapy permits the social worker to treat more than one person at a time, thus being a substantial saving in the use of professional staff.

In essence a group therapist uses the principles of one-to-one counseling (discussed in Chapter 4) and of group dynamics to work with clients to change dysfunctional attitudes and behavior. Generally, a group therapist also uses the principles of certain comprehensive treatment techniques (such as reality therapy or client-centered therapy) and of certain specialized treatment techniques (such as parent effectiveness training and assertiveness training) to help clients resolve personal and emotional problems. The selection of which treatment techniques to use is generally based on the nature of the problems.

SENSITIVITY Encounter groups, sensitivity training, and T (training)-groups (these terms are used somewhat synonymously) refer to a group experience in which people relate to each other in a close interpersonal manner, and self-disclosure is required. The goal is to improve interpersonal awareness. Jane Howard offers a typical description of an encounter group:

Their destination is intimacy, trust, and awareness of why they behave as they do in groups; their vehicle is candor. Exhorted to "get in touch with their feelings" and to "live in the here-and-now," they sprawl on the floor of a smoky room littered with styrofoam coffee cups, half-empty Kleenex boxes and overflowing ashtrays. As they grow tired they rest their heads on rolled-up sweaters, or corners of cot mattresses, or each other's laps.[16]

An encounter group may meet for a few hours or for a longer period of time up to a few days. Once increased interpersonal awareness is achieved it is anticipated that attitudes and behaviors will change. In order for these changes to occur, a three-phase process generally takes place: unfreezing, change, and refreezing.[17]

Unfreezing occurs in encounter groups through a deliberate process of interacting in nontraditional ways. Our attitudes and behavior patterns have been developed through years of social experiences. Such patterns, following years of experimentation and refinement, have now become nearly automatic. The interpersonal style we develop through years of trial and error generally has considerable utility in our everyday interactions. Deep down, however, we may recognize a need for improvement, but we are reluctant to make an effort to seek improvement, partly because our present style is somewhat functional and partly because we are afraid to reveal things about ourselves.

Stewart L. Tubbs and John W. Baird describe the unfreezing process in sensitivity groups.

Unfreezing occurs when our expectations are violated. We become less sure of ourselves when traditional ways of doing things are not followed. In the encounter group, the leader usually does not act like a leader. He or she frequently starts with a brief statement encouraging the group members to participate, to be open and honest, and to expect things to be different. Group members may begin by taking off their shoes, sitting in a circle on the floor, and holding hands with their eyes closed. The leader then encourages them to feel intensely the sensations they are experiencing, the size and texture of the hands they are holding, and so forth.

Other structured exercises or experiences may be planned to help the group focus on the "here-and-now" experience. Pairs may go for "trust walks" in which each person alternately is led around with his eyes closed. Sitting face to face and conducting a hand dialogue, or a silent facial mirroring often helps to break the initial barriers to change. Other techniques may involve the "pass around" in which a person in the center of a tight circle relaxes and is physically passed around the circle. Those who have trouble feeling a part of the group are encouraged to break into or out of the circle of people whose hands are tightly held. With these experiences, most participants begin to feel more open to conversation about what they have experienced. This sharing of experiences or self-disclosure about the here and now provides more data for the group to discuss.[18]

The second phase of the process is "change." Changes in attitudes and behavior are usually facilitated in sensitivity groups by spontaneous reactions or feedback on how a person "comes across" to others. In everyday interaction we almost never get spontaneous feedback, and we tend to repeat ineffective interaction patterns, since we lack knowledge of our effect on others. But in sensitivity groups such feedback is strongly encouraged. The following set of interactions illustrates such feedback:

Carl: All right [in a sharp tone], let's get this trust walk over with and stop dilly-dallying around. I'll lead the first person around—who wants to be blindfolded first?

Judy: Your statement makes me feel uncomfortable. I feel you are saying this group is a waste of your time. Also, this appears to be your third attempt this evening to "boss" us around.

Jim: I also feel like you are trying to tell us peons what to do. Even the tone of your voice is autocratic and suggests some disgust with this group.

Carl: Really? I didn't realize I was coming across that way. I wonder if I do that at work and when I'm at home?

Such feedback provides us with new insights on how we affect others. Once problem interactions are identified, that member is encouraged to try out new response patterns in the relative safety of the group.

The third and final phase is "refreezing." This stage involves incorporating more effective behaviors and interaction patterns into the person's response patterns. Unfortunately, the term *refreezing* is not the most descriptive, since it implies rigidity with a new set of response patterns. The goal of this phase involves the attitude of experimenting with new sets of behaviors so that the person becomes someone who is growing, continually changing, and increasingly becomes more effective in interacting with others. In terminating a sensitivity group, the leader may alert the participants that they have to be "on guard," as old behavior patterns tend to creep back in.

TABLE 17.4

Contrasting Goals of Therapy versus Sensitivity Groups

Therapy Groups	Sensitivity Groups
Step 1 Examine problem(s) in depth	*Step 1* Help each person become more aware of himself or herself and how she or he affects others in interpersonal interactions
Step 2 Explore and then select (from various resolution approaches) a strategy to resolve the problem	*Step 2* Help a person then to develop more effective interaction patterns

Sensitivity groups usually generate an outpouring of emotions that are rarely found in other groups.

The goal of sensitivity groups provides an interesting contrast to those of therapy groups (see Table 17.4). In therapy the goal is to have each member explore in depth personal or emotional problems that she or he has and then to develop a strategy to resolve that problem. In comparison, sensitivity groups seek to foster increased personal and interpersonal awareness and then to develop more effective interaction patterns. Sensitivity groups generally do not directly attempt to identify and change specific emotional or personal problems that people have (such as drinking problems, feelings of depression, sexual dysfunctions, and so on). The philosophy behind sensitivity groups is that with increased personal and interpersonal awareness, people will be better able to avoid, cope with, and/or handle specific personal problems that arise.

Sensitivity groups are being used in our society for a wide variety of purposes: to train professional counselors to be more perceptive and effective in interpersonal interactions with clients and with other professionals, to train people in management positions to be more effective in their business interactions, to help clients with overt relationship

A senior citizens' dance (above) and a halfway house for ex-prisoners (opposite) both illustrate socialization, a primary focus of group work. Motivating the elderly to become more socially active and helping former convicts adjust to life outside prison would seem to have little in common, but both require a special skill for using groups to foster individual growth.

problems to become more aware of how they affect others and to help them to develop more effective interaction patterns, and to train interested citizens in becoming more aware and effective in their interactions.

Although encounter, marathon, and sensitivity groups are popular and have received considerable publicity, such groups remain controversial. In some cases inadequately trained and incompetent individuals have become self-proclaimed leaders and have enticed people to join through sensational advertising. If handled poorly, sensitivity groups may intensify personal problems. Many authorities on sensitivity training disclaim the use of encounter groups as a form of psychotherapy and discourage those with serious personal problems from joining such a group. After re-

viewing the research on the outcome of sensitivity groups, Morton Lieberman, Ervin Yalom, and Matthew Miles conclude:

Encounter groups present a clear and evident danger if they are used for radical surgery to produce a new man. The danger is even greater when the leader and the participants share this misconception. If we no longer expect groups to produce magical, lasting change and if we stop seeing them as panaceas, we can regard them as useful, socially sanctioned opportunities for human beings to explore and to express themselves. Then we can begin to work on ways to improve them so that they may make a meaningful contribution toward solving human problems.[19]

How to Start and Lead Groups

Many students and other people fear taking a leadership role in groups. They are uncertain what a leader actually does, and they fear they do not have the qualities or traits to be a leader. Amazingly, the truth of the matter is that even the most fearful and anxious students have already taken on leadership roles in many groups. Being a designated leader for a group is not that different from taking on leadership roles. This section will focus on providing guidelines on how to start and lead groups. The following aspects will be covered.

1. Doing homework prior to the first session.
2. Planning a session.

3. Relaxing before starting a meeting.
4. Observing cues on entering the meeting room.
5. Making seating arrangements.
6. Making introductions.
7. Clarifying roles.
8. Setting an agenda.
9. Ending a meeting.

DOING HOMEWORK PRIOR TO THE FIRST SESSION   When leading a group, extensive preparation is key to the group being a successful experience for the members (including yourself). Even experienced leaders have to prepare carefully for each group, and for each session that the group meets.

In planning for a new group, answers are needed for the following questions: What is the overall purpose or general goals of the group? What are possible ways in which these general goals might be accomplished? What are the characteristics of the members? Are some members apt to have unique, individual goals and/or needs? What resources do the members need to have in order to accomplish the general goals? What should the agenda be for the first meeting? The group members should have considerable input in suggesting and deciding on the specific goals of the group: How can this best be accomplished? When the group first meets, should an ice breaker exercise be used: If so, what? Should refreshments be provided? How should the chairs be arranged? What type of group atmosphere will best help the group accomplish its tasks? What is the best available meeting place? Why have you been selected to lead the group? What do the members expect you to do?

As you plan for the first meeting, it is very helpful to seek to view the group as a new member would view it. Questions and concerns that a new member may have are the following: What will the goals of this group be? Why am I joining? Will my personal goals be met in this group? Will I feel comfortable in this group? Will I be accepted by other members? Will the other members be radically different in terms of backgrounds and interests? If I do not like this group, can I get out of attending meetings? Will other members respect what I have to say, or will they laugh and make fun of me? Through considering such concerns, the leader can seek to plan the first meeting in a way that will assist the other members to feel comfortable and that will help clarify the members' questions concerning the goals and activities of the group.

When being a leader, it is *absolutely essential* that you do your homework prior to the first meeting to identify as precisely as possible what the group's needs and expectations are. The quickest way to fail as a leader is to seek to have a group go in a different direction than the members desire. For example, I remember going to a workshop with other counselors that was entitled "Grief, Death, and Dying." The counselors expected material on how to more effectively counsel clients who were grieving about the death of a loved one. The presenter instead gave a historical review of how present-day funeral rituals had evolved since the Middle Ages. The audience was very disappointed because their expectations were unmet.

There are a variety of ways to identify what the members want. It may be possible to ask some members, prior to the first meeting, what their expectations are. If you are asked by someone else to lead the group, it is essential to ask that person what the expectations for the group are. The members should generally be asked at the first meeting to give their views about what they desire to get out of the group. Another way (which needs to be done for preparatory reasons anyway) is to "scout" the following about the members:

1. How many members are expected?

2. What are their characteristics—ages, socioeconomic status, racial and ethnic backgrounds, sex mix, educational and professional backgrounds, and so on?

3. How knowledgeable and informed are the members about the topics the group will be dealing with?

4. What are the personal goals and agendas of the various members apt to be?

5. How motivated are the members to accomplish the purposes for which the group is being formed? This can partly be determined by examining how voluntary the membership is. Groups composed of involuntary members (for example, a group that is court ordered to attend because of a conviction of driving while intoxicated) have little motivation to participate or to make changes in their lives. They may even be hostile that they are being forced to attend.

6. What are the underlying value systems of the members apt to be? A group of teenagers who are on juvenile probation is apt to differ significantly from a group of retired priests. (However, it is important to remember to view the members in terms of being unique persons rather than in terms of stereotypes.)

In planning for the first (and additional meetings) it is helpful to visualize (imagine) how you, as leader, want the meeting to go. For example, at the first meeting the following may be visualized:

The members will arrive at various times. I will be there early to greet them, to introduce myself, to assist them in feeling comfortable, and to engage in small talk. Possible subjects of small talk that are apt to be of interest to these new members are _____, _____, and _____.

I will begin the meeting by introducing myself and the overall purpose of the group. I will use the following "ice-breaker" exercise for members to introduce themselves and to get acquainted with each other. I will ask the group to give me a list of four or five items that they would like to know about the other members. Then each member will introduce himself or herself and give answers to the four or five items. I will also answer these items and encourage the members to ask further questions that they have about me and the group.

After the ice-breaker exercise I will briefly state the overall purpose of the group, and ask if the members have questions about this. Possible questions that may arise are _____. If such questions arise, my answers will be _____.

We will then proceed to the items on the agenda for this decision-making group, which has been mailed out to the members. During the discussion of each of these items, the questions that may arise are _____. My answers to such questions, should they arise, are _____.

The kind of group atmosphere I will seek to create is a democratic, equalitarian one. Such an atmosphere is best suited for encouraging members to become committed to the group goals and to then contribute their time and resources. I will seek to do this by arranging the chairs in a circle, by drawing out through questions those who are silent, by using humor, and by making sure that I do not dominate the conversation.

I will seek to end the meeting by summarizing what has been covered and by summarizing the decisions that have been made. We will set a time for the next meeting. I will finally ask if anyone has any additional comments or questions. Throughout the meeting I will seek to establish a positive atmosphere, partly by complimenting the members on the contributions they make.

If a group has met for one or more times, the leader needs to review the following kinds of questions. Have the overall goals been sufficiently decided on and clarified? If not, what needs to be done in this clarification process? Is the group making adequate progress in accomplishing its goals? If not, what are the obstacles that need to be confronted? Has the group selected adequate courses of action to reach its goals, or are there more effective courses of action that might be considered? What items should be placed on the agenda for the next meeting? What activities should be planned? Will successful completion of these activities move the group toward accomplishing its overall goals? If not, perhaps other activities need to be selected. Does each member seem sufficiently interested and motivated to help the group accomplish its goals, or are there some members that appear disinterested? If so, why do they appear disinterested, and what might be tried to stimulate their interests?

PLANNING A SESSION In planning a session, it is essential to be aware of the overall goals for the group. It is also essential to identify for each session what the specific goals are for that session. It is critical to know exactly what you want to accomplish in each session and to make sure that all the items on the agenda relate to the goals you want to accomplish. The following are some suggestions.

1. *Select content that is relevant.* The material should not only be relevant to the specific goals for the session but should also be relevant to the backgrounds and interests of the participants. For example, in a time-management presentation, the timesaver tips you give to college students probably will be quite different than the ones you give to business executives. In the former, the tips should probably focus on improving study habits, whereas the latter should probably focus on improving work activities in an office setting. An excellent way to evaluate the relevance of your material is to define precisely how it will be valuable to members of the group. Ask yourself, "If a group member asks why I should know this, can I concisely give a valid reason?" If you are unable to come up with more than a vague answer, then it may be best to consider discarding that material and selecting other, more relevant material.

2. *Use a number of examples.* Examples help to illustrate key concepts. They also stimulate the interests of the participants. People tend to remember examples much more than statistics. To illustrate, in a presentation on spouse abuse, a few vivid real-life stories of the drastic effects on a woman's life of continued battering by her husband will be remembered much longer than statistics on the extent of spouse abuse.

3. *Present materials in a logical order.* It is generally desirable to begin by summarizing the agenda items for the session. Ideally, one topic should blend into the next. If group exercises are used, they should be placed next to the related theoretical material.

4. *Plan for time.* Once you have the content of the session fairly well arranged, seek to estimate how long each segment will take. Accurate estimations will help you determine if you have too much or too little material planned for the alloted time. It is a good idea also to plan what you will do if the content is covered faster or slower than what you are estimating. (For example, if the material is being covered slower than anticipated, you will then be prepared to revise your agenda when you

realize that you will not have time for everything.) You should also be prepared to cover extra material when things move more quickly than you anticipated. If you are planning to use a film or have a guest speaker for part of the time, you should have plans for appropriate substitute material in case the film projector fails to operate or the guest speaker fails to appear.

5. *Be prepared to be flexible with your agenda.* A variety of unexpected events may make it desirable to change the agenda during a session. The material may be covered much faster than anticipated. Or, interpersonal conflict may erupt between some members that may take considerable time to process. Some members may bring up subjects related to the group's overall purpose that may be more valuable for the group to focus on than the prepared agenda.

6. *Occasionally change the pace.* People will be able to pay attention for longer periods of time if there is an occasional change of pace. Long, long lectures or long discussions bore people. The pace can be changed in a variety of ways: using a group exercise, showing a film, inviting a guest speaker, taking a break, having a debate, showing slides, changing the topics, and so on. In group therapy sessions, one way to change pace is to switch from focusing on one member's problems to focusing on another's concerns. If you are presenting a lecture, you can increase attention by:

   a. Speaking extemporaneously rather than by reading the material.

   b. Occasionally walking around the room rather than standing or sitting in one place.

   c. Drawing out the participants through asking them questions.

(An excellent way to learn how to give more stimulating presentations is to observe the nonverbal and verbal communication patterns of dynamic speakers and then seek to use those patterns in your presentations that you believe will be productive for you.) When changing pace it is critical to use appropriate transitions so that the topics blend into one another rather than the tempo becoming choppy and confusing.

In changing pace, it is helpful to use a variety of methods. There are many methods of conveying information: lectures, discussions, role plays, films, exercises, slide presentations, diagrams, and so on. In selecting methods, it is useful to be aware that people tend to remember for a longer period of time information they receive in an active way (such as through an exercise) than information they receive in a passive way (through listening).

RELAXING BEFORE STARTING A MEETING   Prior to starting a meeting, you are apt to be nervous about how the session may go. Some anxiety is helpful in order to be mentally alert and to facilitate your attending to what is being communicated during the meeting. Some leaders, however, have too high a level of anxiety, which reduces their effectiveness. If your anxiety is too high, you can reduce it by engaging in activities that you personally find relaxing. Relaxation techniques are highly recommended. Effective group leaders generally learn they can reduce their level of anxiety through using one or more of the following techniques: taking a walk, going jogging, meditating, listening to music you find relaxing, and finding a place where you can be alone to clear your mind. Through practice in leading groups, you will gradually build up your confidence that you are an effective group leader.

OBSERVING CUES ON ENTERING THE MEETING ROOM   It is important for you as leader to be on time and perhaps even a little early. By being early, it allows you to check to see that everything is as you planned. By being early, you'll be able to do what needs to be done, such as checking to see that refreshments are available (if refreshments are planned), erasing the blackboard, arranging the chairs in the way you desire, and so on.

By being early you will also have an opportunity to observe the moods of the members. If it is a group you have not previously met, being early will give you an opportunity to gain information about the interests of the participants from their age, sex, clothes and personal appearance, small-talk, and interactions with one another. An effective leader observes such cues and generally finds a way to "join" with such participants. For example, this author was asked to give a workshop on suicide prevention to a high school class. On arriving, I was informed by the teacher that one of the students in the class had recently committed suicide. Instead of beginning with my planned presentation, I acknowledged that I had just been informed about their classmate, and I began by anonymously asking each of them to write down on a sheet of paper one or two concerns or questions that they had about suicide. After they turned in their sheets, we had a lively discussion related to their questions and concerns. Such a discussion was probably more valuable than the formal presentation (which was never given), since the discussion focused on the specific questions and concerns that they had.

MAKING SEATING ARRANGEMENTS   The seating arrangement is important for several reasons. It can affect who talks to whom and have an influence on who is apt to play leadership roles. As a result, it can affect group cohesion and group morale.

It is important in most groups for the members to have eye contact with one another. It is even more important for the group leader to be able to make eye contact with everyone, in order to obtain nonverbal feedback on what the members are thinking and feeling.

A circle is ideal for generating discussion, for encouraging a sense of equal status for each member, and for promoting group openness and group cohesion. The traditional classroom arrangement (with the leader in front and everyone facing that person while sitting in rows) has the effect of placing the leader in a position of authority. It also tends to inhibit communication because members are generally able to make eye contact only with those closest to them.

Tables have advantages and disadvantages. They provide a place to write and to put work materials. Some members feel more comfortable at a table because it gives them a place to lean onto. Disadvantages of tables are that they tend to restrict movement and may serve as a barrier between people.

The leader should carefully consider whether it is desirable or undesirable to have tables. For example, if members are to sift through papers or are expected to take notes, tables should generally be used. In therapy

groups, tables are seldom used because they tend to restrict movement and act as a barrier.

In many settings tables can be arranged to best meet the goals of the meeting. For example, arranging small tables in a circle tends to facilitate communication.

Tables influence the way group members interact with each other. If the table is rectangular, it is customary for the leader to sit at one end, which then is viewed as the "head" of the table. The person who is at the head of the table is often viewed as the "authority" and usually tends to do more talking and to have a greater influence on the discussion. If an equalitarian atmosphere is desired it is helpful to use a round or square table. Two rectangular tables can be placed together to make a square.

Tables also influence interactions by where people sit. People are most apt to talk to those who are sitting at right angles to them and next most likely to talk to those next to them. Those sitting directly across receive less communication, and those sitting elsewhere than mentioned are even less likely to be talked to.

When a group meets for the first time (and often later) members are most apt to sit next to friends. If it is important for everyone in the group to interact with one another, it may be desirable to ask people to sit next to people they do not know. This will counteract any cliqueishness in the group and encourage members to get to know each other.

MAKING INTRODUCTIONS   During the introduction of the leader, his or her credentials should be summarized in such a way that members gain a sense of confidence that she or he can fulfill their expectations. If the leader is being introduced by someone else, a brief and concise summary of the leader's credentials *for the expected role* is desirable. If the leader is introducing himself or herself, the important credentials should be summarized in a nonarrogant fashion. The summary should also be delivered in a way to create the desired atmosphere, whether it be an informal or formal atmosphere, a fun or serious one, and so on. An excellent way in many groups to handle the introductions is to use an ice-breaker exercise, such as the one described earlier in this section.

In meeting with a group, it is highly desirable to learn the members' names as quickly as possible. This requires extra attention on the leader's part. Name tags facilitate this process for everyone. Members appreciate being called by their name: It helps convey to them that they are valued members of the group.

If the group is small, it is generally advantageous for each member to introduce himself or herself, perhaps through using an ice-breaker exercise. It is often desirable during introductions for members to state their expectations for the group. This helps uncover hidden agendas. If a stated expectation is beyond the scope of the group, the leader should tactfully state and discuss it in order to prevent an unrealistic expectation becoming a source of frustration or dissatisfaction for that member.

CLARIFYING ROLES   As leader of a group, you should be clear about your roles and responsibilities. If you are unclear, you may want to discuss with the group their expectations concerning the appropriate roles for the leader and for the other members. One way of doing this is for the group to select goals and then to make decisions about the tasks and responsibilities that *each* member will have in working toward the goals of the group. In most situations it is clearly a mistake for the leader to do the majority of the work. The group will generally be most productive if all members make substantial contributions. The more that members contribute to a group, the more that they are apt to feel a part of the group psychologically.

Even if you are fairly clear about what you would like your role to be, the other members may be confused about what your role is or may have different expectations of you. If there is a realistic chance that the other members are unclear, you should explain carefully what you perceive your role to be. If members indicate they have somewhat different expectations, time should be devoted for the group to make decisions about who will do what.

In explaining what you perceive your role to be it is generally desirable to be humble about your skills and resources. Generally you will want to come across as a knowledgeable "human" rather than as an authority figure who has all the answers.

You should always be prepared to explain the reasoning behind the things you do. For example, if you are doing an exercise, the group should generally be informed about the goals or objectives of that exercise. (If questions arise about whether the goals for the exercise are consistent with the overall goals for the group, you should be prepared to provide an explanation.)

The role that the leader should assume in a group will vary somewhat from situation to situation. For example, there are apt to be marked differences in responsibilities of the leader in a therapy group versus those of the leader in a Boy Scout group.

SETTING AN AGENDA   For most meetings, there should be an agenda. Ideally, all members of the group should have an opportunity to suggest items for the agenda. If possible, the agenda should be sent to the members several days before the meeting to give them an opportunity to prepare for the items that will be considered.

At the start of the meeting the agenda items should be briefly reviewed, prior to consideration of the first item. This review gives each member a chance to suggest additions, deletions, or other changes. In some meetings it may be appropriate for the group to discuss, and perhaps vote, on the suggested changes in the agenda.

ENDING A MEETING   You need to give attention to how to end a session. A few minutes before the session is scheduled to end, or when it appears the group has exhausted a subject, you may conclude with a brief summarization of the key points made by you and the other members. Such a summary emphasizes the major points to be remembered and leaves the group with a sense of achievement. If group members have tasks to perform prior to the next meeting, it is often desirable to summarize what is expected to be done and to ask if there are questions related to performing these tasks.

Through learning how to lead groups effectively, you will become more aware of yourself, grow as a person, become more self-confident, feel good about yourself, develop highly marketable skills that employers are seeking, learn to improve interpersonal re-

Community issues often require professionals to assume more partisan roles. Social workers who become activists are most effective in achieving change when their decisions are guided by rational thinking and planning.

lationships, and help yourself and other members accomplish important tasks. Leaders are not born; they are trained. You have the potential to become an effective group leader. Through gaining a working knowledge of the above concepts, you will become an effective group leader.

COMMUNITY PRACTICE

Students considering a career in social work initially express disinterest in community practice, indicating they would rather work directly with people. Many have the erroneous belief that community practice involves skills and techniques that are too complex and too abstract for them to learn. Also, they view community practice as having too few rewards and as involving a lot of boring, unenjoyable work. As an introduction to social work community practice it should be noted that the above beliefs are erroneous. The realities are (*a*) the most basic skill needed in community practice is to be able to work effectively with people; (*b*) community practice primarily involves working together with individuals and with groups; (*c*) every practicing social worker occasionally becomes involved in community practice projects; (*d*) in working on a community project a worker becomes "ego involved," and seeing that project develop, approved, and implemented is immensely gratifying; and (*e*) community practice efforts are often "fun."

Workers in direct practice with individuals or groups are likely to become involved in community development activities when gaps in services or unmet needs are identified for clients they are working with. For example, if there is a rapid increase in teenage girls becoming pregnant in a community, a school social worker may become involved in efforts to establish a sex education program in the school system. If there are a number of terminally ill patients and their families are complaining about the way they are treated in a hospital, a medical social worker may become involved in efforts to establish a hospice. If a juvenile probation officer notes a sharp increase in juvenile offenses, the officer may become involved in efforts to have juvenile offenders visit a prison and hear the consequences from inmates of what prison life is like (as depicted in "Scared Straight" programs).

Workers involved in developing needed new services are aware of the human benefits that will result. These payoffs and the time and efforts workers put into community practice projects often lead them to become highly "ego involved." Being successful in establishing new services is experienced as a deeply gratifying political victory. On a negative note, a reality is that the development of new services generally involves a number of unanticipated obstacles and requires several times as much time and effort as initially anticipated.

As yet, there is no widely accepted definition of the term *community practice*. The modes of practice performed under this heading have a variety of labels: social planning, community planning, locality development, community action, social action, macropractice, community organization, and community development.

Community practice will be defined here as being the process of stimulating and assisting the local community to evaluate, plan, and coordinate its efforts to provide for the community's health, welfare, and recreation needs. In community practice a worker acts as a catalyst in stimulating and encouraging community action. Community practice activities include encouraging and stimulating citizen organization around one or more issues, specifying the nature of the problem, coordinating efforts between·groups, fact finding, formulating realizable goals, doing public relations and public education, conducting research, planning, iden-

tifying financial resources, developing strategies to achieve a goal, and being a resource person. Agency settings that employ community practice workers include community welfare councils, the United Way, social-planning agencies, health-planning councils, neighborhood councils, city-planning councils, community action groups, and occasionally some other private or public organization.

Community practice workers become involved in a wide variety of social issues, including civil rights, welfare reform, meeting the needs of poor people, education and health issues, housing, improving leisure-time services, race relations, minority-group employment, developing services to counteract alienation of youth, urban redevelopment programs, developing services for teenage runaways and for those experimenting with drugs, and developing services for those who test positive to HIV and to those who have AIDS.

There are a number of other disciplines in addition to social work that provide training in community practice: community psychology, urban and regional planning, health planning, corrections planning, recreation, and public administration.

In recent years American citizens have organized around a number of issues. A few of the issues receiving national attention will be listed: unions striking for higher pay, women's rights issues, farmers wanting higher prices, the abortion question, capital punishment, rights for homosexuals, tax cuts, school closings in many cities, national defense budget, nuclear energy, changing marijuana laws, massage parlors, nude dancing, affirmative action guidelines on hiring, and environmental concerns.

Brief History of Community Practice

For centuries people have organized to change social and political conditions. In the 1700s, for example, Americans organized to revolt against the British and fought what has come to be called the Revolutionary War.

Community practice in social work has its roots in the 1800s in the charity organization society movement and the settlement house movement.[20]

In the 1800s, private philanthropy bore the major responsibility for the relief of poverty and dependence in the United States. During the early 1800s, a wide range of private health and welfare agencies were established to provide funds and services (which were generally combined with religious conversion efforts) to those in need. To avoid several agencies providing similar services to the same families, the Charity Organization Society was formed to *coordinate* efforts and to *plan* for meeting unmet needs.

The reformers associated with the settlement house movement based many of their programs on *social action* to promote social legislation for providing needed services to neighborhoods. The settlement house reformers also encouraged and stimulated neighborhood residents to work together to improve living conditions.

Community welfare councils were first organized in 1908.[21] Continuing the efforts begun by the charity organization movement, these councils served as coordinating organizations for voluntary agencies. The functions of these councils have continued to the present time and include planning, coordination, efforts to avoid duplication of services, setting standards for services, and efforts to improve efficiency and accountability.

Community Chests (now called United Way) were formed around 1920 to be centralized campaigns for raising funds for voluntary agencies.[22] In practically all communities United Way has been combined with community welfare councils for the raising of funds and for the allocation of funds to voluntary agencies.

All social welfare agencies and organizations become involved at times in community practice efforts.

Roles of Organizer

There are several styles or roles for community practice activities. The role that is applied is, ideally, determined by the job to be accomplished. A given community issue may involve a variety of tasks, which usually necessitates the worker assuming different roles. Six of the main roles will be briefly described.

ENABLER   In this role the worker helps people articulate their needs, clarify and identify their problems, and develop their capacities to deal with their own problems more effectively. This is the *classic* or traditional role of community practice. Considerable emphasis is placed on developing constructive relationships with community residents. The focus is to "help people organize to help themselves." The enabler makes extensive use of group dynamic principles. The enabler's role is simply to facilitate the community organization process.

In the enabler role the worker first helps to awaken and focus discontent about community conditions. In order to do this the worker has to spend considerable time in getting acquainted with residents and in securing their trust and respect. After this respect is attained the worker encourages residents to verbalize their concerns.

The second function as enabler is to encourage organization. Apathy and passivity generally cause the community organization process to be painfully slow. Usually, the time taken to identify problems and discontents will provide the motivation to organize. During this phase the worker seeks to have residents with common concerns begin communicating with one another and begin organizing to do something about their concerns. Even when the way has been well prepared, some communities falter at organizing. When this happens the reasons for the faltering need to be examined and dealt with.

The third function of an enabler is to nourish good interpersonal relations. This function is similar to the rapport a counselor seeks to establish with clients. The worker seeks to have organizational meetings run smoothly. The objective is to have the physical and psychological conditions arranged in such a way that people feel comfortable, enjoy themselves, and feel free to verbalize their concerns.

The fourth function of the enabler is to facilitate effective planning. The worker usually does this by asking relevant questions such as, "What are some ways to resolve this?" and "What will be the effects if we try this?" The enabler does not lead or provide answers. Instead, she or he asks questions that stimulate insight and supports and encourages members to develop plans to do something about their concerns.

BROKER   A broker links individuals and groups who need help (and do not know where help is available) with community services. Today, even moderate-sized communities have 200 or 300 social service agencies and organizations providing community services. Even human resource professionals are frequently only partially aware of the total service network in their community. As in the fields of finance and real estate, social service brokers serve the function of negotiating, for their clients, with a complex network of social institutions about which clients are uninformed and with whose workings clients are inexperienced.

Often, all that is required to perform this linkage function is to provide information that puts people in contact with resources. However, if difficulties arise, collective action may be needed to effect the exchange. (For example, a broker may suggest to elderly people that needed services—such as a community center— may be provided if they *collectively* request and document to the city council that such services are needed.) Through such brokerage activity changes in policies and programs may occur that affect whole classes of persons.

A number of governmental agencies (particularly in human services, education, health, and housing) now employ one or more staff persons to work part- or full-time with citizens, educating them to the problems the agency is dealing with and eliciting their ideas for making changes in the delivery system to serve customers better. This broker function acts as a consciousness-raising device to show people what the system is really like and also makes the system more responsive to the needs of consumers.

EXPERT   As an expert the worker provides information and gives advice in a number of areas. An expert may suggest how an organization should be structured,

including how subgroups should be represented. An expert may suggest different responsibilities for members to assume, including that of the leader. An expert may give advice on the goals and subgoals that a group should set. An expert may suggest tactics or strategies to accomplish goals that are set. An expert may give advice on how to do certain tasks, such as conducting a neighborhood survey. An expert should inform the organization about other relevant research and documents that exist and also inform the organization about other resources that may help them accomplish their goals. Also, an expert should give advice on how the organization can set up procedures to evaluate its activities and efforts.

It is important for an expert to remember not to insist on the acceptance of his or her advice. Advice given by an expert should only be viewed as ideas being offered for consideration, with the organization having the responsibility to decide whether to accept these suggestions.

SOCIAL PLANNER   A social planner gathers facts about a social problem and analyzes the facts to arrive at the most rational course of action. The planner then develops a program, seeks funding sources, and strives to secure consensus among diverse interest groups about providing the program. Such consensus may or may not be obtained. If sufficient support is obtained (generally from the power structure), the planner's final task is facilitating the implementation of the plan. Social planners are generally employed, or at least sponsored, by the power structure, for example, city, county, and state governments or the boards of influential private agencies such as the United Way or a community welfare council. Often, social planners are assigned to work with concerned community groups. Planners generally have graduate training in research or planning.

Although the roles of expert and social planner overlap, an expert focuses more on giving advice, whereas a social planner focuses more on doing the tasks involved in developing and implementing programs.

ADVOCATE   The role of an advocate has been borrowed from the law profession. It is an active directive role in which the worker is an advocate for a client or for a citizen's group. When a client or a citizen's group is in need of help and existing institutions are uninterested (and sometimes openly negative and hostile) in providing services, then the advocate's role is appropriate. In such a role the advocate provides leadership for collecting information, for arguing the correctness of the client's needs and requests, and for challenging the institution's decision not to provide services. The object is not to ridicule or censure a particular institution but to modify or change one or more of the service policies. In this role the advocate is a partisan who is serving the interest of a client or of a citizen's group. The impartiality of the enabler and broker roles is absent here.

THE ACTIVIST   An activist seeks basic institutional change; often the objective involves a shift in power and resources to a disadvantaged group. An activist is concerned about social injustice, inequity, and deprivation. An activist seeks to stimulate a disadvantaged group to organize to take action against the existing power structure, which is viewed as being the oppressor. Tactics involve conflict, confrontation, and negotiation. An effective activist is skilled at being an advocate, agitator, broker, and negotiator. Similar to an advocate, an activist takes a partisan role. The constituency of an activist is generally viewed as being a victim of the power structure.

REFLECTIONS ON THESE ROLES   The traditional neutrality role of the social work profession is often desirable. The enabler, expert, broker, and social planner are quite effective when such nonpartisan activity meets the needs of clients and client groups. When it does not the role of an advocate or of an activist may be warranted.

An advocate and an activist cannot be effective if they emotionally overreact, that is, let their actions and decisions be determined by emotion rather than rational thinking and planning. In order to be effective, they must make decisions and plan strategy according to the following guideline: "Is what I'm doing going to be constructive (or destructive) in achieving the desired outcome, and is there an even better way to achieve the desired outcome?"

Models of Community Practice

A variety of approaches have been developed to bring about community change. In reviewing these approaches, Jack Rothman and John Tropman have been able to categorize them into three models: locality development, social planning, and social action.[23] It should be noted these models are "ideal types." Actual approaches to community change have tendencies or emphases that result in them being categorized in one of the above models; yet most approaches have components that are also characteristic of one or both of the other models. Advocates of the social planning model, for example, may at times use community change techniques (such as wide discussion and participation by a variety of groups) that are characteristic of the other two models. At this point we will not attempt to deal with the mixed forms, but for analytical purposes will view the three models as being "pure" forms.

Model A, locality development (also called community development), asserts that community change can best be brought about through broad participation of a wide spectrum of people at the local community level. The model seeks to involve a broad cross section of people (including the disadvantaged and the power structure) in identifying and solving their problems. Some themes emphasized in this model are democratic procedures, a consensus approach, voluntary cooperation, development of indigenous leadership, and self-help.

The roles of the community practitioner in this approach include enabler, catalyst, coordinator, and teacher of problem-solving skills and ethical values. The approach assumes that conflicts that result between various interest groups can be creatively and constructively handled. It encourages people to express their differences freely but assumes people will put aside their self-interests in order to further the interests of their community. The approach assumes people will put aside their self-interests through appeals to altruism. The basic theme of this approach is "Together we can figure out what to do and do it." The approach seeks to use discussion and communication

These young newlyweds (above), reflecting the idealism of the early Kennedy years, teach each other French before their new assignment as Peace Corps volunteers in Togo. A generation later, volunteer Melissa Lang (opposite) examines plans for a spillway and reservoir in Thailand. The philosophy of the Peace Corps—that community change is best brought about through the participation of a cross-section of people at a local level—has made it a model for many other community development efforts.

between different factions to reach consensus about the problems to focus on and the strategies or actions to resolve these problems. A few examples of locality development efforts include neighborhood work programs conducted by community-based agencies; Volunteers in Service to America; village-level work in some overseas community development programs, including the Peace Corps; and a variety of activities performed by self-help groups. A case example of the locality development model is presented in Box 17.4.

Model B, the social planning approach, emphasizes a technical process of problem solving. The approach assumes that community change in a complex industrial environment requires highly trained and skilled planners who can guide complex change pro-

cesses. The role of the expert is stressed in this approach to identifying and resolving social problems. The expert or planner is generally employed by a segment of the power structure, such as area planning agency, city or county planning department, mental health center, United Way board, Community Welfare Council, and so on. Because the social planner is employed by a segment of the power structure, there is a tendency for the planner to serve the interests of the power structure. Building community capacity or facilitating radical social change is generally not an emphasis in this approach.

The planner's roles in this approach include gathering facts, analyzing data, and serving as program designer, implementer, and facilitator. Community

participation may vary from little to substantial with this approach, depending on the community's attitudes toward the problems being addressed. For example, an effort to design and obtain funding for a community center for the elderly may or may not result in substantial involvement by interested community groups, depending on the politics surrounding such a center. Much of the focus of the social planning approach is on identifying needs and on arranging and delivering goods and services to people who need them. The change focus of this approach is "Let's get the facts and take the next rational steps." A case example of this approach is presented in Box 17.5.

Model C, the social action approach, assumes there is a disadvantaged (often oppressed) segment of the population that needs to be organized, perhaps in alliance with others, in order to pressure the power structure for increased resources or for treatment more in accordance with democracy or social justice. Social action approaches at times seek basic changes in major institutions or seek changes in basic policies of formal organizations. Such approaches often seek redistribution of power and resources. Unlike the vision of a unified community held by locality developers, the power structure or opposition is the target of action. Perhaps the best-known social activist was Saul Alinsky, who advised, "Pick the target, freeze it, personalize it, and polarize it."[24]

The roles of the community practitioner in this approach include advocate, agitator, activist, partisan,

BOX 17.4

Case Example of the Locality Development Model

Robert McKearn, a social worker for a juvenile probation department noticed in 1985 that an increasing number of school-age children were being referred to his office by the police department, school system, and parents from a small city of 11,000 people in the county served by his agency. The charges included status offenses (such as truancy from school) and delinquent offenses (such as shoplifting and burglary). Mr. McKearn noted that most of these children were from single-parent families.

Mr. McKearn contacted the community mental health center, the self-help organization Parents Without Partners, the pupil services department of the public school system, the county social services department, some members of the clergy, and the community mental health center in the area. Nearly everyone he contacted saw an emerging need to better serve children in single-parent families. The pupil services department mentioned that such children were performing less well academically in school and tended to display more serious disciplinary problems.

Mr. McKearn arranged a meeting of representatives from the groups and organizations that were contacted.

At the initial meeting a number of concerns were expressed about the problematic behaviors being displayed by children who had single parents. The school system considered these children to be "at risk" for having higher rates of truancy, dropping out of school, delinquency activities, suicide, emotional problems, and unwanted pregnancies. Although a number of problems were identified, no one at this initial meeting was able to suggest a

---

broker, and negotiator. Tactics used in social action projects include protests, boycotts, confrontation, and negotiation. The change strategy is one of "Let's organize to overpower our oppressor."[25] The client population is viewed as being a "victim" of the oppressive power structure. Examples of the social action approach include boycotts during the civil rights movement during the 1960s, strikes by unions, protests by antiabortion groups, and protests by black and Native American groups.

The social action model is not widely used by social workers at present. Many workers find that being involved in social action activities may lead their employing agencies to penalize them with unpleasant work assignments, low merit increases, and refusal to promote them. Many agencies will accept minor and moderate changes in their service delivery systems but are threatened by the prospect of radical changes that are often advocated by the social action approach.

An example of the social action approach is presented in Box 17.6. Table 17.5 presents a summary of the three models that have been discussed: locality development, social planning, and social action.

Essential Skills and Knowledge Needed by Community Practitioners

This section will summarize some of the skills and knowledge needed by community practitioners. This

viable strategy to better serve single parents and their children. The community was undergoing an economic recession, therefore funds were unavailable for an expensive new program.

Three more meetings were held. At the first two of these a number of suggestions for providing services were discussed, but all were viewed as either too expensive or impractical. At the fourth meeting of the group, a single parent representing Parents Without Partners mentioned that she was aware that Big Brothers' and Big Sisters' programs in some communities were of substantial benefit to children who were raised in single-parent families. This idea seemed to energize the group. Suggestions began to "piggy back." The group, however, determined that funds were unavailable to hire staff to run a Big Brothers' and Big Sisters' program. However, Rhona Quinn, a social worker in the pupil services department, noted that she was willing to identify at-risk younger children in single-parent families and that she would be willing to supervise qualified volunteers in a "Big Buddy" program.

Mr. McKearn mentioned that he was currently supervising a student in an undergraduate field placement from an accredited social work program from a college in a nearby community. He noted that perhaps arrangements could be made for undergraduate social work students to be "Big Buddies" for their required volunteer experience. Rhona Quinn said she would approve of the suggestion if she could have the freedom to screen interested applicants for being "Big Buddies." Arrangements were made over the next two months for social work students to be "Big Buddies" for at-risk younger children from single-parent families. After a two-year experimental period, the school system found the program to be sufficiently successful that it assigned Ms. Quinn half-time to supervise the program, which included selecting at-risk children, screening volunteer applicants, matching children with Big Buddies, monitoring the progress of each matched pair, and conducting follow-up to ascertain the outcome of each pairing.

---

listing is not exhaustive but does summarize some of the essential skills and knowledge bases needed by community practitioners.

KNOWLEDGE OF THE COMMUNITY AND ITS VALUES   It is essential that a community practitioner have an understanding of the community—its power structure, economic base, governmental structure, network of social welfare programs, religious organizations and beliefs, racial and ethnic composition, social problems, and cherished values.

Community practitioners need to have such a knowledge base in order to facilitate residents in articulating their needs and in developing strategies that will be acceptable to the beliefs and values of the people being served. For example, if teenage pregnancy is problematic in an area, knowledge is needed of community values to determine whether it would be desirable to consider locating a family-planning clinic in the local high school. Such a proposal may be vigorously opposed by some religious groups.

Community practitioners also need to know community values so that they do not make statements or take actions that would offend community values. For example, in working with Wyoming ranchers, it would be a grave mistake to state any of the following: "Red meat should not be eaten," "Coyotes should be protected," and "Deer hunting should be outlawed." Making statements that gravely offend potential consumers of new services usually results in the community practitioner being ostracized.

BOX 17.5

Case Example of the Social Planning Model

I n the mid-1960s the U.S. Department of Health, Education and Welfare mandated (for several years) that every community in the nation had to provide information and referral (I&R) services about social services. If the I&R services met federal guidelines, the federal government would reimburse local communities for 75 percent of the cost. In Wisconsin, the State Department of Human Services met with local planning agencies and encouraged them to develop I&R services in their local communities. The state agreed to reimburse local communities for an additional 12.5 percent of the cost. This reimbursement schedule meant local communities could provide I&R services for only 12.5 percent of the total cost.

The board of directors of Lincoln County Social Planning Agency authorized its staff to do a feasibility study on establishing a centralized information and referral center. Donald Levi (social planner on the staff) was assigned to direct the study. Mr. Levi collected data showing the following:

> There were over 350 community service agencies and organizations in this largely metropolitan county. Not only clients but also service providers were confused about what services were available from this array of agencies.

> There was a confusing array of specialized information and referral services being developed. (Specialized information and referral services only provided I&R services in one or two areas.) There were specialized information and referral services developing in suicide prevention, mental health, mental retardation, day care, adoption services, and alcohol and drug treatment.

Mr. Levi then designed a program model for providing a centralized information and referral service. The model involved a service that would provide I&R services on *all* human and community services in the county. For example, I&R would provide information not only on available day-care services but also on where to find public tennis courts and whom to call to remove a stray cat killed in front of your house. The centralized information and referral service number would be widely publicized on television, radio, newspapers, bill-

---

INTERPERSONAL AND RELATIONSHIP SKILLS   A community practitioner needs good rapport skills in order to receive the support of potential consumers of new services. Such rapport skills include being perceptive, conveying sincerity and honesty, being personable, being a positive thinker and an encourager, being accepting of differences, being assertive, being able to

"join" and communicate with a wide variety of people, selling oneself as being a knowledgeable and self-confident (but not arrogant) person, and being a good listener. These skills are very similar to those held by competent psychotherapists and group therapists. Successful community practitioners are good at influencing others; that is, they are skilled at selling themselves

boards, telephone directories, and so on. A budget was developed by Mr. Levi for the program costs.

The board of directors of the Lincoln County Social Planning Agency concluded that such a centralized information and referral service would be more efficient and economical than the confusing array of specialized information and referral services that had been developing. The board therefore authorized Mr. Levi to pursue the development of a centralized I&R service.

Mr. Levi conducted a questionnaire survey of all the human service agencies in the county and of all the clergy in the county. The results showed that both groups strongly supported the development of a centralized I&R service. In addition, the Easter Seal Society felt so strongly that such a service was needed that they contacted Mr. Levi to indicate that the organization was willing to donate funds for the new program. Mr. Levi was delighted, and an arrangement was worked out for the Easter Seal Society to fund the program for a three-year demonstration period.

The only remaining barrier was that federal and state guidelines required that the program be approved by the county welfare board before reimbursement would be made. Mr. Levi and two members of the board of the Lincoln County Social Planning Agency presented the new program proposal to the county's welfare board. The presentation included graphs showing the savings of a centralized I&R service over specialized I&R services and contained written statements of support from a variety of sources, including city council members, the United Way, human service agencies, and members of the clergy. It was also indicated there would be no cost to the county for a three-year demonstration period. At the end of the demonstration project there would be an evaluative study of the merits and shortcomings of the program. Mr. Levi fully expected approval. He was speechless when the county welfare board said no. They indicated that they turned the proposal down because they felt a centralized I&R would mean more people would be referred to county social service agencies, which would raise costs to the county, and because they thought there would be pressure on the county to fund the program after the three-year demonstration project ended.

The county continued to be served by less efficient and less effective specialized I&R services. This case example realistically illustrates that some planning efforts are unsuccessful.

and their ideas. They inspire people to believe that working together on community problems will result in a better life for many in the area.

NEWS MEDIA SKILLS   Community practitioners analyze what will be of interest to newspapers and to radio and television stations in the area. Once problems of the potential consumers of services are identified, community practitioners may seek to publicize (in a positive light) the needs and proposed courses of action through the news media. The news media plays an important role in articulating these needs to the broader community. The manner in which concerns of the affected people is delivered to the broader

TABLE 17.5

Three Models of Community Organization Practice According to Selected Practice Variables

	Model A (Locality Development)	Model B (Social Planning)	Model C (Social Action)
1. Goal categories of community action	Self-help; community capacity and integration (process goals)	Problem-solving with regard to substantive community problems (task goals)	Shifting of power relationships and resources; basic institutional change (task or process goals)
2. Assumptions concerning community structure and problem conditions	Community eclipsed, anomie; lack of relationships and democratic problem-solving capacities; static traditional community	Substantive social problems; mental and physical health, housing, recreation	Disadvantaged populations, social injustice, deprivation, inequity
3. Basic change strategy	Broad cross section of people involved in determining and solving their own problems	Fact-gathering about problems and decisions on the most rational course of action	Crystallization of issues and organization of people to take action against enemy targets
4. Characteristic change tactics and techniques	Consensus: communication among community groups and interests; group discussion	Consensus or conflict	Conflict or contest: confrontation, direct action, negotiation
5. Salient practitioner roles	Enabler-catalyst, coordinator; teacher of problem-solving skills and ethical values	Fact gatherer and analyst, program implementer, facilitator	Activist-advocate: agitator, broker, negotiator, partisan
6. Medium of change	Manipulation of small, task-oriented groups	Manipulation of formal organizations and of data	Manipulation of mass organizations and political processes

community plays an important role in determining whether the broader community will support, oppose, or be apathetic about efforts to assist those who are affected.

GROUP FACILITATIVE SKILLS   Much of the work that is done in community change projects is done in small groups. As a result, community practitioners need skills at arranging meetings; motivating people to attend and to become involved in identifying needs; facilitating

group discussions; helping members to use a problem-solving approach; and helping members to reach decisions and to take actions.

PROBLEM-SOLVING AND ANALYTICAL SKILLS   Community practitioners need such problem-solving skills as identifying and articulating problems, identifying possible resolution strategies, analyzing the merits and shortcomings of strategies, selecting and implementing strategies, and evaluating the outcomes. Community

TABLE 17.5

(Continued)

	Model A (Locality Development)	Model B (Social Planning)	Model C (Social Action)
7. Orientation toward power structure(s)	Members of power structure as collaborators in a common venture	Power structure as employers and sponsors	Power structure as external target of action: oppressors to be coerced or overturned
8. Boundary definition of the community client, system, or constituency	Total geographic community	Total community or community segment (including "functional" community)	Community segment
9. Assumptions regarding interests of community subparts	Common interests or reconcilable differences	Interests reconcilable or in conflict	Conflicting interests that are not easily reconcilable; scarce resources
10. Conception of the public interest	Rationalist-unitary	Idealist-unitary	Realist-individualist
11. Conception of the client population or constituency	Citizens	Consumers	Victims
12. Conception of client role	Participants in an interactional problem-solving process	Consumers or recipients	Employers, constituents, members

Source: This chart is reprinted from J. Rothman, "Three Models of Community Organization Practice," in *Social Work Practice, 1968* (New York: Columbia University Press, 1968), pp. 24–25. Reprinted with permission from *Social Work Practice, 1968*, published for the National Conference on Social Welfare by Columbia University Press.

practitioners also need good analytical skills. They need to be able to identify significant information in mounds of data. They also need to analyze through visualization the consequences of various strategies to accomplish community change. A skilled community practitioner is able to visualize the outcomes (including reactions of opposing groups) of each possible strategy.

RESEARCH AND GRANT-WRITING CAPACITIES   Commu-

nity practitioners often need to serve as advisors and consultants to community groups in conducting surveys and need assessment studies to help identify and document existing problems. New programs that are advanced generally need funding. One important method of obtaining funds is through grants. Community practitioners often assist community groups in identifying possible sources of grants, including philanthropic organizations, the United Way, and federal and state government sources. Community practitioners

BOX 17.6

Case Example of the Social Action Model

S aul Alinsky, a nationally noted social action strategist, provides an example of a creative social action effort. The example also shows that social action efforts are often
enjoyable.

*I was lecturing at a college run by a very conservative, almost fundamentalist Protestant
denomination. Afterward some of the students came to my motel to talk to me. Their problem was that they couldn't have any fun on campus. They weren't permitted to dance or
smoke or have a can of beer. I had been talking about the strategy of effecting change in a
society and they wanted to know what tactics they could use to change their situation. I
reminded them that a tactic is doing what you can with what you've got. "Now, what have
you got?" I asked. "What do they permit you to do?" "Practically nothing," they said, "except—you know—we can chew gum." I said, "Fine. Gum becomes the weapon. You get 200
or 300 students to get two packs of gum each, which is quite a wad. Then you have them
drop it on the campus walks. This will cause absolute chaos. Why, with 500 wads of gum I
could paralyze Chicago, stop all the traffic in the Loop." They looked at me as though I was
some kind of nut. But about two weeks later I got an ecstatic letter saying, "It worked! It
worked! Now we can do just about anything so long as we don't chew gum."*

Source: Saul Alinksy, *Rules for Radicals* (New York: Random House, 1972), pp. 145–146.

may also serve as consultants or as primary writers
of grants.

FUND-RAISING CAPACITIES   Some community groups
decide to raise their own funds for the programs
they seek to implement. In such situations community
practitioners often serve as advisors and consultants
to help community groups to determine how much
money needs to be raised, identify targets for the fund-
raising (such as businesses, door-to-door solicitation,
and community groups such as the Kiwanis Club),
design the ads for the fund-raiser, and orient the
people who will do the "leg work" in the fund-raising
campaign.

KNOWLEDGE OF COMMUNITY CHANGE MODELS   Community practitioners need to be knowledgeable about
community change models. Knowledge of a variety of
community change models and processes is needed so
that if one strategy is failing, other strategies can be
suggested, evaluated, and then one or more implemented. It is important that a community practitioner
have a model in his or her mind for helping a community group to identify problems it wants to focus on,
to set goals, and to develop and implement strategies
for reaching the goals. If that model encounters unforeseen obstacles, it is essential that the community
practitioner has a working knowledge of other community change processes that can be suggested and
perhaps implemented.

YOUR FUTURE IN COMBATING HUMAN PROBLEMS

This text has sought to describe social work and social welfare. A major thrust has been to describe the social problems and the diverse fields of practice in which social workers and other human service professionals seek to combat human problems. A number of case examples have been given that are designed to illustrate the type of work and the frustrations and gratifications encountered in social work practice. This final chapter has sought to describe generalist social work practice. All of this information is designed to help you make a career decision about whether social work is a profession you want to pursue.

Test your interest:

1. Do you enjoy working closely and intensely with people?

2. Do you think you could cope with failure?

3. Do you think you would be willing to acquire the knowledge, skills, and values necessary to make life more meaningful to individuals, groups, families, and communities?

4. Do you think you would like a profession dedicated to social change?

If you honestly are able to answer yes to each of these questions, you may well have the potential to become an effective social worker.

Whether or not you decide to pursue a career in social work, the material in this text on social problems and social services is designed to give you a framework for making responsible citizenship decisions. As a voter you help decide which political officials will be elected to work for the expansion or the curtailment of social welfare services. You have the opportunity to be a volunteer for a human service agency, to serve on boards and committees of agencies, to participate in fund-raisers for human service programs, to become involved in legislative processes that affect human issues, and to influence others in daily interactions about controversial social welfare issues. Changes in the structure and functioning of the social welfare system are inevitable. You have the opportunity to work for the improvement of human living conditions. John F. Kennedy in his 1961 Presidential Inaugural Address eloquently stated, "Ask not what your country can do for you. Ask what you can do for your country."[26]

SUMMARY

A generalist social worker is trained to assess and treat people (who have a variety of social and personal problems) with a large number of assessment and intervention techniques. In working as a generalist, it is essential that a social worker be trained to work with individuals, with small groups, and in community practice.

Traditionally, working with individuals in social work is called casework. The primary skill and role of a caseworker is counseling. Other roles include broker, public education worker, advocate, outreach worker, teacher of new information and skills, behavioral specialist, case manager, and consultant. Counseling, from the client's perspective, can be conceptualized as involving these progressive stages:

1. Problem awareness.

2. Relationship to counselor.

3. Motivation.

4. Conceptualization of the problem.

5. Exploration of resolution strategies.

6. Selection of a strategy.

7. Implementation of the strategy.

8. Evaluation.

Questions have in recent years been raised about whether casework and counseling are effective. In actuality, casework is not a single method; rather, there are many theoretical approaches to casework. Some approaches are more effective than others. In future years there will be considerable research on testing various approaches to casework, with the less effective approaches gradually being discarded. An effective caseworker has a working knowledge of a wide variety of treatment approaches.

To be effective at counseling, a caseworker needs skills in (*a*) establishing a working relationship with clients and (*b*) interviewing in order to explore problems in depth. She or he also needs (*c*) a knowledge of various treatment approaches and community resources so that alternative resolution strategies can be explored with clients.

Groups are increasingly being used in social work. Almost every social service agency now provides some group services. The focus of social work groups has considerable variation, including social conversation, recreation, recreation-skill development, education, problem solving and decision making, self-help, socialization, therapy, and sensitivity training.

The goal in therapy groups is generally to have each member explore, in depth, personal or emotional problems that they have and to develop a strategy to resolve that problem. In contrast, sensitivity groups seek to foster increased personal and interpersonal awareness and to develop more effective interaction patterns.

Group therapy is increasingly being used in counseling. In essence a group therapist uses the principles of one-to-one counseling and of group dynamics to bring about positive changes in attitudes and behaviors of clients. Generally, a group therapist also uses the principles of comprehensive treatment techniques and of specialized treatment techniques to help clients.

Guidelines are presented in this chapter on how to start and lead groups. Aspects discussed included doing homework prior to the first session, planning a session, relaxing before starting a meeting, observing cues on entering the meeting room, making seating arrangements, making introductions, clarifying roles, setting an agenda, and ending a meeting.

Community practice is the process of stimulating and assisting the local community to evaluate, plan, and coordinate its efforts to meet the needs of a community. Social work is one of several disciplines that provides training in community practice. Practically all social workers, in one capacity or another, become involved in community practice efforts.

There are several roles for community practice ac-

tivities including enabler, broker, expert, social planner, advocate, and activist. The role that is applied should generally be determined by the task to be accomplished. Because a given community issue may involve several roles, a community practitioner should be skilled in applying all of these roles.

The enabler, broker, expert, and social planner roles are generally nonpartisan. If nonpartisan attempts are not successful in meeting the needs of individuals or groups of people, partisan activity (such as being an advocate or an activist) may be warranted.

Three models of community practice were described: locality development, social planning, and social action. The locality development model asserts that community change can best be brought about through broad participation of a wide spectrum of people at the local community level. The basic theme is, "Together we can figure out what to do and do it." The social planning model emphasizes a technical process of problem solving. The role of the expert is stressed in this approach to identifying and resolving social problems. The theme of this approach is, "Let's get the facts and take the next rational steps." The social action model seeks to organize a disadvantaged group in order to pressure the power structure for increased resources or for treatment more in accordance with democracy or social justice. The basic theme of this approach is "Let's organize to overpower our oppressor."

The chapter summarized a number of essential skills and knowledge needed by community practitioners. These skills and knowledge bases include knowledge of the community and its values, interpersonal and relationship skills, news media skills, group facilitative skills, problem-solving and analytical skills, research and grant-writing capacities, fund-raising capacities, and knowledge of community change models.

A generalist social worker is a multiskilled professional who is able to work effectively with individuals, families, groups, the news media, funding sources, and other community agencies and organizations. This chapter (and this text) ends by noting that regardless of whether or not you choose to pursue a career in social work, you have the opportunity to work for the improvement of human living conditions.

NOTES

1. Joseph Anderson, *Social Work Methods and Processes* (Belmont, CA: Wadsworth, 1981).

2. Louise Johnson, *Social Work Practice, A Generalist Approach,* 3d ed. (Boston: Allyn and Bacon, 1989), p. 436.

3. Joel Fischer, "Is Casework Effective? A Review," *Social Work* 18 (January 1973), pp. 5–20.

4. A. E. Bergin, "The Effects of Psychotherapy: Negative Results Revisited," *Journal of Counseling Psychology* 10 (1963), pp. 244–250; H. J. Eysenck, "The Effects of Psychotherapy," *International Journal of Psychiatry* 1 (1965), pp. 97–144; Joel Fischer, "Is Casework Effective? A Review"; and R. B. Stuart, *Trick or Treatment: How and When Psychotherapy Fails* (Champaign, IL: Research Press, 1970).

5. H. J. Eysenck, "The Effects of Psychotherapy"; G. Heilbrunn, "Results with Psychoanalytic Therapy," *American Journal of Psychotherapy* 17 (1963), pp. 427–435; J. Leo, "Psychoanalysis Reaches a Crossroad," *New York Times,* April 4, 1968, sec. 1, pp. 1, 58; A. Salter, *The Case against Psychoanalysis* (New York: Citadel Press, 1963).

6. Michael S. Olmstead, *The Small Group* (New York: Random House, 1959), pp. 21–22.

7. Gerald L. Euster, "Services to Groups," in *Contemporary Social Work,* eds. Donald Brieland, Lela B. Costin, and Charles R. Atherton (New York: McGraw-Hill, 1975), p. 227.

8. Ibid., p. 227.

9. Ralph Dolgoff and Donald Feldstein, *Understanding Social Welfare* (New York: Harper & Row, 1980).

10. Alfred H. Katz and Eugene I. Bender, *The Strength in Us: Self-Help Groups in the Modern World* (New York: Franklin-Watts, 1976), p. 9.

11. Alan Gartner and Frank Riessman, *Help: A Working Guide to Self-Help Groups* (New York: Franklin-Watts, 1980).

12. Frank Riessman, "The 'Helper Therapy' Principle," *Journal of Social Work,* April 1965, pp. 27–34.

13. Euster, "Services to Groups," p. 220.

14. Kurt Lewin, "Group Decision and Social Change," in *Readings in Social Psychology,* eds. G. E. Swanson, T. M. Newcomb, and E. L. Hartley (New York: Holt, 1952).

15. S. E. Asch, "Opinions and Social Pressure," *Scientific American* 193, no. 5 (1955), pp. 31–35.

16. Jane Howard, *Please Touch: A Guided Tour of the Human Potential Movement* (New York: McGraw-Hill, 1970), p. 3.

17. Steward L. Tubbs and John W. Baird, *The Open Person* (Columbus, OH: Charles E. Merrill, 1976), pp. 48–50.

18. Ibid, p. 48.

19. Morton A. Lieberman, Ervin D. Yalom, and Matthew B. Miles, "Encounter: The Leader Makes the Difference," *Psychology Today* 6 (1973), p. 11.

20. A. Panitch, "Community Organization," in *Contempoary Social Work,* 2d ed., eds. Donald Brieland, Lela Costin, and Charles Atherton. (New York: McGraw-Hill, 1980), pp. 124–125.

21. Neil Gilbert and Harry Specht, "Social Planning and Community Organization: Approaches," *Encyclopedia of Social Work,* 17th ed. (Washington, D.C.: National Association of Social Workers, 1977), pp. 1412–1425.

22. Ibid.

23. Jack Rothman and John E. Tropman, "Models of Community Organization and Macro Practice Perspectives: Their Mixing and Phasing," in *Strategies of Community Organization,* 4th ed., eds. Fred Cox, John Erlich, Jack Rothman, and John E. Tropman (Itasca, IL: F. E. Peacock, 1987), pp. 3–26.

24. Saul Alinsky, *Rules for Radicals* (New York: Random House, 1972).

25. Saul Alinsky, *Reveille for Radicals* (New York: Basic Books, 1969).

26. Quoted in James A. Henretta, W. Elliot Brownlee, David Brody, and Susan Ware, *America's History* (Chicago: The Dorsey Press, 1987), p. 875.

APPENDIX

THE NASW
CODE OF ETHICS

The National Association of Social Workers (NASW) is the professional association that represents the social work profession in this country. Its Code of Ethics summarizes important practice ethics for social workers and is presented as follows:

·

PREAMBLE

This code is intended to serve as a guide to the everyday conduct of members of the social work profession and as a basis for the adjudication of issues in ethics when the conduct of social workers is alleged to deviate from the standards expressed or implied in this code. It represents standards of ethical behavior for social workers in professional relationships with those served, with colleagues, with employers, with other individuals and professions, and with the community and society as a whole. It also embodies standards of ethical behavior governing individual conduct to the extent that such conduct is associated with an individual's status and identity as a social worker.

This code is based on the fundamental values of the social work profession that include the worth, dignity, and uniqueness of all persons as well as their rights and opportunities. It is also based on the nature of social work, which fosters conditions that promote these values.

In subscribing to and abiding by this code, the social worker is expected to view ethical responsibility in as inclusive a context as each situation demands and within which ethical judgment is required. The social worker is expected to take into consideration all the principles in this code that have a bearing upon any situation in which ethical judgment is to be exercised and professional intervention or conduct is planned.

NASW Code of Ethics
(Summary of Major Principles)

I. The Social Worker's Conduct and Comportment as a Social Worker
   A. *Propriety.* The social worker should maintain high standards of personal conduct in the capacity or identity as social worker.
   B. *Competence and Professional Development.* The social worker should strive to become and remain proficient in professional practice and the performance of professional functions.
   C. *Service.* The social worker should regard as primary the service obligation of the social worker profession.
   D. *Integrity.* The social worker should act in accordance with the highest standards of professional integrity.
   E. *Scholarship and Research.* The social worker engaged in study and research should be guided by the conventions of scholarly inquiry.

II. The Social Worker's Ethical Responsibility to Clients
   F. *Primacy of Clients' Interests.* The social worker's primary responsibility is to clients.
   G. *Rights and Prerogatives of Clients.* The social worker should make every effort to foster maximum self-determination on the part of clients.
   H. *Confidentiality and Privacy.* The social worker should respect the privacy of clients and hold in confidence all information obtained in the course of professional service.
   I. *Fees.* When setting fees, the social worker should ensure that they are fair, reasonable, considerate, and commensurate with the service performed and with due regard for the client's ability to pay.

III. The Social Worker's Ethical Responsibility to Colleagues
   J. *Respect, Fairness, and Courtesy.* The social worker should treat colleagues with respect, courtesy, fairness, and good faith.
   K. *Dealing with Colleagues' Clients.* The social worker has the responsibility to relate to the clients of colleagues with full professional consideration.

IV. The Social Worker's Ethical Responsibility to Employers and Employing Organizations
   L. *Commitments to Employing Organizations.* The social worker should adhere to commitments made to the employing organizations.

V. The Social Worker's Ethical Responsibility to the Social Work Profession
   M. *Maintaining the Integrity of the Profession.* The social worker should uphold and advance the values, ethics, knowledge, and mission of the profession.
   N. *Community Service.* The social worker should assist the profession in making social services available to the general public.
   O. *Development of Knowledge.* The social worker should take responsibility for identifying, developing, and fully utilizing knowledge for professional practice.

VI. The Social Worker's Ethical Responsibility to Society
   P. *Promoting the General Welfare.* The social worker should promote the general welfare of society.

The course of action that the social worker chooses is expected to be consistent with the spirit as well as the letter of this code.

In itself, this code does not represent a set of rules that will prescribe all the behaviors of social workers in all the complexities of professional life. Rather, it offers general principles to guide conduct, and the judicious appraisal of conduct, in situations that have ethical implications. It provides the basis for making judgments about ethical actions before and after they occur. Frequently, the particular situation determines the ethical principles that apply and the manner of their application. In such cases, not only the particular ethical principles are taken into immediate consideration, but also the entire code and its spirit. Specific applications of ethical principles must be judged within the context in which they are being considered. Ethical behavior in a given situation must satisfy not only the judgment of the individual social worker, but also the judgment of an unbiased jury of professional peers.

This code should not be used as an instrument to deprive any social worker of the opportunity or freedom to practice with complete professional integrity; nor should any disciplinary action be taken on the basis of this code without maximum provision for safeguarding the rights of the social worker affected.

The ethical behavior of social workers results not from edict, but from a personal commitment of the individual. This code is offered to affirm the will and zeal of all social workers to be ethical and to act ethically in all that they do as social workers.

The following codified ethical principles should guide social workers in the various roles and relationships and at the various levels of responsibility in which they function professionally. These principles also serve as a basis for the adjudication by the National Association of Social Workers of issues in ethics.

In subscribing to this code, social workers are required to cooperate in its implementation and abide by any disciplinary rulings based on it. They should also take adequate measures to discourage, prevent, expose, and correct the unethical conduct of colleagues. Finally, social workers should be equally ready to defend and assist colleagues unjustly charged with unethical conduct.

I. The Social Worker's Conduct and Comportment as a Social Worker

A. Propriety.   The social worker should maintain high standards of personal conduct in the capacity or identity as social worker.

1. The private conduct of the social worker is a personal matter to the same degree as is any other person's, except when such conduct compromises the fulfillment of professional responsibilities.

2. The social worker should not participate in, condone, or be associated with dishonesty, fraud, deceit, or misrepresentation.

3. The social worker should distinguish clearly between statements and actions made as a private individual and as a representative of the social worker profession or an organization or group.

B. Competence and Professional Development.   The social worker should strive to become and remain proficient in professional practice and the performance of professional functions.

1. The social worker should accept responsibility or employment only on the basis of existing competence or the intention to acquire the necessary competence.

2. The social worker should not misrepresent professional qualifications, education, experience, or affiliations.

C. Service.   The social worker should regard as primary the service obligation of the social work profession.

1. The social worker should retain ultimate responsibility for the quality and extent of the service that individual assumes, assigns, or performs.

2. The social worker should act to prevent practices that are inhumane or discriminatory against any person or group of persons.

D. Integrity.   The social worker should act in accordance with the highest standards of professional integrity and impartiality.

1. The social worker should be alert to and resist the influences and pressures that interfere with the exercise of professional discretion and impartial judgment required for the performance of professional functions.

2. The social worker should not exploit professional relationships for personal gain.

E. Scholarship and Research.   The social worker engaged in study and research should be guided by the conventions of scholarly inquiry.

1. The social worker engaged in research should consider carefully its possible consequences for human beings.

2. The social worker engaged in research should ascertain that the consent of participants in the research is voluntary and informed, without any implied deprivation or penalty for refusal to participate, and with due regard for participants' privacy and dignity.

3. The social worker engaged in research should protect participants from unwarranted physical or mental discomfort, distress, harm, danger, or deprivation.

4. The social worker who engages in the evaluation of services or cases should discuss them only for professional purposes and only with persons directly and professionally concerned with them.

5. Information obtained about participants in research should be treated as confidential.

6. The social worker should take credit only for work actually done in connection with scholarly and research endeavors and credit contributions made by others.

II. The Social Worker's Ethical Responsibility to Clients

F. Primacy of Client's Interests.   The social worker's primary responsibility is to clients.

1. The social worker should serve clients with devotion, loyalty, determination, and the maximum application of professional skill and competence.

2. The social worker should not exploit relationships with clients for personal advantage, or solicit the clients of one's agency for private practice.

3. The social worker should not practice, condone, facilitate, or collaborate with any form of discrimination on the basis of race, color, sex, sexual orientation, age, religion, national origin, marital status, political belief, mental or physical handicap, or any other preference or personal characteristic, condition or status.

4. The social worker should avoid relationships or commitments that conflict with the interests of clients.

5. The social worker should under no circumstances engage in sexual activities with clients.

6. The social worker should provide clients with accurate and complete information regarding the extent and nature of the services available to them.

7. The social worker should apprise clients of their risks, rights, opportunities, and obligations associated with social service to them.

8. The social worker should seek advice and counsel of colleagues and supervisors whenever such consultation is in the best interest of clients.

9. The social worker should terminate service to clients, and professional relationships with them, when such service and relationships are no longer required or no longer serve the clients' needs or interests.

10. The social worker should withdraw services precipitously only under unusual circumstances, giving careful consideration to all factors in the situation and taking care to minimize possible adverse effects.

11. The social worker who anticipates the termination or interruption of service to clients should notify clients promptly and seek the transfer, referral, or continuation of service in relation to the clients' needs and preferences.

G. Rights and Prerogatives of Clients.   The social worker should make every effort to foster maximum self-determination on the part of clients.

1. When the social worker must act on behalf of a client who has been adjudged legally incompetent, the social worker should safeguard the interests and rights of that client.

2. When another individual has been legally authorized to act in behalf of a client, the social worker should deal with that person always with the clients' best interests in mind.

3. The social worker should not engage in any action that violates or diminishes the civil or legal rights of clients.

H. Confidentiality and Privacy.   The social worker should respect the privacy of clients and hold in confidence all information obtained in the course of professional service.

1. The social worker should share with others confidences revealed by clients, without their consent, only for compelling professional reasons.

2. The social worker should inform clients fully about the limits of confidentiality in a given situation, the purposes for which information is obtained, and how it may be used.

3. The social worker should afford clients reasonable access to any official social work records concerning them.

4. When providing clients with access to records, the social worker should take due care to protect the confidences of others contained in those records.

5. The social worker should obtain informed consent of clients before taping, recording, or permitting third party observation of their activities.

I. Fees.   When setting fees, the social worker should ensure that they are fair, reasonable, considerate, and commensurate with the service performed and with due regard for the client's ability to pay.

1. The social worker should not divide a fee or accept or give anything of value for receiving or making a referral.

III. The Social Worker's Ethical Responsibility to Colleagues

J. Respect, Fairness, and Courtesy.   The social worker should treat colleagues with respect, courtesy, fairness, and good faith.

1. The social worker should cooperate with colleagues to promote professional interests and concerns.

2. The social worker should respect confidences shared by colleagues in the course of their professional relationships and transactions.

3. The social worker should create and maintain conditions of practice that facilitate ethical and competent professional performance by colleagues.

4. The social worker should treat with respect, and represent accurately and fairly, the qualifications, views, and findings of colleagues and use appropriate channels to express judgments on these matters.

5. The social worker who replaces or is replaced by a colleague in professional practice should act with consideration for the interest, character, and reputation of that colleague.

6. The social worker should not exploit a dispute between a colleague and employers to obtain a position or otherwise advance the social worker's interests.

7. The social worker should seek arbitration or mediation when conflicts with colleagues require resolution for compelling professional reasons.

8. The social worker should extend to colleagues of other professions the same respect and cooperation that is extended to social work colleagues.

9. The social worker who serves as an employer, supervisor, or mentor to colleagues should make orderly and explicit arrangements regarding the conditions of their continuing professional relationship.

10. The social worker who has the responsibility for

employing and evaluating the performance of other staff members, should fulfill such responsibility in a fair, considerate, and equitable manner, on the basis of clearly enunciated criteria.

11. The social worker who has the responsibility for evaluating the performance of employees, supervisees, or students should share evaluations with them.

K. Dealing with Colleagues' Clients.   The social worker has the responsibility to relate to the clients of colleagues with full professional consideration.

1. The social worker should not solicit the clients of colleagues.

2. The social worker should not assume professional responsibility for the clients of another agency or a colleague without appropriate communication with that agency or colleague.

3. The social worker who serves the clients of colleagues, during a temporary absence or emergency, should serve those clients with the same consideration as that afforded any client.

IV. The Social Worker's Ethical Responsibility to Employers and Employing Organizations

L. Commitment to Employing Organization.   The social worker should adhere to commitments made to the employing organization.

1. The social worker should work to improve the employing agency's policies and procedures, and the efficiency and effectiveness of its services.

2. The social worker should not accept employment or arrange student field placements in an organization which is currently under public sanction by NASW for violating personnel standards or imposing limitations on or penalties for professional actions on behalf of clients.

3. The social worker should act to prevent and elimi-

nate discrimination in the employing organization's work assignments and in its employment policies and practices.

4. The social worker should use with scrupulous regard, and only for the purpose for which they are intended, the resources of the employing organization.

V. The Social Worker's Ethical Responsibility to the Social Work Profession

M. Maintaining the Integrity of the Profession.   The social worker should uphold and advance the values, ethics, knowledge, and mission of the profession.

1. The social worker should protect and enhance the dignity and integrity of the profession and should be responsible and vigorous in discussion and criticism of the profession.

2. The social worker should take action through appropriate channels against unethical conduct by any other member of the profession.

3. The social worker should act to prevent the unauthorized and unqualified practice of social work.

4. The social worker should make no misrepresentation in advertising as to qualifications, competence, service, or results to be achieved.

N. Community Service.   The social worker should assist the profession in making social services available to the general public.

1. The social worker should contribute time and professional expertise to activities that promote respect for the utility, the integrity, and the competence of the social work profession.

2. The social worker should support the formulation, development, enactment, and implementation of social policies of concern to the profession.

O. Development of Knowledge.   The social worker should take responsibility for identifying, developing, and fully utilizing knowledge for professional practice.

1. The social worker should base practice upon recognized knowledge relevant to social work.

2. The social worker should critically examine, and keep current with, emerging knowledge relevant to social work.

3. The social worker should contribute to the knowledge base of social work and share research knowledge and practice wisdom with colleagues.

VI. The Social Worker's Ethical Responsibility to Society

P. Promoting the General Welfare.   The social worker should promote the general welfare of society.

1. The social worker should act to prevent and eliminate discrimination against any person or group on the basis of race, color, sex, sexual orientation, age, religion, national origin, marital status, political belief, mental or physical handicap, or any other preference or personal characteristic, condition, or status.

2. The social worker should act to ensure that all persons have access to the resources, services, and opportunities which they require.

3. The social worker should act to expand choice and opportunity for all persons, with special regard for disadvantaged or oppressed groups and persons.

4. The social worker should promote conditions that encourage respect for the diversity of cultures which constitute American society.

5. The social worker should provide appropriate professional services in public emergencies.

6. The social worker should advocate changes in policy and legislation to improve social conditions and to promote social justice.

7. The social worker should encourage informed participation by the public in shaping social policies and institutions.

PHOTO CREDITS

p. 3: Sovfoto

p. 4: (top) Tom Ballard/EKM-Nepenthe; (bottom) Martha Tabor

p. 5: Elizabeth Crews

p. 14: Paul Strand, *Blind Woman, New York, 1916*, Copyright © 1971, Aperture Foundation, Inc., Paul Strand Archive

p. 17: Dorothea Lange, © 1982, The Oakland Museum, the city of Oakland

p. 19: AP/Wide World Photos

p. 32: Terrence McCarthy/NYT Pictures

p. 33: Steve Hansen/Stock, Boston

p. 41: Barnardo Photographic Archive

p. 44: Sophia Smith Collection/Smith College

p. 46: #BC288, Chicago Historical Society

p. 48: Nita Winter

p. 54: Karen Stafford Rantzman

p. 68: Sara Krulwich/NYT Pictures

p. 77: Bruce Davidson/Magnum

p. 80: (top) Culver Pictures; (bottom) George W. Ackerman/National Archives

p. 81: Joan Kelley/ACTION

p. 86: Jacob Riis/The Museum of the City of New York

p. 88: Paul Fusco/Magnum

p. 93: Milwaukee Journal/Sentinel, Inc.

p. 95: Martha Tabor

p. 124: (top) AP/Wide World Photos; (bottom) Shepard Sherbell/Picture Group

p. 125: (top) David Wells/The Image Works; (bottom) Charles Steiner/Picture Group

p. 134: The Museum of Modern Art/Film Stills Archive

p. 135: Nita Winter

p. 142: Courtesy The Samaritans, Boston, Mass.

p. 152: The World Bank

p. 155: (left) Jim Estrin/NYT Pictures; (right) Jill Cannefax/EKM-Nepenthe

p. 165: (left) Ari Mintz/New York Newsday; (right) Jon Simon/NYT Pictures

p. 182: Kit Hedman/Jeroboam

p. 192: Prints Old and Rare, San Francisco

p. 193: Courtesy the San Francisco AIDS Foundation

p. 195: UPI/Bettmann Newsphotos

p. 202: Rhoda Sidney/Stock, Boston

p. 211: Chester Higgins, Jr./Photo Researchers

p. 241: The Bettmann Archive

p. 250: Milwaukee Journal/Sentinel, Inc.

p. 253: Comstock Inc./Lynn Eskenzai

p. 256: AP/Wide World Photos

p. 264: Mark Antman/Stock, Boston

p. 265: Marcia Oliveri/New York State Division of Substance Abuse Services

p. 270: UPI/Bettmann Newsphotos

p. 276: San Francisco Examiner

p. 286: AP/Wide World Photos

p. 291: UPI/Bettmann Newsphotos

p. 304: Denver Public Library, Western History Department

p. 305: Gene Page

p. 306: Danny Lyon/Magnum

p. 308: Rob Nelson/Picture Group

p. 328: Elizabeth Crews

p. 329: Owen Franken/Stock, Boston

p. 334: Bernard Pierre Wolff/Photo Researchers

p. 335: Fred R. Conrad/NYT Pictures

p. 341: Elizabeth Crews/The Image Works

p. 349: Donna Binder/Impact Visuals

p. 358: Martha Tabor

p. 365: Grant Heilman Photography

p. 366: Sophia Smith Collection/Smith College

p. 370: Martha Tabor

INDEX